Personality Types

Revised Edition

BOOKS BY
DON RICHARD RISO

The definitive text of Enneagram theory and descriptions.
PERSONALITY TYPES
Using the Enneagram for Self-Discovery   1987, 1996

Practical applications of the Enneagram in your life.
UNDERSTANDING THE ENNEAGRAM
The Practical Guide to Personality Types   1990

An introduction to the Enneagram with an accurate personality test.
DISCOVERING YOUR PERSONALITY TYPE
The New Enneagram Questionnaire   1992, 1995

Spiritual and psychological help for each type.
ENNEAGRAM TRANSFORMATIONS
Releases and Affirmations for Healing Your Personality Type   1993

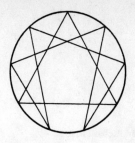

Personality Types

USING THE ENNEAGRAM

FOR SELF-DISCOVERY

Revised Edition

Don Richard Riso
with Russ Hudson

HOUGHTON MIFFLIN COMPANY
Boston New York

For information about permission to reproduce selections from this book, write to Permissions, Houghton Mifflin Company, 215 Park Avenue South, New York, New York 10003.

For information about this and other Houghton Mifflin trade and reference books and multimedia products, visit The Bookstore at Houghton Mifflin on the World Wide Web at http://www.hmco.com/trade/.

This book is the result of the original work of the authors and represents thousands of hours' work conceptualizing and refining the material. The Enneagram of personality is a modern synthesis of both ancient and modern psychological and spiritual teachings. No body of Enneagram material has been passed down in an oral tradition of any kind. The contents of this book have been copyrighted and may not be reproduced in whole or part by any means whatsoever without the express written permission of Houghton Mifflin Company. Please respect the rights and efforts of the authors by not photocopying or otherwise infringing on the copyrighted material. If you would like to obtain multiple copies of this book at a reduced price, please order them in bulk from the publisher. See the last page of this book for ordering information.

Library of Congress Cataloging-in-Publication Data
    Riso, Don Richard.
        Personality types : using the enneagram for self-discovery / Don Richard
Riso with Russ Hudson. — Rev. ed.
        p.   cm.
    Includes bibliographical references and index.
    ISBN 0-395-79867-1
    1. Typology (Psychology).   2. Enneagram.   I. Hudson, Russ.   II. Title.
BF698.4.R57   1996
155.2'6 — dc20   96-22202   CIP

Printed in the United States of America

BP 10 9 8 7 6 5 4 3

Artwork by Mark S. Desveaux

*This book is dedicated to those
who have made it possible.
They know who they are.
They have my love
and deepest gratitude.*

Contents

Authors' Note   xi
Preface   xvii
Acknowledgments   xxi

PART I

1   Understanding Personality Types   3
2   Origins   11
3   Guidelines   27

PART II
THE NINE PERSONALITY TYPES

The Feeling Triad
4   Type Two: The Helper   59
5   Type Three: The Motivator   95
6   Type Four: The Individualist   134

The Thinking Triad
7   Type Five: The Investigator   173
8   Type Six: The Loyalist   216
9   Type Seven: The Enthusiast   259

The Instinctive Triad

10   Type Eight: The Leader   297
11   Type Nine: The Peacemaker   338
12   Type One: The Reformer   376

PART III

13   Advanced Guidelines   413
14   The Theory of the Enneagram   431
15   Postscript   455

Appendix   465
Bibliography   495
Index   499

I am a man:

nothing human is alien to me.

— TERENCE

Authors' Note

for the Second Edition

At the time of this writing, *Personality Types* has established itself as a fundamental source book and as a classic in the field of
Enneagram studies. It is one of the best-selling and most-translated
Enneagram books in the world, having sold over 150,000 copies in
the United States alone. Therefore many might wonder why we
have wanted to revise it.

The principal answer is that the Enneagram is a work in progress, and as such, both the breadth and the depth of our understanding of this remarkable system are constantly expanding. We
are continually finding better terminology, making new discoveries,
formulating more profound questions, uncovering new areas for in-
vestigation, and seeing more fertile connections with other bodies of
knowledge. The possibility for deeper insight into human nature is
always present: human nature is open-ended, and so our work with
the Enneagram is ongoing.

The Enneagram is a work in progress also in the sense that we
are approaching the material in the spirit of scientific inquiry—
there is no "Enneagram bible" or "sacred scripture" that has been
passed down to us to which we can refer. Unfortunately, the first
edition of *Personality Types* was perhaps a source of the mistaken
idea that there was a body of knowledge about the Enneagram

which had been transmitted through an ongoing "oral tradition" of some kind. Nothing could be further from the truth. The Enneagram is largely a modern development, the work of Oscar Ichazo, Claudio Naranjo, the authors, and other contemporary writers. As such, there will be a need to reassess our formulations and ideas in the light of new discoveries.

Since the original version of *Personality Types* was published in 1987, we have conducted scores of workshops and Training Programs around the world in which we have shared our discoveries about the Enneagram with thousands of intelligent, well-informed people. In the process of teaching our material, we discovered that while we were on target, or at least on the right track with many ideas, we could often find more effective ways of expressing the fundamental truths of the Enneagram to our students. At the same time, our interactions with them yielded many new insights and refinements which have helped clarify our understanding of the types and of the Enneagram as a whole.

Moreover, as our own personal development has progressed, we have uncovered deeper truths about the function of the personality and its relationship to our essential, spiritual nature. This has produced a more complete and focused orientation to our understanding of the Enneagram itself, one that illuminates it in exciting and unexpected ways. We are more convinced than ever of the power and efficacy of the Enneagram for transformational work — but only insofar as our language and ideas are accurate and precise. The more clearly and specifically we have insight into ourselves, the more possible it is to let go of old debilitating patterns from the past. As we let go of our old patterns, our awareness expands and our sense of self shifts. Accurate, precise, clear language is therefore vitally important, and we continue to search for the most exact expression that we can.

As our teaching evolved, we began to be aware that it was outpacing the expression of the ideas which had been published in the first edition of *Personality Types*. Moreover, there were also a number of important, original discoveries which could have gone into the first edition, but which were withheld for a variety of reasons. The success of *Personality Types* has afforded us the luxury of being able to include some of these other findings, as well as to enrich and elaborate on the original book. Houghton Mifflin Company has generously allowed us to do so, and we have added some fifty thousand new words to the original text.

In reviewing *Personality Types*, we did not feel so much that it required a major overhaul, but that it would be an even stronger book if we could find a way to include more of the refinements and observations that we had been making. In the nine years since *Personality Types* was first published, we have made many new discoveries which have greatly clarified previously unexplored or unnoticed areas of the types and the Enneagram as a whole. We believe that the inclusion of this new material significantly enlarges our understanding of the types and makes working with the Enneagram easier and more effective. Even so, we have not been able to include all of our new discoveries, since some of them are too advanced for this book, and including them all would strain it to the breaking point.

A noteworthy change in this new edition involves an elusive quality, its tone. We have attempted to give this new edition a softer, warmer voice while retaining the elegance, richness, and precision of the original version's language. As much as possible, we have also attempted to correct any biases or inequalities in our presentations of the nine types. We have wished to be as even-handed and objective in our descriptions as we possibly could. Our intention has been for readers not only to be able to find their type, but to have a less difficult time recognizing and acknowledging the problematic aspects of their character structure. We knew that this would require a compassionate and gentle approach, and we have endeavored to incorporate this in our revised type descriptions.

One of our most important original discoveries that we have included here for the first time is the Core Dynamics (with their Levels of Development) for each of the nine personality types. Prior to their publication here, the Core Dynamics were available only to students who had attended our Professional Training Programs. This new edition now makes these available to the general public as well as to researchers and mental health professionals. The Core Dynamics are explicitly presented in the appendix at the end of this book, as well as implicitly in the descriptions of the Levels of Development in each of the nine type chapters. The Core Dynamics will greatly enhance understanding of the motivations and ego defenses of the types, as well as greatly clarify the inner logic and range of each type's overall pattern of attitudes and behaviors. The Core Dynamics (with their Levels of Development) are a specific measure of each type's state, giving students of the Enneagram an elegant conceptual framework which, we predict, will be used in a wide variety of fields. Therapists, educators, and business consultants—in fact, anyone wishing to make practical applications of the Enneagram—will turn to the Core Dynamics to accelerate the effectiveness of their work.

We have also greatly expanded our discussion of the origins and history of the Enneagram symbol and our account of the modern development of the system. While many are deeply interested in learning about the roots of this typology, the previously available material on this subject has been a source of considerable confusion and misinformation, as already noted here. Although there still are gaps in the long story of the Enneagram's evolution, we have endeavored to give an accurate account based on all of the information now available.

There are many questions about the childhood patterns and developmental origins of the personality types, and we have taken this opportunity to clarify our explanations on this subject. We are now using clearer and more encompassing terminology for the childhood patterns that were first introduced in the original edition of *Personality Types*, and we have gone into greater depth in our discussion of each type's developmental origins here. For instance, rather than describing type Three as "positive to the mother or mother-substitute," we now teach that this type is "connected to the nurturing-figure" (who may or may not be the biological mother, nor is the connection necessarily "positive"). This change of emphasis has broader implications and has resonated with Threes as a more accurate interpretation of their experience.

Another feature is our introduction of new names for some of the types and two of the Triads. Over the years, we have changed "the Status Seeker" to "the Motivator," "the Artist" to "the Individualist," "the Thinker" to "the Investigator," and "the Generalist" to "the Enthusiast." We have made these changes because we felt that the new names help distinguish each type from the others while giving less cause for confusion and mistyping. These new type names also seem to better capture the core issues of each type.

Similarly, we changed the name of the Relating Triad to the Instinctive Triad, and the Doing Triad to the Thinking Triad. These changes help make the Triad names consistent with the names of the three traditional centers of human awareness: namely, thinking, feeling, and instinct. We have also included additional thematic material explaining how each individual type relates to its respective Triad. For instance, we have been more explicit about how resistance plays a major role in types Eight, Nine, and One, and how types Two, Three, and Four all are seeking validation for a particular self-image, and so forth.

Many other features of *Personality Types* have also been expanded and refined. We have included longer descriptions and specific names for each of the eighteen wing subtypes. For example, we have named the Four with a Three-wing "the Aristocrat," and the Four with a Five-wing "the Bohemian." We are the first authors who have done sufficient research into the wings to be able to make these wing subtype distinctions, and we are making them available here for the first time.

We have also enlarged our discussions of the Directions of Integration and Disintegration. Each type chapter now includes a groundbreaking description of the movement of the type in the Direction of Disintegration *Level by Level* so that readers can see precisely how they tend to "act out" under stress as an "early warning signal"—just one of the many uses of the Levels of Development for personal growth. There are also additional original explanations and descriptions of each type's Direction of Integration. Throughout the book, we have presented a more refined theoretical understanding of the Enneagram as a system, including more new information on the wings, the Directions of Integration and Disintegration, the Triads, and the correlations with other theories of personality. For the first time, we offer our own original brief explanation of the instinctual orientations (sometimes called the "Self-Preservation, Social, and Sexual subtypes"), placing them in a larger context and providing a coherent rationale for future research in this area.

We trust that readers will concur that this new edition is a significant improvement on an already solid achievement. By being scholarly and comprehensive we believe that this will be a milestone in the growth of the field. We hope that the efforts that have gone into updating *Personality Types* have produced a text for self-discovery and personal growth that will be useful and enlightening for many years to come.

Nevertheless, our knowledge of human nature is constantly deepening. As this process continues, we may decide that, at some point in the future, yet another revision of this book will be useful. If you are already familiar with *Personality Types*, we hope that you will be rewarded by exploring its many new features and ideas as much as we have enjoyed developing them. If you are new to the Enneagram, we hope that you will find in these pages a foundation for understanding yourself and others which will serve you well for the rest of your life. For all our readers, we thank you for your generous encouragement and your enthusiasm for our work which, after all is said and done, has made this new revised version possible.

Don Richard Riso
Russ Hudson
New York City
March 1996

Preface

The Enneagram and Transformation

If there is a single overriding theme in our interpretation of the Enneagram, it is the need to acknowledge and understand our inner states so that we can begin to move beyond them. Self-understanding is the prelude to transformation, to moving beyond the ego and all that makes up what is called "false personality." Transcending the ego is the gate to every spiritual path, and the Enneagram shows each type (and therefore each of us as individuals) what that gate is and how to pass through it. By helping us know that ego-transcendence and the integration of higher states of consciousness is possible, and by providing us with an understanding of the freer, more expansive qualities of our own being, the Enneagram encourages us to pursue them.

All of us are looking for answers to some of life's most difficult problems. We may well express it in different ways, but at some common human level we all are seeking a way to lead richer, more fulfilling, and graceful lives—and to help others do the same. While the Enneagram does not have all the answers it can help us identify how (and why) so many people often go wrong and bring unhappiness and various kinds of destructiveness on themselves and others.

The personality types of the Enneagram identify the chief features of our inner landscape—where the precipitous cliffs, arid deserts, and treacherous quicksands of the soul lie, as well as where the fertile oases, restful forests, and life-producing springs are within us. We are free to go to those places or not, free to fall into the many potential traps of psychic quicksand or not, free to scale the heights and move into new territory or not. Thus, understood and used properly, the Enneagram is a map not merely of our states of personality, but a map that points the way toward what lies beyond personality, *once we have transcended our egos.*

Moreover, the Enneagram is an interpretation of human personality so encompassing that it takes us to the threshold of the spiritual. It is not out of place to talk about spirituality with regard to the Enneagram, since spirituality manifests itself in our daily lives as an ever changing array of virtues. Indeed, what are traditionally called "virtues" are spontaneous and natural expressions of the human spirit. They are the sources of many of the goods that we seek in our daily lives and are the traits we find in the healthy Levels of Development of each type. The "practice of virtue" (which, in one form or another, is required by all forms of spirituality) is not simply a religious issue. Uncovering our virtues is one of the things we learn from the Enneagram, and this enables us to lead a good life—one that is profoundly fulfilled and that allows us to make valuable contributions to the world. When we are healthy, we are being virtuous and are moving out of ego states toward states of higher functioning and integration. To move in the Direction of Integration is to live out of our "Essence"—as an expression of our best and truest self.

At its deepest, therefore, the Enneagram is not only profound psychology but a means to a deeper, more genuine spirituality. If you are learning to observe yourself and let go of the habits of your personality, then you are already on a spiritual path, whether you call it that or not, because no spiritual path can be followed without self-transcendence. Thus, the Enneagram is itself not a form of spirituality but a means to spirituality of all kinds. It is psychology so profound and encompassing as to have spiritual overtones. Its insights resonate with the insights we find in many different traditions from around the world.

Turning evil into good, the dross of our lives into pure gold, is the most profound alchemy. Gurdjieff claimed that the Enneagram is, in fact, the long-sought "philosopher's stone" that catalyzes lead into gold. From our point of view, the process of turning lead into gold is also what we are concerned with here: the transformation of ourselves and our lives into something more fit for higher purposes—although we cannot, perhaps, always be certain precisely what those purposes are.

In the end, however, the Enneagram is merely a tool and an intellectual system—simply a source of insight—and as such it cannot work magic. Nevertheless, it can provide us with some of the wisdom we need to make good choices in our lives and the objectivity we need to see the truth about ourselves. But these are no small matters, for they enable us to accept the gift of Grace, which alone can transform our lives.

Acknowledgments

for the First Edition

This book did not take long to write, yet in another sense, it has been a long time in the making. It would have been impossible without the following people.

Some twelve years ago, when I started to study the Enneagram, Tad Dunne, S.J., suggested that I read the work of Karen Horney, and Bob Fecas encouraged me to continue to develop the descriptions of the healthy side of the personality types. Both suggestions have proved to be most helpful.

When I began lecturing about the Enneagram, the Reverend Richard Powers was extraordinarily generous about making lecture facilities available to me. Without the give-and-take of public presentations, I doubt that I would have been able to get the kind of confirmation of the Enneagram's validity which was useful and necessary at that time. Also helpful to me in a similar way, but in different circumstances, were Karl Laubenstein, Steve Rodgers, Priscilla Rodgers, Richard Hunt, S.J., and the members of Ruah, in Cambridge, Massachusetts.

Many of my friends have taken an interest in my work. I am grateful to them for their enthusiasm, which nurtured my fragile undertaking in those early years. The encouragement of Ruben St.

Germain, Bob Cabaj, Irwin Montaldo, Robert Moore, Chuck Webb, Rose Mary O'Boyle, and Jeff Posner has been especially important to me. I would also like to thank Hugh P. Finnegan, Ann L. Mac-Dougall, Diana A. Steele, Erwin Mayr, and Dick Kalb for reading early drafts of the manuscript and commenting on them. Thanks also to Mark S. Desveaux for the line drawings and wonderfully realized caricatures of the personality types.

There are a number of other people whose names, for entirely personal reasons, I would like to invoke here. They are Beverly Moreno Pumilia, Jeff and Gertrude Moreno, Dominick and Virginia Riso, Agnes Bazzle, Sister Thérèse of the Angels, Harry Claypool, Rob Bliss, Charles Aalto, Terri Kyller, Brent BecVar, Bruce Mac-Clain, John Lush, Lester Wolff, Philip Stehr, Louisa and Sandy Arico, Bill and Lynette Rice, Robert Drez, Brother Brendan, S.C., as well as August Coyle, Joseph Tetlow, Edward Romagosa, Youree Watson, Daniel Creagan, Pat Byrne, and Peter Sexton—these last of the Society of Jesus.

I have a number of people to thank at Houghton Mifflin, doubt-less many more than I realize. My first editor, Gerard Van der Leun, has since left Houghton. He taught me to say more by writing less. After his departure I was fortunate to be assigned to Ruth Hapgood, who has proved to be a beacon of wisdom, good cheer, and patience. I thank her especially for her forbearance in letting this book become itself. Geraldine Morse, my copy editor, improved the book greatly, saving me from untold error and em-barrassment.

Above all, my thanks go to Austin Olney, the former editor in chief of Houghton Mifflin. Austin saw this book's potential when the manuscript was little more than a sketch. To say that he has been kind, supportive, and understanding is to say much too little. This book would not be in your hands now were it not for him.

Over the years I have received some of the best advice—and innumerable ideas and suggestions—from my agent and lawyer, Brian Lawrence Taylor, and from Patricia D. Walsh and James Peck. Their interest in my work has been more valuable to me than they know. The fact that these three people of rare intelligence also believed in the Enneagram helped sustain me in dark hours. Finally, my most profound thanks go to my family for all that they are. I wish it were possible to reveal everything that they have done for me, but I have not yet fathomed it myself. It will have to be enough to say that without their constant love, help, and understanding, this book would not exist.

Don Richard Riso
1987

Acknowledgments for the Revised Edition

There are always more people to acknowledge than one is aware of: I have been influenced by so many people in so many different ways over the past nine years that it is impossible to know who all of them are, much less mention them here.

Since the publication of the first edition of *Personality Types* in 1987, I have met thousands of people in Enneagram workshops and trainings and have heard from thousands more around the world who have been touched by the book in various ways. They have confirmed what I already knew—that understanding the personality types of the Enneagram is invaluable: by uncovering structures that express reality, all nine impart many actualizing lessons. Properly understood, the Enneagram speaks the truth in a way that touches the human heart. Many have reported that it gave them insights that changed their lives or saved a marriage or helped them understand a child—or even saved their own lives. To have this kind of beneficial impact on people was one of my deepest hopes during the twelve years I was originally writing *PT*. I am grateful that it has helped people around the world understand themselves and others, and I pray that this new edition be the vehicle for even more understanding to flourish in the world.

We have been blessed with many outstanding students whose contributions have gone far beyond helping us to confirm or correct our original insights. The suggestions of students like Tom Markey, who made a case for the parental orientations of the types, were instrumental in pointing us in fruitful directions. Similarly, Joan Jennings had a seminal insight into the structure of the Triads in relation to the process of integration. Other students and colleagues whose contributions we are happy to acknowledge include Elisabeth Auspurg, Joel and Annie Baehr, Marilyn Bernhardt, David Beswick, Catherine Breeding, Katherine Chernick, Phyllis Cloninger, Mona Coates, Kevin Cullen, Remi de Roo, Ben Eiland, Diane Ellsworth, Cathie Flanigan, Paul Gandy, Pearl Gervais, Belinda Gore, Brian Grodner, Orn Gudmundsson, Anita Hamm, Jane Hollister, Andrea Isaacs, Ed Jacobs, Michelle Jurika, Ann Kirby, Jack Labanauskas, Claes Lilja, Lawrence Martin, Damon and Elizabeth Miller, Maurice Monette, Dan Napolitano, Rose Mary O'Boyle, Karen Page, Marie-Anne Quenneville, Joyce Rawlings-Davies, Richard Reese, John Richards, Maggi and Les Saucier, Robert Siudzinski, Robert and Lois Tallon, Wes Van Hee, and Vanessa Williams. My sincere apologies to anyone I have inadvertently left off this list: there are surely many more who also richly deserve to be remembered here.

Special mention must go to Brian Taylor, my lawyer and best counselor, on whose support and advice I constantly rely; Brian has kept me out of a lot of trouble over the years! Also, I have the deepest regard for the memory of William McGrane II for his faith in me and his hearty and heartfelt mentoring and encouragement. Our editors at Houghton Mifflin, Betsey Lerner, Hilary Liftin, and, currently, Marnie Patterson, deserve special thanks, as does our agent, Susan Lescher.

Above all, I take great pride in acknowledging the friendship and great good influence of my teaching partner and coauthor, Russ Hudson. About a year after *Personality Types* first came out, Russ stumbled over the book and sought me out for personal advice. When I first met Russ, it was one of those rare occasions when one gets the strong impression that something momentous is happening: this was a person who would be important in my life and work. And so it happened. When our friendship began in 1988, its focus was on the Enneagram, but over the years it has expanded to include much more as we began to live the subtle inner teachings of this system of human understanding. More than any other person, Russ's wisdom and brilliance have been responsible for the development of many of the ideas presented in this second edition. He has taught me as much as I have taught him, and I'm proud that many of his contributions and new discoveries (although still not all!) are being presented here.

As complete as *Personality Types* now is, we are acutely aware that there is still more to say. There will always be more to learn as we contemplate the intricacies of the human soul: yearning to be free, it falls into slumber and illusions, only to wake up and fall asleep again. With each awakening, however, something invaluable is deposited in us, and over time we are gradually transformed. The Enneagram is extraordinarily valuable because it shows us the pattern of our dreams. What it cannot reveal to us is what we will discover if, finally, we awaken.

Don Richard Riso
New York City
May 1996

In addition to the many extraordinary people that Don has mentioned, I would like to add my thanks to a few more individuals.

First, I would like to thank my parents, Al and Honey Hudson, for their many years of support and sacrifice on my behalf. Their love has been a foundation that has given me the resources to explore this work. Similarly, I want to thank my sisters, Meredith Van Withrow and Lorraine Mauro, as well as their families. I feel truly blessed to have had the opportunity to share this journey with such good friends.

I would also like to acknowledge the love and support of my dear friend, Gay Mehegan, as well as Sean, Eben, and Tara. At a time when I needed it most, Gay was there for me and helped me see what my life might really be about.

A number of other friends have played a critical role in guiding me along the path that led to this book. They offered feedback, counsel, caring, and emotional support in ways too numerous to mention. They include Mindi McAlister, Joan Clark, Richard Porter, Tucker Baldwin, Laura Lau, Jerry and Vivian Birdsall, Claes Lilja, Butch Taylor, Wendy Simmons, Mike and Marianne Eisenburger, Hal and Kathy Von Hoff, Lizzie Goren, Joe Hall, James Massenburg, Randy Nickerson, Joe Koproski, Russell Maynor, William Hicks, George Graham, Sonnie Starr, Budd Hopkins, Lori Fogler, Mark Reichard, Mark Kudlo, John Mack, Jerry Brewster, Alan and Cathy Fors, Gary and Linda Freed, Karen Miller, Maggie Cullen, Mellon Lovrin, Peter and Jamy Faust, the Puzones, the

Holifields, and the Coles. There are certainly many more, and my apologies to anyone I may have omitted.

Last, I would like especially to thank and acknowledge my teaching partner, coauthor, mentor, and my beloved friend, Don Richard Riso. I am moved again and again by Don's extraordinary generosity, humility, and unwavering support. He had faith in me when I had little faith in myself, and our relationship has been the vessel in which I have discovered what it means to be a true "Essence friend." He is that rare person in whom I can confide anything, and his sincerity and compassion have helped me weather some extremely difficult periods. I will always be grateful for the opportunity that he gave me to join him in this work, and pray that I will be able to live up to what I have been given. I feel as though some wonderful and mysterious destiny called us to the Enneagram and to each other's friendship, and I continue to be in awe of its gentle unfolding, each day of my life.

Russ Hudson
New York City
May 1996

Part I

Know then thyself, presume not God to scan;
The proper study of mankind is man.
            —Alexander Pope, *An Essay on Man*

Chapter 1

Understanding Personality Types

What is the point of understanding personality types? Since everyone is unique, the idea of cramming people into categories seems odious. And even if personality types were somehow theoretically valid, they would probably be either too academic to be helpful in our daily lives or too vague to be meaningful—grab bags anyone can read anything into.

These are valid objections, but they miss the mark. There are a number of good reasons to study personality types, the most important of which is that human beings are inherently interesting—and dangerous. Our fellow human beings compel our attention because they are easily the most changeable, infuriating, pleasurable, and mystifying objects in the environment. It would be impossible for most of us to spend a day without coming into direct or indirect contact with dozens of people—family, friends, people on the street, at the office, on television, in our fantasies, and in our fears. People are everywhere, having all sorts of impacts on us—for better or worse.

Most of the time we navigate the shoals of interpersonal life without coming to grief, but there have no doubt been times when we suddenly became aware that we did not really know the people we thought we knew. There may even have been times when we realized that we did not know ourselves. The behavior of others—and even our own behavior—is, at times, strange and unsettling. Odd things keep popping up, or seem to be out of place. Some of these surprises can be pleasant, but some are decidedly unpleasant, having calamitous effects upon us far into the future. This is why, if we are too unthinking about the personality types in which human nature expresses itself, we run the risk of disaster. The person we thought we knew may turn out to be a monster or hopelessly self-centered. We may find that we have been callously used or that our legitimate needs have been selfishly ignored. Unless we have insight, we can be terribly abused. The opposite is equally true: unless we have insight, we may overlook a diamond in the rough, or be too quick to get out of a relationship which is actually worth saving. Without insight, we may be hurt or foolish, and either way end in unhappiness.

Thus, becoming more perceptive is worthwhile, if only to avoid painful consequences. Understanding ourselves and others should make us happier.

The problem is, however, that while everyone wants insight into others, few people are as willing to look so intently at themselves. We want to know what makes other people tick, yet we are afraid to discover anything upsetting about ourselves. Today's competitive culture has shifted the emphasis of the ancient injunction of the oracle at Delphi from "know thyself" to "psych out the other guy." We would like to be able to figure out people as if we had X-ray vision, while not wanting others to see our weaknesses and shortcomings. We do not want anyone, including us, to see us as we really are. Unfortunately, something necessary and valuable—looking at ourselves with the same objective eye with which we view others—has been lost.

We have everything upside down. To correct this, we should remember Kierkegaard's advice. He suggested that we become subjective toward others and objective toward ourselves. That is, when we judge the actions of others, we should put ourselves in their place, trying to understand how they see themselves and their world. And when we judge ourselves, we should see ourselves as others see us, overcoming the ease with which we find extenuating circumstances for ourselves. Of course, Kierkegaard's suggestion is very difficult to put into practice. We need to cut through vanity and self-deception when we look at ourselves, as well as cynicism and defensiveness when we examine others. We must have courage toward ourselves and empathy toward others.

How can we acquire the knowledge and sensitivity we need? How can we begin to make sense of the vast diversity of human personality? How can we develop insight so that we can lead fuller, happier lives?

The answer is paradoxical: we will discover that we cannot really know anyone else until we know ourselves, and we cannot really know ourselves until we know others. The solution to this seeming conundrum is that understanding ourselves and understanding others are really two sides of the same coin—understanding human nature.

Because such a vast amount of territory is covered by human nature, it would be useful to have an accurate map of that familiar yet ever unexplored territory. It would be helpful to have a reliable means of charting who we are and where we are going so that we will not lose our way.

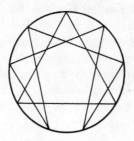

The Enneagram

We believe the Enneagram (pronounced "ANY-a-gram") is the map of human nature which people have long sought. Although the Enneagram symbol is ancient, as are many of the roots of its psychological theory, it is remarkably contemporary because human nature has not changed. The Enneagram, which has been transmitted to us from a variety of history's rich spiritual and philosophical traditions, represents a profound understanding of human nature, something needed as much now as it was in the past. The Enneagram presented here is a distillation of teachings from several profound schools of spiritual wisdom, combined with insights from modern psychology. It is at once ancient and modern, representing a marvelous and dynamic synthesis of old and new. The purpose of this book is to introduce the general reader to this remarkable system.

Psychology has been wrestling with the problem of discovering a workable personality typology (a way of classifying human nature) which is accurate and practical, theoretically comprehensive and elegant. Beginning at least with Hippocrates in the fifth century B.C., Greek philosophers recognized that personality types exist in some form or other. However, no one has been able to discover the *fundamental* categories which human nature assumes, the basic personality types themselves.

Different classifications have been proposed over the centuries, although none has been without problems, inaccuracies, or contradictions. Many typologies do not do justice to the great variety of human nature—they employ too few categories, they are too abstract, or they concern themselves only with different kinds of neurosis and not with normal behavior. Not only has discovering the individual personality types been an enormous conceptual problem, it has been even more difficult to discover a system which indicates how the types are related to each other, thereby revealing how people change and grow. Finding a personality typology which truly does justice to human nature was an unsolved problem— until the development of the Enneagram. That is the argument of this book.

Every psychological system has an organizing principle. If we look briefly at some other systems, we see, for example, that Freud's three different character types emphasize the belief that psychic energy is fixated during early child development around the mouth, the anus, or the genitals. These fixations yield oral, anal, and phallic types which correspond to Enneagram types. Another Freudian approach to character types emphasizes the dominance of the ego, the id, or the superego in the personality. The latter is a more sophisticated application of Freud's concepts, one which theorists have found difficult to apply, although it also correlates with the Enneagram, as we shall see.

Jung's typology delineates eight types based on how a person's psychological *attitude*, extroversion or introversion, is modified by one of four basic mental *functions* which Jung posits—feeling, thinking, sensation, or intuition. Thus, Jung describes an extroverted feeling type and an introverted feeling type, an extroverted thinking type and an introverted thinking type, and so on.

Karen Horney developed character descriptions based on her clinical observations of interpersonal orientations—that a person could be considered as fundamentally "moving toward others," "moving away from others," or "moving against others." She did not work out all of the subtypes within these three general categories, but had she done so, her system would probably have yielded nine personality types, just as the Enneagram does. (There will be more about Freud, Jung, and Horney in the Theory chapter, particularly about the correspondence of their typologies to the Enneagram personality types.)

The organizing principle of the Enneagram is simple: nine personality types result from three personality types in each of three groups, or Triads. The Enneagram's three Triads specify whether your fundamental psychological orientation, which includes positive and negative traits, has to do with your emotions and self-image (if so, you are in the *Feeling* Triad) or with your thought processes and how you find security (if so, you are in the *Thinking* Triad) or with your "gut" instincts and how you relate to the world (if so, you are in the *Instinctive* Triad).

We can characterize the resulting nine personality types very simply for now; they will become more sophisticated later on. In the Feeling Triad, the types are the *Helper* (the Two—the encouraging, demonstrative, possessive type), the *Motivator* (the Three—the ambitious, pragmatic, image-conscious type), and the *Individualist* (the Four—the sensitive, self-absorbed, depressive type). In the Thinking Triad, we see the *Investigator* (the Five—the perceptive, cerebral, provocative type), the *Loyalist* (the Six—the committed, dutiful, suspicious type), and the *Enthusiast* (the Seven—the spontaneous, fun-loving, excessive type). And in the Instinctive Triad, we find the *Leader* (the Eight—the self-confident, assertive, confrontational type), the *Peacemaker* (the Nine—the pleasant, easygoing, complacent type), and the *Reformer* (the One—the rational, idealistic, orderly type).

You may be able to find your own personality type from these brief designations. If not, do not worry. You will learn how to identify your personality type, or that of someone else, in the

Guidelines chapter. Since there is a full chapter about each of the nine basic personality types, there is much more to become acquainted with. (To get a quick idea of any of the personality types, turn to the Caricature and Profile at the beginning of each description. The Profile lists many of the major traits of each type.) There will also be more about the three Triads of the Enneagram and how they produce the nine basic personality types, and many personality subtypes, in the Guidelines, and even more about them in the Advanced Guidelines.

As you might expect, how the Enneagram works is complicated and subtle. Considering your personality type as an expression of one of the fundamental orientations (emotion, intellect, or instinct) is but one possible level of analysis with the Enneagram. By the end of this book you will see that we can approach the nine personality types from Freudian, Jungian, Hornevian, or other viewpoints, because the Enneagram operates on different levels of abstraction simultaneously. It bridges the gap between approaches to personality which emphasize depth psychology and those which emphasize behavior. The insights we can obtain from the Enneagram range from the most abstract generalizations about human nature to highly specific descriptions of each personality type. And yet, as complex as the Enneagram is, paradoxically, it is easy to understand.

Furthermore, while the nine personality types of the Enneagram form discrete categories, you should not think of them as ironclad entities. You will find that the Enneagram is open-ended and extraordinarily fluid, like human nature itself. Movement and change —development toward either integration or disintegration—are essential aspects of this remarkable system. And because the descriptions of the personality types given in this book range from the highest levels of health and integration to the lowest stages of neurosis, they not only describe behavior but predict it as well— something which can be extremely useful.

Because an introductory book should be relatively simple, it is not possible to present all the complexities of the Enneagram here. Many of the most advanced, theoretical aspects of the Enneagram have either been omitted or touched on only briefly.

We have also omitted specific suggestions about how you can use each of the personality descriptions themselves. Even so, interested readers will be able to apply the descriptions to many different situations in their lives. For example, psychologists and psychiatrists will be able to diagnose the problems of their clients more accurately—and those in therapy will be able to save time and money by gaining insight into themselves more quickly. The Enneagram will also give clients and therapists a common language with which to discuss their problems and their progress, no matter which school of psychotherapy they follow.

Lawyers will be better able to understand clients, as well as assess their credibility and their capacity to cooperate in legal matters. The Enneagram will help them particularly in situations such as divorce and child custody cases where personality factors are important. Physicians will have more insight with which to counsel their patients, particularly those whose physical ailments are compounded by psychological problems. Clergy can be more psychologically attuned to others in pastoral situations. While this book does not deal with spiritual direction as such, there are common areas between the psychological and the spiritual, since both build upon the whole person. Teachers can become more perceptive of their students. Different personality types have different natural aptitudes, different approaches to learning, and different ways of interacting with other students.

Personnel directors and businesspeople can become better managers by being more aware of their employees' personality types. Job satisfaction and productivity increase when employees feel that management understands their personal needs and takes them into consideration. Hiring officers and those in charge of building effective teams for all purposes—from the boardroom to the assembly line—will find it valuable to have greater insight into the personality types of the individuals they consider. Understanding personality types can also be useful to journalists, politicians, and those in advertising. In short, understanding personality types is useful to anyone who has a personality (and who does not?) or who is interested in the personalities of others (and who is not?).

Despite its many practical applications, however, this is really a book which has been written for you, the individual, to use in your personal life.

However, we should say that this is not a typical self-help book: it does not promise miracles. It is not possible to write a psychological "cookbook" for becoming a healthy, fulfilled individual. Becoming a whole human being is, by definition, a challenging process which goes on as long as we live. Books can provide valuable information and advice, they can give us new insights, they can encourage. But knowledge alone is not enough to change us. If it were, the most knowledgeable people would be the best people, and we know from our own experience that this is not so. Knowledge would be virtue, and it is not. Knowing more about ourselves is but a means toward a goal of being happy and leading a good life, but the possession of knowledge alone cannot bestow virtue, happiness, or fulfillment on us. Books cannot provide answers to all the problems which confront us or impart the courage necessary if we are to persevere in our search. For these things, we must look both within and beyond ourselves.

Furthermore, this book is not, and cannot be, the last word on either the Enneagram or personality types. There will always be more to be said, new connections to be made, and new understandings to be reached. Perhaps the mysteries of the psyche can never be fully described because they may never be fully understood. How can human beings stand outside of themselves to study human nature in a totally objective way? How can we ever be completely subjective toward others and objective toward ourselves, as Kierkegaard suggests? Psychologists who try to describe human nature are themselves human beings subject to all the distortions and self-deceptions of which humans are capable. No one has a "God's-eye view" of the whole of human nature, so no one can say with absolute confidence what it all means. This is why there will always be an element of faith to psychology, not necessarily religious faith, to be sure, but a set of beliefs about human beings which goes beyond what can be demonstrated scientifically.

This is why attaining some kind of final, objective truth about ourselves is probably impossible. What may be more important than arriving at ultimate answers is being searchers on the quest. Through the process of honestly seeking the truth about ourselves, we gradually liberate ourselves from many painful and limiting behaviors and beliefs about who we are. Thus, gradually and in ways we do not expect, we are transformed into persons who are fuller, more life-affirming, and self-transcending.

Chapter 2

Origins

One of the main problems with introducing the Enneagram is that its exact origins are lost to history. No one really knows precisely who discovered it or where it came from. Some writers maintain that the Enneagram first surfaced among certain orders of the Sufi, a mystical sect of Islam which began in the tenth and eleventh centuries; others speculate that it may have originated as long ago as 2500 B.C. in Babylon or elsewhere in the Middle East. But these are mere speculations.

It seems that men have always been in search of the secret of perpetual self-renewal. We find it in one of the oldest legends preserved by man: in the story of Gilgamesh the Sumerian hero and his pilgrimage in search of the secret of immortality. At about the time that the Gilgamesh epic was compiled from earlier song, some 4,500 years ago, there arose in Mesopotamia a brotherhood of wise men who discovered the cosmic secret of perpetual self-renewal and passed it down from generation to generation. For a long time it was preserved in Babylon: 2,500 years ago it was revealed to Zoroaster, Pythagoras and other great sages who congregated in Babylon at the time of Cambyses (the Persian king who conquered Egypt in 524 B.C.). Then the custodians of the tra-

dition migrated northward and about a thousand years ago reached
Bokhara [in what is now Uzbekistan] across the river Oxus.

In the fifteenth century, [Islamic] mathematicians trained in
their schools discovered the significance of the number zero and
created the decimal system which all the world uses now. It was
observed at the time that a new kind of number appeared when
one was divided by three or seven. This we now call a recurring
decimal. . . .

These properties were combined in a symbol that proved to
have amazing significance. It could be used to represent every
process that maintains itself by self-renewal, including of course,
life itself. The symbol consists of nine lines and is therefore
called the Enneagram. (J. G. Bennett, *Enneagram Studies*, 1–3.)*

Ennea is the Greek word for nine, so *Enneagram* is a Greek word
roughly meaning "a nine diagram." A plausible conjecture about
its origins is that the Enneagram is based on ancient mathematical
discoveries—Pythagorean and Neo-Platonic, or earlier—and was
passed on to the West with other Greek and Arabic learning during
the fourteenth or fifteenth centuries by the Moslems. It is said to
have been used at this time by the Islamic mystics, the Sufis, particularly by the Naqshbandi Brotherhood. If the Enneagram did not
appear in its present form when the Sufis came across it, they may
have developed it according to discoveries in Arabic mathematics
and used it to advance self-knowledge for individuals within their
secret brotherhoods and as a way of establishing harmony in society at large.

I concluded . . . that this symbol and the ideas for which it stands,
originated with the Sarmān [or "Sarmoun" Brotherhood, a wisdom school reputedly in Babylon] society about 2,500 years ago
and was revised when the power of the Arabic numeral system
was developed in Samarkand in the fifteenth century. . . .

There are endless possibilities of interpretation of this remarkable symbol. The simplest is given by numbering the points on
the circumference from 1–9 which gives the triangle numbers 3,
6 and 9, and the hexagon 1–4–2–8–5–7 which is the well-known

---

*Citations for this and all other quotations are given in the Bibliography.

recurrent sequence that gives the remainder when any integer is divided by seven. This property arises only in a decimal number system, which suggests that it was discovered only after the mathematicians of Central Asia had founded the modern theory of numbers by giving zero a separate symbol. Whereas the belief that the number seven is sacred probably goes back to Sumerian times, the form of the enneagram is likely to have been developed in Samarkand in the fourteenth century. This would account for its absence from Indian or European literature. However, Gurdjieff asserted that it was far more ancient and attributed it to the Sarmān Brotherhood. Both versions may be true. (J. G. Bennett, *Gurdjieff: Making a New World*, 293–294.)

While some ideas related to the Enneagram and the Enneagram symbol itself can be found in a few Sufi orders, it is by no means common to all Sufi traditions. In fact, most Sufi orders have never heard of it. Further, it is worth mentioning that the term *Sufi* is used to describe a wide variety of esoteric schools within the Islamic world. These schools range from North Africa in the West to Pakistan in the East, and contain philosophical and practical approaches as diverse as the cultures and geography in which they are found.

There is much to suggest, however, that the origins of the Enneagram and the system of types are not Sufi, and certainly not Islamic. The symbol and its roots seem to have been used much earlier, as Gurdjieff and Bennett suggest. More likely, some Sufi schools preserved the Enneagram and related ideas in much the same way that the Christian monasteries of Europe preserved the classical thought and literature of ancient Greece and Rome. If this is true, calling the Enneagram Sufi is like calling Aristotle and Greek mythology Christian. It is probable that some of the Sufi brotherhoods used the symbol and found it intriguing enough to pass on to subsequent generations, but they did not invent it.

More likely sources of the system can be traced to early teachings in the Judeo-Christian tradition and in early Greek philosophy. The symbol itself, with its fascinating geometry and its basis in the mathematics of ratio and proportion, strongly suggests Greek roots, particularly the teachings of Pythagoras, the founder of a philosophical school which flourished in the fourth and fifth centuries B.C.

Oscar Ichazo, the inventor of the modern Enneagram, supports this view of the Enneagram's lineage, as will be discussed later in this chapter.

While the origins of the Enneagram symbol are elusive, the remote origins of the nine personality types are better documented. The first and most important source of the types comes from the idea of the Seven Deadly Sins, with the addition of two other "sins" to bring the total to nine. The seven deadly sins, which include pride, envy, anger, gluttony, avarice, lust, and sloth, were part of the teachings of medieval Christianity, and were studied and commented on extensively throughout Europe. But even this traditional concept has branches and older roots. Other early sources which seem related to this system can be found in the Kabbala, an ancient body of mystical teachings from the Jewish tradition, the works of the Neo-Platonic philosophers, and the teachings of the Desert Fathers, early Christian ascetics who probably originated the concept of the seven deadly sins.

No matter how or where these various bodies of knowledge were used by the Desert Fathers or the secret brotherhoods of the Sufis, the Enneagram symbol was totally unknown in the West until quite recently. The credit for transmitting the symbol to the West goes to George Ivanovich Gurdjieff (ca. 1877–1949), an adventurer, spiritual teacher, and seeker of what might be called practical secret knowledge about human nature. Despite the many books written about his life and the many investigations into the sources of his teachings, Gurdjieff still remains an enigma: some people think that he was little more than a charlatan, while others feel that his importance as a spiritual guide and practical psychologist has been vastly underrated. It is difficult to get to the truth of these opposing opinions, since Gurdjieff was secretive about his activities, purposely cultivating a charismatic and mysterious aura about himself. What is undoubtedly true, however, is that he had a profound impact upon everyone who met him. His students have been debating about him and the meaning of his vast, complex system of thought since he died.

Although Gurdjieff was unclear about how and where he discovered the Enneagram, it was nevertheless through his transmission that the Enneagram became known in Europe in the 1910s and 1920s, first at group lectures in St. Petersburg and Moscow prior to the Russian Revolution, and later at his school outside Paris near

Fontainebleau, the Institute for the Harmonious Development of Man. The Enneagram was subsequently transmitted, along with the rest of Gurdjieff's teachings, through small private study groups in Paris, London, New York, and around the world.

In his book *The Harmonious Circle*, about Gurdjieff and his immediate group of students, James Webb attempts to sort out the facts of the Enneagram's history.

The most important use which Gurdjieff made of number symbolism is the figure of the enneagram, which he said contained and symbolized his whole System. His enneagram consists of a circle with the circumference divided into nine points which are joined to give a triangle and an irregular six-sided figure. Gurdjieff said that the triangle represented the presence of higher forces and that the six-sided figure stood for man. He also claimed that the enneagram was exclusive to his teaching. "This symbol cannot be met with anywhere in the study of 'occultism,' either in books or in oral transmission," Ouspensky reports him as saying. "It was given such significance by those who knew [i.e., by his Sufi teachers], that they considered it necessary to keep the knowledge of it secret."

Because of the emphasis which Gurdjieff placed on this diagram, his followers have sought high and low for the symbol in occult literature. [J. G.] Bennett claims that it cannot be found anywhere; and if disciples of Gurdjieff have in fact discovered the figure, they have kept it very quiet. (Webb, 505.)*

---

*This is not the place for a lengthy bibliography on Gurdjieff or his work; the interested reader will have no problem finding information about him. For full and critical accounts of Gurdjieff, see Webb, *The Harmonious Circle*, and Moore, *Gurdjieff: The Anatomy of a Myth*. Also see Kathleen Riordan Speeth, *The Gurdjieff Work*, 9, forwarding the Sufi origin of the Enneagram among the Naqshbandi Brotherhood, and Speeth and Friedlander, *Gurdjieff, Seeker of the Truth*, for an informative account of Gurdjieff's travels in the Near East in search of wisdom. Also see P. D. Ouspensky, *In Search of the Miraculous*, 286–290, and Maurice Nicoll, *Psychological Commentaries on the Teaching of Gurdjieff and Ouspensky*, vol. 2, 379 ff., for more on the Enneagram, its structure, and particularly the esoteric meaning of the numerical sequence (1–4–2–8–5–7–1), and related matters. For an attempt at applying the Enneagram to topics other than personality, see J. G. Bennett, *Enneagram Studies*, cited above. Those interested in a strictly Gurdjieffian viewpoint will find this book of interest.

Gurdjieff was perhaps purposely unclear about the origins of the Enneagram because one of his teaching methods was to make everything difficult for his students so they would discover as much as possible on their own. Whatever the truth of the matter, as Webb continues to examine the Enneagram's historical sources, he makes an interesting discovery.

> The enneagram forms the center of the magnificent frontispiece to the *Arithmologia* published in Rome by the Jesuit priest, Athanasius Kircher, in 1665. Kircher (1601–80) is a figure of great significance for the origins of Gurdjieff's ideas. He was typical of the Renaissance man of learning and a prototype of the scholarly Jesuit of later days. . . .
>   In the *Arithmologia*, there is a figure called an "enneagram" composed of three equilateral triangles. (Webb, *The Harmonious Circle*, 505–507.)

Although Webb calls Kircher's figure an "enneagram," it is important to note that it is comprised of three equilateral triangles and is not Gurdjieff's single equilateral triangle with an inner hexagon. This makes a crucial difference, but having noted the difference, Webb glosses over its significance.

Webb continues with a discussion of the Kabbala and the occultist Ramon Lull, then moves on to a discussion of esoteric Christianity, esoteric Buddhism, the occult revival of the nineteenth century in Europe and Russia, including Rosicrucianism, and to other movements, all of which Webb speculates, and in some instances is able to show, had various degrees of influence on Gurdjieff. But at the end of this lengthy discussion, which is certainly beyond the scope of this book even to condense, Webb seems to have lost sight of his attempt to explain the origins of the Enneagram in Gurdjieff's thought and has gone on to other matters.

And in any event, investigating Gurdjieff's sources for the Enneagram, while historically interesting, is something of a digression, since Gurdjieff's delineation of "type" seems only tangentially related to the nine personality types of the Enneagram described here. There is a correspondence between Gurdjieff's "Man Number One, Man Number Two, and Man Number Three"* and

---

*Speeth.

the three Triads of the Enneagram, the Instinctive Triad, Feeling Triad, and Thinking Triad, respectively, but that is as far as it goes. Many of Gurdjieff's fascinating ideas are very relevant to the psychology underlying the current Enneagram system, although they do not directly address a theory of nine types. Central among these is the relationship between the *personality*, the learned or acquired part of a person's behavior and identity, and the *essence*, the innate part of human nature which needs to be addressed for real transformation to occur. (The relationship between the nine Enneagram types and this important topic will be discussed in a future book.)

Despite a number of tantalizing connections and references, it is clear that whatever Gurdjieff knew about type was not transmitted to his students in any complete form, and *was never linked with the Enneagram symbol*. Most of what Gurdjieff taught about the Enneagram was transmitted to his students through sacred dances and movements which were created to give the dancer an inner sense or impression of the dynamism of this diagram. Gurdjieff repeatedly asserted that the Enneagram was a "living symbol" and therefore in constant motion. His teachings on the diagram explain it as a symbol combining three universal laws which can be used for a complete understanding of any particular independent entity or process. (For a definitive discussion of the Gurdjieffian view of the Enneagram symbol, see the references to Ouspensky and Nicoll cited in the footnote on page 15.) Thus, while we must credit Gurdjieff with first making the Enneagram symbol known in the West, and for synthesizing a tremendous body of psychological insights which can be extremely useful and relevant to the study of the Enneagram, saying anything more about his particular interpretation of it at this time would lead us far afield.*

The delineation of the nine personality types presented in this book derives in part from work done on the Enneagram by Oscar Ichazo, the founder of the Arica Institute. While Ichazo agrees with Gurdjieff that the Enneagram is ancient, he has attributed his theories about it to a variety of sources, primarily the Hebrew Kabbala and

---

*For more about Gurdjieff's interpretation of personality types, see Webb, *The Harmonious Circle*, 139 ff., and Speeth, *The Gurdjieff Work*, 31 ff.

Neo-Platonic philosophy, and, to our knowledge, he is the sole originator of the Enneagram of personality types.*

In a rare interview ("The Enneagram Wars," Michael Goldberg, *LA Weekly*, October 15–21, 1993), Ichazo commented on the sources which he drew upon in developing the Enneagram types, or *ego fixations*, as he has called them. He was quick to emphasize that the system was not Sufi in origin. "I know Sufism extensively . . . and I know realized Sufi sheiks. It is not part of their theoretical framework. They couldn't care less about the Enneagon."

In the same interview, Ichazo states rather plainly the sources which inspired his discovery of the modern Enneagram.

> To begin with, Plotinus' Enneads [a Neo-Platonist work from the second century B.C.] hit me with almost inconceivable strength. It describes the nine mystical states, the origin of the doctrines that are studied in the Kabbala as the 10 Sephirot [the ten primary components of the Kabbalistic "Tree of Life," said to be a map of divine and human consciousness]. . . . From there, I went immediately to Pythagoras. I saw Pythagoras from the point of view of the Kabbala. And at that point I really started developing my theory of the Enneagons.

The modern Enneagram, therefore, seems to be the result of Ichazo's brilliant synthesis of a number of related systems of thought about the nature and structure of human consciousness, brought together in the enigmatic Enneagram symbol. It is best described as a contemporary and evolving theory of human nature based on a variety of time-honored sources and traditions. At the same time, it is quite clear that there is no single body of knowledge, no continuous "oral tradition" of the Enneagram handed down from antiquity. Rather, many traditions and innovations, both modern and ancient, have gone into the creation of this remarkable system.

*For more about Ichazo's approach to the Enneagram, see Sam Keen, "We have no desire to strengthen the ego or make it happy," reprinted from *Psychology Today*, July 1973, in *Interviews with Oscar Ichazo*, 8 ff.; Dorothy De Christopher, "I am the root of a new tradition," in *Interviews with Oscar Ichazo*, 144 ff.; John C. Lilly and Joseph E. Hart, "The Arica Training," in *Transpersonal Psychologies*, 333 ff. This article is highly recommended to anyone who is interested in Ichazo's interpretation of the Enneagram. Another significant glimpse of Ichazo's views can be found in an interview and article by Michael Goldberg, originally printed in *LA Weekly*, October 15–21, 1993, entitled "The Enneagram Wars."

Ichazo's focus and contribution has been the assignment of the nine "ego fixations" and "passions" around the Enneagram and the offering of practices which he claims will help students open up the latent spiritual capacities locked in the ego structure of each type. These nine passions are based on the seven deadly sins, with two more passions bringing the total to nine. According to Ichazo, the One's passion is Anger, the Two's is Pride, the Four's is Envy, the Five's is Avarice, the Seven's is Gluttony, the Eight's is Lust, and the Nine's is Sloth. To Type Three, he assigned the passion of Deceit, and to type Six, that of Fear.

Ichazo first began teaching the Enneagram at the Institute for Applied Psychology in La Paz, Bolivia, as part of his larger system of human development, and later, in the 1960s, taught in Arica, Chile. Ichazo came to the United States in 1971, founded the Arica Institute, and continued teaching. According to its brochure, the Arica Institute "teaches a science of human development which systematically develops the full potential of a human being. It synthesizes Eastern mysticism and Western psychological traditions to present a body of theory and method precisely designed to deal with the realities and stresses of our technological society." Among those who first learned Ichazo's system were Americans from the Esalen Institute in Big Sur, California, including John Lilly, M.D., and psychiatrist Claudio Naranjo, M.D.*

The seminal work on the Enneagram, as it is now known, is Ichazo's original work. Having found no clear antecedents, we support his contentions and wish to give him full credit for the tremendous discovery of combining the core ideas of the nine types with the Enneagram symbol in the correct sequence and combination. Ichazo, who calls the symbol the Enneagon, places the system within a larger context of a complete spiritual teaching as did Gurdjieff. There is great wisdom in this perspective, and we agree that studying the Enneagram outside of a serious commitment to psychological growth and spiritual practice will lead to limited results, at best. Nonetheless, it is our hope that this system will help individuals understand themselves, recognize the pitfalls of their type, and maybe stimulate a real interest in some of the more profound implications of Enneagram theory and practice.

*See John Lilly, *The Center of the Cyclone*, 126 ff., for a treatment of his encounter with Ichazo.

However, the interpretation of the Enneagram presented here diverges from Ichazo's perspective approach on a number of important points, particularly in attempting to make the "ego fixations" (as Ichazo calls the personality types) more comprehensive and accessible, as well as to bring the personality types into clearer coherence with modern psychology.

Ichazo's approach to the Enneagram and our approach are really quite different. Ichazo's interpretation of the Enneagram includes material on the ego fixations, "traps" of each ego fixation, the "holy ideas," the passions and virtues, the physical organs and systems of the body as they relate to attaining enlightenment, the "mentations" (symbolic ways of thinking about the body), astrological signs, mantras, and much more, which we do not go into. Furthermore, the basic descriptions of the types as taught in Ichazo's Arica school, and those taught by other contemporary Enneagram teachers, are significantly different. Those who wish to learn more about Ichazo's approach can find Arica groups and publications in most large North American cities.

The next link in the transmission of the Enneagram was certainly Claudio Naranjo, M.D., a noted Chilean-born psychiatrist, who was a member of the first group from Esalen to join Ichazo in Arica, Chile, in 1970. Here, along with many other aspects of Ichazo's philosophical system, he was introduced to the Enneagram, and on his return to the United States he began to teach it to a private group of individuals in Berkeley, California, who, like himself, were deeply interested in exploring techniques for developing and expanding human consciousness. He called this group SAT, an acronym for Seekers After Truth, a name borrowed from and in tribute to a group started by Gurdjieff in the early days of his search.

Naranjo is generally credited with expanding the descriptions of the Enneagram types and finding correlations between them and known psychiatric categories. He did this by organizing the participants at his lectures into groups, based on what he or they knew of their psychological profiles, and using his skills as a psychiatrist and his experience as a Gestalt therapist to interview them and elicit information that might illuminate his understanding of the types. This eventually evolved into the method of using panels of exemplars to illustrate various aspects of the types in Enneagram workshops.

Also in the early 1970s, several American Jesuit priests—most notably the Reverend Robert Ochs, S.J.— learned the material from Claudio Naranjo and his SAT group. Ochs taught it to other Jesuits at Loyola University in Chicago, and from there it spread quickly. Shortly thereafter, the Jesuits began to adapt the Enneagram to their counseling needs for the seminarians and laymen with whom they came into contact. Before the Jesuits became involved with the Enneagram, as far as we can tell, short impressionistic descriptions of the nine types began to be passed around throughout North America. It was only in 1972–1973 that the first brief notes on the personality types were written down and taught in informal seminars at Jesuit theological centers, particularly those at the University of California at Berkeley and Loyola University, Chicago. It was at this point that Don Richard Riso encountered the early Enneagram material. He recalls:

When I encountered the Enneagram in 1974 in Toronto, Canada, the core of the "Jesuit material" consisted of nine one-page impressionistic sketches of the personality types. These pages contained the seeds of this book.

At first I was skeptical about what I saw of the Enneagram. Like most newcomers, I especially disliked being pigeonholed by others who—rather too quickly for my taste—assigned one of the "Sufi numbers" to me. At the time, I was a Jesuit seminarian studying theology at the University of Toronto, and the other Jesuits with whom I lived referred to the Enneagram personality types as the "Sufi numbers" rather than to personality type One, Two, Three, and so forth. They used the Enneagram to get a quick fix on each other much as they might have used astrological signs had they been inclined to that ancient typology.

My first impression was that the Enneagram, like much that was coming out of California in the 1970s, was a fad, and I resisted becoming involved with it. But as I listened to people talk about the Sufi numbers, I began to be intrigued; soon I was able to see beyond the glib use of the system to the genuine insights it contained.

My "conversion" to the Enneagram came suddenly. In the winter of 1974 I woke up one morning before dawn and, for no particular reason, reached for the loose-leaf binder in which I had collected information on the Enneagram from other Jesuits. Back under the blankets, I began to read in earnest, concentrating for the first time on the nine impressionistic sketches of the personality types. I was soon able to spot my own type among them, and before long I began to gain some insights into the personalities of the other seminarians, my family, and friends. When I finally got out of bed a couple of hours later, I realized that there was more to this system than I had thought, and I wanted to know more about it.

Even though many of the details of the Enneagram as a psychological system had not been worked out, I was still able to intuit the essential correctness of the personality types. The Enneagram seemed to categorize people in a way which made sense. For the first time in my life, I could see that there actually are "personality types"—that while people are unique, they also belong to a larger class of which they are particular examples, like different kinds of primates in the animal kingdom. I felt that I no longer was at the mercy of the unknown: it was possible for me to see more deeply into people by understanding which personality type an individual belongs to. This was a revelation.

I was not alone in my enthusiasm for the Enneagram. As more people became acquainted with it, interest in the Enneagram grew. Some Jesuits taught it to their friends and acquaintances informally, while others began to include presentations of the Enneagram on the roster of offerings at retreat houses. Awareness of the Enneagram quickly began to spread beyond Jesuits to other religious and nonreligious circles throughout the United States, Canada, and Europe, particularly among human potential groups. Nevertheless, what was still lacking was a clear conception of how the Enneagram worked, as well as a more accurate description of the personality types themselves.

Since the Enneagram seemed to be valid, I thought that it must be consistent with the findings of modern psychology, because both were trying to describe the same thing—human beings. After using the Enneagram in my personal life for about two years, I was sufficiently convinced of its validity and usefulness to attempt to interpret it according to modern psychology.

I soon found that correlating the Jesuit Sufi numbers to psychology would be difficult for a number of reasons. The development and transmission of the Enneagram has been a long and mysterious affair. There was no one source or tradition to consult. Indeed, it became clear to me that the three main sources of the Enneagram that I was working with—Gurdjieff, Ichazo, and the Jesuits—were quite different. Furthermore, when I began to work full time on the Enneagram in 1975, very little had been written about it.

A diagram of the lines of transmission which we have seen so far may help to clarify the history of the Enneagram.

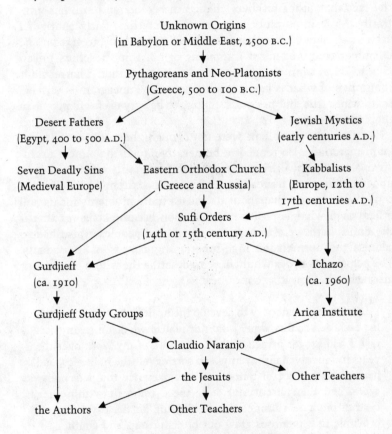

Unknown Origins
(in Babylon or Middle East, 2500 B.C.)

Pythagoreans and Neo-Platonists
(Greece, 500 to 100 B.C.)

Desert Fathers
(Egypt, 400 to 500 A.D.)

Jewish Mystics
(early centuries A.D.)

Seven Deadly Sins
(Medieval Europe)

Eastern Orthodox Church
(Greece and Russia)

Kabbalists
(Europe, 12th to
17th centuries A.D.)

Sufi Orders
(14th or 15th century A.D.)

Gurdjieff
(ca. 1910)

Ichazo
(ca. 1960)

Gurdjieff Study Groups

Arica Institute

Claudio Naranjo

the Jesuits

Other Teachers

the Authors

Other Teachers

The Transmission of the Enneagram

Finding material on the Enneagram was not the only difficulty. As different teachers presented the material, beginning in the 1970s, they usually added something of their own as they passed it on to their students. Students in turn frequently became teachers of the Enneagram and they also added their insights. For better or worse, the material was constantly changing, and many different interpretations began to emerge, even within the Jesuit stream of transmission.

While some of these additions represented an advance in understanding the personality types, others did not. For example, some teachers specify certain colors and animals to symbolize each of the types, an approach which may be poetically allusive were it not for the fact that other teachers change the colors and animals arbitrarily. More important, different interpretations flatly contradict each other about basics, such as the Directions of Integration and Disintegration, and most important of all, some teachers misattribute traits from one personality type to another. The result is that much of what is being taught about the Enneagram is garbled: it still rings true, but not quite enough to be very useful to people in their daily lives.

As if all these problems were not enough, the traditional Enneagram materials also tended to be negative, focusing almost exclusively on the unhealthy aspects of each personality type. Of course, understanding our unhealthy tendencies is extremely helpful, because what is negative about us causes more problems for us and others than what is positive. But it soon became apparent that if the Enneagram were to become valuable to people, it also had to address the normal and high-functioning aspects of individuals. The personality types would have to describe the whole person, not just neurosis. Don Riso continues:

> I therefore decided to try to develop the healthy and average traits for each personality type. I did not realize what a monumental task I had set for myself. Indeed, the bulk of my work over the years has involved discovering and sorting out the hundreds, and perhaps thousands, of traits which characterize the personality types, and then discovering how those traits fit within each type to produce a unified whole. Relying on the psychological principle that neuroses grow out of distortions and conflicts in *normal* modes of behavior, I eventually discovered how the healthy, average, and unhealthy traits form a *continuum of traits* for each type (which is the Levels of Development). (There will be more about the continuum in the next chapter, which gives guidelines to the basic theory of the Enneagram.)

In short, I have retained the essence of the Enneagram—its delineation of the nine personality types—while remaining skeptical of the many garbled interpretations and misattributions which have accumulated around it. I have also eliminated some of the more esoteric elements which were originally part of the traditional teaching, along with whatever interpretations seemed to be neither useful nor accurate.

What did not make sense or what was not helpful has not been retained. Even so, the more I cleared away the accretions surrounding the Enneagram, the more obvious it was that this typology deserved to be more widely known and used.

Finally, there is, at present, no scientific proof for the nine personality types. I have not done any formal research on them other than to use my own observation, intuition, and reading. It has been said that psychology is as much an art as it is a science, and my interests lie more on the humanistic side of the truth of psychology than in its scientific proof.

Each body of knowledge has its own kind of proof. The proof of the truth of a proposition about art is certainly different from that of a proposition about history, just as history's proof is different from that of physics and the other hard sciences. The proof of the Enneagram's accuracy lies not so much in empirical validation as in its ability to describe people in a way which deepens their understanding of themselves and others. In the last analysis, either the descriptions of the personality types in this book have "the ring of truth" about them or they do not; either the Enneagram makes sense in your own experience or it does not. Those who take the time will find themselves in these pages. You will experience a shock of recognition when you discover your own personality type—the most important proof there is of the Enneagram's accuracy.

Some rather good advice comes from Gurdjieff about all esoteric systems. It also applies to a good deal of psychology—and, of course, to the Enneagram.

The fact of the matter is that in occult literature much that has been said is superfluous and untrue. You had better forget all this. All your researches in this area were a good exercise for your mind; therein lies their great value, but only there. They have not given you knowledge. . . . Judge everything from the point of

view of your common sense. Become the possessor of your own
sound ideas and don't accept anything on faith; and when you,
your self, by way of sound reasoning and argument, come to an
unshakable persuasion, to a full understanding of something, you
will have achieved a certain degree of initiation. (Quoted in
Webb, *The Harmonious Circle*, 500.)

It is worthwhile applying Gurdjieff's advice to this book: "Become the possessor of your own sound ideas and don't accept anything on faith." If the Enneagram is to have value in your life, it
will be because *you* have worked through it and made it a part of
yourself. If you find yourself in these pages—if these descriptions
ring true in your own experience—then the effort which has gone
into them will have been worthwhile.

Chapter 3

Guidelines

It is necessary to know merely a handful of concepts to understand how the Enneagram works. Because many distinctions are required to describe personality types, however, the theory of the Enneagram is ultimately subtle and complex. This chapter is not concerned with all the nuances of the Enneagram; instead, it will introduce you to the practical points you must know in order to understand and make use of the descriptions.

The explanations in this chapter have purposely been kept as simple as possible. They will introduce you to the more complex ideas which will be discussed at the end of the book in chapters 13 and 14, Advanced Guidelines and The Theory of the Enneagram.

The Structure of the Enneagram
Although the Enneagram may look confusing at first glance, its structure is actually simple. There are nine equidistant points on the circumference of the circle. Each point is designated by a number from one to nine, with nine at the top, by convention and for symmetry. Each point represents one of the nine basic personality types. They are interrelated with each other in certain specific ways, as indicated by the inner lines of the Enneagram. It will help you to understand how the Enneagram is constructed if you sketch it yourself.

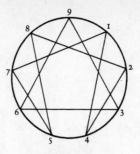

The Enneagram

Note that points Three, Six, and Nine form an equilateral triangle. The remaining six points are connected in the following order: One connects with Four, Four with Two, Two with Eight, Eight with Five, Five with Seven, and Seven with One. These six points form an irregular hexagram. The meaning of these sequences of numbers will be discussed shortly.

The Triads

On the simplest level of analysis, the Enneagram is an arrangement of nine personality types *in three Triads*. There are three personality types in the *Feeling Triad*, three in the *Thinking Triad*, and three in the *Instinctive Triad*, as shown below. Each Triad consists of three personality types which are best characterized by the assets and liabilities of that Triad. For example, personality type Two has particular strengths and liabilities involving its feelings, which is why it is one of the three types in the Feeling Triad. The Seven's assets and liabilities involve thinking, which is why it is in the Thinking Triad, and so forth for all nine personality types.

The three personality types of each Triad are not arbitrary. Each type results from a "dialectic," consisting of a thesis, antithesis, and synthesis, of the psychological faculty characterizing that Triad. In each Triad, one of the types overexpresses the characteristic faculty of the Triad, another type underexpresses the faculty, and the third is most out of touch with the faculty. These relationships are depicted in the illustration that follows.

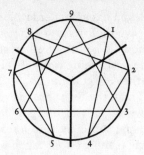

The Triads of the Enneagram

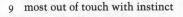

9 most out of touch with instinct

8 overexpresses instinct   1 underexpresses instinct

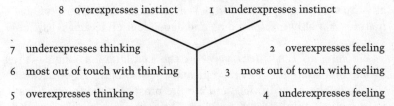

7 underexpresses thinking   2 overexpresses feeling

6 most out of touch with thinking   3 most out of touch with feeling

5 overexpresses thinking   4 underexpresses feeling

The Dialectical Structure of the Triads

By going around the Enneagram Triad by Triad, you will see what this means. For example, in the Feeling Triad, the Two has overexpressed its feelings, expressing only its positive emotions while repressing its negative ones, sometimes histrionically or even hysterically. The Three is most out of touch with its feelings, suppressing them in order to function more effectively and to make a favorable impression on others. The Four has underdeveloped the personal expression of its feelings, revealing itself indirectly through some form of art or aesthetic living. Further, the Four's feelings are highly influenced by and dependent on thinking about their feelings.

In the Thinking Triad, the Five's ability to think is overexpressed: it substitutes thinking for doing, endlessly preoccupied with ever more complex, yet isolated, thoughts. The Six is most out of touch with its own thoughts, thus Sixes look for reassurance and confirmation about what they think, or tend to get stuck in circular thinking patterns that have no grounding in their immediate experience. And the Seven has an underdeveloped thinking style, in that Sevens tend to leave their trains of thought incomplete. They do not finish one thought before another grabs their attention. Also, the Seven's style of thinking is highly dependent on activity, on anticipating what they are going to do.

In the Instinctive Triad, the Eight has overdeveloped its instinctive responses to the world, moving on "gut" hunches and powerful reactions but not pausing sufficiently to foresee the consequences of its actions. The Nine is most out of touch with its instincts, and thus its ability to relate to the environment in an immediate way. Nines disengage from their instinctive drives and from their reactions to the world so as to maintain an inner stability and peace. And the One has underdeveloped its instinctive responses, repressing them with a strict, superego-driven conscience. Instinct is usually the source of drive that propels people into action, but in Ones, instinct is highly influenced by and dependent on feelings, particularly anger.

We refer to the three types on the equilateral triangle—the Three, Six, and Nine—as the "primary" personality types because they have the most trouble and are the most blocked in some way with feeling, thinking, or instinct. The remaining six personality types—the One, Four, Two, Eight, Five, and Seven on the hexagram—are the "secondary" types because they are more mixed and not as out of touch with feeling, thinking, or instinct. In the Advanced Guidelines we will see more of what this means and why making this distinction is important.

No matter which Triad the basic personality type is in, everyone has the ability to feel, think, and respond instinctively to the environment. We become one of the nine personality types because our sense of self, our ego, beginning in early childhood, has become more identified with one faculty than with the remaining two. But this does not mean that the remaining two faculties are not also a part of us. They are, and we are who we are because all three faculties operate in an ever changing balance to produce our personality.

Focusing on your basic personality type within its Triad is but the first place to begin the process of self-understanding. Many other factors are also part of the picture, however, because the Enneagram is, at its most abstract, a universal mandala of the self—a symbol of each of us.

The Basic Personality Type

The simplest way to think of the Enneagram is as a configuration of nine distinct personality types, with each number on the Enneagram denoting one type. Everyone has emerged from his or her childhood as a unique member of *one* of the personality types, and his or her psychological potentials have either developed or deteriorated from that starting point.

The personality types, and their relationships with each other, can be represented schematically. One of the nine points on the circumference of the Enneagram denotes a particular personality type which characterizes you more fully and accurately than any other type. This is your *basic personality type*, which you will be able to identify shortly.

It is commonly accepted by psychologists that personality is highly influenced by the relationship a child has had with its parents or other significant persons. By the time the child is four or five years old, its consciousness has developed enough for it to have a separate sense of self. Although its identity is still very fluid, a child at this age is beginning to establish itself and find ways of fitting into the world on its own. Doubtless, there are hereditary factors which predispose a child to have (practically from birth) a certain temperament, as the physical basis of personality is called. However, science has not been able to say precisely what genetics are involved, and in any event, each basic personality type of the Enneagram represents the overall way in which the child has unconsciously adapted itself to its family and the world. In short, which basic personality type a person has represents the total outcome of all childhood factors that have gone into the formation of the child's personality, including genetics. Since there is more about the childhood origins of each personality type in the descriptions and in the Theory chapter, we will not go into any detail about them here.

However, several more points should be made about the basic personality type itself. First, people do not change from one basic personality type to another. Each person is a unique individual within that larger group and, in the last analysis, remains that type for the rest of his or her life. In reality, people do change in many ways throughout their lives, but their basic personality type does not change.

Second, the descriptions of the personality types are universal and apply equally to males and females, since no type is inherently masculine or feminine. Questions about sexual roles and purely biologically based sexual differences are important, but they are beyond the scope of this book. In any event, much of what we associate with masculinity or femininity results from cultural expectations and learned behaviors which are not inherent in human nature.

Third, not everything in the description of your basic type will apply to you all the time. This is because people fluctuate among the healthy, average, and unhealthy traits that make up their personality type. For example, if you are fundamentally healthy, the unhealthy traits will not be applicable, and vice versa. However, as you get to know yourself more objectively, you will recognize that all the traits of your personality type are genuine tendencies inherent in yourself. If you were to become healthy or unhealthy, you would do so in the way the Enneagram predicts.

Fourth, as we have seen, the Enneagram uses *numbers* to designate each of the personality types. There are several things to understand about the use of numbers. The principal reason for their use is that they are indeterminate. Because they are value neutral, they imply the whole range of traits for each type without indicating anything either positive or negative about it. Using numbers is an unbiased, shorthand way of indicating a lot about a person. Unlike the diagnostic labels used in psychiatry, numbers are helpful without being pejorative.

In psychiatric terminology, for example, personality types are always designated by their pathological characteristics: the obsessive type, the depressive type, the psychopathic type, the antisocial type, and so forth. While the Enneagram encompasses the pathological aspects of each personality type, it also indicates the healthy and average traits—and it is clearly not appropriate to use pathological labels for average or healthy people. Furthermore, it is more encouraging to think of yourself as a Six, for instance, rather than as a paranoid type, or as an Eight rather than as an antisocial type, and so on, especially if you are reasonably well-functioning in your life. In short, because the Enneagram comprehends *more* than the standard psychiatric designations, it is appropriate that its categories be as neutral and unbiased as possible. The use of numbers fulfills this function.

The last point to make about numbers is that the numerical

ranking of the personality types is not significant. A larger number is no better than a smaller number; it is not better to be a Nine than a Two because nine is a bigger number.

Fifth, no personality type is inherently better or worse than any other. Each type has its particular strengths and weaknesses, and it is extremely useful to know what they are. While all the personality types have assets and liabilities, some types are usually more desirable than others in any given culture or group. You may not be pleased with your personality type; you may feel that your type is "handicapped" in some way which dissatisfies you. However, as you learn more about all the personality types, you will discover that each is limited in particular ways and each has its unique capacities. If some personality types are more highly esteemed in modern society than others, it is because of the qualities which society rewards, not because of any superior value of those types.

For example, the aggressive, self-assured, extroverted types are highly valued in our competitive, materialistic, success-oriented society, while the introverted, shy, easygoing types tend to be regarded as second-class citizens. If you feel that your personality type is in the latter group, remember that the more socially desirable types also have limitations, while the types that receive fewer social rewards have assets which make them valuable, too. The ideal is to become *your best self*, not to envy the strengths and potentials of others.

Identifying Your Basic Personality Type
Applying these concepts to yourself will make them more concrete. Which of the following nine roles fits you best most of the time? Or, to put it differently, if you were to describe yourself in one word, which of the following words would come closest?

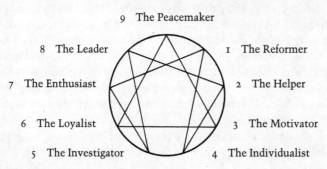

9 The Peacemaker
8 The Leader
7 The Enthusiast
6 The Loyalist
5 The Investigator
1 The Reformer
2 The Helper
3 The Motivator
4 The Individualist

We will now expand these one-word descriptions. Read the following four-word descriptions to see if you still feel comfortable with the type with which you have just tentatively identified yourself. Keep in mind that these traits are merely highlights and do not represent the full spectrum of each personality type.

The *Two* is caring, generous, possessive, and manipulative.
The *Three* is adaptable, ambitious, image-conscious, and hostile.
The *Four* is intuitive, expressive, self-absorbed, and depressive.
The *Five* is perceptive, original, detached, and eccentric.
The *Six* is engaging, committed, defensive, and paranoid.
The *Seven* is enthusiastic, accomplished, uninhibited, and manic.
The *Eight* is self-confident, decisive, dominating, and combative.
The *Nine* is peaceful, reassuring, complacent, and neglectful.
The *One* is principled, orderly, perfectionistic, and self-righteous.

We will now look at the main assets and liabilities of each type to discover why each is in the Feeling, Thinking, or Instinctive Triad. Although the following short descriptions are still simple, see if the personality type you have tentatively chosen still fits you best. If it does not, consider the next most likely possibility.

In the Feeling Triad: Personality Types Two, Three, and Four

These three personality types have common assets and liabilities which involve their *feelings*. When these types are healthy, their feelings are the focus of what is admirable about their personalities, enabling them to become highly valued for their interpersonal qualities. When they are unhealthy, however, their emotions are out of balance in one way or another.

The strengths of healthy Twos result from the ability to sustain positive feelings for others. Healthy Twos are compassionate, generous, loving, and thoughtful; they go out of their way to be of service to people. However, average Twos are possessive, controlling, and needy, but not able to express their needs directly. They want to be loved, but often intrude on others too much. And unhealthy Twos deceive themselves about the presence of their negative feelings, particularly rage and resentment. They want others to see them as loving and good all of the time even when they manipulate people and act selfishly.

The strengths of healthy Threes involve the desire to improve themselves and their ability to adapt to others. Healthy Threes quickly learn how to make the best of most situations, and they are interested in building and maintaining high self-esteem. They are able to motivate others to want to be like them because they are genuinely admirable in some socially valued way. Average Threes, however, are the most out of touch with their emotions and with their individuality. They suppress their feelings in order to perform more effectively and to make others like them. They lose touch with their feelings as they try to get the success and affirmation they crave. Unhealthy Threes can become hostile and extremely malicious if they do not get the admiring attention they desire.

The strengths of healthy Fours involve intuitive self-awareness. Healthy Fours are very personal, revealing and communicating their feelings in ways that enable others to get in touch with their own emotions. However, average Fours become too aware of their feelings, especially their negative ones, withdrawing from others and living too much in their imaginations. And unhealthy Fours are extremely depressed and alienated from others, tormented by self-doubt and self-hatred. They become suicidal when they can no longer cope with reality.

The Two, Three, and Four have common problems with their *identity* and with *hostility*, which they may take out either on themselves or on others, or both. Their problems with identity stem from a rejection of their own authentic self in favor of a persona that they believe would be more acceptable in some way. Although all of the nine types are involved in maintaining a "false self-image," this is the central problem for these types. Thus, all three are highly concerned with issues of self-esteem, personal value, appreciation, and shame, and with getting others to validate the self-image they have created.

We can examine in a little more detail the different ways that these three types cope with their common issues. Twos have problems with their self-image in the sense that they reject many of their true feelings and qualities, especially their hurt, need, and shame, in order to see themselves (and have others see them) as entirely loving, generous people. Twos may well be loving and generous, but, as they become more disappointed with others and more lonely, they increasingly suppress their real feelings to maintain their "loving" self-image. This leads them into self-deception, suppressing their anger, manipulation of others, and increased frustration and sadness.

The underlying problem is that Twos look primarily outside themselves to other people for validation of their "selfless" self-image. They seek specific responses that let them know that they are loved and appreciated. If these responses are not forthcoming, Twos repress their disappointment and redouble their efforts to get the positive reactions they want. To the degree that their self-esteem has been damaged, however, Twos become caught in a pattern of trying too hard to win people over, eventually driving them away, and becoming more resentful and heartbroken themselves.

In a sense, the issues of Fours are virtually the reverse of those found in Twos. Fours have problems with their identity because they are never quite sure who they really are. Fours do not identify much with other people, and so turn inward to the world of feelings and imagination to construct a self-image. Unfortunately, this self-image may have only a passing resemblance to many of the realities of their lives, so Fours come to reject their real life in favor of the idealized self-image that exists in their imaginations. To their continual frustration, they can never live up to the self-image they have constructed for themselves.

Furthermore, Fours are almost the opposite of Twos in that they look primarily inward, rather than to other people, to maintain their sense of self. Also, while Twos need to suppress many of their negative feelings to maintain their self-image, Fours suppress many of their positive feelings to keep their self-image as a "victim" intact. The self-image of Twos is bolstered by a sense of closeness and connection with others. Fours, however, derive a stronger sense of self by seeing how *different* they are from other people. They have developed a self-image which heightens their uniqueness, even to the point of alienation, while suppressing the aspects of their personality which seem to them "ordinary" or "regular."

Threes, in the center of the Triad, both look to others to validate a positive self-image, like Twos, and, like Fours, look inward to their imaginations to create an idealized self that they try to actualize. Of these types, Threes are potentially the most estranged from their own feelings and needs because their image concerns are both externally and internally generated. Threes look outside themselves to determine what activities or qualities are valued by the people who matter to them, and they try to become the kind of person who has those qualities. At the same time, they engage in a lot of inner dialogue and imagination about the kind of person they would like to become. This can be as simple as having inner "pep talks," or may involve long-term fantasies of success and adulation. But as with the Two and the Four, Threes have rejected their authentic self with the result that none of their accomplishments can really affect or satisfy them.

In the Thinking Triad: Personality Types Five, Six, and Seven

These three personality types have common assets and liabilities which involve *thinking*. When these types are healthy, their remarkable insights, ideas, and ability to understand things is unequaled by the other personality types: they are frequently responsible for outstanding practical, creative, or scientific achievements. When they are unhealthy, however, their thinking gets out of balance in one way or another.

The assets of healthy Fives make them the most profoundly perceptive of the personality types. Healthy Fives are extremely knowledgeable about some aspect of their environment, and are capable of brilliant, original, inventive solutions to problems. However, average Fives feel more at home with thinking and imagining than with doing, and so get lost in the mazes of their minds while their lives and opportunities diminish. As a result of thinking too much, unhealthy Fives create more problems for themselves than they solve because they have become so completely isolated from reality. They are unable to know what is real or unreal, true or untrue.

The strengths of healthy Sixes involve the ability to think systematically and to foresee potential problems. When healthy Sixes act, it is to everyone's mutual benefit. As loyal, and faithful friends, they are committed to others, and they look for the same qualities from others. Average Sixes, however, look outside themselves too much for "permission" to act from an authority figure or belief system which will tell them what to do. Unsure of themselves unless the authority is on their side, they nevertheless feel they must assert themselves *against* the authority to prove their independence, at least from time to time. Unhealthy Sixes succumb to anxiety and feelings of inferiority and insecurity, self-destructively bringing about the very consequences they most fear.

The assets of healthy Sevens involve their remarkably quick and avid minds, which give them the ability to do many things exceptionally well. Healthy Sevens are exuberantly enthusiastic about the environment, becoming extremely accomplished in a wide variety of activities. However, the thinking of average Sevens becomes extremely restless, moving from one topic to the next before anything can be completed, engaged in an unending search for new experiences. This causes them to do more of everything, although, ironically, the more they do, the less they are satisfied. They want to keep their minds occupied at all times so that their anxiety will not get to them. They constantly imagine that they are "missing out" on something that would be more enjoyable than their current activity, and greedily want more of everything so they will not feel deprived. Unhealthy Sevens become self-centered, dissipated escapists, flying impulsively out of control.

The Five, Six, and Seven have common problems with *insecurity* and *anxiety* which they handle in different ways, depending on the personality type. In all three types, a pervasive fear or anxiety arises from a profound feeling of lack of support, either from others or from the environment. Because they are anxious about not having the support they feel they need, the types of this Triad each use a different solution to gain some degree of security as a defense against their fear.

Fives are anxious about the world around them and their ability to cope with it. They experience the environment as potentially threatening and overwhelming, and view themselves as unable to meet many of life's demands. In response to these fears, Fives seek security in two main ways: first, by developing expertise in some area of knowledge or activity as a way of reinforcing their self-confidence, and second, by reducing their connections with and dependencies on others as much as possible. Fives begin to view most aspects of the external world as overpowering, and so increasingly withdraw into the safety of their minds and imaginations. Basically, Fives deal with their fear of the environment by retreating from it until they can develop the skill or knowledge to cope with it.

In type Seven there is virtually a reverse of the strategy of the Five. Sevens, at first glance, do not appear to be afraid of very much at all. They approach life with great gusto and exuberance, and do not seem to hesitate to explore new experiences, activities, or relationships. A closer look, though, will reveal that Sevens are anxious about their *inner* reality. Not wanting to feel their anxiety and pain, they plunge into activity as soon as any degree of fear arises into awareness. Sevens doubt their ability to cope with their losses and grief, and so turn to the environment for support and to defend themselves against intolerable feelings. Whereas Fives retreat from the external world of activity into the security of their minds, Sevens flee from the anxiety in their minds by finding security in the external world of activity.

Sixes, in the middle of the Thinking Triad, have anxieties about both the external environment and their inner world of fear and grief. Thus, Sixes try to establish support systems in the world that they hope will fend off real world dangers. At the same time, they attempt to establish a consistent belief system which will also give them a sense of security and defend them from their inner demons. Often, Sixes will be more direct in the ways that they seek security and support, turning to things outside of themselves as sources of reassurance. What Sixes depend on for security could be anything from a secure job to a good friend to a philosophical or religious system of thought. In any of these cases, Sixes illustrate clearly the central themes for the whole Triad: anxiety, a feeling of being without adequate support, and a search for security.

In the Instinctive Triad: Personality Types Eight, Nine, and One

These three personality types have in common assets and liabilities which involve *instinct*. When they are healthy, these types relate to their environment and to others exceptionally well, responding from a deep wisdom within themselves, frequently as leaders of one kind or another. However, when they are unhealthy, they become out of balance with how they relate to the world and other people.

The strengths of healthy Eights are based on a tremendous vitality and a keen intuition that can see possibilities in situations and in people that others often miss. They feel strong and capable, and can use their immense self-confidence, courage, and leadership abilities to inspire others to great accomplishments. Average Eights, however, tend to dominate everything in the environment too aggressively, asserting themselves impulsively and indulging their instinctual needs for control and satisfaction without much regard for the consequences. Unhealthy Eights relate to their environment as bullies and tyrants, ruthlessly tearing down anyone and anything that stands in their way.

The assets of healthy Nines are based on their openness, their ability to identify intimately with a person or belief, and a centeredness that enables them to remain calm even when others around them are reacting hysterically. The receptiveness, optimism, and peacefulness of healthy Nines are reassuring to others, enabling others to flourish because Nines create a harmonious atmosphere for everyone. However, average Nines undermine their own development (and their ability to deal with reality) by disengaging from a real, grounded connection with their own drives, with others, and with the environment. To maintain their tranquillity, Nines begin to idealize the other—whether a person or an abstraction—too much. And unhealthy Nines become dangerously fatalistic and neglectful as they cling to what have become little more than illusions about reality from which they have dissociated themselves.

The strengths of healthy Ones involve the ability to relate impartially to the environment; they are consequently able to act with wisdom and conviction. Healthy Ones are reasonable, fair-minded, and conscientious, guided by principles and an inner "knowing" which give them strong consciences and a clear understanding of right and wrong. However, average Ones are out of balance with their natural drives, feelings, and instincts, which they try to control too much. They strive for nothing less than absolute perfection, finding it difficult to accept anything as it is since it can always be better. Unhealthy Ones are intolerant and self-righteous, becoming obsessed about the corruption they find in others while ignoring their own contradictory actions. In the name of the highest ideals, they can become extraordinarily cruel to themselves and others.

The Eight, Nine, and One have common problems with *repression* and *aggression* which they handle in different ways, depending on the personality type. All three of these types can also be seen as resisting some part of their experience to maintain ego-boundaries, especially by defensively resisting the influence of others in different ways.

Eights are perhaps the most openly aggressive or assertive of the nine types. They express their instinctive energy directly, standing up for themselves and saying what they mean. Their powerful connection with their own vitality gives them great self-confidence, and they are less intimidated by conflicts than the other types. Essentially, Eights resist the external world, especially other people. They do not want to be too influenced by others for fear that others would get control over them and harm them. To prevent this from occurring, Eights develop a tough, defiant stance against the world, aggressively asserting their wills to prove to themselves that others cannot "get to them." To do this, though, Eights must repress their vulnerability, their tenderness, and their desire to be close to others—a cost that eventually takes its toll on their health and their spirit.

In many ways, the pattern of Ones is almost the reverse of that of Eights. Ones are also aggressive, but more subtly so. Much of the aggression of Ones is directed at themselves in a steady stream of self-criticism and demands for better behavior. Ones are quite capable of being aggressive with others as well, but when they are, it is usually because they are trying to deflect the attacks of their own superego. While Eights give free rein to their instinctive drives and intuitions, Ones tend to repress them, becoming tense and angry from the resulting inner conflict. Just as Eights resist the external world, Ones primarily resist their inner world. They are afraid that their impulses, desires, instincts, or other irrational parts of themselves may betray them, so they stay vigilantly in control of their responses and reactions as much as possible. Ironically, the more they do this, the more volatile their reactions and the more out of control they become. Ones ultimately become worn down and dispirited from their endless inner war.

Nines are the center of this Triad, and therefore resist both the influence of the outer environment, like Eights, and their inner world of instinctive drives, like Ones. Eights, however, are able to use their instincts to defend against the world, but since Nines repress their instincts, their responses become "frozen." They try to maintain a balance between the demands of the external environment, especially people, and the potential turmoil of their inner reactions and responses to those demands, especially anger. The result is a kind of cancellation of their own instinctual life and drives, with a resulting apathy and loss of vitality. Thus, as much as possible, they attempt to inhabit a safe middle ground in which nothing can get to them, creating an idealized version of reality that they find less disturbing. Nines use their imaginations to relate to their image of others in a way that does not threaten their inner stability and peace. Thus, Nines gain some freedom from conflicts and upsets, but they sacrifice a real and vibrant experience of their own lives. Like Eights and Ones, they also suffer a loss of health and motivation as a result of continually resisting life.

If you still cannot decide what your personality type is, at least try to narrow the possibilities to two or three of the most likely candidates. Your basic personality type should finally become clear when you read the full descriptions.

A common problem is that people tend to pick the personality type they would like to be rather than the one they actually are. You can avoid this by trying to be objective about yourself, although this is one of the most difficult things to achieve. However, the more you understand the descriptions—and yourself—the more you will see that one personality type really does describe you better than any of the others. Give yourself time to find out which one it is.

You may find yourself responding to several traits from each type, seeing yourself in all of them but in no one type in particular. While you may be able to find a little of yourself in all the types, when you read the description of your own personality type, *you will know it.* You may feel chills run down your spine, or an uneasy feeling in the pit of your stomach. This will be your subconscious telling you that something is hitting home.

On one level, it is true that we have aspects of all nine of the types within us, and it is certainly instructive to explore each chapter carefully, even if you are fairly sure of your own basic type. The understanding that we can derive from the other types is greatly enhanced, however, when we know our own type and are familiar with it. There is a simple reason for this. While we do "visit" characteristics of the other types from day to day and at different times in our lives, our own type is the "home base" to which we always return. It is the lens through which we interpret our experiences, even those that come from behaviors associated with another type. Thus, the more we understand our own basic type, the less its particular lens distorts our perceptions. We begin to see ourselves and others with an increasing clarity. The first time we recognize the degree to which our personality type affects every aspect of our lives can be a powerful, even earthshaking, experience.

While the descriptions are therefore not difficult to understand intellectually, they may be difficult to deal with emotionally. Some people have found that they become anxious or depressed as they read the description of their type. Seeing yourself revealed in these pages can be elating. It can also be disturbing.

If you become anxious as you read the description of your type, it might be useful to put the book aside until you have thought about what you found upsetting. One of the most helpful things about reviewing the descriptions is that it will help you recognize the changes you need to make in your life. Changing yourself takes time and the willingness to confront unpleasant truths about yourself, but it is the only way to be free of troublesome habits and self-defeating patterns of behavior. And, as you will see for yourself, the very process of reflecting on the description of your personality type can be cathartic: the more you go over this material and apply it to yourself, the more freeing the process becomes.

The Wing

Now that you have tentatively identified your basic personality type, we can begin to make some refinements. It is important to understand that no one is a "pure" personality type. Most people are a unique mixture of their basic type and one of the two types adjacent to it on the circumference of the Enneagram. One of the two types adjacent to your basic type is called your "wing."

Your basic type dominates your overall personality, while the wing complements it and adds important, sometimes contradictory, elements to your total personality. The wing is the "second side" of your overall personality, and you must take it into consideration to understand yourself or someone else. For example, if you are a personality type Nine, you will have either a One-wing or an Eight-wing, and your total personality can best be understood by considering the traits of the Nine in some unique blend with the traits of either the One or the Eight.

In some cases, people will show a very strong influence from their wing, while in others, even of the same basic type and wing combination, the influence may be slight. Some people, familiar with the Enneagram, insist that they have a degree of influence from both wings, and in a certain number of instances this may be so. Moreover, everyone has both wings in the sense that to some extent we all have all nine types in our personality. Thus, if you were a Three with a Two-wing, you would naturally expect to have some influence from the other wing, type Four, because Four is one of the other eight types, all of which will be part of your personality to some degree. Nonetheless, there may be a number of individuals who are equally influenced by both wings.

In our experience, however, the vast majority of people that we have encountered have a *dominant* wing, and they can be distinguished from members of the same type who have the other wing.

The basic type and wing result in a blend which is distinct from the other type-wing combination. For instance, a Four with a Three-wing is noticeably different from a Four with a Five-wing, in fact, so much so that they can be viewed as separate subtypes. Indeed, the resulting eighteen wing subtypes are so distinct and so important that we have done what no other authors have attempted — we have developed extensive descriptions of these subtypes that can be found in each of the individual type chapters. We have also given each a particular name and are publishing them here for the first time in the type descriptions and in the Enneagram below.

Obviously, it is necessary to determine your basic personality type *before* you can determine which wing you have. In order to determine your wing, you have to know which traits comprise the two types adjacent to your basic type. The best way to diagnose your wing is by reading the full descriptions of the two possible types, and by seeing which one best applies to you. The extensive descriptions of the wing subtypes found at the end of each descriptive chapter on the types should confirm your diagnosis.

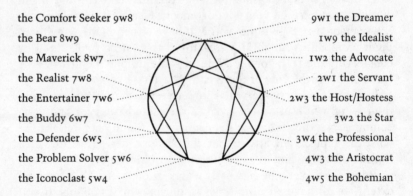

the Comfort Seeker 9w8 — 9w1 the Dreamer
the Bear 8w9 — 1w9 the Idealist
the Maverick 8w7 — 1w2 the Advocate
the Realist 7w8 — 2w1 the Servant
the Entertainer 7w6 — 2w3 the Host/Hostess
the Buddy 6w7 — 3w2 the Star
the Defender 6w5 — 3w4 the Professional
the Problem Solver 5w6 — 4w3 the Aristocrat
the Iconoclast 5w4 — 4w5 the Bohemian

The 18 Riso-Hudson Wing Subtypes

You will see much more about the wing in the Advanced Guidelines, since it is one of the major elements which explains why two people who have the same personality type can still be very different.

The Levels of Development

There is an overall structure to each personality type. As you will see, the analysis of each type begins with a description of its healthy traits, then moves to its average traits, and then to its unhealthy traits. That structure is the Levels of Development which forms the personality type.

The Levels were discovered by Don Riso in 1977 and formed the basis of the description of the types that he wrote for the first edition of this book. The nine internal Levels for each type provide an elegant conceptual framework for all of the constituent traits and motivations for each type. The Levels also make it obvious when traits are misattributed and when they are internally consistent for each type.

To understand an individual accurately, you must perceive not only his or her basic type and wing, but also *where the person lies along the Levels of Development of the basic personality type.* In other words, you have to diagnose (to simplify for a moment) whether the person is healthy, average, or unhealthy. This is important because, for example, two people of the same basic personality type and wing will still differ significantly if one of them is healthy and the other unhealthy. (Where a person lies along the Levels of Development of his or her *wing* is also important, but since this can be difficult to perceive, it is not emphasized here.)

The concept of a personality continuum is not an academic one; it is something we intuitively use every day. One of the things we have no doubt noticed about ourselves (and others) is that we change constantly—sometimes for the better, sometimes for the worse. Understanding the concept of the Levels makes it clear that when we do so, we are shifting within the spectrum of traits which make up our personality type. You will see more about how and why we move along the Levels in the Advanced Guidelines chapter.

The Levels of Development for each of the basic personality types may be thought of as pictured below.

It may help you to think of the Levels of Development as a photographer's gray scale, which has gradations from pure white to pure black with many shades of gray in between. On the continuum of the Levels, the healthiest traits appear first, at the top, so to speak. As we work down through the continuum, we progressively pass through each Level of Development, marking a distinct shift in the personality's deterioration to the pure black of neurosis at the bottom.

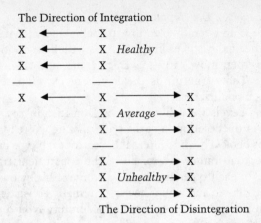

The Direction of Integration

The Direction of Disintegration

The Levels of Development

Briefly, there are nine Levels of Development within each personality type—three in the healthy section, three in the average section, and three in the unhealthy section. Moreover, the traits which appear at each of the Levels of Development are not arbitrary; they are arrayed in related clusters at each Level. As you read the description of each personality type, you will, in effect, be seeing some of the most important traits from each of those clusters at each Level as you proceed along the continuum from health to neurosis.

The Levels help make sense of each personality type as a whole by providing a framework upon which to place each healthy, average, and unhealthy trait. The Levels are also worth understanding because it is in the healthy range of the continuum that we are able to move in the Direction of Integration (see below), just as it is in the average to unhealthy range that we "act out" in the Direction of Disintegration. It is worth noting that movement in the Direction of Disintegration is the "path of least resistance" and is the result of acting on the habitual mechanisms of our personality. On the other hand, the Direction of Integration always involves conscious choice and effort, although not the effort of striving and straining, or condemning ourselves for our failures. Indeed, most of these efforts usually result in inner conflict, increased anxiety, and may even cause a descent into lower Levels of the continuum. Rather, the effort required to move in the Direction of Integration is the effort of letting go of our old personality patterns. As the Enneagram assists us in seeing the habitual nature of many of our thoughts, reactions, and behaviors, and as we see that they often work against our best interest, we find the serenity and freedom to let go of them, thus opening the possibility of a richer, more fulfilling life. Indeed, observing our fears, hurts, and weaknesses without judgment and without justification is one of the most compassionate things we can do for ourselves, and it frees us to extend this gift to others.

Directions of Integration and Disintegration

The next important concept to understand is what the lines on the Enneagram mean. The nine personality types are not static categories; they are open-ended, allowing for psychological growth and deterioration.

The numbers on the Enneagram are connected in a specific sequence. The way the numbered points are connected is significant psychologically because the lines between each of the types denote the Direction of Integration (health, self-actualization) and the Direction of Disintegration (unhealth, neurosis) for each personality type. In other words, as you become more healthy or unhealthy, you can move in different "directions," as indicated by the lines of the Enneagram, *from your basic type.*

The Direction of Disintegration for each type is indicated on the Enneagram by the sequence of numbers 1–4–2–8–5–7–1. This means that types in their average to unhealthy range of behaviors, under conditions of increased stress and anxiety, will begin to exhibit or "act out" some of the average to unhealthy behaviors of the type in their Direction of Disintegration. Thus, an average to unhealthy One will exhibit average to unhealthy behaviors of the Four; an average to unhealthy Four will exhibit average to unhealthy behaviors of the Two; an average to unhealthy Two will exhibit average to unhealthy Eight behaviors; an Eight will exhibit average to unhealthy Five behaviors; an average to unhealthy Five will exhibit some Seven behaviors, and an average to unhealthy Seven will exhibit average to unhealthy One behaviors. Likewise, on the equilateral triangle, the sequence is 9–6–3–9: under conditions of stress or increased anxiety, an average to unhealthy Nine will exhibit some of the average to unhealthy behaviors of the Six, an average to unhealthy Six will exhibit some of the average to unhealthy behaviors of the Three, and an average to unhealthy

Three will exhibit some of the average to unhealthy Nine behaviors. You can see how this works by following the direction of the arrows on the Enneagram below.

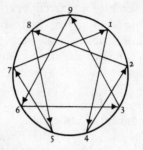

The Direction of Disintegration

1–4–2–8–5–7–1
9–6–3–9

The Direction of Integration is indicated for each type by the *reverse* of the above sequences. Each type moves toward increasing integration in a direction which is the opposite of its unhealthy direction. Thus, the sequence for the Direction of Integration is 1–7–5–8–2–4–1: an integrating One goes to Seven, an integrating Seven goes to Five, an integrating Five goes to Eight, an integrating Eight goes to Two, an integrating Two goes to Four, and an integrating Four goes to One. On the equilateral triangle, the sequence is 9–3–6–9: an integrating Nine will go to Three, an integrating Three will go to Six, and an integrating Six will go to Nine. You can see how this works by following the direction of the arrows on the Enneagram below.

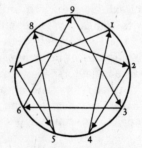

The Direction of Integration

1–7–5–8–2–4–1
9–3–6–9

Separate Enneagrams for the Direction of Integration and the Direction of Disintegration are unnecessary. Both directions can be shown on one Enneagram by eliminating the arrows and connecting the proper points with plain lines.

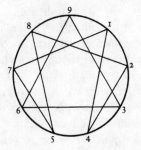

The Direction of Integration	**The Direction of Disintegration**
1–7–5–8–2–4–1	1–4–2–8–5–7–1
9–3–6–9	9–6–3–9

It will be helpful for you to memorize both sequences of numbers so that you know the Direction of Integration and the Direction of Disintegration for any given personality type.*

It is important to understand that the Directions of Integration and Disintegration are metaphors for psychological processes occurring in everyone. There is no literal movement around the Enneagram; rather, this is a symbolic way of indicating how a specific personality type will either integrate or disintegrate beyond the state it is in.

A brief example will illustrate what these movements mean. At personality type Six, one line is drawn to Nine, and another to Three. This means that if the Six were to become healthy and begin to actualize her potentials, she would move to Nine, the Direction of Integration specified by the Enneagram, activating what the healthy personality type Nine symbolizes for the Six. When the Enneagram predicts that a healthy Six will move to Nine, we find

---

*An easy way to memorize both sequences of numbers is to remember the *unhealthy* sequence and then reverse it for the healthy one. A trick to help you remember the unhealthy sequence (1–4–2–8–5–7) is to group these six numbers in pairs: each pair is approximately twice the preceding pair. Thus, the first two (1–4, or "14") when doubled is "28," and when that is doubled, it becomes "57." (It is really 56, of course, but this does not harm the mnemonic. So: 14–28–57, or 1–4–2–8–5–7.)

that this is precisely the kind of psychological development we see in individuals who are Sixes. Many of the Six's problems have to do with insecurity and anxiety, and when the Six moves to Nine, he or she becomes relaxed, accepting, and peaceful. The Six at Nine is more self-possessed and less anxious than ever before.

Conversely, the line to Three indicates the Six's Direction of Disintegration. Average to unhealthy Sixes are anxious and insecure, and feel inferior, especially about their ability to function in the world without stable external support, which can be from their employment, their family and friends, or from a belief system. When Sixes feel that their security is threatened, their anxiety may bring out behaviors associated with average to unhealthy Threes. Depending on the situation and the degree of stress, Sixes may become driven and competitive while trying to retain the good regard of others, like average Threes. They may become disengaged from their feelings and more identified with tasks and the quality of their performance, while relating to others in a brisk, "professional" tone. They may also attempt to overcompensate for their inferiority feelings by becoming arrogant and self-promoting like Threes. If the degree of anxiety is overwhelming, Sixes may plunge into the neurotic aspects of the Three, covering their mistakes, deceiving others, and relentlessly driving after whatever they believe will restore their security and self-esteem.

It is important to note that a person tends to act out the behavior of the type in his or her Direction of Disintegration at roughly the same Level in the Levels of Development as the Level at which they are functioning in their own type. For example, a Six at Level 5 will tend to act out some of the characteristics of a Three at Level 5. An Eight at Level 4 will tend to act out some of the characteristics of a Five at Level 4, and so on. In the section on the Direction of Disintegration in each of the individual type chapters, we include a full description of how the type moves in its Direction of Disintegration, Level by Level, down the continuum.

No matter what your basic personality type, be aware that the types in *both* your Directions of Integration and Disintegration have an influence on you. To obtain a more complete picture of yourself (or someone else), you must take not only your basic type and wing into consideration, but also the two types in your Directions of Integration and Disintegration. The traits of those *four* types blend into your total personality; a unique mixture of these four types gives you the fullest picture of yourself. For example, no one is simply a personality type Two. Anyone who is a Two has either a One-wing or a Three-wing, and the Two's Direction of Disintegration (Eight) and its Direction of Integration (Four) also play important parts in its overall personality.

If you want more information than is given in the descriptions of the Directions of Integration and Disintegration for any of the personality types, you can read the appropriate section in each type's Direction of Integration or Disintegration and make the application yourself. For example, to know more about what it means for a Two to integrate to Four, read the description of the healthy Four with the healthy Two in mind. Or, if you want to know more about what is involved in a Nine disintegrating to Six, read the description of the average to unhealthy Six, applying the traits to the Nine, and so forth for all the types. The basic idea is that when a type integrates, it appropriates the healthy traits of the type in its Direction of Integration, and when it deteriorates, it appropriates the commensurate average to unhealthy traits of the type in its Direction of Disintegration.

The Enneagram is able to predict integrated or disintegrated traits because these states are foreshadowed in the dynamics of the person's basic personality type. The Direction of Integration for each personality type is a natural outgrowth of the healthiest qualities of that type, so it is connected to another type by a line on the Enneagram to indicate that interrelationship. In a sense, then, you can think of each personality type as flowing into the next, because the type in the Direction of Integration marks a further development of the prior type, just as the type in the Direction of Disintegration marks its further enmeshment in conflicted ego states.

Ultimately, the goal is to move completely around the Enneagram, integrating what each type symbolizes and acquiring the active use of the healthy potentials of *all the types*. The ideal is to become a balanced, fully functioning human being, and each of the types of the Enneagram symbolizes different important aspects of what we need to achieve this end. Therefore, which personality type you begin life as is ultimately unimportant. What matters is what you do with your personality type, and how well (or badly) you use it as the beginning point for your development into a fuller, more integrated person.

Getting Started

We can now turn to the descriptions of the nine personality types, which may be read in any order.

It might be helpful to understand the organization of the descriptions. Each chapter opens with a Caricature and Profile of the type to give you an impression of its most important traits. The Profiles are particularly useful, since they give you over a hundred key adjectives which you can use as a checklist to see if the personality type under consideration applies to you or someone else.

Next comes to Overview, a short essay presenting the principal psychological dynamics of the type being described. In the Overview, you will see how the personality type compares and contrasts with other types in its Triad, what its parental orientation and childhood patterns are, how it correlates to the Jungian and other typologies, and most important, the major themes that will be developed more systematically in the longer analysis which follows. The Overview can be read as an independent short essay on each type or as a review after you have finished the analysis.

The more systematic description—the analysis of the personality type—follows the Overview. It begins with the *healthy* traits, then moves into the *average* traits, and then into the *unhealthy* traits. In other words, the description *gets progressively more negative* as it traces the deterioration of the type along the Levels of Development.

The analysis ends with a discussion of what will happen to the type if it continues in its unhealthy direction on the Enneagram—its Direction of Disintegration—as well as a description of what it will become if it moves toward increasing health—its Direction of Integration. Following these two sections is a description of the two major subtypes for each personality type—its wings—with examples of famous people, real or fictional, and some final thoughts about the type as a whole.

The examples of well-known people are educated guesses based on intuition, observation, and reading. They are offered as illustrations of the diversity of the personality types, with no implication about their state of health or neurosis. Remember that each of these people may have been healthy, average, or unhealthy at various times in their lives, and that each may have moved to his or her Direction of Integration or Disintegration. Above all, remember that there is an enormous amount of individual diversity, including intelligence, talent, and experience, among those illustrating any given type. But even taking these various factors into consideration, the famous people are included because by understanding how they exemplify the different personality types, you will be able to see both what is common to them all and what a vast range of psychological territory is covered by each type. Of course, in their private lives, a few of these people may be substantially different from their public persona, and may even be another type. However, these examples were chosen because their public personalities were illustrative of a type, whatever their private selves may be.

The last point about the descriptive chapters is that the quotations in parentheses are included to give the personal flavor of each of the types. Unless otherwise noted, these statements are not specific quotations.

You may be able to figure out your own type and those of a few close friends very quickly, or you may find it difficult to "categorize" people and not know where to begin. Either state is normal. It is not always apparent which type someone is, and it takes time to sharpen your skills. Remember that you are like a beginning medical student who is learning to diagnose a wide variety of conditions, some healthy and some unhealthy. It takes practice to learn to identify the major symptoms and apply them to the proper syndromes.

You might also keep in mind that while some people have an aptitude for psychological insight, others do not. If you find that your psychological aptitude is undeveloped, do not be discouraged. Read the descriptions carefully, going back to them when you need to check something or as new insights occur to you. You will probably be surprised at how quickly you get better at it.

There is really no secret to learning how to "type" people. You must learn which traits go with each type and observe how people manifest those traits. This is tricky, because there are many subtypes and quirks to the personality types, as you will see. Also, different types can sometimes seem similar. For example, several of the types can be bossy. Even though they order people around, they do so in different ways and for different reasons. Eights boss people around as if saying, "Do as I say because I have power over you and I will punish you if you disobey me!" while Ones boss others around as if they were saying, "Don't argue with me: just do as I say because I am right." Under various circumstances, other types can also be bossy. Twos can be domineering, bossing people around as if they were saying, "You really don't want to hurt me, do you? You may as well do what I'm asking." Sixes can exhibit a blustering aggressiveness toward people, and Sevens can boss others around by demanding that others give them what they want, and so forth.

Similarly, Fours are described as depressive, often feeling misunderstood. Many people quickly jump to the conclusion that they are therefore Fours. In fact, all nine types have the capacity for depression and feeling misunderstood.

These examples illustrate why it is unwise to focus on a single trait in isolation and to try to make a diagnosis based on that. It is necessary to see each type as a whole—its overall style and approach to life, and its basic motivations. A lot of elements must be put together before you can type someone accurately.

For better or worse, there is no easy, automatic way to diagnose either yourself or others. It takes time, sensitivity, the ability to observe, and an open mind—unfortunately, more than most people are willing, or able, to bring to their relationships, although these are among the very qualities you will be able to develop with the help of the Enneagram.

The ultimate purpose of the Enneagram is to help each of us become a fully functioning person. It helps us to see ourselves more clearly so that we can become better balanced and integrated individuals. However, the Enneagram does not promise perfection, nor does it counsel us to become world-denying ascetics. In the real world, healthy people do not live in a constant state of Zen-like enlightenment, nor do they ever achieve total personhood—whatever that might mean. No matter how healthy or happy we become, we will always be incomplete and limited. Instead of fleeing from life into Nirvana or trying to become superior to life in a quest for an impossible perfection, we must learn to rise to the tremendous challenge of becoming, and being, fully human.

Attaining the goal of a full, happy life, ripe with experiences well-used, means that each of us will become a paradox—free, yet constrained by necessity; shrewd, yet innocent; open to others, yet self-reliant; strong, yet able to yield; centered on the highest values, yet able to accept imperfection; realistic about the suffering existence imposes on us, yet full of gratitude for life as it is.

The testimony of the greatest humans who have ever lived is

that the way to make the most of ourselves is by transcending ourselves. We must learn to move beyond self-centeredness to make room within ourselves for others. When you transcend yourself, the fact will be confirmed by the quality of your life. You will attain— even if only momentarily—a transparency and a radiance of being, which result from living both within and beyond yourself. This is the promise and the excitement of self-understanding.

Part II

The Nine Personality Types

Chapter 4

Type Two: The Helper

THE TWO IN PROFILE

Healthy: Empathetic, compassionate, feeling with and for others. Caring and concerned about their needs. Outgoing and passionate, they offer friendship and kindness. Thoughtful, warm-hearted, forgiving, and sincere. / Encouraging and appreciative, able to see the good in others. Dedicated and supportive of people, bringing out the best in them. Service is important: they are nurturing, generous, and giving—truly loving people. *At Their Best:* Deeply unselfish, humble, and altruistic, giving unconditional love to self and others. Feel it is a privilege to be in others' lives. Radiantly joyful and gracious.

Average: Engage in "people pleasing" in order to be closer to others, becoming overly friendly, emotionally demonstrative, and full of "good intentions." Bestow seductive attention on others: approval, "strokes," flattery. Talkative, especially about love and their relationships. / Become overly intimate and intrusive: they need to be needed, so they hover, meddle, and control in the name of love. Want others to depend on them: give, but expect a return. Send mixed messages. Enveloping and possessive: the self-sacrificial, parenting persons who cannot do enough for others, wearing themselves out for everyone, creating needs for themselves to fulfill. / Increasingly self-important and self-satisfied, feel they are indispensable, although they overrate their efforts in others' behalf. Seek specific forms of repayment for their help. Hypochondria, becoming a "martyr" for others. Overbearing, patronizing, presumptuous.

Unhealthy: Manipulative and self-serving, instilling guilt by making others feel indebted to them. Abuse food and medications to "stuff feelings" and get sympathy. Undermine people by making belittling, disparaging remarks. Extremely self-deceptive about their motives and how selfish and/or aggressive their behavior is. / Domineering and coercive: feel entitled to get anything they want from others and are bitterly resentful and angry. Somatization of their aggressions results in chronic health problems as they vindicate themselves by "falling apart" and burdening others.

Key Motivations: Want to be loved, to express their feelings for others, to be needed and appreciated, to get others to respond to them, to vindicate their claims about themselves.

Examples: Mother Teresa, Archbishop Desmond Tutu, Eleanor Roosevelt, Barbara Bush, Robert Fulghum, Leo Buscaglia, Luciano Pavarotti, Barry Manilow, Richard Simmons, Sammy Davis, Jr., Pat Boone, Doug Henning, Ann Landers, Florence Nightingale, "Melanie Hamilton Wilkes" in *Gone with the Wind*, the "Tin Woodsman" in *The Wizard of Oz*, and the "Jewish Mother" stereotype.

AN OVERVIEW OF THE TWO

Because it has so many facets, love is difficult to define. It means different things to different people in different kinds of relationships. The word can be used to cover a multitude of virtues as well as vices. Of all the personality types, Twos think of love in terms of having positive feelings for others, of taking care of others, and of self-sacrifice. Twos may also see love in terms of intimacy and achieving closeness with others. These aspects of love are undoubtedly important parts of the picture. But what Twos do not always remember is that, at its highest, love is more closely aligned with realism than with feelings. Genuine love wants what is best for the other, even if it means risking the relationship. Love wants the beloved to become strong and independent, even if it means that the Two must withdraw from the other's life. Real love is never used to obtain from others what they would not freely give. Love outlives a lack of response, selfishness, and mistakes, no matter who is at fault. And it cannot be taken back. If it can be, it is not love.

A central thing to understand about Twos is that although on the surface they seem to be offering love, on a deeper level they are really searching for it. Twos believe that if they love others enough, surely others will love them in return. Again and again, as we shall see, Twos extend themselves to others with affection, gifts, services, and many other things, but are often disappointed by the responses they receive. However, until Twos learn to properly love themselves, none of the responses they get, however loving, will make them feel loved.

Twos believe deeply in the power of love as the prime source of everything good in life, and in many ways they are right. But what some Twos call "love" and what is worthy of the name are very different things. In this personality type, we will see the widest possible meanings of love, from disinterested, genuine love, to the flattering effusions of "pleasers," to desperately needy manipulation and the dangerous obsessions of the "stalker." There is tremendous variety among those who march under the banner of love, from the most selfless angels to the most hate-filled devils. Understanding the personality type Two will help us understand how they got that way.

In the Feeling Triad

Although Twos have strong feelings for others, they have potential problems with their feelings. They tend to overexpress how positive they feel about others, while ignoring their negative feelings altogether. They see themselves as loving, caring people, yet all too often they love others only to manipulate others to love them in return. Their "love" is not free: expectations of repayment are attached. Twos are often hampered in their ability to truly love others because their self-image is highly invested in having only certain positive feelings for people, and not having other "unpleasant" feelings.

Healthy Twos, however, are the most considerate and genuinely loving of all the personality types. Because they have strong feelings and sincerely care about others, they go out of their way to help people, doing real good and serving real needs. But if they become unhealthy, Twos deceive themselves about the presence and extent of their own emotional needs as well as their aggressive feelings, not recognizing how manipulative and domineering they can be. As we shall see, unhealthy Twos are among the most difficult of the personality types to deal with because they are extremely selfish in the name of utter selflessness. They can do terrible harm to others while believing that they are completely good.

The essence of the problem is that even average Twos have difficulty seeing themselves as they really are, as persons of *mixed* motives, conflicting feelings, and personal needs which they want to fulfill. This is because their superegos tell them that if they pursue what they want directly, they are being selfish and will be punished. Thus, Twos must convince themselves that they have no needs, and that what they do for others is without self-interest. They must see themselves only in positive terms, laying the groundwork for self-deception. What is difficult to understand about less healthy Twos is how they can deceive themselves so thoroughly; what is difficult to deal with in them is the indirect way in which they go about getting their needs fulfilled. The more unhealthy they get, the more difficult it is for others to square their perceptions of them with the Twos' increasingly virtuous perception of themselves. They constantly exonerate themselves and demand that others do the same—indeed, they demand that people accept their interpretation of their actions, sometimes even when that is contrary to the plain facts.

Twos correspond to the extroverted feeling type in Jung's typology. Unfortunately, it is not one of his most insightful descriptions; nevertheless, the following characteristics are worth noting.

Depending on the degree of dissociation between the ego and the momentary state of feeling, signs of self-disunity will become clearly apparent, because the originally compensatory attitude of the unconscious has turned into open opposition. This shows itself first of all in extravagant displays of feeling, gushing talk, loud expostulations, etc., which ring hollow: "The lady doth protest too much." It is at once apparent that some kind of resistance is being over-compensated, and one begins to wonder whether these demonstrations might not turn out quite different. And a little later they do. Only a very slight alteration in the situation is needed to call forth at once just the opposite pronouncement on the selfsame object. (C. G. Jung, *Psychological Types*, 357–358.)

What Jung describes is the ambivalence of the Two's feelings — the ability to shift from apparently totally positive feelings for others to highly negative ones. As we trace the deterioration of the Two along the Levels of Development, we can see that healthy Twos really do love others genuinely. But average Twos have mixed feelings: their love is nowhere near as pure or selfless as they want it to be. And in unhealthy Twos, the opposite of love is operative: hatred finds fuel in burning resentments against others. Jung is not correct in saying that "only a very slight alteration in the situation is needed to call forth at once just the opposite pronouncement on the selfsame object," since hatred is at the other end of the spectrum from genuine love. But what is true is that step by step, as Twos deteriorate along the Levels toward neurosis, this is precisely what happens.

Problems with Hostility and Identity
Twos, Threes, and Fours have a common problem with hostility, although they manifest it in different ways. Twos deny that they have any hostile feelings whatsoever, concealing their aggressions not only from others, but also from themselves. Like everyone else, Twos have aggressive feelings, but they protect themselves from realizing their existence and extent because their self-image prohibits them from being openly hostile. They act aggressively only if they can convince themselves that their aggressions are for someone else's good, never for their own self-interest. Average to unhealthy Twos fear that if they were ever openly selfish or aggressive, not only would their negative behavior contradict their virtuous self-image, it would drive others away from them. They therefore deny to themselves (and to others) that they have any selfish or aggressive motives whatsoever, while interpreting their actual behavior in a way which allows them to see themselves in a positive light. They eventually become so practiced at this that they completely deceive themselves about the contradiction between their expressed motives and their real behavior. Unhealthy Twos become capable of acting both very selfishly and very aggressively, while, in their minds, they are neither selfish nor aggressive.

The source of their motivation is the need to be loved. However, Twos are always in danger of allowing their desire to be loved to deteriorate into the desire to control others. By gradually making others dependent on them, average Twos inevitably arouse resentments against themselves while demanding that others confirm how virtuous they are. When interpersonal conflicts arise, as they inevitably do because of their attempts to control others, average to unhealthy Twos always feel "more sinned against than sinning." They see themselves as martyrs who have sacrificed themselves selflessly without being appreciated for it in the least. Their repressed aggressive feelings and resentments eventually manifest themselves in severe psychosomatic complaints and physical illnesses which force others to take care of them.

Gaining the love of others is important to Twos because they fear that they are not loved for themselves alone. They feel that they will be loved only if they can earn love by always being good and by constantly sacrificing themselves for others. In a word, they fear that others would not love them *unless they made others love them.* (Twos could be briefly characterized as persons who, fearing that they are unlovable, spend their lives trying to make people love them.) Naturally, that creates a deep source of hidden aggression, and if people do not respond to them as they want, average to unhealthy Twos become increasingly resentful. But since they cannot consciously own up to their aggressive feelings, they express them indirectly, in manipulative behavior they disavow. It is astonishing to see how badly unhealthy Twos can treat others while justifying everything they do. But no matter how destructive their actions are, unhealthy Twos must persuade themselves that they have nothing but love and the purest of good intentions at heart.

One of the major ironies of all Twos is that, unless they are healthy, the focus of their attention is essentially on themselves, although they neither give this impression to others nor think of themselves as egocentric. Assertions to the contrary, even for average Twos the welfare of others is not primary. Rather, their positive feelings about themselves—as reinforced by the positive reactions of others—is what is important to them and what they are always angling for.

In a real way, Twos are dependent on the loving responses of others to validate their self-image—the good, selfless, loving person. The problem is that as long as Twos are focused on others to find indications of their own value and lovability, they fail to be fully aware of all of their own feelings and cannot recognize the lovable qualities within themselves. As Twos deteriorate, the situation worsens, because they also fail to recognize loving responses in others. Average to unhealthy Twos start looking for very specific signs of others' affection for them, and any differing indications of love do not count. Thus, Twos must figure out what kind of person they need to be and what they will have to do in order to elicit from others the specific responses that "count" as love.

This is why Twos have a second problem in common with Threes and Fours — a problem with their identities. Other people do not see Twos as they really are, and, more important, Twos do not see themselves as they really are. There is an ever increasing disparity between the loving self-image and the actual needy person, between the claims of selfless generosity and the claims they make on the love of others.

In a real way, Twos have learned to reject themselves and their own legitimate needs, believing that the idealized self-image they have created—the selfless helper and friend—will be more acceptable than their own authentic feelings and responses. And because their identity is dependent upon others affirming and appreciating their goodness, Twos become trapped in behaviors that increasingly frustrate them and alienate others. For Twos to escape this trap, they need to recognize the degree to which they ignore their own needs as well as their grief and shame. They can then apply their extraordinary nurturing skills to someone who desperately needs them—themselves.

Parental Orientation

As children, Twos were ambivalent to the protective-figure, the person in their early development who was responsible for guidance, structure, and discipline. This is often the father, but other people can also play this role, including the mother or even an older sibling. Twos did not identify strongly with the protective-figure, but they also did not psychologically separate from the person entirely. As a result, Twos felt that they could best fit into the family system by creating an identity that was complementary to the protective-figure. Since the orientation is toward the protective-figure who represents the qualities associated with patriarchy—

authority, structure, discipline, guiding the child in the ways of the world—the child began to identify with the complementary, matriarchal role. Young Twos learned to become "little nurturers" as a way of gaining safety and security in the family system. In other words, they believed that if they could nurture others in their family sufficiently, they could win the affection and protection of the protective-figure. This relationship with the protective-figure sets the stage for a similar orientation toward everyone who can give Twos the love they want.

This ambivalent orientation to their protective-figure helps explain why Twos' self-esteem is conditional. Twos do not love themselves unconditionally, and this is really the source of all the suffering that Twos will experience or cause. Their self-esteem is based on the condition that they be absolutely good and "unselfish." They must see themselves in this way because they believe that only by being extraordinarily good and generous people will they ever obtain love from others. Further, the more dysfunctional the Twos' family systems were, the more they will feel that they must sacrifice and repress their own needs in order to get love.

Unfortunately, the more Twos see their own needs as selfish, the more they must find indirect ways of meeting them. Twos' superegos are ever vigilant, judging not only the "selfishness" of the Two, but the responses of others to the Two's help. ("That was a nice thing Brenda said, but if you were *really* a lovable person, she would have given you a hug.") In average to unhealthy Twos, very little can satisfy the superego. The Two cannot be self-sacrificing enough, and no response from others is sufficient to make Twos believe that they are loved. Ironically, Twos try to maintain their psychological survival by trying even harder to convince themselves and others (as well as their punitive superegos) that they truly are being good, selfless, and without needs.

While there is certainly nothing objectionable about Twos seeing themselves as good and loving people when they are genuinely good, problems begin when they need to feel that they are good all the time. Even when they are far from good, Twos *must* see themselves as good for others. The irony is that their need to think of themselves as all-good and helpful is never more urgent than when they are frantically needy, self-centered, and manipulative.

However, when they are healthy, Twos are able to move beyond their desperate search for love by learning to nurture themselves.

They understand that self-nurturance is not selfish: in fact, it is essential if they are going to be of any real help to anyone else. They know that to the degree that they can love themselves unconditionally, they do not have to get love from others by being good all the time. They can then be caring, unselfish, and disinterested, in the most positive meanings of those words, because their love is truly without agenda. Unfortunately, at the lower end of the personality continuum, the "love" of unhealthy Twos is nothing more than a veneer for the desire to create dependencies so that they can hold on to others. Because of the intensity of their neediness, unhealthy Twos do evil in the name of good and can no longer tell the difference.

ANALYZING THE HEALTHY TWO

Level 1: The Disinterested Altruist

At their best, healthy Twos are amazingly unselfish and altruistic, able to offer others a truly unconditional, continuing love with no strings attached. Their unconditional love allows Twos to love without concern for themselves and without necessarily being loved in return. "Getting a return" on their love is not what matters to them.

Truly unconditional love is both free and freeing: healthy Twos are free to love or not, and others are free to respond or not. Others are allowed to grow on their own terms, even if it means that they will grow away. Healthy Twos always remember that it is an immense privilege to be allowed to be a part of someone's life, a gift others bestow on them, not something they can rightfully claim for themselves.

This is possible because at Level 1, Twos have learned to focus on their own real feelings and to truly nurture themselves. Healthy Twos are able to do good for themselves without feeling that they are being selfish or fearing that doing so will alienate people. By learning to love and nurture themselves, Twos no longer have to try to get love from others. They can honestly assess their own needs and deal with them and so can more objectively see and respond to the needs of the people in their lives. Sometimes they see that the best thing they can do is to do nothing. For very healthy Twos, giving is a choice, not a compulsion.

Very healthy Twos are as altruistic as human beings can be.

They are unselfconscious about their goodness, not letting "their right hand know what their left hand is doing." They have immense reservoirs of good will and are absolutely delighted at the good fortune of others. Their attitude is that good is to be done, no matter who does it or who gets the credit for it. Very healthy Twos are not angry if someone else takes credit for something they have done. Good was done, other people have benefited, and that is all that matters.

At their best, therefore, healthy Twos are completely disinterested in the truest sense of the word: they do not help others out of hidden self-interest, because they are directly attending to their own needs. Their intentions and actions are purely directed toward the good of the other, with no ulterior motives. Their disinterest allows Twos to see the real needs of others clearly, without ego or their own unmet needs clouding the picture. As a result, an extraordinary directness is possible in all their relationships, because ego and self-interest do not get in the way.

The paradox of very healthy Twos is that the more they learn to give to themselves, the more they enjoy giving to others. The more revered they are, the more humble they become. The more power people give them in their lives, the less they want. The less they look for love from others, the more others love them. Furthermore, virtue is not simply its own reward: the enduring reward of virtue is happiness. Very healthy Twos are happy to be good, and are filled with an outflowing joy. They are among the most radiant human beings one can hope to find in life—radiating the inexpressible happiness which comes from truly being good and doing good for others.

Few people rise to this level of sustained altruistic love, and those who do, do not advertise it. Those few who do come as close to being saints as anyone becomes, although they are too humble to think of themselves this way. They would be embarrassed by any suggestion that they are saints because, good as they are, they know perfectly well that their virtue does not truly belong to them. And besides, their sights are no longer on their own qualities. Even so, when they are at their best, very healthy Twos present us with an example of the heights which human nature can attain. They have been victorious in the never-ending battle to transcend the ego to make room for both the self and the other. They have truly learned to love.

Level 2: The Caring Person

Even if they do not live at this high peak of disinterested altruism all of the time, healthy Twos remain personally concerned for the welfare of others. Emotionally attuned to other people, they are the most empathetic of the personality types.

Empathy is the quality of being able to feel with another person, to experience his or her feelings as if they were your own. Empathy makes the feelings of others your feelings, their needs your needs. Being highly empathetic, healthy Twos are able to put themselves in the place of others, feeling compassion and concern. They have the strength to empathize with those who suffer. For example, when they hear about a disaster on television, their hearts go out to those who have been affected. The marital or job problems of their friends touch them deeply. Just knowing that someone else knows how you feel, that someone weeps with you, cares about you, takes your needs seriously, and will do all he or she can to help you, is itself a source of great comfort in times of trouble.

At this Level, Twos are extremely healthy, extraordinary people, but they have lost some of the freedom they experienced at Level 1. This is because Twos have begun to shift their focus more toward others and so lose contact with some of their own feelings. They also begin to see themselves as people who have good feelings for others, rather than simply allowing whatever feelings are present to be felt. At Level 2, this self-consciousness is rather benign, and much good still comes from Twos because most of their positive feelings for others remain genuine and deep.

Because their emotions are engaged so strongly and so positively for others, healthy Twos are aware of themselves as empathetic, caring people. Their hearts rather than their heads are their main faculty, and because they are led by their hearts, they do not judge others or concern themselves with keeping a strict account of right and wrong.

Healthy Twos see themselves as good because, in fact, they are good. They rightly see themselves as loving persons because, in fact, they are loving. They are well meaning, sincere, and warm-hearted—and they recognize these strengths in themselves. Moreover, realizing that they sincerely care for others gives Twos an enormous amount of self-confidence, allowing them to venture "where angels fear to tread." Their confidence, however, is not primarily in themselves but in the value of the goodness they so deeply believe in.

It almost goes without saying, but healthy Twos are extremely generous. One of the most important forms of their generosity is their generosity of spirit, not primarily a material generosity (since a particular Two may be poor or of modest means), but more an attitude toward others. They are charitable and put a positive interpretation on everything, emphasizing the good they find in others. This is, in a sense, an irrational gift, because it goes beyond reason: healthy Twos do not find fault with others even when there is fault to be found, not because they are not perceptive (far from it), but because they are much more attracted to what is positive and want to support those values. They are able to "love the sinner, not the sin," a saving distinction.

Level 3: The Nurturing Helper

Healthy Twos like to express how much they love others. Their strong, positive feelings for others naturally impel them into action. Service therefore is the keynote at this stage, and healthy Twos become giving people who take great satisfaction in helping others in many tangible ways. They serve those who are in need and cannot take care of themselves, feeding the hungry, clothing the naked, visiting the sick, volunteering for philanthropic work, using whatever means are at their disposal to help others.

Healthy Twos reach out to people, giving substantial help even if it means going out of their way when it is inconvenient or difficult to do so. They are exceptionally thoughtful about the material, psychological, emotional, or spiritual needs of others. Twos are extraordinary in crisis situations because others know that they can count on them. They are the kind of people you know you can call in the middle of the night for help. They are generous with their time, attention, money, and other resources—self-sacrificial in the best sense of the word. Indeed, people seek out healthy Twos because of their unique mixture of personal concern and practical helpfulness.

Of course Healthy Twos do not spend all of their time running around looking after other people's needs. Nonetheless, they experience in themselves a sense of bounty that they enjoy sharing with others, and there are many ways that Twos can express this beyond overt caretaking. Twos like to share whatever they have, and this can include talents like singing or performing, cooking, personal possessions, or simply their time. Healthy Twos are gratified by being able to give something of value to others and seeing others grow.

All of this is possible because healthy Twos have a clear sense of their own boundaries and their own needs. And while they are sincerely interested in helping others in whatever ways they can, they know their physical and emotional limits, and do not exceed them. While attending to others, they attend to themselves. While looking after someone else's health, they look after their own health. While counseling others to get enough rest and recreation, they make sure that they do, too.

Having clear boundaries also enables Twos to have enough energy to enjoy their lives. They make stimulating companions because they are good listeners, emotionally attuned to others, and have a genuine sense of fun. And because they are realistic and honest about their needs and limitations, they are much more free and relaxed about their relationships.

Healthy Twos also have uniformly good effects on people because their love is so particular: they make others feel that someone really sees them and cares about them as an individual. They divine the good in others and, armed with this knowledge, they are able to encourage and praise others sincerely, uplift spirits, and instill confidence. They build self-esteem because they give people the attention and appreciation they need to thrive.

Without trying to do so, healthy Twos exert an immense influence over others, because few things in life are as powerful as instilling the feeling in others that someone good cares about them, believes in them, and is on their side. Expecting good from others and appreciating what they do nurtures self-confidence and creates a climate of expectation which enables others to do wonderful things.

Thus, healthy Twos are an archetype of the good parent, acting as parent figures, in the best possible sense, to everyone they meet. Good parents want what is best for their children. They actively look out for their welfare. Similarly, healthy Twos actively look out for the welfare of others—nurturing them, encouraging them, and empowering them to grow and discover their own strengths.

In a word, they are the embodiment of the ideal of charity in action. Healthy Twos may be saints—or not quite saints—but in either case, they try to be caring, loving, and helpful. This is their ideal, and to one degree or another, healthy Twos attain it.

ANALYZING THE AVERAGE TWO

Level 4: *The Effusive Friend*

While healthy Twos are genuinely good, average Twos do less real good while talking more about their feelings and good intentions. Some reverse gear in their psyches has become engaged, and the attention they previously directed toward others begins to be focused on themselves. Their attention shifts away from doing real good for others to seeking reassurance that others love them and have good feelings about them.

Average Twos have begun to fear that they are not doing enough for others to really "win them over," and they begin to equate love with personal intimacy and closeness. While intimacy is certainly an essential quality of any good relationship, Twos begin focusing on it to the exclusion of many other things, and sometimes in situations in which it may be inappropriate. Nonetheless, Twos want people to notice how much they care and how deeply they feel for others. In conversation, they like to talk with people about the relationship they share as if to remind the person of how special the relationship is. ("Isn't it wonderful how close we are?") In truth, Twos are trying to get closer to others and to convince themselves that others really want them around.

At Level 4, Twos may still be helpful and generous, but they seem more interested in being seen as generous persons. They are friendly and talkative, and want to be on good terms with everyone they encounter. Twos at this stage can be quite sentimental— wearing their hearts on their sleeves and unapologetically telling everyone how they feel. They have a knack for meeting people, instantly regarding them as friends rather than acquaintances. Tactile people, they frequently give others a reassuring squeeze of the hand or an arm around the shoulder. They like to be physically close; kissing, touching, and hugging are natural extensions of their outgoing, effusive style.

At this stage, average Twos are people pleasers, gratifying others so that others will love them in return, although average Twos would have difficulty admitting this motive. They are convinced that they simply want to love others and to express how much they like people. But when they overstate their appreciation of others, genuine appreciation deteriorates into flattery, the purpose of which is not appreciation of the other, but that the flatterer be appreciated for his praise.

Average Twos are confident that they have something valuable to share with others: *themselves* — their love and attention. They are completely convinced of the sincerity of their good will toward everyone, putting a favorable interpretation on everything they do. However, they are not so much good as they are faultlessly well-intentioned. An inflation of ego is involved, although they take pains not to let this show, especially to themselves.

Religion often plays an important part in their lives. Average Twos may well be sincerely religious and want to do good for others because of their religious convictions. However, religion is also very congenial to the way they view themselves. Religion reinforces their self-image of being well-intentioned and gives credibility to their assertions of sincerity. Religion also gives average Twos a vocabulary and a respected value system in which to talk about love, friendship, self-sacrifice, goodness, what they do for others, and how they feel about others — all of their favorite topics. On another level, Twos often develop a connection with religion or focus on psychic abilities because these can become very valuable gifts Twos can bestow upon others. Also, religion or psychic abilities become "value-added" aspects of the Two's persona to which others may be attracted. Furthermore, religion puts average Twos on the side of the angels so that few people, including, of course, average Twos themselves, will dare to question their motives. Religion also appeals to their pride: they would secretly like to be thought of as savior figures, miracle workers, and rescuers. They have fantasies of their love conquering all, of killing the other person with kindness, and of winning over others through sheer goodness — all religious themes which make average Twos feel good about themselves.

The genuine appreciation of others that we find in healthy Twos has deteriorated into the beginning of an egocentricity which draws attention to itself in subtle ways. In all circumstances, Twos assert the depth of their feelings and how sincerely well-intentioned they are. And while their fine words seem to be for others' benefit, average Twos are in fact trying to get others to acknowledge their goodness. They begin to cultivate friendships, giving more and more attention to people whose love and appreciation they want to win, and encouraging them to reveal their inmost thoughts and intimate details about their personal lives. Average Twos want to be the "special friend," the confidant, the person to go to when one is troubled, because they believe that being such a person would surely mean that they are lovable.

Many people like the attention of average Twos, and average Twos know it. Their ability to lavish praise and flattery on people is a source of power, particularly over those who are hungry for approval. The approval they give, however, is not without cost.

Level 5: The Possessive "Intimate"

Given their interpersonal talents, it is not unusual for average Twos to gather a circle of people around themselves who become increasingly dependent on them. Average Twos would like to create an extended family, or a community, with themselves at the center so that others will regard them as important figures in their lives. They envelop people, making others feel that they are both part of a family and indebted to them for being invited to join it.

At this stage, Twos are like the stereotypical Jewish Mother who cannot do enough for others, although average Twos of all religions and sexes are equally inclined to this behavior. They are forever feeding people both literally and emotionally, something which has a powerful effect on others. Few things are as disarming as a seemingly sincere interest in oneself, and average Twos are never more effective than with those who, for their own psychological reasons, are searching for a mother's love. Because of this, average Twos are on the lookout for people who will need them, but this sets up a serious problem. Since Twos are taking care of others to get appreciation and in the hopes of eventually getting their own needs satisfied in return, selecting dysfunctional, emotionally needy people makes the chances of getting sufficient feedback remote at best. Twos end up being drawn to the people who will be least able to reciprocate their attention—addicts, the infirm, the emotionally wounded.

This would not be an issue if it were not for the fact that Twos are looking for specific signs of appreciation from the objects of their affection. Tragically, Twos have begun to fear that the people they care about will love others more than them, and they believe that they must be *needed* by others in order to stay in their lives. To this end, Twos increasingly look for ways to be needed by the people they love. Their superego does not allow them to acknowledge this, though, so Twos must continue to convince themselves that they are only motivated by selfless love.

Of course, love remains their supreme value, and they want to love everyone. Love becomes their excuse, their rationale, their every motive, their only goal in life. If there is any type which is a Johnny-one-note about anything, it is the average Two talking about love. But it is also clear that when average Twos talk about love what they mean is that it is *their* love which is the solution to everybody's needs.

Thus, average Twos see everyone as needy children hungry for love and attention, which they begin to press on others whether they seek it or not. They hover and interfere, giving unrequested advice, intruding into situations, and imposing themselves on people—making pests of themselves in the name of self-sacrificial love. The difficulty is that they are self-sacrificial to a fault, martyrs who invent needs to fulfill so that they can assume a greater position of importance to others. In short, they need to be needed.

They become busybodies, intrusively nosing into people's affairs. In adopting the role of the loving parent even to their peers, Twos make it their business to solve everyone's problems, from matchmaking to finding a job to giving advice about decorating an apartment. Because they want others to need them (their love, advice, approval, guidance), they do not hesitate to jump into people's lives to help out. Others often experience this as meddling, and begin to distance themselves from the Two—the very thing Twos want to avoid.

The intimate conversations of Level 4 have also deteriorated into gossip, which serves as a way to let others know how many friends the Two has and how close the relationship with them is. They talk incessantly about their friends (and about friendships) in embarrassingly explicit detail. ("Let's talk about us.") They also think nothing of asking very pointed personal questions. Most people are usually too embarrassed (or too dependent on them) to rebuff their inquiries. The problem is that the flow of information is one-sided: average Twos always pry more out of others than they reveal about themselves. After all, they do not have problems: they are there to help others solve *their* problems.

Average Twos insinuate themselves into other people's lives very quickly; others invariably find it difficult to pull away. Unfortunately, average Twos begin to inflict their ego agenda on others, who have to bear the burden of the Two's love—or really, of the Two's need to feel loved. Not surprisingly, their intrusiveness has negative effects on the very people Twos think they love. (The smothering mother's love suffocates.) But because their love is so relentlessly self-sacrificial, the beneficiaries of it are constrained from complaining about the quality of the Two's help.

Since they are sacrificing themselves for others, average Twos begin to feel that they have proprietary rights over them. They become possessive and extremely jealous of their friends, constantly hovering and "checking in" on the telephone. Twos become increasingly insecure about others' affection for them and are afraid that if they let their loved ones out of their sight, their loved ones would probably leave them. They do not introduce their friends or encourage them to get to know one another because they fear that they might be left behind. They begin secretly to like it when other people are in a crisis: this gives them a role to fulfill and guarantees that they will be needed—at least for a while. Average Twos do not know how to let go of people, a problem which only gets worse as they continue to deteriorate toward unhealth.

Average Twos look for tangible responses from others as signs of success in their relationships. As they become more fearful that they are not lovable, it takes more to convince them that people do love and appreciate them. By Level 5, Twos evaluate the responses of others to their overtures of friendship and help, and only very specific responses are recognized as love. Twos expect people to know what the Two wants and needs. After all, haven't Twos made it their business to know what others need? They may expect to receive phone calls, or invitations to dinner, or cards for every conceivable occasion, or thank-you notes—constant reassurance that people miss and love them. But only the specific response counts. A card will never do if what the Two really wants is a hug. Twos often deal with this by projecting their desire onto the other. ("You look like you could use a good hug.") More often, though, they will simmer with frustration and find more ways to be "helpful." Their superego will not allow them the "selfishness" of asking for what they want directly. In their pride, Twos cannot admit to the depth of their hurt and need.

Twos compensate for their growing fears by acting as if they were holding court. It flatters Twos to be treated like a guru, someone to whom others come for advice about all sorts of personal matters. Naturally, others are expected to keep them informed about everything significant in their lives: they want to be the social switchboard through which every piece of important information must pass. Twos are frantic to get positive feedback, to hear that their love and attention is valued and appreciated. To keep the flow of responses going, they stay in touch with old friends, spending a considerable amount of time maintaining their relationships—letting people know that they are thinking of them, worrying about them, praying for them, and so forth. Thus, while average Twos may still be thoughtful, it is in increasingly superficial ways: they remember birthdays and call frequently on the phone, but they begin to avoid getting tied down to the real needs of others so they can influence more people.

Ironically, their overinvolvement in the lives of others takes a toll on their genuine obligations, especially if Twos have families of their own. A problem with commitment surfaces. They become fickle, not so much because they drop one person to become deeply involved with another, but because they are constantly looking for love from yet another source. Since they want to be loved and appreciated by everyone, average Twos are constantly widening their circle of friends and acquaintances, doing yet more for others and inventing more needs to fulfill. When those who depend on them turn to them for help, they find that the Two is no longer there—they are off helping someone else.

Average Twos inevitably overextend themselves, helping too many people, sitting on too many committees, giving advice to too many friends, until they begin to feel *burdened* and physically worn out by their charity. Yet it is difficult for them not to be so involved, since that is how they maintain their sense of self. Furthermore, histrionic qualities have begun to surface, and as average Twos sacrifice themselves for others, they feel that they suffer because of their goodness. They dramatize every ache and pain, every inconvenience and problem which their kindliness has cost them. Illnesses, little breakdowns, and hypochondria become part of the picture.

The fact is that at this stage average Twos are not as loving as they think they are. They have strong egos, something they probably would not deny. (They have never claimed that they have no ego but that they are always well-meaning and loving.) They also have aggressive impulses on which they cannot act directly, as well as personal needs. Since they cannot risk being selfish and driving others away, they convince themselves that what they do is never for themselves but for everyone else. ("I was just doing it for you, trying to make your life easier.") Even the simplest, seemingly most spontaneous acts of kindness become loaded with unacknowledged ulterior motives.

Unfortunately, average Twos feel that they will be loved only if they are constantly doing things for people—in effect, bribing others to love them. Of course, Twos want a sincere response, but instead of allowing others to take the initiative, they prime the pump to get the kind of response they want. The irony is that when Twos receive the response they have maneuvered for, they never know whether they would have received it without their own prompting, so the response does not mean much. This raises a new anxiety: How much are they appreciated for themselves? It is a problem which Twos create—and then begin to chafe under.

Level 6: The Self-Important "Saint"

Their point of view is understandable: average Twos feel that they have done many good things—they have taken a well-meaning interest in people, they have sacrificed themselves, they have taken care of people's needs—and they simply want to be appreciated for it. It seems to them that others completely take for granted the efforts they have made. They feel that no one values them, that others do not think about their needs or sacrifice themselves for them the way they have. Twos feel that others are ungrateful and thoughtless and must be reminded of how good they are.

The reason for this kind of behavior is that it is difficult for Twos to appreciate themselves—and to keep their aggressive impulses under control—unless their value is reinforced by others. The person who was once so seemingly other-oriented has, at this stage, become egocentric under a veneer of modesty calculated to draw attention to itself. Twos at this stage are now altogether too self-important, patronizingly regarding themselves as indispensable to others, praising themselves, and becoming shamelessly self-congratulatory—modestly talking about their many virtues.

Vainglory is the capital sin of average Twos. Very pleased with themselves, they never allow an opportunity to slip by without reminding others of how much people love them, or how many friends they have, and what good works they have done. ("Imagine someone like me becoming friendly with someone like you! People have told me that you are lucky to have me as a friend.") They drop the names of everyone they know, particularly if these are people of prominence. (Dropping names impresses others with how important Twos are as friends, sending the message that others had better value them since so many other people already do.)

Self-satisfied Twos may well not be aware of the extent of their pride. They like to impress others as selfless saints, calling attention to their virtue so that their good deeds will not go unnoticed—for the edification of others, of course. They like to shine in the eyes of others, be acclaimed for their virtues, and told what fine people they are, or even better, overhear themselves discussed in the most glowing terms. (Twos can, of course, proclaim their little human foibles, but God help anyone who accuses them of any serious faults.) The fact is that by now others have become mere appendages to their egos, little more than sources of gratification for their pride.

Pride is also destructive to Twos in the sense that it prevents them from acknowledging the intensity of their resentments or the depth of their emotional suffering. Twos believe that were they to admit to these "negative" feelings, they would be quickly abandoned. In fact, just the opposite is true. While Twos may not want to admit to their growing hurt and rage, others certainly feel it and are repelled by the mixed signals Twos send. Some open communication would be helpful, but at Level 6, they are too invested in maintaining their false self-image.

The servant has become the master. The underlying wounds to their self-esteem and narcissism are so deep that Twos need others to be grateful to them constantly: an unending stream of gratitude, attention, and praise must flow in their direction. They expect others to do favors for them as signs of their importance and feel that others should repay them—in cash or kind—for their previous self-sacrifices, real or imagined. Having done a good deed sometime in the past, self-important Twos feel that the beneficiary is forever in their debt. The problem is that they grossly overvalue what they have done for others, while undervaluing what everyone else does for them. What others find particularly galling is that Twos at this Level take credit for everything positive in their lives, as if they alone were responsible for whatever success or happiness others have. Twos feel that they are indispensable and that others could not have done anything without their help ("You have me to thank for that"), and do not hesitate to say so.

At the same time, Twos at Level 6 are still extremely needy for affection, and they are far less discriminating about where and how they get it. Their emotional needs are intense, and all the more so for being repressed. For all of their pride and self-importance, they are willing to chase after anyone who gives them the slightest hint of the kind of attention and contact they are looking for, and when they are at this Level or lower, what they recognize as love can be abusive and destructive.

Their tendency at Level 5 to take on too many obligations has escalated into an indiscriminate pursuit of attention. Before, they often left their primary loved ones unattended because of all of the "friends" that they had to help. Now they are eager to be part of any situation that promises to get them some attention or emotional connection. They want to be part of every social get-together they hear about, and can spend long hours on the phone in rambling conversations. Under certain circumstances, they may pursue various kinds of sexual escapades. Indeed, the ability to attract others sexually becomes an indication of their lovability. They can resemble Sevens in their scattered lack of focus, but while Sevens are running around to avoid their anxiety, Twos are running around because they are magnetized by any situation that even potentially offers to make them feel needed and loved. Thus, the people closest to them may feel abandoned by them, a particularly ironic turn of events given the Two's desperate need for appreciation.

Unfortunately, Twos do not see that their expectations of appreciation are much too high. They are bound to be disappointed and furious if others do anything short of handing over their very lives to them. But this creates a serious conflict: they are furious with others if others do not love them in return. Yet rehashing their claims to force others into loving them will likely only drive others away, making Twos feel the bitter sting of rejection even more acutely because of their inflated self-importance. Often they will attempt to "stuff" their feelings by abusing food, alcohol, or prescription medications, but this only makes them feel more hopeless and unlovable. Resentments smolder, becoming the prelude to manipulation, coercion, and revenge.

ANALYZING THE UNHEALTHY TWO

Level 7: The Self-Deceptive Manipulator

It usually takes a background of chronic abuse or a major catastrophe in people's lives to precipitate a fall into the unhealthy
Levels, but when this does occur, Twos take a particularly nasty
turn for the worse. Their aggressions have been strongly aroused,
but because their aggressions conflict with their all-good self-
image, Twos cannot express how they actually feel. The upshot is
that unhealthy Twos have to express their aggressions indirectly,
by manipulating others to give them the kind of loving response
they desperately want. The irony is, however, that if they manipulate others, the responses they receive will never satisfy them.

Not feeling that they are loved not only hurts unhealthy Twos
terribly, it calls into question their whole value system—the value
of "love." If love does not have the power to get them what they
want, then what does? Having loved and lost, they are furious
about it. The answer is, of course, that what passes for love in unhealthy Twos is not love, but extreme forms of codependency and
desperate need. By Level 7, Twos are too neurotic to even recognize
love, let alone give or receive it. While they still use the vocabulary
of love, their words are self-serving, designed to get something from
others without appearing to do so directly. Manipulation is the
name of the game.

Manipulative Twos are the maestros of guilt; they can play
others like an orchestra, upping the level of guilt into a disturbing crescendo or dampening it down to a whisper, as needed. They
play people against each other, and worse, they are able to play
others against themselves. It is shocking to people to realize how
much the unhealthy Two's manipulations pull them off their own
center. Grown men and women, heads of households and corporations, are reduced to so much emotional wreckage by being
manipulated into enlisting part of themselves against themselves.
But by casting others into self-doubt and making them feel guilty
and confused, unhealthy Twos throw others off the scent of their
own manipulations.

They undermine others while presenting themselves as "help-
ers" who can heal the pain they have subtly caused. They prick at
tender spots with one hand while soothing the hurt with the other;

they put people down and then bolster their self-confidence with left-handed compliments; they never let people forget their problems, making their future seem hopeless while promising to remain with them forever; they reopen old wounds, then rush in to stitch them up. They become one's best friend and, unwittingly, one's worst enemy.

At the same time, unhealthy Twos still feel compelled to do things for others to be needed. They are too unhealthy to really be of assistance, but still they cannot stop themselves, which inevitably leads to problems with their physical health. This often begins as hypochondria at Level 6. Getting sick allows Twos to take a break from wearing themselves out for everyone without feeling like a bad or selfish person. But over time, as Twos continue "stuffing" their anger and frustration and abusing food and medications, they really do get sick and begin to use their illness as a way of eliciting attention. In the unhealthy Two, pity comes to substitute for love.

Naturally, unhealthy Twos are difficult to help and notoriously resistant to therapy. They put themselves in a morally superior position, no matter what they have said or done. And by insisting on the absolute purity of their motives, they call those of others into question. No one can question their behavior or motives without Twos ascribing evil-mindedness to them. Even tangible evidence has no effect on them since it can be dismissed as irrelevant to their good intentions. Unhealthy Twos can always be depended on to defend themselves by appealing to good intentions and the laws of the heart to sanction anything they do. They use religious rationalizations to extricate themselves from guilt or responsibility for their actions; they make another's attempt at an objective analysis of a situation seem niggling and petty by comparison to their superior ethics, which follow a higher morality. They have turned the dictum "love, and do what you will" into a license to do whatever they want in the name of "love."

All of this destructive behavior stems from the tremendous rage which unhealthy Twos are suppressing, and the struggles of their fragile ego to survive. Convinced that everyone is leaving them or would leave them if they were less dependent on the Two, unhealthy Twos use whatever means they can to hold on to people at all costs. They are terrified of being left alone, but also furious at the people they "love" for causing them to suffer so much. But again, they cannot admit to their hatreds or even to the idea that they might have any self-interest.

Self-deception is the defense mechanism which allows unhealthy Twos to avoid seeing the discrepancy between the virtues they think they possess and their actual behavior. No matter how destructive they are, unhealthy Twos, through self-deception, are able to interpret whatever they do as good. In their minds, they always remain well-intentioned, loving human beings. Their consciences are always clear.

It is important to understand that unhealthy Twos are at peace with being manipulative because they do not have to rationalize individual acts. With the help of self-deception, they have managed to rationalize their entire lives. Once they have defined themselves as "good," they are able to justify whatever they say or do without feeling guilty, and without feeling that they are no longer good. Others have caused them to suffer. They are only helpless victims. In fact, if they are at Level 7 or lower, Twos have likely been victimized by others in very serious and damaging ways. The wounds to their self-esteem are so great that they must constantly rationalize their behavior to justify their existence. Further, they are so afraid that people will not love them that they are desperate to hang on to any emotional connection with others, even if it is painful and destructive.

At Level 7, the joyously radiant qualities so evident in healthy Twos are nowhere to be found. Twos are bitter and in great pain, neither spreading joy nor experiencing it. Their behavior can be deeply frustrating and painful for those around them, but their aggressions are still primarily psychological. Unfortunately, without help, their behavior may get markedly worse.

Level 8: The Coercive Dominator

The possessiveness we saw in average Twos has deteriorated into coercively demanding love from others on their own terms—and neurotic terms at that. What emerges is a delusional sense of entitlement, the feeling that they have an absolute right to get whatever they want from others. From their viewpoint, everyone else owes them whatever they want because of the self-sacrifices unhealthy Twos insist they have made in the past.

Neurotic Twos are nearly hysterical in their fears of being unloved and can be highly irrational and extraordinarily difficult to deal with. Their ability to conceal the depth of their need breaks down. Twos at Level 8 lack the energy to maintain their image of selflessness in any consistent way. They are tired of being selfless. They now insist that others put their needs first. Their egos, whose needs were formerly met indirectly through various kinds of service to others, are thrust into the foreground, making demands on others with a vengeance.

Twos at this Level pursue their emotional gratification with a reckless abandon. They want love and they will turn to almost any source to find it. Often, a person at this level of unhealth will have suffered a highly dysfunctional childhood environment, quite possibly being physically, sexually, or emotionally abused. As a result, unhealthy Twos would not know genuine love if they fell over it. Instead, they compulsively seek out whatever kind of connection they had with their protective-figure as children, whether abusive, violent, or neglectful. The kinds of relationships they compulsively engage in are frequently clear indications of their root anxieties. Promiscuity, destructive affairs, and other forms of sexual acting out are not uncommon.

Nor are their emotional needs the only aspect of their personalities to be exposed at this Level. Twos have been harboring deep and painful resentments for a long time, and now their hatred and anger boils to the surface. They express their contempt and rage at others in a variety of ways, and yet what remains of their fragile ego demands that they justify their aggressions and keep their few remaining loved ones from deserting them completely.

Their aggressions often take the form of an unnerving and frustrating knack for belittling people in the name of love. Neurotic Twos can make the most derogatory remarks about others, both behind their backs and to their faces, if need be, "for their own good." They may also punish others by withdrawing their love. ("Well, you can just try to get along without me!") They do not hesitate to make dire predictions about others' possibilities without them. ("You're not going to be happy; you're going to fall right on your face without me.") By denying that they take any personal satisfaction in telling people what they think of them, or in having any ulterior motives whatsoever, they are free to do and say anything they please. ("I can say anything I want about him, because I love him.")

They are furious with others and it shows. The veneer of love drops away, and neurotic Twos let loose a torrent of bitter complaints about how they have been treated, how their health has suffered, and how unappreciated they are. They endlessly dredge up things from the past, harping on how much they have helped people, how hopeless others are without them, and how they made others who they are today. ("Remember what I did for you? Is this the thanks I get?")

While their incessant complaints and disparaging remarks bring them attention, it is the wrong kind of attention—the resentment and anger of others. Of course, unhealthy Twos are aware of this and it becomes a source of fresh complaints. The vicious circle of recrimination continues. However, they feel that anything offensive or hurtful they may do to others does not reflect on them as deeply loving human beings, but is justified by the unloving treatment they have received. Hence, they can do the most awful things to people without a qualm of conscience. ("If one judges love by most of its results, it is closer to hatred than friendship."—La Rochefoucauld)

Indeed, neurotic Twos want to be loved so much that they may attempt to coerce others to love them in the most damaging ways. It is possible that some forms of pedophilia and child molestation have their roots here, and that Twos, as a group, figure disproportionately in this kind of destructive behavior. It is worth remembering that Twos typically enjoy the trust and admiration of family and friends. They may be teachers, clergy, daycare workers, or nurses—those whose word and integrity is usually not suspected by anyone. But, at this stage, since Twos are neurotic and in all probability lack satisfactory intimate relationships with their peers, it is possible that they will turn to children or other inappropriate sources of "love" to fulfill their emotional and sexual needs.

Moreover, since they are already extremely manipulative and self-deceptive, neurotic Twos are more than capable of taking advantage of the powerlessness of children. Indeed, their helplessness is one of the qualities which attracts Twos to children: they can comfort the very child they have terrorized, playing the role of savior once again.

Level 9: The Psychosomatic Victim

If demanding love from others has gotten them nowhere, unhealthy Twos unconsciously try another avenue. They want to be loved, to be shown concern, and to be appreciated more desperately than ever. Physical illness seems to be a reliable way of ensuring that they receive the appreciation which they have been seeking. Becoming an invalid is the solution: others will have no choice but to take care of them. While being cared for is not the same as being loved, it may be as close to love as they are going to get.

Neurotic Twos try to obtain the love of others, which has always been their fundamental desire, by unconsciously desiring to go to pieces. They fear being held responsible for their words and deeds. They also fear that their aggressions have revealed some hypocrisy about themselves which would make them unlovable, their greatest fear. They therefore unconsciously attempt to escape responsibility for themselves by having a physical breakdown which will, in a sense, exempt them from further punishment. And, in their minds at least, physical suffering will conclusively prove many of the most important claims they have made about themselves: that they have been selfless, that they have been victimized by others, that they have worn themselves out for others, and so on, all of which may have some degree of truth to them.

Their health falls apart because, as formidable and willful as neurotic Twos are, the strain of living under enormous contradictions becomes unbearable. The stress of trying to control and justify their hatred of others takes its toll physically. Furthermore, their superego is so toxic and relentless that the only way unhealthy Twos feel that they can get some attention—or even some relief—is to become ill.

Psychosomatic illnesses are the result of the process known as hysterical conversion reaction. In psychological terms, neurotic Twos are hysterics who convert anxiety into physical symptoms. They usually fall victim to a wide array of mysterious illnesses, including skin eruptions, gastrointestinal problems, arthritis, and high blood pressure—all diseases in which stress plays an important role. (Even average Twos may develop mysterious illnesses; however, by the time a Two is fully neurotic, the list of diseases has become long, and being an invalid has become a way of life.) Because Twos are ill so often, others may suspect a masochistic enjoyment of their sufferings, but, strictly speaking, this is not the case. They do not actually enjoy suffering because the suffering is real; instead, they enjoy the benefits suffering affords them. Horney describes it vividly.

Suffering is unconsciously put into the service of asserting claims, which not only checks the incentive to overcome it but also leads to inadvertent exaggerations of suffering. This does not mean that his suffering is merely "put on" for demonstrative purposes. It affects him in a much deeper way because he must primarily prove himself to his own satisfaction that he is entitled to the fulfillment of his needs. He must feel that his suffering is so exceptional and so excessive that it entitles him to help. In other words this process makes a person actually feel his suffering more intensely than he would without its having acquired an unconscious strategic value. (Karen Horney, *Neurosis and Human Growth*, 229.)

Physical suffering is also a permanent, guilt-instilling rebuke to those who have not provided neurotic Twos with the love and appreciation they have always wanted. It is an unending source of demands for attention, care, concern—for love. The "saint" has become a drain on everyone. The most other-oriented person either drives away family and friends or makes their lives unbearable.

ANALYZING THE DYNAMICS OF THE TWO

The Direction of Disintegration: The Two Goes to Eight
Starting at Level 4, average to unhealthy Twos will sometimes respond to stress and adversity by exhibiting some of the traits of the average to unhealthy Eight. Because Twos repress many of their negative and aggressive feelings, the move to Eight can be seen as a way of acting them out when the Two's normal ego defenses fail.

At Level 4, Twos tend to be friendly and well-meaning, expressing their positive feelings about everyone in their lives. When they go to Eight, they suddenly become more direct and, in a sense, "cut to the chase." They can seem shrewd and pragmatic, in marked contrast to the image of sweetness they usually project, and can be downright blunt. They also respond to stress by working harder, getting more deeply engaged in the projects they have established, and getting concerned about their family's survival needs.

At Level 5, Twos want to be needed, and try to make themselves indispensable to people. Here, the move toward Eight underscores their need to be appreciated for their efforts. They begin to draw attention to their importance, bluffing and boasting and making big promises to people. This mixes with the Two's gossiping and name-dropping in a way that is intended to communicate to others, "I hope you are aware of how important I am in your life." Twos at this Level can also pick up some of the Eight's swaggering and domineering qualities. In response to the frustrations entailed in their self-sacrifices, they are starting to throw their weight around.

At Level 6, when patronizing and self-importance collapse, Twos can become more flagrantly aggressive and controlling in the manner of Eights at Level 6. They may make threats and attempt to undermine the confidence of the people around them as a way of getting them to stay, but also of exerting control. When Twos act out Eight traits at this Level, the pretenses of being loving and friendly disappear and the underlying rage and feelings of betrayal are exposed. Although Twos will tend to rationalize these episodes and even forget them, others will not.

By Level 7, Twos have become deeply neurotic and are using all of their strength to repress their growing rage and hostility in order to preserve the illusion that they are still good, selfless people. The movement toward Eight here is indicative of a failure to "keep the lid on" any longer. The tempers of Twos at this Level can be frightening, as their anger and disappointment come to the surface. They may strike others, or scream viciously and abusively at the people they feel are frustrating them.

At Level 8, even the pretenses of sweetness have vanished, and when Twos go to Eight now, they release their aggressions, going after whatever they want with feelings of entitlement. Their suppressed desires can emerge wildly out of control, and Twos can be relentless and brutal in pursuit of whatever they believe has been denied them. They feel powerful, justified, and unstoppable in the rush of lust that explodes in them.

The essential problem with unhealthy Twos is that they have not come to grips with their aggressive feelings. Even in the depths of their illness and suffering, neurotic Twos realize that they are still coercing the attention of others, and this thought continues to enrage them. They may be bedridden or hospitalized because they are physically ill, but they are not deranged or dissociating from reality.

Thus, at Level 9, while unconsciously having a physical breakdown has been adaptive (since illness and physical incapacitation take the possibility of violence against others out of their hands), this form of adaptation may not last for long. After all, they may actually recover and something else may precipitate a move to Eight, the eruption of their aggressive feelings into seriously destructive behavior.

Because they are still neurotic, however, unhealthy Twos are in no position to deal constructively with their aggressive impulses. Their bitterness and rancor, their desire for revenge and self-vindication, are directed to those who have frustrated their desire to be loved. When they move to Eight, neurotic Twos strike out at those who have not responded to them as they have wanted. The hatred they have suppressed comes pouring out, and is openly expressed against those who Twos feel have not loved them sufficiently in the past. Love completely turns into hatred, and smoldering hatred into violence and destruction.

A deeply neurotic Two at Eight can become physically violent, even murderous. Those in the immediate family are usually the people most at risk, the very ones for whom, Twos are convinced, they had nothing but good intentions and undying love. The invalid, the self-sacrificial martyr, the suffering saint becomes a monster, sacrificing others.

The Direction of Integration: The Two Goes to Four
When healthy Twos go to Four, they get in touch with their feelings, especially their aggressive ones, and become aware of themselves as they really are. They graduate from an unwillingness to examine themselves and their motives, and move toward self-knowledge.

Integrating Twos accept the presence of their negative feelings as fully as they accept their positive feelings. This does *not* mean that they act on their negative feelings when they are at Four, but that they are willing to acknowledge these feelings in themselves. Because Twos at Four become emotionally honest, they are able to express the full range of their emotions—not just their loving side, although it is certainly still present and more genuine than ever before.

For the first time, integrating Twos unconditionally accept themselves, just as they unconditionally accept others. It is therefore possible to give something deeper and more personal to others than they have ever done in the past. And when they are loved by others, it is all the more gratifying because others love the whole of them. Integrating Twos can rightly feel that they are no longer loved just for what they do for others, but for who they are.

There is also the possibility of harnessing their fuller, more authentic feelings into forms of creativity. They become more self-aware and reflective human beings, who have intuitions into the depths of the human condition. Whatever they give to others is now all the more valuable because integrating Twos are more genuine as human beings, whether as artists, or as parents, or as friends.

THE MAJOR SUBTYPES OF THE TWO

The Two with a One-Wing: "The Servant"

Both the Two and the One are strongly oriented to their superegos, so we see a heightened sense of altruism in the Two with a One-wing. At the same time, the Two's traits and those of the One tend to conflict with each other: Twos are emotional, interpersonal, and histrionic, while Ones are rational, impersonal, and self-controlled. The empathy and interpersonalism of the Two are counterbalanced by the restraint, objectivity, and idealism of the One. Thus, the Two with a One-wing strives for love through goodness and selfless service. The One-wing contributes a degree of circumspection and severity which is less pronounced in the Two's other subtype. The sense of obligation and duty is also stronger, while the Two's more interpersonal qualities are typically more muted. In this respect, this subtype can be misidentified as Type Six, or vice versa. There is a strong conscience and a desire to act on principles so that people of this subtype will try to treat others fairly, no matter what their emotional needs are, although because Two is the basic type, they will probably feel conflicts between their principles and their heart. Noteworthy examples of this subtype include Mother Teresa, Eleanor Roosevelt, Archbishop Desmond Tutu, Danny Thomas, Alan Alda, Ann Landers, Florence Nightingale, Lewis Carroll, "Melanie Hamilton Wilkes," and "Jean Brodie."

Healthy persons of this subtype can do a great deal of good for others, partly because of the One-wing's principles. Teaching others, improving their lives, and working for a cause are noteworthy traits. Many charities and religious and philanthropic organizations are probably begun and staffed by this subtype. They want to give the best possible service to others, and they do so with less self-regard and more altruism than the Two's other subtype. They often feel a seriousness of purpose and are drawn to search for their life's task. They may be particularly fine teachers, since they not only have an objective, intellectual orientation to facts and values, but the emotional warmth to bring ideas to life. As teachers and parents, they are also very encouraging and appreciative of those in their charge. In their personal style, they like to keep things simple and functional, in contrast to the more flamboyant Two with a Three-wing.

In average persons of this subtype, there is a tension between personalism and idealism. As Twos, they empathize with people, but if they have a strong One-wing, their abstract ideals conflict with their feelings, making it difficult for them to empathize with others wholeheartedly. At least some part of them remains judgmental, ready to make moral pronouncements. Yet both components cause people of this subtype to feel strongly driven to serve others, and they experience great difficulty saying no to people. Average persons of this subtype can also be very controlling, both of others and of themselves. They are egocentric, although this is hidden by their ideals, especially the ideal of love. We see the conflicting tendencies of the two subtypes most clearly in the desire to be important to others versus the desire to be reasonable and objective. They feel awkward about drawing attention to themselves and prefer working in the background, yet as Twos they want to feel significant in others' lives. Persons of this subtype are also more subject to guilt and to self-condemnation than Twos with a Three-wing, since they tend to be more highly critical of themselves when they fail to live up to their own moral standards. They often feel that they already have too much, and have more trouble asking for what they want than the other subtype of the Two.

Unhealthy people of this subtype are self-righteous, inflexible, and moralistic about whatever they think is the right thing to do. Self-righteousness and the desire to justify themselves combine with self-deception and manipulation to produce a strongly entrenched mind-set which is very difficult to change. Persons of this subtype are quick to condemn others and are able to justify themselves on moral grounds. They cannot allow themselves to be proved wrong, nor can they allow themselves to be proved selfish, and they completely deny their aggressive feelings. People of this subtype are subject to hypochondria and psychosomatic disorders—obsessions and compulsions focused on their bodies.

The Two with a Three-Wing: "The Host/Hostess"

The Two's traits and those of the Three tend to reinforce each other: both types relate easily to people. The Three-wing adds elements of charm, "personality," and adaptability; thus, Twos with a Three-wing seek love through the creation of intimacy and personal connection. This is also the more "seductive" side of the Two: this subtype employs charm and social graces to win the affection of others. The Three's desire for acceptance and validation blends with the Two's drive for appreciation and closeness to form a personality in which relationships are the central focus. Noteworthy examples of this subtype include Luciano Pavarotti, Barbara Bush, Barry Manilow, Richard Simmons, Sammy Davis, Jr., Leo Buscaglia, Kathy Bates, Doug Henning, Tommy Tune, John Denver, Pat Boone, and Lillian Carter.

Healthy people of this subtype are charming, friendly, and outgoing. They enjoy the attention of others, are self-assured, and exude an aura of well-being and wholesome self-enjoyment. They possess a free-spirited, worldly attitude that can easily be confused with the joie de vivre of the Seven. There is genuine warmth in people of this subtype, as well as the ability to communicate that warmth to others. The "giving" of this subtype is less likely to take the form of overt caretaking. They enjoy bestowing whatever talents they possess upon their friends and admirers: cooking, entertaining, singing, and listening are all experienced as an inner bountifulness to be shared. The Two with the Three-wing is more a "gift giver" than a "servant." Social qualities are valued more than moral or intellectual ones. They are less task-driven than the other subtype, but also less likely to engage in self-questioning and self-criticism.

Average Twos with a Three-wing want to project an image of outstanding warmth and friendliness. It is important for them to be perceived as extraordinary, desirable people. Twos use others to validate their goodness; Threes, to validate their desirability, which in this subtype is often expressed as a focus on physical attractiveness and sexual desirability. Also, to the extent that the Three-wing is operative, they are hard working and want tangible signs of achievement and success. The image-consciousness of average Threes can begin to manifest in Twos as excessive friendliness, "cuteness," and exaggerated sentimentality. They are also more prone to flattery and gossip than the other subtype. Whereas none of these behaviors are necessarily harmful, they tend to cause others to reject them as serious intimates—exactly the opposite of what Twos want. They are also highly aware of what others think of them and how they come across to others. When combined with the Two's possessiveness, this can cause them to be overly concerned with their desirability in a way that can lead both to strong attractions and big disappointments. Having the right friends, dropping names, and cultivating people is typical. We also find the tendency to be self-important and narcissistic, although the Three's calculation of his or her "image" and the Two's self-sacrificial persona will mask this to some degree. The Three-wing helps Twos be more direct about what they want, but also causes them to draw more attention to the services they have provided. A person of this subtype fears being humiliated and losing status rather than feeling guilty over the violation of his or her moral ideals.

If people of this subtype become unhealthy, they can be emotionally devastating to others since they become both manipulative and exploitative, deceptive with respect to others and self-deceptive, opportunistic and neurotically feeling entitled to get whatever they want from others. Hostility toward others can be extremely strong and all-consuming: beneath their apparent charm lies viciousness. They are potentially psychopathic in the destructiveness they are capable of wreaking. In them we find elements of emotional obsession—even stalking behavior—that can lead to malice and the tendency to ruin what they cannot have, especially relationships. Twos with a Three-wing are capable of pathological jealousy and violent crimes of passion.

SOME FINAL THOUGHTS

As we look back, we can see that Twos have conflicts between their desire to love and their need to be loved, between their genuine self-esteem and their need to manipulate others to feel good about themselves. What is unfortunate is that, to paraphrase Othello, average to unhealthy Twos have loved neither too wisely nor too well. But at least according to their own lights, they have tried to love others. Therein lies the nobility of their goal and their tragedy if they fail to attain it.

The irony is that unhealthy Twos compulsively bring about the very thing they most fear: they want to be loved, but end up being hated, or at least unwanted by anyone. A second, darkly comic irony lies in the likelihood that the only person who may be attracted to the unenviable position of caring for an invalid, neurotic Two may be another Two. If the second Two is manipulatively self-sacrificial about the help which he or she gives, a pathetic duel of wills may play itself out between these two likeminded, draining souls. The result is a macabre dance of death.

If we draw a lesson from this personality type, it is that Twos can be right in their belief about the value of love, yet wrong in their manner of loving others. If they intrude upon people with "love," Twos unwittingly prove that what they force on others is not love, and, for that very reason, is doomed to failure. As soon as ego masquerades behind love, love becomes tainted and eventually corrupt — with all the consequences which we have seen in this personality type.

Chapter 5

Type Three: The Motivator

THE THREE IN PROFILE

Healthy: Self-assured and energetic, with high self-esteem: they believe in themselves and their own value. Adaptable, well-adjusted, and charming, often attractive and popular. Realistic and purposeful with a good sense of their potential. / Ambitious to improve themselves, to "be all that they can be" — often become outstanding, a kind of human ideal, embodying widely admired qualities. Others are motivated to be like them in some positive way. High-spirited, goal-oriented, and persistent. They are effective, industrious people. *At Their Best:* Inner-directed and authentic, everything they seem to be. Accept their limitations and live within them. Self-deprecatory sense of humor and a childlike innocence emerge. Charitable, genuinely modest, and benevolent.

Average: Highly concerned with performance, doing the job well, being superior, and rising above others. Compare themselves with others in search for status and success. Become driven careerists and social climbers, invested in achievement, exclusivity, and being a "winner." / Become image-conscious, highly concerned with how they are perceived. Begin to present themselves according to the expectations of others and what they need to do in order to be successful. Pragmatic and efficient, but also studied, losing touch with their own feelings beneath a smooth façade. Problems with intimacy, credibility, and expediency emerge. / Want to impress others with their superiority: constantly promoting themselves, making themselves sound better than they really are. Narcissistic, with grandiose, inflated notions about themselves and their talents. Exhibitionistic and seductive, as if saying, "Look at me!" Arrogance and contempt is a defense against feeling jealous of others and their success.

Unhealthy: Fearing failure and humiliation, they misrepresent themselves, distorting the truth of their accomplishments. They can be extremely unprincipled, covetous of the success of others, and willing to do "whatever it takes" to preserve the illusion of their superiority. / Exploitative and opportunistic, but also deceptive so that their mistakes and wrongdoings will not be exposed. Pathological lying, extreme hostility, and delusional jealousy: betraying and sabotaging people in order to triumph over them. / May become vindictive, attempting to ruin what they cannot have. Relentless, obsessive about destroying whatever reminds them of their own shortcomings and failures. Psychopathic tendencies: murder.

Key Motivations: Want to feel valuable and worthwhile, to be affirmed, to distinguish themselves, to have attention, to be admired, and to impress others.

Examples: Bill Clinton, Christopher Reeve, Michael Landon, Richard Gere, Shirley MacLaine, Jane Pauley, Paul McCartney, Sting, Tom Cruise, Sharon Stone, Tony Robbins, Bryant Gumbel, Dick Clark, Vanna White, Brooke Shields, Kathie Lee Gifford, Denzel Washington, Sylvester Stallone, Arnold Schwarzenegger, Truman Capote, O.J. Simpson.

AN OVERVIEW OF THE THREE

The United States is fast becoming a dysfunctional "Three" culture: driven, narcissistic, image-oriented, emphasizing style over substance, symbols over reality. The pursuit of excellence (as exemplified by the healthy Three) is being replaced by the celebration of the artificial as everything is treated like a commodity — packaged, advertised, and marketed. Politics is becoming less concerned with principles or the use of power for the common good than with the display of personalities. Politics serves public relations, selling candidates with their calculated positions to a public which can no longer tell a fabricated image from a real person.

The communications media, particularly television, are primarily concerned with attracting attention so that the public can be sold something. The shallow values and the beguiling glitter of "show biz" have become the norms by which everything is measured. The only guideline is the ability to gain attention: what is noticed and in demand has value. People are so seduced by the slick package that they often do not realize that there is nothing in it. To paraphrase McLuhan, the package is the message. Calculated images successfully masquerade as reality, from the programmed friendliness of television personalities to the rehearsed sincerity of beauty contestants to the hard fluff of "evening magazine" shows.

Exhibitionism and self-promotion are becoming acceptable as people do whatever it takes to be noticed in an increasingly competitive marketplace. The ideal is to be a winner—to be successful, famous, and celebrated. The quest for success and prestige is everywhere. Every day, a new book tells us how to dress for success, eat for success, or network for success. We are being sold a narcissistic fantasy: that we will be "somebody" if we are like everybody else, only better. If you manage your image properly, you too can become a star—or a god.

The personality type Three exemplifies the search for the validation of the self, and so Threes look to esteemed others to determine who they must be, what they must do, in order to feel valuable and worthwhile as human beings. With this particular focus, Threes frequently become successful in the eyes of their society because they make it their business to achieve those things which their peers find valuable. This is no less true in a Buddhist monastery in Thailand than in a fast-track corporate culture. Threes will strive to exemplify whatever qualities are honored in their given milieu. Thus, in an unhealthy society which manipulates such fears and motivations, Threes stand to gain the most attention and success from the society, but also end up among its greatest victims—estranged from their own heart's desire, empty, and emotionally isolated, while never knowing what has gone wrong.

In the Feeling Triad
Threes, the primary personality type in the Feeling Triad, are the most out of touch with their emotional lives. This is because

Threes have learned to put their own feelings and their own true desires aside in order to function more effectively. Threes believe that they will be valued only for what they do, so they put their energies into performing well, "getting the job done," and becoming successful in their endeavors, however "success" may be defined. Further, Threes want positive responses from others, so they learn to behave in ways that they believe will create a good impression. Whereas this can be a useful orientation in certain situations, it can become a habitual way of being—even in circumstances where such behavior would be inappropriate, or at least limiting. Over time, as Threes continually postpone dealing with their own real feelings, they begin to have trouble accessing them. A profound split develops between who they seem to be and who they are, between the image they project to others and the reality behind it. Eventually, their image becomes their only reality. They become so distanced from their own feelings and needs that they no longer know who they are. They believe that the image is all they have. At this point, since whatever affirmation they are receiving is in response to an image, and not to themselves, no amount of praise or achievement will make them feel better. The great challenge for people of this personality type is to become inner-directed, to develop themselves as persons according to their genuine feelings and their own true values. Most Threes are unaware of the extent to which they have abandoned themselves, and it can be a very difficult realization when they discover that the dreams they have been so relentlessly pursuing are not their own.

When they are healthy, Threes are loved and admired, even idolized by others because they have taken pains to acquire the qualities and skills they embody virtually to an ideal degree. Ironically, though, healthy Threes feel worthwhile and valuable not because of others' validation but because they are in touch with their own heart and are guided by it. Of course, the attention and praise of others is wonderful to have, but healthy Threes are not swayed by it. They would pursue their goals even without the admiration. The overwhelmingly positive self-esteem of healthy Threes is real, and therefore cannot be affected by the opinions of others. The freedom and purposefulness of this way of living is very attractive to others who hold them in high regard. Also, because healthy Threes have more fully integrated their feelings, they are warm and genuine both in their personal lives and in their careers. Healthy Threes are outstanding, human nature's stars.

However, average Threes do not feel self-esteem, they believe that they will feel good about themselves only if they achieve, only if they become big successes and stars—number one in the class. This leads them to be intensely competitive with others for all forms of success and prestige, since they are convinced that this will give them a sense of value. To the degree that they repress feelings of worthlessness, Threes will be driven to become "winners." Unfortunately, they also look outside themselves to determine what qualities a winner must have. Instead of developing themselves, they resort to projecting images, which are meant to make a favorable impression. Pragmatic and calculating, they are able to change their image to get what they want. As they become more desperate and empty, they begin showing off and hyping themselves to attract more admiration, but since they are not expressing who they really are, all of the attention in the world cannot touch them.

If they become unhealthy, Threes deceive themselves and others so they can maintain the illusion that they're still on top—still superior people. They are extremely devious if they are in danger of being exposed and humiliated. Unhealthy Threes are like any other type with deep psychological problem: they have difficulty functioning. Yet for Threes, functioning, or at this stage, even the appearance of functioning, is everything. They are terrified that anyone will discover the degree of their disorder. They can become extremely dangerous as they strike out at anyone who they perceive threatens the crumbling image which they now identify with entirely.

Problems with Hostility and Narcissism

Like the other personality types of this Triad, Threes have a problem with hostility, which can manifest in less healthy Threes as vindictive malice toward anyone who they believe threatens their self-image. While Twos and Fours are indirectly hostile, average to unhealthy Threes are more directly hostile in a wide variety of ways, from arrogantly distancing themselves, to snide humor at others' expense, to sarcastic putdowns, to sabotaging and betraying people. Hostility serves Threes in two ways: first, it compensates for their own feelings of inadequacy, and second, it keeps away people who, for one reason or another, undermine their fragile self-esteem. In this latter regard, less healthy Threes may even be hostile to people who they admire or to whom they are attracted.

Average Threes are the most narcissistic of the personality types. While healthy Threes justly possess high self-esteem, average Threes build their identities around an increasingly inflated self-regard: they appear to be utterly in love with themselves. But, more precisely, they are in love with their inflated image rather than their actual selves. Instead of loving themselves as they really are, including a realistic acceptance of their limitations, they love a false façade which bears little resemblance to the undeveloped person beneath.

Because Threes adapt themselves to the desires and expectations of others to validate themselves, they can lose a clear sense of who they actually are and what they want from their lives. In average to unhealthy Threes, the drive to get recognition for themselves becomes so great that it drowns out other legitimate needs they may have. Further, because their sense of their authentic self becomes increasingly blocked, average Threes begin to engage in internal "pep talks" to convince themselves that they actually are the outstanding person they are trying to become.

Narcissists care principally about themselves—and about others only to the degree that they reflect well upon themselves. They remain intensely self-centered, with a limited ability to empathize with anyone else's feelings or needs. This is why they have little capacity for love and why—once they have become narcissistic—average Threes have little capacity to form lasting, mutually satisfying relationships. Relationships are one-sided because both parties are in love with the same person: the Three.

Of course, their narcissism puts them in constant conflict with people. Because they believe so much in their superiority, average Threes are competitive with the very people from whom they want admiration. They show off as if others were no more than an adoring audience endlessly ready to applaud their every move; if others do not applaud, Threes give them "attitude" or otherwise reject them. Worse, narcissistic Threes add insult to injury by demanding that people admire them even when they are contemptuous of the people whose admiration they want.

The problem is that narcissism is not the same thing as genuine self-esteem. Although average Threes seem to be coolly self-contained, they are not really secure with themselves because their self-esteem is based not on the development of their real capacities but on the ability to capture the attention of others. Threes are finely attuned to people's reactions to them, and can respond by projecting whatever image they need at the moment. But since their repertoire of images does not have a corresponding measure of reality behind it, everything they do is done for affirmation, not because they are personally committed to, or deeply involved with, whatever they are expressing (being "politically correct").

The irony is that behind the façade is a deeply hidden dependency on others, a dependency they cannot acknowledge because of the demands of their narcissism. Once narcissism takes over, Threes cannot live with people and they cannot live without them, because they are hostile toward the people on whom they depend, and because they feel like "nobody" without the attention of others.

Parental Orientation

As young children, Threes were connected to the nurturing-figure, the person who in their early development mirrored them, cared for them, and provided affection and a sense of the Three's personal value. Young Threes are highly adaptable and responsive to the emotional states of others, and so learn to adjust themselves to the reactions and subconscious expectations of their nurturing-figure. This person is usually the Three's mother or a mother-substitute, but not always. In some cases, the mother may have been largely absent, physically or emotionally, and it fell upon the father or a sibling to nurture the baby. In other cases, a nanny or grandparent may have fulfilled this role. In any case, it is important to understand that the nurturing-figure is the person who cared for the child and who provided mirroring.

In their formative years, Threes learn to tune in to the desires and hopes of their nurturing-figure. The expectations of the nurturing-figure need not be expressed explicitly. With the remarkable intuitive gifts of children, young Threes know what will please their nurturers and which behaviors produce approving looks and smiles. All of this is quite natural, and if the nurturing-figure is reasonably healthy, he or she mirrors the child's true qualities and the Three will mature into a well-balanced person with good self-esteem. But to the degree that the nurturing-figure has unresolved narcissistic needs of his or her own, the Three will have to make much greater adaptations. To please the troubled nurturer, young Threes will have to abandon themselves to become the person who *will* be approved. In cases where the nurturer was more pathological and needy, Threes will have to disconnect from their own feelings and needs almost entirely. Because the nurturing-figure's expectations are so unrealistic, the child is doomed to fail. Little that the child can do will get the nurturing-figure to approve of them or validate their existence. The result is a desperate individual with deep narcissistic wounds and an intense underlying hostility for being forced to abandon his or her own heart.

As adults, Threes continue to play out this pattern learned in early childhood. They seek out people whom they admire and esteem to give them validation and admiration. Threes are not interested in indiscriminately getting everyone to like them: rather, they focus on specific individuals who they themselves view as valuable, successful people. Although this motivates Threes to do those things which will make them seem worthwhile to others, this also leaves them highly vulnerable to fears of rejection. They will work tirelessly to avoid ever being rejected, ever being seen as a "loser." The admiring gaze which they sought from their nurturing-figures made them feel that they were loved and valued, and in one form or another, they are always seeking that look in the eyes of others. Admiration makes them feel alive and worthwhile—at least for a while. Without it, they feel empty and hostile because their underlying feelings of not being valued *for who they are* begin to surface.

Average Threes perceived as children that they were generally valued for what they accomplished, for the quality of their performance, not for themselves. In adult Threes, this can lead to highly effective work habits, but it can also lead to powerful fears of intimacy. They may initiate relationships, but then end them before the other person gets to know them well, or have relationships with people other than the person they most want to be near. This protects their fragile self-image, but at a great cost to their happiness and connection with others. Threes believe that others will love them only for their image and for their success, but if people were really to get to know them, they would see the person beneath the image and they would be rejected. Because of difficult childhood experiences with their nurturing-figure, average Threes cannot accept the idea that others could love them just as they are. It seldom occurs to them that the most important person who has rejected them is themselves.

To give up their performance and risk exposing the vulnerable self within feels like an enormous risk to Threes. They feel that their authentic self has been rejected in the past and are secretly terrified of having it happen again. They also become convinced that their real self is relatively undesirable and that only their performance is worthwhile. Having put so much effort into it, to give it up seems unthinkable. Yet, if Threes never take that risk, they may become successful in the eyes of others, but will never know what it really is to be themselves, nor will they be able to relate to, much less feel love from, anyone else. Sadly, newspapers and magazines are full of stories about highly successful people who "have everything going for them," but who suddenly contradicted their popular image in startling and tragic ways. One can imagine the anxiety and desperation of a person who has tirelessly worked to accomplish what they believed would make them feel good about themselves, only to discover that their feelings of emptiness remained and were more painful than ever.

ANALYZING THE HEALTHY THREE

Level 1: The Authentic Person

At their best, very healthy Threes transcend their desire to be affirmed by others and accept themselves as they are. They are no longer motivated by a concern for what others think of them or a desire to obtain applause or admiration. Rather, very healthy Threes shift their center of gravity to become inner-directed and self-generating; in so doing, they plant the seeds of their own interiority, their own feelings, their own identities. Their development becomes interior and personal, a matter of discovering their own values rather than overt, outward behavior.

Like many of the qualities of the very healthy Three, the ability to be inner-directed may not sound like much at first, but this is only a testament to the degree to which the illusions of the modern world have entranced us. To be truly inner-directed is a rare accomplishment. It does not mean that one is led by emotional reactions or fantasies, by avoidance or fear or compensations, any more than it means being influenced by the opinions of others or by prevailing tastes and mores. To be inner-directed is to follow the truth of one's own heart and to act and speak from that place.

When healthy Threes do this, they are inspiring and genuinely affecting. They communicate in a way that touches others and motivates them to pursue higher purposes. Their self-expression is direct and entirely authentic. Healthy Threes feel deeply, but they are not sentimental or effusive. Rather, theirs is an openness of heart that takes in the truth of themselves and others with a child-like simplicity and compassion. Being authentic is an extraordinary accomplishment, especially when we consider how few moments in life we express our genuine feelings and perceptions to others. These moments are usually rare and precious, and entail a profound acceptance of self and others.

Self-acceptance is a way of viewing one's self compassionately, without condemnation or justification. It is a starting point in life which makes other things possible. It celebrates the fullness and joy of being alive and of being who we are: accepting ourselves, however, does not mean embracing our neuroses or bad habits and celebrating them as if they were virtues. On the contrary, self-acceptance involves loving ourselves enough to accept painful truths about ourselves. It helps us to abjure the world of grandiose fantasies and to cease to listen to the temptation to be false about ourselves in any way. Self-acceptance is, at its simplest, the experience of one's self, here and now, as a complete human being, with all the glories and problems that condition entails. By accepting themselves, very healthy Threes take responsibility for developing themselves as they truly are, both to realize their many gifts and talents and to gracefully acknowledge their weaknesses and limitations.

At this stage, healthy Threes are modest and direct about themselves because their energy is invested in being only who they are. Threes are practical even when they are less healthy, but at Level 1, they are also deeply contented. They often possess a disarming sense of humor about themselves because they are wise to their own tricks and can laugh at them, rather than act on them. Far from having some of the intimacy problems which develop further down the continuum, healthy Threes are tender and loving. They can listen to others attentively and communicate their feelings clearly and simply: they are nothing more and nothing less than what they seem to be. Their reality and their image converge, giving them a firm foundation upon which to develop as persons. Their feelings originate from within and are connected to their immediate experiences, not simulated or postponed until a time when they will not have to "function." Healthy Threes are continually touched and amazed by the love that others extend to them, and because they are present to their own feelings, they are able to take others' love in. Other people and their hurts and triumphs are intensely real to them because very healthy Threes are real to themselves.

Very healthy Threes often become extremely benevolent and charitable, not because of the positive impression this will make on others, but because they have opened their hearts and are truly concerned about the welfare and success of others. Truly wishing good for others, they take actions to guide people less fortunate than themselves toward their own goals. They are no longer concerned with "getting ahead" and distinguishing themselves. They begin to experience themselves as part of the greater human family, and are moved to take a responsible role within it, while modestly using whatever talents and position they may have to contribute something worthwhile.

Level 2: The Self-Assured Person

Even healthy Threes are not always this healthy. Instead of being inner-directed, they more typically start looking outside themselves to find out what others value. They become adept at determining what qualities are esteemed by people who are important to them, and adapt themselves so as to become a person with those same qualities. Although Threes are still authentic people, they have begun to shift from following their own hearts to seeking validation and recognition from others.

At Level 2, Threes have begun to seek the positive regard of others because they have succumbed to their Basic Fear that they are worthless, without value in and of themselves. In a way that is similar to the dilemma of a Two, Threes feel they can only get a sense of their own value by obtaining the praise and recognition of significant others in their lives. To the extent that Threes were not seen or valued for themselves in childhood, they will begin to turn their focus away from their own needs and feelings to determine what behaviors, qualities, and attitudes will make them valued within their world. To this end, Threes develop their ability to adapt along with their talent for reading others' expectations to a fine degree.

Since they possess the most exquisite social instincts, healthy Threes are extraordinarily well adapted to other people, effortlessly responding to attention the way leaves turn their faces to catch sunlight. Every shift of emotion, every variation of warmth or cooling by others registers immediately in the Three's psyche, in the same way that a sunbather can tell when the thinnest cloud comes between him and the sun. Healthy Threes possess a talent parallel to the Twos' empathy in their ability to read people and situations. Upon entering a room, Threes immediately sense the prevailing mood of others and are able to respond effectively and sensitively to the situation. This ability puts others at their ease and usually causes them to respond favorably to the Three's presence. When Threes bask in the approving attention of others, they positively glow. The affirmation of others makes them feel alive and good about themselves.

Their psychic dynamics are difficult to analyze precisely because there is a subtle interaction continually taking place between Threes and other people. The affirming attention of others makes Threes feel desirable, and they respond to people by adapting themselves to the values they perceive in others. Others, seeing their ideal selves reflected in Threes, continue to shower them with attention, and the interaction is sustained. When they are healthy, Threes are able to maintain this "feedback loop" because they really are embodying qualities that others admire, and they are secure enough in themselves to give genuine affirmation and positive attention to others. However, because Threes are not entirely inner-directed, this self-esteem requires maintenance. Not only do Threes feel the need to adapt themselves to others, they begin to require self-affirmation, designed to keep them feeling convinced of their own worth, as if to continually remind themselves, "I am a valuable, significant person."

One way that Threes convince themselves of their worth is by focusing on what they begin to see as their unlimited potential. Healthy Threes really work at maintaining a "can do" attitude and feel that they are able to accomplish goals and get things done. They took to heart the often repeated message from childhood, "You can be anything you want to be if you set your mind to it." Indeed, Threes often function as the "hero" in their family, the child who is an athletic star or gets straight A's on report cards or gets cast as the lead in the school play. In one way or another, young Threes strive to make their families proud of them. In healthy Threes, however, this sense of potential and possibility is tempered by a well-grounded realism and a steadiness of purpose which gives Threes the ability to actually achieve many of their goals.

Their apparent self-assurance and positive attitude make healthy Threes extremely attractive, which encourages more interactions and more affirmation. Other people are also attracted to Threes because, as a group, they are often physically attractive, and even if they are not particularly attractive by a culture's standards, Threes usually know how to put their best foot forward, making the best of whatever positive attributes they do possess. In any event, Threes learn to be attractive in the broader sense of the word. They know how to attract other people, how to get others interested in them, and how to have others enjoy being in their presence. They possess a magnetism and an aura of desirability which is exciting to be around.

Desirability and attractiveness (both physically and personally) are important qualities for human beings because, on a biological level, we must attract others for the propagation of the species. But we are also social creatures and, to a certain degree, we all need the good regard of others in order to accomplish things in life. And people of no other personality type are more suited to attracting favorable attention to themselves than healthy Threes.

Level 3: The Outstanding Paragon

Just as negative feelings about oneself reinforce each other, so do positive feelings. Because healthy Threes want to feel good about themselves, they engage in constructive activities that will increase their self-esteem. Having worked to convince themselves of their own value and worth, they begin to fear that others will reject them or be disappointed by them. As a result, healthy Threes invest time and energy developing themselves, making themselves into outstanding individuals.

Healthy Threes are ambitious and eager to improve themselves in any number of ways—academically, physically, culturally, professionally, and intellectually. They are not ambitious for money or fame or social standing, but to make more of *themselves*. There is much to admire in healthy Threes because they really do embody something excellent. They are worthy of the admiration of others because they are outstanding, frequently model persons in whatever sphere of activity they enter—whether the Olympics, or West Point, or medical school. They are well-adjusted, well-rounded boys and girls, men and women who embody the values that the culture admires. (Of course, a particular Three may not embody the values you personally admire or would like to possess, but what he or she always embodies are those values which are affirmed by the Three's own cultural and social environment.) Thus, Threes are living models of the culture's values, the paragons by which we see and assess ourselves.

Because they possess outstanding qualities, healthy Threes are also able to motivate other people to develop themselves. Others see in Threes what they could be like if they made the effort to develop their potential as Threes have. Moreover, healthy Threes are willing to help others attain the qualities that they embody. If they are terrific dancers, they will teach you how to dance; if they are bodybuilders, they will share helpful tips while working out with you at the gym; if they have made a killing on the stock market, they will help you get into the market too.

In the workplace, healthy Threes are extremely capable and competent. They focus on goals and like to see projects through from start to finish. They also inspire team morale with their high spirits and industriousness. Threes persist through adversity, because they are convinced that hard work will pay off in accomplishing the goals that they have set for themselves. They are also effective communicators, able to motivate others to take on tasks or contribute money to worthy causes. Indeed, healthy Threes are often sought out by organizations as spokespersons to represent them to the public. In such positions, their poise, charm, and confidence act as powerful incentives to others who wish to emulate them.

Not every moment is geared toward effectiveness and self-development, however. Healthy Threes are highly energetic, youthful, and rambunctious, like healthy animals frisking in the sunlight. Their sense of humor admits a degree of self-mockery, an enjoyment of their own foibles and minor pretensions, which is as disarming as it is charming. These traits, added to their attractiveness and other admirable qualities, result in healthy Threes' being in great social demand, because they are so stimulating to be around.

Almost everyone would like to be a healthy Three, at least in some way. Who would not like to be attractive and at ease with themselves and with others? Who would not like to be self-assured and endowed with the energy and motivation to make the most of their potential? Who would not like to enjoy being themselves as healthy Threes so evidently do? When they are healthy, Threes are truly stars. When people are in their presence, they are aware of something special about them.

ANALYZING THE AVERAGE THREE

Level 4: The Competitive Status-Seeker

A shift in attitude now takes place: Threes begin to want to distinguish themselves from others. It is no longer a question of working hard to feel worthwhile: average Threes want to be noticed. They begin to compare themselves with others, fearing that they may be overshadowed by others' accomplishments. This inevitably sets up a need to compete with people, although at this point, the competition is mostly subtle and covert. Average Threes want to demonstrate to themselves and to their peers that they are extraordinary, superior people. They do this by working harder than others and by acquiring whatever symbols represent success and achievement to them: diplomas, raises, a prestigious address, a recording contract, a special position with their teacher or guru. Rising above others reinforces their self-esteem, defending Threes from deeper feelings of worthlessness by temporarily making them feel more desirable and more worthy of attention and admiration.

To this end, Threes literally throw themselves into their projects, their careers, and whatever else they are doing to enhance their self-esteem. They are truly Type A personalities, driven and potentially workaholic. Of course, not all Threes are in fast-track Wall Street careers; nevertheless, whatever "career" a Three has chosen will be a major focal point of their energy. A Three who is a homemaker and parent will work within the framework of his or her economic means to create a "model home." Threes will strive to make their children outstanding, providing them with lessons and sending them to the best schools possible. A Three who is a Buddhist monk will work to become the most holy and selfless of his brothers. Average Threes want to excel at whatever they are involved with, and if possible, they want to be the best.

For example, they may be good swimmers or tennis players, but they begin to feel that this is not enough to suppress their fears of worthlessness, so they must outdo everyone else. Average Threes therefore create rivalries where none existed. Unfortunately, creating these comparisons puts all their relationships on an entirely new footing because they have put themselves in the position of competing with people whose positive regard they need.

Indeed, average Threes are more directed by the values of others, and work even harder to achieve goals they believe to be sanctioned as worthwhile by their peers. This begins to result in a growing estrangement from their own desires and feelings. After all, it is difficult to stay focused on goals when one's heart does not entirely support them. Feelings then become a distraction, something that interferes with the Three's ability to function, to stay "on track." Average Threes are not concerned with what they have or do because they enjoy it, but because it makes them feel that they are "getting ahead."

Average Threes pursue success with an efficiency unrivaled by any other personality type. (We can characterize average Threes in a nutshell by the three things they value most highly: career, success, and recognition.) Success to Threes means being number one, a "winner," constantly improving their position or status. To be sure, average Threes work hard to get and stay on top. They value professional competence and aim at being the best at what they do, mainly for the prestige of being at the top of their profession. For better or worse, theirs is the world of the résumé and the "rat race."

At this stage, they are careerists, since professional success becomes the primary gauge by which they measure their value as persons. Plotting career moves relentlessly, they want to advance as quickly as possible and are willing to make big sacrifices to achieve the success they seek. Unfortunately, these sacrifices can include a marriage, family, or friends, not to mention their emotional health. Having a prestigious title or profession is important to average Threes because it reinforces their sense of themselves as successful. (For the same reason, their self-esteem is highly threatened if they do not have a prestigious career, and doubly so if they are unemployed.)

Because success is so important to average Threes and because they have begun competing with others, they learn to present themselves more favorably and acquire the skills of diplomacy.

While being diplomatic can be useful in many situations, in average Threes it marks the beginning of a move away from authentic self-expression. Threes are starting to mask their motives and to communicate with others to produce a desired response, not to express what the Three is actually thinking or feeling. Further, this orientation can lead them to become strategic about their friends and associates. To maintain "upward mobility," good political sense and having the right friends and associates is critical. They are forever networking, making contacts, and cultivating people to further their careers and add to their social luster. Their healthy talent for sensing people's states is now used to size up others quickly according to their prestige value, as if to ask, "How can you help me achieve my goal? Are you worth pursuing?"

Thus, average Threes become highly status-conscious, and are constantly assessing whether they are "moving forward" or not by looking for tangible symbols of their progress. But even these can fail them if one of their peers suddenly has something more valuable or gets greater respect or admiration ("keeping up with the Joneses"), They are still highly organized and goal-directed, but their focus is becoming distorted. What are the Threes' goals? Is it their own self-improvement and the accomplishment of specific tasks or is it winning the recognition and attention of others? Increasingly, it is the latter.

Level 5: The Image-Conscious Pragmatist

Fearful of losing the positive regard of others because of their increasing competitiveness, average Threes begin to submerge their feelings and authentic self-expression even further, and become preoccupied with creating a favorable impression of themselves. This marks a significant stage in a Three's development or deterioration. Healthier Threes may be competitive, but they are primarily focused on their own actual efforts and achievements. They are interested in genuine self-improvement. From Level 5 down, however, Threes are primarily interested in improving their self-presentation, their image. They want to make a favorable impression, whether or not the image they project reflects who they actually are. Style over substance—how one comes across to others—becomes their overriding concern.

Fear of rejection causes average Threes to increasingly abandon themselves as they search for the "right combination" of factors which they believe will enhance them and make them more acceptable. Their self-presentation becomes smooth and professional, their appearance more calculated. The Three's tremendous energy is poured into developing a polished veneer which will hopefully "pass muster" and win them the success they desire. Of course, such attention to image betrays an underlying lack of authentic self-esteem. Average Threes have rejected themselves, and are determined to come up with a "package" which will be more worthwhile and valuable than they perceive their authentic selves to be.

Ironically, the result is that average Threes become less desirable as genuine human beings and more desirable as commodities. Image-conscious Threes correspond, in part, to the personality type described by Erich Fromm as the marketing orientation.

> [This] character orientation . . . is rooted in the experience of oneself as a commodity and of one's value as exchange value. . . .
>
> Success depends largely on how well a person sells himself on the market, how well he gets his personality across, how nice a "package" he is. . . . A stockbroker, a salesman, a secretary, a railroad executive, a college professor, or a hotel manager must each offer different kinds of personality that, regardless of their differences, must fulfill one condition: to be in demand. . . .
>
> The marketing orientation . . . does not develop something which is potentially in the person (unless we make the absurd assertion that "nothing" is also part of the human equipment); its very nature is that no specific and permanent kind of relatedness is developed, but that the very changeability of attitudes is the only permanent quality of such orientation. In this orientation, those qualities are developed which can best be sold. Not one particular attitude is predominant, but the emptiness which can be filled most quickly with the desired quality. This quality, however, ceases to be one in the proper sense of the word; it is only a role, the pretense of a quality, to be readily exchanged if another one is more desirable. (Fromm, *Man for Himself*, 76–77, 84.)

Because average Threes experience themselves as commodities, they become obsessed with how they come across to others. They worry about what impression they are making and constantly wonder what people think of them. Issues of being successful enough, competent enough, and attractive enough continually re-play in their minds. They feel as if every eye is on them and they must always be prepared with the right look, the right thing to say, the right level of affect. Naturally, this orientation does not allow them to express their own genuine feelings and responses. In fact, average Threes have increasing difficulty even knowing what their own feelings are.

The problem is that they act according to the needs of the image they are projecting, not according to their own real needs and not because they sincerely believe in what they are saying or doing. Average Threes learn to project one simulated emotional state after another, each appropriate to the situation and each equally convincing. They may appear to be sincere, friendly, modest, kindly, repentant, virtuous, and truthful, although they may not be. They may have only adjusted their image to meet the demands of the moment so that others will think well of them. What they appear to be and what they actually are begin to be quite different. Thus, there is an element of slickness, an emotional hollowness about average Threes because much of what they say and do is not a true reflection of who they are. "Who they are" is becoming ever more difficult to identify, both for others and for themselves.

Average Threes know how to package themselves to fit into their environment successfully. Entire industries have been devoted to this aspect of human behavior: the advertising and fashion industries understand and manipulate these fears particularly well. The professional and corporate worlds are full of highly paid image consultants who teach others how to put together the right look, master professional jargon, and erase any annoying regionalisms in the person's speech or style. Like the changing coloration of a chameleon, an image is useful to the degree that it allows one to fit into the environment perfectly. Their image allows Threes to do just that, only one better: they do not merely fit into the environment, they may perfect their image to the extent that it becomes the standard by which others judge themselves. The image assumes a reality of its own once others accept it as desirable.

It is important to stress how subtle average Threes can be in projecting a believable image, and how difficult it is for others to detect whatever degree of inauthenticity is involved, especially if a particular Three is intelligent and well-educated. This personality type is by no means limited to vacuous television game-show hosts, beauty contestants, or cloned yuppies. Average Threes can be found everywhere, in every profession, from MBAs to self-help instructors, from sports figures to politicians, from artists to network anchorpersons.

The clue to others that they are dealing with an image rather than a person is the average Three's apparent perfection. Threes come across extremely well (the cool, composed, "friendly" professional is typical), although others may notice a somewhat rehearsed, studied quality about them. Threes, however, are aware of others' reactions to them even if they are largely unaware of their own reactions. If others seem put off, they will redouble their efforts and make further adjustments, or apologies, if necessary.

It is precisely because their behavior is so well-considered that it is difficult for others to put their finger on what Threes lack. If, however, others look deeply enough, they will find almost nothing "essential" about average Threes—they express few genuine feelings and have few deeply held personal convictions. They seem to have no idiosyncrasies and no passion beneath the smoothly polished surface. Although everything about them seems perfect, the various images do not add up to a whole person. What is missing is a personal sense of engagement and commitment. Average Threes are not connected with themselves, with their own feelings. They are like perfectly engineered machines which perform precisely as expected and therefore continue to be in demand.

As one might expect, there are difficulties with this orientation. Average Threes fear genuine intimacy lest anyone discover their inner emptiness. They fear (probably unconsciously) that their authentic self is worthless and they become increasingly unwilling to let others see the vulnerable self beneath the image. It is an extraordinary sign of trust and respect when an average Three dares to reveal himself to someone. More often, however, with their considerable charm and ability to adapt to people, Threes are able to create the impression of intimacy, seemingly revealing more of themselves than they really do. This is why average Threes are typically concerned with their credibility, with whether people believe the idealized image they are constructing.

Despite all of the attention and effort that average Threes have put into their image, they are increasingly unconvincing because their emotional disengagement becomes evident to others. However, being disconnected from their feelings allows Threes to be extremely efficient at work and unusually able to focus their energy on attaining professional objectives. Expedient and goal-oriented, they are good at practical problem solving because their pragmatism allows them to respond to situations without being constrained by abstract principles or turbulent emotions. When feelings do arise, average Threes tend to feel out of control and lost. They deal with their feelings privately. They emote quickly and strongly, but want to get "back to business" as soon as possible. Their feelings are increasingly strange and unfamiliar territory to them—threatening to destroy their focus as well as their image of efficiency.

As a result, Threes become unsure of what they feel about things. They have spent so much time trying to become someone else that they have difficulty accessing their own beliefs and responses. They can take either side of an issue—and switch to the opposite side with incredible ease—because their passions and personal convictions have become foreign to them. Instead, they learn to rely on techniques and formulas, whether in their careers or their personal lives. Average Threes are masters of jargon, supreme manipulators of symbols to effect their ends, whether to elect a president, sell a toothpaste, or promote themselves. Others begin to sense that the friendliness of average Threes is often out of expediency. They have places to go and things to accomplish, and become increasingly brisk, efficient, and emotionally detached.

Because they are losing contact with their own heart's desire, the only source of guidance for Threes at this Level is "what works." While they are well suited to mastering technical problems, average Threes are usually not good leaders because they lack personal vision, have few strongly held values, and little empathy for others. Unfortunately, however, average Threes are often attracted to positions of leadership because prestige is involved. The upshot is that they lead by following, by telling people what they want to hear rather than what they need to do. Once the image becomes the reality, it takes on a false life of its own.

Level 6: The Self-Promoting Narcissist

After meticulously crafting a "new, improved" self that others can affirm and accept, Threes may fear that others will see through them and discover that they are not really the fantastic, "all-together" image they are trying to project. At this point, to be exposed as less than their idealized image would cause complete humiliation, so Threes "up the ante" and shift into an overdrive of self-promotion to impress others. They want others to admire and envy them, to think that they are absolutely outstanding in every way, that they have it all, that they are nothing less than perfect. But most importantly, Threes want to forget the increasingly needy inner self that continues to cause them shame and pain. They want to become their image.

As a compensation for their growing fears of worthlessness, their self-image has become grotesquely inflated and grandiose. They begin to advertise themselves relentlessly, bragging about their accomplishments, dropping important-sounding names, "hyping" their achievements or letting others know about the great success they are about to have, making themselves sound incredibly wonderful and making whatever they do seem better than whatever anyone else does—and better than it actually is.

At this stage, average Threes begin to oversell themselves, making extraordinary claims about their achievements. Narcissistic self-inflation marks a degree of dissociation from their actual selves, with all their real neediness and limitations, to claims about a glorious self which does not exist. There is actually less than meets the eye here, although this is still difficult to perceive because their sales pitch is usually quite convincing. Nevertheless, although they are desperate to convince themselves and others that they are outstanding, others may begin to sense that they are too good to be true: much of what they say about themselves just does not add up.

Everything they do at this stage is for show, to get people to notice and admire them. Their self-displays all have the subtext "Look at me!" They become shameless braggarts, showing off their culture, their education, their status, their bodies, their intelligence, their careers, their spouses, their sexual conquests, their wit—whatever they think will garner admiration. Their only subject of conversation is themselves, and they act as if others were, or should be, enthralled by everything they say and do. Naturally, this often has the effect of boring others, who then withdraw their attention—exactly what Threes want to avoid.

Conflicts with others also begin, and get progressively worse, as a result of their now overt competitiveness. Because it is difficult for Threes at this Level to have positive feelings for anyone with whom they compete, they begin to have problems making friends with their peers. Competitiveness makes them see others as threats and obstacles to their own success. They feel comfortable around people only if they feel superior to them in some way, either because others have less status than they do, or because Threes have beaten them in some kind of open or covert contest.

Because Threes at Level 6 have deep wounds to their sense of worth, they feel that only huge success will be sufficient to satisfy them. The ultimate mark of success for average Threes is to become rich and famous, especially famous. Fame has a deep appeal to them because it means being known by a large number of people. With fame, their existence is affirmed: they are not nobodies. If everyone knows who they are, they must be truly valuable people.

They also typically pursue and promote status symbols as a way of creating new social values. Average Threes give possessions their status by adopting them, then using them as the basis for competition with others. Exclusivity is a very important adjunct to competitiveness because by excluding less desirable people from their social circle, average Threes make themselves arbiters of who is "in" and who is "out." Status is thus the game of one-upmanship played by those who idolize success. As self-styled arbiters of status, Threes need to ensure that whoever else plays the game will fail, yet still come back for more.

It goes without saying that narcissistic Threes are self-involved, arrogant, and highly impressed with themselves. They begin to believe their own press and convince themselves that they actually are superior people. By adopting a contemptuous attitude toward others, Threes are able to reinforce their delicate self-esteem. Feeling superior to others also ensures that they will not be rejected by anyone, and if for some reason they are, the rejection will not bother them, since they feel that those who reject them are inferior and do not count anyway. In short, they look at others only to see if others are looking at them.

Looking good, literally and figuratively, has always been extremely important to Threes, but physical attractiveness is never more important than when they are openly narcissistic. They strike poses, displaying "attitude" both as a way of being exclusive (and unapproachably better than anyone else), and of drawing attention to themselves (without seeming to do so constantly). Male or female, Threes at this stage are exhibitionistic and seductive, using their sex appeal to increase their desirability. Hypermasculine or hyperfeminine sexual displays, such as being a hunk, or stud, or beauty queen, are typical. Of course, not all Threes are physically attractive. Nevertheless, physical qualities are important to them, and those who are not attractive may substitute such narcissistically self-enhancing traits as a reliance on intelligence and cleverness, money and success, fame and prestige to impress others.

Narcissism is essentially passive, and the sexuality of Threes has a passive element to it as well: they want to be the object of desire. Narcissistic Threes want others to admire them, although they are not concerned with gratifying anyone else, either sexually or psychologically.

Narcissistic passivity shows up in other ways. Having won others over, they begin to "rest on their laurels" and become arrogantly complacent. They are so caught up in short-term boosts to their narcissism that they are increasingly unable to focus on real, long-term goals and accomplishments. They begin to coast through life, relying on sex appeal and charm. Whatever energy they may have expended in cultivating relationships stops: having charmed or seduced others, Threes can now take them for granted. Or they lose interest in others altogether: having made a conquest, they drop people once they receive the boost to their narcissism that they sought. They also enjoy frustrating those who attempt to get close to them, as if to say, "You can look, but you can't touch. You can worship me, but you can't have me." All of this arises because their great fear of intimacy is at odds with a tremendous need for affirmation of their desirability.

Conflicts with others also result from their pretensions, because Threes begin to believe their own hype, puffing up their achievements to ludicrous extremes. ("My discovery will win the Nobel Prize." "My first art exhibit will sell out on opening day.") The trouble is that the more pretentious they are, the most easily offended they are by anyone's pointing out how unrealistic their evaluation of themselves or their expectations for success have become. The irony is that, because of their grandiose expectations, they actually set themselves up for disappointments. And the more narcissistic they are, the quicker Threes are to feel slighted by others. They are very touchy about their self-worth precisely when their narcissism is most inflated, a sure sign that narcissism is covering up a profound lack of genuine self-esteem.

Indeed, if their narcissism is not constantly reinforced, average Threes begin to get hostile, quickly losing whatever sense of humor about themselves they may once have had. They become contemptuous and sarcastic about everyone else. Under the guise of being honest with others, Threes put people down to stay on top, at least in their own minds. Those few friends they still have come in for shabby treatment: they are ignored, stood up on dates or for appointments without apology, and made to feel inadequate and inferior in different ways. The deteriorating Three at this Level is a far cry from the outstanding, exemplary person we saw in the healthy Three. No longer focused on real goals or genuine self-improvement, they are consumed by a desperate need for recognition, although they do not know why. But having rejected their own hearts, and seeing that their hard work has failed to make them feel better about themselves, they are filled with disappointment and rage, which they try their best to suppress. If Threes can get in touch with their shame and self-alienation, they can begin to recover the authentic self and become healthier. However, if they continue to deceive themselves about their true condition, they risk completely severing the connection with who they really are.

ANALYZING THE UNHEALTHY THREE

Level 7: The Dishonest Opportunist

Failure is one of the most humiliating prospects for Threes. If they continue to overextend themselves and cannot make good on their claims, they will attempt to maintain the impression that they are still "winners" by deceiving others.

Their fear of failure, and thus of humiliation, makes unhealthy Threes more than willing to be dishonest to get what they need to maintain at least the illusion of superiority. We have already seen that they are pragmatists: at Level 7, Threes are determined to survive, and since they are completely identified with their image, that means ensuring that their image survives. Consequently, unhealthy Threes detach from their core, and have no direction other than what works for them at the time. Their pragmatism has degenerated into an unprincipled expediency in which Threes will do almost anything to convince others that they are still exceptional people. But because they actually are having severe psychological difficulties it is almost impossible for them to do this without distorting the truth of their situation: they lie on their résumés, plagiarize, cut corners, take credit for the work of others, or recount accomplishments that never occurred to make themselves seem more outstanding then they are. Unhealthy Threes are determined not to be losers, no matter who must pay the price for their success.

They are ready to sell out, lie, change their "loyalties," or take advantage of others to come out on top. Because they are almost completely cut off from their conscience and their ability to discern the truth, they seem not to know what the truth about themselves is, and so do not feel guilty about deceiving others. Their underdeveloped and vulnerable inner self is disappearing beneath a personality structure that has only one agenda—its own inflation and survival. All of their energies are directed toward getting what they need to hold their self-image together.

Unhealthy Threes must now use exploitation of some sort to maintain their inflated self-image. Ironically, they have become superior not only to everyone else, but even to themselves by overshooting the limits of their talents. Either they must come down to earth and recognize the grandiosity of their expectations, not to mention their intense psychological distress, or they must take what they need from others to maintain their "superiority." It often goes unnoticed, however, especially to the unhealthy Threes, that one person who is being repeatedly exploited in all this is themselves. Threes "sell themselves out," often sacrificing their futures on the altar of short-term payoff. Their health, their careers, their integrity are all expended in the pursuit of narcissistic "fixes." In colloquial terms, unhealthy Threes have become hustlers, people "on the make," opportunists taking advantage of situations while unwittingly making their own situations worse. Their disconnection from their feelings has other severe consequences. Unhealthy Threes are unable to feel much about themselves or to have empathy for others. Because they do not see other people as real or as having value without reference to themselves, others become merely providers of attention and admiration, what are called "narcissistic suppliers," as objects to be used to aggrandize themselves.

This is why there is absolutely nothing reciprocal about relationships with unhealthy Threes. They will keep a relationship going as long as they get what they want, but will drop someone without a second thought, particularly if someone more desirable comes along. One of the tip-offs that, despite appearances, there is something wrong with unhealthy Threes is precisely their lack of long-term relationships. They run through a staggering number of friends and acquaintances, exploiting people and dropping them once they have gotten what they want. The same can be said for their work habits. There is little of the goal-orientation of the healthy Three in evidence here. Unhealthy Threes seem to be continually responding to situations as if their own sense of values, the part of themselves that could give coherence and meaning to their activities, is missing. Nonetheless, their energy is still directed at their performance, and unhealthy Threes will not let others get close enough to see the cracks in their façade.

Unfortunately, Threes are able to maintain the illusion that they are highly functional even when they are unhealthy. (It is axiomatic that Threes always seem to be healthier than they really are.) This ultimately works against them as it prevents Threes from getting the kind of help that could turn their situation around. Often, a catastrophe in their lives will cause their defense to fail, at least temporarily. Their inner desolation and emptiness are then exposed as Threes collapse into a depressive breakdown. Most unhealthy Threes will hide themselves when this happens so that others cannot see the extent of their deterioration.

Level 8: The Malicious Deceiver

Having seriously distorted the truth of their claims about themselves and concealed their pathology, unhealthy Threes become increasingly fearful that they will be caught and that their deceptions will be exposed. However, rather than face the fact that they are having major psychological problems and must seek help, Threes may go one step further in their deterioration by doing whatever they deem necessary to support their false claims. As a result, they get involved in even more seriously destructive activities while covering their tracks, concealing their true motives and actions as much as possible.

The ability to project an image, which we saw in average Threes, is relied upon more desperately than ever. Unhealthy Threes now become completely deceptive, because they need to hide whatever wrongdoings and previous deceptions they may have been involved with. ("False face must hide what the false heart doth know."— *Macbeth*, I, vii, 82) The image they now project is still convincing, but beneath it they have become extremely unhinged and potentially treacherous. Others almost always find out how deeply neurotic Threes are only after they have already done their damage.

It goes without saying that neurotic Threes are pathological liars. Neurotic Threes seem unable to stop lying even if nothing significant depends on it since, at this Level, Threes are completely compulsive about making an impression. Many times, however, their lies are far from insignificant, causing others enormous harm, financial loss, or emotional torment. Threes who have deteriorated to this degree of pathology are unable to tell what the truth is. They feel that it can be whatever they want it to be. Many of their lies will be connected to the objective they are pursuing at the time. They will say whatever gets them what they want with the least trouble, although they risk even greater trouble if they are discovered.

This way of living only heightens their terrors, although they will use whatever parts of themselves still function to convince others that they are calm and in possession of themselves. Beneath the surface, however, unhealthy Threes feel cornered and are barely able to suppress their panic. Their growing fear of being caught and punished can make them extremely dangerous. They become remorseless, and are quite capable of betraying friends, playing people off each other, or destroying evidence to keep their wrongdoings concealed. They sabotage what others have worked for and hurt those who love them because seeing the downfall of others is the only way that they are able to feel superior. ("It is not enough that I succeed, but that others must fail."—Oscar Wilde) Of course, one crime begets another, and Threes find themselves more and more entangled in the webs of their own deceptions. They make it almost inevitable that they will be discovered and held accountable for their actions. To avoid this state of affairs, Threes may descend into complete maliciousness and madness.

Level 9: The Vindictive Psychopath
Deeply pathological Threes fear that their falseness and emptiness—not to mention their wrongdoings—will be exposed. They

have every reason to believe that if such an event were to occur, they would be completely ruined. There would be no chance for them to ever escape their unbearable feelings of worthlessness and inferiority. Indeed, the success and apparent superiority of others mocks them and humiliates them at every turn. It seems to them that others are, and will always be, superior to them. At this stage, they move beyond deception into unmitigated vindictiveness, in effect saying, "I will triumph over you no matter what it takes!" And, if they have nothing to lose, neurotic Threes will stop at nothing. Since they now have no capacity to empathize with anyone, nothing restrains them from seriously harming others. Indeed, destroying anyone or anything that reminds them of the wretchedness they are still trying to fend off becomes a monomaniacal obsession.

> The need for a vindictive triumph then manifests itself mainly in often irresistible, mostly unconscious impulses to frustrate, outwit, or defeat others in personal relations. . . .
> Much more frequently the drive toward a vindictive triumph is hidden. Indeed, because of its destructive nature, it is the most hidden element in the search for glory. It may be that only a rather frantic ambition will be apparent. In analysis alone are we able to see that the driving power behind it is the need to defeat and humiliate others by rising above them." (Karen Horney, *Neurosis and Human Growth*, 27–28.)

While moments of hostility have erupted from time to time in the past, their hostility has now grown into an irrational malice, the result of the extreme jealousy they feel toward anyone who has anything they want. Despite their outward contempt for people, pathological Threes are secretly intensely jealous of others, precisely because others have attained worthwhile goals instead of chasing after narcissistic illusions. Therefore, anyone who is authentic or capable of feeling or who loves and is loved—in short, anyone who is a normal human being—is a threat to their shattered self-esteem and an object of their malice. Maliciousness may reach dangerous proportions as neurotic Threes become obsessed with ruining others so they can triumph. This is the dark, hidden side of themselves which they cannot show to others nor even to themselves.

Others who may sometimes be aware of their situation are usually afraid of confronting them about it. Unhealthy Threes count on the fact that others dare not say or do anything about their behavior for fear of retaliation. Their complete lack of restraint makes it nearly impossible for others to defend themselves against Threes because they sense that unhealthy Threes will go lower than they are willing to descend.

At this stage, Threes can become utterly psychopathic, ignoring the normal limits of behavior, acting out their cruelest fantasies of revenge. Having no internal brakes on their behavior, they do whatever they can until their fury is spent, others are ruined, or someone stops them. Their dissociation may be so complete, however, that after striking out viciously, they may actually have no conscious recollection of having done so. It is as if they were using the last vestiges of their sanity to buffer themselves from the intensity of their hatred and rage—as well as from the horror of the crimes they may be committing.

In addition to crimes like assault, arson, and sabotage, psychopathic Threes are entirely capable of murder. They are capable of killing a human being with as little remorse as normal people have in killing a fly. Their psychopathic behavior may seem unmotivated because of the randomness of their violence, as in the case of a sniper shooting at people on a street below. But from the psychopath's point of view, the crime is motivated by the constant need to regain superiority by destroying others.

It is also worth noting that male psychopaths' victims are frequently women, and since Threes often identified with their mothers, this fits the pattern. To arrive at Level 9, it is extremely likely that Threes experienced incredible abuse as children. Nothing they could do or be could win the affection or positive regard of their nurturing-figure. But since Threes depend upon gaining the affirmation of their nurturing-figure, and since a small child cannot consciously hate their parent and survive psychologically, their rage is displaced onto substitute figures who somehow remind the psychopath of their original torments. Rape, torture, and sexual mutilation are frequent outcomes.

Despite their duplicity and deviousness, psychopathic Threes may trip themselves up because part of their need for vindictive triumph includes the desire for their victims to know who victimized them. Their need for attention and affirmation, which we have seen from stage to stage in different forms, becomes their nemesis. However, psychopathic Threes do not care. Public condemnation and notoriety give them the attention they crave: being feared or despised affirms that they still exist as "somebody."

ANALYZING THE DYNAMICS OF THE THREE

The Direction of Disintegration: The Three Goes to Nine

Starting at Level 4, Threes will begin to respond to stress by acting out some of the qualities of average to unhealthy Nines. Threes are highly driven and identified with what they do, so the move to Nine can be seen as a way of disengaging from their relentless activity and pursuit of success.

At Level 4, Threes are usually focused on developing their careers, achieving, and getting ahead. They are competitive with peers and eager to prove themselves to others. When they push too hard, or their competitiveness becomes apparent to others, they move to Nine, becoming conciliatory and apologetic. Threes want to stand out from "the pack," but not too much. When anxiety arises that they may be alienating others, they begin to take on more conventional roles, lowering their profiles and conforming to group norms.

At Level 5, Threes are constantly working at a variety of projects in order to get ahead and make a favorable impression. This frequently leads them into situations in which they are uncomfortable or into work that they do not necessarily want to do. Average Threes deal with the stress of this denial of their own desires by disengaging their attention from their activities. They lose themselves in busywork and routine and hope to get through difficult situations without being directly affected by them. Threes are usually quick and effective in dealing with demands on them, but when they go to Nine, they become strangely unresponsive and unfocused. Over time, this can lead to a complacency which appears in marked contrast to their usual industriousness.

At Level 6, Threes are incessantly promoting themselves and their accomplishments. They want everyone to know that they are a "somebody." But maintaining the energy of this self-deception is exhausting and collapses are inevitable. They are particularly vulnerable to setbacks in their careers at this stage, and if they are experiencing disappointments on that front, they may move to

Nine for lengthy periods of time. No longer able to maintain their grandiose views of themselves, their underlying self-doubt breaks through and they can suddenly become apathetic and aimless. Formerly effective and goal-oriented, Threes now collapse into a listless resignation, avoiding the realities of their problems and resorting to wishful thinking and fantasies of their next big success. Drinking and substance abuse may enter the picture.

At Level 7, Threes have become deeply neurotic, and attempt to keep the illusion of their superiority alive through deception and false claims about themselves. They may engage in unethical, even illegal, activities in order to save their sinking self-esteem. Too unstable to function well, their "success" depends on convincing themselves and others that they've "got it together," which, in fact, they do not. When the stress of keeping up the ruse overwhelms them, they can fall into deep apathy and depression. They become unwilling to look at the disasters in their lives, and seem to give up on themselves. They are highly ineffectual and have difficulty performing even basic tasks. Unhealthy Threes may spend months or even years in this condition rather than fall into Level 8 or 9.

At Level 8, Threes are desperately trying to cover up their misdeeds as well as the depth of their dysfunction. They are cut off from their feelings, and in the interest of saving their image, are capable of dangerous and criminal actions. Although they may be successful at concealing their true condition for a while, they are too broken down to avoid periods of collapse. When they go to Nine, the full extent of their distress and their lack of development are laid bare. They may regress to earlier parts of their life, replaying childhood triumphs or traumas. They may also alternate between depressive, dissociative periods and sudden hysterical outbursts. They will, if at all possible, avoid letting anyone see them like this, and, as long as they have the strength to do so, will restore their image whenever they interact with others.

At Level 9, unhealthy Threes are full of rage and hostility and want to attack whoever they feel has wounded what remains of their self-esteem. When the horror of their compulsive behaviors registers, or when others discover what they have been up to, they go to Nine, deteriorating into a psychotic-like condition, into a dream world from which they think they will not awake. Everything becomes unreal, including the horrible acts they may have perpetrated on others. They no longer feel enraged or hostile or vindictive. When they go to Nine, neurotic Threes unconsciously dissociate themselves from the only feelings they have, their hostile feelings, so completely that they feel absolutely nothing. Their depression manifests as "deadness," flatness, having no energy or interest in anything, even themselves.

When deteriorated Threes become this depersonalized, the extent of their true alienation from themselves becomes apparent. The inflated illusions with which their narcissism allowed them to maintain their sense of self has collapsed, exposing their emptiness. They stop taking an interest in themselves, may gain weight, and sink into a vegetative state. At Level 9, they may break from reality altogether, fracturing into subpersonalities or retreating into a state resembling catatonia.

The Direction of Integration: The Three Goes to Six

Going to Six can be frightening for Threes because in doing so, they commit themselves to someone else, exposing themselves to the fear of being rejected. Genuine intimacy with others is especially threatening to Threes because they have come to believe that only their image and accomplishments are valuable. They feel that their authentic self is too undeveloped and vulnerable to be worthwhile.

When healthy Threes go to Six, however, they become committed to something or someone outside themselves, realizing that their value is not diminished by being part of something greater than they. Integrating Threes discover that by their commitment to something outside themselves, they paradoxically begin to grow as persons within themselves. Identifying with others allows solid values to take root.

Their commitment to others also allows Threes to do what they are so afraid of doing: letting others see their real feelings and vulnerabilities. When Threes go to Six they find the courage to explore their fears and genuine emotional needs and, because they often do so within a committed relationship, they find that they are still accepted and therefore have a firm foundation upon which to begin to develop their authentic selves. (A spiritual conversion may be extremely helpful in this regard.) What also helps healthy Threes to go to and remain at Six is the experience of falling in love with someone who is clearly more developed than they are. If Threes can admire and feel loved by others with whom they are not competitive, relationships have a real chance of lasting. Once Threes have established a committed relationship, the relationship draws qualities from them which may well help them to remain healthy.

When they move to Six, Threes no longer worry about impressing others with their prestige, success, or status, nor do they aggrandize themselves at the expense of others. They use their talents to affirm the value of others, which allows them to experience their own true value. Last, by learning to work for and serve causes which will not necessarily bring them direct attention or praise, Threes begin to open up their hearts and discover real sources of self-esteem. They are fulfilled by the rich satisfactions of cooperating with others for shared goals and discover that their commitment to others brings them more affirmation, love, and support than their drive for success and competitiveness ever could. Most profoundly, though, without even noticing it, Threes have stopped focusing on their own image, and as it drops away, bit by bit, their real self emerges: being in touch with the goodness of their own hearts fills them with more joy and serenity than they ever could have imagined.

THE MAJOR SUBTYPES OF THE THREE

The Three with a Two-Wing: "The Star"

In general, the Three's traits and those of the Two reinforce each other. Threes with a Two-wing have extraordinary social skills: they like to be among people and enjoy being the center of attention; they are often extremely charming, sociable, and highly popular. They pride themselves on their interpersonal charm, humor, and attractiveness, which adds considerably to their social desirability as well as to their stimulating effect on others. With the Two-wing, the emphasis is more on personal touch and personal presentation. There is also a greater interest in reaching out to others and making interpersonal contact. Noteworthy examples of the Three with a Two-wing include Bill Clinton, Prince Andrew, Elvis Presley, Paul McCartney, Brooke Shields, Jane Pauley, Whitney Houston, Denzel Washington, Shirley MacLaine, Jack Kemp, Kathie Lee Gifford, Dick Clark, Vanna White, Tony Robbins, Joe Montana, Sylvester Stallone, Arnold Schwarzenegger, O.J. Simpson, "Hedda Gabler," and "Lady Macbeth."

Depending on how much the Two-wing is operative, healthy Threes of this subtype are generally more outwardly emotional and friendly than Threes with a Four-wing. They possess some degree of warmth and positive feelings for people. Threes are not completely affectless, of course. They care about those few people they are close to. They can encourage and appreciate others, and their feelings can be touched and hurt. There is a perky, vivacious quality about them that can resemble the energetic qualities of the Seven. They can be talkative, helpful, and generous like Twos, while maintaining the sense of poise and self-control characteristic of Threes. They usually want a particular kind of affirmation from others: besides receiving attention, they want to be loved. This encourages them to be more responsive to the needs and desires of others.

Average Threes of this subtype wish to convince themselves and others of their desirability, so they energetically reach out to others, attempting to engage them and garner attention. The Two-wing heightens their ability to project their feelings, or the illusion of feelings, as the case may be. Actors, models, and singers are frequently of this subtype. They know how to "turn it on" when they feel they need to impress someone, and as they become more unhealthy, this becomes their continuous preoccupation. People of this subtype care a great deal about what others think of them: competitiveness, comparing themselves to others, and success in their relationships are particularly important. They not only desire an enviable relationship with a spouse, they want the spouse to be a catch, sexually and socially desirable, one who reflects well on themselves. Children are also typically narcissistic extensions of the self, as is the home, hobbies, vacation spots, and other values in their lives. The narcissism of this subtype is more open than that of Threes with a Four-wing. They begin to use their "charms" excessively and inappropriately, often unaware that their efforts are backfiring. Exhibitionism and seductiveness are also more pronounced in people of this subtype. As they deteriorate, Threes with a Two-wing may court publicity, even negative publicity, to get attention, while shielding what is left of their fragile inner emotional life from any and all examination. Since their attention seldom visits this inner world, they are sometimes unaware of the anger and resentment they feel toward others who do not respond to the "sacrifices" they are making in order to be accepted.

Unhealthy Threes of this subtype are not only deceptive about getting what they want from others; they can be self-deceptive as well. They can be manipulative and feel entitled, which whets their appetite for revenge against those who do not give them the attention and love they feel they deserve. Both the Three and the Two have a problem with aggression: Twos feel aggressive when others do not appreciate them, and Threes are hostile when there is any slight to their narcissism. The combination produces particularly hostile people if they are not on top. The jealousy we see in unhealthy Threes is also present in unhealthy Twos, motivating these people to coerce others to give them what they want. When their hostility does break through, the intensity of their rage can reach dangerous levels, surprising everyone, including themselves. Threes with a Two-wing become malicious toward others, even psychopathically destructive. They are charming psychopaths, attractive men and women who seem to have had everything going for them until they suddenly become violent, usually toward those with whom they are closest, but who, for whatever reason, have frustrated their narcissistic needs.

The Three with a Four-Wing: "The Professional"

The traits of the Three and those of the Four produce a complex subtype whose traits often conflict with each other. The Three is essentially an "interpersonal" type, whereas the Four withdraws from contact with others. In this subtype, there is less emphasis on interpersonal skills and more focus on work, achievement, and recognition. To the degree that the Four-wing is operative, some persons of this subtype seem more like Fours then Threes: they can be quiet, rather private, subdued in demeanor, and have artistic interests and aesthetic sensibilities. They can be more emotionally vulnerable than Threes with a Two-wing, but are more restrained in their self-expression. Noteworthy examples of the Three with a Four-wing include Jimmy Carter, George Stephanopoulos, Sting, Richard Gere, Barbra Streisand, Meryl Streep, Tom Cruise, Michael Tilson Thomas, Dick Cavett, Bryant Gumbel, Truman Capote, Andy Warhol, Somerset Maugham, and "Iago."

Healthy Threes with a Four-wing have some amount of intuition which they can direct both toward themselves and others. Because some self-awareness is also part of the picture, people of this subtype have more potential for gaining self-knowledge and developing their emotional lives than Threes with a Two-wing. They may have artistic sensibilities and creative ability, and often possess a strong sense of style, especially in regard to their homes and their personal appearance. They usually emphasize intelligence over personal attractiveness in their self-image and social dealings. In addition to the degree that the Four-wing is operative, there will be a strong attraction to aesthetic objects and a love of fine things. Hard workers, they generally present a more serious and overtly task-oriented persona than Threes with a Two-wing. Many people of this subtype spend a great deal of time honing their craft and make it their business to master whatever technical knowledge and skill is necessary to excel in their chosen field of endeavor. For this reason, they can easily be mistyped as Fives or Ones. People of this subtype are self-assured and outstanding in some way, yet also introspective and sensitive.

Since Three is the basic type, however, average Threes with a Four-wing will still be interested in success and prestige, although in more subtle ways than the other subtype. The competitiveness of the Three and the self-doubt of the Four combine in ways which inevitably create tremendous pressures for the Three with a Four-wing. They begin to base their self-esteem on the reactions of specific others to their work, and often feel as though they are putting their entire self-worth on the line with every project they take on. Their imaginations and feelings will play a more active role, but as Threes, they are still, as much as possible, suppressing their feelings in order to function more effectively and to "make the right impression." Under such pressure, they are bound to make mistakes sooner or later, and when they do, the Four-wing adds a component of self-accusation which can be difficult to endure. The relentless drive for achievement of the Three combined with the self-reproach of the Four make the idea of failure truly terrifying for this subtype. Threes with a Four-wing tend to be more moody and pretentious than the other subtype, and also more aloof and conscious of how others treat them. They put great stock in their ideas and demand that others do likewise. Narcissistic feelings of superiority and arrogance mingle with the Four's feelings of exemption and self-indulgence. They can be subtle showoffs, but showoffs nonetheless.

Unhealthy Threes of this subtype alternate wildly between the ego-inflation of the Three and the self-doubt of the Four. Since Three is basic, self-satisfaction and grandiose fantasies are the rule. To the extent that the Four-wing comes into play, they may also begin to suffer depressions in which they shut down emotionally and physically for periods of time. Threes can come out of these states with a renewed sense of purpose, but often fall right back into the same routines that got them in trouble in the first place. This can happen several times until the Three gets the message and makes significant life changes, burns out, or sinks into truly pathological behavior. (People of this subtype may be misidentified as manic-depressives since their moods may change rapidly, an element which Threes with Four-wings have in common with the manic-depressive disorder. However, the underlying problem here is not anxiety but narcissism and the lack of fulfillment of their grandiose expectations.) It is possible that people of this subtype will also be self-destructive and suicidal if constantly frustrated by reality.

SOME FINAL THOUGHTS

Looking back at Threes, we saw that they go astray by abandoning themselves, rejecting their own heart's desire in order to become the kind of person that they believe will be more acceptable and worthwhile. As a result, Threes develop only certain parts of themselves, like bodybuilders who focus on the development of only one aspect of their physique instead of seeking overall balance. While the qualities healthy Threes develop are real, they are parts, not the whole, of themselves. In average Threes we saw the overdevelopment of a much more insubstantial part of themselves, their image, which served their narcissistic need for affirmation. And we saw that unhealthy Threes sacrifice their true selves, destroying their integrity and causing others a great deal of harm to keep their own inflated self-image alive.

Unhealthy Threes unwittingly bring about what they most fear. They fear being worthless and without value, but because of their narcissism, exploitativeness, and malice, they end up cut off from the only source of true value a human being can have, their own inner life. Their desperate bid for success leads to a gnawing desolation and terrifying feelings of deficiency. The person so desirous of being affirmed by others has done things that are despised by others. So much of what others admired turns out to have been a false front, a façade, which has collapsed, revealing the inner emptiness.

Because Threes are so adept at promoting favorable impressions of themselves, it is not apparent that they may be very undeveloped human beings beneath their image. The irony is that they are more and more dependent on others to affirm their value when there is progressively less and less of value about them to affirm. Yet when Threes brave their fears of worthlessness, stop the performance, and reveal the more simple, vulnerable human beings they really are, they become profoundly affecting and powerful.

Chapter 6

Type Four: The Individualist

THE FOUR IN PROFILE

Healthy: Self-aware, introspective, engaged in a "search for self," aware of feelings and inner impulses. Sensitive and intuitive both to self and others: gentle, tactful, compassionate. / Highly personal, individualistic, true to their feelings. Self-revealing, emotionally honest, humane. Ironic view of self and life: can be serious and funny, vulnerable and emotionally strong. *At Their Best:* Profoundly creative, expressing the personal and the universal, possibly in a work of art. Inspired, self-renewing, and regenerating—able to transform all their experiences into something valuable: redemptive and self-creative.

Average: Take an artistic, romantic orientation to life, creating a beautiful, aesthetic environment to cultivate and prolong personal feelings. Heighten reality through fantasy, passionate feelings, and the imagination. Long for the idealized partner. / To stay in touch with feelings, they interiorize and personalize things, becoming self-absorbed, hypersensitive, shy, and self-conscious. Temperamental and moody, they play "hard to get," but still feel like outsiders. / Feel that they are different from others and are therefore exempt from living as everyone else does until their emotional needs are met. Become melancholy dreamers, disdainful, decadent, and sensual, living in a fantasy world. Self-pity and envy of others leads to self-indulgence. Become increasingly impractical, unproductive, and pretentious—yet, waiting for a rescuer.

Unhealthy: When dreams fail, become self-inhibiting and angry at self, depressed and alienated from self and others, blocked and emotionally paralyzed. Ashamed of self, fatigued and unable to function. Stay withdrawn to protect their self-image and to buy time to sort out feelings. / Tormented by delusional self-contempt, self-reproaches, self-hatred, and morbid thoughts: everything about them becomes a source of torment. Blaming others, they drive away anyone who tries to help them. / Despairing, feel hopeless and become self-destructive, possibly abusing alcohol or drugs to escape. In the extreme: emotional breakdown or suicide is likely.

Key Motivations: Want to be themselves, to express themselves in something beautiful, to find the ideal partner, to withdraw to protect their feelings, to take care of emotional needs before attending to anything else.

Examples: Tennessee Williams, Jeremy Irons, Rudolf Nureyev, Ingmar Bergman, J. D. Salinger, Johnny Depp, Bob Dylan, Joni Mitchell, Martha Graham, D. H. Lawrence, Maria Callas, Edgar Allan Poe, Judy Garland, Michael Jackson, Yukio Mishima, Anne Rice, Leonard Cohen, Roy Orbison, Marcel Proust, Virginia Woolf, "Blanche DuBois," and "Laura Wingfield."

AN OVERVIEW OF THE FOUR

In the artist of all kinds I think one can detect an inherent dilemma, which belongs to the co-existence of two trends, the urgent need to communicate and the still more urgent need not to be found. . . .

What more fruitful way to redressing the balance than by portraying one's inner world in a work of art and then persuading other people to accept it, if not as real, at least as highly significant? Part of the satisfaction which a creative person obtains from his achievement may be the feeling that, at last, some part of his inner life is being accepted which has never been accorded recognition before. Moreover, since art became an individual matter rather than a task for anonymous craftsmen, creative work is generally recognized as being especially apt for expressing the personal style of an individual (which is of course closely related to his inner world). The value we place upon authenticity is often exaggerated; yet there is a sense in which it is justified. However good a painting or a piece of music may be, taken quite apart from its creator, the fact that it is or is not another expression of the personality of a particular artist is important. For it either is or is not an addition to our knowledge of that artist; a further revelation of that mysterious, indefinable and fascinating thing— his personality. (D. W. Winnicott, quoted in Anthony Storr, *The Dynamics of Creation*, 58.)

The nature of creativity will probably always remain mysterious because its basis is irrational—in the feelings and unconscious of those who create—and because, as Winnicott notes, part of the motive for creating is to remain concealed, to be unfound by others. Yet the motives given for artistic work—to communicate and to conceal the self—are but two possible motives which any person may have for creating. These two motives are, however, particularly appropriate to the Four, the artistic temperament among the personality types. Of course, members of any other personality type can become artists in the sense of making a livelihood by producing works of art, however that is defined. Fours, however, are in search of their identities, and by taking an artistic or at least aesthetic orientation to life they hope to find out who they are and what about themselves is significant.

In the Feeling Triad
The Four is the personality type which emphasizes the subjective world of feelings, in creativity and individualism, in introversion and self-absorption, and in self-torment and self-hatred. In this personality type we see creative artists, romantic aesthetes, and withdrawn dreamers, people with powerful feelings who feel different from others because self-consciousness blocks them from getting outside themselves.

Fours are the most self-aware of the types, and this is the basis of what is most positive and negative about them. The constant conflict we see in Fours is between their need to be aware of themselves, so they can find themselves, and, at the same time, their need to move beyond self-awareness, so they will not be trapped in self-consciousness. The tension between self-awareness and self-transcendence can be resolved in creativity. In the creative moment, healthy Fours harness their emotions without getting lost in them, not only producing something beautiful but discovering who they are. In the moment of inspiration they are, paradoxically, both most themselves and most liberated from themselves. This is why all forms of creativity are so valued by Fours, and why, in its inspired state, creativity is so hard to sustain. Fours can be inspired only if they have first transcended themselves, something which is extremely threatening to their self-image. In a sense, then, only by learning not to look for themselves will they find themselves and renew themselves in the process.

The problem with average Fours, however, is that they try to understand themselves by introspecting on their feelings. As they move inward in a search for self, they become so acutely self-conscious that their subjective emotional states become the dominant reality for them. And, because even average Fours are so involved with their emotions, they do not usually express their feelings directly. Instead, they communicate their feelings indirectly and symbolically.

The overall direction of their personalities therefore is inward, toward increasing self-absorption, because Fours feel that they are different from other people and they want to know why they feel this way. Ironically, however, they try to find their place in life by withdrawing from it so they can trace the labyrinth of their emotions. But the result of their withdrawal is that even average Fours have noticeable difficulties coping with life, while unhealthy Fours have some of the most severe emotional difficulties of all the personality types.

Fours tend to compound their emotional difficulties in some striking ways. Because Fours have identified themselves with their feelings, they begin to look for intensity of feeling in all of their activities. The more intensely they feel something, the more real they feel. Thus, average Fours begin to employ their imaginations to "stir up" their emotional life. They can take even the most transitory encounter with a person and dwell on it for hours to extract all of its "emotional juice." The problem is that it becomes difficult for Fours to sustain their moods and fantasies if they are still interacting with others or taking care of practical needs. Their feeling states and self-image become rarefied to a degree that reality will not support. Increasingly, they begin to withdraw from life and real relationships and experiences, both to prevent others from interfering with their strong reveries and moods, and to avoid potential embarrassment and humiliation. Eventually they will only interact with those few people who support their identities and emotional needs. As they draw the curtains and turn away from life, however, they cut themselves off from the wellspring of their feelings and their creativity—participation in the world.

In healthy Fours, however, the rich life of the unconscious becomes accessible and is given shape. More than any other personality type, healthy Fours are the bridge between the spiritual and the animal in human nature because they are so aware of these two sides of themselves. They sense in themselves the depths to which human beings can descend, as well as the heights to which they can be swept up. No other personality type is as habitually aware of the potentials and predicaments of human nature: human beings are spiritual animals occupying an uneasy place between two orders of existence. Fours sense both sides of their potentially conflicting natures, and they suffer intensely or are ecstatic because of them. This is why, at their best, healthy Fours create something which can move others deeply, because they have been able to get in touch with the hidden depths of human nature by delving deeply into their own. By doing so, they transcend themselves and are able to discover something universal about human nature, fusing personal conflicts and divergent feelings into art.

But, like everyone else, most Fours do not live at the peak of their potential. In response to anxiety, they turn inward, becoming self-conscious, particularly about the negativity they discover in themselves. To offset their negative feelings, they use their imaginations to make their lives more bearable. As a result, average Fours begin to withdraw from ordinary life. They become self-absorbed and do not learn how to relate to people or how to manage in the practical world. They feel like outsiders, somehow flawed and different from others, unable to break through the barrier of self-consciousness that separates them from easy commerce with the world.

And if they are unhealthy, their negative feelings feed upon themselves because Fours have closed themselves off from any other influences. Unhealthy Fours are so completely alienated from others, and ironically, even from themselves, that they despair of ever finding a way out of their excruciating self-consciousness.

They realize that their search for self has led them into a world of useless fantasies and illusions. Understanding only too clearly what they have done to themselves, and fearing that it is too late to do anything about it, unhealthy Fours hate and torment themselves, turning against themselves to destroy what they have become.

Problems with Identity

Fours find it difficult to transcend self-consciousness because just the reverse is what they want: to become more conscious of their states and feelings so that they can find themselves and arrive at a firm sense of identity. But as they become more self-conscious, Fours become increasingly drawn into unresolved, contradictory, and irrational feelings which they want to sort out before they dare express them.

Self-discovery is an extremely important motive for Fours because they never feel that their sense of self is strong enough to sustain their identities, particularly if they need to assert themselves. Because their feelings change so readily, their sense of identity is not solid, dependable, in their own hands. They feel undefined and uncertain of themselves, as if they were a gathering cloud which may produce something of great power or merely dissipate in the next breeze. Fours can never tell how the next moment will affect them, so it is difficult for them to count on themselves. Something is missing in the self, something they cannot quite put their finger on, but which they feel they lack nonetheless.

The difficulty is that average Fours may not know what their feelings are until after they have expressed them personally or artistically. But if they express all that they feel, they fear that they may reveal too much, exposing themselves to shame or punishment. On the other hand, by not expressing their feelings, average Fours undermine the possibility of discovering themselves by getting caught in endless self-absorption. They become aware of being aware of themselves—their consciousness is filled with little more than fantasies and memories, ultimately leading to illusions, regrets, and a wasted life.

As Fours become more fearful that they cannot find a solid identity in themselves, they begin to create one out of whatever random tendencies they find. Thus, matters of taste, likes and dislikes, and

emotional reactions become the materials which Fours use to construct an identity. Because their sense of self is so tenuous, however, Fours begin to put a great deal of weight on what would be for
others relatively unimportant traits. ("I only wear black." "I listen
to classical music, *never* country and western.") It is important to
note that most of these personal traits function by negation. Fours
may not know who they are, but they certainly believe they know
who they are not. While these idiosyncrasies can be fairly harmless
in and of themselves, as Fours increasingly depend on them to
figure out who they are, they begin to paint themselves into a
corner. In the interest of maintaining a narrowly defined self-
image, Fours may refuse to engage in many basic activities necessary to live their lives. ("I'm a poet. *I* can't work in an office.")

Fours maintain their sense of identity through a continuous
inner dialogue and referencing of their emotional reactions. Of
course, Fours want someone to validate their self-images, too, but
they are less dependent on the affirmation of others than Twos or
Threes. In fact, much of their identity is tied to their feelings about
not having the affirmation of others. Feeling different and misunderstood is as central to the Four's self-image as being only good
and loving is to the Two's or being a totally competent "winner" is
to the Three's.

Parental Orientation
Fours are disconnected from both parents. As children, they did not
identify with either their mothers or their fathers. ("I am not like
my mother; I am not like my father.") They may have had either
unhappy or solitary childhoods as a result of their parents' marital
problems, divorce, illness, or simply because of personality conflicts within the family. In some cases, Fours may have had relatively "normal," uneventful childhoods. Nonetheless, even with a
supportive environment, they did not see themselves reflected in
either parent: they felt that their parents did not see them as they
actually were or that what their parents conveyed to them was
somehow irrelevant. The advice and reactions they got seemed to
them to apply to a generic child, not to themselves. Lacking definitive role models, Fours as children turned inward to their feelings
and imaginations as the primary sources of information about
themselves from which they could construct their identities.

From childhood, Fours felt essentially alone in life. It seemed to them that, for reasons they could not understand, their parents had rejected them, or at least that their parents did not take much interest in them. Fours therefore felt that there must be something deeply wrong with them, that they were somehow defective because their parents did not give them the kind of nurturing attention which, as children, they needed. As a result, they turned to themselves to discover who they are.

Self-knowledge became their most important goal, the means by which they hoped to find some self-esteem. Fours felt that if they could discover who they are, they would not feel so different from others in the deep, essential way that they do. However, instead of creating themselves through introspection, Fours ironically become trapped in self-consciousness. Their self-consciousness alienates them, making them feel vulnerable, and arouses their aggressions at themselves and others, particularly their parents. But because they also feel powerless to express their aggressions or to do anything about their condition, they withdraw from their parents and from others, turning their aggressions mostly against themselves.

Because the formative relationship with their parents was primarily one of disconnection, Fours also begin to develop a sense of ego identity based on their *difference* from others. There were few qualities in their parents that they identified with, so Fours began to inventory all of the ways in which they were unlike the people around them. Eventually, this sense of difference becomes a strongly developed and defended part of their self-image, and many Fours have difficulty seeing the many ways in which they are like everyone else. To be "ordinary" becomes a frightening prospect, since a sense of "being unique" feels like one of the only stable building blocks of their identity. Ironically, although Fours cling to their "differentness," they also envy and resent people who seem to enjoy a more normal existence.

Their disconnection from their parents also produces a longing for the "good parent"—the person who will see them as they truly are and validate the self they are trying to construct. Fours usually experience this as a longing for an ideal mate or partner. They will often project this role onto new acquaintances, idealizing them and fantasizing about the wonderful life they will have together. Unfortunately, as Fours get to know the person better, they become disenchanted, realizing that the other is not the perfect parent who will rescue them from all their problems. Fours see very quickly that the person is just an ordinary human being: the other's "blemishes" soon become the focus of the Four's attention, and they lose interest in the person. Before long they are back to their search and fantasies again, but generally with more desperation to find the person "of their dreams."

Problems with Hostility and Despair

Like Twos and Threes, the other two personality types of the Feeling Triad, Fours have a problem with hostility. They direct their hostility at themselves because, like Twos and Threes, Fours have rejected their real self in favor of an idealized self-image. However, because of their self-awareness, Fours are always becoming conscious of all of the ways in which they are *not* like their idealized self. They come to disdain many of their real qualities, which they see as barriers to becoming the self of the imagination. Angry with themselves for being defective, Fours inhibit and punish themselves in the many ways which we will see.

Of course, Fours also experience hostility toward others. They can become enraged if others seem to question or dismiss their self-image or emotional states, but they tend to express this by "dropping" people, suddenly and without explanation. The creativity of Fours can also be employed in sarcastic, withering remarks directed at those who have wounded their "sensitivities." Fours also can experience intense hostility toward the very people they have idealized. When others fail to live up to Fours' hopes of the "good parent," they may relive the original pain they felt at not being able to connect with their parents and project this onto the new love interest. They may dramatically express the rage and emotionality that they could not with their own parents, but usually withdraw quickly before the intensity of their feelings overwhelms them or does further damage to their relationships. More often, Fours will simmer and seethe in silence.

On a deep, unconscious level, Fours are hostile toward their parents because they feel that their parents did not nurture them properly. Fours feel that they were not welcomed into the world; they feel out of place, unwanted—and they are deeply enraged at their parents for doing this to them. However, their rage at their parents is so deep that Fours cannot allow themselves to express it. They fear their own anger, and so withhold it, trying to come to terms with it themselves. While some of the types may well feel the same degree of rage at their parents, Fours tend to have more difficulty getting on with their lives because they dwell on these old hurts. On a subtle level, Fours do not want to let go of their pain, lest others, especially their parents, not realize how much they have been hurt.

As awareness of their hostility and negative feelings gradually wears them out, however, average to unhealthy Fours sink ever more deeply into self-doubt, depression, and despair. They spend most of their time searching for the courage to go on living despite the overwhelming sense that the essential flaw in themselves is so deep that it cannot be healed. Indeed, the feeling of hopelessness is the current against which they must constantly swim. And if the undertow of hopelessness is too strong, unhealthy Fours either succumb to an emotional breakdown or commit suicide, because they despair of ever breaking free of it.

As soon as Fours devote themselves to a search for self by withdrawing from life, they are going in the wrong direction. No matter how necessary this search may seem to them, they must become convinced that the direct search for self is a temptation which eventually leads to despair.

On the other hand, what makes healthy Fours healthy is not that they have freed themselves once and for all from the turbulence of their emotions, but that they have found a way to ride that current to some further destination. Healthy Fours have learned to sustain their identities without exclusive reference to their feelings. By overcoming the temptation to withdraw from life to search for themselves, they will not only save themselves from their own destructiveness, they will be able to bring something beautiful and good into existence. If they learn to live this way, Fours can be among the most life-enhancing of the personality types, bringing good out of evil, hope from hopelessness, meaning from absurdity, and saving what appeared to be lost.

ANALYZING THE HEALTHY FOUR

Level 1: The Inspired Creator

Of all the personality types, very healthy Fours are most in touch with impulses from their unconscious. They have learned to listen to their inner voices while remaining open to impressions from the environment. Most important, they are able to act without self-consciousness, and if they have the talent and training, are able to give their unconscious impulses an objective form in a work of art worthy of the name.

Having transcended self-consciousness, very healthy Fours are free to become creative in the root sense of being able to bring something new into the world. Of course, profoundly creative moments come and go, because creativity is difficult to sustain. Nevertheless, at their best Fours are able to sustain creativity because they have transcended their self-consciousness, opening up the way to inspiration. They draw inspiration from the widest variety of sources, filtering the raw material of experience through the unconscious. In doing so, inspired Fours are like oysters, transforming all their experiences, even painful ones, into something beautiful. In their inspired creative work, healthy Fours become wellsprings of revelation for others, as if they were conduits through which the sublime passes into the world.

Their creativity is paradoxical, because Fours are able to express the personal universally, in something that has resonance and meaning beyond what they intend when they create. By opening themselves to their hidden depths, Fours are able to express something true about themselves. Yet it is difficult for them to explain where their creativity has come from. Much of their knowledge about themselves and others has the quality of being an inspiration, something which comes to them spontaneously, completely, mysteriously, and beyond their conscious control.

Being creative is not limited to artists, but is an important quality which everyone should try to awaken within themselves. The most important form of creativity is self-creation — renewing and redeeming the self by transcending the ego. It is the process of turning all your experiences, good and bad, into something more for your growth as a person. ("Be the kind of person on whom nothing is lost." — William James)

[Otto] Rank did not glorify the artist as such, but rather the creative individual, whose expressions varied with the cultural conditions in which he found himself. . . . In fact, Rank argued, the creative artist is still seeking in art a refuge which it would be better to give up and return to real life. Once he does that, he becomes the new man whom psychoanalysis is seeking to create. (Reuben Fine, *A History of Psychoanalysis*, 271.)

By acting in the moment of inspiration, which is not primarily a moment of feeling, Fours paradoxically create and discover themselves in what they bring into the world. The problem with their identities begins to be solved. Fours are "told" who they are not by their parents, but by what they discover in their creativity, and in the richness of the lives they live from day to day, from moment to moment. This is why Fours at their healthiest are not merely artists, as Rank indicates, but creative, life-enhancing individuals, who may also be artists.

Fours at this Level embrace life profoundly: they are truly connected with their authentic selves and with the world. They stop restricting the kinds of experiences that they will allow themselves and learn to say "yes" to life. As they open to more of life's possibilities, they begin to experience themselves freshly in each moment—and their true identity is gradually but endlessly revealed. To be able to renew the self constantly is the highest form of creativity, a kind of "soul making," which requires a higher state of integration than making a painting or a book or a dance. This is the state the other personality types can learn from healthy Fours, and the state to which Fours constantly aspire.

Level 2: The Self-Aware Intuitive
Even relatively healthy Fours do not always live at such a high level of consciousness. When they draw back from the inspired, creative moment to reflect upon it, or to enjoy their creativity, they lose the unselfconsciousness that is necessary to sustain it. Inspired creativity can be maintained only in the act itself, by continuing to transcend self-consciousness. It requires a constant renewing of the self with each moment. In truth, the self is more like a process than like an object. Fours, however, begin to fear that they cannot find themselves in their constantly shifting feelings and impressions. They cannot locate their identity, so they begin to self-reflect rather than allow their experiences to flow freely. Thus, as soon as they try to grasp a specific identity, they become conscious of themselves and lose the spontaneous quality of inspiration. Fours become self-aware and introspective.

As we saw in the Overview, one of their basic motivations is to understand who they are, since they were not mirrored by their parents in a way that felt real to them. ("Who am I? What is my life all about?") To establish a self-image, a basic identity that they can rely on, Fours turn not to other people, but to their inner feelings and emotional responses. This provides healthy Fours with intuitive gifts and a rich inner life but also introduces a problem. Of all aspects of the human psyche, feelings are perhaps the most changeable and volatile. By trying to create a consistent identity from the world of feelings, Fours, like all other types, have embarked on a path that cannot provide what they are looking for. In fact, as we shall see, the more Fours identify with their feelings, the more confused they become about their identity. At this Level, Fours still have some objectivity about their feeling states and a high degree of emotional equilibrium. Still, this subtle shift from Level 1 will have profound consequences for Fours that can lead into the lower Levels of Development. They have stopped *having* their feelings and have begun to *be* their feelings.

Awareness of their feelings also creates the problem of automatically distancing even healthy Fours from their environment. Life becomes a kind of theater in which, for better or worse, they are both spectators and actors. While this awareness allows healthy Fours to use the distance they sense between themselves and everything else as a framing device to understand themselves more clearly, it also makes it difficult for them to be self-assertive or sustain practical activities. Moreover, they realize that there is nowhere for them to hide. Fours are forced to acknowledge disquieting realities (about themselves, others, and life) because their awareness makes them sensitive both to the feelings of others and to their own subconscious impulses. Nevertheless, healthy Fours are not afraid of what their feelings are telling them, even though those feelings may be painful and disturbing.

Fours are not only sensitive to themselves, they are sensitive to others because they are intuitive. Intuition gives Fours the ability to understand how others think and feel and see the world. Intuition is not some sort of useless sideshow telepathy but a means of perceiving reality by way of the unconscious. It is like receiving a message in a bottle which has washed up on the shore of consciousness.

Self-awareness is the psychological basis of intuition. Fours are conscious of themselves, the world, and other people by way of the unconscious. And it is by seeing how their experiences affect them that Fours hope to discover their own dimensions. (Or more poetically, "I note the echo that each thing produces as it strikes my soul."—Stendhal)

Fours correspond to Jung's introverted intuitive type.

> Introverted intuition is directed to the inner object, a term that might justly be applied to the contents of the unconscious. . . .
>
> Although his intuition may be stimulated by external objects, it does not concern itself with external possibilities but with what the external object has released within him. . . .
>
> In this way introverted intuition perceives all the background processes of consciousness with almost the same distinctness as extroverted sensation registers external objects. For intuition, therefore, unconscious images acquire the dignity of things. (C. G. Jung, *Psychological Types*, 398–399.)

Because the richest part of their conscious life is outside their control, even healthy Fours are aware that they are not completely in control of themselves. Their intuitions come and go like ghosts which cannot be summoned at will. Moreover, their intuitions can be unsettling, making them aware of feelings which are difficult to identify or resolve. Intuitions are also difficult for Fours to express rationally—precisely because intuitions are irrational and have unconscious roots. For better or worse, their intuitions make them conscious of an endless stream of positive and negative feelings about themselves and the world. It therefore takes Fours time to identify and understand their intuitions, and courage for them to accept what their intuitions are telling them.

Level 3: The Self-Revealing Individual

Healthy Fours need to express what they feel so they can know what their intuitions are telling them about themselves. They are the most personal of the personality types, revealing themselves to others with directness and authenticity. They do not put on masks, hiding their doubts and weaknesses, nor do they deceive themselves about their feelings and impulses no matter how unseemly or unflattering these are. Healthy Fours willingly reveal their flaws and irrationalities to others, since they feel that these things are not merely incidental to who they are, but reflect their personal truth. It would be dishonest to communicate themselves to others if they did not communicate the whole of themselves, the bad along with the good, doubts along with certainties. There is something very human about this: theirs is a genuineness and depth of feeling, a willingness to be touched, even at the expense of pain, if that is the authentic thing to do.

Healthy Fours are concerned with being true to themselves as individuals, even at the risk of being censured by those who value tradition or convention over self-actualization. The emotional honesty we find in healthy Fours may well antagonize, or sometimes embarrass, others, who may wish that Fours were not so candid about themselves. But what healthy Fours bring to society is the example of their humanity, the message that everyone is valuable because they are individuals.

Thus, just as healthy Fours want to be true to themselves, they also want others to be true to themselves. ("This above all: to thine own self be true, / And it must follow, as the night the day, / Thou canst not then be false to any man." —*Hamlet*, I, iii, 78–80) They are respectful of the individuality of others, sensitive about their feelings, considerate of their privacy and their needs. Fours willingly allow others to find their own way in life without trying to control them, one reason why they make good parents, friends, listeners, and therapists. They see other people as "other," not as functions of themselves or as objects to be used for their own gratification.

Healthy Fours are willing to be touched by the pains and feelings of others and are not easily thrown off balance by others' "revelations." Because they have been thoroughly engaged in exploring their own emotional terrain, they are able to listen to others in a way that is supportive and compassionate. There are few states of consciousness which healthy Fours have not entertained, so they can help others come to difficult truths which might otherwise overwhelm them. Others see in them a quiet, emotional strength which feels safe and well-grounded.

Because healthy Fours are grounded in reality and interested in interacting with others, they can be quite astute in their observations and eloquent in their expression. If they have been blessed with creative talent, their work can be deeply affecting. By diving deep within their own subconscious and wrestling with the truths they find there, Fours emerge with works of art in which others can recognize feelings and impressions which they had not been able to articulate themselves.

Fours at this Level are also acutely aware of themselves as individuals: they have a sharp sense of their unique otherness as well as the otherness of everything. Although they are not lonely, they understand that they are alone in life, an individual consciousness. From this point of view, healthy Fours are not merely individualists but existentialists, aware of their existence as individuals.

While there is a certain seriousness about all of this, healthy Fours are not serious about everything. They have a rich sense of humor because they see the poignant absurdity of much of human behavior in the light of the larger questions of life. Healthy Fours have a kind of double vision on human nature: they can see the devil and the angel, the sordid and the noble in human beings, especially in themselves. The ironic juxtaposition of such opposites is as funny as it is deeply touching. The incongruities of the human condition are what make healthy Fours shake their heads in amusement, and nowhere are they more aware of human incongruities than in themselves.

ANALYZING THE AVERAGE FOUR

Level 4: The Imaginative Aesthete

Average Fours fear that they will not be able to sustain the flow of feelings, impressions, and inspirations that are the basis of their identity. They believe that their creativity and, on a deeper level, their very sense of self, will not be sustained unless they feel them more intensely and more consistently. To this end, Fours begin to use their imaginations to stir up their feelings and to hold onto certain moods that they feel express who they really are. Whereas this can lead to a fertile fantasy life and is still relatively harmless, it marks a major shift away from interaction with life, and deeper into a potential morass of self-involvement.

Average Fours still want to be creative, but their creativity becomes somewhat self-conscious and therefore less universal. We can see that healthy Fours are artistic whereas average Fours think of themselves as artistic. At Level 4, they pursue various outlets for their self-expression, but less spontaneously and less consistently. Since more of their energy is being used to create moods from which they believe they will be inspired, their work becomes sporadic. More of their creativity begins to occur only in the realm of their imaginations.

Of course, not all average Fours are artists, and certainly not all artists are Fours. Nevertheless, since revealing their feelings remains essential to their emotional health, any artistic activity average Fours engage in is especially valued because art and beauty become a substitute for themselves, a means of expressing the self through a kind of proxy to the world.

If they are professional artists, they must have discovered which medium is best suited for their talents; they also must have learned their craft so that they can express themselves adequately. If Fours are not professional artists, or are in professions that do not allow an artistic outlet for self-expression, they will typically regard their work merely as a way of supporting themselves while their real interest lies elsewhere—in beauty and some sort of *aesthetic* self-expression. If they were given a "magic wish," the vast majority of average Fours who are not artists would choose to become painters, singers, ballet dancers, poets, novelists, sculptors, filmmakers, designers, or some other kind of artist.

If they do not have the ability to make works of art, average Fours try to make their environments more beautiful, for example, by decorating their apartments tastefully, by collecting art, or by dressing well. Fours are powerfully attracted to beauty, whether in people or in things, because aesthetic objects stimulate their feelings and reinforce their sense of self. Moreover, aesthetic objects symbolize the perfection and wholeness that Fours would like to find in themselves. Having sensed that something is missing in the self, they attempt to replace this inner loss by heightening the impact of beauty upon their emotions. They are romantics, idealizing beauty.

Creating an aesthetic environment serves another important function: it helps average Fours hold on to certain feelings and moods that reinforce their sense of self. Atmosphere becomes important, and they are most at home when there is an air of mystery and romance. Certain music, lighting, color schemes, particular objects which have strong emotional associations, all become supports for the moods that average Fours want to sustain. Clothing, especially when it is in some way "tastefully different," becomes another means of indirectly expressing their identity.

Little in the homes or the wardrobes of average Fours is casually selected. Everything is designed to support the Four's feelings and to announce quietly to the world, "This is who I am."

However, because average Fours are using their imaginations to intensify their emotions, they are also increasingly shifting their attention away from reality as they rework the world in their fantasies. They want to be swept away by grand passions, lyrical longings, and stormy emotions which, by elating, keep the sense of self alive. The romantic imagination may dwell on nature, or God, or the self, or the idealized other, or some combination of these, looking for portents and meanings, fascinated with death and the passing of all things. But because average Fours use them so often, their imaginations become powerful and seductive, an endless source of solace and gratification.

Fours are also strongly attracted to those who stimulate their feelings and sense of beauty. However, they begin to relate to people in their imaginations as if others were aesthetic objects, to be contemplated like works of art rather than as persons in their own right. Fours also become easily infatuated with others, holding long conversations with their lovers and friends in their imaginations. Scenes of love and longing, courtship and romance, possessing the other in sexual ecstasy, and the bitter sorrows of letting go of the beloved play themselves out.

From this stage on, Fours long for a deep and intimate relationship with someone who will "recognize" them for who they are. They want someone to see them and validate their identity in the way they feel their parents did not. They are therefore always on the lookout for love. Fours spend a great deal of time recalling brief meetings with acquaintances or casual glances across a crowded street, searching for the potential meanings of these encounters and wondering if the other is the special person who will see them and accept them. Most Fours at this Level like to see themselves as loners, but actually, they are constantly looking to get into a relationship with whoever has engaged their feelings and sense of beauty.

Unfortunately, the great part of their relationships takes place almost solely in their imaginations, without others ever being aware of their attention or the degree of their ardor. By using their imaginations, average Fours heighten the emotional impact of relationships, making them into something extremely exciting, while sparing themselves the problems of self-exposure and rejection.

Naturally, this approach to people is fraught with difficulties, not the least of which is that others inevitably turn out to be quite different from what Fours imagined them to be.

While there is nothing wrong with being imaginative, once the desire to heighten emotions in fantasy takes root, things start to become imbalanced because average Fours relate to their fantasies instead of to reality. The intuition we saw in healthy Fours has deteriorated into the unlimited use of the imagination as a way of making up to themselves for experiences they do not actually have.

Level 5: The Self-Absorbed Romantic

As average Fours become more involved in cultivating their moods and romantic fantasies about themselves and others, they begin to believe that too much interaction with the world, and especially with other people, will cause the fragile self-image they are creating to fall apart. They control access to themselves because they fear that other people will shame them or point out all of the ways that they are not like the image of themselves they are forming in their imaginations. For example, they may imagine themselves to be great artists, but do not spend much time actually creating art or may have doubts about the quality of what they are producing. In their imaginations, however, anything is possible, and average Fours want to surround themselves only with those people and situations that will support their self-image.

At this stage average Fours are reserved, shy, and extremely private—melancholy outsiders, painfully self-conscious. They want to let others know about who they believe they really are, but fear that they will be humiliated or laughed at. This is not an entirely unreasonable fear, because Fours probably have developed a persona which has little connection with their own background or experience (like the person from a small, Midwestern town who affects a British accent to feel more refined and sophisticated). Fours have now begun to reject themselves, but rather than trying to impress others with an idealized self-image, like Threes, Fours' self-doubt causes them to withhold their idealized self—including most of their authentic thoughts and feelings—from all but a few close confidants. Fours rationalize their withholding from others by viewing others as incapable of appreciating the subtlety of their feelings. ("There's no point throwing pearls before swine.")

They begin to avoid many people rather than risk the emotional problems involved with communicating anything about themselves. Instead, they seek the company of individuals who they see as kindred souls and exclude those who do not share their sensibilities. When Fours do find someone who they feel understands them, they pour out their hearts in long conversations that can stretch late into the night. At last, they are not alone—someone has come to share their world.

The ardor and excitement average Fours feel in encounters of these kinds is an indication of how deeply they long to be understood, and even rescued. They want to have someone in their lives who will alleviate their loneliness and, above all, be the good parent they are secretly seeking. However, if they are to continue eliciting the attention of a rescuer, average Fours must also continue to have problems and not allow themselves to become too functional. Although they typically see themselves as loners, they actually require "high maintenance" from other people. In fact, average Fours begin to evaluate how much they mean to others by how much others are willing to tolerate their emotional ups and downs and their neediness. They can be difficult and sometimes play "hard to get," but not to the extent of driving the other away, or so they hope.

In any case, average Fours will only allow people who support their ephemeral self-image to be around them. They insist that others respect the delicacy of their feelings, and by being temperamental and emotionally volatile, may cause others to "walk on eggshells" so as not to upset their fragile equilibrium. While it is certainly true that average Fours are experiencing emotional confusion and doubts about their identity, they also use their vulnerability to get attention and to control others. They demand that others tolerate their peccadilloes and mannerisms while generally being highly impatient with the habits of others.

Few people are willing to spend much time with average Fours because their relationships are often little more than long discussions about the Four's feelings and problems. While healthy Fours are stimulating company because they are attentive to others and are curious about the world, average Fours are uninterested in anything that does not immediately impact on their feelings and their quest for identity. They do not really want to know about other persons' experiences unless they relate directly to something they have been brooding about. Of course, the reasons for this are not difficult to understand. Fours are becoming worn out by their self-doubt and their frustrating search for a self-image that feels true to them. They feel that they simply do not have sufficient emotional resources to deal with other people's problems.

Nonetheless, Fours are still self-aware enough to recognize the discrepancies between their fantasized ideal self and the realities of their life. This only adds further confusion and causes them to be more unsure of themselves. It is difficult for them to meet people, to make small talk, or to work with anyone else. Average Fours feel socially inept and uncomfortable around most people, not so much because they do not like people—quite the contrary, they long to have intimate, intense relationships, as we have seen—but because they are so self-conscious that they cannot function well.

Naturally, social requirements and the needs of others become a burden to them. Thus, Fours do not go out of their way to meet others; rather, they secretly want people to seek them out. They project an aura of silence and aloofness, hoping that someone will notice them and take the trouble to approach them. While others may think that they are mysterious, or perhaps profound, Fours at this Level are simply attempting to disguise their growing emotional vulnerabilities behind the protective haze of exotic mystery. If someone has hurt their feelings and Fours have withdrawn to lick their wounds, their withdrawal is as aggressive an act as average Fours allow themselves, a denial of their presence to the other, although it annoys Fours greatly if the offender does not realize that they have done so.

Many of their problems stem from the fact that average Fours take everything personally. They must interiorize their experiences—feel their feelings—for their experiences to have meaning to them. But by interiorizing everything, average Fours become vulnerable and uncomfortably self-conscious—"hypersensitive." For example, a curt reply by a cab driver can ruin their day, and a perceptively critical comment from a friend can become a thorn in their side for months. If anyone should tease them or prick at their defenses, average Fours feel "cut to the quick" and do not know how to respond. ("What does so-and-so mean by that?") In many cases, Fours begin to hear negative reviews even in compliments. If a friend congratulates them on losing weight, they may spend hours feeling insulted that the person was actually commenting on how fat they had been. They simply cannot be easygoing or spontaneous, since their increasing self-absorption does not allow it.

Because they internalize all their experiences, everything seems to be connected with everything else. Every new experience affects them, gathering associated meanings until everything becomes overloaded, full of private associations. If they are healthy, this richness of emotional connections feeds their creativity, because their internalized and augmented experiences become available as inspirations. But the ironic result of self-absorption is that average Fours begin to lose touch with their emotions. They feel confused, amorphous, unanchored to anything permanent in themselves.

Rather than help to sort out their feelings, constant self-absorption makes average Fours feel more inadequate. They begin to doubt their ability to sustain contact with the environment, or to defend themselves adequately, since they feel so vulnerable and storm tossed. They become extremely conscious of not fitting into the environment as easily as others seem to and they begin to envy others and secretly resent them. It is a short step from "Why do I feel this way?" to "What is wrong with me?" Self-doubts assail them, as do problems with self-esteem and hostile feelings about others.

While healthy Fours can be quite comfortable when they are alone, average Fours often feel lonely. They feel that, at best, they are only tolerated by others (seldom really liked), and any problems in their relationships will invariably result in rejection, something which will only confirm their worst fears about themselves. Their assessment of their social situation may or may not be accurate, but average Fours give themselves few opportunities to find out.

This is not a satisfying way to live, even for Fours. To solve their problems, they begin to withdraw, feeling that they are being called away from the environment by something inside themselves, although they are not sure by what. It is as if they have been physically wounded and were bleeding to death. Before they can resume their lives, Fours feel they must obtain the first aid they need. Some inner disorder must be attended to before they can give their attention to anything else.

They brood about themselves. And because they are emotionally vulnerable to real or imagined slights, they become extremely moody. This becomes the precondition for every action as average Fours constantly introspect on their feelings to see how they feel before they do anything. They put off writing letters, going to the grocery, or looking for a job until they are in the right mood. But since Fours never know when they are going to be in the right mood, things either do not get done, or they are done against internal resistance, producing no pleasure.

This would not be as much of a problem for Fours if not for the fact that most of their moods are unpleasant. They dwell on their own shortcomings or simmer with resentment at the slights to their self-image from the "crude and insensitive" people in their lives. They may spend hours or even days rehashing old conversations and reliving their wounded feelings or endlessly imagining all the forms of revenge they will visit upon those who have frustrated them. More and more, Fours are frittering away their days in fantasy instead of taking constructive actions for themselves.

Level 6: The Self-Indulgent "Exception"

The longer they remain self-absorbed, the more practical and emotional difficulties Fours unwittingly create for themselves. They have not developed their social and professional skills, and their self-esteem has suffered from constant self-questioning. They feel vulnerable and unsure of themselves. In a word, average Fours feel different from others because by withdrawing to pursue their own private fantasies, they have become different. And because they are different, they feel they have needs that must be satisfied in unusual ways. They therefore want to compensate themselves for what they feel they lack by indulging their desires. They feel they are exceptions to the rule, exempt from expectations, totally free to "be themselves." The result is that they become completely undisciplined, luxuriating in whatever emotional and material pleasures they can afford.

Fours have been trying to create a specific and consistent self-image, but at Level 6, it is so narrow that Fours have "painted themselves into a corner." Because they have defined themselves largely by all of the things they are not, by all of the things they dislike, they reject many of the normal day-to-day experiences that comprise a normal human life. They may be unwilling to hold down a regular job or even look for one, to cook or clean for themselves, or to involve themselves in any social or community affairs. They defend against their uncertainties about their identity by feeling contempt for "the rabble," the faceless herd of which they will never allow themselves to be a part. Their sense of aesthetics becomes a weapon, a way to insult and dismiss others who fail to appreciate what the Four appreciates.

At the same time, while Fours have disdain for the lives of the common masses, they are filled with envy and resentment. Although they tell themselves that they want nothing to do with the pathetic lives of others, deep down the Four's self-awareness reveals the truth of whose life has become pathetic. They see the simple happiness of others in their "ordinary" jobs, marriages, and friendships, and realize the depth of their own unhappiness. Fours at Level 6 perceive others as shallow, lacking the real depth that they believe they possess, yet every instance of others' joy, unself-consciousness, and spontaneity is like a slap in the face. If Fours could see that their "depth" has become a pretension and an illusion, that their self-absorption is costing them a real, meaningful life, they might discover a way out of their emotional quagmire. Unfortunately, many turn their back on the world and try to succor themselves for all that they believe they have been missing.

Average Fours may once have attracted interest, and even some sympathy, from those who found their reserve and self-consciousness endearing, or at least intriguing. Others may have been touched by their shyness and vulnerability. But now the picture has changed. Self-indulgent Fours antagonize others because they are so perversely willful. They have no sense of social responsibility; they cannot be counted on for anything; and they resist all obligations, becoming petulant if anything is forced upon them either by events or by people. They take a special pride in maintaining the freedom to do things in their own way, in their own time, or not at all. ("I do what I want to do when I want to do it.")

Because they feel different from others, they feel special and exempt from living as everyone else does, free from any obligation to follow the ordinary conventions of social life. They feel that everything is allowed because of their emotional needs: their time is their own, and they resent any intrusion whatsoever. They resist everything, from having a job to employing healthy self-discipline to cooperating with others, if they think that doing something else will make them feel better about themselves. But rather than being strengthened by their self-indulgences, average Fours are further weakened by them. By definition, self-indulgence does not satisfy real needs, only transient desires. However, because self-indulgent Fours often depend upon the support of others to maintain the freedom of their lifestyles, they do not want anyone to know the full extent of their indulgences or to call them to task for them.

By insisting on the freedom to do as they please, they become increasingly precious and totally impractical, manifesting an effete disdain for reality. Affectations and mannerisms substitute for genuine self-expression, giving some Fours a certain dramatic "prima donna" quality. If they are still artists, their art becomes as self-indulgent and self-referential as they are. And because they are self-indulgent, they usually do not work seriously at much of anything, lapsing instead into eroticism and languorous, overwrought fantasies. Brilliant poetry, heart-rending music, and portentous winter novels pour from their imaginations—as long as they never try to write them down.

At this stage, average Fours are still self-aware enough to know that they are missing out on many important aspects of life, particularly relationships. Consequently, they feel sorry for themselves. They may become minor hypochondriacs, worrying about themselves—since no one else does. Self-pity is among the least attractive of traits, yet average Fours indulge in it excessively because it allows them to rationalize whatever they want. It allows them to feel that life owes them something. They can revel in their tragic existence without trying to change or say no to themselves.

Wallowing in their feelings gives self-indulgent Fours something to do, a way of occupying their time. The problem is, however, that their imaginary pleasures can never be satisfying because they are always unreal. The imagination is enticing nonetheless because it keeps their feelings at a fever pitch. By indulging their imaginations, their sense of self is kept alive, even as the life is being drained out of it.

To make up for their lack of achievement, Fours at this stage typically give themselves over to sensuality as a way of deadening the too-sensitive self to its growing unhappiness. They may become sexually licentious, engaging in anonymous sexual activities for release, for fleeting human contact, and for excitement. Or they may lose themselves in sexual fantasies, sinking into erotic daydreams rather than making any real efforts at anything. They may masturbate frequently, virtually a symbol for their self-referential, ingrown way of life. They may become obsessed with those with whom they have fallen in love in their imaginations, providing themselves with an endless source of pain and pleasure, desire and frustration, violent and wasteful feelings. Or they may sleep excessively or abuse food, drugs, and alcohol.

Their dependency on their imaginations has brought Fours to an overripe, unsavory state. Their emotions are too lush, as if they were rare orchids that have been kept in a hothouse all their lives—the hothouse of self-absorption. At this state, average Fours are decadent, at least in the estimation of others. Naturally, Fours do not see themselves this way—they are simply making up for their many deprivations.

Of course, they cannot admit that they are deprived because they have deprived themselves of contact with reality. The sad fact is that by now they have abandoned the search for self, and have substituted self-gratification for the discovery of an identity which is growing ever more nebulous.

ANALYZING THE UNHEALTHY FOUR

Level 7: The Alienated Depressive

As we have just seen, self-indulgent Fours consider themselves exempt, free to live in a world of self-gratification. In time this creates a new source of anxiety: the fear that they may lose the possibility of attaining their hopes and dreams, especially their hope of self-actualization. Actualizing themselves is what Fours have always wanted, but if something happens to make them feel that that dream has been lost, they suddenly feel cut off from themselves. Something they have done or failed to do now comes home to roost, and suddenly they "spiral in" to some core of themselves, both in shock and to protect themselves from even more loss.

Unhealthy Fours are angry at themselves for what they have done to themselves. They realize that they have wasted precious time, missed opportunities, and have fallen behind others in almost every way—personally, socially, and professionally—and they feel acutely ashamed. They envy others—everyone else seems to be happy, accomplished, and successful in the many ways in which Fours feel they are not. They see, much to their sorrow, that withdrawal into self-absorption has not turned out to be a way of finding themselves. Instead, things have gone wrong: they are wasting their lives, and they know it. They feel terribly confused and racked with self-doubt. They feel like failures—they have not accomplished anything worthwhile, and fear that they never will.

Unhealthy Fours unconsciously inhibit themselves from having any kind of meaningful desires because they do not want to be hurt any more, especially by having desires and expectations for themselves. The result is a sudden total blockage of all feelings, as if life had suddenly been drained from them. Whatever fulfillment they may once have found in their creative work, whatever hopes they may have had suddenly vanish. They instantaneously become fatigued, apathetic, alienated from themselves and others, sinking into emotional paralysis, barely able to function.

Exerting themselves in any way is extraordinarily difficult. They cannot bring themselves to sit in front of an easel or a typewriter until their creative juices begin to flow again; nor can they call friends or go to a movie. Looking for work or finding a therapist is out of the question. They feel like staying in bed all day, and often do. Ironically, unhealthy Fours can no longer be self-indulgent even if they wanted to, because they simply cannot bring themselves to get involved with anything.

As angry at themselves as they are, unhealthy Fours fear expressing their anger lest it make things worse. If they are angry at someone else—a romantic interest, for example—for disappointing their expectations, unhealthy Fours are so enraged that they cannot stand being in the same room with the former beloved, the object of such recent erotic obsessions. They are so angry that they hold themselves back from showing reactions of any kind, insofar as it is possible. (Others, however, can see that they look desolate, sigh deeply, and are close to tears.)

Fours at this Level often feel that everyone has let them down. They are furious with their families, their friends, the world, and themselves, and view their problems as, if not insurmountable, certainly worse than everyone else's. Fours have always wanted to see themselves as unique, but unhealthy Fours can find uniqueness only in the degree of their suffering: they suffer more than anyone else. (It often comes as a humiliating shock to Fours in therapy or recovery to discover that others have suffered as much as they have, and in some cases even more.) However, the fact that others are also suffering does not discount the fact that unhealthy Fours really are in a great deal of pain and cannot find ways to express it or release it. Their anger and grief feel too vast to experience in their entirety, so Fours use whatever energy they have left to hold it back.

Unhealthy Fours are still self-aware, and they realize that they are depressed and on the verge of becoming even more depressed. They know that only with the greatest difficulty will they be able to keep themselves from going under emotionally. An inner light is going out, one which they fear may never be rekindled. Everything seems to be futile and dying.

Level 8: The Emotionally Tormented Person

Depressed and alienated from themselves and others, unhealthy Fours go from bad to worse. They fear that because of their depression and inability to function, they are doomed. Their disappointment with themselves intensifies into a consuming self-hatred.

Neurotic Fours turn against themselves with an absolutely withering self-contempt, seeing only the worst in themselves. They excoriate themselves about everything: the mistakes they have made, the time they have wasted, their unworthiness to be loved by anyone, their worthlessness as human beings. They are caught in the grip of obsessionally negative thoughts, and their relentless self-reproaches become a form of delusional thinking into which no ray of hope can intrude.

Morbid fantasies become obsessions. They are convinced that they are outcasts in life, sacrificial victims, endlessly suffering for what their parents have done to them and what they have done to themselves. They feel pathetic, rightly rejected by everyone. They also feel guilty for existing: they have contributed nothing, and people would be better off without them. Their self-hatred is like an electron accelerator whipping incidents of virtually no significance into formidable forces, smashing them into what little self-esteem remains.

Not only are unhealthy Fours convinced that they are utterly and permanently defective, they are also convinced that others regard them as contemptuously as they regard themselves. They have absolutely no self-confidence, and no reason to hope that they will ever be able to acquire any. A chasm of inner darkness has opened inside them, like a black hole draining whatever life they have. They are extremely distraught, yet unable to shake themselves free of the self-accusations and feelings of hopelessness plaguing them. They may sit alone for hours, barely breathing and yet violently tormented. They may burst into tears and uncontrollable sobbing, then retreat once again into silence and intense inner suffering.

They sabotage themselves in various ways, wrecking what few opportunities remain for them and hurling irrational accusations at their remaining friends and supporters. They still hope that someone will see their plight and rescue them, that the "good parent" may still appear, but that hope seems increasingly remote and eventually becomes another source of self-torture. If there has been drug or alcohol abuse it is rapidly escalated. Their fantasies, such as they are, become morbid and death-obsessed.

Everything becomes a source of torment to them: the whole of life becomes an unbearable reminder of their alienation from it. If they were once artists, their unfinished work mocks them; if they were once in love with someone, their failure in love mocks them; if they once had a family or a job, their failures there mock them as well.

Unfortunately, some of their self-accusations may have a basis in fact. Because of their self-absorption and self-indulgence, Fours may have missed many opportunities to do something positive with their lives. To some extent, they are responsible for bringing their anguish upon themselves, and they know it—which is why their self-accusations cut so deeply. But rather than truly expiate guilt by punishing themselves, their self-hatred only destroys whatever inner resources they still possess. The only way out is to do away with their tormented consciousness altogether.

Level 9: The Self-Destructive Person

If conditions do not change for the better, their despair becomes so deep that neurotic Fours will attempt to destroy themselves, one way or another. When they become hopeless, what remains to be seen is the form their despair will take—whether they will kill themselves directly or indirectly, through drugs or alcohol or some other means.

It is difficult for other personality types to understand that because of their self-hatred, neurotic Fours feel cut off from life itself. Everything in the world—everything positive, beautiful, good, and worth living for—has become a rebuke to them, and they cannot bear the thought of living that way for the rest of their lives. They must do something to escape from their crushingly negative self-consciousness. In essence, neurotic Fours must rid themselves of themselves, since they feel defeated by life and see no way of coming to life again.

While suicide attempts as a way of eliciting help are possible, many neurotic Fours believe that they are utterly hopeless, and so intend to have their suicide work. Despairing Fours may embrace death as the final solution to the ongoing problems of their lives. Death is a welcome chance to leave their sorrows, a hoped-for annihilation of their painful self-consciousness.

Suicide is not only a way of escaping from their intense mental suffering, it is a rebuke to others for not helping them enough, for not understanding their needs, for not caring about them. From the Four's point of view, others' lack of love and understanding has driven them to take their own life. Suicide is the ultimate act of withdrawal, an aggressive act by which Fours inflict suffering on others without having to be aggressive, or guilty, or responsible.

Although Fours are far more likely to destroy themselves, in their emotional torment they are also capable of murdering the people they feel are responsible for ruining their lives. If a major disappointment in love played a role in the Four's descent, their jealousy may overwhelm them, causing them to impulsively commit a crime of passion, killing the object of their unrequited love before taking their own lives.

Suicide also holds another attraction: it is the one thing in life over which despairing Fours still feel they have any control. By contemplating suicide, they feel that they remain the masters of something, even if it is only the possibility of saying no to life, of refusing to go on being tormented. The mere thought that, if they wished, they could put an end to themselves is a source of comfort.

Before they have reached this stage, Fours have doubtless thought about suicide many times. The danger is that the more they think about it, the more they may become infatuated with death as a solution to their problems. When they are in despair, having rehearsed suicide so often in their imaginations, they may act without any more consideration or warning to others.

THE DYNAMICS OF THE FOUR

The Direction of Disintegration: The Four Goes to Two

Starting at Level 4, Fours under stress will begin to exhibit many of the qualities of average to unhealthy Twos. Although they are usually withdrawn from people, average Fours have always wanted and needed people, and their move to Two is an ironic, unintended acknowledgment of this. Fours are drawn to Two because they need to overcome their alienation from themselves and others by finding someone who will love them. By so doing, Fours hope that they will, in time, be able to love themselves and actualize the good that is in them.

At Level 4, Fours spend a great deal of time in romantic fantasies about themselves and others. They are not withdrawn, but they are more focused on their imaginations than on real people and events. They feel stress when others try to engage with them more directly, and usually respond with a slightly forced effusiveness. Relationships, either actual or potential, also become a major source of stress for Fours, and they think about them frequently. Like average Twos, Fours want to be reassured that the relationship is working, that the other person likes them, so they frequently talk about how much they care about the other, and remind him or her of how meaningful their relationship is.

At Level 5, Fours are highly self-absorbed and have difficulty relating to others because of their self-consciousness. They dwell on their feelings and fantasies and have trouble maintaining interest in others except inasmuch as they may want to talk about their issues and desires. This causes others to avoid Fours, which inevitably produces stress and fears of abandonment. Fours respond by hovering around and intruding themselves into others' lives like average Twos. They become clinging and possessive of those people whom they still feel comfortable with and who are willing to support the Four's fantasies. They begin to find ways to "be needed" and do not like to let the people they care about out of their sight for long.

At Level 6, self-indulgence and exemption are taking their toll, and Fours soon realize that they need support, especially financial support, to continue their "artistic" lifestyle and search for self. Anxieties about money and "slipping through the cracks" cause them to exaggerate their importance in others' lives. Fours at this stage are so self-absorbed that the slightest gesture or gift they may offer feels like a major act of generosity. In fact, Fours may not have been particularly generous, but they want to remind others of whatever acts of kindness they have done as a way of discouraging them from leaving. At this Level, Fours become obsessed about getting acknowledgment for services rendered or just for the "unique pleasure" of having their company. They want others to respect them as gifted, undiscovered talents, while the reality may be that they are merely dreaming their lives away, dissipating themselves in idle sensuality.

At Level 7, unhealthy Fours are too depressed and fatigued to care for themselves, let alone hold down a job. They are increasingly dependent on the good will of others, but can be extremely difficult to deal with because of their deep feelings of resentment and anger. Losing others at this point is truly terrifying to them — without the support of their friends and relatives helping them out, Fours fear that they would be out on the street, destitute. Thus, in the shift toward Two, they begin to manipulate others, playing on guilt and undermining others' confidence to keep their "supply lines" flowing. This problem only adds to the self-reproaches and resentments of Fours, because they are often left in the care of people they want to get away from — their families. Consequently, they are never more desirous of having a wonderful relationship with someone who will understand them, who will be patient with them and save them from their problems. Unfortunately, however, neurotic Fours are almost completely incapable of entering into and sustaining a genuine relationship with anyone.

At Level 8, unhealthy Fours are tormented by their delusional self-hatred and morbidity. When they reach their limit, they may go to Two and break through their smothering self-inhibitions, acting out their repressed rage and sexual impulses. They feel that they have been suffering long enough, and are therefore entitled to get their needs met by others. They may go on a binge of drugs or alcohol or look for solace in compulsive sexuality. Further, they may stalk a person who has become the object of their sexual obsessions or, if they have the means to do so, take advantage of people who are more helpless and defenseless than they are. Their fury at others may also burst open, causing them to physically attack persons who they feel are responsible for their miserable condition.

At Level 9, when neurotic Fours go to Two they may well have some sort of nervous breakdown, indirectly coercing someone, but almost certainly not the beloved of their imaginations, to take care of them. Eliciting pity from others substitutes for being loved. They may also be without financial resources, and therefore need to live off someone else in what is little more than a parasitic existence and an extension of the feeling of exemption which we have already seen. Furthermore, since they are broken down, deteriorated Fours also feel exempt from having any expectations placed on them, even the expectation that they get well.

Ironically, Fours at Two will likely begin to hate the very person they have become dependent upon, since their dependency is a constant reminder of their defects and lack of self-esteem. Conflicts will escalate as Fours alternate between intense feelings of aggression toward themselves and aggression toward the other. Others will no doubt also be infuriated with deteriorated Fours because many of their problems were either caused or greatly exacerbated by their own actions. Fours will therefore probably destroy the very relationship they so desperately depend on. The prognosis for deteriorated Fours is bleak indeed: if they do not receive adequate professional help, they may well eventually go mad, commit suicide, or both.

The Direction of Integration: The Four Goes to One

Healthy Fours actualize themselves by focusing upon something objective, something beyond their feelings and their imaginations. When very healthy Fours go to One, they move from the world of subjectivity to the world of objectivity, from self-absorption to principled action. They have found the courage to act without reference to their feelings and have thus freed themselves from the relentless tug of self-absorption. They are no longer controlled by their feelings, but by their convictions, acting on principles rather than moods. Like healthy Ones, integrating Fours are people of action, mobilizing their energies in the service of something beyond their personal interest and emotional gratification.

Fours at One acknowledge that there are values to which it is necessary to submit. They willingly become self-disciplined, working consistently toward actualizing their potentials so they can contribute to the world. Ironically, integrating Fours find the freedom they have sought by desiring to do what they need to do instead of doing whatever they please in a misguided search for self. By being part of the world, they find a context in which to discover themselves. Furthermore, integrating Fours do not lose contact with their feelings; rather, their feelings become connected with what is happening in reality.

And since they receive satisfaction from reality, they are no longer tempted to be self-indulgent, nor do they think of themselves as different from others. Instead, integrating Fours submit both to reality and to the dictates of conscience, willingly putting limits on themselves, thereby overcoming the tendency to exempt themselves from social and moral obligations. Like healthy Ones, integrating Fours are exceptional teachers, objective about themselves and yet, because they are Fours, able to bring the riches of the subjective world to the light of day. Their intuition is reinforced by excellent discernment, personal insight by clarity of mind.

Finally, because integrating Fours have transcended themselves, what they create is objective, something from which they can learn what is true about themselves. Integrating Fours are able to contemplate their creation, whether it is a work of art, an act of kindness, or a successful relationship, not only learning who they are, but giving themselves reasons for genuine self-esteem. They learn that to the extent that their creation is good, the person who created it must also be good.

THE MAJOR SUBTYPES OF THE FOUR

The Four with a Three-Wing: "The Aristocrat"

The combination of Four and Three traits produce a subtype which is both emotionally volatile and contradictory. (This is true for the Three with a Four-wing as well.) While the two component types may on the surface appear to be opposites, they have much in common, and if properly used can do much to offset some of their individual weaknesses. Fours are often introverted, withdrawn, and self-absorbed, whereas Threes tend to be extroverted, interpersonal, and goal-oriented. The Four's fear of exposing itself (in a sense, a "fear of success") is the opposite of the Three's self-display and competitive desire for success. The Four's introverted self-consciousness contrasts with the Three's charm and other extroverted social skills. As conflicting as these two component types are, both are nevertheless concerned with self-image and self-esteem issues. Fours tend to develop a self-image which is largely a private matter: Fours are trying to become their self-image through their imagination and feelings. Threes develop a more public self-image and try to get others to validate its reality through their achievements. Both opposing sets of traits can coexist in the same person, although uneasily. Noteworthy examples of the Four with a Three-wing include Tennessee Williams, Maria Callas, Rudolf Nureyev, Judy Garland, Michael Jackson, (The Artist Formerly Known as) Prince, Frederick Chopin, Jeremy Irons, Marcel Proust, Martha Graham, Edith Piaf, Paul Simon, Harold Pinter, Walt Whitman, Albert Camus, E. M. Forster, Gustav Mahler, Tchaikovsky, and "Blanche DuBois."

Because of the Three-wing, healthy people of this subtype can be sociable, ambitious, and accomplished, particularly in the arts: they possess both creativity and the drive to "make their mark." They are in touch with who they are and who they are becoming, but with a more extroverted, energetic dimension to them. In general, Fours tend to be private and not particularly action-oriented, but with a healthy Three-wing, this impulse is tempered by a desire to accomplish and to improve the self. To do this, Fours with a Three-wing know that they must produce, and that they must be involved with people. Thus, the Three-wing tends to be more goal-oriented, sociable, and aware of interpersonal "politics" than the Five-wing. Healthy Fours with a Three-wing want to be successful, but distinctive, and are willing to put in the necessary work to actualize their dreams. Both subtypes can be highly creative, but the Four with a Three-wing is more aware of creating with an audience in mind. They are adaptable, sensitive to others, and have a good sense of humor.

Average people of this subtype may be helped out of their self-absorption by a concern for what others think of them. Since people of this subtype have the ability to project a favorable image, they are able to conceal their real emotional condition more effectively than the other subtype: others may not realize how vulnerable or emotionally troubled they may be. Fours with a Three-wing are competitive and interested in making something of themselves in the world, but they fear success, self-exposure, and possible humiliation. However, to the degree that the Three-wing is operative, this subtype also has a strong need for attention and admiration which may serve as partial motives for their behavior. There is a strong sense of the romantic in both subtypes, and their combination tends to heighten the sense of drama, to the point of even exhibitionism. And, to the degree that their narcissistic needs are unfulfilled in reality, their desires for triumph can both play a part in their fantasy life and become a focal point for disappointments. They tend to be more practical than the other wing subtype, but also more emotionally and financially extravagant. As befitting their nickname, average Fours with a Three-wing like to surround themselves with objects and settings which provide them with a sense of refinement and culture. Having "good taste" becomes a prerequisite for a close association with this subtype, and regardless of their economic background, less healthy Fours with a Three-wing will see themselves as more sophisticated and "high class" than the people around them—especially their families. The Three component adds a strong desire to be pleasing others, so Fours with a Three-wing tend to be more responsive to others' suggestions, help, and criticism than the other subtype, but can also be more resentful because of the suppression of their deeper emotional responses.

Since unhealthy persons of this subtype are still fundamentally Fours, they take out their aggressions principally on themselves. They are self-inhibited and alienated from others, depressed, self-contemptuous, and so forth. However, to the degree that the Three-wing plays a part in the overall personality, there will be moments when they act like unhealthy Threes. People of this subtype can be hostile and malicious; their secret envy of others will be reinforced by the Three-wing's jealousy. Exploitativeness, opportunism, and duplicity may also be present, although these traits increase their shame and guilt if they should succumb to them. The desire to ruin others which we find in Threes is frequently contemplated but rarely acted upon by this subtype. If it ever is, however, neurotics of this subtype will punish themselves even more severely than they inflict pain on anyone else. Crimes of passion and suicide are possible.

The Four with a Five-Wing: "The Bohemian"

The traits of Fours and Fives tend to reinforce each other. Both are "withdrawn" types: Fours withdraw to protect their feelings; Fives, to protect their security. Thus, this subtype is more reclusive and less ambitious than the Four with a Three-wing. Fours with a Five-wing will be markedly more observant of the environment, particularly of other people. There is an intellectual depth and intensity here which is not found in the other subtype, but also a corresponding social insecurity. This subtype can be more insightful and original, but also less likely to do consistent, concrete work. Noteworthy examples of the Four with a Five-wing include Virginia Woolf, Edgar Allan Poe, Anne Rice, Ingmar Bergman, D. H. Lawrence, Yukio Mishima, J. D. Salinger, Johnny Depp, Bob Dylan, Joni Mitchell, Saul Steinberg, Søren Kierkegaard, Hermann Hesse, William Blake, and "Laura Wingfield."

Healthy, gifted individuals of this subtype are probably the most profoundly creative of all the types because they combine intuition with insight, emotional sensitivity with intellectual comprehension, frequently with stunningly original, even prophetic, results. Fours with a Five-wing burn lighter than Fours with a Three-wing, but at the risk of burning themselves out faster. They are often drawn to the arts and to social sciences, where their insights into the human condition can be expanded and explored. Because of the Five-wing, healthy individuals of this subtype care less about the opinions of others, so they tend to follow their muse wherever it leads them. Their self-expression is highly personal and can be somewhat idiosyncratic. They tend to create more for themselves than for an audience.

Average persons of this subtype are given not merely to self-absorption but to philosophical and religious speculation. Their emotional world is the dominant reality, but with a strong intellectual cast. People of this subtype tend to be loners, more lacking in social connectedness than the other subtype. Thus, their artistic expressions more completely substitute for the person than in Fours with a Three-wing. They often display brilliant flashes of insight, but have trouble sustaining their efforts. These people also frequently have an otherworldly, ethereal quality about them; they are extremely independent and unconventional to the point of eccentricity. They also tend to be secretive, intensely preoccupied with their thoughts, and purposely enigmatic in their self-expression. Their creative ideas may also be somewhat unusual, emphasizing the mysterious, even the surreal. They are very attracted to the exotic and the symbolic and tend to be more unusual in their personal presentation—bohemian or, at least, casual. Members of this subtype care little for communicating with those who cannot understand them. Rather, they are interested in expressing their inner vision, whether sublime or terrifying, bleak or lyrical. They tend to choose a simpler lifestyle than Fours with a Three-wing, but can also get caught up in the Five's minimizing of needs. Aspects of the Five's eccentricity begin to manifest, as well as a high-strung nervous energy. Less healthy Fours with a Five-wing can become very reclusive, daydreaming through life with baroque fantasies and ideas, but increasingly tormented by self-doubt and unable to galvanize themselves into constructive action.

Unhealthy persons of this subtype inhabit a particularly barren and terrifying inner world. There is a self-denying, even life-denying, element of inner resistance to everything outside the self, throwing all of the Four's existential problems into sharper relief. They may have great understanding of their problems, but can more easily become lost in emotional turmoil—fatigue, depression, and hope-lessness. Indeed, pondering the nature of their torment leads Fours with a Five-wing around in circles, heightening both their self-contempt and their nihilism. Since Four is the fundamental per-sonality type, Fours with a Five-wing are assailed by self-doubt, alienation from others, inhibitions in their work, and self-contempt. To the degree that the Five-wing plays a part in the overall person-ality, unhealthy Fours of this subtype will also resist being helped by anyone, thus increasing their alienation from others. They also tend to project their fears into the environment, resulting in dis-torted thinking patterns which may include hallucinations and pho-bias. Not only are people of this subtype subject to torment from their self-hatred, they can see very little positive outside them-selves, and become very pessimistic about the apparent meaning-lessness of life. Of all the personality types, people of this subtype are potentially the most isolated from themselves and from reality. They are prone to the depressive forms of schizophrenia.

SOME FINAL THOUGHTS

Looking back on their deterioration, we can see that neurotic Fours have made the worst and most crippling aspects of their self-image into the whole truth of who they are. Ironically, their idealized self-image becomes so out of touch with reality that they reject many of the positive qualities that they actually possess. The pity is not that they always have been as damaged as they feel they are, but that they have become profoundly damaged because they hate themselves. They have created a self-fulfilling prophecy and suffer the consequences.

From our present perspective, we can also see that one of the most important mistakes Fours make is to equate themselves with their feelings. The fallacy is that to understand themselves they must work through their feelings, particularly their negative ones, before acting. Fours do not see that the self is not the same as its feelings, or that the presence of negative feelings does not preclude the presence of good in themselves. However, as they deteriorate, the bad drives out the good: their negative feelings about themselves gradually obliterate any positive ones they might have developed.

Fours must make a leap of faith that, despite their lack of a clear sense of themselves, they will discover themselves most surely by acting positively toward others. They must love others even if they do not feel that they have been loved adequately. When they love others, Fours will begin to discover who they are, and self-esteem will follow. They will also discover that because they can love, they must have learned to love from somewhere. What they have been given has perhaps been enough after all.

Chapter 7

Type Five: The Investigator

THE FIVE IN PROFILE

Healthy: Observe everything with extraordinary perceptiveness and insight. Are mentally alert, curious, have a searching intelligence: nothing escapes their notice. Display foresight and prediction abilities. Able to concentrate: become engrossed in what has caught their attention. / Attain skillful mastery of whatever interests them. Excited by knowledge: often become expert in some field. Innovative and inventive, producing extremely valuable, original works. Highly independent, idiosyncratic, and whimsical. *At Their Best:* Become visionaries, broadly comprehending the world while penetrating it profoundly. Open-minded, take things in whole, in their true context. Make pioneering discoveries and find entirely new ways of doing and perceiving things.

Average: Begin conceptualizing everything before acting — working things out in their minds: model building, preparing, practicing, gathering resources. Studious, acquiring technique. Become specialized and often "intellectual": involvement in research, scholarship, and building theories. / Increasingly detached as they become involved with complicated ideas or imaginary worlds. Become preoccupied with their visions and interpretations rather than reality.

Are fascinated by offbeat, esoteric subjects, even those involving dark and disturbing elements. Detached from the practical world, a "disembodied mind," although high-strung and intense. / Begin to take an antagonistic stance toward anything which would interfere with their inner world and personal vision. Become provocative and abrasive, with intentionally extreme and radical views. Cynical and argumentative.

Unhealthy: Become reclusive and isolated from reality, eccentric and nihilistic. Highly unstable and fearful of aggressions: they reject and repulse others and all social attachments. / Get obsessed with yet frightened by their threatening ideas, becoming horrified, delirious, and prey to gross distortions and phobias. / Seeking oblivion, they may commit suicide or have a psychotic break with reality. Deranged, explosively self-destructive, with schizophrenic overtones.

Key Motivations: Want to be capable and competent, to master a body of knowledge and skill, to explore reality, to remain undisturbed by others, to reduce their needs.

Examples: Albert Einstein, Stephen Hawking, Friedrich Nietzsche, Stanley Kubrick, Georgia O'Keeffe, Emily Dickinson, Simone Weil, Bill Gates, Jean-Paul Sartre, Jacob Bronowski, James Joyce, Gary Larson, David Lynch, Stephen King, Tim Burton, Clive Barker, Laurie Anderson, Meredith Monk, John Cage, Glenn Gould, Charles Ives, Bobby Fischer, and Vincent van Gogh.

AN OVERVIEW OF THE FIVE

The connection between genius and madness has long been debated. These two states are really poles apart, the opposite ends of the personality spectrum. The genius is someone who fuses knowledge with insight into the nature of reality, someone who has the ability to see things with utter clarity and with awe-inspiring comprehension. What separates the genius from the madman is that the genius, in addition to extraordinary insights, has the ability to see them correctly, within their context. The genius perceives patterns which are actually present, whereas the madman imposes patterns, projecting erroneous perceptions onto every circumstance. The genius may sometimes seem to be out of touch with reality, but only because he or she operates at a more profound level. The madman, however, is truly out of touch with reality, having nothing but delusions to substitute for it.

The Five is the personality type which most exemplifies these extremes. In the Five, we see the genius and the madman, the innovator and intellectual, the mildly eccentric crackpot and the deeply disturbed delusional schizoid. To understand how these widely diverse states are part of the same personality type is to understand the Five.

In the Thinking Triad

Fives are members of the Thinking Triad. Their potential problem results from the fact that they emphasize thinking over doing, becoming intensely involved with their thoughts. Fives think so much that their mental world becomes all-engrossing, virtually to the exclusion of everything else. This is not to say that Fives do nothing at all, but that they are more at home in their minds, viewing the world from a detached vantage point, than they are in the world of action.

All three members of the Thinking Triad—Fives, Sixes, and Sevens—focus their attention on the world outside themselves. This may seem to contradict the statement that Fives are engrossed in their thoughts, but it actually does not. Fives focus their attention on the external world for a variety of reasons, one of the most important of which is that the material they think about comes through their sense perceptions—the accuracy of which they can never be completely sure of because they are not certain about what lies outside themselves. The only thing they know with certainty is their own thoughts. Hence, the focus of their attention is outward, on the environment, while identifying with their thoughts about the environment. The source of many of their problems is their need to find out how their perceptions of the world square with reality so that they can act in it—and *do* things with confidence.

Problems with Security and Anxiety

Like the other two members of the Thinking Triad, average Fives tend to have problems with insecurity because they fear that the environment is unpredictable and potentially threatening. Further, they feel powerless to defend themselves against the world's many dangers: they believe they are not capable of functioning as well as others and so make it their number one priority to acquire the skills and knowledge they feel are necessary for them to be able to operate adequately in life.

Their Basic Fear, of being helpless and incapable, influences their behavior in significant ways. Fives believe that their personal resources and capacities are limited, so they respond to their anxiety by downscaling their activities and needs. The more anxious they feel, the more they minimize their needs. While this can be a sensible approach to problems at times, anxious Fives may reduce themselves to living in extremely primitive conditions in order to allay their fears of inadequacy. Naturally, given this orientation, Fives feel easily overwhelmed by others' needs as well, and try to avoid situations in which others will expect more from them than they feel able to give. As their fears increase, Fives begin to "shrink away" from the world and from connections with others.

When Fives are healthy, they are able to observe reality as it is and are able to comprehend complex phenomena at a glance because they are participating in life and testing their perceptions. In their search for security, however, the perceptions of even average Fives tend to become skewed. Their thinking becomes more convoluted, elaborate, and increasingly fueled by anxiety. As they withdraw from the world, it only heightens their fears that they cannot cope with it. Eventually, even basic living requirements seem overwhelming and frightening. And if they become unhealthy, Fives are the type of persons who cut themselves off from most human contact. Once isolated, they develop their eccentric ideas to such absurd extremes that they become obsessed with completely distorted notions about themselves and reality. Ultimately, unhealthy Fives become utterly terrified and trapped by the threatening visions which they have created in their own minds.

Their problem with anxiety, one of the issues common to the personality types of the Thinking Triad, is related to their difficulty with perceiving reality objectively. They are afraid of allowing anyone or anything to influence them or their thoughts. Because they doubt their own ability to do, they fear that others' agendas will overwhelm them or that people who are more powerful than they are will control or possess them. Ironically, however, even average Fives are not unwilling to be possessed by an idea, as long as the idea has originated with them. Nothing must be allowed to influence their thinking lest their developing sense of confidence be diminished, although by relying solely on their own ideas and perceptions, and without testing them in the real world, Fives can become profoundly out of touch with reality.

The upshot of this is that average to unhealthy Fives are uncertain whether or not their perceptions of the environment are valid. They do not know what is real and what is the product of their minds. They project their anxiety-ridden thoughts and their aggressive impulses into the environment, becoming fearful of the antagonistic forces which seem to be arrayed against them. They gradually become convinced that their peculiar and increasingly dark interpretation of reality is the way things really are. In the end, they become so terrorized that they cannot act even though they are consumed by anxiety.

The basis of their orientation to the world is thinking; personality type Five corresponds to Jung's introverted thinking type.

> Introverted thinking is primarily oriented by the subjective factor. . . . It does not lead from concrete experience back again to the object, but always to the subjective content. External facts are not the aim and origin of this thinking, though the introvert would often like to make his thinking appear so. It begins with the subject and leads back to the subject, far though it may range into the realm of actual reality. . . . Facts are collected as evidence for a theory, never for their own sake. (C. G. Jung, *Psychological Types*, 380.)

Although they correspond to Jung's introverted thinking type, Fives are perhaps more precisely characterized as a subjective thinking type because the aim of their thought is not always introverted (that is, directed toward themselves); rather, it is directed often outward toward the environment, which Fives want to understand so that they can be safer in it. The impetus for their thinking comes, as Jung says, from "the subjective factor," from their need to know about what lies outside themselves, as well as from their anxiety when they do not understand the environment. This is why thinking is the method Fives use both to fit into the world and, paradoxically, to defend themselves against it.

One of the results of the way Fives think is that even healthy Fives are not very deeply rooted in visceral experience. They are the type of people who get a great deal of intellectual mileage out of very little experience because they always find something of significance where others see little or nothing. This may lead to great discoveries. However, when they stop observing the world and focus their attention on their interpretations of it, Fives begin to lose touch with reality. Instead of keeping an open mind while they observe the world, they become too involved with their own thoughts and dreams. This leads them further away from the world of constructive action—the very arena in which their self-confidence needs to develop. They may spend a great deal of time playing around with ideas or visions of alternative realities which have almost no practical impact on their lives, leaving them more fearful about themselves and feeling more vulnerable to the predations of the world.

Parental Orientation

As a result of their formative experiences, these children became ambivalent to both parents. Fives, like Twos and Eights, were in search of a niche within the family system, a role that they could fulfill that would win them protection and nurturance. For whatever reasons, though, they perceived that there was no place for them to fit in—that nothing they could do was wanted or needed by their family. As a result, Fives withdrew from active participation in the family to search for something that they could "bring to the table." Fives want to find something that they can do well enough to feel like an equal of others. Unlike other types, however, since Fives' underlying fear is of being helpless and incapable, they generally look for areas of expertise that others have not already explored. In a sense, their agenda is to focus on the search for and mastery of subjects and skills, until they feel confident enough to "reenter" the world.

In the meantime, Fives strike a kind of unstated bargain with their parents which carries over into all of their subsequent relationships: "Don't ask too much of me, and I won't ask too much of you." Fives feel that they need most of their limited time and energy to acquire the knowledge and skills that they believe will make them capable and competent. Thus, average Fives come to resent intrusions upon their space, their time, and certainly upon their persons. What to another type might feel like a comfortable distance can feel uncomfortable to an average Five. The reasons for this may relate to the Five's feeling of not having a place in the family. They may have felt crowded out or figuratively or literally intruded on by their parents and their agendas. Their parents may have nurtured them erratically, or may have been emotionally disturbed or alcoholic or caught in a loveless marriage, and therefore not dependable sources of love and reassurance. The result is that these children become ambivalent not only toward both parents, but ambivalent toward the world.

Fives attempt to resolve their ambivalence by not identifying with anything other than their thoughts. They feel that their thoughts are "good" (that is, correct, and can be safely identified with), while outside reality is "bad" (and must therefore be vigilantly watched), so that it can be repulsed at a moment's notice. In average to unhealthy Fives, the sense of being crowded may have resulted in their feeling unsafe in their bodies. They then become profoundly detached, indifferent to physical comfort, and extremely cerebral, as if the quality of their material existence was irrelevant to them. Fearful Fives are willing to jettison many comforts and even needs in order to protect the space and time they feel they need to pursue their interests — that is, those areas they are trying to master.

They continue to find their parents, the world, and other people fascinating and necessary, but Fives also feel that they must keep everything and everyone at a safe distance lest they be in danger of being overwhelmed by some outside force. Thus, from the very way they think — their "cognitive style" — Fives set up a strict dualism between themselves and the world: they see everything as essentially split into two fundamental areas — the inner world and the outer world, subjects and objects, the known and the unknown, the dangerous and the safe, and so forth. This sharp split between themselves as subjects and the rest of the world as objects has tremendous ramifications throughout their entire lives.

Problems with Detachment and Phobia

When they are healthy, Fives do not have to detach themselves from the environment, because they feel secure and confident enough to fully participate in the world around them. Because they are interacting with the environment, their observations are accurate and balanced. But as they deteriorate down the Levels of Development toward unhealth, their perceptions become more intensely focused on what seems to be threatening and dangerous in the environment. As a result of their preoccupation with things they find fearful and dark, their mental world becomes filled with anxiety.

Ironically, however, the more fearful Fives become, the more compelled they feel to investigate the very things that terrify them.

In the end, since they invariably focus on what is threatening, Fives turn their terrifying projections into their *only* reality, and in so doing, turn their minds against themselves, literally scaring themselves out of their minds. They become completely defenseless against the environment, which they find supremely dangerous because their minds have made it so. They become so phobic—and their sense of capability becomes so fragile—that it is extraordinarily difficult for them to function or turn to anyone for help. Yet, unless deteriorating Fives can reach out to someone, they have few ways of getting back in touch with reality.

If they live like this for long, their thought processes become so delusional and terrifying that they must separate themselves not just from the world but even from their own thoughts. Neurotic Fives become schizoid, unconsciously splitting themselves off from their teeming minds so that they can continue to live. Their reality has become hellish: dark, painful, and without hope. Recoiling in horror, they retreat into emptiness—and yet more horror.

ANALYZING THE HEALTHY FIVE

Level 1: The Pioneering Visionary

At their healthiest, Fives have the paradoxical ability to penetrate reality profoundly while comprehending it broadly. They are able to take things in whole, perceiving patterns where others see nothing but confusion. They are able to synthesize existing knowledge, making connections between phenomena which no one previously knew were related, such as time and space, the structures of the DNA molecule, or the relationship between brain chemistry and behavior. If they are artistically inclined, they may develop entirely new art forms, or revolutionize the form they are working with in ways that have not been seen before. These innovations often become the new platform from which others will learn and create.

The healthiest Fives do not cling to their own ideas about how the world works. Instead, they encompass reality so profoundly that they are able to discover unanticipated truths they could not have arrived at by mere theorizing. They make discoveries precisely because they are willing not to know the answers, keeping an open mind while they observe reality.

Because they do not impose their thoughts on reality, very healthy Fives are able to discover the internal logic, the structure, and interrelated patterns of whatever they observe. As a result, they have clear thoughts into obscure matters, and are able to predict events, often far in advance of the ability of others to verify them. Fives operating at the peak of their gifts may seem to be prophets and visionaries, although the explanation is simpler. They possess foresight because they see the world with extraordinary clarity, like a weaver who knows the pattern of a tapestry before it is completed.

The result is that they transcend rational thought to reveal objective reality, and in so doing they move toward the ineffable, to a level of comprehension where words, theories, and symbols are left behind. They perceive the world in all its complexity and simplicity with a vision that seems to come from beyond themselves. They are closer to contemplatives than thinkers. This is the quality of the "quiet mind," discussed in Buddhism and other spiritual traditions. When the mind becomes still and quiet it becomes like a mirror which accurately contains and reflects whatever it turns toward. Healthy Fives are not using their minds to defend against reality; rather they are allowing reality in, understanding that they are not separate from it.

Very healthy, gifted Fives so perfectly describe reality that their perceptions and discoveries seem simple, even obvious, as if anyone could have thought of them. But the genius's insights are obvious only in hindsight. To have made the leap from the known to the unknown, and to describe the unknown so clearly and accurately that the discovery accords perfectly with what is already known, is a great achievement. Similarly, anyone can "create" a new form of artistic expression, but to do so in a way that is powerful for others changes the way that others perceive reality, is both rare and extraordinary.

Thus, very healthy Fives are intellectual pioneers who open up new domains of knowledge and creativity. An individual Five, if sufficiently gifted, may well be a genius of historic dimensions, able to make staggering intellectual breakthroughs for mankind. A genius of the highest caliber may understand the way the world works for the first time in history. Less gifted individuals may have a sense of the genius's excitement when they first understand calculus or how to use a computer. Their understanding is new to them, and can be thrilling. Others can only imagine how exciting it must be for someone to discover something totally new—when the discovery is new not only to that individual, but to humanity.

Yet, at Level 1, the brilliance of very healthy Fives is entirely unselfconscious. What Fives themselves are most aware of is feeling at home and at peace in the world. Because they have transcended their fears of being incapable and helpless, they are also freed from their relentless pursuit of knowledge and skill. They no longer feel overwhelmed by other people or by challenges and are able to bring their hearts and minds together for the compassionate use of their knowledge and talents.

Level 2: The Perceptive Observer

Even though Fives are not always this healthy, they are still extraordinarily conscious of the world around them, its glories and horrors, incongruities and inexhaustible complexities. They are the most mentally alert of the personality types, curious about everything. Healthy Fives enjoy thinking for its own sake; possessing knowledge—knowing that they know something, and being able to turn it around in their minds, to play with ideas—is extremely pleasurable for them. Knowledge and understanding are exhilarating. They are fascinated by people, by nature, by life, by the mind itself.

Given sufficient intelligence, healthy Fives penetrate the superficial, getting to profound levels very quickly. Their insights can be brilliant because they have the uncanny ability to see into the heart of things, noticing the anomaly, the curious but heretofore unobserved fact or hidden element which provides a key for understanding the whole. Because they see the world with unfailing insight, they always have something interesting and worthwhile to say. The act of seeing is virtually a symbol of their entire psychological orientation. If something can be seen, that is, apprehended either by the senses or by the mind, Fives feel that it can be understood. Once something is understood, it can be mastered. Then Fives can act with the confidence they desire.

Nothing escapes healthy Fives unnoticed because they do not merely observe the world passively, they concentrate on it, noting how things go together to form patterns and have meaning. People and objects are perceived in detail, as if Fives were training a magnifying glass on the environment. Since their minds are so active and they find everything around them fascinating, healthy Fives are never bored. They like learning what they do not know and understanding what is not obvious. No matter how much they know, they always want to learn more, and since the world is, for all intents and purposes, infinite in its complexity, there is always more to know.

Healthy Fives are also able to perceive far more than others because they have the ability to sustain concentration; they are not easily distracted. They quickly become deeply involved in the object of their scrutiny so they can understand how it works — why something is as it is. Their intellectual curiosity leads them to expend considerable effort to find out more about those things which have caught their attention. They are incredibly hard workers who will patiently attack a problem until they solve it, or until it becomes clear that the problem is insoluble. They will labor in obscurity for many years because they are excited about what they are exploring or creating. Because healthy Fives are accustomed to pursuing their interests with little support or attention, they are not dissuaded by others' indifference or lack of comprehension. The process of exploring, learning, and creating is more enjoyable to Fives than achieving a final goal. They take delight in questioning reality and tinkering with familiar forms until they become almost unrecognizable, especially in the arts. They are also very good conceptualizers, asking the right fundamental questions and defining the proper intellectual boundaries for the problems with which they are involved. They do not attempt to do the impossible, only to understand what they have not understood before.

Regardless of their actual intelligence, most Fives consider themselves "smart" and perceptive, and see these as defining characteristics. Many Fives are not intellectuals or scholars, but all focus their attention in the world of ideas, perceptions, and ways of looking at reality. They are constantly on the lookout for something that they have not noticed before, or a way of connecting disparate ideas or activities they have been exploring. Having a new insight into a question or creative problem they have been grappling with gives them a sense of confidence and goads them into deeper explorations.

Fives are aware that others may view them as "unusual." This may be due to their intelligence, a highly developed sensory acuity, idiosyncratic behavior, or perhaps their penetrating gaze. Fives are not interested in being "different" like Fours are; instead, they view their status as outsiders with a shrugging acceptance. They tend to be unsentimental about life, and this lack of sentiment extends to their own circumstances as well. Fives can also appear to be unusual because they are willing to follow their curiosity and their perceptions wherever they lead. They are relatively unconcerned with social convention; rather, they want to be unencumbered by activities that take them away from what they are really interested in.

Healthy Fives want to feel competent and capable in the objective world, and yet, the very act of inquiring into things begins to shift them away from active participation and toward the role of an outside observer. Even at this stage, healthy Fives are subject to a certain amount of anxiety about the environment if they do not understand it. (And, of course, because they cannot understand it until they deal with it, they are caught in a conundrum.) Therefore, the habit of observation reflects not simply a dispassionate curiosity but a deep personal need.

Level 3: The Focused Innovator

Once Fives have identified themselves as intelligent and perceptive, they begin to fear that they might lose their perceptiveness or that what they are thinking may be inaccurate. So they begin to focus their energies intensely into those areas that they are most interested in with the goal of really mastering them. In this way, Fives hope to develop an ability or a body of knowledge which will ensure that they will have a place in the world. They are not interested in merely acquiring facts or skills, but in using what they have learned to go beyond what has previously been explored. They want to "push the envelope," both because it is a greater test of their competency, and also because they want to create a niche for themselves which no one else could have come up with.

Sometimes the results of their explorations are ingenious inventions and technological marvels which yield highly practical results. At times, their tinkering may produce startling new discoveries or artistic works. At other times, few things may result from their original ideas, although in time, those ideas, too, may have practical applications. What is impractical in one era often becomes the underpinning of an entirely new branch of knowledge or technology in another, such as the physics which made television and radar possible, or a few scraps of ideas which later produce a novel or a movie.

Because they are looking for new areas to explore and master, healthy Fives are generally open-minded people. They are not attached to particular points of view, and are curious to learn what other people think about things. They believe that there is almost always something interesting to learn from another person's perspective. They are also patient about explaining their own thoughts to others, even when their thoughts are complex or the other person is slow to understand. Healthy Fives want to communicate, and they want others to understand what they are saying.

Because Fives understand things so perceptively, their profound knowledge enables them to get to the heart of difficulties so that they can explain problems, and possible solutions, clearly to others. Healthy Fives like sharing their knowledge because they often learn more when they discuss their ideas with someone else. This is why healthy Fives make exciting teachers, colleagues, and friends. Their enthusiasm for ideas is infectious, and they enjoy fertilizing their own areas of expertise with those of other intellectuals, artists, and thinkers, or, really, with anyone who is as interesting, curious, and intelligent as they are.

As much as they like being among those who can understand and appreciate their insights, healthy Fives are nevertheless extremely independent. For the most part, innovating, learning, and creating are solitary adventures best embarked on alone. Because they never know where their projects and discoveries will lead, Fives value their independence very highly; they are willing to be as unorthodox as their inquiries require, pursuing their interests and discoveries regardless of the sanctions of others or of society. They are not afraid to challenge existing dogmas, if need be.

Their innovations can be revolutionary, overturning previous ways of thinking. Owing to the nature of their interests and the scope of their intellects, healthy Fives give us powerful ideas which can literally change the course of history. The worlds of art, dance, cinema, and music have many times been "scandalized" by the strange new creations of Fives—which later on become widely accepted standards of "how things are done."

Healthy Fives are also in possession of a whimsical sense of humor. They are attuned to life's many absurdities and ironies and enjoy sharing their wry observations with others. They have a way of distorting the picture of reality just enough to highlight some assumption or way of looking at life that has no logical underpinning. They are fascinated by strange, offbeat subjects and love tinkering with objects, images, and words. There is a taboo-breaking quality to the humor of even healthy Fives, because they are attracted to looking at subject matter that others would reject or turn away from. Their imaginations are powerful and they use them to visualize the solution to a problem or to create an alternative reality. For this reason, many artistic Fives become filmmakers, cartoonists, or authors of genre fiction (science fiction, horror, black humor). The aesthetic sense tends to run in two extremes: minimalist and spare on one end, and surreal and fantastic on the other. Most Fives who are involved in the arts are not interested in simple "human interest" stories or narratives. They want to direct their audience's attention beyond their daily concerns toward truths which are more absolute—especially those that are hidden in the "ordinary world."

In the process of mastering those areas which interest them, healthy Fives accumulate knowledge. People of this personality type develop expertise in various disciplines, whether in the arts (for example, abstract expressionist painting, electronic music, or Egyptian hieroglyphics), or in the sciences (how to build a computer or put a satellite into space). Healthy Fives are usually polymaths, possessors of knowledge in a wide range of subjects and expert in them all. Healthy Fives know what they are talking about and share their knowledge with others, enriching the whole of society with their learning. They are also relatively confident because they are actively doing things with their insights, and it is precisely because their insights are so on target that both healthy Fives and their ideas are especially valuable to the rest of society. Where would we be without the computers and antibiotics, the sophisticated communications media and the technological innovations of all sorts which make up the modern world?

ANALYZING THE AVERAGE FIVE

Level 4: The Studious Expert

The essential difference between average Fives and healthy Fives is that average Fives begin to fear that they do not know enough to act or take their place in the world. They feel that they need to study more, to practice more, to acquire better technique or run further tests, to involve themselves even more deeply with their subject. ("The more you know, the more you know you don't know.") For whatever reason, they fear that they will not be able to put their concepts and ideas into action. Convinced that they are insufficiently prepared to put themselves on the line, they retreat into an area of their experience where they feel much more confident and in control—their minds. Every personality type deals from its strongest suit, and the intellect is what Fives are gifted with and what they favor in their development. Rather than innovating and exploring, however, average Fives begin conceptualizing and preparing. In a word, healthy Fives use knowledge, whereas average Fives are in pursuit of it.

Because Fives have become adept at playing with concepts and their imagination, they are more sure of themselves when they are "in their heads," and from this Level down they begin to avoid more direct contact with the world. They can spend many hours conceptualizing a problem or an idea for a song, but hesitate to put their ideas out as real, concrete forms. Average Fives get stuck in "preparation mode," endlessly studying, gathering more background information, and practicing. Or they may simply develop the idea for a book or an invention in their imagination and never actualize their projects in reality. "I need a little more time" is a repeating refrain from average Fives. They are not being reluctant for no reason, however: their hesitation belies their growing lack of faith in their ability to cope with the world.

Because they are beginning to experience themselves as somehow less prepared for life than other people, average Fives feel compelled to gather whatever information, skills, and resources they believe they will need to "build themselves up." To this end, Fives begin to disengage from social activities and spend more and more of their time and energy acquiring these resources. Their homes become a reflection of their minds, storage areas for their collections of books, tapes, videos, CDs, gadgets, and so forth.

Average Fives are typically bookish. They haunt bookstores, libraries, and coffeehouses catering to intellectuals who discuss politics, films, and literature far into the night. They love scholarship, and are fascinated with the technical appurtenances by which they acquire knowledge. And while they will spend money to obtain whatever tools they need to pursue their intellectual interests, be they medieval manuscripts or computer equipment, average Fives are usually loath to spend money on themselves or their own comfort because they identify with their minds and their imaginations, not with their bodies.

In their pursuit of mastery, average Fives tend to become highly specialized in some field, delving into a body of knowledge not understood by most. (As specialists, they take pride and pleasure in their ability to say, in effect, "I know something that you don't know.") Some Fives may become specialists within an academic discipline—analyzing genetic structures, or the mathematics of snowflake formation, or the migration patterns of birds in the Amazon Delta. Others may specialize in less academic areas, becoming specialists in antiques, stamp collecting, comic books, or jazz. Their approach to collecting becomes a metaphor for their whole approach to life: gathering in more material and incorporating it into the body of what they believe they know or can do.

Their predilection for collecting can combine with their desire to specialize in surprising ways. Fives may have a complete video collection—organized by director, of course—of every major horror or science fiction film between 1950 and 1990. The completeness of the collection and the thorough knowledge of its contents becomes important. An average Five would feel superficial if he or she had only a few Beatles albums or only three Beethoven symphonies. They want to acquire the complete Beatles catalogue, including rare bootleg recordings, and have all nine Beethoven symphonies as recorded by various orchestras. To observe the chronological progression of the Beatles' music or to compare and contrast the different recordings of Beethoven's Third Symphony become enjoyable pursuits for Fives, and a certain degree of knowledge is gained by these activities, to be sure. But Fives might well wonder how profitably they are spending their time in these endeavors. They achieve at least a temporary feeling of competency by mastering these narrow areas of interest, but are beginning to avoid the kind of activities that might really help develop their confidence.

Average Fives have begun to identify more completely with their minds, and although this is not entirely problematic, it is not without consequences. As we have seen, healthy Fives are highly observant of the environment and attuned to the world around them, but because of their increasingly cerebral approach to life, average Fives begin to miss things. They focus intently upon certain details and may overlook other relevant information entirely. They tend to make a science of whatever they are interested in, whether history, linguistics, stereo equipment, jogging shoes, or the sociology of ape families. It is here that we see the beginning of their tendency to abstract from reality, concerning themselves with only those aspects of reality which capture their attention. They are by no means out of touch with reality in any unhealthy sense yet. They are, however, narrowing the focus of their perceptions so that they can pursue their interests in more depth.

Although they may not be aware of it, average Fives begin to approach most new experiences by trying to analyze them or to find their context in relation to what they already know. This is the shy person who tries to learn how to do a dance by watching people dancing and trying to analyze and memorize the different steps and movements. The easiest ways to learn to dance is to jump in and start moving, but average Fives fear to enter an activity until they have worked it all out in their minds. Usually, the dance is over by the time the Five is done "figuring it out." This can be a cumbersome way of learning things, but it does have some positive aspects. Because their method of learning is so systematic, and because they are observing and memorizing every step of any process they engage in, many Fives can explain to others how they arrived at certain conclusions or achieved specific results. And at Level 4, Fives enjoy sharing their expertise with others. They can discourse enthusiastically and at length on the projects they have been pursuing. Unfortunately, average Fives may not be comfortable talking about much else. Their personal lives, their hopes, desires, and disappointments, and especially their feelings become private matters, and they are reluctant to share these parts of themselves with others. They prefer to discuss subjects of interest to them, and to arrive at deeper "truths" through intelligent conversation.

Level 5: The Intense Conceptualizer

As average Fives retreat into the apparent safety of their minds, they ironically begin to heighten their insecurities about their abilities. After all, they are putting less and less time into anything outside of their narrowing interests, and are less willing to try new activities. They shift into mental high-gear, using whatever internal and financial resources they have to gain a sense of confidence and strength that would allow them to move forward with their lives. Unfortunately, average Fives often misapply this energy, getting increasingly bogged down in what others would see as trivia and losing perspective on which activities will actually help them in their lives. They spend endless hours engaged in their projects, but are unable to come to closure, both because they are more uncertain of themselves and their ideas and because they are afraid to leave the security of their cerebral constructs.

As a result, Fives believe that they have no inner resources to spare. They fear that other people and their emotional needs will overwhelm them, or at the very least, sidetrack them from their projects. Fives believe that everything depends upon their acquiring a skill or ability that would give them a chance to survive in what they increasingly perceive as a world without pity or mercy. They may deeply want to connect with others, but feel that this is not possible until they can develop the sense of confidence and mastery they seek. Average Fives begin to view most of their social interactions as intrusions upon their time and space—time and space they believe they must devote to their quest for mastery. To defend themselves against these potential "intrusions," they withdraw further into their own inner worlds by intensifying their mental focus and activity. If Fives began to create alternative realities in the healthier levels, they begin to inhabit them at Level 5. Average Fives do not want anyone or anything to distract them from whatever they believe they are gaining by exploring those realities.

Strangely, though, average Fives begin to distract *themselves*. If all of their energies were devoted to constructive projects, their behavior might be more comprehensible to others, but their growing insecurity causes them to spend much of their time engaged in any sort of activity which might provide some temporary sense of confidence and competence. In their minds, Fives can feel capable and fully in control of their situation, which begins to compensate for their fears about being powerless and incapable in the real world.

They plunge into complex intellectual puzzles and labyrinthine systems—elaborate, impenetrable mazes by which they can insulate themselves from the world while dealing with it intellectually. They get involved in highly detailed, complicated systems of thought, immersing themselves in obscure theories, whether these have to do with the abstruse regions of such traditional academic studies as astronomy, mathematics, or philosophy, or with esoteric topics such

as the Kabbala, astrology, and the occult. They are endlessly fascinated with intellectual games (such as chess, computer simulation
games, or Dungeons and Dragons), making areas of study into a kind
of game, and games into an area of study. They often develop a strong
affinity for genre fiction, especially science fiction and horror. Exploring the dark and fantastic realms of the imagination gives Fives
the feeling of mastering something—even if it is only an image
in their imaginations. Their interest in strange, disturbing subject
matter is both a further search for "turf" unclaimed by others and a
counterphobic reaction to their feelings of helplessness.

The thinking of average Fives becomes increasingly uncensored:
they are willing to entertain *any* thought, no matter how horrible,
unacceptable, or taboo it may seem to others. Fives are in pursuit of
the truth, and if the truth is unpleasant or upsets existing conventions, so be it. In healthy Fives, this tendency is laudable and
the source of many great discoveries. In average Fives, however,
it starts to create problems. Because they are not participating
as actively in the world, they are getting fewer "reality checks."
Consequently, their exploration of potentially unsettling subject
matter begins to add fuel to their anxieties about the world and
themselves.

Because of these fears, and because their imaginations are causing
them to see ominous implications in almost everything, average
Fives are typically fascinated with power. They feel that knowledge
is power and that by possessing knowledge, they will be secure
because they perceive more than others do—and hence, can protect
themselves. They are attracted by areas of study which deal with
some form of power, whether in nature, or in politics, or in human
behavior. However, Fives are also ambivalent about power and suspicious of those who have power over them. They feel that whoever
has power may use it against them, rendering them completely
helpless, one of their deepest fears.

One way that average Fives maintain their independence and
avoid the potential control of others is by becoming more secretive.
They become increasingly unwilling to talk about their personal or
emotional lives, fearing that to do so would give others power over
them. Additionally, speaking about such things might well plunge
them into a more direct experience of their own fears and vulnerability—a prospect that average Fives distinctly wish to avoid. In
any event, Fives begin to control others' access to them, not by

overt deception but by offering little information about themselves; they can be terse, cryptic, or totally uncommunicative. They also control access by compartmentalizing their relationships and different aspects of their lives. A Five will tell one friend about his professional life, while another friend will learn of his fascination with insects. Still another will know about his romantic life, while another knows where the Five likes to go late at night. No one gets the complete picture, however, and as much as possible, average Fives will make sure that these different friends do not meet to "share notes."

This state of affairs would be difficult to maintain if Fives had too many friends, but to keep their life simple and to allow more time for their private pursuits, at Level 5 they do with relationships what they do elsewhere in their lives, they begin to reduce their needs. Average Fives become more determined to continue their projects and want to avoid any involvements or dependencies that might hinder them. They begin to "cut back" on creature comforts, activities, and relationships. Anything that might compromise their independence and their freedom to continue with their interests becomes expendable. Fives at this point are so caught up in their mental world that even basic amenities and comforts become almost irrelevant to them. They can become extremely Spartan and minimal in their existence, requiring less of others so that others will require less of them. Average Fives will often take employment far beneath their capabilities because they want to avoid becoming entangled in the demands of a more challenging career. Ironically, they are avoiding living their lives so they can devote time to preparing to live their lives. They live for whatever pleasures and small victories they may derive from their cerebral preoccupations.

The problem is that average Fives have stopped observing the world with any consistency, and have instead focused their attention on their ideas and their imagination. This is a turning point in their development. Rather than investigate the objective world, average Fives at this stage become preoccupied with their own interpretations of it, mentally detaching themselves from the environment or even their own emotional experiences by becoming more intensely involved with their ideas. Healthy Fives are extraordinarily perceptive and aware of their environment. To the degree that Average Fives are absorbed in their own thoughts, they perceive very little of the world around them.

As Fives speculate and theorize, turning their ideas around in their minds, examining them from every angle, endlessly producing new interpretations, they lose the forest for the trees. With every new conjecture, they have no sense of certitude that their speculations are final: everything remains hanging in the air, in a cloud of possibilities. For example, the more they write, the more complex the exposition becomes, until it is virtually incomprehensible. As brilliant as they may be, average Fives do not easily publish their ideas because they cannot bring them to a conclusion.

Furthermore, all ideas seem equally plausible to Fives, since they can make a convincing case for almost anything they think of. Anything thinkable seems possible. Anything thinkable seems real. They are intellectually and emotionally capable of entertaining any new thought, even horrifying or outlandish ones, since speculating on new possibilities is virtually all they do. Their ideas, however, begin to have no direct connection with the outside world. (The problems of epistemology not only fascinate them, average Fives unwittingly live them out.) But establishing a relationship between their ideas and reality is no longer the primary function of the thinking of average Fives. Instead, speculation and imagination maintain the sense of self by keeping the mind active.

Moreover, for all the time they spend thinking, average Fives at this Level do not communicate to others clearly, because their thought processes are so complex and convoluted. They get into too much detail; their ideas become highly condensed. The stream of consciousness floods out in elaborate monologues, making it difficult for others to follow their train of thought. They go off on tangents, jumping from one point to another without indicating the intervening steps in their logic. A perceptive observation about Jackson Pollock's painting technique may be followed by a disquisition on modern media and the hazards to biological systems of higher levels of chemicals in the environment. Their monologues may well be fascinating, and possibly breathtaking in the sweep of their intellectual range; however, their discourses may also be strange and tedious, because the mental exertion required to follow them is exhausting. Nor is it always clear that the trip will be worth the effort, although average Fives think that whatever they have to say is as interesting to others as it is to themselves.

They begin to function as disembodied minds because, as far as they are concerned, the body is merely the vehicle for the mind. At this Level, they do not pay much attention to their physical condition except when that gets in the way of their thinking. They become so deeply involved in projects that they forget to eat or sleep or change their clothes. They frequently look like the proverbial absent-minded professor, missing a button when putting on their shirts or forgetting to tie their shoes. No matter. To them such considerations are insignificant: the life of the mind, the excitement of pursuing their interests, is what counts.

Both for better and for worse, they are extremely high-strung, as if their nervous systems were tuned to a higher pitch than those of the other personality types. (Nines also become more cerebral and imaginative in the average Levels, but their affect is very different. Nines become placid and passive, while Fives become agitated and intense.) Fives seem to lack the ability to repress the unconscious impulses which erupt into their minds, fueling their intense involvement in their perceptions, their work, and their relations with others. They find it difficult to do things casually, and find close relationships with others particularly taxing.

The more detached average Fives are, the more ambivalent they are to just about everyone—they are attracted to people, yet suspicious about them. They want to figure out what makes other people tick, just as they analyze other objects of intellectual interest. ("What you just said was fascinating—you're incredibly angry at men, aren't you?") Yet they usually try to avoid getting deeply involved with others because people are unpredictable and potentially demanding. Average Fives believe there must be a catch. They cannot imagine why anyone would be interested in them personally and fear that others may expect something from them which they will not be able to deliver. Further, emotional involvements arouse strong feelings which average Fives find difficult to control: the passions flood too easily into their minds. But because most Fives also have strong sexual impulses, they cannot avoid involvements altogether, as much as they would like to. Thus, though Fives find people and relationships endlessly fascinating, they remain wary.

It is therefore typical of average Fives either to be unmarried or to have stormy relationships with people. Intimacy with others gets so involved, so complex and exhausting, that they stop trying to make contact with others and become reclusive, ever more completely burying themselves in their work and ideas. Doing so only fuels their feelings of helplessness, though, and as Fives become more isolated they are increasingly prey to their own growing fears about themselves and the world. Their view of reality grows ever more bleak and doubtful. They have great difficulty accepting the idea of a benevolent universe, let alone a benevolent God. Moreover, the problem of evil is an enormous stumbling block: the horror and uncertainty of the world is so apparent to Fives that any God who allowed the world to be as it is must be sadistic, an evil God, a God they refuse to become involved with.

Level 6: The Provocative Cynic

In time, the complexities Fives create in their minds cause new and more troubling problems for them. Nothing is clear or certain; anxiety increases. They are more desperate than ever about whatever projects and ideas they are trying to develop and fear that other people will demand that they give up their pursuits before they are ready. They fear that they will be drawn "off course" by the intrusions of life and are determined to defend against whatever they perceive as a threat to their fragile niche. At Level 6, through their style of speech, their manner of dress, and the subjects that they involve themselves with, Fives are saying to the world, "Leave me alone!" If others could not get the message before, Fives become more aggressive in their efforts to scare people away.

On the surface, Fives at this Level may seem intellectually arrogant, but they are actually less certain of themselves. Even their most valued ideas and projects begin to seem futile to them, and they alternate between defending them aggressively and finding them worthless. They begin to take more extreme and unorthodox positions, as if they were trying to extract more confidence from ideas that are becoming meaningless for them. Fives may not be entirely convinced of the radical views they express, but express them they do, wielding them like cutting tools. Further, their own subconscious fears about their inability to cope with the environment are frequently erupting into their minds, and they live in growing terror of the world and others. They feel uncertain and uneasy about nearly everything, and it infuriates them that other people seem to be content or oblivious to the horrors which they notice. They therefore begin to undermine others' certainty or contentment by "sharing" their provocative views. ("So you're going to the beach? I was just reading the latest report on the ozone layer. Studies show that the chances of getting skin cancer have gone up by nearly one hundred percent.") There is often an element of truth in what Fives express at this point, but their intention is no longer to arrive at the truth. It is to use their knowledge as a way of unsettling others. And because they have spent so much time gathering information, they can easily use it both to reinforce their conviction that the world is rotten and to subvert other people's sense of security.

A certain extremism is as typical of their social style as it is of their intellectual viewpoint. In political or artistic matters, antagonistic Fives are usually radicals, populating the avant-garde. They love to take ideas to their furthest limits—for their shock value, to defy what has conventionally been thought or done, or to puncture and demolish popular opinions. (And even if they are not as correct as Fives think they are, their provocative ideas virtually force others to react to them, stirring up debate or even hostility.) As dyed-in-the-wool nonconformists and dissenters, they rebel against all social conventions, rules, and expectations, whether these involve feminism, politics, child rearing, sexual liberation, or all of them in some peculiar combination. They have an ax to grind. Understanding has been abandoned for polemics.

At Level 6, Fives use their entire lifestyle as a statement of their views and as a rebuke of the world. They may choose to live an extremely marginal existence to avoid "selling out." At this Level, "selling out" may mean any kind of regular employment or even having a relationship. They may wear intentionally provocative clothing or groom themselves in nonconformist ways. Of course, social protest can be a vital and healthy impulse in any culture, and healthier Fives (as well as other types) may well use provocative language, art, or style of dress to make a point. But with lower average Fives, the point is that there is no point. Life is futile. People are stupid. My own life is meaningless. Although other types are certainly part of the picture, this attitude is common in many of the "alternative" cultures that have developed in the latter part of the twentieth century. Grunge, cyberpunk, heavy metal, and other youth subcultures embrace this ethos.

Ironically for those so given to complex thought, Fives at this Level have also become more reductionistic, oversimplifying reality and dismissing more positive, alternative explanations of things. For example, dismissing the flower, reductionistic Fives focus on the ooze from which it sprang, as if the brightest blossom were "nothing but" mud in some significantly altered state; painting is nothing but the desire to smear feces; God is nothing but a projection of the father into the cosmos; human beings are nothing but biological machines, and so forth. The result is that their ideas mix legitimate insights with extreme interpretations, while Fives themselves have no way of knowing which is which.

An irrational element—a kind of perverse resistance to reality—has begun to taint their thought processes. Fives at Level 6 are not crazy, even though their ideas may be strange and extremely unorthodox. Healthy originality, however, has deteriorated into quirky eccentricity; the genius has become little more than a crank. (They may assert that arcane secrets are hidden in numerical codes derived from the names of characters in their favorite TV show, or that all rational thought is meaningless.) Others may well have entertained outlandish ideas, but lower average Fives dwell on them, sometimes using all of their time and energy to "prove" them. Their extreme ideas are so much a part of their sense of self that Fives will defend their ideas at all costs, asserting them vigorously and attempting to demolish all counterarguments. Contentious and quarrelsome, they also worry about establishing their intellectual priority and protecting their ideas, threatening lawsuits if they think that someone has stolen one of their brilliant theories.

Even so, as radically extreme and reductionistic as many of their ideas are, average Fives are not necessarily completely off the mark. They are usually too intelligent not to have something interesting to say. The problem is knowing which of their ideas are valuable and which are not. This is because, at a deeper level, Fives are becoming cynical and hopeless about all of their ideas and projects. A profound pessimism is creeping into their thoughts, and they begin to see all viewpoints as equally irrelevant. They can argue any point because everything seems equally true or untrue, and therefore equally worthless. Fives at Level 6 may even enjoy arguing viewpoints which they find repugnant just to reaffirm their intelligence while simultaneously proving the futility of making any further efforts.

Fives at this stage give the appearance of being extremely involved in their projects, but a closer inspection usually reveals that they are spending much of their time in relatively inessential activities. They may need to put together a résumé, take care of bills, or complete a project for work, but will instead devote their efforts to reading a book on ants, creating a detailed computer database for their record collection, or studying strategies to improve their chess game. They put more and more of their time into activities which will do little to improve their situation, and which actually become harmful because they are distracting Fives from what they really need to do. They are so unsure of themselves that they feel completely unable to engage in many activities—especially those that might improve their quality of life—and keep gravitating to situations that give them the temporary feeling of having their lives "under control." Average Fives may not be able to face a job interview or learn to drive a car, but they can conquer the world, survive a nuclear holocaust, or wield awesome occult powers in the world of their imaginations.

At this Level, Fives feel profoundly unsettled and anxious about their apparent helplessness in what seems to them a dark and hostile reality. They feel that it is extremely unlikely that they will ever find a place for themselves in the world, and in fact, their abrasive behavior is making this a real possibility. Fives desperately want to find something they can do that will make them feel more connected with the world, but their fear and anger cause them to retreat further and further from any contact with others. They are tormented by their tempers and by their teeming imaginations: insomnia is not uncommon. If they could reach out to others and acknowledge their own suffering, Fives could turn around their difficulties and reconstruct their lives. If they continue to turn away from the world, however, they may eventually cut off what few connections remain in their lives and plunge into a much more terrifying darkness.

ANALYZING THE UNHEALTHY FIVE

Level 7: The Isolated Nihilist
The need to keep others at a safe distance to protect their frantic search for mastery sets the stage for Fives to become extremely antagonistic toward anyone who they believe threatens their world. Unfortunately, as they become more unhealthy, their self-doubt becomes so great that almost everything threatens them. It seems to them that the only way that they can be safe is to cut off their connections with others and "go it alone." They feel hopelessly ill-adapted for life and are profoundly disgusted with the world.

Unhealthy Fives are convinced that they are never going to find a place for themselves in society, and so they turn their back on it. They become extremely isolated and prey to growing eccentricity and nihilistic despair.

Their aggressions are aroused when people question their ideas— or worse, if their ideas are ridiculed or dismissed. To maintain what little remains of their self-confidence, which is thoroughly wedded to their ideas, unhealthy Fives go on the offensive: individuals must be discredited, their ideas shown to be worthless, their solutions to problems an illusion, their world a fool's paradise. Thus, unhealthy Fives unwittingly provoke others into rejecting them, and then become cynical about the value of all relationships. But in so doing, they become profoundly cut off from others and extremely hopeless about the possibility of ever relating to anyone.

Indeed, their need to reject what others believe is so strong that they take pleasure in debunking whatever is positive in life, trying to prove the virtual impossibility of human relationships and the complete rottenness at the core of human nature. Unhealthy Fives take delight in deflating what they see as the bourgeois illusions by which others get through life so comfortably, and to which they have not fallen prey because of their greater intellectual honesty.

As usual, there is a half-truth operating here. While others may well be living too comfortably for their own good, while some people may be self-deceptive, while some families and some relationships may be tainted by hypocrisy, jealousy, and struggles for power, it does not necessarily follow that cynicism is the best response. Unhealthy Fives throw out the baby with the bath water: faith, hope, love, kindness, friendship—all are extraordinarily difficult for them to believe in because of their fear of involvement with others. Attachment to others is too threatening at this stage, so unhealthy Fives must justify their isolation by becoming nihilistic and cynical about all relationships, indeed, about the value of humanity itself.

Just as an intense stream of water from a fire hose can hold back a crowd, the intensity of their minds, overheated by their erupting aggressive impulses, repels everything that might influence them. They "burn their bridges behind them," ending friendships, quitting jobs, and emptying out all but the barest of necessities in their lives. ("To hell with everything!") It is as if unhealthy Fives were attempting to purge themselves of everything but their most basic life-support systems so that they will not be dependent, and there-fore potentially overwhelmed by anyone or anything. This process may be taken to extreme degrees. Unhealthy Fives may end up living out of a car, or squatting in a condemned building so that they will not be part of "the system." They neglect themselves physically, paying no attention to their appearance, eating poorly, and going unwashed. Alcoholism and other forms of substance abuse are quite common at this stage, and the rebellious side of Fives has no hesitation about using illicit drugs. Their experi-mental nature may also lead them into trying new "designer drugs" or substances known to be dangerous, such as heroin. Drugs are harmful for any type, but for Fives they can be particularly debili-tating. Unhealthy Fives are already having great difficulty facing even the basic maintenance of their lives, and their connection with reality is extremely tenuous. Drugs further erode their confi-dence and drive them further into isolation, thus accelerating their deterioration.

At this Level, unhealthy Fives believe they must maintain their isolation so that they will not be influenced by anyone. While usu-ally not violent, they may rant and rave, write long diatribes and denunciations, or suddenly withdraw into a glowering, hateful silence. Since most people are repulsed by this kind of behavior, the isolation of Fives rapidly deepens, which is exactly what unhealthy Fives want. Yet, for that reason, they are vulnerable to ever wors-ening distortions in their thought processes. They are no longer getting "reality checks" from others, no longer comparing their per-ceptions to reality, and what few forays into the environment they do have are tainted with their growing terror. All of their experiences become confirmations of their helplessness and of the utter mean-inglessness of life. Unhealthy Fives feel besieged by even minor prob-lems and view all interactions with others as invasions upon their fragile space. Aggressions—and fear—continue to escalate.

Some of the personality types are able to conceal the degree of their distress in the unhealthy Levels, but Fives are clearly and unmistakably unstable. Others can see their disintegration and are both saddened and horrified, but unhealthy Fives' aggressive defense of their isolation makes interventions difficult. Even the hint that they may "need help" may trigger their fears of helpless-ness and incompetency and drive them deeper into pathology. Un-healthy Fives also retain their ability to reason to some degree, and can cleverly argue away any positive input, dismissing any possibility that their dark and corrosive view of life may be in error. They have no expectations of themselves or others and retreat into a reality as bleak in its actuality as it is in its outlook.

Because unhealthy Fives are terrified of the world and of their own inability to cope with it, they stew in a destructive mixture of dark, twisted fantasies, feelings of contempt for others, and horror at the emptiness of their lives. They want to act, to do something that would discharge the relentlessness of their teeming minds, but they feel crippled by fear and have no belief in themselves or others. Consequently the intense force of their irrational thoughts keeps building without relief. They are filled with rage at a world which they believe has rejected them, but feeling powerless to do anything about it, they avoid all contact with others, let alone reach out for help. It is as if they cannot stop cutting themselves off at the knees. Unhealthy Fives may still be brilliant or talented, but their nihilism destroys any chance of their doing anything constructive with their abilities, and thus building up their confidence. Instead, they tear down everything in their lives, devaluing and rejecting all their attachments to the world. Yet, unhealthy Fives are worse than merely isolated; they are filled with aggressions and impulses which cannot be discharged, because they do not want to get into violent conflicts with others. Unhealthy Fives are thus trapped in a terrible dilemma: they are obsessed by their aggressions yet unable to act on them because they fear the consequences. They want to accomplish something in the world, but their bleak, cynical attitude does not allow them to engage in any activities that might improve their situation. The result is that they do nothing, and the intensity of their own minds begins to devour them.

Level 8: The Terrified "Alien"

As unhealthy Fives retreat further and further into their isolation, their belief in their ability to cope with the world disintegrates. Further, their lack of contact with other people allows their fearful thoughts to run rampant without being checked. They begin to feel that the world is closing in on them, and that it will show them no mercy. At this stage, Fives have reduced their activities and their living conditions to the point where there is nowhere left to retreat. They may be living in a single room and almost never venture forth from it, or literally hiding out in the basement of a friend's or relative's house. The only place left to go is deeper into their own minds, but because their minds are the true source of their terrors, this becomes their ultimate undoing.

At Level 8, Fives have tremendous difficulty distinguishing between the sensory impressions generated by the environment and those which have their origin in their fearful thoughts. Thus, unhealthy Fives see all of reality as an implacable, devouring force. The world appears to them like a delirious fever dream—an insane landscape, like something out of a Hieronymus Bosch painting. Almost nothing in the environment is a source of comfort or reassurance. The more Fives look at the world through their distorted perceptions, the more horrified and hopeless they become.

As their fears spread and grow in intensity, they encompass and distort more of reality until doing anything becomes impossible, because everything is charged with terrifying implications. Thus, neurotic Fives may begin to be incapacitated by phobias. Inanimate objects take on a sinister appearance—the ceiling is about to collapse on them, their armchair may swallow them up, the television is giving them brain cancer. They may also experience hallucinations—hearing voices or having grossly distorted visual perceptions. They begin to experience their bodies as alien, perceiving their physical selves as turning against them just as the environment has seemed to turn against them. Neurotic Fives cannot rest or sleep or distract themselves, because they must be vigilant—and because they cannot turn off their minds. As a result, they become physically exhausted, which only compounds their problems.

Even average Fives can have trouble sleeping, but unhealthy Fives literally cannot sleep. They are afraid of being more vulnerable to malevolent forces while they sleep and are also afraid of their dreams, which can be intensely violent and disturbing. They may increase their drug or alcohol use as a way of shutting down their minds, but this only adds to their exhaustion. Sleeplessness heightens the intensity of their thoughts, leading to hallucinations. The childhood monsters in the closet become real for them. Their fear and insomnia wear them down physically, leaving them emotionally volatile and physically fragile.

What begins to frighten neurotic Fives even more is that their thoughts seem to have a life of their own. Their thoughts are uncontrollable, scaring them when they do not want to be scared. Their minds race wildly and they become terrified by fears from which they cannot possibly escape, since, after all, their fears originate in themselves. Like Dr. Frankenstein, they are in danger of being destroyed by processes to which they themselves have given life.

Their healthy ability to find connections and to draw conclusions from disparate facts now works against them. Mental connections go haywire; they relate things which have no basis in fact, yet neurotic Fives are absolutely convinced that they are related. The behavior of birds becomes indicative of political trends. The number of raisins in a bowl of cereal portends the number of months to global cataclysm. Unhealthy Fives see existence as pointless and horrifying, yet constantly assign sinister meanings to trivial daily phenomena.

Unhealthy Fives are unable to stop the destructive force of their distorted thinking because they have cut themselves off from almost all of the constructive outlets for their tremendous mental energies. Their minds have become like a light bulb with more electricity coursing through its filament than it is designed to handle—five hundred watts through a one-hundred-watt bulb. Their thoughts blaze with a terrifying intensity which is rapidly burning them up. They cannot stop their horrific thoughts and fantasies and are almost completely incapable of doing anything positive for themselves. Worse, they resist all help from others, fearing that they will become even more powerless by accepting assistance. Getting help would also be the final confirmation of their own uselessness, their own inability to cope. They are likely to avoid or flee anyone reaching out to them.

Unhealthy Fives would like to destroy *everything*, so detestable has the world become in their eyes. Their rage, fear, and aggressions have become all-consuming and overwhelming, yet Fives are still unable to act or to discharge their destructive impulses and feelings. Their actions become erratic and irrational, even frightening, but they are still only minor responses to the eruptions of chaos in their psyches.

Life becomes unbearable: they seem to see too much, as if their eyelids had been removed. But the truth is that their minds are devouring them. The world becomes filled with terrors because their minds are filled with terrors. No part of their mind offers any solace or comfort.

Level 9: The Imploding Schizoid

To exert what little control remains over their growing terror and despair, neurotic Fives attempt to use the same defenses they have used all along—detachment and compartmentalization—but at this stage of pathology, these methods are ineffective at holding their fears at bay. They become increasingly schizoid, splitting off from terrifying parts of their psyches and identifying with whatever remaining ideas or fantasies offer some sense of power over their disintegration. But the relentless force of their fear keeps breaking through, leaving Fives feeling that they have no safe space left, even in their minds.

Ultimately, neurotic Fives come to believe that they can no longer defend themselves from hostile forces in the world or from the terrors in their own minds. In fact, most Fives at this Level cannot distinguish between these two realms: they have collapsed into one continuous experience of pain and horror. At this point, Fives want everything to stop. They want cessation, to end all experience in oblivion. There are two main ways that they are likely do this.

The first and most obvious of these is suicide. Like unhealthy Fours, neurotic Fives are likely to take their own lives, although for somewhat different reasons. Fours destroy themselves out of self-hatred and to silently accuse those who they feel have let them down. Fives tend to commit suicide because they see life as meaningless and horrifying. There is simply no point in continuing to exist. (Of course Fives with a Four-wing and Fours with a Five-wing will display some combination of these motivations.) All that unhealthy Fives perceive in themselves and the world fills them with terror and nausea. They conclude that the only way to stop their horrible experiences is to stop all experience. Like Hamlet, the prospect of "not being" becomes a "consummation devoutly to be wished."

If they do not commit suicide, unhealthy Fives "solve" the problem of how to control their minds, especially the overwhelming anxiety produced by their consuming phobias, by unconsciously splitting consciousness into two parts. Neurotic Fives retreat into that part of themselves which seems safe, regressing into an autistic-like state which resembles psychosis.

At this final Level, Fives may defend themselves from reality by unconsciously cutting themselves off from every connection with it. To put this another way, unhealthy Fives are so terrorized by their thoughts that they must get rid of them somehow. They do so by identifying with the emptiness that remains within themselves when they detach from their remaining identifications. In effect, they detach themselves from themselves, like parents who, to stop being tormented by the memories of a dead child, throw away everything that reminds them of the child. The result is that neurotic Fives live in a totally empty house—the self which has been purged of everything that reminds them of their terrifying and painful attachments to the world.

Thus, neurotic Fives deteriorate into a state of inner emptiness and, if they continue to live this way, in all probability into a form of schizophrenia.*

All their former intellectual intensity and capacity for involvement is gone. Fives at this stage are utterly isolated from their environment, from other people, and from their inner life—from their ability to think, to feel, and to do.

Unhealthy Fives have finally succeeded in putting distance between themselves and the environment, although at the price of completely removing themselves from it through suicide or a schizoid break. The irony is, however, that Fives retreat from reality to gain the time and space to build their confidence and ability to deal with life, but they ultimately destroy their own confidence and talents, even their own life, through their fear and isolation. Those

---

*Because of the importance of schizophrenia, we should consider the hypothetical links between this disease and the Five. It seems likely that schizophrenia is one of the possible outcomes of a neurotic Five's way of coping with the world. The stress caused by social isolation and the physical exhaustion brought about by a hyperactive mind may eventually cause a change in the chemical balance in the brain, resulting in the thought disorders of schizophrenia. Of course, not every unhealthy Five is schizophrenic, and not every schizophrenic is a Five. But this personality type does seem to be more prone to schizophrenia than any other. It is possible that the hereditary factors which leave an individual prone to schizophrenia may be related to the hereditary factors which contribute to an individual's becoming a Five. Further research in this area might shed new light on both schizophrenia and "Fiveness."

A way of conceptualizing a possible relationship between the Five and schizophrenia is to think of these two entities as if they were on parallel mental tracks. At some point when the brain can no longer function within the neurotic Five's life situation, it skips tracks from neurosis to schizophrenia. From a mainly psychological maladjustment, the person jumps into a different realm: into a chemical and physical disease which, of course, has psychological ramifications. This might explain why some neurotic Fives remain neurotic while others develop into schizophrenics, and why some schizophrenics become ill without being either Fives or neurotic.

Fives who do not take their own lives may end up living a life of helplessness, dependency, or incarceration—the very situation they most feared—as a result of severe psychotic breaks with reality. In a final effort to escape from the horrors around them, Fives attempt to remove themselves from the environment. But what they have removed themselves from is not actually reality, but the projection of their anxieties about reality. They have succeeded only in removing themselves from their thoughts and feelings. Once neurotic Fives have done this, they become unable to cry out to anyone from the void they have created within themselves. All is emptiness within the abyss of the purged self.

THE DYNAMICS OF THE FIVE

The Direction of Disintegration: The Five Goes to Seven

Starting at Level 4, Fives under stress will begin to exhibit many of the qualities of average to unhealthy Sevens. Average Fives tend to retreat from connection with others and from activities in the world which they fear they will be unable to accomplish. Thus they become increasingly narrow in their focus and concerns. The move to Seven can be seen as an unconscious reaction to this shrinking of the Five's world, albeit in the scattered, hyperactive discharge of anxiety found in the average to unhealthy Seven.

At Level 4, Fives are focusing their energies in studying, practicing, and preparing. They do not feel confident to enter the arena of life and believe that further developing their knowledge and skills will give them the protection they need to survive. Along with this, however, comes a desire for variety and a restlessness of mind characteristic of type Seven. Also like Sevens, Fives at this Level are constantly acquiring information, building their collections of music, books, and videos, or whatever else captures their interest. They move from one topic to another, looking for the subject that will satisfy them, for the project they can really get involved with. But in this state of restlessness, none of their pursuits are entirely satisfactory to them.

At Level 5, Fives have become even more preoccupied and involved with their projects and ideas. They are beginning to isolate themselves socially and to become more focused on their thoughts than on the world around them. Fives begin to be starved for stimulation, and under stress may begin to involve themselves with a wide variety of experiences which do not relate directly to their central projects or motivations. They distract themselves with video games, movies, and science fiction and horror novels. They love to let their minds free-associate, and can enjoy moments of silliness and offbeat humor which often surprise the people around them. Fives under stress may also develop a taste for nightlife, exploring restaurants, bars, and nightclubs—often as voyeurs. They will usually be secretive about this, however, and few of their friends will be aware of this aspect of their lives. As their anxiety escalates, so does their desire for distraction and stimulation.

At Level 6, Fives are becoming more fearful, and despair of ever finding a niche for themselves. They become threatened by most interactions with others and can be antagonistic and provocative in defense of their intellectual or creative "turf." They get into high gear in their avoidance of anxiety, and can be insensitive and aggressive in their pursuit of whatever they want at the time. The jaded, calloused qualities of the Seven only reinforce the Five's growing cynicism, making them impatient with people and extremely hardened in their view of the world. Some may find them wild and exciting at this level, but most people are put off by their intense, bristling energy. Further, Fives under stress will not hesitate to use drugs or alcohol to quell their anxieties. They will pursue whatever offers them relief from their pain and fears, even if their escape is costly and short-lived.

At Level 7, unhealthy Fives are extremely isolated, cut off from contact with others and the world, and consequently have no constructive outlets for their inner intensity. When they go to Seven, they discharge this energy in a variety of escapist behaviors, which only makes them more dissipated and incapable. Unhealthy Fives lurch from an isolated, fearful state to one of wild activity. Their minds are beginning to run out of control, and when they can no longer contain their fear, this enormous mental turbulence gets acted out in impulsive and often irresponsible ways. They lunge into mindless activity, by which they succeed only in getting themselves into worse trouble and more serious conflicts with the environment. They are irrational, have extremely poor judgment, and make poor choices about which actions to take. When others question their self-destructive escapism, their responses can be abusive and infantile.

At Level 8, Fives are full of terrors and cannot distinguish the horrific images that erupt from their unconscious from reality. Under increased stress, their behavior becomes manic and reckless. Moving to Seven now, deteriorated Fives go totally out of control. Some of the terrible things they have feared may actually happen as a result of their erratic and irresponsible behavior. And as fearful as Fives have become, they are often heedless and unaware of real dangers. For example, they may be killed—not because they are devoured by their furniture or exposed to death rays from their television, but because, not watching where they are going, they get run over by a truck. Out-of-control Fives are reckless and accident-prone: they may be poisoned, not by the KGB but because they mistakenly ate something they should not have. Neurotic Fives need to reestablish contact with reality (particularly the positive aspects of it), although at this Level they are completely incapable of doing so. They act impulsively, erratically, and hysterically, like a manic-depressive Seven, becoming increasingly unstable and unpredictable.

At Level 9, Fives are consumed with terror and are desperate to escape the horrors they perceive around them. Similarly, they cannot find anything in themselves which inspires confidence or gives them any sense that they will be able to cope with the rest of their lives. Fearing that they have reached some sort of horrible dead end, they may compulsively do permanent harm to themselves or someone else. Even if they do not kill themselves, their reckless activities may well have severely damaged their health and limited their ability to pursue any further activities. Like unhealthy Sevens, they are debilitated, burned-out, and paralyzed with fear. As anxiety reaches an ever new pitch, they may do something irrevocable, such as impulsively killing someone or committing suicide.

The Direction of Integration: The Five Goes to Eight

Fives typically do not feel that they know enough to act: there is always more to know. They will always feel insecure until they have mastered the real world and are not simply masters of their own minds. From a psychoanalytic point of view, their egos are typically too weak for the ids—their aggressions and other impulses tend to overpower their minds.

This no longer happens to healthy, integrating Fives because they have incorporated their perceptions of the world into themselves by identifying with them instead of merely observing them. They no longer identify just with their thoughts, but also with the objects of their thoughts. Thus, integrating Fives have overcome their fear of the environment and are learning to trust it. Hence their self-confidence grows, after the manner of healthy Eights.

When they go to Eight, Fives also realize that, as little as they think they know, it is still more than almost anyone else. They also realize that they do not have to know absolutely everything before they can act. They will learn more as they do more; they will be able to solve new problems as they arise. They understand that they will know what they need to know when they need to know it. Their confidence will come not from some collection of skills or some vast body of information that they have memorized, but from a real connection with their presence in the world. They then experience themselves not as separate from the world, not as a helpless speck, but as a powerful, integral part of it.

Integrating Fives act from a realization of their own genuine mastery. While they do not know everything, they know enough to lead others with confidence. The correctness of their ideas has been so well confirmed by reality that they no longer fear acting. They acquire the courage it takes to put their ideas, and consequently *themselves*, on the line. Thus, integrating Fives realize that they are able to contribute something worthwhile to others. As a result, their thoughts are finally given expression in action and possibly in leadership. Integrating Fives show others how to do what only they know how to do. And, as we have seen, the practical value of their ideas may be incalculable.

THE MAJOR SUBTYPES OF THE FIVE

The Five with a Four-Wing: "The Iconoclast"
The traits of the Five and those of the Four reinforce each other in many ways. Both Five and Four are withdrawn types: they turn to the inner world of their imagination to defend their egos and to reinforce their sense of self. They both feel that something essential in themselves must be found before they can live their lives completely. Fives lack the confidence to act, and Fours lack a strong, stable sense of identity. Thus, Fives with a Four-wing have difficulty connecting with others and staying grounded. People

of this subtype are more emotional and introverted than Fives with a Six-wing, although paradoxically, they tend to be more sociable than the other subtype. As a result of their Four component, they are also more interested in the personal and intrapsychic. The two types also have some significant differences in their approach. Fives are cerebral, holding experience at arm's length, while Fours internalize everything to intensify their feelings. Despite these differences—or because of them—these two personality types make one of the richest subtypes, combining possibilities for outstanding artistic as well as intellectual achievement. Noteworthy examples of this subtype include Albert Einstein, Werner Heisenburg, Friedrich Nietzsche, Georgia O'Keeffe, John Cage, John Lennon, k. d. lang, Laurie Anderson, James Joyce, Emily Dickinson, Stanley Kubrick, David Lynch, Buster Keaton, Gary Larson, Stephen King, Tim Burton, Clive Barker, Franz Kafka, Umberto Eco, Jean-Paul Sartre, Oriana Fallaci, Glenn Gould, Peter Serkin, Hannah Arendt, Kurt Cobain, and Vincent van Gogh.

In healthy people of this subtype, we find the union of intuition and knowledge, sensitivity and insight, aesthetic appreciation and intellectual endowments. Fives with a Four-wing are likely to be involved in the arts as writers, directors, designers, musicians, composers, choreographers, and so forth. This subtype has been somewhat overlooked in many descriptions of Fives because they do not fit the stereotype of the academic/scientific Five (the Five with a Six-wing). This subtype is more synthetic in its thinking, pulling things together and seeking out new ways of looking at things. Also, Fives with a Four-wing tend to utilize their imaginations more than the analytic, systematic parts of the mind which are more the domain of the other subtype. If they are involved in science, Fives with a Four-wing are drawn to those areas in which there is less emphasis on experimentation and data collection than on intuition and comprehensive vision. This subtype is particularly aware of—and on the lookout for—the beauty in a mathematical formula, for example. For this subtype, beauty is one of the indications of truth, because the order which beauty represents is a confirmation of the objective rightness of an idea. One of the foremost strengths of healthy Fives with a Four-wing lies precisely in their intuition, since intuition helps them uncover areas of knowledge where their conscious thoughts have not yet ventured. The Four-wing adds a desire to find a unique, personal vision to the curiosity and perceptiveness of the Five, and the result is a propensity to "tinker" with familiar forms until they become something almost unrecognizable. In talented Fives with a Four-wing this can lead to startling innovations in their chosen fields of endeavor.

In Average Fives with a Four-wing, the Four-wing adds emotional depth, but causes difficulties in sustaining efforts and in working with others. Fives with a Four-wing are more independent than Fives with a Six-wing and resist having structures and deadlines imposed on them. There can be an off-putting detachment from the environment, both because they are involved in their thoughts and because they are introverted and emotionally self-absorbed. Analytic powers may be used to keep people at arm's length rather than to understand them more deeply. Emotionally delicate, people of this subtype can be moody and hypersensitive to criticism, particularly regarding the value of their work or ideas, since this impinges directly upon self-esteem. Both component types tend to withdraw from people and be reclusive. They can be highly creative and imaginative, envisioning alternate realities in great detail, but can get lost in their own cerebral landscapes. The Four-wing gives a propensity to fantasizing, but with the Five with the Four-wing, the subject matter tends toward the surreal and fantastic rather than the romantic. Individuals of this subtype can become highly impractical, spending most of their time reading, playing intellectual games, or specializing in trivia. There is often an attraction to dark, forbidden subject matter or to any way of self-expression which would disturb or upset others. Some Fives with a Four-wing become fascinated with the macabre and the horrific. As they become more impractical and fearful about their possibilities in life, one typical solution is to find emotional solace in various forms of self-indulgence—in alcohol, drugs, or sexual escapades.

Unhealthy persons of this subtype may fall prey to debilitating depressions yet be disturbed by aggressive impulses. Envy of others mixes with contempt for them; the desire to isolate the self from the world mixes with regret that it must be so. Intellectual conflicts make their emotional lives seem hopeless, while their emotional conflicts make intellectual work difficult to sustain. Moreover, if this subtype becomes neurotic, it is one of the most alienated of all of the personality types: profoundly hopeless, nihilistic, self-inhibiting, isolated from others, and full of self-hatred. Unhealthy Fives with a Four-wing retreat into a very bleak, minimal existence, attempting to cut off from all needs. The self-rejection and despair of the Four combines with the cynical nihilism of the Five to create a worldview that is relentlessly negative and terrifying. Social isolation, addiction, and chronic depression are common. Suicide is a real possibility.

The Five with a Six-Wing: "The Problem Solver"

This subtype is the one that has been most often associated with Fives—the intellectual who is interested in science, technology, acquiring facts and details. Fives with a Six-wing are the "analysts" and "cataloguers" of their environments; they are problem solvers and excel at dissecting the components of a problem or thing to discover how it works. The traits of the Five and those of the Six-wing combine to produce one of the most "difficult" of the personality types to contact intimately or to sustain a relationship with. Both components, the Five and the Six, are in the Thinking Triad, and Fives with a Six-wing are perhaps the most intellectual of all the subtypes. They also tend to be more disengaged from their feelings than Fives with a Four-wing. Persons of this subtype have problems trusting others, both because they are essentially Fives and because the Six-wing reinforces anxiety, making any kind of risk taking in relationships difficult. However, the coping mechanisms of the Five and Six are somewhat at odds, creating an inner tension between the two components. Fives find security by withdrawing from others while Sixes find security by working cooperatively with others. Hence, their interpersonal relations are erratic, and in general are not an important part of their lives. Noteworthy examples of this subtype include Bill Gates, Stephen Hawking, Sigmund Freud, Simone Weil, Jacob Bronowski, Charles Darwin, Edward O. Wilson, Karl Marx, James Watson, Ursula K. LeGuin, Alfred Hitchcock, Doris Lessing, Cynthia Ozick, Bobby Fischer, B. F. Skinner, Isaac Asimov, Howard Hughes, Ezra Pound, and Theodore Kaczynski.

Healthy people of this subtype are more extroverted and focused on the external world than Fives with a Four-wing. They are not particularly introspective, preferring to observe and understand the world around them. Healthy Fives with a Six-wing observe the world with extraordinary clarity, combining the Five's drive for mastery with the Six's quest for certainty. The result is a gift for drawing meaningful conclusions from disparate facts, and an ability to make predictions based on those conclusions. They are often drawn to technical subjects, engineering, science, and philosophy, as well as inventing and repair work. The Six-wing gives this subtype a greater ability to cooperate with others and to bring a disciplined, persistent approach to their endeavors. There is more aptitude for and interest in the practical matters of life, and with sufficient talent, Fives with a Six-wing can combine their innovation with business savvy, sometimes with very lucrative results. Their attention is more often directed at objects than at people, although they identify strongly with key people in their lives. They may feel things deeply, but are extremely restrained in their emotional expression. In them we find an intellectual playfulness, a good sense of humor, as well as other attractive, lovable qualities. If others have been tested and permitted to come closer, they discover that people of this subtype have a deep capacity for friendship and commitment. There is also an endearing element in their desire to be accepted by others, and even if they are sometimes socially clumsy, others cannot help but be touched by their eagerness to reach out to people.

However, average persons of this subtype generally have problems with relationships. The Six-wing provides good organizational abilities and an endearing personal quality, but also adds to the Five's anxiety and fearfulness. They do not seem to know what to do with their feelings, much less how to express them directly. Hence we find an insensitivity to their own feelings and emotional needs, as well as to the feelings and emotional needs of others. They have little awareness about how they communicate themselves to others. (They are the classic intellectual nerd, the socially inept oddball.) Average Fives with a Six-wing can become extremely preoccupied, theoretical, and absent-minded. They are totally wrapped up with intellectual pursuits and live completely in their minds, immersing themselves in their work to the exclusion of everything else. When interpersonal conflicts arise, average Fives with a Six-wing avoid resolving problems by burying themselves even more deeply in their intellectual work, and by employing passive-aggressive techniques, putting off people and problems rather than dealing with them directly. They can be rebellious and argumentative for no apparent reason, although something may have touched off unconscious emotional associations. Fives with a Six-wing tend to cling more tenaciously to their views and theories (reductionism) and to antagonize people who disagree with them, whereas Fives with a Four-wing tend to reject all meaning (nihilism) and to disturb the certainty of people who seem secure.

Unhealthy people of this subtype tend to be suspicious of people and to have counterphobic, contentious, and volatile reactions to others. They are extremely fearful of intimacy of any sort and can be highly unstable, with paranoid tendencies. Unconsciously seeking rescue, they also fearfully reject and antagonize their supporters. The isolation and mental distortion we see in unhealthy Fives are reinforced by the Six-wing's paranoia, inferiority feelings, and conviction of being persecuted. Neurotic Fives with a Six-wing ultimately become extremely phobic, projecting dangers everywhere while retreating from all social interaction. They may lash out at imagined enemies, sometimes with lethal results. Psychotic breaks and madness are possible.

SOME FINAL THOUGHTS

Taking an overall view of the Five, we can see that there has been a struggle between various pairs of polar opposites: between thinking and doing, between a fascination with the world and a fear of the world, between identification with others and rejection of them, between love and hate. This process of attraction to and repulsion from the environment as a whole began with their ambivalence toward their parents. But unfortunately, what happens is that Fives gradually become so obsessed with defending themselves from potential threats from the environment—that is, from whatever they see as harmful and dangerous—that they also exclude the good. Eventually, there is nothing in the world with which Fives can identify, nothing true or valuable in which they can believe. The final result is total nihilism: there is nothing left to which they can attach themselves.

Like every other personality type which becomes gripped in the downward spiral of neurosis, Fives bring about the very thing they most fear: that they are helpless, useless, and incompetent. The irony is that they have become helpless and incompetent because they have rejected attachment to everything. And by intensifying their involvement with their mental processes, instead of finding security or power, Fives have brought about their own insecurity and powerlessness.

It is a tragic end. If there is something perverse and dark—even demonic—about Fives, it is that to protect themselves they have relentlessly repulsed the world and other human beings. What then is left? Only a fascination with—and a terrifying attraction to—the darkness.

Chapter 8

Type Six: The Loyalist

THE SIX IN PROFILE

Healthy: Able to engage others and identify with them; steadfast, earnest, and affectionate. Trust important: bonding with others, forming relationships and alliances. / Dedicated to individuals and movements in which they deeply believe. Community builders: responsible, reliable, trustworthy. Good foresight and strong organizational ability: natural troubleshooters. Hardworking and persevering, sacrificing for others; they create stability and security in their world, bringing a cooperative spirit. *At Their Best:* Become self-affirming, trusting of self and others, independent yet symbiotically interdependent and cooperative, as an equal. Belief in self leads to true courage, positive thinking, leadership, and rich self-expression.

Average: Start investing their time and energy into whatever they believe will be safe and stable. Organizing and structuring, they look to alliances and authorities for security and continuity. Make many commitments to others, hoping they will be reciprocated. Constantly vigilant, anticipating problems. They seek clear guidelines and feel more secure when systems and procedures are well-defined. / To resist having more demands made on them, they react against others passive-aggressively. Become evasive, indecisive, cautious, procrastinating, and ambivalent. Strong self-doubt as well as suspicion about others' motives. Are highly reactive, anxious, and complaining, giving contradictory "mixed signals." Internal confusion makes them react unpredictably. / To compensate for insecurities, they become belligerent, mean-spirited, and sarcastic, blaming others for problems. Highly partisan and defensive, dividing people into friends and enemies while looking for threats to their own security. Authoritarian, prejudiced, and fear-instilling to silence their own fears.

Unhealthy: Become clingingly dependent and self-disparaging, with acute inferiority feelings. Seeing themselves as helpless and incompetent, they seek out a stronger authority or belief to resolve all problems. Submissive and masochistic. / Feeling persecuted, that others are "out to get them," they lash out and act irrationally, bringing about what they fear. Fanaticism, violence. / Hysterical, and seeking to escape punishment, they become self-destructive and suicidal. Alcoholism, drug overdoses, "skid row," self-abasing behavior.

Key Motivations: Want to have security, to feel supported, to have the approval of others, to test the attitudes of others toward them, to defend their beliefs.

Examples: Robert F. Kennedy, Malcolm X, George Bush, Walter Mondale, Tom Hanks, Bruce Springsteen, Candice Bergen, Gilda Radner, Patrick Swayze, Princess Diana, Julia Roberts, Phil Donahue, Jay Leno, Johnny Carson, Diane Keaton, Woody Allen, Andy Rooney, Jessica Lange, Marilyn Monroe, Oliver North, J. Edgar Hoover, Richard Nixon, Rush Limbaugh, "George Costanza," and "Archie Bunker."

AN OVERVIEW OF THE SIX

Sixes are full of contradictions. They can be dependent on others, yet value their independence. They want to be trusted and to trust others, yet constantly test others to allay their own suspicions. They want the protection of authority, yet fear it. They are obedient, yet disobedient; fearful of aggression, yet sometimes highly aggressive themselves. They search for security, yet feel insecure. They are likable and endearing, yet can be mean and hateful. They are reassured by traditional values, yet may subvert those values.

They want to escape punishment, yet may bring it on themselves. Sixes are full of contradictions because anxiety makes them rico-chet from one psychological state to another. And in response to anxiety, Sixes look to structures, beliefs, allies, and authorities to put their anxiety to rest.

> Our system of education teaches us to put our faith in something else—a corporation, a marriage, a trade, a profession, a religion, politics, something, one might almost say *anything*, which offers us a set of rules we can obey and rewards us for obedience to them. It's safer to be a domestic animal than a wild one. (Michael Korda, *Power*, 254.)

For Sixes, security comes from a rock-of-ages allegiance and an investment of themselves in something outside themselves which they believe will give them stability and safety. Sixes want to feel protected and secure by having something bigger and more pow-erful than they guiding them. IBM will do, but so will the Commu-nist party, or the Republican party, or the church. The doctrines Sixes believe in are important to them, but so is having someone to trust and believe in.

In the Thinking Triad

Sixes are the primary personality type in the Thinking Triad. They are the most out of touch with the ability to make decisions and act on their own without reference to a trusted person, an institution, or a belief system. In a sense, Sixes have difficulty trusting their own minds, their own ability to know what to do without reference to ideas that are not their own. Thus, once Sixes have found some system of thought that seems reliable to them, they must con-stantly evaluate any new ideas that either contradict or alter what they have understood to be true. They are looking for something—a set of guidelines, an authority—to supply them with a direction in life, to tell them what they can and cannot do, to give them more clarity, to put limits on them—in a word, they are looking for secu-rity. Of course, in one way or another, all nine personality types have some kind of relationship with authority figures and need some guidance and reassurance in life, but whether supporting authority, rebelling against it, or fearing it, Sixes seem to have the most issues in this area.

Sixes are among the most puzzling of the nine personality types because they are reactive, fluctuating from one state to another — sometimes the virtual opposite — very quickly. Sixes can be baffling and frustrating because their emotional states and attitudes can be so contradictory: they can be engaging and funny, then cranky and negative; they can be decisive and self-assertive, then, almost in the next moment, indecisive and self-doubting. While they seek the approval of those who are important to them, they resist being in a position of inferiority. They may be obedient, and then openly disobedient, intentionally deviating from what the authority has told them to do. As a result, because Sixes are the most contradictory of the personality types, they are one of the most difficult to understand. They often remain so enigmatic, even to those closest to them, that the most others can say about them is that they are "easy to like but hard to get to know."

The key to understanding Sixes is that they are ambivalent: the two distinct sides of their personalities oscillate between aggressive and dependent tendencies. They feel both strong and weak, dependent and independent, passive and aggressive, sweet and sour. It is difficult to predict the state Sixes will be in from moment to moment. At each Level, they display a personality substantially different from what has gone before and what will follow.

To make matters more complicated, Sixes are not only ambivalent toward others, they are ambivalent toward themselves. They like themselves, and then disparage themselves, feeling inferior to others. They have confidence and then feel hopeless and defeated, as if they could not do anything without help from someone else. They feel weak-kneed and cowardly, then suddenly fill with rage and strike out at others. A double set of dependent and aggressive impulses operates in them, continuously interacting in various complex combinations since Sixes react ambivalently not only to the external authority but to the internal authority, their superego.

As much as possible, Sixes want to avoid being in this anxious, ambivalent state, so they work hard to build structures into their lives to give them stability and continuity. As long as they know what the rules of the game are, and have some sense that they are supported by others in their lives, they can be a consistent, steady presence and accomplish a great deal. But herein lies the problem. Sixes make their internal stability dependent on the stability of their external environment: in other words, as long as everything in their lives is running reasonably well, they feel secure and able to cope with things. As soon as problems or areas of uncertainty arise, however, they are quickly thrown into a storm of confusion and emotional reactions. (For this reason, many Sixes mistake themselves for Fours.) Their self-doubt and suspiciousness arise and Sixes are right back into their ambivalence and unsteadiness.

It is impossible to understand Sixes without understanding their oscillating nature. Maintaining their sense of self requires that *both* sides of their psyches interact with each other. Sixes cannot emphasize one side of themselves and ignore the other—for instance, they cannot become independent by suppressing their dependent side. For better or worse, they are an amalgam of both sides of themselves. When they are healthy, both sides work hand in hand with each other. However, if tension between their two sides increases, so does anxiety, and therein lies the source of many of their problems.

Problems with Anxiety and Insecurity

All three personality types of the Thinking Triad have a problem with anxiety, but Sixes, as the primary type, have the greatest problem with it. They are the type which is most conscious of anxiety—"anxious that they are anxious"—unlike other personality types who are either unaware of their anxiety or who unconsciously convert it into other symptoms. Fives, for example, displace anxiety by distancing themselves from their own experience; Sevens repress it through constant activity. On the other hand, Sixes are aware that they are anxious: sometimes they are able to resist it, and sometimes they succumb to it.

Sixes tend to use two different methods of coping with their anxiety: a *phobic* response or a *counterphobic* response. Sixes who are more phobic often deal with their fears through a dependent stance. They are more aware of their anxiety and turn quickly to others, particularly authority figures, for support. They are more self-doubting and emotionally vulnerable and can resemble type Four. Phobic Sixes believe in keeping a low profile and not causing trouble, especially in those situations to which they have turned for security. They will often pursue a course of appeasement when conflicts arise, and like to stay within well-defined guidelines and procedures. Phobic Sixes are fearful that the people on whom they depend will abandon them.

Sixes who are more counterphobic are much more likely to question, or even rebel against, authorities. They are quicker to confront others and are often more suspicious than phobic Sixes. They are more determined to be independent and resist turning to others for support. In this respect, counterphobic Sixes can resemble Eights. They try to repress their anxiety through action, and in the average Levels, can react strongly and defensively if questioned. They want to know where others stand and may aggressively provoke a response from them to find out. Counterphobic Sixes are fearful that others will try to trick them or take advantage of them. When conflicts arise, they can be highly confrontational and even belligerent. Nevertheless, beneath their bluster, they are just as fearful and anxious as phobic Sixes, but their aggressive behaviors are a reaction to the anxiety rather than a direct expression of it.

It is important to note that no Six is entirely phobic or counterphobic. Rather, each individual person who has personality type Six has some mixture of these attitudes or response patterns, and they are likely to appear in different areas of their lives. For example, one Six may be very aggressive and counterphobic with his or her spouse, but more phobic and dependent in the workplace. In another Six, the exact opposite might be the case. Much of the preference for one of these approaches over the other comes from early childhood. In some cases, the basic approach they were taught was to "turn the other cheek," to be obedient, and to walk away from bullies and antagonists. Other children are taught to be tough, to not let anyone push them around, and to fight back against bullies and enemies. In either case, Sixes, like everyone else, will carry these lessons and experiences into adulthood, but their responses to fear and to potential danger will be a more central issue than for other types. Sixes in general also tend toward being more phobic at certain Levels of Development, and more counterphobic at others. In fact, the two responses seem to alternate, Level by Level, as we will explore later in this chapter.

All Sixes protect themselves by being extraordinarily vigilant so they can anticipate problems in the environment, particularly problems with other people. Their need to question, their attention to details and problems, their need to know where others stand with them—and eventually, their paranoid tendencies—are all attempts to defend themselves from real or imagined dangers.

As a result, Sixes learn to live in a state of constant alertness about their environment. Because of their fear, they train themselves to watch people and the environment in general so that they can foresee events and take protective steps accordingly. Ironically, Sixes must have "danger" on their minds to feel safe: the more paranoid they become, the more completely defended they try to be.

At the root of their anxiety is a continual feeling of being unsupported. Most fundamentally, Sixes doubt that they can support themselves. They do not trust their ability to know what to do, especially when their decisions affect their security. At the very least, they tend to second-guess themselves, making a decision and then fearing that they made the wrong choice. Because they feel unsure of themselves, Sixes look outside themselves for something to support and reassure them. This could be a spouse, a job, trusted friends, the military, a religion or belief system, a therapist, a spiritual practice, a guru . . . the possibilities are as varied as the individual circumstances of Sixes' lives.

Consequently, Sixes must continually monitor their support systems to make sure that they are stable and secure. They worry about how things are going at work, about their investments, about potential legal problems—literally anything that could upset the safety of their world. Particularly, Sixes are compelled to "touch base" with their allies and supporters to make sure that they are still "on the team." Average Sixes often do not know how others feel toward them: they want people to like them, but often doubt that they do. As a result, they test others to discover the attitudes of others about them, constantly looking for evidence of approval or disapproval. And if average Sixes deteriorate into neurosis, they become so suspicious of others that they become paranoid, anxiety-ridden, and so insecure that they cannot function.

Sixes correspond to Jung's introverted feeling type. Even though they belong to the Thinking Triad, Sixes are also emotional, because their feelings are affected by anxiety. Unfortunately, Jung's description of this type is not one of his clearest. Possibly to explain his difficulty in describing this type, Jung says,

> It is extremely difficult to give an intellectual account of the introverted feeling process, or even an approximate description of it, although the peculiar nature of this kind of feeling is very

noticeable once one has become aware of it. (C. G. Jung, *Psychological Types*, 387.)

As we have just seen, it is difficult to describe this personality type in simple terms, because its psyche continually changes. It may be helpful to think of Sixes as "ambiverts," a mixture of extroverted and introverted feelings. This is why they react to whatever they have done, especially if anxiety has been aroused, by doing the opposite to compensate. They then react to this state, and then to the next, ad infinitum. For example, they may be affectionate toward someone; then, fearing that they will be taken advantage of or abandoned, they become suspicious of the very person who has just been the object of their warmth. But, becoming anxious about their suspicions, they seek reassurance that the relationship is still all right. As soon as they receive reassurance from the other, Sixes wonder if they have not been too ingratiating, so they overcompensate by becoming defensive, acting as if they did not need the other person. And on it goes. If you have difficulty understanding someone who is a mass of contradictions, you are probably dealing with a Six.

It is also important to understand that while Sixes are emotional, they do not show their emotions directly—as Twos do, for example—even to those they are closest to. Similarly, Sixes are seldom sentimental, preferring to take a less "rose-colored" view of people and the world. Most healthy to average Sixes are, however, fairly clear about how they feel about things. They know who they love and who they dislike. They are uncertain about what they *think* about things, and they are especially uncertain when it comes to deciding what to *do*. Because of this uncertainty, they become afraid of taking the wrong action or sending the wrong signal. Their minds turn round and round with conflicting thoughts about what they should be doing while they simultaneously try to figure out what the others in their lives are *really* up to. Consequently, ambivalence toward both themselves and others causes them to give mixed signals. Or, to put this another way, Sixes react to their feelings—particularly anxiety—and communicate their reactions rather than their feelings. Except when Sixes are very healthy, others can rarely be certain of what is really on their minds.

This is why achieving independence and emotional stability, especially freedom from anxiety, is so important to them. If they are too compliant, their self-esteem suffers: they feel inferior to others, like someone who can be pushed around. On the other hand, if they are too aggressive in their search for independence, they fear that they will alienate the very people who provide them with security and will be punished in some terrible way. The challenge Sixes face is to find a way of maintaining both sides of their personalities, gradually reducing the tensions between their conflicting sides until they form a reciprocal unit—themselves as healthy persons.

Parental Orientation

As the result of their formative experiences, Sixes became connected with their protective-figures. The protective-figure was the adult in the child's early environment who provided guidelines, structure, and sometimes discipline. This was the person who occupied the traditional patriarchal position in the family. Most often this was their fathers, or a father figure, such as a grandfather or teacher, but in many cases the mother or an older sibling may actually be the protective-figure. As children, Sixes wanted the security of approval by their protective-figures, and felt anxious if they did not receive it. As they grew up, their connection with their protective-figure shifted to an identification with substitutes for this person, such as civil authorities or belief systems from which they could obtain security.

From the perspective of depth psychology, the role of the protective-figure is to help the child break away from the mother so that the child can function independently. Unconsciously, Sixes are looking for people or structures that will help them be more independent. Ironically, the more unsure of themselves Sixes are, the more dependent they become on the people or systems they have turned to for assistance in becoming independent.

Because they are connected to the protective-figure, Sixes powerfully internalize their relationship with that person, whether it is a loving, supportive one, or a difficult, destructive one. They continue to play out in their lives the relationship with the person who held authority in their early childhood years. If Sixes as children perceived that their protective-figure was benevolent, and a reliable source of guidance and encouragement, as adults they will continue to look for similar direction and support from others, be it their spouse, their job, their therapist, or a mentor. They will do their best to please this figure or group, and will dutifully observe the rules and guidelines they have been given. In this case, though, Sixes will feel extremely disappointed and betrayed if the other person or situation violates their trust or fails to live up to their expectation of support.

On the other hand, if Sixes experienced their protective-figures as abusive, unfair, or controlling, they will internalize this relationship with authority and feel themselves always at odds with those who they believe have power over them. They walk through life fearing that they will be "in trouble" and unjustly punished, and adopt a defensive, rebellious attitude as a protection from the cruel protective-figure they project into many of their relationships. Sixes who suffered extremely dysfunctional childhood environments may have been so devalued or ill-treated by their protective-figure that they end up leading self-destructive, wasted lives as they unconsciously live out their protective-figure's negative image of them.

Furthermore, just as Threes abandon themselves to varying degrees to become more acceptable to their nurturing-figures, Sixes abandon themselves to gain the support of their protective-figures. They believe that if they get enough support, they can become independent. This is because Sixes feel cut off from an internal guidance, their own ability to move forward in the world with confidence. They may act this out directly, through a phobic, dependent approach to life, or they may react against it with assertive, counterphobic behavior. Either way, Sixes are not really experiencing their own inner capacity and strength, and must constantly look outside themselves for reassurance, support, and evidence of their ability to successfully engage with life. As Sixes deteriorate, however, either their dependency on allies and authorities or their hysterical reactions to them increase, until they actually destroy their own security.

Because they have been taught not to trust their own inner guidance, Sixes internally question their activities to see whether they will meet the internalized standards of the protective-figure — their superego. Like Ones, Sixes are often trying to figure out the "right" course of action, and they attempt to do this by thinking about how their various mentors, allies, and authority figures would respond to their choices. Sixes may go around and around in this process for days if the decision is a major one, because they are afraid of alienating any of their supporters. It is as though Sixes must regularly hold committee meetings in their imagination to "check in" with the different people with whom they have identified. Highly counterphobic Sixes may well bluster at authorities they see as unfair, but they too need their support network, and do not want to take actions which might jeopardize it. Of course, less healthy Sixes may undermine their system of support because of their hysterical reactivity and paranoia, but they will then go to great lengths to reconnect with some other source of security. In all Sixes, the pattern of orienting themselves to life by obtaining the reassurance and approval of others is one which is deeply ingrained in their nature.

ANALYZING THE HEALTHY SIX

Level 1: The Valiant Hero
At their best, very healthy Sixes learn to rely on themselves. They are in touch with their own inner authority and are able to trust themselves without the nagging self-doubt which plagues average Sixes. They thus have a positive basis for forming balanced relationships with others and, paradoxically, with themselves. They feel secure, accepted, and comfortable with themselves.

Self-reliance is internal, a process of staying connected with one's own inner strength, one's own inner knowing. Once this connection has been made, Sixes are possessed of a clarity of mind that lets them know exactly what they need to do from moment to moment. Furthermore, very healthy Sixes experience in themselves the fortitude and will to accomplish whatever life requires of them. The self-reliance of the healthy Six is a real quality of groundedness in life and in a kind of support that can only arise in the deepest part of a person's soul. It is emphatically not the same thing as reacting aggressively out of fear. The self-reliance of very healthy Sixes arises from a realization of their own intrinsic capacity and value without reference to anyone else. Their self-reliance marks a shift from seeing protection and security residing outside themselves, especially in authority figures, to finding a sustaining faith in themselves and in life that is not a belief but a deeply felt, lived experience. Very healthy Sixes are no longer reactive but mature, their own persons. They have faith that their world is not going to fall apart and that they will be able to cope with whatever life brings. Centered in their own being, and as a result are capable of facing even major crises with equanimity, determination, and grace.

Healthy Sixes are also able to give confidence and courage to others because of their own positive thinking and reassuring presence. Their demeanor communicates calm, decisiveness, and a willingness to work tirelessly for a greater good. They find an indomitable courage within them. Thus, very healthy Sixes are willing to face great dangers to champion others' welfare or to speak out against injustice. (In this respect, they can resemble healthy Eights or Ones.) They are also flexible in their approach to challenges, and can work wonderfully with others, or just as easily tackle problems on their own.

In their relationships, very healthy Sixes achieve a dynamic interdependence, a true reciprocity, which brings out the best in both parties. No one dominates the relationship, and no one is inferior in it. Healthy Sixes are able to support others and be supported by them, to love and be loved, to work by themselves and with others. They are fully cooperative, coequal partners, able to interact with others without anxiety. They feel genuinely secure, because they trust themselves and are consequently able to trust those who are worthy of their trust.

Their deepest feelings are free to emerge, because they have tapped the inner springs of courage—faith in themselves. They no longer reflexively react to situations or their own feelings and so are able to express themselves effectively both personally and in their work. If they have the talent and training, they may become outstanding artists or leaders because they are able to do for themselves those things which sustain and nurture their spirit. Very healthy Sixes are particularly effective leaders because they know what it is like to feel insecure and to look to someone else for help. They are now able to help create genuine security for others. Becoming courageous is a high achievement for Sixes, which is why we see it only in their healthiest state. The courage of very healthy Sixes is all the more praiseworthy because it has been won not merely against external difficulties but against chronic inner doubt. ("The only security is courage."—La Rochefoucauld)

Because anxiety is part of the human condition, it is useful for even very healthy Sixes to remember that they will never be entirely relieved of it. Of course, the more integrated Sixes are, the less anxious they feel, but they also understand that they cannot count on always being totally free from anxiety. Human beings cannot insure themselves against disease, loss, or any of the thousand mishaps of fate. Healthy, self-reliant Sixes therefore do not expect that they will always be absolutely secure, since this is an impossible goal. Rather, they learn to harness the inevitable degree of anxiety which goes with the territory of being human to achieve higher goals.

Level 2: The Engaging Friend

Even relatively healthy Sixes do not always rely on themselves; nor do they feel quite the equal of others. They begin to look for security outside of themselves because, for one reason or another, they fear being abandoned and alone in life. They have lost touch with the support of their own inner strength and believe that they lack the internal resources to survive on their own. They therefore feel they need support from others and that their well-being depends on maintaining secure relationships and structures that will enhance their safety.

Simply put, Sixes are looking for someone or something to trust, because they have begun to lose faith in themselves. At Level 2, this is very subtle, but they have made a distinct change of direction from the self-reliance of Level 1. Sixes begin to scan the environment, trying to find potential allies and supporters or looking for situations that would enhance their security and self-confidence. They move out into the world, looking for ways they can connect with others or get involved with projects. To this end, healthy Sixes develop the capacity to engage others emotionally.

Healthy Sixes have an endearing, personable quality which unconsciously appeals to others. It is sometimes difficult to say exactly what this quality is or how healthy Sixes can so easily engage people. In any case, healthy Sixes know how to arouse strong emotional responses in others, engaging their emotions unconsciously. They have the capacity to get people to respond to them, even though they are usually unconscious of this process themselves.

It may well be that Sixes are able to engage people because of their own genuine curiosity about others and their desire to find mutually beneficial connections. It is as if Sixes were silently asking, "Can we be friends? Can we work together?" Others sense that their friendliness is genuine and so respond positively. Sixes have an inviting, ingratiating quality which stimulates relationships. Even so, their appeal is not always easy to identify, precisely since it can be very subtle—a matter of eye contact, of smiling a lot, and of subliminal body cues—nor is it necessarily overtly seductive or ingratiating in a fawning way.

We might understand their appeal better by observing the same process in children: the qualities of trust, expectation, and love which children display to their parents are the qualities by which healthy Sixes engage others. They are able to communicate the nonverbal message "There is nothing to fear here." They can be extremely winsome, playful, even silly, with a childlike mischievousness about them. Healthy Sixes also possess a droll, self-deprecating sense of humor, teasing those with whom they want to form a relationship. Good-natured bantering is a sign of affection from Sixes, a sign that they feel secure with others and want to become closer.

Besides their natural affability, healthy Sixes are nothing if not reliable and trustworthy. They make it their business to back up their promises or offers with prompt, consistent action. (In this regard, they can be mistaken for healthy Ones.) They do their best to be the person that others can count on, always offering steadiness and common sense. There is a solid, down-to-earth quality to healthy Sixes that is distinct from the healthy qualities of the Five and the Seven, the other two Thinking types. In their search for support, healthy Sixes make it clear that they offer unwavering support themselves.

Along with this steadiness and reliability, Sixes possess an ability to perceive potential threats and problems before they become unmanageable. Their desire for security attunes them to hazards and pitfalls, so they develop a vigilant alertness, scanning their environment for possible problems and taking measures to make sure everyone around them is safe. This talent serves healthy Sixes and the people in their lives well because the world does present many dangers and difficulties that must be addressed.

Naturally, their attempt to build relationships with others can be mutually beneficial and flattering. Others are asked, more by deed than by word, for their friendship, trust, and support, and are offered friendship, trust, and support in return. Further, in close personal relationships with others, spontaneous nurturing and affectionate qualities emerge which can be delightful and emotionally rewarding for both parties. Note, however, that the desire to engage the other automatically puts the other person in the superior position, something which will have significant consequences later on.

Level 3: The Committed Worker

Once healthy Sixes have begun their search for security and have found some people, ideas, or situations which seem reliable and safe, they naturally begin to fear that they will lose their connections with these things, their feelings of protection and belonging. The very act of engaging someone else at least raises the possibility that the attempt will be rejected or that the relationship will not go well. Having to engage others is sure to raise at least a glimmer of anxiety, even in healthy Sixes. They cannot help but realize that, by seeking security outside themselves in the good will and acceptance of others, they are bound to feel some insecurity. They consequently want to strengthen the friendships, alliances, and security structures they have made to ensure that their safety will be maintained. They do this by fully committing themselves to others and to the jobs and projects in which they have involved themselves.

To this end, healthy Sixes become highly practical, responsible people. They bring discipline and persistence to all of their pursuits, as well as a meticulous attention to detail and craft. Sixes want to feel proud of their work, and proud of the contribution they are making to the projects they have committed to. They are highly effective at keeping organizations running, be they major corporations, small businesses, or family budgets. They are the sort of people who make sure the bills are paid and that there is enough money to pay taxes. They are thrifty, industrious, and hard working, making themselves a valuable asset to any company or partnership. In this way, Sixes seek to make sure that there will be a place for themselves in the world, and that their work will keep them relatively safe and secure.

Many Sixes, particularly if they are talented and educated, have a skill for analysis and troubleshooting. Their vigilance translates well into a facility with details and an ability to both give and take directions well. In general, Sixes enjoy working within structures in which the parameters are clearly defined and understood. Within these structures, Sixes feel safe to work creatively and inventively, whether they are computer programmers, engineers, legal professionals, CPAs, or musicians. They often display a highly developed craftsmanship in their work, which indicates the care and skill they put into their projects. For these reasons, and because they are so likable, healthy Sixes, if they are sufficiently talented, frequently rise in their professions. They succeed like the tenacious tortoise who beats the faster, flashier hare.

Healthy Sixes also help the enterprises they have created or joined by bringing an egalitarian spirit and a strong sense of community welfare. They are respectful of others and are able to create a collegial atmosphere in which everyone feels like a partner or a coworker rather than a superior and a functionary. They understand that their security is largely dependent on the well-being of their place of employment and their community. They therefore work cooperatively with others to maintain the institutions and structures which make their community stable and healthy. They will often get involved in local political matters, joining the school board or committees for improving their town or apartment building. Public service appeals to many Sixes because it gives them an arena for many of their positive values. Similarly, Sixes often become interested in politics at some level, not always on a national level, but at least within their profession or local community. They often see themselves as stewards of their work and their environment, and want to do what they can to protect and preserve them.

At the same time, and for the same reason, healthy Sixes are not afraid to raise questions if they sense there is some impropriety going on around them, or if they perceive that others are abusing power within the systems they are part of. Healthy Sixes will work to rally support against injustices or to inform others of problems in the community or environment. As we will see, however, average Sixes tend to lose their nerve in these situations, using passive-aggressive techniques to confront people or situations they do not like, or actually becoming fear-instilling saboteurs of community stability themselves. In healthy Sixes, though, the willingness to question authority reflects a genuine interest in the general welfare and a commitment to integrity and honesty.

On a personal level, healthy Sixes are able to commit themselves deeply to those with whom they have formed special emotional bonds. They devote their energies to the well-being of others and want to have others respond to them in kind. This is why being part of a family of some kind is often important to them, even if it is only a "family of friends." The family is virtually a symbol of the kind of emotional support and stability which Sixes seek. They want to have people they can depend on, to have unconditional acceptance, to have a place where they belong. Having close ties with family and friends makes them feel that they are not alone. Being committed to others diminishes the fear of being abandoned.

Some of the virtues of healthy Sixes are not in vogue in today's "Me first!" "Looking out for number one" society. However, the assets of this personality type—perseverance, faithfulness, honesty, hard work, commitment to family and friends, and to the general welfare of the group—speak for themselves and need no apology.

ANALYZING THE AVERAGE SIX

Level 4: The Dutiful Loyalist

Once Sixes become committed to a person or a group, they may begin to fear doing anything that would jeopardize the stability of the relationship. They become afraid of "rocking the boat," of moving strongly in any direction for fear of wrecking their security. Sixes feel that they have worked hard to put together a lifestyle that seems solid and steady, and they begin to worry about all the things that could go wrong. They consequently try to further strengthen their "social security" systems by working harder to be accepted and approved by their allies and authorities.

Thus, average Sixes take on even greater commitments and obligations, insisting that they can follow through and get the job done. Their anxiety causes them to load themselves down with responsibilities because they want to ensure that their position is secure and that they will not be left without the structures they have labored to build up around them. They want to "cover all the bases," to have all of the angles considered and accounted for, and be ready for any possible problems in the future. The Boy Scout motto, "Be prepared," is quite suitable for average Sixes. At this stage, they may take on multiple sources of employment, or spend their free time maintaining their homes and checking over the family finances. Others wonder if they resent the workloads and pressures they seem to be under, yet Sixes seem eager to fulfill their obligations and duties, finding more work for themselves as soon as their pressure lightens.

In a similar manner, average Sixes become preoccupied with investing themselves, their resources, and their energy in situations and institutions which will continue to support them in the future. For this reason, they are not interested in involving themselves with work, organizations, or institutions that lack a "track record." They will carefully check the credentials of their doctor, their therapist, their lawyer: they will meticulously inspect the background of a car or home before they purchase it. They want to know that if they commit today, the thing they have committed to will be around for the foreseeable future. A certain cautiousness has begun to color their thinking and consequently limit their choices.

At Level 4, much of the self-reliance seen in the healthier Levels of the Six begins to disappear, and average Sixes become more attached to and identified with particular systems of thought and belief which offer answers or make them feel more sure of themselves. At the same time, they may begin to question and doubt their own ideas and thoughts. As this occurs, Sixes start to seek out the reassurance of people who "seem to know what they are talking about," as a way of convincing themselves that their ideas are correct. Simply put, they look for confirmation that what they believe is true.

Most of their need for reassurance can be seen as a symptom of their lack of trust in their own decision-making ability. Instead of making decisions themselves, average Sixes increasingly look for precedents and answers in documents, authoritative texts, or in rules and regulations—"scriptures" of one sort or another. (Average Sixes who function as leaders most likely do so by forming committees and governing through consensus rather than by making decisions independently.) Even when they are observing guidelines and protocols, Sixes second-guess themselves and wonder if they are getting it right. They check in with friends or authorities to make sure that their interpretation is "on track." This can be anyone or anything that the Six sees as authoritative, from a drill sergeant who interprets the army's rules, to a priest who interprets the church's rules, to the law itself, which interprets society's rules. Sixes feel that if they understand the rules, they will be able to avoid criticism and possible punishment. They may choose to break the rules at some point, but they want to know exactly what those rules are and how much they must stretch them before they do.

This does not mean that average Sixes cannot make decisions in some matters, but that they become more conflicted and self-doubting when major decisions arise. Career choices, or decisions which directly affect their families or the stability of their employment become sources of major anxiety. Of course, important decisions are not easy for anyone, but average Sixes can get themselves into real emotional knots over them as they continually reach a conclusion about what to do, and then doubt or negate it. The situation is further complicated because average Sixes resent other people making decisions for them. Thus, they are compelled to go through a storm of anxiety, consultation, and doubt every time an important choice presents itself.

Despite some difficulty with decision-making, however, Sixes at this level are not spineless milquetoasts. They are true believers, who, from their point of view, are merely observing legitimate precepts which should be respected because they have the weight of authority and time-tested traditional values on their side. Average Sixes therefore do not mind getting some form of "permission" before doing things, nor do they mind following rules and official procedures. (Indeed, average Sixes are adept at making the rules and regulations laid down by the authority work for them: having the law or the organization on their side can frequently be very convenient.)

Thus, many average Sixes are comfortable with being traditionalists, organization people, and team players, the main personality type which populates most institutions and bureaucracies—the backbone of groups of all sorts. Instead of being oppressed by having rigorous structure in their lives, average Sixes feel strengthened by it. Belonging to something larger than themselves makes them feel they are not alone but that they are stronger and more secure precisely because they are part of something that is likely to endure. (A fraternity or club or large corporation has this appeal, as do political parties, universities, unions, and religious paths and affiliations.) The security which groups and institutions provide far exceeds the strength of any individual member, and groups are able to achieve many things which individuals alone cannot. Also, close friendships arise ("bonding" on sports teams or among women in an office, for example) which are emotionally satisfying to average Sixes. There are, however, two major drawbacks: first, average Sixes tend to do things because they feel obligated to. Their sense of responsibility begins to wear on them, and they frequently find themselves taking on tasks that they do not really want to do.

Second, identifying one's self with a group, or a political or religious view, tradition, or organization encourages a parochial way of looking at the world, in which everyone is divided into "them" versus "us" groups. Of course, the world is greatly simplified when people know who thinks like they do, who has the same values, who shares the same convictions about religion, country, and politics. But parochialism also creates unnecessary divisions between people. And even within their own group, average Sixes make it their business to find out who is pulling their weight and who is not. They do not like it when others do not take their duties and obligations as seriously as they do. If others are not as loyal or committed, it not only makes them angry, it threatens them.

The loyalty of average Sixes for the people with whom they have identified is almost without bounds. They find it extremely difficult to break their emotional bonds, even should they desire to do so. ("Once a friend, always a friend.") If Sixes have given their hearts away, their love may, in time, turn to hatred but never to indifference. For better or worse, they are never entirely free of their attachments, whether to an individual, a football team, a country, or a church. Their commitments last because their commitments are not superficial choices but deep identifications which become important parts of who they are. Consequently, average Sixes become slower to commit to anyone or anything because they are aware of the tremendous energy they will invest in their commitments. They begin to ask themselves who is worthy of their loyalty.

Level 5: The Ambivalent Pessimist

If they have overextended themselves with the duties and commitments they have taken on, Sixes begin to fear that they will not be able to meet the pressures and demands placed on them. However, they are also fearful of losing the security of their alliances and support systems, and do not want to alienate them. This creates a major problem for them. How can they reduce the pressure and stress they are experiencing without disappointing or even angering the people they have committed to? Sixes then begin to walk a narrow path between the expectations of their allies and authorities and their need to resist having any further demands placed on their shoulders.

Eventually, Sixes realize that they cannot be there for all the people they have committed to equally. Clearly, some people and situations are more central to their needs than others, but the difficulties in making decisions become even more painful as Sixes are forced to decide who to "let down." They therefore want to find out who is really on their side and who will really be a reliable source of support. At this stage, Sixes test others (including their allies and authority figures) to find out how others feel about them. They are anxious about themselves and anxious about others, sometimes reacting defensively toward others, sometimes compliantly. Sometimes, it seems, both ways at the same time.

This dilemma is heightened because average Sixes begin to react strongly to their own thoughts, feelings, and actions. This is actually an intensification of the second-guessing Sixes do at Level 4, but here the emotional content is stronger and more volatile. Average Sixes want to keep a cool head, and as long as things are running smoothly, they generally do; however, when problems arise, their inner order can quickly spin into a high level of nervousness and confusion which often leads to impulsive reactions. In this state, Sixes seem unable to arrive at an appropriate response to their problems. They may decide that they are too obedient, and begin to wonder what others in their group think of them. They may then conclude that maintaining their self-esteem requires that they react *against* people (including the authority), at least occasionally. Average Sixes begin to suspect that they are being taken advantage of or wonder if others really respect them. So they become more guarded and suspicious. While healthy Sixes are reliable and consistent, average Sixes are increasingly evasive and unpredictable, sometimes in small ways, sometimes by denying responsibility and being openly defensive.

Because of these opposing tensions in themselves and their relationships, average Sixes are deeply ambivalent. As the opposing sides of their alternating psyches surface, average Sixes fluctuate between compliant and aggressive impulses, feeling that others like them and then do not. Or Sixes feel that they like others and then that they do not. Knowing their ambivalence toward others, they cannot help but feel that others are equally ambivalent toward them. And knowing how quickly they can turn on someone else, Sixes feel that others may well turn on them. So they become guarded and evasive.

Healthy Sixes are fairly open-minded and curious, and search for ways to connect with others, but Sixes at Level 5 feel overloaded with their responsibilities and are reluctant to take on any more ideas or acquaintances. They become skeptical of new views and ideas, feeling that they have already put a lot of effort into understanding the perspectives and approaches they already know. Thus, they begin to fear and resist change, seeing it as a potential threat to their security and requiring that they add even more to a mind that to them feels overcrowded. Their thinking and their views therefore become more positional and entrenched. They become more out of touch with the ability to reason clearly, and increasingly resort to sputtering assertions and specious arguments.

Because average Sixes are losing touch with their own inner authority, they now have difficulty doing things on their own, making decisions by themselves, or leading others if they are called upon to do so. They go around in circles, unable to make up their minds, unsure of themselves and what they really want to do, dithering around and procrastinating. If they must act, they are extremely cautious, making decisions timidly, covering all bases with legalisms and precedents which both guide and protect them. When something must get done, they wait until the last moment to get started, and then work under great pressure to meet their obligations.

Ambivalence has been described by psychologists, probably because indecision and anxiety bring a lot of patients into therapy.

The ambivalence of passive-aggressives intrudes constantly into their everyday life, resulting in indecisiveness, fluctuating attitudes, oppositional behaviors and emotions, and a general erraticism and unpredictability. They cannot decide whether to adhere to the desires of others as a means of gaining comfort and security *or* to turn to themselves for these gains, whether to be obediently dependent on others *or* defiantly resistant and independent of them, whether to take the initiative in mastering their world *or* to sit idly by, passively awaiting the leadership of others; they vacillate, then, like the proverbial donkey, moving first one way and then the other, never quite settling on which bale of hay is best. (Theodore Millon, *Disorders of Personality*, 244.)

While ambivalence allows Sixes to evade pressure and responsibility for their behavior, it also generates a great deal of emotional stress, causing them to become tense and tired. It is as if they simultaneously had one foot on the accelerator and the other on the brake. Whenever they are under tension of any sort, they complain a lot, and get grumpy and negative. The families and friends of average Sixes know well that their dinner conversations tend to be litanies of complaints about their day and about the people who they believe are causing them problems. They seem grim and fretful, as if everything in their lives was difficult and unpleasant. They "make mountains out of molehills" and can find a problem in any situation or a reason why an idea will not work. Drugs and alcohol, in particular, may be used to ease tensions. However, if Sixes overuse either as a solution to their anxieties, they risk becoming dependent, ironically trading dependency on authorities and belief systems for dependency on something else, perhaps much worse.

At this Level, Sixes become extremely frustrating to deal with because they force others to take responsibility for decisions while sending out mixed signals about their own intentions. One result is that no one can get a straight answer from them: yes means no and vice versa. They may say that they would like to meet someone for dinner, for example, but never agree on a date. They seem to be friendly but are defensive, holding on to people with one hand while putting them off with the other. Their evasiveness forces others to take the lead in everything, while average Sixes continue to react unpredictably, either by going along with or by rejecting what has been decided. If something goes amiss, they complain loudly about it, while avoiding any responsibility for the poor decision.

By being aggressive to others indirectly, average Sixes express the aggressive side of their passive-aggressive nature. For example, a Six who is angry at someone may put that person on hold on the telephone and "forget" to come back. A passive-aggressive employee may frustrate the boss by "forgetting" a deadline or by losing materials. Because of their indirection, passive-aggressive aggressions are never open, so Sixes can avoid responsibility for them.

Passive-aggressive indirection shows up in all their social inter-actions, even in their humor, which now has an edgy, sarcastic note. Passive-aggressive humor allows Sixes to get in a jab at people indirectly, by saying the opposite of what they mean. ("Of course I respect you—I treat you with all the respect you deserve.") People may not understand how caustic Sixes' jokes are until the aggres-sive subtext sinks in sometime later on.

This Level is a turning point in the deterioration of average Sixes. For the first time they realize that their attitudes toward themselves and others are confused. They begin to be suspicious of others and of themselves. The are not sure of their allegiances to others or how others feel about them. They do not know either their thoughts or their feelings; they are not sure what to do or not do. In short, all kinds of doubts and anxieties enter their minds, and once they do, they are difficult to put to rest.

Level 6: The Authoritarian Rebel
Rather than attempt to resolve their doubts and anxieties, average Sixes react against them, shifting to another reversal of behavior. They fear that their ambivalence and indecision may be costing them the support of their allies and authorities, so they overcom-pensate by becoming overzealous and aggressive in an effort to prove that they are not anxious, indecisive, or dependent. They want to let others know that they cannot be "pushed around" or taken advantage of. In fact, their fear and anxiety have reached a critical point, and Sixes are attempting to "pull themselves to-gether" and control their fear through bold, forceful actions. To demonstrate their strength and value to their allies and their enemies, they strongly assert the aggressive side of their passive-aggressive ambivalence in an attempt to repress the passive side.

At this stage, whether they are fundamentally phobic or counter-phobic, Sixes become more openly counterphobic, trying to master their growing anxieties by battling with whatever seems to have aroused them. In its innocent forms, counterphobia is well em-ployed by people to master their fears—for example, children who are afraid of the dark might purposely go into a dark room to over-come their fear. But at this Level, average Sixes are far from inno-cent. Counterphobia makes them overcompensate: they blame and berate whatever threatens them. They become rebellious and bel-ligerent, harassing and obstructing others however they can to prove that they cannot be pushed around. Sixes at this stage are full of doubts about themselves and are desperate to latch onto a position or a stance that will make them feel stronger and dispel their feelings of inferiority.

Their overcompensating aggressions are not a sign of true strength, but a way of feeling superior to others by frustrating or isolating them in some way. Ironically, Sixes, who have been afraid of being cut off from others and left without support, start isolating others and cutting off others' support. At this level, Sixes become masters of intrigue and office politics, and work to knock potential rivals or threats to their security "out of the race." If they are in positions of power over others, they become exactly the sort of authority figure they detest themselves: arbitrary, unjust, and vindictive. They are caricatures of authority, martinets and petty tyrants, full of bombast and bluster, dangerous but weak—and therefore especially dangerous. Instead of being truly strong, average Sixes at this stage make life difficult for people since they are petty and mean-spirited.

We have already seen that average Sixes identify with groups and positions, but at this Level they are extremely partisan and authoritarian, strictly dividing people according to those who are "for us" and those who are "against us." Everyone is reduced to bare dichotomies of them against us, outsiders versus insiders, friends versus enemies. Their attitude is "My country (my authority, my leader, my beliefs) right or wrong." Should their beliefs be challenged, average Sixes see it as an attack on their very way of life. While anxiety is still their underlying problem, at this stage irrational fear and hatred of others is its manifestation.

Authoritarian Sixes are extremely prejudiced and closed-minded in the defense of whatever or whoever they believe is creating their security, reacting with a siege mentality to all outsiders, whom they look on with suspicion as potential enemies. Fearing conspiracies, they will conspire against others. They will use all of their abilities to turn popular opinion against people they perceive as enemies—even against members of their own group who seem to them not to be completely on their side. But because of the dynamics of overcompensation, Sixes ironically often deviate from the very beliefs they have embraced. Sixes who so firmly believe in freedom and democracy become rabid bigots and authoritarians, eager to deny civil rights to fellow citizens. Christians hate, thereby contradicting their beliefs as Christians. The law-and-order person becomes a lawbreaker in the name of the law.

Sixes who are leaders are particularly dangerous at this stage. Less healthy Sixes crop up in politics periodically because they are able to tap into the fears and anxieties of a group and express them, often blaming others for problems but seldom offering substantial, realistic solutions. They may have been sought after as leaders precisely because of their apparent aggressiveness and willingness to go to any length to uphold the group's "traditional values." Unfortunately, they usually turn out to be demagogues, inciting insecurities in others so they can acquire the strength of a mob behind them. Insecurity, not courage, is the impetus here.

At Level 6, it is very difficult for a Six to work *for* something. Instead, their energies are galvanized by being *against* people and things. They are the classic revolutionaries who, having overcome their enemies, find themselves uninterested in the work of setting up a more just system. Indeed, Sixes at this stage *need* enemies to discharge their anxieties. If there was no one to blame for their problems, their guilt and fears about themselves would escalate—a prospect intolerable to them at this Level. If there is no clearly defined enemy, overcompensating Sixes will find one, settling on a scapegoat of some sort as the focus for their aggressions. One of the uglier aspects of Sixes at this stage is their need to have a person or group on whom they can release their pent-up anxieties. Their scapegoats are always assigned the basest motives so that Sixes will feel justified in dealing with them in whatever way satisfies their emotional needs. This can occur in office politics, in a family system, between the sexes (or sexual orientations), or in national politics. Often, unpopular authorities become the scapegoat, the sole cause of all of the Sixes' problems. In other cases, people who are weaker and less supported than the Six become the target. Ironically, the people they typically hate—blacks, Jews, homosexuals, foreigners, "outsiders" of all sorts—often embody the very vulnerabilities and insecurities Sixes fear in themselves. As long as someone must be marginalized it will not be the Six. It is also worth remembering that militancy and bigotry cut in many directions. Obviously, many Sixes are members of minority groups themselves, but at Level 6, they too will find someone to blame and marginalize.

From the Sixes' perspective, their aggressions are justified because they feel that they have been handed a "raw deal." They believe that there are powerful forces who are exploiting them, if not out to destroy them. They feel small and helpless in the face of frustrating and seemingly overwhelming odds. Sixes at this Level believe that there must be some cause for their distress. There must be someone who is ruining their lives and they are determined to defend themselves from that threat. Average Sixes agree with the well-known complaint from the film *Network:* "I'm mad as hell, and I'm not going to take this any more!" Sixes feel besieged by problems and riddled with self-doubt. They are angry about their past and are terrified about their futures. Unfortunately, at Level 6, they take their anxieties out on others, and not only on "outsiders," but also on people in their immediate environment: their families, their pets, weaker coworkers or schoolmates—even strangers who happen to be in the wrong place at the wrong time.

As in the other types, to be functioning at this Level or lower usually indicates that there were extremely dysfunctional elements in the child's environment. Since the Six's issues relate to the connection with the protective-figure, it is likely that the young Six experienced their protective-figure as unjust and dangerous. As a result, the adult Six projects this relationship into the world, seeing threatening, overpowering bullies at every turn. Ironically, because lower average Sixes have unconsciously defined themselves by this troubling early relationship, they end up using many of the same aggressive tactics on others. This is like the person who, as a child, was beaten for crying and who, as an adult, feels aggression and the desire to strike out arise whenever he or she hears a child crying.

It would be difficult to persuade others who did not know them before they became so belligerent and authoritarian that they are, or once were, capable of being likable, endearing people. They are so mean and petty now that they are anything but endearing. Moreover, since the strength of their authoritarian belligerence is built on a shifting psychic foundation, it is not a permanent state. But unfortunately, because their aggressions are real, they may last long enough for Sixes to do serious mischief, or worse harm, to others. As with all of the types at this Level, it is unfortunate that Sixes are in so much suffering, but it is even more unfortunate that their fear causes them to make others suffer as well. If they persist in this behavior for long, however, they will ultimately succeed in alienating many of their allies and making real enemies for themselves. Once this has happened, their position becomes truly threatened and tenuous.

ANALYZING THE UNHEALTHY SIX

Level 7: The Overreacting Dependent

If they act too aggressively or give in to ill-considered episodes of defiance or threat, Sixes may begin to fear that they have jeopardized their security by ruining relationships with their supporters, allies, and authorities. Furthermore, they realize that their words and actions may have created powerful enemies and they will suffer some sort of serious punishment as a result. At the very least, they fully expect to be abandoned by everyone they have depended on. Although they may not have actually run afoul of their supporters, they fear that they have. As a result, they become prey to intense anxiety, seeking reassurances that, no matter what they have done in the past, their relationship with their allies and authority is still intact. (Beneath the armor of the tough authoritarian is a frightened, insecure child.)

Average Sixes who once exhibited a blustering toughness, at moments even feeling that they no longer needed the support of others, have shifted abruptly. Tearful and obsequious, they are disgusted with themselves for not having been tough enough to stand on their own two feet, to defend themselves, to be independent. They feel cowardly because they have not been able to sustain their aggressive stance, although not because they have not tried.

Sixes become trapped in an unhealthy pattern of self-disparagement and massive insecurity which reinforces intense feelings of inferiority and worthlessness, a marked deterioration from the indecision and evasiveness we saw in average Sixes. Unhealthy Sixes are convinced that they are incompetent and unable to do anything on their own. Increasingly anxious, they become clingingly dependent on their allies or authority figures, or, if their friends and protectors have deserted them, on anyone who will take them in.

Healthy loyalty to those they are committed to has deteriorated into dependency. Unhealthy Sixes are massively relieved just to get through their day: taking any decisive, constructive actions for themselves feels impossible to them. As much as they can, they fall back on whatever support systems are available to them. They lean heavily on spouses, friends, or if possible, family, waiting for someone to come along and direct them. They are terrified of making a mistake, lest their few remaining authorities abandon them in disgust. Consequently, they take almost no initiatives, and avoid taking any responsibility for themselves. ("I was just doing what you told me to do"; "The priest said it was all right"; "But my friends were doing it, too.") But while avoiding responsibility frees average Sixes from much anxiety, it tends to jeopardize their own hope of becoming independent, since they increasingly depend upon someone else to make the key decisions in their lives.

Unhealthy Sixes feel absolutely worthless. They whine and complain and disparage themselves so much that they weaken whatever remaining self-confidence they have and become an emotional drain on everyone. Those around them begin to feel insecure and anxious themselves, because Sixes have the uncanny ability to induce their anxieties, as well as other feelings, in others. Their despondency gets people down, virtually forcing others away. Of course, this only makes unhealthy Sixes all the more clinging, more "morbidly dependent," in Karen Horney's phrase, and more difficult to deal with.

They put themselves down constantly, and truly feel inferior to everyone else. ("Anyone who likes me must have something wrong with him.") By disparaging themselves, they seem to be saying "You ought to love me because I am helpless and no good without you." They do not believe in themselves, and they cannot believe that anyone else could either. If someone should encourage them, unhealthy Sixes immediately discount anything positive said to them. They are not so much looking for a pep talk, although that helps momentarily, but for the promise that someone strong and decisive will take over for them—a "good" protective-figure.

At the same time, unhealthy Sixes are still suspicious of people, and are often confused by true acts of kindness toward them. In many cases, Sixes who are this unhealthy suffered from extremely abusive authority figures in their youth, and still respond most strongly to people who treat them in a similar manner. Wise counsel, gentleness, or compassion directed toward them feels alien. While unhealthy Sixes may recognize mentally that good advice and help are being offered to them, they seem unable to trust that anyone would really be kind to them, and passive-aggressively push away those who are trying to get them on their feet.

Sadly, unhealthy Sixes seem to be attracted to the same sorts of people who have caused them to suffer in the past. They fall in with "bad company"—people who make them more dependent, encourage their paranoia, or prey on their insecurity in other ways. Sixes often feel a misplaced sense of camaraderie with other disgruntled "outsiders" with whom they can commiserate and complain. They will also seek out abusive or indifferent people for their romantic relationships, again because they cannot trust benevolence at this point. It is too unfamiliar: it increases their anxiety. ("What does she *really* want from me?") Bullies, addicts, hysterics, and rogues they at least understand.

At work, their colleagues cannot help but notice their insecurity and anxiety. The quality of their performance is poor, because they are too anxious to concentrate and are frequently absent from work due to mysterious psychosomatic problems, little physical breakdowns which put them in bed for a day or two, or on the bottle for somewhat longer. (Any previous problem with alcohol now worsens considerably because unhealthy Sixes need alcohol—or some other drug—to deaden anxiety and take the edge off insecurity.)

Depression becomes a serious problem for unhealthy Sixes. They are terribly anxious, boiling over with fear and tension; yet they are frightened to express what they are feeling, both for fear that their friends will abandon them and because they might lose control of themselves completely. By repressing their anxiety, however, they become increasingly lethargic, depressed, and incompetent. Day by day, their life passes by with their insecurity and dependency growing and their confidence and prospects for the future diminishing. And underneath their depression, their rage and paranoia are growing, too.

The longer Sixes remain like this, the more hopeless and insecure they feel and the more hopeless and insecure they genuinely become. Others may suspect that they are not really interested in solving their problems, since "having problems" and complaining about them function as ways of obtaining reassurances from others. In fact, unhealthy Sixes have a vested interest in maintaining their problems so that someone will come to their aid and give them the security they crave. If that does not happen, or if the person who does come is as unhealthy as the Six is, the picture becomes frightening indeed.

Level 8: *The Paranoid Hysteric*

The oscillating nature of their psyches once again makes itself felt: unhealthy Sixes shift from self-disparagement to become overreacting and hysterically anxious. At the previous stage, unhealthy Sixes were anxious because they disparaged themselves and felt inferior. Now, in addition, neurotic Sixes are anxiety-ridden because they have lost the ability to control their anxiety. They are irrational and panicky when they think about themselves, hysterical and paranoid when they think about others.

Insecurity has escalated into a state of free-floating anxiety so great that neurotic Sixes irrationally misperceive reality, turning everything into a crisis. Neurotic Sixes unconsciously project their own aggressions onto others, becoming paranoid about the aggressions they find. This marks yet another "reversal" in their deterioration, because neurotic Sixes no longer see their own inferiority as the main problem, but the hostility which others apparently have toward them. To put this differently, they shift from fearing themselves to fearing others.

In a sense, the fears of average Sixes are replayed in a more intense form when they become neurotic. Average Sixes want to test others to find out how they feel about them. Neurotic Sixes are positive that the verdict is negative, and are sure that others are out to get them. If their boss is gruff, neurotic Sixes irrationally overreact, becoming certain that they are going to be fired. If they get into a conflict with their landlord, they are sure he will evict them, or hire a hit man to retaliate. They see conspiracies plotted against them everywhere; they feel persecuted by everyone, especially by authority figures who, they are convinced, are trying to punish them for their failures. In fact, neurotic Sixes are in a particularly terrible conflict about authority: because they are so anxious, they need the reassurance of authority figures more than ever; yet, because of their paranoia, neurotic Sixes believe the authority is out to destroy them.

At this level, Sixes are furious with the people they have counted on for letting them down, betraying them, or harming them. They are seething with rage and hatred, but are so fraught with anxiety that they are unaware that they are the source of the terrible feelings they are having. Instead, they project them onto others, since their hypervigilant attention is constantly focused outward, expecting danger at any moment. They believe that their hateful, destructive thoughts and feelings are actually the attitudes of others toward them, and they are determined to save themselves from the hostile "others" that seem to surround them. Their mind has become like a sentry that must stay on guard twenty-four hours a day, lest any intruder get through and destroy what remains of their security.

As a result of projecting their fears and aggressions onto others, neurotic Sixes become terrorized by what they find. Everyone and everything seems dangerous. Mere coincidence becomes conclusive fact for them. Even the most innocent remarks confirm their paranoia. They think a stranger walking toward them on the street is a policeman come to arrest them, or a spy who has them under surveillance, or a madman about to attack. Unfortunately, their delusions only succeed in making their fears all the more consuming. Mere suspiciousness has deteriorated into true craziness— insane paranoid delusions.

Paranoid delusions of persecution may alternate with compensating delusions of grandeur and delusions of reference, the notion that they are being watched by someone important—God or the ghost of a childhood hero, for example—providing neurotic Sixes with a sense of importance. Paranoid elements may also be mixed with grandiose delusions: the FBI is out to get them because they alone know about research into a nuclear antigravity device. Or the paranoid elements alone may dominate their delusional thinking: they become convinced that the telephone is bugged, their mail is being read by the CIA, their food is poisoned, their friends are secretly plotting against them. However, more than ever, paranoid Sixes think that they are more realistic than anyone else. They alone see what is really going on.

They fulminate and rant about their enemies, often picking out individuals that they have never met, or whole groups of people, and characterizing them as monsters that must be stopped. Sixes have always had a taste for politics, but here it can become ugly. Terrified individuals, feeling rejected and fearing that other rival groups will destroy what little security they have left, band together in conspiracies whose only mission is to attack or weaken others. If unhealthy Sixes do not join such groups, or have friends who support such extreme ideas, they often become loners, quietly developing their paranoid theories and waiting for an opportunity to strike back at their perceived oppressors.

It is important to understand that neurotic Sixes are bundles of irrational fears; they look for reasons to be afraid. They live under the cloud of dread, absolutely certain that something horrible is about to happen to them, blowing the smallest incidents completely out of proportion. It is, of course, impossible to reason with them. Everything seems like the end of the world to them, and since they undoubtedly have genuinely serious problems, they are thrown into a panic about everything. Precisely when their problems and failures are multiplying, they cannot cope.

The danger here is that unhealthy Sixes are no longer able to restrain their anxiety and may precipitously lash out at their allies or at strangers who represent what the Six most fears, or even at a hero the Six believes has let him down. In its most harmless forms, this can be a hysterical outburst or attack on a spouse or coworker that may result in an estrangement or dismissal. They may smash furniture, scream, or actually get into physical violence with a friend, associate, or relative who has frustrated them or become a symbol for their fears. In its darkest forms, however, this can manifest as an assassination of a political or popular figure the Six has become obsessed with, the random attack of a gunman in a public place, or the collective insanity of mob violence, gangs, and hate groups.

Fortunately, most Sixes do not get trapped at this level of neurosis, and many of those that do have sufficient support and help to prevent them from allowing their fear to lead them into irreversibly destructive actions. But even if neurotic Sixes do not engage in acts of violence, their terror and paranoia have been unrelenting. This condition becomes insufferable, and Sixes may go one step further to escape their anxiety.

Level 9: The Self-Defeating Masochist

If Sixes really have overreacted to their fears with some precipitous action, or if they cannot stop projecting their fear and hostility onto others, they may self-destructively hasten their downfall to provoke some kind of attention from and connection with others. Further, unhealthy Sixes are certain that punishment from their authority figures is inevitable, so they punish themselves both to expiate for any guilt and to escape, or at least lessen, the wrath of the authority.

They become self-defeating, another reversal. Instead of continuing to be anxiety-ridden, living in dread that something awful will happen to them, neurotic Sixes seek to reduce the threat of the environment by punishing themselves first. They bring defeat and degradation on themselves. Ironically, just as they may once have scapegoated and persecuted others, they now turn their aggression against themselves with the same hatred and desire for revenge.

Neurotic Sixes bring disaster of some sort on themselves not to end their relationships with authority figures, but to reestablish a protective one. By bringing defeat on themselves, they at least save themselves from being defeated by someone else. As painful and humiliating as whatever they do to themselves may be, it eases their guilt and defuses the self-condemnations which might push them to suicide. In a sense, then, they defeat and humiliate themselves so they can be rescued from a worse fate.

This does not always work. Sixes at this level of dysfunction are far from rational, and the methods they employ to punish themselves may result in severe debilitation or even death. They may drop out, abasing themselves as vagrants and living in skid row conditions, thus allowing their health and minds to deteriorate to the point of no return. Other Sixes may similarly punish themselves with excessive alcohol and drug intake, literally flirting with death. Still others may engage in suicide attempts that work more effectively than they had planned.

It is also important to understand that neurotic Sixes are masochistic not because they take pleasure in suffering as such, but because they hope their suffering will draw to their side someone who will save them. Masochistic suffering seeks union with another, as if to say, "Punish me because I have been bad. Then you can love me again."

Wilhelm Reich agreed that behind the masochist's behavior lay a desire to provoke authority figures, but he disagreed that this was in order to bribe the superego or to execute a dreaded punishment. Rather, he maintained, this grandiose provocation represented a defense against punishment and anxiety by substituting a milder punishment and by placing the provoked authority figure in such a light as to justify the masochist's reproach, "See how badly you treat me." Behind such a provocation is a deep disappointment in love, a disappointment of the masochist's excessive demand for love based on the fear of being left alone. (Leland E. Hinsie and Robert J. Campbell, *Psychiatric Dictionary*, 452.)

Even if neurotic Sixes succeed in being punished by someone else, they nevertheless retain an element of control. Hence, their self-esteem is not at absolute zero. They have elicited punishment and gotten the reassurance that they have not been completely abandoned. They are still connected with someone, even if the connection is a painful one. For neurotic Sixes, to be punished by the authority is still to be loved. Someone still cares. This sadly recalls the child who is being beaten and abused by their protective-figure. The relationship may be terrible, but any small child prefers the presence of a horrible parent to being cut off and left without anyone at all to guide them. Thus, masochism avoids the much more threatening problem of being rejected and abandoned, and gives neurotic Sixes a degree of security. When that too is gone, they see little recourse but to end their lives.

THE DYNAMICS OF THE SIX

The Direction of Disintegration: The Six Goes to Three
Starting at Level 4, under conditions of stress, average to unhealthy Sixes begin to act out some of the characteristics of average to unhealthy Threes. Average Sixes are plagued by self-doubt, social insecurity, and a lack of confidence. When they feel particularly unsure of themselves, they compensate for their insecurity by behaving in ways they believe others expect them to, like average Threes. Also like average Threes, they become determined to convince themselves and others of their value, excellence, and capability.

At Level 4, Sixes invest themselves in those alliances, situations, or structures which they believe will enhance their security. They feel obligated to meet others' demands of them, and want their approval and support in return. Increased stress causes them to move to Three, where they become more intent on developing their careers, achieving recognition, and "getting ahead"—all of which serve as buffers against potential loss of safety. Similarly, they know that resources are limited and that there are only so many opportunities to go around, so they become competitive to secure the desired prestige or position for themselves. Also, because of their identifications with their allies and with whatever systems they have turned to for security, they use the esteem they derive from that identification to bolster their egos, and feel competitive with other systems. ("Harvard is better than Yale"; "I use a Mac, not an IBM clone"; "My Cowboys won the Super Bowl again!") Sixes at this Level can begin piling up responsibilities and burying themselves in work as ways of repressing their anxiety. Basically, when their insecurity arises, like average Threes, they start working harder.

At Level 5, Sixes feel pressured by their many obligations, and are ambivalent about many of their work situations and the alliances they have made. However, like average Threes, Sixes do not want to alienate others, or to let others know that they are unsure of themselves or the situation. Thus, they turn on the charm, becoming more "friendly" or "professional" as needed. Like Threes, these adaptations are driven by fear of rejection—Sixes believe there is some behavior that would be more appropriate than their genuine response. They try to win people over by adapting themselves to their expectations, and then gauging their responses. Such efforts are usually unsuccessful: Sixes are not Threes, and others can read the uneasiness under the friendly, professional demeanor. Their positive attitude and cheerfulness seem rehearsed and inauthentic. As Sixes realize that others are seeing through their efforts at appearing confident and "together," they become even more anxious and self-doubting.

At Level 6, Sixes become defiant and aggressive in their attitudes and behavior. They put everyone on notice that they cannot be trifled with, but tend to go too far and bully others. The move to Three at this Level can be seen as a kind of arrogance and high-handedness. Sixes get "big-headed," overestimating their abilities and inflating their accomplishments to compensate for their growing inferiority feelings. They promote themselves, their business, or the causes and ideologies to which they have attached themselves, assuming a superior position and belittling the people they perceive as rivals. They insist that others recognize their talents or achievements, and can become hostile when such appreciation is not forthcoming. Also, like Threes at this level, Sixes may resort to hyping their meager successes or to sexual conquests to fortify their sagging self-esteem. At the same time, the group competitiveness seen at Level 4 has degenerated into hostility and aggression at Level 6. People get into heated fights over football teams, or tear down rival spiritual or political views. Pride in their affiliations has become a frenzied contest for supremacy.

At Level 7, Sixes fear that they have gone too far and have eroded their base of support. They are terrified that their allies or superiors will call them to task for their wrongdoing. Like unhealthy Threes, Sixes attempt to cover their mistakes and will deny any involvement with problems they have created. Often, unhealthy Sixes will continue to offer assistance to others, both personally and professionally. ("I'll get that done for you.") But they are actually too dysfunctional to get much accomplished, and so must deceive people by saying that they have done things that they have not done. They do not necessarily deceive others maliciously, but to escape punishment or abandonment. They believe that they may be able to repair the damage they have caused, or do the work they have claimed to have done, if they can placate others long enough. The fact is, though, that unhealthy Sixes are being untruthful and setting themselves up for greater anxiety and loss of security. Their fabrications become yet another source of pressure and stress, requiring more work and causing more panic.

At Level 8, paranoid Sixes may be getting involved with activities and obsessions which are potentially dangerous and destructive for themselves and others. They live in constant fear that their obsessive hatred as well as any plans of revenge will be uncovered by others. As a result, they become devious and duplicitous, like unhealthy Threes. They are the proverbial "nice, quiet person down the block" who no one pays much attention to until their paranoia erupts in some horrible incident. On a less dramatic level, they may give no indication that they are unhappy with a job or a relationship until they unexpectedly disappear one morning without explanation. Their paranoia may also cause them to create false identities for themselves, or to present themselves to new acquaintances as quite different from who they actually are. It is as if unhealthy Sixes were terrified of being seen without camouflage— one of the last sources of security they feel they have.

At Level 9, Sixes try to punish themselves to avoid being punished by others, but under greater pressure, that may act out the lowest Level of Three behavior, in which their anxiety and rage explode in psychopathic fury. Sixes who go to Three no longer masochistically turn their aggression against themselves; instead, they turn it against others to see them suffer. The authoritarian bigotry and hatred seen in average Sixes returns in a much more aggressive and dangerous form. Deteriorated Sixes strike out at others violently to overcome their inferiority feelings once and for all. They vindictively hurt others, even though their victims may not have been the actual cause of their suffering.

But Sixes at Three remain fundamentally Sixes, and their psychopathic violence is merely another form of self-defeat, but one which demands the strictest punishment. If they have broken the law, Sixes at Three will not succeed in eliciting a response which reconciles them to the other. Instead, they may be imprisoned or executed, or themselves become the object of hatred and revenge.

The Direction of Integration: The Six Goes to Nine

In the simplest terms, Sixes need to resolve their ambivalence and their anxiety about themselves and others. This is precisely what happens when they go to Nine.

Sixes at Nine are much more emotionally open, receptive, and sympathetic toward people, and as a result, their emotional spectrum grows much wider. Integrating Sixes are emotionally stable, peaceful, and self-possessed. They fully overcome their tendencies to be dependent, and instead become autonomous and independent persons on whom others can and do rely. Integrating Sixes are able to reassure and support others rather than seek reassurance and support from others, as we have seen throughout their Levels of Development.

In fact, Sixes at Nine are quite different from even healthy Sixes. A revolutionary change for the better has taken place in the integrating Six: he or she becomes independent and yet, paradoxically, is closer to others than ever before.

One unexpected payoff of this development is that integrating Sixes develop a greater number of friends than they had when they looked to others for protection, either as authority figures or as members of their in-group. No longer reactive to people, they are able to form a stable union with others. Others seek them out because they are so healthy, mature, and well-disposed to people. The playfulness and sense of humor we saw in healthy Sixes has not been left behind, although added to these qualities are the

Nine's sunniness of disposition, optimism, and kindheartedness, traits for which Sixes are not usually known but which they now possess in abundance.

Integrating Sixes at last attain not only security but the ability to trust others, something which has always eluded them. Further, because they now trust themselves, they finally transcend their anxiety and feel grounded and truly at ease in the world.

THE MAJOR SUBTYPES OF THE SIX

The Six with a Five-Wing: "The Defender"

The traits of the Six and those of the Five are in some degree of conflict with each other. The general orientation of Sixes is toward affiliation with others, while the orientation of Fives is toward detachment from people so that they can avoid being influenced by anyone. Sixes and Fives are both looking for safety, but Sixes look to alliances with others and commitment to systems of thought for security, while Fives tend to retreat from others and to tinker with, or even dismantle, established systems of thought. Both tendencies exist in the Six with a Five-wing, producing a subtype which sees itself as fighting for the "little person," while at the same time being drawn to systems, alliances, and beliefs which often contain strong authoritarian elements. Sixes with a Five-wing can seem like Ones because they are serious, self-controlled, and committed to specific moral, ethical, and political beliefs. Like Eights, they can also be rather outspoken and passionate in the expression of their beliefs, with less concern about being liked than the Six with a Seven-wing. Noteworthy examples of this subtype include Richard Nixon, Robert F. Kennedy, George Bush, Malcolm X, Robert Redford, Michelle Pfeiffer, Diane Keaton, Jessica Lange, Bruce Springsteen, Phil Donahue, Rock Hudson, Billy Graham, Walter Mondale, Alexander Haig, Bob Dole, Joseph McCarthy, J. Edgar Hoover, Oliver North, Meir Kahane, and John Hinckley, Jr.

Healthy people of this subtype combine the Six's capacity for organization and personal engagement with the Five's perceptiveness and curiosity. They may have a strong intellectual streak, depending on how much the Five-wing is in their overall personality. Healthy Sixes with a Five-wing often develop technical expertise and are valued as practical problem solvers; they are good communicators, educators, and pundits. They are also attracted to professions such as medicine, law, and engineering; they desire to master a system of knowledge but within a field where the rules and parameters are established and known. They often get involved with political causes and community service. There is a strong identification with the underdog, and Sixes with a Five-wing may become the spokespeople or champions for groups or individuals they see as disadvantaged. Sixes with a Five-wing possess greater powers of concentration and focus than the other subtype, although they can sometimes be perceived as too narrow in their concerns. They are usually shrewd observers of the environment, particularly people, and put a premium on foresight and predicting how others will react. Their perceptions are more original than those of Sixes with a Seven-wing, but because Six is the basic type, they do come across not as intellectuals but as extremely competent, knowledgeable individuals.

The anxiety we see in average Sixes also causes people of this subtype to be more intense than Sixes with a Seven-wing. Sixes with a Five-wing are more independent than Sixes with a Seven-wing, and are less likely to go to others for reassurance, advice, or to solve their problems. They may have one or two mentors or confidants, but in most cases they will "gut out" their problems and anxieties alone. They can be very hardworking and loyal to the systems or people with whom they have identified, but this can lead to strong partisan stances and a competitiveness with rivals. Persons of this subtype tend to be constricted in the expression of their emotions, and are usually more detached, cerebral, and pessimistic. The Five-wing also adds a tendency toward secretiveness and compartmentalization which fuels the suspiciousness of the average Six. As their insecurities escalate, they tend to see the world as dangerous. They become more reactive and aggressive, and will denounce or scapegoat any perceived threat to their security. They see others as potential enemies and fear that people may be conspiring to ruin them. Ironically, they may respond by hatching plots against others.

Unhealthy persons of this subtype become increasingly paranoid and obsessed with maintaining their security, and may go to great lengths to protect their position. They are extremely needy, and may abuse alcohol or drugs as a way of dealing with anxiety and paranoid delusions, as well as of bolstering their inferiority feelings. The Five-wing adds elements of cynicism and nihilism to the fearful mentality of the unhealthy Six, resulting in growing isolation, desperation, and a capacity for sociopathic actions. Intense stress will likely lead to outbreaks of rage and extremely destructive behavior accompanied by breaks with reality. Self-sabotaging, self-destructive actions bring about humiliation and punishment to atone for guilt, although the extent and nature of their self-destructiveness will be hidden from others because of their reclusive nature. There may be strong propensity for violence as well as sadomasochistic tendencies in sexual expression. Murder and suicide are both real possibilities.

The Six with a Seven-Wing: "The Buddy"

The traits of the Six and the traits of the Seven reinforce each other. This subtype is more clearly extroverted, more interested in having a good time, more sociable, and, for better or worse, is less intensely focused upon either the environment or itself than Sixes with a Five-wing. In this subtype, there is also a dynamic tension between the main type and wing. The Six focuses on commitment, responsibility, and sacrifice of personal pursuits for the sake of security, while the Seven focuses on experience, satisfaction of personal need, and keeping options open. (People of this subtype can sometimes seem like Twos.) They can be affable, supportive, and strongly identified with others. Sixes with a Seven-wing are more eager to be liked and accepted by others than the Six with a Five-wing and are also more hesitant to speak out. The Seven-wing adds sociability, playfulness, and enthusiasm, but the Six component can be uneasy with this, so Sixes with a Seven-wing frequently monitor the reactions of others to see if they are behaving acceptably. Noteworthy examples of this subtype include Jay Leno, Tom Hanks, Johnny Carson, Sally Field, Candice Bergen, Gilda Radner, Princess Diana, Marilyn Monroe, Julia Roberts, Mikhail Baryshnikov, Reggie Jackson, Patrick Swayze, Tom Selleck, Ted Kennedy, Andy Rooney, Rush Limbaugh, "Fred Mertz," "Archie Bunker," and "the Cowardly Lion."

Healthy persons of this subtype desire to feel not only accepted and secure with others, but also happy, particularly with regard to material well-being. They have broad areas of interest and often have one or more hobbies or pastimes. People in this subtype are friendly and sociable, taking neither themselves nor life that seriously, or at least not solemnly. Many Sixes with a Seven-wing are attracted to the performing arts (acting, popular music) or other professions that allow them to combine their energetic, interpersonal qualities with discipline and craft (advertising, marketing, managing, law). They tend to be self-deprecating, and if possible, turn their fears into occasions for reassurance, further bonding with others, or even humor. Healthy Sixes with a Seven-wing are usually extremely playful and funny, since a sense of humor is one of their most salient means of coping with life and its tensions. They are generally more extroverted than the other subtype.

Average Sixes with a Seven-wing are also hardworking and loyal, but begin to have problems with procrastination and initiating projects. They tend to depend more on others for reassurance and will usually seek advice from a number of sources before coming to an important decision. If they get conflicting advice, they tend to be more indecisive than the Sixes with Five-wings. They do not handle anxiety, tension, or pressure well and often react by becoming impulsive, grumpy, and peevish. Their sense of humor is used to deflect others, and their passive-aggressiveness to get them out of unpleasant situations. Increasingly, the subtype complains, frets, and turns the Seven's propensity for envisioning options into a tendency to conceive of everything that can go wrong in a situation. At the same time, the Seven-wing causes them to succor themselves with various distractions and compensations. Overeating, drinking, and substance abuse may enter the picture, along with nonproductive "hanging out" (the good ol' boy, the gal who hangs out at the local bar or club). Sixes with a Seven-wing may not take the strong political stands of Sixes with a Five-wing, but they tend to become highly opinionated and quite vocal about their likes and dislikes. Because they are afraid of confronting the real sources of discontent in their lives, however, their anxieties about personal failings or important relationships are often displaced onto helpless "third parties"—the "kicking the cat" syndrome.

Unhealthy persons of this subtype are more disposed to becoming dependent on others, and do not attempt to disguise the depth of their emotional needs. They may become stuck in abusive working conditions while dependent upon other people, addictive substances, or both. Inferiority feelings combine with the desire to escape from themselves. Unhealthy Sixes with a Seven-wing have few means of dealing with anxiety, and as anxiety gets worse, they become increasingly emotionally erratic. People of this subtype are in a flight from anxiety, tending to become manic rather than para-noid. They act out their unconscious fears, flying into hysterical overreactions much more readily than the other subtype, mak-ing them highly unpredictable and reckless. They may alternate between desperately clinging to destructive relationships and lash-ing out at their supporters. This subtype is also subject to debili-tating panic attacks, since anxiety, rather than aggression, has the upper hand. Suicide attempts, as a way of eliciting help, are likely.

SOME FINAL THOUGHTS

Looking back on the deterioration of Sixes, we can see that they have ruined their desire for security. Unhealthy Sixes are self-defeating persons who are their own worst enemies. If they persist in masochistic, self-defeating behavior, neurotic Sixes will likely drive away everyone on whom they depend. They will be aban-doned and alone, the very things they most fear.

There is nothing wrong with forming alliances with others, but it is crucial for Sixes to be aware of the character of their allies, since they have such an important influence on them. Commit-ment to a good person goes far in helping Sixes to be good them-selves; commitment to a person who brings out their aggressions and insecurities will have very bad effects on them indeed.

Sixes fear being abandoned and alone because without at least one other person in their lives they would be completely at the mercy of anxiety. Other people put boundaries on them, governing their fluctuations between anxiety and their response to it, aggres-sion. However, Sixes need some tension in their psyches to main-tain their sense of self. Ironically, then, Sixes interact with people both to control anxiety and to stimulate it. But, of course, anxiety is unpleasant and aggression dangerous, so Sixes also look to others to save them from the consequences of both states should they get out of hand. Thus, their psyches present an insoluble conundrum unless Sixes can find a way to completely break out of it. They must learn that they do not have to react to people or depend on them if they trust themselves. Sixes can trust themselves only if they learn that they have a quiet source of inner guidance within themselves. And by trusting that inner guidance, they find the security, support, and direction they have been looking for.

Chapter 9

Type Seven: The Enthusiast

THE SEVEN IN PROFILE

Healthy: Highly responsive, excitable, enthusiastic about sensation and experience. Most extroverted type: stimuli bring immediate responses—they find everything invigorating. Lively, vivacious, eager, spontaneous, resilient, cheerful. / Easily become accomplished achievers, generalists who do many different things well: multitalented. Practical, productive, usually prolific, cross-fertilizing areas of interest. *At Their Best:* Assimilate experiences in depth, making them deeply grateful and appreciative for what they have. Become awed by the simple wonders of life: joyous and ecstatic. Intimations of spiritual reality, of the boundless goodness of life.

Average: As appetites increase, become acquisitive, materialistic, "worldly wise," constantly amusing themselves with new things and experiences: the sophisticate, connoisseur, and consumer. Money, variety, keeping up with the latest trends important. / Become hyperactive, unable to say no to themselves, to deny themselves anything. Uninhibited, doing and saying whatever comes to mind: storytelling, flamboyant exaggerations, wisecracking, performing. Fear being bored, so keep in perpetual motion, but do too many things—become superficial dilettantes. / Conspicuous consumption and all forms of excess. Self-centered and greedy, never feeling that they have enough. Demanding and pushy, yet unsatisfied, crude, jaded. Addictive, hardened, insensitive.

Unhealthy: Become offensive and abusive while going after what they want. Impulsive and infantile: do not know when to stop. Addictions and excesses take their toll, leaving debauched, depraved, dissipated escapists. / In flight from self, they act out impulses rather than deal with anxiety or frustrations: go out of control, have erratic mood swings, and act compulsively (manias). / Finally, their energy and health is completely spent: become claustrophobic and panic-stricken. Often give up on themselves and life: deep depression and despair, self-destructive overdoses, impulsive suicide.

Key Motivations: Want to be happy and satisfied, to have a wide variety of experiences, to keep their options open, to enjoy life and amuse themselves, to escape anxiety.

Examples: John F. Kennedy, Leonard Bernstein, Steven Spielberg, Malcolm Forbes, Marianne Williamson, Elizabeth Taylor, Mozart, Arthur Rubinstein, Federico Fellini, Dr. Richard Feynman, Timothy Leary, Robin Williams, Jim Carrey, Bette Midler, Elton John, Liza Minnelli, Bruce Willis, Jack Nicholson, Joan Collins, Noel Coward, Larry King, Joan Rivers, Regis Philbin, Susan Lucci, Geraldo Rivera, Howard Stern, Liberace, John Belushi, "Auntie Mame," and "Martha" in *Who's Afraid of Virginia Woolf?*

AN OVERVIEW OF THE SEVEN

It is no great difficulty to see why the life of diverse hedonism is unsatisfactory even on its own terms. Boredom, its ultimate enemy, is unavoidable.... A life devoted to the collection of enjoyable or "interesting" experiences is an empty life. It is not a life of spirit, but one in which spirit disappears in the multitude of diversions.... When we think of it, we all know that those who are in a position to sample life's sweet diversions are no better off in any fundamental way than those who are not. We know that those who have thrown themselves into lives of self-indulgence are often racked with emptiness, loneliness, self-hatred, nostalgia, and yet are unwilling to change. Knowing all this, however, we would be reluctant ourselves to pass up the opportunity for such a life. Why is this so? Because we convince ourselves that we would be judicious in our use of pleasure. We would practice restraint. . . . The life of superficial diversions has great attraction, as does the pastry table for the child. In the latter case it is, we know, because the child is not serious about his eating habits. So it is, also, with us. . . . To throw oneself into indulgence is to say, "All I am is a potential for pleasure. The more pleasure that exists, the greater I am." No one can believe this in earnest, of course, and this is why such a life must rest upon self-deception. (John Douglas Mullen, *Kierkegaard's Philosophy*, 100–101.)

Some of those blessed with the sweetest pleasures of life are in fact *not* "racked with emptiness, loneliness, [and] self-hatred." Some are truly happy and know how blessed they are. Then there are those who seem to be quite happy—at least, they think they are—but they are merely amused and distracted, grabbing after the pleasures of life rather than experiencing happiness on its deeper levels. Finally, there are those who, despite having everything, are bitter and disappointed. For some reason, the possession of wealth and all the good things of life has not been enough for them. Why the differences among these three kinds of people?

All the personality types are faced with the issue of how to "use" the world to its best advantage, although the Seven is the type which most exemplifies this universal problem. How to enjoy pleasure without living for pleasure? How to possess the good things of life without being insensitive to the needs of others? How to live in the world without getting lost in it? For better or worse, the Seven lives out these questions.

In the Thinking Triad

Sevens are one of the three personality types in the Thinking Triad. The nature of their potential problem begins with one of their strongest assets—their agile minds: their thinking is quick and mercurial. Sevens are curious, easily stimulated, and eager for new ideas and experiences. However, the degree to which they are anxious about themselves or their lives is the degree to which their minds race out of control, leading them into a widening circle of unfocused behaviors. There is a powerful link in Sevens between their thinking and their doing. If they entertain an idea about an activity which they believe will be interesting and enjoyable, they want to do it as soon as possible. Ultimately, their minds are speeding along about two steps ahead of them, and they are moving fairly quickly! They tend to spin out of control trying to realize all of their ideas, in a search for satisfying experiences and happiness.

Sevens are readily excited by the environment: they respond to stimuli strongly, throwing themselves into the world of experience with enormous vitality. It is worth noting that, unlike Fives, Sevens focus their thoughts primarily on this world and on the things they want to do in it. Thinking about their possibilities and future activities makes them feel good, and wards off potentially painful emotions and anxiety. Sevens react to everything with such immediacy that whatever they do rapidly leads to more exciting ideas and consequently, more doing.

Experience is their guide to life. Sevens are at home among the tastes, colors, sounds, and textures of the material world. Their identities and self-esteem depend on their obtaining a steady stream of stimulating ideas and impressions. Their personality traits, their defense mechanisms, and their motivations all reflect the fact that to Sevens everything desirable exists outside of themselves in the world of things and experiences. Sevens therefore have very little interest in what they cannot immediately sense. Generally speaking, they are neither profoundly introspective nor especially person-oriented. Instead, they are experience-oriented—extroverted, practical, and urbane. They feel that the world exists for their enjoyment, and that it is up to them to get what they want for themselves.

When they are healthy, their experiences are a source of immense satisfaction to them, and they learn to do many things well because the focus of their attention is on producing something in the environment. However, the focus of average Sevens shifts away from productivity to the possession and consumption of more goods and experiences. They stay busy to keep their level of stimulation high. However, hyperactivity makes happiness ultimately elude them because they do not appreciate anything they do or have. This is why, if they become unhealthy, Sevens are little more than dissipated escapists, acting impulsively and increasingly out of control.

Sevens correspond to the extroverted sensation type in the Jungian typology.

As sensation is chiefly conditioned by the object, those objects that excite the strongest sensations will be decisive for the individual's psychology. The result is a strong sensuous tie to the object.... Objects are valued in so far as they excite sensations, and, so far as lies within the power of sensation, they are fully accepted into consciousness whether they are compatible with rational judgments or not. The sole criterion of their value is the intensity of the sensation produced by their objective qualities....

No other human type can equal the extroverted sensation type in realism. His sense for objective facts is extraordinarily developed. His life is an accumulation of actual experiences of concrete objects.... What he experiences serves at most as a guide to fresh sensations.... Sensation for him is a concrete expression of life—it is simply real life lived to the full. His whole aim is concrete enjoyment, and his morality is oriented accordingly. (C. G. Jung, *Psychological Types*, 362–363.)

Jung's description of the extroverted sensation type applies exceptionally well to Sevens. No personality type is more practical or more widely accomplished than they are. Their positive, even joyous, orientation to the world produces a great deal of happiness for themselves and others. But if their appetites get the better of their ability to control them, average Sevens consume more than they need and more than they can possibly appreciate. They begin to enjoy their experiences less while becoming anxious about obtaining more of everything.

Problems with Anxiety and Insecurity
Like types Five and Six, the other two types of this Triad, Sevens have problems with anxiety, and develop a pattern of thinking and behaving as a defense against it. We have seen that Fives are fearful and anxious about their ability to cope with the external environment and so retreat from it. Sevens are almost the exact opposite: they are fearful and anxious about their ability to cope with their *inner* environment—their grief, loss, and anxiety. As a result, they flee outward into the external environment and seek to interact with it sufficiently to avoid dealing with their internal emotional pain.

Sevens attempt to control their level of anxiety by keeping their attention occupied with ideas and possibilities that excite them.

They keep their mind full of activities that they can look forward to, positive experiences that they know they will enjoy. Every time anxiety rears its head, Sevens are ready with a new adventure, a new book, a workshop they plan to attend, or an exciting new relationship. As long as they can keep their attention occupied with positive expectations, Sevens can hold their pain and anxiety at bay. They do not want to deal with their anxiety or examine its causes in their lives because doing so draws them inward, making them more anxious, while extroversion pulls them outward, toward the environment, repressing anxiety, at least temporarily. They discover that the distractions which their activities provide repress anxiety whenever it threatens to erupt into consciousness, but that they need to keep searching for exciting activities to keep themselves safe from their inner distress. They therefore throw themselves into more and more experiences to avoid having to face anxiety or any feeling of unhappiness.

The problem is that the more Sevens fill up their minds anticipating the fun they will have in the future, the less they are in touch with whatever experience they are having in the present. Consequently, the experience they are currently having cannot really affect them, cannot really satisfy them. This is like the person who has always wanted to see the pyramids in Egypt; however, on arriving at the pyramids, the person is anticipating an exciting dinner in Cairo that night, or thinking about showing friends back home pictures of the trip, and so "misses" actually *seeing* the pyramids. The person's attention is elsewhere, not on the experience that he or she is having. Naturally, this decreases the enjoyment of the experience, leaving the Seven hungry for more.

As enjoyment decreases, average Sevens feel anxious and insecure, leading them to overdo their activities all the more. But as they become hyperactive, average to unhealthy Sevens not only do not enjoy what they do, they become even more anxious and are tempted to dissipate themselves even further. They do not realize that it will become increasingly difficult for them to break out of this vicious circle once they become addicted to staying in motion.

Furthermore, the more anxious Sevens are, and the more pain they are repressing, the more their minds will be "revved up" and the less they will be able to be satisfied by the experiences they are going to great trouble to have. It is as if their minds are walking two or three steps ahead of them. The more anxious they get, the more they distract themselves by anticipating the future and the less their experiences serve to quell their anxiety. Sevens keep fleeing outward into the world of experience as they try to outrun the fear and hurt inside them. But the more they flee, the bigger the thrills they need and the harder they are to sustain.

The flaw in this pattern is that the more average to unhealthy Sevens do, and the more they distract themselves to avoid their pain, the less satisfaction their experiences are able to provide. They do not see that their happiness is precarious and easy to lose, because they neither interiorize their experiences nor control their appetites. Ultimately, if they invest little of themselves in their experiences, Sevens cannot be satisfied by what they do. To their mounting panic, they discover that nothing makes them happy. They then become enraged and terrified because it seems that life has cruelly deprived them of happiness.

Parental Orientation

As young children, Sevens were disconnected to the nurturing-figure, the person in their early development who mirrored them, cared for them, and provided affection and a sense of personal value. This person is often the mother or a mother-substitute, but not always. In some family systems, the father, or an older sibling, provided nurturance to the infant. In any event, Sevens perceived that there was some problem with their nurturing-figure. They did not feel bonded with this person, or feel that the person was a safe and consistent source of nurturance. For a wide variety of possible reasons, Sevens felt frustrated by their nurturing-figures: they did not feel that they could depend on getting what they needed from them. As a result, Sevens try to compensate for the nurturance they feel they did not receive by getting things for themselves.

It is probable that, in most cases, their nurturing-figures did not intend to frustrate them when they were children. Some other childhood deprivation, such as poverty, war, being orphaned, or a long illness, may have shaken their expectation that the good things of life would be given to them. There may have been an absence of the nurturing-figure at a critical stage, or some accident that shook the child's faith that he or she would be adequately supported. It may also be that Sevens naturally need a great deal of contact and stimulation which may be more than the nurturing-figure can provide. Thus, for whatever reasons, the fear of deprivation becomes the fundamental motivation for this personality type. The other side of the psychic coin is that Sevens begin to demand that all their desires be satisfied. Possessing whatever they think will make them happy becomes symbolic of having the nurturing and sense of well-being they feel is always just beyond their grasp.

Problems with Appetites and Aggressions

Average Sevens want instant gratification. They place few limits on themselves and do not want to deny themselves anything. If they see something they want, they must have it. If something occurs to them to do, they must do it right away. If something gives them plea-sure, they want more of it immediately. Their appetites are strong, and the lengths to which they go to gratify their desires allow us to characterize Sevens as aggressive personalities. However, since they are also insecure, the picture is mixed: they enlist their aggressive impulses to stave off their anxieties and insecurities.

Sevens also typically get into conflicts with people by putting others in the position of having to place limits on them instead of doing it themselves. Whatever self-control average to unhealthy Sevens have must come from outside themselves, either from others who are forced to say no to them, or from reality itself, which may well frustrate their desires. If they are frustrated, Sevens become enraged because it unconsciously raises the memories of their real or imagined childhood deprivations. Those who frustrate average to unhealthy Sevens are not likely to forget the anger they arouse, or the depth of the need Sevens unwittingly display.

When Sevens are healthy, however, they concern themselves with the satisfaction of their genuine needs rather than the gratifi-cation of every desire. They are productive, adding to the world instead of merely consuming it. They become accomplished, mak-ing the environment yield more of its riches for themselves and for others. They are also unusually happy people because they are able to truly assimilate their experiences, getting in touch with their feelings and with themselves.

But as they deteriorate toward unhealth, Sevens allow their appetites to run amok, and they become greedy, selfish, and insen-sitive to the needs of others. They care only about their own gratifi-cation. The terrible irony is that since unhealthy Sevens interiorize nothing, nothing can satisfy them. They are like drug addicts who need a larger and larger "fix" to maintain their artificial highs. In the end, unhealthy Sevens become so indiscriminate in their search for happiness that they fly totally out of control, both in their actions and their ability to repress their ever mounting anxiety. Panic overwhelms them because they have nothing solid within to anchor themselves to. The type which affirms life so completely when it is healthy becomes, when it is unhealthy, the type which is most terrified by the very conditions of life.

ANALYZING THE HEALTHY SEVEN

Level 1: The Ecstatic Appreciator

At their best, very healthy Sevens have enough faith in reality to allow themselves to have contact with the environment without attempting to make it supply them with anything. Rather than escaping from themselves into the chattering "entertainment" of their minds, they stay present to their experiences, moment by moment. In this way, each moment of their lives becomes a source of nourishment and profound joy. They discover that whatever life holds is enough to satisfy them—if they assimilate it into themselves. Moreover, reality deeply experienced makes them not merely happy but ecstatic, impelling them to go beyond the mere acceptance of reality to affirm life as it is. ("I love life unconditionally!"—Arthur Rubinstein)

In affirming life, they allow the mystery, and the precariousness, of human existence to make an impression on them. But rather than feel anxious over the inherent fragility of existence, very healthy Sevens celebrate life for what it is. Possibly for the first time, they are able to perceive something beyond the outer surface of life to the possibility of a metaphysical reality they have never glimpsed before. Affirming reality in the depths of their souls is a special achievement for Sevens, sweeping them up into something beyond mere psychological happiness into an ecstasy that goes beyond words and feelings. They sense that there is something holy about life which is to be revered and respected. Filled with wonder, lost in admiration, they fall on their knees to give thanks, and praise.

They are tremendously grateful for everything, starting with the inexplicable fact of existence itself. Life is so wonderful, awe inspiring, and astonishing that very healthy Sevens can find something good in everything, even in those things which they never thought would make them happy. The incredible richness of existence has a profound effect on them, transforming Sevens from within. Their inner life—the spiritual life—becomes a reality to them. Thus, even the dark side of life, and the fact that life will end in death, is no longer so terrifying because this, too, is part of the existence they now embrace. Paradoxically, just when Sevens are able to embrace life most, they are least attached to it or to anything in it.

Because they understand that everything is a gift, not something which exists for their own gratification, they learn to appreciate things as they are in themselves rather than as objects to be consumed. They stop putting conditions on life. ("I'll be happy when I get that new car.") Life ceases to be about waiting for things that will make them happy and becomes an appreciation of all the gifts and experiences which are available right now. Thus, very healthy Sevens acquire faith in the essential goodness of life. ("Consider the lilies of the field . . . they toil not, neither do they spin.") And they discover that, when all is said and done, no matter what they have, it is enough to make them profoundly happy if they use it rightly. They do not have to push to acquire experiences or possessions, since each moment, if it is comprehended, holds the possibility of satisfying their deepest needs. They will not be unhappy if they focus on what is truly best in life—not apparent goods, but real goods, things of value which endure.

When very healthy Sevens are in this state of ecstatic affirmation, they are continually surprised by reality, since there are dimensions to it which they have never experienced before, a wonderful irony for those who think they have experienced everything. Their ecstasy, the greatest high they have ever had, can be experienced over and over because reality cannot be exhausted. There will always be enough for them. They cannot be deprived.

Level 2: The Free-Spirited Optimist

Even healthy Sevens do not always live at the high degree of psychological balance found at Level 1. Some degree of anxiety enters the picture: Sevens begin to lose faith in life's abundance and begin to fear that there will not be enough of what they need. This change is very subtle, since Sevens at Level 2 are still extremely positive, energetic people. However, rather than fully assimilating their present experiences, they begin to anticipate future experiences. They begin to think about the things that they want to do, or about how to acquire the experiences or things that they believe they need to be happy. Thus, they remove themselves one step from the immediacy of their experiences, and so are less satisfied by them.

Because they are so outwardly focused on the world around them, healthy Sevens are open to experience in a way unparalleled by any other personality type. The sensory world excites them, and they want their excitement to continue for as long, and in as many pleasurable ways, as possible. Their psyches are charged by the tangible world, immediately closing access to their unconscious experiences because they are instantly aware of, and respond to, external reality.

Healthy Sevens see themselves as happy and enthusiastic. They like being happy and make psychological happiness, the feeling of euphoria, the goal of their lives. They are delightful company because they are almost always in high spirits. Their vitality, vivacity, and joie de vivre are infectious, making people feel stimulated by being in their company. They are genuinely fun to be with since they are so upbeat and exuberant. Other people simply cannot help but be caught up in their high spirits. ("Energy is eternal delight." — William Blake)

Sevens at this Level have remarkably quick, avid minds. Like Fives, they are extremely alert, have a wide-ranging curiosity, and enjoy learning about new things. Given sufficient intelligence, Sevens have wonderful linguistic skills: they are adept at languages, witty and quick with repartee, and gifted with the ability to apprehend form and structure quickly, from the language of music to that of the eye — color, shape, and design. Sevens often have excellent memories, since everything registers on their minds like light on film: one brief exposure and they have it. Instantly, and effortlessly, they remember stories, anecdotes, musical scores, lines from movies, and history. They tend to learn things quickly and easily, which sometimes becomes a problem for them in the lower Levels. When things come too easily to them, they sometimes fail to appreciate or develop the many gifts they possess. On the positive side, however, their eagerness to explore the world around them leads them to try many things, and gives them a wide variety of skills. Sevens, in general, enjoy thinking about doing things, thinking about experiences rather than abstract concepts. In many ways, their inner life is a catalogue of their experiences.

Although healthy Sevens have strong likes and dislikes, they are extremely positive about everything, as long as they remain healthy. They "think young" and have a remarkable youthfulness about them, even when they have grown older. They are also extremely resilient, able, like a phoenix rising from the ashes, to rebound from unavoidable setbacks and disappointments. Sevens never let things get them down for long; they seem to have a way of making the most of whatever situation they are in. ("If life gives you lemons, make lemonade.")

Along with their positive attitude, healthy Sevens are extremely free-spirited. They have a wonderful spontaneity, and can respond rapidly to changing situations. When they are healthy, they are not particularly wed to any specific plans, often preferring to "see what comes up." They have a strong sense of adventure, and are not afraid of trying something new. Sevens at this Level also are easily able to laugh at themselves, and so are not embarrassed when they cannot do something well. Falling down on the ski slope or playing a new instrument awkwardly is OK with them. They are not self-conscious about these things, seeing them all as part of the learning process.

In short, Sevens seem to be blessed with an enormous physical vitality, with the capacity to be recharged by everything that happens to them. Their every contact with the world invigorates them; every experience seems to enlarge their capacity for more experience.

Level 3: The Accomplished Generalist

Healthy Sevens begin to worry that they will not be able to sustain their happiness and excitement. The fear of deprivation is never far away, and they want to make sure that they will be able to obtain whatever experiences or things will make them happy. As a result, healthy Sevens develop a realistic, pragmatic attitude about life. They know that if they want to have the freedom and financial means to have a satisfying life, they are going to have to be productive, and at Level 3, Sevens are amazing in their creative output and in the amount of work they generate.

Combining their great vitality and enormous enthusiasm with practical good sense, healthy Sevens contribute something valuable to others by being extraordinarily productive and creative people, achievers who do well at whatever they focus on. They are generalists, multitalented, enjoying a dazzling array of skills. They are so good at what they do that Sevens become bridge builders from one area of experience to another. They know a tremendous amount about a wide variety of subjects, particularly practical ones, cross-fertilizing their many areas of interest.

As a group, healthy Sevens are probably the most capable of the personality types. If they are exceptionally intelligent, they may have been precocious children. But whether or not they are out-standingly gifted, Sevens are usually much more accomplished than their years or experience would lead others to expect. A large part of this is a consequence of the extroversion of their psyches: virtually all their attention and energy is focused outward into the world. Sevens are not distracted by introspective ruminations which might cause them to withdraw from practical action. On the contrary, they are eager to get on with new projects. In fact, as we have seen, one of their defining hallmarks is that they are not afraid to try something new. Their delight with the world always leads them back to the world. The result is that they constantly acquire new interests and new skills, as if by osmosis.

Healthy Sevens are enviably at home in everything: they may know several languages, play a number of musical instruments, be exceptionally competent in their professions, and cook well, ski, know their way around art, music, the theater, and what have you. Quite literally, the whole world seems to be at their disposal. In fact, Sevens develop many of these skills because of their willing-ness to jump into activity and because they are realistic about the skills they will need to accomplish things. A Seven scanning the want ads in a newspaper will not be discouraged about the require-ments for typing and word-processing skills: they will learn how to type and use a word processor.

The more healthy Sevens accomplish, the more they are able to accomplish—skills beget more skills. Exercising a skill leads them into new areas, and their abilities mount exponentially as Sevens do more and more with them. For example, a Seven may learn to play the piano and a singer might ask him to accompany her. The Seven might then become interested in vocal coaching, and an oppor-tunity might arise to direct a local opera company or conduct an orchestra—and a career might be launched. Another Seven might enjoy telling stories to his or her brothers and sisters and decide to write some of them down for publication. Before long the short sto-ries grow into a book, then to novels or movie scripts, which may lead to screenwriting or becoming an actor. One thing always leads to another, and as long as Sevens are involved with what they are doing, then not only do they delight themselves, but what they produce is a source of delight and enjoyment for others as well.

One of the enduring sources of their pleasure involves introducing their enthusiasms to others. Whether the object of their enthusiasm is a painting, a favorite dish, a piece of music, or an idea, healthy Sevens enjoy sharing their excitement. Healthy Sevens want others to have a good time and to appreciate what they appreciate. This delightful trait rightly endears them to many people.

It is important to understand that healthy Sevens can accomplish a great deal because they can prioritize their activities and set limits for themselves. They know where satisfaction and fulfillment lie, and are willing to make the sacrifices necessary to achieve them. As long as Sevens are prioritizing and really allowing themselves to get fully involved with their projects and experiences, this can be a fruitful and healthy approach to life. However, anxiety in Sevens starts to cause a restlessness, a fear that what they are doing is not satisfying enough.

ANALYZING THE AVERAGE SEVEN

Level 4: The Experienced Sophisticate

Since their experiences are so gratifying to them, Sevens begin to fear that if they focus on only one or two things, they will miss out on others, so they begin to want more of those things which have made them happy. This is not an unreasonable desire, but in colloquial terms, "their eyes get bigger than their stomachs," and all their appetites increase. The result is that average Sevens literally become more experienced, trying everything at least once so they can see and do it all, and therefore not feel the anxiety which results from depriving themselves of anything.

The difference between healthy Sevens and average Sevens is that healthy Sevens are more interested in producing and creating, while average Sevens are more interested in consuming and entertaining themselves. They cast their net wider to have more and different sensations. Average Sevens place a premium on their freedom to go places and do things. They lament that there is not enough time in life to do all of the things they want to do, and they begin to fear that they will lose the possibility of having the things and experiences they believe will make them happy. Their desires increase for ever new and better things, from owning a large house and a fine car to traveling and entertaining extensively. In short, average Sevens want more experiences and more possessions, because they think that more of everything will make them happier.

Again, the basic problem for average Sevens is the anxiety that they are missing out on something more exciting than what they are doing. ("The grass is always greener on the other side of the fence.") Further, they worry that the activities they are already engaged in may not remain sufficiently stimulating to hold their anxieties in check. When this occurs, Sevens become restless, and want to move on to another activity or experience which promises to be more interesting. This is like the person who is engaged in a fascinating conversation at a party, but begins to overhear another intriguing conversation nearby. At this point a choice arises: does the person stay focused on the conversation she is already having, or does she excuse herself and join the other conversation? Average Sevens will attempt to listen to *both* conversations for a while, but in the process, they will get less satisfaction out of either of them. Thus, anxiety causes average Sevens to move from one interesting area to another, but does not allow them to linger with any of them long enough to really assimilate them.

Sevens at this stage are usually unaware of their anxiety, labeling it instead as "boredom." Ironically, for a type so positive and engaged with life, Sevens talk about boredom more than any other type. This is because boredom means more to Sevens than it does to other types. When Sevens say they are bored, what they are often actually saying is that there is insufficient energy or stimulation in their environment to keep them from feeling anxious. Painful feelings or discomfort threaten to emerge into consciousness, so Sevens feel they need to "change the scenery."

As a result of this orientation, average Sevens begin to accumulate a lot of experience. They are the people to consult to learn about the latest movies, the best local restaurants, or the most interesting personal-growth workshops. Sevens love to talk, and they enjoy telling stories and sharing their adventures with others. They may travel a great deal, and often enjoy compiling lists of the many places they have been, taking satisfaction in the growth of the list. If they enjoy reading, their purchases of books will exceed the rate at which they can finish them, often resulting in a stack of partially finished volumes on their nightstands.

Sevens at Level 4 are still productive, although they are less focused. They tend to keep themselves busy, filling up their schedules and creating backup plans if one of the main events of the week should fall through. Sevens are generally good at multi-tasking, and at this Level, enjoy the thrill of juggling the different activities, tasks, and diversions that comprise their lives. The sheer variety of their activities is extremely appealing to Sevens, and they do their best to keep their experiences fresh and diverse.

In some Sevens, the quest for experiences translates into a love of acquiring material possessions. Generally speaking, however, it is the *acquiring* of the possession that Sevens enjoy. Thus, shopping, looking at catalogues, and fantasizing about a new car or fur coat or stereo system is often more satisfying than actually having the item. Once the object has been purchased, it loses its excitement, its newness, and Sevens are busy looking for something else. If they have sufficient funds, they may become worldly sophisticates and connoisseurs in the process, people who have "class" and know how to live a life of glamour and elegance. Those Sevens who have less money may acquire less, but they are not necessarily any less acquisitive.

On the lower levels, this type is the lover of tangible reality, with little inclination for reflection. . . . To feel the object, to have sensations and if possible enjoy them—that is his constant aim. He is by no means unlovable; on the contrary, his lively capacity for enjoyment makes him very good company; he is usually a jolly fellow, and sometimes a refined aesthete. In the former case the great problems of life hang on a good or indifferent dinner; in the latter, it's all a question of good taste. Once an object has given him a sensation, nothing more remains to be said or done about it. It cannot be anything except concrete and real; conjectures that go beyond the concrete are admitted only on condition that they enhance sensation. The intensification does not necessarily have to be pleasurable, for this type need not be a common voluptuary; he is merely desirous of the strongest sensations, and these, by his very nature, he can receive only from outside. What comes from inside seems to him morbid and suspect. . . . If normal, he is conspicuously well adjusted to reality. That is his ideal, and it even makes him considerate of others. As he has no ideals connected with ideas, he has no reason to act in any way contrary to the reality of things as they are. (C. G. Jung, *Personality Types*, 364.)

As Jung notes, average people of this type are by no means unlovable; they are bons vivants, unashamedly in search of the good life. Sophisticated banter, lightheartedness, and gaiety are the order of the day. Sevens are typically excellent hosts; they love to throw cocktail and dinner parties, entertaining their guests in as fine a style as they can afford. They know fine food and how to cook well—or which caterer is best. Within their means (or a little beyond them), they are always fashionable, and usually stylish. Average Sevens know the best and take pleasure in creating a rich, luxurious atmosphere for themselves, their families, and friends. Their dream is to have so much money that they do not have to worry about having money.

However, the style and level of opulence can vary greatly among average Sevens, depending upon how refined their pleasures are, the amount of money at their disposal, their socioeconomic group, education, and intelligence. Some Sevens may be debonair and chic, socialite trendsetters at the newest restaurants or at opera and theater openings. On the other hand, if their finances do not permit it, some average Sevens may have to settle for something less lavish, although they still acquire whatever possessions and experiences they can afford. They may go to movies instead of the theater, or to Europe only once a year instead of three or four times, as they would like. Instead of nightclubs, they may go to ball games and shopping malls. Instead of diamonds, rhinestones. The important thing to average Sevens is the constant acquisition of new, enjoyable experiences. ("I want it all!") Yet none of their prizes ever seems to deliver what it promises: nothing they acquire seems to be quite what they are looking for.

The danger for all average Sevens is that as their appetites grow, they become less discriminating about their experiences, and become mere consumers rather than connoisseurs. Their appetites always increase faster than they can be satisfied.

Level 5: The Hyperactive Extrovert
The more they do, the more average Sevens become indiscriminate about the variety and quality of the experiences they allow themselves. They fear the slightest moment in which nothing is going

on because anxiety may have a chance to register in their minds (the dreaded "B" word). They shift from sophistication to uninhibitedly throwing themselves into constant activity to maintain their stimulation and, therefore, their sense of self. They are in perpetual motion, flinging all their energy outward in a centrifugal flight from themselves as they search for ever new experiences. Their credo becomes "I do, therefore I am."

Because they do not say no to anything, average Sevens cram as many experiences into a day as twenty-four hours will allow. They want constant variety and are always looking for something new and different to do to amuse themselves. The faster the pace, the better. They are not interested in thinking about their behavior or in pausing for a moment's reflection amid the swirl of their activities. They literally do everything fast—eat fast, talk fast, think fast—so they can get on with the next event. Average Sevens get so used to life at 120 mph that cutting back to merely 100 would be boring and frustrating.

The pleasure principle is their guiding principle. Everything should be *fun*! If it is not, they immediately lose interest and move on to something else. Sevens are gregarious, outspoken, and flamboyant, public personalities who like nothing more than to be in the company of other "fun people." To hear them tell it, everything they do is "wonderful!" "fabulous!" or "sensational!"—three of their favorite all-purpose adjectives. ("The play was sensational and the acting was fabulous and the staging was absolutely wonderful; then we went to a fabulous restaurant and had a sensationally fabulously wonderful time!") The pace of their activities may leave others a little breathless, but average Sevens like staying active and "on the go" and wonder why others cannot keep up with them. After all, they feel that there are only so many hours in the day, and there are so many new things yet to do.

There is an unmistakable oral quality to Sevens, and many of their favorite activities center around the mouth. Talking, eating, drinking, smoking, laughing, wisecracking, and gossiping are typical—usually undertaken at the same time, if at all possible. They are, for example, the most talkative of the personality types, saying anything that pops into their heads. Their lack of inhibition makes Sevens very funny, and since they have usually done so many different things, they have a raft of stories which they tell in colorful language and with great verve. Sassy and irreverent, they take nothing seriously, and turn everything into a joke as a way of dealing with their anxieties and problems.

There is also something of the performer and comedian in average Sevens. Many professional comedians are Sevens; the source of much of their comedy is the insecurity and anxiety which underlies their feelings about life. Their humor, like their lives, depends on staying uninhibited and censoring themselves as little as possible. There is nothing subtle about average Sevens: they let others know precisely what is on their minds, even at the risk of shocking other people's sensibilities. While they may offend some, others find their brashness and outrageousness refreshing.

As funny and gregarious as they are, average Sevens are not usually the best conversationalists because they do not listen to anyone. They want to be the center of attention, to have others listen to them, laugh at their jokes, and be interested in what they are interested in. But they do not reciprocate with genuine interest. ("Oh, that's nice. Now, let me tell you what *I* did today.") They also jump around from one topic to another as new thoughts cross their minds, interrupting others to keep the flow of talk moving. Even getting into heated arguments is a way of creating excitement, of keeping up the level of stimulation, and of having fun.

All of this intense activity can be understood if we remember that Sevens at this Level are working harder to repress their growing emotional pain and anxiety. In a sense, they are trying to distract and entertain themselves so that their attention will stay occupied. However, they want the environment, including other people, to distract and entertain them too. If their surroundings are not sufficiently exciting to keep them "up" and distracted, they pump out more energy and razzle-dazzle to "jump-start the environment." They want to whip up other people's energy so that they too will be a source of fun and entertainment.

The problem with their hyperactivity is that it encourages superficiality and triviality, since average Sevens do too many different things to do anything well. Ironically, for all they do, average Sevens are not very perceptive about their experiences because they do not stay with them for long. They are either doing something else (reading the program during a play) or they are off to the next event, too busy to reflect on what they have just done. At most, they give something a one-line review, and that's the end of it. ("The food was all right, but I've had better.")

As gifted and intelligent as they often are, average Sevens throw away many opportunities to do something worthwhile. Instead, they stay on the surface and dabble around. Although they do not like to admit it, they can be frivolous and glib. The great capacity for accomplishment which we saw in healthy Sevens has deteriorated into merely being facile. They are no longer connoisseurs but dilettantes. (They may still sing, but not well, since they do not practice; they learn a few phrases of French, then move on to Russian; they take up needlepoint, then painting, then photography, then the piano. But they never become accomplished at anything because they do not stay with it long enough.) Once an activity requires concentration or effort, average Sevens get bored and move on to something new. They rationalize their superficiality by thinking of themselves as jacks-of-all-trades but, as the saying aptly goes, they are now really masters of none.

The bright, swift minds of Sevens now work against them. Repressed anxiety causes their quickness and openness to become a tangential thinking style. Their thoughts and ideas ricochet off one another in a lightning-fast frenzy of free association. In certain situations, this can be harnessed for brainstorming or for entertaining others, but Sevens at this Level begin to walk around in this state of mental flux all the time. Concentration and focus become increasingly difficult for them, and they possess a limited attention span. This begins to undermine their capacity to be productive, because they are unable to follow through with their many good ideas. Lots of exciting creative projects are hatched in the minds of average Sevens, but unless someone else steps in to manage them, few of them are ever realized. Average Sevens still have tremendous energy and substantial creativity, but they are frittering it all away, scattering their force, and on some level, they know this.

A noteworthy degree of neediness begins to enter the picture. Healthier Sevens are independent and enjoy striking out on their own adventures. If others want to join them, so much the better. But average Sevens begin to fear being alone because they are afraid of the feelings that might emerge if they were by themselves. Furthermore, their characteristic banter, jokes, and hyperactivity would be strange without an audience. Without someone else to react to them, Sevens would realize how hollow many of their activities have become.

Their professional work also suffers, because doing a good job requires concentration, and average Sevens do not give their time or attention to anything routine. Their minds are elsewhere, on more pleasurable activities. Or they are off on long lunch breaks, shopping, or on vacation because they are exhausted from their whirlwind schedule. This is a turning point in their development because their high level of activity is not so much productive as it is merely busy and restless. They cannot sit still; they must have something to do every minute, even on vacation. (Being in a cabin by the seashore would drive them crazy, unless the cabin were in downtown Rio.) They are easily distracted. Indeed, they build in distractions for themselves to avoid becoming bored. They cannot stand silence—the stereo and the television are both on while they talk on the telephone. Sometimes they are on even when they sleep.

Personal assimilation is now largely missing in average Sevens. They have little grasp of the subjective element, how their experiences affect them. They are more interested in how many movies they attended in a week than in what the movies meant to them. Since they consume experiences only to keep their level of stimulation high, average Sevens appreciate very little of what they do. And because they do not assimilate their experiences in any depth, Sevens ironically become less interesting—less developed and more infantile—as human beings. Interpersonal conflicts often result because their company is less satisfying to others. Relentless activity gets tiresome.

Level 6: The Excessive Hedonist

At this stage, average Sevens feel the tremendous pressure of their growing grief and fear trying to erupt into consciousness. They become extremely anxious about being frustrated in any way, so they demand more of everything, especially more of whatever once distracted or pleased them. (No longer content with a Cadillac, they must have a Rolls and a Jaguar; one vacation is not sufficient, they must have two or three.) They now become greedy and pushy, insisting that others cater to them so that all their cravings are satisfied immediately. ("I want *more*—and I want it *now*!") They have no tolerance for physical or emotional discomfort, or for any kind of inconvenience. They demand the instant gratification of all of their desires.

Having a lot of money is a very important value to most Sevens at this Level so they can get whatever they want whenever they want it. They typically spend most of their money on themselves, usually running up large debts in the process. They cannot say no to anything, and they see no reason to delay gratifying themselves when, with credit cards, they can have anything they want. Sevens who do not have a lot of money will make acquiring it their top priority, either by marrying money or by making enough money to support themselves in the style to which they have become accustomed. Marrying for love may be a fantasy ideal for them, but materialistic Sevens do not let love, or the absence of it, stand in the way of getting what they want.

Their lifestyle is frankly excessive, one of conspicuous consumption and ostentatious display. By this stage, average Sevens are voracious consumers. ("I see what I want and I go after it until I get it.") Greed is the capital sin of the Seven, and nowhere is it more apparent than in a gluttonous pursuit of pleasure so immoderate as to be obscene. They go too far with everything, pushing beyond actual need and good taste into the realm of wretched excess. ("If one thing is good, two are better.") Ironically, the sophisticated connoisseur becomes garish and vulgar as he or she deteriorates into the crasser forms of extravagance.

Excess touches every area of their lives, including the measures Sevens take to protect their health and youthfulness, which are very important to them. ("You can never be too rich or too thin." — the Duchess of Windsor) They tan themselves until their skin looks like leather and they need cosmetic surgery. They eat and drink so much that they need to go to a fat farm or get a tummy tuck, or dry out at a sanatorium. Female Sevens tend to overdress and wear so much makeup and jewelry that they look cheap and brassy, even though they may have spent a fortune on their wardrobes. Male Sevens usually look nouveau riche and flashy, sporting loud colors and patterns—all very expensive, but reflecting doubtful taste.

Of course, any of the personality types can be excessive once in a while, but excessiveness is a hallmark of Sevens at this stage because they consciously put no limits on themselves, even when their hedonism would be well served by a degree of moderation. At this stage, Sevens are purposely immoderate and inordinate. ("Nothing succeeds like excess.") Profligate and wasteful, they consume and then cast aside once they have gotten what they want. Their attitude is, "I have mine, so what do I care about anyone else?"

Even so, average Sevens still need others around them because they cannot stand being alone. However, friends and people in general are essentially incidental to Sevens at this Level: they continue relationships that contribute to their enjoyment and drop without regret those which do not. Their marriages may last only a year or two; less serious relationships a considerably shorter time. Once the newness wears off, Sevens want to move on to something else.

Despite all they have, they are jealous of those who seem to have more than they do. They are also extremely self-centered and insensitive about the welfare of others, except as it bears on their own convenience or comfort. Sevens at this stage are not interested in sharing what they have with anyone else, and they do not want others to depend on them. They feel that others should take care of themselves just as they do. Beneath whatever veneer of sophisticated manners may remain, they are as hard as nails.

At this Level, Sevens are unwilling to deal with the consequences of their actions. They leave many messes and hurt feelings in their wakes, expecting that others will clean up after them. They respond to criticism with a cavalier attitude that denies any responsibility for the damage they may have done. ("It's not my problem.") In fact, their resistance to feeling their own pain makes them insensitive to the pain of others: whether they have inflicted it or not is almost irrelevant to them. They are determined not to let others "bring them down," and as far as they are concerned, guilt or remorse are just bad feelings they do not want to deal with.

It goes without saying that putting their own gratification before everything else makes them poor parents, because they are too self-centered to really care about the needs of their children. (At this Level, male Sevens are certainly not sensitive, and female Sevens are far from the mothering type.) Rather than allow children to interfere with their lifestyle, they may choose to have an abortion or put a child up for adoption. Having a family ties them down and makes demands on them, circumstances they want to avoid.

The problem Sevens unwittingly create for themselves is that they become so used to immoderation that nothing *can* satisfy them unless it is taken at an excessive dosage. They need more and more of every kind of stimulation for anything to have an impact on them. To get the kind of high they want but are unable to attain naturally, they may begin to be sexually promiscuous or use drugs (especially cocaine and alcohol), or spend great sums of money for new, more expensive toys. But here again, they create problems for themselves because they are addictive. Sevens easily become dependent on a source of stimulation, no matter what it is—television, going out, sex, or drugs. Once they get used to something, they are hooked—and suddenly cannot do without it.

The pity is that average Sevens at this stage completely lack a sense of real happiness. They have much more than they really need, and have done more than most, yet they are not enlarged by their experiences. In fact, just the reverse is true: they are emotionally hardened and increasingly unsatisfied. Unfortunately for them, they are also insatiable. Habitual excess has made them literally "unsatisfiable." What was at healthier Levels a pursuit of pleasure is now really a flight from pain. Although they still like to talk about all of their "fabulous" exploits, others cannot help but notice the anguish and desperation driving all of their "fun."

ANALYZING THE UNHEALTHY SEVEN

Level 7: The Impulsive Escapist
At some point Sevens may begin to notice that the activities they are pursuing are not bringing them much pleasure. In fact, the reverse is more often the case: their excesses are causing them more misery all the time. The recognition of this fact could get Sevens out of their dilemma, but if their avoidance of anxiety gets the upper hand, or if they are already carrying around more emotional pain than they can cope with, they may fly into a state of impulsive escapism, discharging their anxiety by acting it out in aggressive and irresponsible ways.

Since they do not reflect on their experiences, unhealthy Sevens are usually at a loss to figure out why they are so unhappy and dissatisfied, particularly since they are spending most of their time doing the things they want to do. But they are only aware that they are unhappy, so they begin to strike out at whoever or whatever seems to have frustrated them and denied them what they want.

Unhealthy Sevens continue to stay in motion—actually, in flight—like a surfer riding the crest of a wave before it breaks. They become utterly dissipated escapists. The uninhibited hyperactivity we saw in average Sevens has deteriorated into completely indiscriminate behavior, the feeling that anything goes if it promises to make them happy or to help them relieve their pain and anxiety.

They may throw themselves into sexual escapades and drinking or drug binges until they are utterly debauched. They may try increasingly depraved sexual practices because unhealthy Sevens are always looking for new thrills, and a new avenue of escape from themselves. They become so dissipated that they cannot, and do not want to, center themselves or make real contact with anything.

At Level 7, even the appearance of enjoyment has vanished. Although they may still crack jokes and talk about "having fun," their voice has an unmistakably angry edge to it. Unhealthy Sevens are hostile and bitter, and they go about their "pleasures" joylessly and automatically, as if they were merely going through the motions. They are even more anxious about being alone, and so have no qualms about pressuring others to participate in their self-destructive debaucheries. ("If you don't want to get drunk with me, get the hell out of here.")

We have already seen that Sevens are addictive personalities in that they become dependent upon whatever has given them pleasure or has eased their anxiety. The potential for addiction to various forms of "uppers" (so that they can enjoy themselves) and "downers" (so that they can relax and lose consciousness without feeling anxious) becomes very great. By now Sevens will almost certainly have abused every kind of stimulant and tranquilizer they could get their hands on in their pursuit of happiness, gradually becoming unhappier every step of the way.

At this stage Sevens are so terrified of their subconscious grief and suffering that they are even afraid of falling asleep. They want to avoid the window of vulnerability, the state of openness to their unconscious that occurs just before they fall fully asleep. They often run themselves to exhaustion, staying up days at a time if necessary, so that when they finally stop, they will quickly lose consciousness. If that is not enough, they will also employ sleeping pills or alcohol, then jolt themselves into action again the next morning with major doses of caffeine or more powerful stimulants. Like Sixes and Fives, unhealthy Sevens have become hypervigilant guards, but in this case, the frontier they are scanning for danger is their own subconscious.

If they are frustrated for the slightest moment, they become extremely angry, saying and doing things which are insulting, coarse, and ill-considered. They are like spoiled children becoming rude and offensive if others do not give them what they want, impulsively saying whatever comes to mind, no matter how untrue or hurtful. Others usually find their behavior obnoxious and abusive, not that they can do very much about it. Unhealthy Sevens do not give a damn whether they hurt anyone's feelings or ruin an occasion. If something is not to their liking, they throw tantrums, start screaming, or otherwise create a "scene" to vent their rage.

Having no capacity to inhibit their impulses, they act out, doing whatever they are motivated to do at the moment. If they are angry, they will grab something and throw it across the room; if they are sad, they will burst into tears. If they feel like insulting someone, they will do so without hesitation or embarrassment. Unhealthy Sevens hold nothing back because their only way of dealing with anxiety, aggression, or any other disturbing feeling is to give in to it, discharging it right away.

Of course, acting like this not only often gets them their way (others are embarrassed into silence or shocked into acquiescence) but provides another form of instant gratification by discharging tensions. Nevertheless, by acting out their feelings, unhealthy Sevens reinforce impulsiveness, making things worse for themselves in the long run. Furthermore, impulsiveness reveals how infantile and emotionally immature they are. As a result, few people can stand being around them for long—which only frustrates and infuriates unhealthy Sevens all the more.

Lastly, at this stage the defenses that Sevens have erected against their pain are breaking down. For significant periods of time, their grief and hurt emerge into awareness, and they are not able to muster enough energy and activity to suppress them. Without the full capacity of their energetic minds to protect them, Sevens do what others do when faced with feelings they are unable to process—they get depressed. And because Sevens have spent most of their lives avoiding pain and depression, their dark periods are all the more debilitating because they have not developed many ways of coping with these states. Sevens may not stay as chronically depressed as some of the other types, but they feel their depressions acutely, because such emotional territory is alien to their sense of self.

Consequently, unhealthy Sevens want to get out of their pain and back on their feet as soon as possible. They see nothing romantic about their suffering, and want to reconnect with the environment so as to escape their depression. Unfortunately, at this

Level they may be too emotionally distraught to get back into action in a balanced way, and instead become manic.

Level 8: The Manic Compulsive

Because of their bouts with depression and the diminishing enjoyment of their favorite pastimes, unhealthy Sevens fear that they may be completely losing their capacity for pleasure. They are losing even the possibility of real happiness. As a result, they deteriorate from impulsiveness to mania, into a total flight from themselves. Unhealthy Sevens are willing to do *anything* in order to feel something. As much as possible, they hurtle into wild activity in an effort to remain functioning well enough to keep from experiencing the full brunt of their anxiety and shame. And more than many of the other types, they may be able to give the impression that they are somewhat functional, at least for a while. Nevertheless, neurotic Sevens wreak havoc in the environment and their relationships because they are completely out of control and extremely unstable, both in their behavior and in their moods. They are as erratic as the path of a tornado, and just as unpredictable.

The hyperactivity we saw in average Sevens has deteriorated into a neurotic mania where moods, ideas, and actions shift rapidly. Their mood may swing from belligerent hostility to tearful remorse to a feeling of elation, all in the space of a few minutes. Naturally, others find this sort of thing very difficult to cope with, and if they try to reason with neurotic Sevens, or put limits on their "high spirits," Sevens react in any number of unpredictable and dangerous ways.

Although their mood is usually high, Sevens are actually delusionally elated, having a characteristically unnatural, compulsive quality to their temperament. They feel higher than high, on top of the world, giddy with excitement. They talk loudly and rapidly, as if they are on amphetamines. They feel that they can do anything, and so may squander great sums of money on grandiose plans they cannot actually carry out. Or, because they do not stop to consider the consequences, they may use dangerous doses of drugs and alcohol to maintain their feelings of elation.

It is also typical for manic Sevens to throw themselves compulsively into all kinds of different activities so that they can maintain their defenses against becoming depressed. These compulsive activities can take many different forms—from compulsive shopping or gambling, to nonstop, compulsive alcohol and drug binges, to compulsive eating, to compulsive sexual activities. Their compulsive behaviors can also result in serious accidents for themselves or others, such as drunk driving, drug overdoses, or mishaps from various "daredevil" escapades. Even formal "manias" such as kleptomania (the neurotic impulse to steal) may be part of the picture, depending on which objects their impulses are directed toward.

If neurotic Sevens do not realize that they have become delusional, it is because they do not understand the degree to which they are out of control. From their point of view, their only defense against anxiety is to act it out before it has a chance to register in their minds. There is a certain logic to this, since, through their manic activities, neurotic Sevens are able to create new (although delusional) sources of experience against which they can discharge their anxiety. Thus, completing their plans is not the point: having avenues of escape is.

However, what neurotic Sevens cannot appreciate is that they are now in a very dangerous situation. Their minds are like beads of water skittering on a hot iron—slowing down would be the end of them, or so they believe. If they were to lose the ability to stay in constant anxiety-dissipating motion, they would become even more seriously depressed, precisely what their manic activity is staving off and why this is called the manic-depressive defense. Moreover, the compulsiveness of their activities inevitably begins to get them into trouble of one sort or another. Other people (and reality itself) must necessarily frustrate them, eliminating the routes which they can take to escape from themselves.

Level 9: The Panic-Stricken "Hysteric"
Manic Sevens eventually reach a point where they have "consumed" everything in their environment, leaving them nothing upon which to ground themselves. The anxiety they have been able to repress by staying in motion finally breaks into consciousness. But now there is nowhere to go, nothing to hold on to. The result is that they become hysterically afraid, as if they were being pursued by a raging beast. They are "hysterical" in the popular sense of the term—panicked, trembling, unable to act or do anything to help themselves, so great is their terror.

Those hardened, worldly people who seemed entirely capable of taking care of themselves are suddenly devastated by a flood of anxiety from which they can no longer escape. Their defenses crumble instantly and completely, leaving neurotic Sevens prey to an overwhelming amount of anxiety. Of course, any amount of anxiety is extremely threatening to even average Sevens since it comes from their unconscious, a territory unknown to them. But this is all the more true of neurotic Sevens and they suddenly feel as if they were being swallowed up. The tangible world which once seemed so solid is not solid enough to save them from the unnameable dread engulfing them as their unconscious breaks into consciousness.

Once their final defenses collapse, all of the painful, terrifying subconscious material assails them: grief, guilt, trauma, desolation, confusion, and anguish all come crashing into awareness. Further, because unhealthy Sevens have spent almost all of their energies avoiding these feelings, they are completely at a loss for how to cope with them. The result is an absolutely paralyzing terror. Sevens are afraid to move, afraid to think lest they increase their suffering more.

In times of panic such as these, neurotic Sevens experience in their waking hours the kind of terror normal people experience momentarily in nightmares, from which they fortunately awaken. And it is precisely by waking up that normal people recontact reality and are thus able to re-repress their terror. But this is not possible for neurotic Sevens at this Level. They are already fully awake, and there is nowhere for them to hide. They feel claustrophobically paralyzed with fear, terrified of annihilation, of going mad, and of being trapped in endless torment with no way out.

The manic and reckless activities which are common to the unhealthy Levels of this type often push their physical endurance to the limits and beyond. Many unhealthy Sevens find themselves in conditions of severe physical breakdown. Whether the source is an accident caused by their heedless mania, drug or alcohol abuse, sexually transmitted diseases, or breakdown caused by overtaxing the body, the result is the same. Sevens are no longer able to flee their anxiety by leaping into action, and their options for "escape" are severely curtailed.

One of the most terrifying aspects of their anxiety is that the source of their terror is still unnameable—and is therefore extremely difficult to deal with, much less resolve. The reason is that Sevens have habitually given themselves to an externalized life, to one of ever increasing experiences and stimulations, and they have, as a result, become totally unequipped to get in touch with themselves. As they deteriorated down the Levels, they were, in a sense, "buying time," hoping that their unwillingness to deal with their fear and pain would have no negative consequences. Now they realize that they were wrong.

THE DYNAMICS OF THE SEVEN

The Direction of Disintegration: The Seven Goes to One

Starting at Level 4, average to unhealthy Sevens under stress begin to act out some of the characteristics of average to unhealthy Ones. We have seen that average Sevens resist having restrictions placed on them and want to be free to pursue whatever excites them at the moment. On some level, they recognize that they are going to have to focus their energies if they wish to continue having the means to enjoy themselves. When their calendar of activities starts to get out of hand, however, Sevens begin to feel the need to work harder and restrain themselves like an average One. Although some measure of self-restraint is useful to Sevens at this point, it is coming from the wrong motivation, and therefore has limited effect. Sevens feel obligated to impose limits on themselves, but then feel frustrated and rebellious about these impositions. The usual result is that Sevens end up doing more of what they were trying to limit.

At Level 4, Sevens are interested in acquiring a wide variety of new experiences and entertaining themselves. They are eager to explore whatever seems exciting and fresh to them. Like average Ones, they like to educate others about their experiences, zealously reporting on a new workshop or book, or warning their friends about an inferior restaurant. Their enthusiastic conversation, however, can quickly turn into debate, particularly if the other person does not seem to appreciate the excellence of what the Seven has found. At the same time, because they want to ensure that they will have the means to pursue the many exciting possibilities they see around them, they begin to force themselves to stay on track. They do this not because they genuinely are engaged in a particular activity like exercise or homework, but because they feel they should be. Consequently, Sevens feel more frustrated and anxious. They are certain that they are missing out on something more enjoyable.

At Level 5, Sevens are becoming more indiscriminate and restless. Their energies are scattered and some of their spontaneous outbursts are causing others to react negatively to them. When they go to One, they feel they need to rein themselves in and so become more self-controlled and rigid as a way of holding their impulses in check. They can swing suddenly from a boisterous irreverence to a grim seriousness. They can become brusque and impersonal with people, and increasingly impatient with what they see as others' incompetence. Ultimately, their self-control does not work very well because it is actually another way of resisting their real feelings. The only feeling that does emerge from the move to One is increased anger and resentment that their needs are not being met.

At Level 6, Sevens are determined to satisfy their cravings and quell their anxiety. They are self-centered and demanding, and under stress, as they move to One, can become highly critical and sarcastic with people who do not drop everything to take care of their desires. They also become very perfectionistic, both in their expectations of the service they expect to receive from others, and of their own accomplishments. Average Sevens know that they are losing the opportunity to achieve things with their lives, but end up judging their own efforts as inadequate before giving them a chance. Similarly, they become increasingly perfectionistic about their environment. Nothing is ever satisfactory. No one ever gets it right. They find themselves in a continual state of frustration, seeing little that they can take delight in. They scold and nitpick at others for disappointing them and vent their frustration with condescending, sarcastic comments.

At Level 7, unhealthy Sevens are desperate to escape their fear and pain, and engage in self-destructive, dissipative behavior. Here, the move to One exacerbates their bitterness and resentment. When others confront them about their irresponsible lifestyle, they respond with vitriol and rage. They are absolutely inflexible about their activities: no one can change their minds. Further, despite the almost total lack of direction or self-control in their own lives, unhealthy Sevens are extremely intolerant of others' quirks and weaknesses. The once joyful person has become a nasty misanthrope, detesting people and seeing only the worst in them.

At Level 8, the impulsiveness of Level 7 has degenerated into mania and recklessness. Unhealthy Sevens are careening out of control and are dangerous to both themselves and others. When they go to One, they throw all their energy into some direction or plan by which they hope to regain a sense of control. Self control— a way of centering themselves and of finding emotional stability— is what they most need, and going to One seems to offer it. They may try to impose an order on their wild impulses through some obsessive activity or fetishistic belief. They may become completely fixated on an idea that they believe will rescue them from their disintegration, or they may come to believe a particular person or object is causing all their distress. In either event, the move to One at Level 8 signals a last-ditch effort to stop the juggernaut of their anxiety, but because it is usually based on delusions and does not bring a balanced focus to their energies, at best it only buys them some time.

Moreover, going to One does not work, because the rallying point around which deteriorated Sevens hope to find some kind of salvation for themselves is entirely outside themselves, acting ironically as a kind of psychological lightning rod for their destructive impulses. Rather than help Sevens suppress their destructive impulses or deal with them constructively, the person who has become the expected means of salvation becomes instead the focus of the hatred which Sevens have for those who have frustrated their desires in the past.

Thus at Level 9, all the energy they formerly invested in the environment in the pursuit of happiness implodes into a core of hatred, both for reality and for those who have frustrated them. They suddenly streamline their existence, intensifying their interest in a person or thing into an obsession. Going to One supplies them with a rationale by which they can mercilessly root out anyone or anything that seems to be the origin of their frustration and pain. Punitive impulses and the vilest condemnations of others are all part of the picture.

Deteriorated Sevens are dangerous not only because they are impulsive and violent, but because their thinking is disturbed. Now, in a fit of hysterical passion or a moment of temporary insanity, they may well kill or severely injure the very persons they turn to. Even if they are not homicidal, deteriorated Sevens may become violently abusive to their children or spouses. If they succeed in killing or injuring others, their manic defense may finally give way to severe depression, with suicide the ultimate result.

The Direction of Integration: The Seven Goes to Five

Because they have already attained psychological balance, integrating Sevens no longer fear that they will be deprived of happiness. When healthy Sevens go to Five, they become involved with things in depth. By internalizing their experiences, integrating Sevens create the anchors they need to find stability and security in their lives.

The gratitude they feel for life when they are very healthy leads integrating Sevens to want to know more about what has made them so extraordinarily happy. It is no longer enough just to experience the world, they want to know more about it. The focus of their attention has shifted away from themselves (their experiences and their immediate happiness) to the world around them. Integrating Sevens become more respectful of the integrity of everything, understanding the world as existing for purposes other than their personal gratification. They are no longer the consumers of the world but its contemplators. Their sense of gratitude blossoms into a feeling of wonder and curiosity about creation.

Integrating Sevens have by now progressed far from their tendency to be dissipated escapists. Sevens at Five concentrate on their experiences and are rewarded for their efforts, gaining vastly in the satisfactions they receive. New depths of experience become available to them as they center themselves. They become more expert, more profoundly penetrating reality and allowing reality to penetrate them. Integrating Sevens bring the full force of their considerable skills and talents to bear upon their experiences. They do not lose their healthy enthusiasm or productivity when they go to Five. On the contrary, integrating Sevens may well become even more productive by contributing something original to the world.

THE MAJOR SUBTYPES OF THE SEVEN

The Seven with a Six-Wing: "The Entertainer"

The traits of the Seven and those of the Six are in a certain amount of tension with each other: Sixes are oriented toward people, while Sevens are oriented toward things and experiences, quite capable of fulfilling their own needs themselves. In both types, however, there are dependencies; Sixes depend on finding approval and security from others, while Sevens depend on the environment to make them happy. People of this subtype will attempt to find satisfaction for themselves, while looking to other people as additional sources of stimulation and happiness. Sevens with a Six-wing are perhaps the most gregarious and outgoing of all the subtypes. The adventurous search for experience in the Seven combines with the desire for security through connection in the Six, and the mix produces individuals who enjoy encountering and interacting with other human beings. Sevens with a Six-wing are more relationship-oriented than Sevens with an Eight-wing, who tend to be more experience-oriented. Noteworthy examples of this subtype include Robin Williams, Steven Spielberg, Arthur Rubinstein, Mozart, Leonard Bernstein, Elizabeth Taylor, Marianne Williamson, Dr. Richard Feynman, Timothy Leary, Bette Midler, Liza Minnelli, Elton John, Peter Ustinov, Carol Burnett, Shelley Winters, Jim Carrey, Jonathan Winters, Bob Hope, Sid Caesar, Mel Brooks, Zero Mostel, Mickey Rooney, Regis Philbin, Liberace, Zsa Zsa Gabor, John Belushi, and "Miss Piggy."

Healthy Sevens with a Six-wing are highly productive individuals with an infectious joie de vivre. They can be noticeably playful, childlike, engaging, silly, and despite difficult experiences, tend to retain a certain innocence and belief in life's goodness. They can also be highly creative and entertaining—as the subtype nickname suggests—and tend to have a more positive outlook on the world (like Nines) than the Sevens with an Eight-wing. They often have quick minds and an inspired sense of humor, but when healthy can utilize the Six's discipline, cooperative spirit, and organizational abilities to accomplish a great deal. While they are essentially assertive, they also want others to like and accept them. If they have money, they tend to be generous with others, particularly in their socializing, party giving, and traveling. They use their optimism and high spirits to connect with others and forge bonds with them. People of this subtype have a soft, sweet side which can be very appealing. They are a kaleidoscope of contrasting traits—ingratiating and sassy, vulnerable and resilient, spontaneous and dependable, adult and childlike.

Average Sevens with a Six-wing may still be productive, but the Six-wing's fears fuel the tendency of the Seven to lose focus and become scattered. They have problems with insecurity and are more aware of their anxieties than the other subtype. Sevens with a Six-wing can often appear to be nervous and flighty, revved up and fidgety, and they tend to have more trouble with follow-through than Sevens with an Eight-wing. Average people of this subtype are defensive and impulsive. They want approval and are afraid of being anxious or alone, and have high expectations of their paramours. They want to be loved and they fall in love easily. But they also fall out of love easily as soon as the romance has worn off. Being in love is a powerful experience, which average people of this subtype enjoy having: they are always either in a relationship or looking for one. They can still be quite funny, but an underlying note of anxiety is closer to the surface. They may act like cheerleaders, attempting to rouse others and create a more exciting environment, but often become excessive and, to others, tiresome in the process. When others do not meet their expectations for stimulation, the Sixish tendency to sulking and pessimism may come out. Lower average Sevens with a Six-wing become caught between the Seven's desire to move on to "greener pastures" and the Six's fear of losing their safe connections with others. They are gregarious but insecure about what people think of them; impulsive but anxious about their decisions; extravagant yet anxious about money. As their anxieties increase, people of this subtype tend to become increasingly insensitive toward others, without being aware of it. They also become self-centered, demanding that others help them through bouts of anxiety. Thus, for better or worse, while the Six-wing softens the Seven's aggressive nature, it also reinforces its anxiety. As in the Six with a Seven-wing, there is a strong propensity for substance abuse

Unhealthy Sevens with a Six-wing display the erratic, manic qualities of the unhealthy Seven along with the fearful, clinging qualities of the Six, and engage in a restless search for "playmates"—people who will be "coconspirators" in their misadventures and keep them distracted from their mounting fear and distress. They want to have the approval and affection of others, and will likely experience acute problems with inferiority and anxiety, traits which are problems for each of the component subtypes. They will turn to other people, tearfully but obnoxiously demanding that others solve their problems for them. They may stay up night after night, staying on the telephone or hanging out in nightspots with anyone who will talk to them. If this does not work, people of this subtype become hysterical and helpless, alternately thrashing around and lashing out, driving away others and seeking to bring them back to their sides. This subtype is also highly prone to self-destructive behaviors and dramatic, masochistic episodes, such as suicide attempts. Eventually, overwhelmed physically and emotionally, they succumb to addictions or completely break down.

The Seven with an Eight-Wing: "The Realist"

The traits of the Seven and those of the Eight produce a personality combination which is very aggressive, since each component type is aggressive. Persons of this subtype are aggressive in two ways: in the demands they make on the environment and in the strength of their egos to enforce those demands. No one frustrates people of this subtype without hearing about it. They are extremely assertive and industrious, and are also more goal-oriented, pragmatic, and ambitious than the other subtype. They use their drive and high energy to maintain an intense, active lifestyle, and are less worried about having others around for the ride. Their ego strength is considerable, and the Eight-wing provides more focus on tasks and objectives. Noteworthy examples of this subtype include John F. Kennedy, Malcolm Forbes, Cary Grant, the Duchess of Windsor, Federico Fellini, Marlene Dietrich, Joan Collins, Joan Rivers, Phyllis Diller, Helen Gurley Brown, George Plimpton, Noel Coward, Cole Porter, David Niven, Larry King, Lauren Bacall, Judith Krantz, Jacqueline Susann, Susan Lucci, Geraldo Rivera, Howard Stern, and "Martha" in *Who's Afraid of Virginia Woolf?*

Healthy people of this subtype are exuberant and enthusiastic, since they are fundamentally Sevens. They are people who truly enjoy the world and the things it offers—materialists in the broadest sense of the word. They enjoy the good things of life and combine the Seven's avid intelligence with the Eight's daring and drive in a way that often results in material success. The Eight-wing adds elements of self-confidence, willpower, and self-assertion to help them overcome obstacles and endure whatever hardships might be in their paths. This subtype also has a capacity for leadership. Persons of this subtype who are leaders are known for their quick minds and the brilliance of their personal style. They are noticeably adult, earthy, businesslike, persistent (especially with difficult tasks), tenacious, and give an impression of bemused worldliness. Sevens with an Eight-wing know that they can get what they want from life: they think strategically and can rapidly reorganize their internal and external resources in pursuit of something they want.

Average people of this subtype are more practical, worldly, and cosmopolitan than Sevens with a Six-wing. They apply their energies in many directions, multi-tasking or even "multi-careering." The Eight-wing adds a degree of workaholism not as evident in the other subtype. They seek out intense experiences of all sorts, enjoying the rush of adrenaline they supply. There is also a stronger desire to accumulate possessions or "toys"—new cars, fine clothing, jewelry, stereo equipment, TVs, and other gadgets. The subtext is "I'm worth it!" Of course, Sevens with an Eight-wing also enjoy travel and new experiences, but focus more on activities than on socializing with others. People of this subtype are certainly not immune to romance but tend to be hard-nosed realists about their relationships. They are not afraid of being alone, and are very clear about their needs, expectations, and weaknesses. Their directness can verge into a crude bluntness in the lower Levels, and less healthy Sevens with an Eight-wing are not above "pushing to the front of the line" to get what they want. They make their desires known, and pursue them with less regard for the needs, desires, or feelings of others, and sometimes without regard for law or morality. Individuals of this subtype do not try to avoid conflicts; indeed, the reverse is usually the case: they are stimulated by confrontations because of the excitement which conflicts produce. They begin to adopt a jaded, world-weary attitude in contrast to the childish, hyperenthusiasm of the Seven with a Six-wing. They are also stronger willed, resisting anything that might control them, and are therefore somewhat less likely to succumb to substance abuse than the other subtype. At the same time, they tend to be more hardened and willful than the Seven with a Six-wing.

Unhealthy Sevens with an Eight-wing suffer both the Seven's compulsive mania and the Eight's destructive antisocial tendencies. They tend to involve themselves in dangerous scenes in the search for escape from their anxiety. Gambling, involvement with the underworld, extreme sexual practices, and "living on the edge" rapidly deplete their physical, emotional, and financial resources. They can become ruthless, particularly if they believe someone has what they want, whether a person or a thing. Because unhealthy Sevens fly out of control and unhealthy Eights overestimate their power, unhealthy people of this subtype are extremely reckless and dangerous. They may become physically destructive when they act out, with possibly devastating effects for others. Their erratic behavior can quickly lead to circumstances which result in either death or mental breakdown.

SOME FINAL THOUGHTS

Looking back at their deterioration, we can see that unhealthy Sevens have brought about the very thing they most fear. They are deprived of the happiness they seek, not because the world is bent on frustrating them, but because they have not trusted life enough. They have consumed their experiences, tasting them superficially as if everything existed merely for their pleasure. Living for their own immediate gratification has not brought about the happiness they have been seeking, but rather its reverse.

It is also worth noting that while Sevens fear being deprived, it is exceedingly rare to find Sevens who are actually deprived, at least for long. Because they fear deprivation, they do everything they can never to be the victim of it. Because they are aggressive, they usually succeed in getting what they want. But also precisely because they are aggressive, they tend to go overboard, ruining themselves through excess and destroying the possibility of achieving happiness.

If Sevens do not "experience their experiences," whatever they do will be worthless and wasteful. The most exquisite possessions and the most potent experiences will mean nothing if Sevens do not assimilate them. In the end, if Sevens fail to overcome their fear of being deprived, they will continue to consume yet remain dissatisfied. There is no way to convince them of this truth, because the most valuable experiences in life can be realized only after people are psychologically and spiritually prepared for them. Unless Sevens internalize their experiences in the depths of their souls, they will forever bar themselves from the most sublime experiences life has to offer. They will unwittingly trade true gold for lead.

Chapter 10

Type Eight: The Leader

THE EIGHT IN PROFILE

Healthy: Self-assertive, self-confident, and strong: able to stand up for what they need and want. A resourceful, "can do" attitude and passionate inner drive. / Decisive, authoritative, and commanding: the natural leader others look up to. Take initiative, make things happen, champion people, providing, protective, and honorable, they carry others with their strength. *At Their Best:* Become self-restrained and magnanimous, merciful and forbearing, mastering self through their self-surrender to a higher authority. Courageous, willing to put self in serious jeopardy to achieve their vision and have a lasting influence. May achieve true heroism and historical greatness.

Average: Self-sufficiency, financial independence, and having enough resources are important concerns: become enterprising, pragmatic, "rugged individualists," wheeler-dealers. Risk-taking, hardworking, denying own emotional needs. / Begin to dominate their environment, including others: want to feel that others are behind them, supporting their efforts. The "boss" whose word is law: swaggering, boastful, forceful, and expansive. Proud, egocentric, want to impose their will and vision; not seeing others as equals or treating them with respect. / Become highly combative and intimidating: confrontational, belligerent, creating adversarial relationships. Everything becomes a test of wills, and they will not back down. Use threats and reprisals to get obedience from others, to keep others off-balance and insecure.

Unhealthy: Defying any attempts to control them, they become completely ruthless, dictatorial, "might makes right." The criminal and outlaw, renegade and con artist. Hardhearted, immoral, and potentially violent. / Develop delusional ideas about their power, invincibility, and ability to prevail: megalomania. Feel omnipotent, invulnerable. Recklessly overextend themselves. / If they get in danger, they may brutally destroy everything that has not conformed to their will rather than surrender to anyone else. Vengeful, barbaric, murderous. Sociopathic tendencies.

Key Motivations: Want to be self-reliant, to resist their weakness, to have an impact on the environment, to assert themselves, to stay in control, to prevail over others, to be invincible.

Examples: Martin Luther King, Jr., Franklin Delano Roosevelt, Lyndon Johnson, Mikhail Gorbachev, G. I. Gurdjieff, Pablo Picasso, Richard Wagner, Indira Gandhi, Kathleen Turner, Marlon Brando, John Wayne, Charlton Heston, Sean Connery, Ernest Hemingway, Norman Mailer, Mike Wallace, Barbara Walters, Ann Richards, Lee Iacocca, Donald Trump, Frank Sinatra, Bette Davis, Roseanne, Leona Helmsley, Ross Perot, Fidel Castro, Saddam Hussein, Napoleon, Jim Jones, and "Don Vito Corleone."

AN OVERVIEW OF THE EIGHT

Everyday language comments regularly on the reasons for which power is being pursued. If it is narrowly confined to the interest of an individual or group, one says it is being sought for selfish ends; if it reflects the interest or perception of a much larger number of people, those involved are thought inspired leaders or statesmen. . . .

Much less appreciated is the extent to which the purpose of power is the exercise of power itself. In all societies, from the most primitive to the ostensibly most civilized, the exercise of power is profoundly enjoyed. Elaborate rituals of obeisance — admiring multitudes, applauded speeches, precedence at dinners and banquets, a place in the motorcade, access to the corporate jet, the military salute—celebrate the possession of power. These rituals are greatly rewarding; so are the pleas and intercessions of those who seek to influence others in the exercise of power; and so, of course, are the acts of exercise—the instructions to subordinates, the military commands, the conveying of court decisions, the statement at the end of the meeting when the person in charge says, "Well, this is what we'll do." A sense of self-actuated worth derives from both the context and the exercise of power. On no other aspect of human existence is vanity so much at risk; in William Hazlitt's words, "The love of power is the love of ourselves." It follows that power is pursued not only for the service it renders to personal interests, values, or social perceptions but also for its own sake, for the emotional and material reward inherent in its possession and exercise. (John Kenneth Galbraith, *The Anatomy of Power*, 9–10.)

It is difficult to describe power without roaming into ambiguous matters—into a consideration of leadership, authority, will, courage, self-reliance, and destructiveness. What is the difference between willfulness and self-assertion, for example? "Will" can be thought of as good or bad, although more by its use than by what it is. It is difficult to say what gives a person authority or makes someone a particularly able leader. Is it proper to call the use of power with which we agree healthy, while condemning its use by those with whom we disagree? We cannot possibly begin to do justice to the complexities of power here, although they will, of course, be touched on because this chapter concerns itself with the personality type which most exemplifies power.

In personality type Eight, we see courage, will, self-reliance, leadership, authority, self-assertion—and the dark side of power, the ability to destroy what power has created.

In the Instinctive Triad

Eights are one of the three types in the Instinctive Triad. All three personality types of this Triad attempt to keep the environment from affecting them in different ways—Eights by dominating it, Nines by ignoring it, and Ones by striving to perfect it. Eights tend to assert themselves powerfully in the environment so that no one and nothing in it can have power over them.

Of all the types of the Enneagram, Eights are the most openly aggressive personality. They possess a powerful connection with their instinctive drives which gives them tremendous energy, self-confidence, and the desire to impact their world in some significant way. They are take-charge people who want to test their wills against the environment, including, of course, other people. No one can ignore Eights, and others do so only at their own risk. Because they are so strong-willed and forceful, Eights are among the easiest types to identify, although for the same reason they can be the most difficult to deal with because getting their way is so important to them. If they are healthy, they use their immense self-confidence and will to remake the environment in some constructive way. But if they are unhealthy, whatever power Eights have deteriorates into the desire to prevail over others, no matter what the cost, even if it means destroying anyone who stands in their way.

One of the major themes of the Instinctive Triad is that of resistance. All three of the types in this Triad resist some part of themselves and their environment. Type Eight's particular form of resistance is being in conflict with the environment. They see the world around them in terms of struggle and endurance, and believe they must continually test their mettle against their environment if they are going to survive. This outlook leads them to a powerfully assertive style of self-expression, and because they assert themselves so readily, and usually with such favorable results for themselves, they develop a sturdy feeling of confidence in their own powers. Eights have more steely determination and single-mindedness than any other personality type. What Eights do not recognize, however, is that their capacity to assert themselves can become immensely destructive if they allow their willfulness to get out of hand. When this happens, others are often galvanized into action against them, and their lives then are actually torn asunder by conflicts and strife. Their fears of being rendered helpless in a harsh and unforgiving world come true.

Eights correspond to the extroverted intuitive type in the Jungian typology.

The [extroverted] intuitive . . . has a keen nose for anything new and in the making. Because he is always seeking out new possibilities, stable conditions suffocate him. . . . Neither reason nor feeling can restrain him or frighten him away from a new pos-

sibility, even though it goes against all his previous convictions. . . . Consideration for the welfare of others is weak. Their
psychic well-being counts as little with him as does his own. He
has equally little regard for their convictions and way of life, and
on this account he is often put down as an immoral and unscrupulous adventurer. Since his intuition is concerned with
externals and with ferreting out their possibilities, he readily
turns to professions in which he can exploit these capacities
to the full. Many business tycoons, entrepreneurs, speculators,
stockbrokers, politicians, etc., belong to this type. . . .

It goes without saying that such a type is uncommonly important both economically and culturally. If his intentions are good,
i.e., if his attitude is not too egocentric, he can render exceptional
service as the initiator or promoter of new enterprises. He is the
natural champion of all minorities with a future. Because he is
able, when oriented more to people than to things, to make an
intuitive diagnosis of their abilities and potentialities, he can also
"make" men. His capacity to inspire courage or to kindle enthusiasm for anything new is unrivalled, although he may already
have dropped it by the morrow. The stronger his intuition, the
more his ego becomes fused with all the possibilities he envi-
sions. He brings his vision to life, he presents it convincingly and
with dramatic fire, he embodies it, so to speak. But this is not
play-acting, it is a kind of fate. (C. G. Jung, *Psychological Types*,
368–369.)

Eights are confident that they can assert themselves until they
achieve their goals and, as Jung notes, if they are not too egocentric,
their personal goals will be extremely beneficial to others. They
may build skyscrapers, cities, or nations which, while personal
expressions, are also necessary for the well-being of others. Eights
are the natural leaders among the personality types, and may even
achieve some measure of historical greatness if their goals extend
far enough beyond themselves to the common welfare. Their enormous self-confidence inspires others so that everyone's energies
can be harnessed in a worthwhile undertaking.

Unfortunately, as Jung implies, Eights tend to become egocentric. They get carried away by the momentum of their egos and the
projects they have set in motion. Even average Eights begin to pit
themselves against others in a struggle for power and dominance,

as if the welfare of others automatically means that their own welfare must suffer. Average Eights feel that there can be only one person in charge, and they intend to be that person. They feel that the world must adjust itself to them and that others must fall in line to help them accomplish their goals.

Given this disposition, it is not surprising that if they become unhealthy, Eights can be extremely dangerous. They become ruthlessly aggressive in the pursuit of their goals, even if it means, as it ultimately does, that the rights and needs of others will be sacrificed so that they alone can prevail. Thus, the two ends of the spectrum of their traits are starkly contrasting: when healthy, no other personality type has as great a capacity for exerting a constructive influence in the lives of so many people. But the reverse is that no other personality type can so completely misuse power or become so totally destructive as unhealthy Eights.

Problems with Aggression and Repression

The three personality types of the Instinctive Triad have common problems with aggression, and with a lopsided development as a result of repression. Each of these types has aggressive impulses which are either totally repressed (the Nine), sublimated into idealistic work (the One), or forcefully expressed (the Eight). Also, each of these three types represses some aspect of the self, resulting in a characteristic effect on their personalities: in general, none of these three types thinks there is anything wrong with them. They think that all significant problems lie outside themselves in the environment, which they attempt either to dominate (Eights), ignore (Nines), or improve (Ones). Moreover, repression protects these types from feeling anxiety about the consequences of their actions, so they are able to go about their lives relatively unencumbered by emotional conflicts or self-doubt. In the short term, such a disposition simplifies matters for these types, but it can make life difficult for others.

At first glance, it is difficult to see what Eights might be repressing. They certainly have few problems asserting themselves and their ideas, and they like to get straight to the point when they are communicating with people. They can be courageous, and will take on battles for the sake of the people they love, the things they believe in, or simply for their own self-interest. They have hearty

appetites and enjoy their pleasures—so what are Eights not allowing in themselves?

Basically, Eights are driven by the fear of being dominated,
harmed, or controlled by others. As we have just seen, they view
the world as a fairly dog-eat-dog place, and they do not intend to
be eaten. Consequently, Eights believe they must keep up their
guard and toughen themselves against the harsh realities of life,
but in order to do this they must repress their own tenderness and
vulnerability.

Eights are usually very sensitive as children, although their high
energy and natural exuberance are often resisted or even feared
by adults. Their vitality attracts friends, but also engages others
who are threatened by it and who attack young Eights in subtle and
not so subtle ways. As a result, Eights learn to steel themselves
against life, to armor themselves, but they do so at the expense of
their innate sensitivity and gentleness. Most Eights recall some
pivotal childhood crisis in which they realized that they could no
longer afford to be so open, and feel this intensely as one of the
greatest tragedies of their lives.

But tragedy or not, Eights have made the decision to toughen
themselves, and so their vulnerability, their softness, their need for
affection, and their ability to ask for help must all be repressed.
Most of all, Eights must repress their own fear, because it is potentially the greatest threat to their independence and strength. Of
course, beneath the surface, Eights are as afraid as everyone else,
but they have learned to limit the degree to which their fear registers consciously. When it does, Eights will intentionally take on
challenges which confront this fear directly. If they fear heights,
they will learn to climb mountains or go skydiving. If they are
afraid of animals, they will go hunting and trekking in the wilder-
ness. Although we have mentioned the counterphobic aspect of
the Six, the Eight really represents the counterphobic approach to
life par excellence. Ironically, though, Eights who fear being controlled and dominated end up being controlled and dominated by
this very fear.

Another casualty of the Eight's repression of vulnerability is
their connection with other people. In healthy Eights we see the
big-hearted, jovial disposition which reflects their natural feeling
state, but as they succumb to their fears, they begin to believe that

they cannot afford to let others get close to them. They find it difficult to trust, and so try to convince themselves that they do not
need people. They also harden their hearts by telling themselves
that others are around because the Eight has something they need.
This is particularly sad, because in fact, while Eights may recognize
that people need them, they often do not believe that people love
them, and they are afraid to admit the degree to which they want
and love others.

Parental Orientation

As young children, Eights were ambivalent to the nurturing-figure,
the person in their early development who mirrored them, cared for
them, and provided affection and a sense of personal value. This is
often the mother or a mother-substitute, but in some families, the
father or an older sibling may serve as the nurturing-figure. Eights
did not strongly bond with or identify with their nurturing-figure
(like Threes), nor did they psychologically separate from them
entirely either (like Sevens). As a result, Eights learned that they
could maintain some kind of connection with the nurturing-figure
and fit into the family system by functioning in a role that was
complementary to the nurturing-figure. The nurturing-figure represented (and therefore "owned") the qualities associated with
motherhood: warmth, caring, nurturance, approval, gentleness, and
sensitivity. Thus, the Eight identified with the complementary
patriarchal role, and learned that the best way to get some sense of
value, affection, and nurturance was to be "the strong one," the
little protector, the one that others turn to for strength and guidance, especially in a crisis. Eights then identified completely with
this role, feeling that to give it up would be to lose their identity as
well as any hope of ever being loved or cared for.

Like Twos and Fives, the other "ambivalant" types, Eights feel
that their well-being and survival are dependent on fulfilling their
role in life. Twos believe that they must always selflessly nurture
and care for others; Fives believe that they have no role to play and
must find one; and Eights believe that they must be the decisive,
strong person who can handle the big problems and who is indifferent to hardship and suffering. As with all of the types, the
healthy manifestations of these roles can lead to extremely important contributions to the people around them, or even in the world.
However, as fear and insecurity grows, these roles become prisons

which trap the types and prevent them from expressing the full range of their humanity.

As we have seen, Eights begin to repress their fear and vulnerability so that they will be strong enough to meet whatever challenges they must. In highly dysfunctional families or in otherwise dangerous childhood environments, those challenges may be considerable, and in Eights, the result is a tough, aggressive person with a limited capacity to get close to others or to acknowledge their hurt. It is as if Eights must construct a tough shell of aggressive ego defenses so no one will ever again be able to get at the soft, vulnerable person inside.

If Eights have suffered serious abuse in childhood, their faith in others and in the world becomes so damaged that they live in constant anticipation of rejection and betrayal. Unlike Sixes, who also have trust issues and who may develop an aggressive style of defense against the world, Eights do not believe they can rely on anyone or anything outside themselves. Within their family system, they experienced themselves as independent people striving to assert their own authority. Either there was no one else to turn to for reassurance or guidance, or they pitted themselves against whatever authority figures there were in their environment—parents, teachers, older kids, the police. Eights were unwilling to allow their destiny or decisions to be placed in anyone else's hands. ("The buck stops here.")

If there was some degree of warmth, nurturance, and mutual support in the Eight's early childhood environment, chances are good that as an adult, the Eight will take a strongly protective role, especially with the few people that they trust and are close to. If there is little support or nurturance available, Eights may grow up with an "every man for himself" attitude. They feel as though they have had to struggle and fight to survive on their own, and if others are going to make it, they had better be able to take care of themselves. Looking out for number one is a full time job, and caring too much about others becomes a survival risk.

We can see very clearly in this type how a child's natural qualities—in this case, high energy, physical endurance, and willpower—combine with a family constellation to crystallize a particular pattern of behaviors and attitudes that determine a person's identity. In the discussion of the Levels that follows, we will also see how these natural qualities, when positively encouraged and expressed, lead to constructive, empowering human beings who leave a lasting legacy behind them. At the other end of the scale, where these energies have been twisted and distorted by abuse, we see vengeance, destructiveness, and a legacy of a different kind.

ANALYZING THE HEALTHY EIGHT

Level 1: The Magnanimous Heart

At their best, healthy Eights are big-hearted, compassionate people who are able to surrender their own willfulness to serve something greater than their own ambitions. They become truly selfless: not in a passive, ineffectual way—they retain all of their tremendous energy and vitality—but in the sense of acting utterly without self-interest. Healthy Eights see exactly what needs to be done for the greater good, and do it.

They also learn not to act automatically on their own impulse toward self-assertion. Rather, they learn to become more internally quiet, and to wait for a deeper, truer impulse to arise in their hearts, one that is not based on their fears and reactions. They master themselves and their passions, proving the depth of their genuine strength by not acting when they could act forcefully against others if they chose to do so. Paradoxically, Eights never seem as strong as when they act with self-restraint. They become forbearing, attaining the quality of magnanimous dominion rather than domination.

Healthy Eights are not pushovers, however, nor are they in any danger of losing their independence. In fact, healthy Eights know that they really are free and independent at the deepest level of their being. They are possessed of enormous inner resources and vitality and are more able than ever to take on life's challenges. This is because very healthy Eights are also better able to take care of themselves. At the same time, they realize that "no man is an island." They are realistic about asking for help when they need it, and are extremely generous in the help they offer others. This removes a lot of the burden from their shoulders, and allows their natural gusto and love of life to spring forth.

Self-mastery manifests great courage, and the depth of their courage is tested because what they do, or do not do, may well put their own lives in jeopardy. Very healthy Eights possess not only physical courage but moral courage, putting themselves on the line for what they believe in. Thus, they may be thought of as heroes whom others look up to and deeply respect.

Eights have the psychological potential to enable them to do the greatest good for the greatest number of people. Very healthy Eights are invariably charismatic, emanating an aura of absolute self-mastery and compassion which inspires others to gather around them for guidance, safety, and protection. Their largeness of spirit uplifts and ennobles everyone. Very healthy Eights are in the best possible position to achieve something truly great, because they have gotten past their egos to actualize an objective value, such as achieving peace, building schools, or helping others in important, concrete ways.

The essence of their greatness lies in their ability to find ways of alleviating the burdens of others, making life better for everyone. Very healthy Eights take it on themselves to solve problems by using whatever personal resources they possess for the common welfare. They are therefore inevitably seen as benefactors—to their immediate circles, to their countries, or to the world. People are enormously grateful to them for creating the opportunities in which they can improve their lives in peace and prosperity. As a result, people are extremely loyal to healthy Eights, responding to them with almost worshipful devotion.

Even though healthy Eights are often the object of this kind of attention, they remain unaffected by it. There is an innocence and simplicity in their manner, a purity of spirit which is very moving to people. Unlike their less healthy counterparts, they are forgiving, gentle, and possessed of a deep and unshakable faith in life. Their straightforwardness manifests as an ability to contact profound levels of truth.

Eights may be judged as great even if they do not personally succeed in their quest. They may see little of their vision become reality while still having an enormous effect on the world, because the example of their heroism and their vision inspires millions to carry on their work, accomplishing great things in their name. And if Eights of this caliber should die before they complete their life's work, their death leaves others feeling desolate. People feel that their protectors have been taken away, and that without them, they are without a defender before the uncertainties of fate. No other personality type has this kind of elemental, passionate effect on others, who are proud to be called their followers.

Thus, heroic Eights achieve immortality by earning a permanent place in the hearts and minds of their fellow human beings. They make a very particular kind of mark on the world—a mark possible only to those who are loved and revered.

Level 2: The Self-Confident Person

Healthy Eights do not always remain as healthy as they are at Level 1. If they succumb to their fear of being harmed or controlled by others, they desire to protect themselves and to become self-reliant. They want to make their own way in life, so they assert themselves against the environment, creating and reinforcing their willpower. Eights want to feel that they are in control of their own destiny, the "master of their fates," and want to make sure that they have the freedom and space to pursue their objectives. They almost never question their ability to overcome obstacles, giving healthy Eights enormous self-confidence.

Their sense of self as a strong individual comes from experiencing the full weight of their wills meeting the challenges of the world outside. Eights feel they are solid, and communicate their inner strength to others by their self-confidence. They know that they are able to struggle with adversity and come back stronger. ("That which does not destroy me makes me stronger."—Friedrich Nietzsche) They know that they have the ability to stand up for their own rights and needs and the willpower to resist whatever pressure may be put on them.

The more they assert themselves, the more healthy Eights believe in themselves and their ability to overcome difficulties. They have the knack of turning apparent setbacks into new opportunities, thriving on and learning by adversity. Rather than ask why something cannot be done, healthy Eights feel confident that they can do whatever they set their minds to. Unlike some of the other personality types, healthy Eights seldom suffer from self-doubt, anxiety, or insecurity, nor are they given to excessive introspection or concern about their identities.

Throughout the entire spectrum of traits, we will see their endurance, enormous willpower, and ability to assert themselves. There is nothing subtle or indirect about Eights: since their sense of self is reinforced the more they overcome adversity in the environment, they have every incentive to assert themselves at every possible opportunity.

Healthy Eights also have highly developed intuition, although it is usually focused externally, toward the environment. Eights get "hunches"; they see possibilities in people and in situations that others do not recognize. They are the sort of people who can look at a garage full of junk and suddenly realize how it can be put together in some useful way. They look at a burned-out tenement and see a new home or office building. They look at a person struggling with hardships and see potential leadership. Indeed, their intuition makes them excellent judges of character. They are able to look at the raw material of a person and see what he or she can become, or alternatively, they can sense dishonesty or insincerity a mile away.

Their self-confidence, intuition, and self-reliance also make healthy Eights highly resourceful. Self-motivated, they take the initiative when things must be done. Meeting such challenges excites them and motivates them. In a word, they are confident that they can make their way in the world. This is an extraordinarily effective psychological foundation to build upon—the perception of themselves as strong, confident, capable, secure, having will and ego and the ability to affect the environment. The Eight is the only personality type which has such inner solidity. And as long as Eights are healthy, it is a very desirable disposition to have.

Level 3: The Constructive Leader
Once Eights identify themselves as strong, assertive, independent people, they may begin to fear ever being weak, timid, dependent people. Thus, they go out into the world and take on challenges to prove their strength and independence to themselves. They become constructive, authoritative leaders, rising to new challenges, using their strength to achieve worthwhile goals.

While the qualities which make up leadership are complex and difficult to define in the abstract, the Eight is the personality type to whom people naturally turn to find these qualities embodied. Healthy Eights exhibit a masterliness and authority, a decisiveness and sense of honor. They are believed in, trusted, and looked up to—people who can be called on to solve problems or use their strength to do battle on behalf of others. People rightly see healthy Eights as empowering coaches and leaders, protectors and providers who take care of others' needs.

Healthy Eights exude the aura of natural leaders, taking a justifiable pride in themselves and their genuine accomplishments. Healthy Eights at this Level are not without ego, but their egos are in the service of something outside of themselves, influencing others to obtain goals which will be valuable for everyone. When Eights are on the scene, they are in charge. When Eights are healthy, others do not mind having them in charge because Eights are clearly honorable and have everyone's best interests at heart. While Eights are resolute and decisive, their decisions are also fair. Moreover, they are very effective leaders because they are extremely persuasive. As we have seen, their enormous self-confidence and belief in the importance of what they do enable them to motivate others, who willingly support their leadership. ("Leadership is the ability to get men to do what they don't want to do, and like it." —Harry Truman)

Another key aspect of their leadership is the ability to make decisions. In personal style, Eights are direct and impassioned, and they bring these qualities to the challenges of running the projects they have taken on. They are not afraid to take a stand, even an unpopular one, and will make difficult decisions, taking full responsibility for their choices. Others may not always be pleased with the choices that healthy Eights make, but they are respected, nonetheless, as honorable people who are willing to "take the heat."

Having the respect of others is very important to healthy Eights. They strive to be honorable and trustworthy in their dealings—their handshake or their word is sacred to them, and they often will close business deals on a handshake alone—and they expect others to behave in a similar fashion. They are far from naive, however, and will quickly terminate dealings with people they believe are dishonorable or unjust. In fact, injustice of any kind affects them viscerally. Ones are also sensitive to issues of justice and fair play, but they tend to evaluate their own and others' behavior by an internalized standard—a code of ethics. With Eights, the response is more from their gut. When they see others abused, or if they feel that their own interests are being violated, they respond instinctively with swift action, often surprising himself in the process. More than one Eight has found himself unexpectedly the focus of local news for stopping a mugging or intervening in a criminal situation.

Eights at this Level are also people of vision: their intuition is used constructively to create possibilities for others. They may use this gift literally, constructing things such as buildings, public works, parks, and social programs, or they may use it to build up individuals. They offer challenges and incentives to people as a way of building others' strengths and character. ("If you learn how to play the guitar, I'll buy you a good one"; "If you can take care of this arm of the business, I'll promote you to vice president.") Healthy Eights can do this easily because they are not threatened by others' strength. In fact, they understand the necessity of teamwork and delegating tasks, and so they want the people around them to be as strong as they are. Healthy Eights will also work to build up the strength of their children, much like a lioness nudging her cubs along or teaching them the ways of nature. People look up to healthy Eights with affection and gratitude because although they seem powerful, their actions are caring and authoritative rather than authoritarian.

This kind of respect and affection touches Eights, even if they sometimes have difficulty showing it. In their heart of hearts, Eights want to leave some kind of legacy: they want to be remembered as people who had a positive impact on the people in their lives, and if possible, on their community, or even globally. They are aware of the trust that others have in them, and they do not want to let them down. While this provides them with some of their greatest satisfactions, it is also the source of many of their greatest burdens. For better or for worse, healthy Eights see themselves as people with a destiny.

By looking at the characteristics of good leadership, in effect, we see the traits of healthy Eights. Good leaders give people a clear and worthwhile sense of direction as well as the means to attain common goals. Good leaders create and maintain a stable social order on whatever scale of influence they have, from a family to a corporation to a nation. They inspire others to want to work for something larger than themselves, such as winning a war or launching a space station or building a city. They know how to create a community or a people, and in rare circumstances they become the symbol and embodiment of the aspirations of that community or people. They help build self-esteem, courage, and self-confidence in others by inspiring them to accomplish more than they thought they could. And while good leaders enjoy preeminence, they are willing to take ultimate responsibility for the actions of their followers and to suffer the consequences of failure. As long as they are good leaders, as judged by their effects on others, Eights are worthy of loyalty, honor, and support.

ANALYZING THE AVERAGE EIGHT

Level 4: The Enterprising Adventurer

Once Eights have taken on the big challenges and goals they have set for themselves, there is always the possibility that they will not achieve them. Although they would never let anyone else know it, underneath their bold, self-confident exterior, little fears and doubts about their ability to "pull off" their undertakings begin to nag at them. If they succumb to these fears, they begin to lose confidence in their own ability to triumph in the situation, and so begin to focus their energies on building up the resources they feel they need to carry off their plans to maintain the safety and well-being of the people in their "charge."

This entails a definite shift in their priorities, which may be subtle at first, but which has far-reaching consequences. Healthy Eights were guided by an enthusiasm for life and its challenges, a love of truth and justice, and a vision of greater possibilities for themselves and for others. Average Eights have lost some of the focus of that perspective, and instead begin to operate out of pragmatism and the simple desire to keep their enterprises going and growing.

Instead of holding a vision which benefits all, Eights begin to view the environment as a harsh, competitive, dog-eat-dog world. They want the best for themselves and "their people," and unlike Threes, do not mind being up-front about it. They start to see things not as exciting challenges and possibilities for growth, but in terms of profit and loss, winning and losing—and they are determined never to be on the losing side of the equation.

Healthy Eights have an infectious self-confidence and exuberance about life. They are warm-hearted and jovial people who genuinely enjoy others. Average Eights may still have their moments of warmth and levity, but a driven, "no nonsense" quality has entered the picture. Average Eights are hard working, rugged, and businesslike in their communications. Even if they are not actually business people, they will tend to run their families and their affairs as if they were a business. If they lack material resources, they will often take on multiple jobs to make sure that their families will have enough money. It is as if their insecurity about their ability to lead is causing them to construct fortifications and to stockpile their resources.

Eights at Level 4 are preoccupied with running their affairs, but they are still fiercely protective of the few people they care about. The scope of those they concern themselves with or care for is narrower, perhaps again indicative of their insecurities, although the circle of people they deal with may be large indeed. Average Eights are still friendly, but they do not easily give their respect to others, and even less easily give their affection.

Because of their growing anxieties, though, average Eights tend to be more impulsive about their self-assertion. They are shrewd in their assessments of others and do not hesitate to engage in a conflict if they suspect that others are "up to something." They demand absolute honesty and straight talk from everyone around them, and while it is true that average Eights usually do tell people what they think, increasingly there are subjects about which Eights are unwilling to communicate—particularly those areas which open them to their feelings and their fears of vulnerability.

They often like to see themselves as self-sufficient, "rugged individualists," who believe in a free-enterprise system that allows them to pursue their own interests and others to do the same. Average Eights are less cooperative, not very good team players, and not much concerned with the welfare of others unless others contribute to the success of their efforts or are supporting one of the people they feel responsible for. As entrepreneurs, average Eights are particularly plentiful in the business and political worlds as the movers and shakers of society.

Business, real estate, industry, and finance—anywhere that entrepreneurial skills are valued, especially businesses that people see as indispensable, are fertile grounds in which Eights thrive. Of course Eights, like any type, can be found in a wide variety of careers. There are Eights who are health professionals, homemakers, chefs, athletes, artists, and entertainers. What they have in common though, is that average Eights will want to direct their own activities as much as possible, and will be extremely frustrated in situations where they have little or no say in what takes place.

Although their career focus can cause them to be confused sometimes with Threes, the differences are striking. Threes are more interested in having a career with some degree of visibility and, ideally, prestige or glamour attached to it. This is because they are motivated toward success to build their self-esteem and enhance their personal value. Eights, on the other hand, want control and

independence. An Eight would be very interested in owning or running a lucrative garbage dump or a company that manufactures
light switches. This is because Eights know that people in the foreseeable future are going to have to get rid of their garbage and use
light switches. The glamour element is less important than the fact
that these resources offer Eights a reliable base of power.

Therefore, acquiring money becomes important to many average
Eights as the means by which they can become more self-sufficient
and not have to depend on or submit to anyone else. Money allows
average Eights to get involved in whatever projects they want to,
without regard to the loyalty or devotion of others. With sufficient
funds, they can buy what, and whom, they need. ("I believe in
Rhett Butler. He's the only 'cause' I know."—from the 1939 movie
Gone With the Wind) They are often extremely persuasive
salesmen, and at the lower Levels, the more unscrupulous individuals of this type are outright con artists.

Even if they do not start out in life with a lot of money, average
Eights are so enterprising and have so much drive that it is not
unusual for them to substantially improve their financial status
rather quickly. They are effective negotiators and deal makers
because they go after what they want until they get it. They can
withstand pressure and can say no to others. They can also compromise when it is in their interest to do so. They are *Homo economi-
cus*, always ready to buy, sell, trade, and make a deal. They are also
careful consumers, always on the lookout for a good bargain. Their
line of work does not matter much to them as long as they see
that their undertaking is successful, and in many cases, this means
turning a profit. They could be manufacturing shoes or computers,
mining gold, or selling pizza. The important thing is not what they
do but the bottom line, making money and building up their
resources.

Average Eights are competitive with others, although strictly
speaking, Eights are more properly "enterprising," a form of self-
assertion. They assert themselves in the environment, and they
would prefer it if others would capitulate to them immediately. If
others cede the lion's share to them right away, Eights get what
they want and do not have to waste time and energy engaging in
competition.

Risk taking is a necessary aspect of the quest for success in any venture, and average Eights take risks so they can reap the financial and psychic rewards. They love danger and excitement, not only in the business world but in all their activities. They enjoy the high feeling they have when they prevail in challenging situations. Average Eights want to do the impossible, to succeed where others have failed, to do what cannot be done. They may fly airplanes, sail, scuba-dive, or race cars for the thrill of putting themselves in danger and triumphing over the risks. Eights, however, are not interested in wild, irresponsible gambles. They calculate their odds of success, and if they feel reasonably sure of coming out on top, they will take a chance and enjoy the excitement. Most Eights would not be described as cautious, but they are not foolhardy either. In the end, they are interested in surviving and having their legacy continue.

Average Eights usually succeed both at business and in their other goals because they work constantly and enjoy doing so. Work offers an arena in which to assert themselves, and hence to prove their strength and independence. Making deals and taking risks is not only a way to make money, it is a way of literally making more of themselves, and further ensuring that no one will ever get the upper hand on them.

Level 5: The Dominating Power Broker

At this point, Eights are in high gear with their many projects, schemes, and enterprises. They are driving themselves in an effort to "bring home the bacon," or to run their world in a way that mirrors back to them their power and competency. If their projects are not going well, however, or if they feel that others are not respecting them or appreciating their efforts, they may assert themselves more aggressively, not to win resources but to show others their power and importance. Eights want to convince everyone in their sphere that they are the "big shot," "the boss," and they want to convince themselves that they are up to the job.

Consequently, average Eights begin to shift their focus again, this time from their projects to themselves. Eights want to have a personal impact on the environment; they want to see themselves—their wills and egos—extended in it. They want their environment to be a reflection of themselves, a testament to their will power and greatness. It may well be that Eights at this Level or lower received erratic nurturing in childhood, and like Fours are trying to create an environment that supports their self-image. Since the self-image of Eights is one of being powerful, independent, and in control, they assert themselves more powerfully in their world so that they can look at their accomplishments, their activities, and their effect on the people around them to confirm that they are indeed the ones in control. Further, their basic fear of being harmed or controlled by others has escalated to the point where Eights cannot tolerate any competition in their spheres of activity. Others' strength or importance begins to be a threat, so Eights at this Level put everyone on notice that they are in charge.

A typical way of demonstrating their importance is their "edifice" complex. The epic scale appeals to them, both literally and figuratively. They enjoy building, whether a house or a financial empire, as long as it reflects themselves. In their private lives, average Eights would like to be monarchs ruling a large and powerful family dynasty which perpetuates their influence for generations. The wider their influence, the more they can have an impact upon the environment and ensure themselves of immortality, a goal which in various forms average Eights begin to seek.

Eights at Level 5 want others to support them in their efforts, but they are still healthy enough to use persuasion rather than intimidation to get their way. They may dole out favors with the suggestion that there will be more good things to come if the other person will play along. They engage in lots of "big talk," often bluffing or making big promises in an effort to get people on board with their agendas. ("If you come over to work on this project with me, I can guarantee that you'll be making over a hundred grand in the first year.") Their promises may or may not have much substance to them, but their pragmatism has led them away from their honesty and integrity, and they are not above conning people if it gets them to cooperate or removes an obstacle to their plans.

Similarly, they can be rather unsubtle in their means of letting others know how important they are and that they cannot be trifled with. They may ostentatiously throw money around, insisting on paying for everyone's dinner at a restaurant or tipping lavishly. They may provoke or tease others just to show them that they can get away with it. Or they may relish using coarse language so that others will know how "real" and "street-smart" they are. Average Eights are proud and rather impressed with themselves, although their swagger often betrays a growing insecurity and an expectation of rejection.

Just as Eights engage in behavior that is intended to inform others of their centrality and importance, they also look to others for signs that the message has been heard and responded to. They expect perks and privileges, and signs of respect and obedience from the people around them. If they are parents, they expect the other family members to follow their dictates without question. If others do not respond to their satisfaction, they can become heavy-handed and insistent, and are not above throwing their weight around to get people to comply with their wishes.

Average Eights at this stage have an innate sense of the use of power, and they do not hesitate to wield it. "Power people," they exercise power in whatever form is at their disposal. They understand that power is not a thing but the ability to get things done, to shape events, and to make the environment conform to their vision. Power is not something which can be enjoyed in the abstract: it must be continually used if it is to be maintained.

Surprisingly, though, average Eights are often unaware of the amount of force or power they use in their interactions. What seems to them like a simple conversation about an important decision can seem like a heated argument to others. Eights may feel that they are restraining themselves and maintaining their calm while others can feel blown out of the room by their intensity. Similarly, their blunt style of self-expression can come across as insulting or even threatening to people who are less sure of themselves.

Since each of the personality types tends to think that others are more or less like themselves, average Eights think that others are as capable of defending their self-interest as they are. Eights think that others enjoy the rough and tumble of confrontation and conflict as much as they do. But of course, different personality types are not alike, and everyone is not as capable as Eights of working their wills in the environment. As they deteriorate, Eights are less likely to take into consideration the feelings of others, or their physical, economic, or emotional handicaps.

Much of this occurs because their level of anxiety has reached the point where average Eights are beginning to feel that every interaction with others is a potential challenge to their power and independence. Believing that the best defense is a good offense, they assert themselves as soon as they sense any threat to their position. There is a certain territoriality in their attitude, as if they were insisting that certain property, certain behavior, even certain feelings were their prerogative alone. The message is clear. "This is my area. Stay out."

Their style of power is expansive. Average Eights move forcefully to fill a void wherever they perceive one, taking over situations in their desire to continue expanding and to be free of any limitations. Increasing their sphere of influence increases their sense of self, particularly the sense of their own greatness. And because average Eights would feel anxious if they were not expanding and impressing themselves on the environment, they constantly look for ways to do so.

Indeed, average Eights are expansive in every area of their lives, including their sexual lives. Male Eights see themselves as extremely macho, a man's man, although others may regard them as merely boastful and arrogant. In psychoanalytic terms, they are phallic exhibitionists ("I am the biggest and the greatest!"), wanting to prove their superiority by what and whom they control and dominate. At home, they are the undisputed lord and master of their castles, making everyone aware that others are present to serve their needs, not the other way around. Since aggression and sexuality are interrelated in their psyches, average male Eights often have stormy relationships with the opposite sex; they are frequently womanizers, treating their women either as whores or madonnas, but in either case as possessions who exist primarily for their pleasure and to gratify their egos.

Female Eights may also dominate their spouses, since they can be just as aggressive as male Eights. However, outside the home, female Eights have more difficulty expressing themselves aggressively because the culture discourages them from doing so. Many female Eights suffer from extreme stress and frustration because society offers them few outlets for their powerful energy. Therefore, they may limit the expression of their aggressive impulses to the domestic front, where they dominate their husbands, control the finances, demand sexual and psychological gratification, and so forth.

Men are often threatened by powerful women, and it is not uncommon for female Eights to be characterized by others as "dragon ladies," "pushy broads," "castrating bitches," and other unpleasant epithets. While it may be true that less healthy female Eights may have aggressive qualities, they are often condemned for the same characteristics which are applauded in men. (A parallel state of affairs exists for type Two males.) In any event, society's repression of Eight energy in women has probably not done much to bring out their healthier qualities, and the whole issue of gender and the Enneagram types is one which is bound to uncover many imbalances in cultures throughout the world.

It is a great temptation for average Eights who are powerful to begin to believe in their own "larger-than-life" image of themselves. They think of themselves as big shots, swaggering around like Mafia dons or four-star generals. The more they dominate everyone and everything, the more likely it is that conflicts with others will arise because they are no longer supporting and empowering the people around them. In fact, they are beginning to suppress and control others in subtle and in not so subtle ways. They do not delegate authority; they do not allow anyone to threaten their preeminence, and they trust no one. They want total obedience. As much as they enjoy exercising their wills, average Eights ironically are threatened by anyone else doing so.

The greater their dreams for glory, however, the more average Eights need the cooperation of others to achieve them. Average Eights therefore typically offer subordinates patronage in some form, usually money or protection. Ironically, Eights unwittingly become dependent on others to carry out their orders precisely when they are loath to share power or glory with anyone else. This stage is a turning point in their deterioration because the use of power to dominate others begins to dehumanize everyone, making aggression and destructiveness all the more likely.

Level 6: The Confrontational Adversary
If Eights continue to assert themselves against others, dominating the people around them and pushing their agendas, they are likely to get complaints and protests. This can be particularly unsettling for them if the complaints come from the people "under their wings"—the people they had thought they were providing for. The situation can rapidly lead to a crisis for Eights. They fear they are losing control of their situation, and worse, that the people they

have been protecting may challenge their authority. At the very least, they are convinced that others are not backing them up. They are marching into battle, but the troops are not behind them.

When this occurs, their anger rapidly boils to the surface. They feel challenged in the competitive world, and they feel challenged on the home front. Everything in their lives becomes a struggle, and average Eights feel that they must pressure everyone around them into "shaping up" and falling in line with their agendas. They are deeply frustrated, and feel that they cannot trust anyone. They have to push and force things to happen. (This can sometimes manifest quite literally in an impatience with mechanical things. Frustrated Eights may break a clock or snap a knob off trying to force an object to "cooperate," without having checked the instructions.)

Thus, average Eights turn everything into an adversarial relationship, attempting to make others back down rather than do so themselves. They see themselves as fighters, purposely creating conflicts even out of those things which have very little objective importance to them. What is always important to them, however, is their ego: Eights do not back down, because their pride is at stake.

Everyone, from business associates to the greengrocer, becomes an opponent. Eights start putting pressure on people, no longer merely dominating them but threatening and intimidating them until they get what they want. Eights at this Level become belligerent, strong-arming people if that will get them their way. Bullies who make no apologies, they order people around, exploding in a rage if their orders are not carried out immediately. They relish menacing people into submission, making others cower before them. ("What I say goes!")

Through their enterprise, which we saw at the previous Level, average Eights have already built a "power base" whose effectiveness is in proportion to the amount of leverage it gives them over others. Their power is most effective when average Eights make it their business to have what others need. They attempt to control such necessities of life as food, shelter, and security so that people will be compelled to do what they want. Of course, one of the primary needs of people is money, so to the degree that Eights regard money as power, they will make having a lot of it an even higher priority. For those Eights, money becomes the yardstick by which they measure themselves and their success in life. Above all, since it is in their control, money is one of the few things they can depend on to feel self-sufficient. It is the source of their security and independence. The love of a spouse, the devotion of children, the loyalty of friends and associates are all undependable. Only money and power seem certain, the sure means by which they can get their way.

Confrontational Eights are increasingly proud of their combativeness. Their egos are so involved with getting what they want that they cannot compromise with anyone. No other personality type is as headstrong. Prevailing in every contest of wills becomes all-important because it is by doing so that Eights continue to defend their sense of self.

It is also a source of pride to get others to concede to them what they want without having to fire a shot, as it were. Eights usually prevail because they are able to bring more pressure on their opponents than their opponents can bring on them. They can shout longer and louder and threaten others more convincingly, never letting up until others give in. This is why no personality type is better at waging psychological warfare than average Eights. No type is better at bluffing others to make concessions without having to resort to violence. There is, however, always the implicit threat of violence if their commands are not carried out. ("You *don't* want to make me angry.") People fear that they will be punished swiftly if they do not knuckle under to what Eights want. Others rightly sense that Eights have the will and the audacity to back up their threats. Eights at Level 6 make it clear that they will retaliate against actions that they believe interfere with their objectives. The healthy Eights' sense of fair play and justice has degenerated into "an eye for an eye, and a tooth for a tooth."

But Eights at this Level are far from just with others. Whereas healthy Eights take great satisfaction in championing and empowering the people around them, and enjoy inspiring and uplifting their "team," average to unhealthy Eights exert almost the exact opposite effect. Their own egos are too fragile to share the glory with anyone else, and they are too afraid of being controlled or caught off guard to allow anyone close to them to be powerful or confident. So they gradually undermine the confidence of the other people in their lives, creating dependencies and reinforcing their dominance and control. Eights may be aware that they are doing this, but not always. Their insecurity and fear of "letting others get away with anything" may simply drive them to oppress the people around them to the degree that others cannot assert themselves or even give voice to their frustrations or desires.

Indeed, Eights believe in being tough with everyone around them. They hate softness in themselves and even more so in others. Not only do business associates and rivals come in for forceful treatment, so do spouses and children. Eights at this Level use fear to motivate people, employing the "carrot and the stick," promising rewards for obedience and threatening reprisals for disobedience. When they say jump, they expect immediate compliance: the message they give others is "Take it or leave it!" They brook no disobedience or disloyalty and forbid all questioning of their commands. Their word is law.

There is, however, an irony here: average Eights usually intimidate only those they are sure they can beat. Before they act, they find some weakness in their opponent, and strike at the most vulnerable point. Only if their backs are to the wall do Eights confront someone whose strength is equal to or greater than their own. This is not to say that they are all bluster and no substance. Far from it. But belligerent Eights would rather get their way by bluffing than by risking defeat. If they should ever lose, it would be catastrophic. Not only would they lose whatever is at stake, but their sense of self, their pride, would be crushed.

A further irony is that by bullying others so much, Eights make enemies of the very people on whom they depend to carry out their orders, creating a vast pool of resentment against themselves. As they intimidate everyone around them, Eights cannot help but wonder what others might do if they could act freely. Having pushed people around, Eights must either brace themselves to be pushed back or maintain the level of intimidation. They can never relax once they have taken an adversarial stance toward others.

It is frightening not to know how far Eights will go with intimidation. Confrontational Eights are not psychopaths; they recognize limits on their behavior, the limits of their self-interest. They will push others until they see that their self-interest is no longer being served, then push no more. But each situation is different, and the degree to which Eights intimidate others depends on their perception of their opponents. If they think their opponents are weak, Eights will go much further than if they think they are strong. But of course, they may misjudge. Violence may erupt.

ANALYZING THE UNHEALTHY EIGHT

Level 7: The Ruthless Outlaw

Eights have been waging a war of intimidation and confrontation with the world around them. The huge chip on their shoulders has caused them to push almost all of their relationships to the breaking point and beyond. At this juncture, they may rightly perceive that others are turning against them, and either deserting or openly opposing them. This turn of events may well cause pragmatic Eights to stop and reconsider their tactics. If, however, they are overwhelmed by crises, or if they have suffered exceptionally abusive childhoods, they may escalate their war with the world one step further. They are now prepared to do almost anything to survive and to prevail over their enemies. Sadly, their perceptions may not be entirely delusional. If Eights have provoked others seriously enough, it is likely that others will have banded together against them. Prevailing in what has become a life or death situation—certainly figuratively and perhaps literally—is all that matters.

The pragmatism of average Eights has become ruthlessness and brutality in the unhealthy Levels. At this stage, they have deteriorated into a might-makes-right philosophy. The law of the jungle and the doctrine of survival of the fittest give unhealthy Eights a rationale for using force when it suits their ends. They are now a law unto themselves, cynically living in the world of realpolitik, where what matters is having the might to prevail, regardless of right or wrong. Expedience is all.

Because of childhood abuse and deprivation or more recent losses and broken relationships, Eights at this Level feel utterly betrayed and rejected. They trust no one and see the world as a cruel, pitiless place. They see themselves as outcasts, society's "rejects." They believe that they have somehow crossed a line from which there is no going back. They have gone beyond the bounds of what society would ever find acceptable—or so they believe—so there is nothing to lose. Once you have committed one crime, there is less anxiety about committing another. One's status as a criminal has already been established.

And unhealthy Eights are quite capable of criminal behavior. So great is their fear of being controlled by others, almost any restriction placed on them is an invitation to be defied. Any line drawn in the sand is sure to be crossed. There are no rules to which an unhealthy Eight will bow, and if they are still in a position to make rules, there is no limit to the control they will exert over others. Unhealthy Eights are completely ruthless, despotic, and tyrannical: they oppress people, taking away their rights, their freedom, and their dignity.

It is impossible to be intimate with and dangerous to trust unhealthy Eights since they take every sign of friendliness or cooperation as a sign of weakness, and therefore as an invitation to take advantage of others. Treacherous and immoral, unhealthy Eights have little compunction about lying, cheating, stealing, or reneging on their promises. They will resort to any illegality or ruse to get what they want. (They are the most frequent perpetrators of the Big Lie, a blatant and outrageous falsehood repeated so endlessly and vehemently that it begins to be accepted as the truth.) The honesty, straightforwardness, and compassion of the healthy Eight have become distorted into their opposites.

What is especially dangerous at this stage is their willingness, even eagerness, to use violence with very little provocation. The smallest hint of aggression from others will bring an avalanche of retaliation from unhealthy Eights. While some of the other personality types also resort to violence, they usually do so if there are no alternatives for defending themselves. And when the other personality types use violence, they generally feel guilty and fear retribution from others.

This is not so of unhealthy Eights, who use violence almost reflexively, without thought and without guilt. Eights are *capable* of feeling guilty for their actions, but they defy guilt feelings as something they believe would weaken them and leave them vulnerable to the predations of others. They cannot afford to be soft or empathetic, so they intentionally make themselves pitiless.

Power as a means of combating guilt feelings is easily comprehensible; the more power a person has, the less he needs to justify his acts. An increase in self-esteem means a decrease in guilt feelings. In the same way that "identification with the aggressor" is of great help in fighting anxiety, guilt feelings, too, may be refuted by "identification with the persecutor" by stressing the point: "I alone decide what is good and what is evil." However, this process may fail because the superego actually is a part of one's own personality. Thus the struggle against guilt feelings

through power may start a vicious circle, necessitating the acquisition of more and more power and even the commitment of
more and more crimes out of guilt feelings in order to assert
power. These crimes may then be committed in an attempt to
prove to oneself that one may commit them without being
punished, that is, in an attempt to repress guilt feelings. (Otto
Fenichel, *The Psychoanalytic Theory of Neurosis*, 500.)

To put this less technically, defying guilt and other emotions,
such as empathy for others and fear of retribution, allows unhealthy Eights to act ever more ruthlessly. By escalating the abuse
of power, they become so immoral that they must do increasingly
immoral things to avoid feeling guilty. Very simply: the more terrible they are, the more terrible things they must do so as not to
feel guilty about doing them.

Unhealthy Eights inflict some of their worst abuses on those
closest to them: they demean others, subjecting them to verbal, and
possibly physical, abuse. Rape, child molestation, and wife beat-
ing are common expressions of aggression, especially damaging to
those who are unable to defend themselves. Unhealthy Eights play
for very high stakes—for the control of families, fortunes, businesses, or nations—literally for matters of life and death.

Moreover, once unhealthy Eights have begun to defy the law,
morality, and common decency, there is almost no way they can
stop. Indeed, unhealthy Eights do not want to stop, because they
are in too deeply. If they did stop, they would be terrified of retaliation from those they have wronged. Having begun to violate
others, they are desperate to hold on to their power at all costs. To
do otherwise would jeopardize not just their way of life but their
very lives.

It is perhaps as difficult for others to empathize with the plight
of unhealthy Eights as it is for unhealthy Eights to empathize with
others. Their behavior seems so brutal and dehumanized that it is
easy to forget that unhealthy Eights did not get this way by accident or out of a desire to be "evil." It can be quite sobering to
imagine the kind of experiences which shape such a mentality,
remembering that perpetrators of violence were often the victims
of violence as children. Whatever happened to young Eights, they
have resolved that no human being will ever harm them or even get
close to them again.

Level 8: The Omnipotent Megalomaniac

Unhealthy Eights who inhabit a world of illegality, violence, and revenge against society are almost certain to create powerful adversaries, not the least of which may be the powers of the state. If they have acted with violence against others, the threat of retaliation against them becomes a real and ever present possibility. Even if violence is not part of the picture, Eights may have been involved in unscrupulous activities and be pursued by creditors or opponents who wish to ruin them financially. Healthy Eights were able to evoke passionate responses from others. The same can be said of unhealthy Eights, although the nature of that passion is quite different.

Living under such pressures, Eights become obsessed with protecting themselves and making themselves invulnerable to attack. They will often take some realistic steps in this direction—changing their phone numbers, hiring private eyes, or disappearing. However, over time, the stress of living with constant threat, and the reality that they have not been defeated yet, begin to produce a delusion of invincibility. They start to believe that they cannot be harmed, and develop delusional ideas about themselves and the extent of their power. They become megalomaniacs, feeling omnipotent and invulnerable—godlike in the scope of their absolute power.

Eights at this Level consolidate whatever power they have by keeping others terrorized and afraid for their own safety. Average Eights may well issue threats and attempt to intimidate people, but neurotic Eights may punish or harm innocent people to show that they mean business. They want to send a warning to others that they are more than capable of escalating their use of force to horrific levels.

Also, by relentlessly exercising their power, Eights gradually persuade themselves that human limitations do not apply to them. Not having previously submitted to any limits on themselves, neurotic Eights become convinced that fate has given them privileges which other people do not have. They think of themselves as supermen who are beyond morality and who can do whatever they please. Having always gotten their way, neurotic Eights find it difficult to believe that they are not invincible. Since no one has stopped them before, there is no reason for them to think that they will be stopped now.

With no capacity for self-restraint, neurotic Eights play God in ever more outrageous ways for a momentary confirmation of their absolute power. An obscene fascination with death manifests itself at this stage. The fear of death, a reflection of their more basic fear of being harmed by anyone, impels unhealthy Eights to defy death by killing others if it is within their power to do so. They may put others to death not so much for sadistic pleasure but as a magical way of warding off their own death, thinking that they will be invincible if they can kill without being killed.

> Amin claims to believe he is God's instrument. But you feel, as you watch him, that he doesn't believe in anything except his own survival. He will use anything—show off, clowning, flattery, seductive promises, threats, the Big Lie, murder—to remain in control. Yet he sweats like a cornered beast while proclaiming his invincibility. The threat of death hangs thick around him. No one is an individual to Amin. All are potential victims. (Silvia Feldman, *Psychology Today*, December 1976, review of Barbet Schroeder's movie *General Idi Amin Dada*.)

Neurotic Eights are out of touch with reality, especially the reality of their power. Their egos have completely taken over, like a cancer destroying them from within. In fact, their egos have become so inflated that the self has no grounding in reality. The judgment needed to make shrewd decisions to guarantee their own survival is undermined. The irony is that the more delusional they are about their invincibility, the more overextended and reckless they become—sowing the seeds of their own ultimate destruction.

Delusional Eights are thus in a conflict: they must isolate themselves from an increasingly hostile environment while they convince themselves, and those in their entourage, if there are any left, that they are the absolute masters of their world. They may try to reconcile this conflict by using whatever power they still retain to degrade others psychologically or physically, and to increase the level of violence. But since they are reckless, they are doomed to fail, especially once they become killers. They must and will eventually be stopped.

Level 9: The Violent Destroyer

Even megalomaniacal Eights realize that they cannot hold out forever against the forces amassed against them. They will therefore attempt to destroy before they are destroyed. Neurotic Eights are the most widely destructive and antisocial of all the personality types, just as when they are healthy, they are the most constructive of the types.

Since survival is the only thing which matters to them, they will sacrifice anyone and anything to this end: wife, children, friends, business associates, and everything they have built or achieved. The dark side of power is its willingness to destroy, and if the world does not conform to their wills, neurotic Eights will destroy it so that nothing is left. They become barbarically destructive on as great a scale as is within their power.

It is as if they were on a death trip. Their willingness to sacrifice everything for their own survival is absurd and irrational, especially since Eights, like everyone else, will eventually lose their lives anyway. The deaths of others will not assure them of their survival. Just the reverse: by the horror of what they do, destructive Eights bring destruction on themselves. They also lose their bid for greatness and immortality, becoming accursed and, at best, infamous.

It is ironic that what ends in destruction began as a desire for self-preservation. Thus, creation and destruction are the opposite ends of the spectrum of the Eight's personality. The desire to create and the desire to destroy originate from the same impulse; but when the impulse for life becomes defined as saving one's own life at any cost, it becomes corrupt and turns destructive.

Neurotic Eights are able to destroy because they have never identified with anyone else. Their egocentricity allows them to see only themselves in the world, and if the world does not reflect them, they eventually hate the world so much that they want to destroy it. Yet what kind of world would it be if it actually did reflect them? To paraphrase the philosopher Hillel, "If you are not for yourself, who will be? But if you are for yourself alone, what are you?"

THE DYNAMICS OF THE EIGHT

The Direction of Disintegration: The Eight Goes to Five

Beginning at Level 4, Eights under stress begin to act out some of the average to unhealthy characteristics of the Five. Average Eights tend to run on impulse, reacting to challenges and asserting themselves in the environment. This sometimes gets them into situations in which they feel they are in "over their heads." The main enticement for Eights to go to Five is that they see such a development as a tactical retrenchment from assertive action into the safety of thought. They think that they will be able to maintain their power by being shrewder and more premeditated. Instead of acting recklessly, they will attempt to act with more foresight; by being more secretive, they will be able to strike without warning; by being more wily, they will be able to hide from their enemies until they are ready to defeat them utterly. In short, the temptation for Eights to go to Five lies in the union of power and safety, a seemingly unbeatable combination.

At Level 4, Eights are busy building up their enterprises and projects. They are pragmatic, want simple, direct answers or solutions, and move quickly on their decisions. Eights may suddenly find themselves somewhat overwhelmed with the projects and challenges they have set for themselves, or may find that their impulses have led them off course. They will suddenly retreat and start to gather information and resources that they believe will bolster their position, like average Fives. They may do the research themselves, spending long nights acquiring new skills or tracking down the information they need. If they have the financial means, they may hire others to analyze their situation or do some preliminary research, but they will want to review the findings themselves.

At Level 5, average Eights have become more domineering and bold, but much of their blunt, rough behavior belies an expectation of rejection and lack of confidence in social matters. Eights may retreat from others, getting lost in their projects, emotionally detached, and preoccupied like average Fives. They become increasingly uncommunicative, secretive, and high-strung. They may also compartmentalize their friendships and activities to prevent any single person from knowing too much about them, and thereby gaining an advantage.

At Level 6, Eights intimidate others and see most of their relationships as adversarial. They trust almost no one and only want people around them that they can dominate. The move to Five here adds a tendency to provoke others and to hold dark, extreme views of the world. The Five's cynicism and rejection of prevailing values reinforce the Eight's feelings of being an outsider, angry and misunderstood. Their contempt for human weakness is exacerbated by the Five's intellectual arrogance.

At Level 7, Eights have become profoundly antisocial and ruthless, rejecting society and its laws and trusting only in their own wits and their will to survive. Eights may aggressively turn on people they feel have betrayed them, or assert themselves in ways that provoke aggressive responses in others. When they go to Five, they may retreat from the world, hiding out and minimizing their needs so as not to depend on anyone. Under stress, they may cut off what few ties with others they have left, burning their bridges and living like a recluse. And, the unhealthy Five's nihilistic view of life may often be used to justify their suppression of guilt.

At Level 8, neurotic Eights are delusionally convinced that they have omnipotent powers, and that they have a special destiny and cannot be harmed. They overextend themselves and their activities, leaving themselves wide open to attack by other predators or by their enemies. Eights have been able to maintain this behavior, however, largely by repressing their unconscious fears. At Level 7, some cracks in their inner defense may appear, but at Level 8, their energies are taxed to the limit, and they are no longer able to resist the terrors they have been suppressing. As they go to Five, the eruption of fear throws the Eight's mind into sudden chaos and horror, precipitating more irrational and potentially devastating behavior.

At Level 9, neurotic Eights moving to Five become extremely phobic about their continued survival and increasingly detached from their feelings. By going to Five and isolating themselves from others, they can no longer act effectively either in defending or in asserting themselves. What power they still possess swiftly crumbles, giving deteriorated Eights real reasons for at least some of their irrational fears.

As their terror increases, so does their isolation, and their isolation feeds their terror, a vicious circle. For the first time in their lives, Eights become extremely anxious, because their defense mechanisms, especially counterphobia and denial, no longer protect them. They are terrified of being punished for their many crimes, some of which may have been so heinous as to warrant their death. If their paranoia and phobia continue, they may break more or less completely with reality and lose whatever ability they have to defend themselves. (It is difficult to say whether all deteriorated Eights would become true schizophrenics. Probably not, although if this condition lasts for long, a genuine schizophrenic illness may well result.)

If their enemies have not been able to defeat them before, they certainly will have the opportunity now that Eights have deteriorated into such an extremely vulnerable condition. The irony is that the person who was once so mighty lives in abject terror—terrorized not only by the vengeance of others but by the anxiety which floods their minds. This is no omnipotent god but a pathetic devil in torment.

The Direction of Integration: The Eight Goes to Two

Growth for Eights lies in the direction of opening themselves to others rather than dominating them. When healthy Eights go to Two, they learn to use whatever power they have to nurture others as individuals. Healthy Eights, as we have seen, are heroic and magnanimous, but principally to groups of people from whom they stand apart. But when healthy Eights integrate to Two, they put aside their lofty position, relating to others as individuals and as equals.

When healthy Eights move to Two, they identify with others rather than against them, realizing that others are not unlike themselves and are therefore worthy of the same rights and privileges. Integrating Eights have empathy and compassion. They are nurturing, generous, helpful, and genuinely concerned for the welfare and aspirations of others. Integrating Eights no longer care about self-interest, but about the needs of others as if they were their own. Thus their newly emerging capacity for love crowns their other leadership capacities. They learn the power of love rather than being obsessed with the love of power.

They also discover a wonderful truth: that it is in their most profound self-interest to love others. As we have seen, if their power is not used for others, it quickly turns destructive. And even it if is not used brutally, dominating others will never bring Eights what they ultimately need most, to be loved for themselves. On the other hand, by using their power for others, they discover that they are not diminished or in jeopardy. They create something truly new, extending themselves in the world by that most powerful force, love itself.

The greatest and most noble of Eights learn the higher lessons of love at Two, ultimately seeing themselves as the servants of others. Putting themselves in this humble yet exalted position is an extraordinary act of heroism, especially for those whose orientation has been to take pride in self-sufficiency. To open themselves to others, to identify with them, and to take their burdens on themselves—indeed, to sacrifice themselves for the sake of others—are the most courageous and difficult things anyone can do, especially Eights. Rising to this level of heroism will truly make them immortal.

THE MAJOR SUBTYPES OF THE EIGHT

The Eight with a Seven-Wing: "The Maverick"

The traits of the Eight and those of the Seven reinforce each other to produce a very aggressive subtype. Eights with a Seven-wing are the most openly assertive of all the subtypes because each of the component types is aggressive—Eights in their quest for power and autonomy and Sevens in their acquisition of experiences and possessions. They are generally more blunt, realistic, and extroverted than Eights with a Nine-wing, and somewhat more consistent in their self-presentation. They tend to be the same at work as they are at home, and tend to treat all people in their lives similarly. There is a "cut to the chase," no-nonsense quality about Eights with a Seven-wing, and they do not hesitate to express what they really think or feel. They are definitely people of action, and are strongly compelled to interact intensely with the environment and with others. Noteworthy examples of this subtype include Mikhail Gorbachev, Franklin Delano Roosevelt, Lyndon Johnson, G. I. Gurdjieff, Lee Iacocca, Donald Trump, Henry Kissinger, Richard Burton, Sean Connery, Harvey Keitel, Barbara Walters, Ann Richards, Bella Abzug, Ernest Hemingway, Norman Mailer, Frank Sinatra, Mike Wallace, Bette Davis, Roseanne, Leona Helmsley, Muhammad Ali, Aristotle Onassis, Richard Wagner, John DeLorean, Al Capone, Ferdinand Marcos, Joseph Stalin, Mao Tse-tung, Muammar Qaddafi, Idi Amin, and the Reverend Jim Jones.

Healthy people of this subtype will be highly extroverted, action-oriented, and extremely energetic, combining the Seven's quick mind with the Eight's vision for practical possibilities. They take the initiative almost all the time—from business deals to romantic engagements—with great gusto and confidence of success. Eights with a Seven-wing are attracted to entrepreneurial endeavors, creating businesses and projects. They are perhaps the most independent subtype and are generally uninterested in working for others unless doing so would lead them to a situation of greater independence. The healthy Eight's charisma combines with the healthy Seven's capacity to enjoy life, producing an extraordinarily outgoing personality, often attracting many people and involving them in their hopes and plans. They create opportunities for others and enjoy challenging people to make something of themselves. There is a joyful enthusiasm for living life and sharing their experience and fortitude. Their inner strength and vitality may be so outstanding as to allow Eights with a Seven-wing to have a public, and possibly historical, impact. Their magnanimity will have a practical focus in the concern they show for the material well-being of others.

Average people of this subtype are very interested in power and experience, two motivations which reinforce each other. They have a strong business sense, and because they are so extroverted, they possess an enormous drive which they pour into their work, interests, and adventures. These are robust, earthy, and materialistic people whose feet are firmly planted on the ground, although they are not beyond seeking attention and regaling people with stories and "straight talk." Even if they are of limited financial means, Eights with a Seven-wing like to throw money around and have "nights on the town." The Seven-wing also adds a degree of hyperbole, so they tend to make big promises and exaggerate situations in an effort to recruit others into their schemes. Members of this subtype more openly display their attitudes and feelings, and are not particularly concerned with people's reactions to them. They can become impatient, impulsive, and are more likely to be led by their passions. They easily dominate their environments, particularly other people. At the lower Levels, they can become extremely aggressive and belligerent, bullying others to get their way and walking around with a chip on their shoulders. People of this subtype may also use their resources to manipulate others, attempting to pressure them into bending to their agenda. They have little compassion for others and do not feel guilty for their actions. Nevertheless, they betray a certain insecurity about money and power, since they never feel that they have enough of either to make them fully independent or secure in life.

Unhealthy persons of this subtype are ruthless and impulsive: they can say and do things which will later be regarded as either a stroke of genius or a fatal mistake. They can be offensive and tyrannical, verbally and physically brutish to others, lashing out at whoever has frustrated them or dared to resist their wills. They have

explosively violent tempers and quickly get into a rage. They easily
feel betrayed and resist any restraints upon their behavior. Their
manic tendencies reinforce their delusions of omnipotence: they
may spend vast sums of money to feed their inflated notions of
themselves. They tend to get out of control when they are anxious
or feel threatened. Since they are susceptible to anxiety, they
defend themselves against it by acting out, impulsively striking
first, attempting to destroy before they are destroyed.

The Eight with a Nine-Wing: "The Bear"

The traits of the Eight and those of the Nine are in some degree of
conflict with each other. The Eight tends toward assertiveness and
taking on challenges and conflicts, whereas the Nine tends toward
the suppression of aggression and the avoidance of conflicts and
upset. Eights with a Nine-wing enjoy their comfort and peace, and
tend to be much more domestic than Eights with a Seven-wing, but
still make it clear to all in their sphere that they are in control.
Depending on the Nine-wing's strength, individuals of this subtype
are somewhat more oriented to people and less to possessions and
experiences than the other subtype. They have a softer, more accepting quality, and tend to relate to people more easily and with
less confrontational or aggressive undertones. They still get things
done their way, but more likely with a soft, firm voice and more
casual demeanor. They are also less self-assertive, exuding an aura
of quiet strength and of power held in reserve. In general, this is a
less openly aggressive overall personality pattern, although since
Eight is the basic type, persons of this subtype can still be quite
aggressive, especially when they need to be. They tend to maintain
a "poker face" with others, somewhat stolid and impassive, although when aroused they can suddenly become passionate and
angry. Like Nines, Eights with a Nine-wing are often unaware of
their own strength or the force of their anger. Noteworthy examples of this subtype include Martin Luther King, Jr., Golda Meir,
Janet Reno, Charles de Gaulle, Indira Gandhi, Pablo Picasso, Marlon Brando, Paul Newman, John Huston, Robert Altman, Barbara
Stanwyck, John Wayne, Charlton Heston, Johnny Cash, Fidel
Castro, Leonid Brezhnev, "Darth Vader," "King Lear," and "Don
Vito Corleone."

Healthy persons of this subtype possess a quiet power and an
understated wisdom. They are strategic planners like the other sub-

type, but tend to be more steady and inexorable in the execution of their goals. They are not easily perturbed, and are noticeably more at ease with themselves and with other people, not feeling that they must assert themselves at every moment or in every situation. There is less of a wheeler-dealer quality than in the Eight with a Seven-wing, although Eights with a Nine-wing also prefer to run their own enterprises. They are, at times, more open to concerns beyond their immediate self-interest, particularly those involving members of their own family. They are the kinder, more benign patresfamilias or matriarchs, strong-willed but mild-mannered, who tend to assert leadership more through support and protectiveness. Eights with a Nine-wing are able to forge a personal, almost mystical bond between themselves and others. They may be involved with the arts, nature, animals, and children.

Average people of this subtype begin to show a definite split between the two sides of themselves—the aggressive side (which they show in public and in competitive situations) and the passive, more accommodating side (which they reveal to very few, principally their families). The discrepancies in their attitudes toward people can be striking—warm and affectionate at home, hard-nosed and aggressive at work. People of this subtype usually do not seek publicity actively, and like to live quietly, privately, and unobtrusively, preferring to control their affairs from behind the scenes. Their expansive forcefulness is grounded on some inner fortress of imperturbable strength which others are not allowed to breach. This inner sanctum is undisturbed and at peace, although it is doubtful that people of this subtype benefit from that inner part of themselves as much as they might. Others often experience this quality in them as a form of stubbornness and an ability to turn out anxieties. Since Eight is the basic personality type, people of this subtype dominate others, although with a velvet glove over an iron fist. There is a sly, watchful quality in average Eights with a Nine-wing—as if they are daring others to underestimate them. They tend to speak more slowly, but are attuned to the nonverbal cues and body language of the people around them. They can seem friendly and agreeable while secretly sizing people up and assessing their character. In the lower levels, Eights with a Nine-wing move from stubbornness to a quietly menacing quality. However, their moods and reactions tend to be unpredictable. They can be intimidating and belligerent, and then accommodating and kindhearted, especially to those who are close to them. Those around them are never quite sure when their explosive tempers are going to erupt.

Unhealthy Eights with a Nine-wing become reclusive, depressed, and dissociated, but if they have access to power, they can also be extremely vengeful. Since this subtype is almost immune from anxiety, unhealthy Eights with a Nine-wing can be destructive without remorse, combining ruthlessness with indifference. They can get into a strangely dissociated frame of mind, acting in a depersonalized way, as if they were some sort of cosmic force which swatted people aside, crushing them without personal feelings entering the picture. People in this subtype tend, in general, to be less violent and destructive than those in the other subtype. However, if necessary they may be violent toward others, personally regretting the suffering they cause but not feeling any empathy or having any real understanding of what they do. They may make up for the lesser degree of violence they wreak on the environment by generally living longer, thus possibly doing more damage in the long run to those who have the misfortune to live with them.

SOME FINAL THOUGHTS

Looking back on their deterioration, we can see that from the average Levels downward, the self-esteem of Eights came from being increasingly destructive rather than constructive. But is the ability to destroy a reflection of real power? Who is more genuinely powerful, the person who destroys a city or the person who builds one?

We can also see that Eights have brought about the very thing they most feared: having destroyed all they could, they have depleted their resources and become vulnerable to the just retaliation of others who, they rightly fear, may treat them without mercy. They have succeeded in creating a self-fulfilling prophecy: they feared being harmed or controlled by others, and now this comes to pass.

How to stop a tyrant without becoming a tyrant oneself is an age-old problem. Must one become ruthless to fight ruthlessness, unjust to fight injustice? How far can one go to protect oneself from predators, from those who destroy without remorse? In searching for an answer, no other personality type makes others consider what they really believe the ultimate values of life to be. Is the ultimate value self-interest? Is getting your way by trampling on others really all that matters?

If there is no God, then Eights are the most expedient and shrewd of people: self-interest is indeed all that matters. Since we cannot be certain about God, or what form God's justice might take, at least this is certain: no matter how Eights have lived, they cannot escape mortality. Like everyone else, they will have to submit to death, and ultimately to the judgment of others.

The last irony is one of the most poignant: if they have been destructive, they will not have remade the world in their image. They will ultimately be frustrated in one of their deepest desires.

Chapter 11

Type Nine: The Peacemaker

THE NINE IN PROFILE

Healthy: Deeply receptive, accepting, unselfconscious, emotionally stable and serene. Trusting of self and others, at ease with self and life, innocent and simple. Patient, unpretentious, good-natured, genuinely nice. / Imaginative and creative, attuned to nonverbal communication. Optimistic, reassuring, supportive: have a healing and calming influence—harmonizing groups, bringing people together. A good mediator, synthesizer, and communicator. *At Their Best:* Become self-possessed, feeling autonomous and fulfilled: have great equanimity and contentment because they are present to themselves. Paradoxically, at one with self, and thus able to form more profound relationships. More alive, awake, alert to self and others.

Average: Become self-effacing and agreeable, accommodating themselves, idealizing others and "going along" with things to avoid conflict. Have a "philosophy of life" that enables them to quiet their anxieties quickly. Submerge themselves in fulfilling functions for others. In their reactions, they are unresponsive and complacent, walking away from problems and "sweeping them under the rug." Become passive, disengaged, unreflective, and inattentive.

Thinking becomes hazy and ruminative, mostly about their fantasies, as they begin to "tune out" reality, becoming oblivious. Emotional indolence, unwillingness to exert self (and stay focused) on problems: passive-aggressive and indifferent. / Begin to minimize problems to appease others and to have "peace at any price." Become fatalistic and resigned, but also stubborn and resistant to influence. Practice wishful thinking and wait for magical solutions. Inadvertently create conflicts with others by their denial and obstinance.

Unhealthy: Can be repressed, undeveloped, and ineffectual. Do not want to deal with problems: become depressed and listless, dissociating self from all conflicts. Neglectful and dangerously irresponsible. / Wanting to block out of awareness anything that could affect them, they dissociate so much that they eventually cannot function: become numb, depersonalized. / Becoming severely disoriented and catatonic, they abandon themselves, turning into shattered shells. Multiple personalities possible.

Key Motivations: To have serenity and peace of mind, to create harmony in their environment, to preserve things as they are, to avoid conflicts and tension, to escape upsetting problems and demands on them.

Examples: Abraham Lincoln, Joseph Campbell, Carl Jung, Ronald Reagan, Gerald Ford, Queen Elizabeth II, Princess Grace of Monaco, Walter Cronkite, Walt Disney, George Lucas, Garrison Keillor, Sophia Loren, Kevin Costner, Keanu Reeves, Woody Harrelson, Ron Howard, Ringo Starr, Whoopi Goldberg, Janet Jackson, Nancy Kerrigan, Linda Evans, Ingrid Bergman, Perry Como, Jim Henson, Marc Chagall, Norman Rockwell, "Edith Bunker," and "Marge Simpson."

AN OVERVIEW OF THE NINE

The inner landscape of the Nine resembles someone riding a bicycle on a beautiful day, enjoying everything about the flow of the experience. The whole picture, the entire situation, is what is pleasant and identified with rather than any particular part. The inner world of Nines is this experience of effortless oneness: their sense of self comes from being at one with their experience. Naturally, they would like to preserve the quality of oneness with the environment as much as possible.

Their receptive orientation to life gives Nines so much deep satisfaction that they see no reason to question it or to want to change
anything essential about it. Because Nines develop psychologically
this way, we should not fault them if their view of life is open and
optimistic. But we may fault Nines when they refuse to see that
life, while being sweet, also has difficulties which must be dealt
with. Their refusal to fix the tire when it goes flat, so to speak, is
symbolic of their problem. They would rather ignore whatever is
wrong so that the tranquillity of their ride will not be disturbed.

In this personality type, we will see the personal cost of the philosophy of peace at any price. Refusing to deal with problems does
not make them go away. Moreover, the peace Nines purchase is
inevitably at the expense of others, and ultimately at the expense of
their ability to relate to reality. With all the good will in the world,
Nines still may do terrible harm to others while coasting along,
turning a blind eye on what they do not want to deal with.

In the Instinctive Triad

The Nine is the primary personality type in the Instinctive Triad—
the type most out of touch with their instinctual drives and their
ability to relate to the environment. This occurs because Nines do
not want to be affected by the environment. They have established
within themselves a kind of equilibrium, a feeling of peace and contentment, and they do not want their interactions with the world
or with others to disturb them. Similarly, they do not want to become unsettled by powerful feelings that their instincts would stir
in them. Nines have sufficiently dissociated from the intensity of
their passions, their drives, and their anger to allow them to remain
tranquil and even-tempered.

Thus, when they are healthy, they work to create a peaceful,
harmonious environment around themselves. They may do this
directly by soothing others and healing conflicts and hurts, or indirectly through creativity and communication which appeals to the
idealistic side of human nature, to innocence and gentleness. In
this way, Nines contribute to their world, but also influence it so
that it will support their inner peacefulness. When Nines are less
healthy, they maintain peace for themselves by ignoring those
aspects of the environment which they find disturbing or upsetting.
Eventually, this can lead to a highly dissociated approach to life in
which Nines do not relate to others or the environment as they

really are, but instead relate to an inner, idealized image of others which is more pleasant and less threatening. At the same time, while they are "tuning out" many aspects of the world around them, they are also tuning out many aspects of themselves. As a result, unless they are very healthy, Nines do not develop an awareness of themselves as individuals or even a well-defined awareness of the world around them.

Basically, Nines are in search of autonomy and independence, just like the other two types of this Triad, the Eight and the One. They want the freedom and space to pursue their own objectives and to be the way they want to be. Unlike Eights and Ones, however, Nines are blocked to some degree in their ability to assert themselves and their need for independence. They are afraid that such demands would ruin the harmony and equilibrium they have in their relationships with others. So they repress their desires for independence and space and attempt to find their freedom by dissociating—by breaking contact with the other and "inhabiting" the safety of their imaginations and their dreams. They relate to the idealized impression of others rather than to actual people, and similarly keep their own self-image in "soft focus." They put themselves and their own real development in the background so they can maintain the sense of harmony and stability they feel. This approach can give them a temporary sense of ease and freedom from the difficulties and challenges around them, but if it becomes ingrained as a way of life, Nines risk never becoming independent, fully functioning human beings with clear identities of their own.

As long as Nines are idealizing other people, they will also tend to devalue themselves. It is as though they project all of the qualities that they feel they cannot have onto the idealized other. Strength, self-assertion, poise, self-confidence, and many other positive qualities are perceived as present in the other and lacking in the self. Nines are not necessarily anxious about the qualities they believe they lack; in fact, they are not particularly focused on themselves at all. Their attention is drawn far more to what they see as the positive qualities of the other. Of course, the specific qualities will vary from Nine to Nine, but all will seek to identify with people who have or express the mental, emotional, or physical qualities which Nines feel they lack. Most Nines will not be aware of this dynamic, but they will be aware of their strong identifications with certain figures in their lives and their repeated attraction to persons with assertive, energetic qualities. Subconsciously, they desire to merge with someone else in order to incorporate through that person the qualities in themselves that they have repressed or rejected. However, by identifying with someone else, their sense of self eventually becomes ill-defined and incomplete, so they do not relate to the world as individuals. Moreover, by identifying with someone else, Nines do not develop their potentials. Preserving their inner peace becomes their all-important motivation.

Only healthy Nines achieve an awareness of themselves as distinct persons who actively choose what they need and want. Healthy Nines know how to take direct positive actions for themselves. By contrast, average Nines have a relatively passive orientation to life. They still have substantial vitality and willpower, but their willpower is used to deflect others, to resist, to fend off reality. Average Nines use most of their energy to maintain and defend two boundaries against the environment. One is against the outer environment: Nines do not want their inner stability to be affected or influenced by other people. The second is against aspects of their *inner* environment: this can include feelings, memories, thoughts, or sensations which would be jarring or upsetting, thus ruining their balance and harmony. These boundaries do protect the Nine's inner world, but they do so at a high price. What average to unhealthy Nines do not see is that they cannot really contribute to others, or even love them, if they do not develop themselves as persons, and that real development requires risking discomfort, questioning or even jeopardizing one's inner "balance," and sometimes facing truths which are unpleasant and uncomfortable. Ironically, many Nines are attracted to personal-growth books, seminars, and practices, but often gravitate to disciplines or philosophies which comfort rather than challenge. In other cases, they may selectively "edit" the teaching to make it more palatable to them.

Problems with Repression and Aggression

Nines, like Eights and Ones, have a problem with the repression of some part of their psyches. All three of these personality types overcompensate in one area for an underdevelopment in another. The problem Nines have with instinct is that they have repressed the ability to assert the self so they can be more receptive to the other. Eventually, their sense of self can become so repressed that they are barely functional as individuals, so totally do they discount themselves and live through someone else, or, just as bad, so completely do they live in a world of hazy illusions. By repressing themselves, their awareness of themselves, of other people, and of the world gradually becomes leveled out so that nothing can bother them. They become disengaged—at peace, but unrelated to the reality.

While there is certainly nothing wrong with wanting to be at peace, the problem is that average to unhealthy Nines tend to go too far to avoid all exertion and conflict. They do not see that it is sometimes necessary to assert themselves, since Nines equate self-assertion with aggression, as if asserting themselves automatically threatens their relationship with others. In truth, they also are afraid of asserting themselves because to do so allows powerful feelings to surge through them, and powerful feelings are not helpful in maintaining a state of peacefulness. The result is that Nines repress their aggressive impulses so thoroughly that eventually they are not aware of having them. However, just because they are not aware of their aggressions does not mean that these feelings do not exist or that these impulses do not affect their behavior.

Nines typically "solve" the problem of having aggressions by ignoring them out of existence. When Nines inadvertently act aggressively, they simply deny that they have done so. To a certain degree, the peace of average to unhealthy Nines is therefore something of an illusion, a form of willful blindness, a kind of self-deception. They do not realize that to maintain their peace, they have dissociated themselves from themselves—and from reality. However, the irony is that their passivity and denials, their inattention to others, and their increasing disengagement from the environment are all negative forms of aggression—passive resistance—an aggressive withholding of themselves from reality. Nines are far more aggressive than they think they are, and the effects of their denied and repressed aggressions can be devastating to themselves and others.

Parental Orientation

Nines are connected with both parents, in the sense that they have powerfully identified with and incorporated into their psyches the agendas and issues of both their nurturing-figure and their protective-figure. Much of their mental and emotional energy must then be used to deal with keeping all of these identifications in some kind of inner harmony. Thus their inner world is largely a balancing act as they attempt to accommodate their identifications with their nurturing-figure, their identifications with their protective-figure, and hopefully a few of their own needs as well.

Healthy Nines are extraordinarily sensitive and open to their environment, and as children they absorbed a great deal from the people around them, primarily their parents. If they came from a peaceful, harmonious household, the messages and feelings they incorporated were relatively easy to manage, and Nines had sufficient attention available to deal effectively with their world. If their early childhood was torn by strife and dysfunction, holding all of the painful and conflicted feelings and messages inside them was almost intolerable, so average to unhealthy Nines learned to dissociate—to remove themselves from the immediacy of their feelings and thoughts so that the inner turmoil they absorbed did not overwhelm them. At the same time, they learned to tune out the conflicts and pain of the external environment, a strategy familiar to many children. This is like the young person who blocks out the sound of her parents fighting in another room by singing a song to herself or remembering happier times.

Connection with both parents gives at least healthy to average Nines a sense of support and identity because their identity is more or less "given." However, in the process of psychological and spiritual development, Nines may come to see that the identity they have assumed is not who they really are (like Threes) and that they are often dependent on something outside themselves for support (like Sixes). Furthermore, if their psyches are accommodating the issues of both parents, what space is left for them? It is as if Nines have been crowded out of their own selves by the agendas first of their parents and later of other significant people in their lives.

Trying to find some independence and autonomy, claiming some part of their lives for themselves alone, becomes very important. What Nines choose to do as their own may seem trivial to others, but Nines will defend these activities fiercely. Once they understand the nature of their inner accommodations, Nines are able to let go of some of these habits or rituals because they feel safe to claim their own needs in more central areas of their lives.

Finally, we can see that this orientation compels Nines to maintain harmonious relationships with and between the people in their lives. As children who developed their sense of self by bonding and identifying with both parents, the prospect of discord or separation between the parents is terrifying. For young Nines it is the same as having discord and conflict within themselves. Discord or separation between the parents is deeply disturbing to the Nine's inner stability. Basically, Nines feel whole and good as long as the people they have identified with are whole and good. When Nines are healthy, they use their many gifts to help maintain the wholeness and well-being of others. When they are less healthy, they imagine that others are well and whole, even if they are not. Once this occurs, Nines ironically have begun to lose the very people they want to stay connected with.

Problems with Awareness and Individuality

Whether or not they want to recognize it, Nines are individuals and they have an impact on others. They cannot ignore themselves and allow their potential to go undeveloped without paying a serious price: rather than find harmony with others, they will inevitably lose it while living in a dreamy half-awareness in which their relationships are little more than idealized illusions.

The personality type Nine corresponds to Jung's introverted sensation type. Jung describes what we would regard as average to unhealthy Nines, people who maintain their peacefulness and connection with others not as they are, but through an idealization of them. The other person may feel "devalued," as Jung says, for the following reasons:

He may be conspicuous for his calmness and passivity, or for his rational self-control [especially, for example, if the Nine has a One-wing]. This peculiarity, which often leads a superficial judgment astray, is really due to his unrelatedness to objects. Normally the object is not consciously devalued in the least, but its stimulus is removed from it and immediately replaced by a subjective reaction no longer related to the reality of the object. This naturally has the same effect as devaluation. Such a type can easily make one question why one should exist at all. . . .

Seen from the outside, it looks as though the effect of the object did not penetrate into the subject at all. This impression is correct inasmuch as a subjective content does, in fact, intervene from the unconscious and intercept the effect of the object. The intervention may be so abrupt that the individual appears to be shielding himself directly from all objective influences. . . . If the object is a person, he feels completely devalued, while the subject has an illusory conception of reality, which in pathological cases goes so far that he is no longer able to distinguish between the real object and the subjective perception. . . . Such action has an illusory character unrelated to objective reality and is extremely disconcerting. It instantly reveals the reality-alienating subjectivity of this type. But when the influence of the object does not break through completely, it is met with well-intentioned neutrality, disclosing little sympathy yet constantly striving to soothe and adjust. The too low is raised a little, the too high is lowered, enthusiasm is damped down, extravagance restrained, and anything out of the ordinary reduced to the right formula — all this in order to keep the influence of the object within the necessary bounds. In this way the type becomes a menace to his environment because his total innocuousness is not altogether above suspicion. In that case he easily becomes a victim of the aggressiveness and domineeringness of others. Such men allow themselves to be abused and then take their revenge on the most unsuitable occasions with redoubled obtuseness and stubbornness. (C. G. Jung, *Psychological Types*, 396–397.)

At the lower end of the continuum, Nines are a "menace to [their] environment" because, like everyone else, they have a characteristic form of selfishness, although it is more difficult to perceive in Nines than in other types since Nines are so apparently accommodating to others. The particular form which their selfishness takes is their willingness to sacrifice a great many values — in a sense, their willingness to sacrifice all of reality — so they can maintain their inner serenity. Being anxious or emotionally stimulated can be extraordinarily threatening for average to unhealthy Nines because they are unused to being aware of their feelings. Virtually any kind of emotional reaction disrupts the fullness of their repression, whether the reaction is caused by anxiety, aggression, or something else. The result is that average Nines seek peace at any price, although the price they unwittingly pay is that they lose contact with everyone and everything, including themselves.

As they cling desperately to peace by "burying their heads in the sand," they eventually become unable to deal with anything. In their haste to get problems behind them, nothing is faced squarely and problems are never solved. They become disoriented, as if they were sleepwalking through life. They exercise poor judgment, sometimes with tragic results. Moreover, the consequences of their inattention and disengagement cannot be ignored forever, at least by others. Unhealthy Nines may be forced to come to grips with what they have done, although they will try to avoid doing so at all costs. They would rather turn their backs completely on reality than make what seems to them to be the impossible effort of putting their world right again.

Healthy Nines, however, can be the most contented and pleasant people imaginable. They are extraordinarily receptive, making people feel accepted as they are. Their peace is so mature that they are able to admit conflict and separation, growth and individuality into their lives. They are their own persons, yet they delight in giving themselves away. But once they begin to seek peace of mind inappropriately, average Nines become self-effacing, complacent, and fearful of change. They do not want to deal with reality—either the reality of themselves or of others. And unhealthy Nines totally resist anything which intrudes upon them. They live in a world of unreality, desperately clinging to illusions while their world falls apart.

ANALYZING THE HEALTHY NINE

Level 1: The Self-Possessed Guide

At their best, very healthy Nines allow themselves to become fully empowered, independent persons. Having overcome their fear of loss and separation from others, they become self-possessed and truly autonomous. They feel extraordinarily fulfilled and enjoy a profound contentment and an unshakable equanimity because they are in union with someone from whom they can never be separated: themselves. They achieve the peace they are always seeking because they are truly at one with themselves. This sort of wholeness and inner integrity is indeed rare in the world, and a source of great beauty, true creativity, and joyfulness when it occurs.

Although extraordinarily serene, they are also paradoxically vital and alive, in touch with their thoughts, feelings, and desires. Very healthy Nines are aware of even their aggressive feelings without being alarmed by them. They realize that having aggressions is not the same as acting aggressively or being destructive toward others. Thus, self-possession enables Nines to bring more of themselves to others than they ever could before, and so their relationships become more satisfying as they acquire new depth.

Self-respecting, they have enormous dignity because they are aware of their true worth without the faintest whiff of egocentricity or self-congratulation. They are fully present as individuals. And because they can see themselves as they really are, they are able to see others as they really are. People are no longer idealized, and so they become truly other to Nines—and for that reason they are loved much more realistically.

Very healthy Nines are firmly in their own center, dynamic, powerful, and enormously capable of dealing with problems because of the deep inner unity they have achieved. They feel fulfilled, if not as persons who have completely developed all their potentials, then as persons who are able to bring themselves to bear on the world, the moment, and the other. They actively inhabit their own consciousness, as it were, possessing themselves and taking control of their lives. This is an extremely private, almost spiritual event, difficult to observe directly or describe. But it is a real, decisive event nonetheless. Very healthy Nines are being born psychologically, as mature centers of awareness. A new force is entering the world—a new being, an ancient child, an indomitable spirit.

At their best, therefore, very healthy Nines are an example to all the personality types of what it means to be at one with the self and at one with the world. They are an example of the profound unity which is possible for human beings—the unity of the self as well as the unity of the self and the other. They teach us of a self-possession and self-surrender so profound as to have mystical overtones. They are so effortlessly themselves and so completely receptive that very healthy Nines must reflect what human beings were like before the Fall into self-consciousness and alienation. They are a living reminder that, when all is said and done, we are each a gift to the other, just as the other is a gift to us. To be completely ourselves and yet fully related to the other is a mystery to be surrendered to in silence.

Level 2: The Receptive Person

Unfortunately, even healthy Nines are not always so healthy. Self-possession is difficult to sustain, and the fear of losing the sense of balance and harmony they feel with the environment and with the people who are important to them always remains in the shadows of their minds. If they succumb to it, Nines desire to create peace of mind for themselves by becoming unselfconscious. Instead of bringing the fullness of their awareness to themselves, others, and the moment, they subtly begin to lose themselves in their impressions, to begin to forget that they are an active part of what they are experiencing. In the desire to merge harmoniously with the other, they begin to lose their center. Basically, to maintain a sense of peace, Nines begin to diffuse their own awareness, losing touch with the grounding of their sensations and instincts.

Because Nines developed their sense of self by identifying with both parents, they also are able to identify with others, giving positive attention to those who are central in their lives. They are extraordinarily receptive, capable of identifying with others so completely that they are not self-conscious, self-doubting, or self-centered. Not only are healthy Nines free to give their full attention to others, they positively want to do so. Because of their ability to identify with people, healthy Nines have a great capacity for loving and sustaining others.

Since they are so unselfconsciously accepting, there are few conflicts either in their emotional lives or in their relationships. Nines see themselves as peaceful, and as long as they are healthy, they really are at peace with the world. They have a high tolerance for stress and irritation; they are patient, imperturbable, relaxed, and tranquil. They do not fly off the handle over the little annoyances of life. There is also an unmistakable innocence and simplicity about healthy Nines. They are guileless, the kind of people to whom lying or trying to take advantage of others would never occur. (It is incomprehensible to them how others can be guilty of this sort of thing.)

Their receptivity allows healthy Nines to be the most trusting of the personality types. They trust others, they trust themselves, and they trust life. Because they communicate the feeling of nonjudgmental acceptance, Nines serve as emotional anchors for people; stable and solid, they are always there when others need them.

Modest, gentle, and approachable, they are sanctuaries of peace to whom others come for solace, rest, and comfort. Uncritical and unthreatening, they do not have unattainable standards either for themselves or for anyone else. They are easy to please and make few demands on anyone. (Healthy Nines are not, however, totally uncritical and equally receptive to everyone. Some people repel them, of course, but healthy Nines are more gracious to those they dislike than is any other personality type.)

Although healthy Nines feel at ease among people, they also love to commune with nature. Sailing, hiking, camping, gardening, or taking care of animals makes them feel very much at peace. Nature—especially its mystical and mythological side—strikes a receptive chord in them because by identifying with nature, Nines feel at one with something larger than themselves. Moreover, since they are used to identifying with others, personalizing them in their minds, nature, animals, and even abstract ideas and symbols have a deep emotional resonance for them. For example, Nines do not think of their country as an abstraction but as a living thing; their pets are people to them; the countryside is populated by mythological creatures; mountains, trees, and rivers are archetypal forces; elves, ghosts, and leprechauns inhabit their living room or favorite shady spot.

The archetypal imagination we find in healthy Nines also has a deep appeal to other people, since it taps the desire for union with the cosmos which, at some level, everyone desires and needs. Healthy Nines supply the personality types with a vision of the magic of the world. They have a way of looking at the world through innocent eyes. Their mythological imagination recalls the consciousness of childhood in which everything seemed to glow with enchantment. Healthy Nines never lose the contemplative side of themselves or their sense of wonder.

Correspondingly, Nines have an affinity for nonverbal communication. They are at home in the world of pictures and symbols, and they often tend to think in colors and impressions rather than in words. Many Nines are also attuned to music, and derive great fulfillment from singing or playing an instrument. The quality of music is very supportive of their state of awareness: playing or listening to music is an experience in which one can lose one's self in the process. Further, the sense of harmony, tone, and vibration all feed the Nine's feeling of oneness and flow with their environment.

Finally, since Nines see themselves as part of nature, the physical processes of sex, birth, aging, and death itself seem natural to them, things which should be accepted as part of the way things are. Their acceptance of nature and nature's ways is yet another source of their peacefulness, because they are not at odds with existence as many other personality types are. Nines are not defiant of the natural order, but happy to be part of it, yielding themselves to it.

Level 3: The Supportive Peacemaker

Because their peace of mind is threatened by any tension between them and others, healthy Nines want to ensure that peace reigns everywhere in their lives. Achieving and maintaining peace motivates them to become peacemakers, mediating disputes and conflicts between those they are close to. Nines want to reconcile people to each other so that everyone will be at peace, just as they are with themselves.

They are also good mediators because they take the complaints of others seriously. They understand real differences between people, why others are upset and concerned about whatever is on their minds. Healthy Nines also are able to see areas of common ground, and they work toward achieving reconciliation because they feel that there is much more to be gained by cooperation than by divisiveness.

The list of their positive qualities is a long one: healthy Nines have a healing touch and go out of their way to pour oil on troubled waters. They have a soothing effect on others because they are so calm themselves. Others find that they are mysteriously at peace simply for being in the Nine's presence. Nines are also optimistic and reassuring, and whenever they can responsibly do so, they stress the positive, believing that looking on the bright side of things is preferable to dwelling on the negative. They are able to forgive and forget, to put conflicts completely behind them and get on with their relationships and their responsibilities. They are extremely affable, pleasant people, the kind others spontaneously (and rightly) call "nice" or the "salt of the earth." They are jovial and have sunny dispositions, a natural, unaffected sense of humor, and a warm, easy laugh. They are unpretentious, treating everyone with the same honest directness no matter whether the person is royalty or a cab driver. They are easygoing and as comfortable as an old shoe. It must be the rarest of persons who does not like a healthy Nine.

Healthy Nines are not simply good-natured, however. They bring other qualities to society, particularly the support which they give others so that they can thrive. Whoever is significant to Nines—spouses, children, close friends—will be the beneficiaries of their unstinting love and generosity. And since healthy Nines possess a gut instinct about others (as a result of their identification with them), what they do for people is both appropriate and valuable for their development.

When Nines feel something important needs to be said, they can be extremely candid, perhaps saying more than other types would find it politic to say, although Nines do so without desiring to hurt anyone. Their candor can be very valuable, since they distinguish themselves by their uncommon common sense, a combination of simplicity and guilelessness so true as to be extraordinary. They have no ulterior motives, no pretensions, no large ego to protect or inflate, no concern for status or prestige, no desire to impress or condemn others. Hence, they speak with the honesty of children and the wisdom of adults.

Their serenity is certainly soothing to others, and a great help to them in negotiations of all sorts, but it also serves them very well in a crisis. Healthy Nines can maintain a levelheaded calm, even in highly stressful or dangerous circumstances. They often combine this composure with their healing touch in the medical professions or in related fields of health and nutrition. Of course, Nines can be found in a wide variety of professions, but even if they are not pursuing a career in the healing arts, many high-functioning Nines are interested in healing and holistic approaches to life.

In a similar vein, healthy Nines are often students of metaphysics and human development. They are at home with a global, transpersonal perspective and are frequent attendees of workshops on meditation, energy and body work, yoga, and relaxation techniques. Nines enjoy exploring the world of dreams, symbols, and images, and they are frequently attracted to the ways of indigenous peoples who emphasize life in harmony with nature. They also are adept at synthesizing different perspectives or traditions in a way that finds the common threads in them all but also produces new insights.

Nines can be wonderfully creative in more traditional ways as well, and delight in sharing their visions of an enchanted, utopian world with others. When they are healthy, their unselfconsciousness allows them easy access to their creative process (although this changes in the average Levels of the continuum). Not surprisingly, much of the art they produce has qualities similar to their personal style: that is, positive, reassuring, and full of a sense of wonder about the world.

Last, even though healthy Nines are easygoing, they may become extremely successful in their professions because of their ability to bring out the best in others by creating a nurturing environment. But precisely because they are not competitive and rarely call attention to themselves, others tend to underestimate them. People take Nines for granted, until they realize how much they have contributed to everyone's welfare.

ANALYZING THE AVERAGE NINE

Level 4: The Accommodating Role-Player

Outwardly, average Nines seem little different from healthy Nines, although a shift has taken place, not so much in their actions as in their attitudes. The difference between healthy Nines and average Nines is that healthy Nines are in touch with themselves and others, whereas average Nines begin to lose touch with themselves and others by subordinating themselves to roles and social conventions. They do not want to stand out too much, putting themselves in the background so as not to disturb their environment.

In the healthy Levels, Nines are dynamic individuals who work to create a positive, harmonious environment. But in so doing, they may begin to fear that asserting themselves or their desires will create conflicts with others, thus spoiling their peace. When they begin to fear getting into conflicts with people, Nines are being swept into the average Levels of the continuum. Ironically, this strategy is the genesis of many of the conflicts that Nines will have with others. People want attention and responses from Nines, but as they reflexively avoid possible conflicts and repress their opinions, their input is not forthcoming. ("Where would you like to go for dinner tonight?" "I don't care. Wherever you want to go.")

At this stage the basic pattern we see is that Nines lower their expectations of life and of themselves, and begin going along with other people's wishes to avoid conflicts with them. In fact, the expectations of society and of their peers begin to create a role into which Nines can disappear. Everyone plays various roles in life, but in the case of average Nines, the role is created by others and exists to fulfill their expectations and needs. Average Nines want to blend in and to be unthreatening. Becoming too expressive or assertive feels to them like "making a scene."

Self-effacement becomes the main way by which average Nines blend in with their peers and minimize the risk of conflicts. In contrast to Threes, who want to be outstanding in their social roles, average Nines do not want to stand out, lest they draw fire. The result is that they can become "generic" versions of their social role—the boy or girl next door, the nine-to-five worker, the journeyman musician, the pleasant doctor. As with average Threes, it becomes difficult to distinguish the person from the role they believe they are supposed to fulfill.

Self-effacement affects Nines in other ways as well. Average Nines willingly accommodate themselves to others because their sense of self depends on it. Average Nines begin to idealize the people they identify with, so that the more wonderful the qualities of the other, the better Nines feel about themselves. The more the other is idealized, the stronger the emotional bonds and the more at one with themselves Nines feel. In fact, this action creates the opposite effect. Nines feel better about themselves because of their connection with such wonderful people. But they are devaluing themselves to do this. Or more precisely, they are beginning to forget themselves and neglect their own development. They become like a mother who lives for her children or a wife for her husband. Of course, it is appropriate for a mother to accommodate herself to the needs of her children when they are infants and cannot do without her. But it becomes a problem if, as they get older, she continues the same pattern of self-effacement. The essential problem is that average Nines go too far in identifying with the other, losing too much of themselves in the process. Too readily do the wishes of others become their wishes, the thoughts of others their thoughts.

A reciprocal motion occurs: as they accommodate themselves, they idealize the other. If the other is a person, he or she can do no wrong; if it is a value or belief, it is never questioned. Thus, average Nines easily fall into conventional roles, defining themselves as persons whose place in life is to fulfill the functions—as husband, wife, breadwinner, parent, citizen—which have been assigned by someone else or by the culture in which they live. Getting married, having children, and holding down a job, among many other things, are expected of them—so they accommodate themselves. Their lifestyle, their religious and political beliefs, their expectations for themselves and their children are all defined by the conventions which they have accepted.

This is why average Nines are so aptly thought of as the archetypal common man. They are the glue of society, which by its very willingness to be molded into whatever niches are needed is valuable to society, although at a cost to the individuals involved. Without a thought about developing themselves, average Nines embrace the values and ways of thinking and living of the culture in which they find themselves. Even if they are part of an "alternative culture," they will dress, behave, and live their life in the way they feel is "normal" for that culture. (Nines in a spiritual community will be conscientious about observing the practices and protocols of that community.) Respectability is therefore very important to them. Nines are not so much interested in keeping up with the Joneses as in being respectable members of their society, doing what is proper, and not doing what they imagine a person of their society would not do. In this sense, average Nines are also usually conservative, not necessarily politically conservative, but conservative in the sense of being resistant to significant changes in their world.

Because they are conservative, average Nines also tend to be past-oriented. The past is always more comfortable than the present or the future, since the past is a known quantity. It is less threatening because it has already been lived through. Moreover, average Nines can be nostalgic about the past, getting sentimental or idealizing it because doing so creates a source of good feelings for themselves and others. Further, happy memories from the past become a reliable source of positive feelings when conflicts and problems erupt in their world.

It is difficult to quibble with many of the particular values of average Nines. The problem is not so much with their values as with their not thinking them through. They simply adopt their way of life wholesale, naively accepting everything at face value.

Level 5: The Disengaged Participant
Because their emotional stability depends on maintaining their inner world of beliefs and idealizations, average Nines at this stage

fear change. They do not want to do anything which would upset them, and therefore want to maintain the status quo as much as possible. Rather than exert themselves in any deep, essential way, they let everything simply work out on its own, without their intervention or response.

The irony is that average Nines must actually do something to do nothing: they must disengage themselves from anything in the environment which they perceive as a threat to their peace. Their healthy unselfconsciousness has become a certain unreflective disconnectedness, a lack of awareness of aspects of the world around them. They remain on friendly terms with reality, but not slavishly so. A sluggish complacency, intellectual laziness, and emotional indolence set in. ("Oh, well, we don't have to worry about that . . .") They become passive: life begins to happen to average Nines.

There is a distinctive vagueness about Nines at this stage because they maintain an uninvolved distance between themselves and their activities, an impassiveness, which does not allow anything to get to them or upset them. They are extremely easygoing, but they do not make real contact with the environment—or with those in it—becoming matter-of-fact, even about things which would ordinarily call for a more impassioned response. They slip into an indifferent "I can take it or leave it" attitude, which prevents them from getting too excited about or involved in anything. They move from one thing to another, equally content and neutral about it. In short, average Nines are mellow and "laid-back" to a fault, the classic phlegmatic temperament personified. Being "on cloud nine" takes on new meaning.

Because they do not allow themselves to feel anything very deeply, their highs are not high and their lows are not low, as Jung noted. Everything is kept on an even keel. Average Nines are not even aware that their feelings are dampened, since they have disconnected themselves from their feelings. At this stage, average Nines begin to be so vague and undefined that others cannot help but notice that something is missing in them, as if they were not all there. They are unfocused and spacy, a million miles away, as if grooving on some inner trip or secret thought—or on nothing at all.

Nothing seems particularly important or urgent to average Nines, and they put no particular mental energy into anything unless they absolutely have to. Details do not interest them, they forget things, and they do not concentrate on their work for more than a few minutes before mentally floating off. Their conversation rambles or they change the subject abruptly, revealing their lack of attention to what is being said. Average Nines are life's dreamers, enjoying the contemplation of their inner vision of whomever or whatever they have idealized. But, unfortunately, because their attention is inward on their contemplation, they become inattentive to the real world. If they are intelligent and well-educated, they may enjoy talking about philosophy, theology, the arts, or science, although even so, much of their thinking is frankly little more than vague woolgathering, the purpose of which is to pass the time rather than actively engage themselves with anything requiring intense involvement or effort.

Increasingly, to convince themselves that they are doing something constructive with their time, average Nines engage in "busy work." They involve themselves in all sorts of projects, errands, and activities which help maintain their world to some degree, but which have little real impact on them. Furthermore, Nines at Level 5 begin to have difficulty galvanizing themselves to do things that would substantially improve their lives. They feel an enormous inner resistance to leaving the comfort of their routines, as if they were trying to swim through molasses. Everything seems like too much trouble, so average Nines soon switch on "autopilot" and disappear into their routines again.

Their healthy simplicity has deteriorated into obliviousness, a permanent absentmindedness, as if they were constantly daydreaming about nothing in particular, perceiving the world like someone who looks at a clock without seeing the time. Indeed, the way most people have trained themselves to ignore television commercials is how average Nines experience a lot of reality, disconnecting themselves from whatever they do not want to see or hear until inadvertence becomes habitual. They are like sleepwalkers, physically present but not aware of what is going on around them.

Their energy is spent maintaining their peace, ignoring anything which would excite or trouble them. Physical and emotional comfort is an important value, and average Nines do not push themselves too hard intellectually or physically lest they get either too stimulated or too exhausted. They pass the time in undemanding ways, puttering around the house, going on errands, collecting knickknacks, or mindlessly watching television. At this stage, they become accustomed to living in a state of semiawareness, like people who have been on tranquilizers so long that they forget what it is like to be off them.

It is important to understand, however, that psychological passivity is not the same thing as complete inactivity, although it is a precursor to it. Average Nines may be the heads of multimillion-dollar corporations, leading vast enterprises while still maintaining an inner disconnectedness from their activities. Nines are able to be uninvolved because one of their defense mechanisms is compartmentalization (isolation), which allows their subjective experiences to be broken into unrelated segments so that they can move from one thing to another without engaging themselves. As a result, reality has little impact on them. They can be relatively busy while remaining emotionally and intellectually detached from their activities.

Moreover, the social roles they have been fulfilling are now used to keep others from affecting them. They relate to others through their roles but without much investment in the interaction. Instead, their attention is disengaged from the immediacy of their experience, as they withdraw into a safe inner sanctum where the events of their lives will not strongly impact them.

Because they disconnect from their experiences, average Nines do not make the cause-and-effect connections one would normally expect: cause and effect simply do not seem to go together for them. They do not think of the consequences of their actions, or of the fact that their omissions will also have consequences. They do not think through anything, unquestioningly feeling that everything will work out for the best.

Their lack of self-awareness is at the root of what is going on here. Inattention arises because, unless they are healthy, Nines never learn to focus on anything, including themselves. Just the opposite: their entire orientation is to be unselfconscious and receptive to the other, as we have seen. Because they are unable to sense themselves as discrete individuals, they get used to perceiving all of reality vaguely. When practical problems arise, especially with other people, their inability to attend to reality only makes things worse. Average Nines increasingly become part of the problem rather than part of the solution.

The problem is that average Nines have made many accommodations to others to avoid conflicts and to be left in peace. But these accommodations are not without cost, and underneath the passivity, Nines are angry both at others for not seeing them and their needs (although they may be uncertain as to what they are or how to express them to others) and at themselves for their inability to assert their desires. They are convinced, however, that this anger would ruin their inner stability, their peace of mind, so they repress it, not realizing that it is the very energy that would enable them to assert themselves. To repress their anger and anxiety, they begin to disconnect from all of their feelings.

They also disconnect from interpersonal conflicts by compartmentalizing their relationships, splitting people into two major groups: those with whom they have identified and everyone else. The second group of people has little meaning to average Nines because they are essentially unreal, little more than an abstraction. Average Nines can be surprisingly callous and indifferent about this group of people. They may as well not exist.

Nor do average Nines put much energy into their relationships even with those in the first group, with whom they have identified. Nines idealize these people, and then shift their attention from the real people to their idealization of them. The result is that others sense a lack of attention to themselves or to their real needs. Ironically, others may also begin to lose interest in average Nines because there is so little energy or relating going on in the relationship. As Nines drift off, others drift away.

Level 6: The Resigned Fatalist

If doing nothing does not succeed and they must face their problems or conflicts with others, average Nines at this stage attempt to minimize their importance. They underestimate the seriousness of the consequences of their passivity and underestimate how difficult it will be for someone else to correct the problems they refuse to deal with. In fact, they underestimate the necessity of doing much of anything at all.

By this stage, it is likely that average Nines have a number of genuine problems in their lives, but they take pride in their ability to endure whatever happens: they know that they can get through problems by tuning them out. Thus, rather than exert themselves, they become fatalistic, feeling that nothing can be done to change things, and that in any event, whatever the problem is, it is not so much a problem after all. ("Well, it doesn't really matter anyway.") Their healthy receptivity has deteriorated into resignation, a giving up rather than a mature letting go. This is not optimism but self-ishness. ("I don't want to hear it—I just don't want to be upset.")

They begin to trudge through their lives as if life were something to "get through" rather than live. They will stay in a bad marriage or a poor work environment rather than risk upsetting their situation. Apathy has replaced compliance. At this Level, Nines are not even interested in going along with others' wishes. They develop a profound indifference about themselves, their lives, and the people and events around them.

The problem is that Nines refuse to see the problem. As far as they are concerned, no matter what happens, they are resigned to their fate. They show little interest or understanding about what is at stake either for themselves or for anyone else. If others get angry at them because of their refusal to act, Nines quickly try to appease them. They want peace at any price, and will make whatever concessions are necessary to "get their problems behind them," a typical phrase. Once they have appeased others, they feel the crisis has passed, and they can continue as before. But because Nines do not want to deal with anything upsetting, it is hard to resolve difficulties with them. They forget how problems were settled. The following week the problems still exist: nothing that was supposedly worked out has actually sunk into their heads or made a real, permanent difference.

At this stage, they are so eager to avoid conflicts that they water down conflicting positions, give a false sense of hope by minimizing issues, and tell people prematurely to "calm down—everything will be all right." Others are frustrated with Nines because they are so disengaged that it is almost impossible to connect with them in any meaningful or emotionally satisfying way. Ironically, Nines who feared losing their sense of connection and harmony with others have withdrawn their attention from them. Moreover, when others attempt to make helpful suggestions or try to get some kind of a response from them, average Nines can be extremely stubborn and angry, not seeing what all the fuss is about. ("Why can't you accept me as I am?") They want to downplay problems so that everyone can get back to a more peaceful, harmonious existence and so that whatever threatens their tranquillity will go away.

But in doing so they can be penny wise and pound foolish. Their judgment becomes extremely poor. If they are forced to deal with a problem which they alone can solve, they will go only as far as they absolutely must and then drop it. They lack staying power; they simply do not see a problem through to the end. If forced to act, their every tendency is to think that they have done enough once they have made a little effort. Thus, they often undo the good they may have begun and disappoint others who may be counting on them.

Average Nines are often able to endure unpleasant situations for a long time because they live in a world of wishful thinking. They believe in magic: someone will come along and "fix" their problems or, if they are patient and long-suffering, their problems will be taken away. They dream of a better future without doing anything to bring it about. ("Someday my ship will come in"; "Someday my prince will come.") In this state of disengagement, day after day goes by, and Nines find the possibility of actualizing their dreams and longings slowly fading away.

Furthermore, others realize that they will have to suffer the consequences of the fatalism and unwillingness of Nines to exert themselves. Even so, it is frustrating for others to confront fatalistic Nines. They are still so nice that few people are willing to press them or get them upset. People tend to leave Nines alone because Nines want to be left in peace.

The nature of their selfishness is now clear: without being aware of it, Nines are able to put their peace above the more serious needs of others, in effect, above reality and the harm they do by ignoring it. Their appeasement of others is a defense against changing anything essential about themselves or the idealization of their important relationships. By minimizing reality, average Nines, in a sense, sacrifice others to continue the illusion of union with them, so that they can maintain their identities and their tranquillity. In this way, they are able to sacrifice their spouses, their children—and themselves—to the god of peace.

There is much aggression in this, but it is so subtle that other people usually do not even notice it. However, others are no longer real to Nines. Their lives have been taken away—not literally but psychologically. Nines have created a relationship with a fantasy and have turned their backs on reality, particularly the reality of others. There can scarcely be a more pervasive kind of aggression.

Nines have been using all of their internal energy to block out of awareness their fears and anxieties, but now their anxieties are too great to ignore. They have become compliant with others to avoid conflicts, but now everyone seems to have a grievance with them, and they do not seem to be able to keep their easy relationships and peaceful feelings going.

ANALYZING THE UNHEALTHY NINE

Level 7: *The Denying Doormat*

Unhealthy Nines become adamant about not facing conflicts and problems. They actively resist seeing their problems (denial) so they can protect themselves from emotional pain and anxiety and maintain their relationship with their illusions. As a result, unhealthy Nines are obstinate and neglectful and absolutely impervious to pressure to change. Problems can even have the most obvious and relatively easy solution, yet unhealthy Nines do not do anything *and do not want to.*

All their energy goes toward maintaining their defenses against dealing with reality so that nothing will get to them. This defense, known as repression resistance, is extraordinarily frustrating to deal with and makes it almost impossible to get through to unhealthy Nines. It is as if they have bolted shut some inner door, preventing anyone from having access to them. Ironically, those who were once so open and receptive have become impenetrable. They are furious with others for trying to force them to do anything, and hence for arousing their anxiety. But the only way unhealthy Nines can express anger is to resist others and block them out all the more. Passive resistance is as aggressive as unhealthy Nines become, except perhaps for an occasional inadvertent eruption of rage when the repression momentarily fails.

More typically, however, unhealthy Nines tend to be victims and "doormats." The self-effacement and accommodation we saw in the average Levels has deteriorated into allowing themselves to be exploited and abused. Unhealthy Nines are so fearful of conflict and of losing the other—and have such low self-esteem—that they will not defend themselves from either psychological or physical abuse. From another perspective, unhealthy Nines are, of course, profoundly outraged at being abused, but continue to repress their rage and even their self-preservation instincts because their tenuous emotional equilibrium and sense of self would be overwhelmed by such powerful feelings. The repression of their rage is extremely tiring, leaving Nines depressed, confused, and unable to function. As a result, they are more dependent than ever on their oppressors and less capable of taking constructive action for themselves.

Since they feel incapable of taking any decisive action, they become seriously neglectful not only of their responsibilities toward others but even toward themselves. They will not go to a doctor if they are ill, much less recognize the medical or emotional problems of their spouses or children. They cannot do their work at the office if it upsets them in the least. Those who depend on them realize very clearly that they are completely unreliable. Getting unhealthy Nines to do anything for themselves is like running into a stone wall.

Because repressed Nines obstinately resist contact with reality, they become inadequate and undeveloped as persons, virtually helpless about doing anything on their own. Ironically, for people who exert themselves so little, unhealthy Nines have little energy because of their repressed rage, as we have seen. They are often fatigued because their energy goes into warding off reality rather than dealing with it. The usual result of this is depression. They become listless and dependent, able to function in only minimal ways. Unhealthy Nines cannot cope with any tension or pressure whatsoever because everything upsets them (or rather, they think it will) or demands more attention and effort than they are able to muster. Others—sometimes those they have harmed by their neglect—must step in to save them from themselves, correcting the problems unhealthy Nines have refused to face.

Serious interpersonal conflicts are certain to arise at this point, if they have not already done so. When hostilities break out, unhealthy Nines are invariably mystified by the intensity of other people's negative feelings toward them. They do not realize how much their inattention has cost others.

Having to face the fact that through their negligence they have harmed someone with whom they have identified would provoke extreme anxiety and guilt in unhealthy Nines. They would be plunged into despair and possibly driven toward suicide. However, repression spares them from being aware of their failures and inadequacies, although not from all realization. Moments of insight into the finality of their actions—or more properly, the consequences of their neglect—break in on them now and then. They realize that their omissions have had consequences which cannot be undone. It is too late to go back. The horror of this is like a beast pounding at the door of their unconscious. How to keep it out?

Level 8: The Dissociating Automaton

Pressure from reality and antagonism from others may get so strong that to protect themselves from having to face the awareness of what they have done, neurotic Nines cut themselves off entirely from everything. They blank out subjectively so that they do not make contact with reality and so that reality does not make contact with them. Their fear of anxiety is so intense that neurotic Nines dissociate themselves from reality, becoming depersonalized. They regress to an infantile state as if they desired to return to the womb. They block out so much that they withdraw into a numb, affectless condition as if in amnesia, completely dissociating from the self.

Neurotic Nines are like automatons: they do not feel or react to anything. It is as if the self had been removed from the body which functions on its own. The extent of their denial of reality can be astounding. They may have lost a limb, but either deny that it happened or think that the arm or leg will grow back. They may think that they were not really fired or that a divorce or death did not really happen. As pathetic as this state is, there is a poetic appropriateness to their condition, since Nines have been increasingly absent from themselves for some time. By now, however, their dissociation from themselves has become habitual, a way of life, or more precisely, a way of not living.

They are in the fog of dissociation, feeling that life is a bad dream, a sort of make-believe from which they must take flight so that reality will not really happen to them. Of course, in times of severe loss and trauma, other personality types also react by denying reality until they can begin to deal with what has happened. However, neurotic Nines dissociate because they feel that they cannot deal with reality ever again.

Nines at this level resemble trauma victims in shock in the aftermath of an accident. They seem lost, confused about their identities and sometimes even their whereabouts. Depressions which may have developed at Level 7 settled into a chronic condition. Unhealthy Nines are desolate and numb, yet their anguish and anger may continually and unexpectedly break through to the surface. They may be blank and depersonalized one moment, and sobbing hysterically the next. It is as though they are regressing to earlier and earlier memories in an attempt to escape the terrors of their current condition. Nines at this stage are also full of tremendous rage at others, although they are completely unaware of it. What glimmers of it do arise are extremely threatening. Neurotic Nines fear that releasing any of it would destroy whatever inner refuges they retain. Nonetheless, hysterical outbursts and temper tantrums can be part of the picture.

Indeed, there is a hysterical element in their flight from reality, although this is difficult to perceive since the hysteria is repressed out of consciousness. Nevertheless, their unconscious anxiety has reached such a pitch that neurotic Nines must stay in flight both from themselves and from reality. But this means that they have nowhere to go, either outward to the world to find refuge or inward to seek their own comfort and counsel. Life has become like a terrible nightmare from which Nines hope they will soon awaken, but at this point, their problems are often very real. The only way out is to push dissociation one final step in the direction of self-abandonment. In flight both from anxiety and reality, neurotic Nines dissociate themselves from themselves as completely as possible.

Level 9: The Self-Abandoning Ghost
If something pushes them over the edge (if, for example, reality puts pressures on them from which they cannot flee), neurotic Nines may well suffer a psychotic break with reality as well as schizoid breaks within their psyche. They disintegrate as persons into the most extreme state of dissociation from who they are. As we have seen, their receptive orientation to life has facilitated their flight from self-awareness. Now, they completely flee from themselves, retreating into a state that resembles autism.

If Nines suffered chronic and extreme abuse as children, they may be particularly prone to multiple personality disorder. This is not to say that all multiple personality cases are Nines or that all unhealthy Nines will develop multiple personalities, but there does seem to be some overlap of these two conditions. In such cases, we can see how multiple personalities can result from the individual's attempting to accommodate highly conflicting emotional material and attempting to build an identity from it.

In most cases, neurotic Nines unconsciously abandon themselves as whole persons, reinvesting consciousness into various fragments of themselves, each of which may represent an aspect of the self which has been repressed and denied and undeveloped. Memories, dreamlike trances, and emotional reactions seem to come and go at random. It is as though the very structure of the personality has come "unglued" or broken apart, and only its constituents remain to interact with the environment.

To abandon themselves as persons, retreating into complete dissociation and fragmenting their personalities, is a "solution" of sorts, because then it is not really they who live but someone else through whom they can live. We have seen that average Nines tend to live through the other; now we see that they live through the other-self, the fragments of the self which are little more than the disconnected identifications and relationships with significant others from the Nine's past. The core self has been so traumatized that it is as though in a dream without a dreamer. This can hardly be called living. Furthermore, because one of the subpersonalities can do harm to other people or to itself, this is neither a safe nor truly adaptive way to live.

Fragmenting into subpersonalities is, however, an ironically appropriate outcome for neurotic Nines because they have never shown much interest in themselves as individuals. Now they are truly not individuals: they are many different "people" — and no one. Moreover, Nines who so feared losing or separating from others have not only psychologically done so, they have also separated from and lost themselves.

THE DYNAMICS OF THE NINE

The Direction of Disintegration: The Nine Goes to Six
Beginning at Level 4, Nines under stress will begin to act out some of the characteristics of average to unhealthy Sixes. Average Nines are disengaging from the environment and from their anxiety in order to maintain a peaceful equilibrium within themselves. When events around them become too stressful for this defense to work, they begin to experience the full intensity of their anxiety and may become reactive and insecure, like average Sixes. Nines need to engage in constructive action on their own behalf, and they need to stay in touch with their feelings, but when they are further down the Levels of Development, they tend to do both of these things in erratic, imbalanced ways.

At Level 4, Nines are busy accommodating themselves to the wishes and expectations of others. They put their own agendas on the "back burner" and comply with other people's demands in order to reduce the possibility of conflicts. When circumstances cause their anxieties to increase, they may well go to Six and engage in lots of "organizational activity." Like average Sixes, they attempt to stabilize their environment and their relationships in order to make them safer. They may get into intensive periods of work, investing their time and energy in activities they believe will enhance their security, and thus their peace of mind. These actions are guided not by positive intention, however, but by anxiety. They also begin to identify more strongly with protectors, supporters, groups, or ideas that increase their self-confidence and give them a feeling of purpose and direction.

At Level 5, Nines are disengaging from the environment. They want to remain well within their "comfort zone" and stay with activities which will not disturb them. They may well be busy, but they will be busy doing tasks and routines that do not threaten to draw them out of their safe inner world. When their stress is such that this is not possible, they go to Six and become negative and defensive. Average Nines have been complying with others to avoid having conflicts with them—to keep the peace—but now the things that others expect of them may cause them to leave the emotional security of their disengagement. At this Level, the anger and anxiety of Nines are escalating, so their defenses against both must also become greater. They use passive-aggressive tactics to assert their own needs, but in ways which they hope will not alienate their supporters. They keep saying yes to people's demands on their time, then doing what they want to do. They feel pressured, complain, and are evasive like average Sixes.

At Level 6, Nines are digging in their heels to resist the environment and hold on to what remains of their inner stability. They have a resigned, fatalistic attitude, and have entrenched themselves in comforting routines and habits that they hope will keep the world, others, and their own anxiety from bothering them. When others continue to disturb their "slumbers," Nines develop a siege mentality and can react aggressively to people like average Sixes. They may blame others as the cause of their problems, or they may react defiantly to the people around them who have been trying to get through their self-defeating defenses. Displays of temper and angry outbursts are not uncommon, though they are often as much of a surprise to Nines as they are to the people who know them. Their belligerent reactions create more conflicts and escalate their anxiety.

At Level 7, Nines are likely to have serious problems in their lives. To maintain their peacefulness now requires a huge amount of energy, and a willful turning away from reality. Nines at this level feel that they simply cannot cope with the world, and so repress themselves to the point of numbness. Now their move to Six reflects a growing dependency on others, feelings of helplessness, and a desire to hand their lives over to someone else who will "fix everything." However, the central problem is that Nines are too frightened, and too full of rage about the accommodations they have made, to risk confronting and dealing with their problems. But unless they do, their problems will only get more unmanageable, and it will become less likely that anyone else will want to untangle them, especially without some participation from the Nine.

At Level 8, Nines are starting to shut down. They are highly dissociated and detached from themselves and from their environment. Depression that may have developed at Level 7 becomes chronic at Level 8. But underneath the blank surface, Nines are terrified and enraged. Their feelings of aggression are enormous, but to entertain them even for a moment feels like the destruction of whatever shreds of peacefulness they retain. When they can no longer remain numb, however, their anxiety and rage can explode hysterically in irrational rants, random acts of violence, or paranoid delusions about the people around them, in the manner of unhealthy Sixes. They may suddenly throw dishes, wreck furniture, or physically attack people. They simply cannot repress their anger and frustration any longer.

At Level 9, when unhealthy dissociated Nines go to Six, anxiety finally and completely breaks through their massive repression. All the feelings and realizations they have been warding off come crashing down upon them. The person who was once so easygoing becomes an overreacting hysteric, anxiety ridden, fearful, agitated, apprehensive, tearful, panicked. More then ever, deteriorated Nines need someone else to take care of them and to save them from whatever threatening situation they have gotten into. To elicit help from others, they may become abjectly self-abasing ("morbidly dependent" in Horney's phrase) and masochistically self-destructive so that others will have to care for them.

Deteriorated Nines at Six may also do something self-defeating and humiliating, putting themselves in worse positions than ever before. The motive behind this is twofold: self-punishment to expiate the intense guilt they feel for letting others down and making them suffer; and self-abasement to repair the separation from others by drawing people back to them.

These psychological tactics do not work, however, because besides anxiety, deteriorated Nines have also unwittingly let loose aggression toward themselves and others from the Pandora's box of the unconscious. No longer able to repress aggressive feelings, they become self-punishing and full of self-hatred. They also become intensely hostile toward others, lashing out at anyone who increases their anxiety rather than immediately relieving it. If others do not magically restore peace, they become the enemy.

Unfortunately, deteriorated Nines have no defenses with which to handle anxiety or aggression. They can no longer repress the particularly acute anxiety of being rejected by those who have been significant to them. They will likely turn to alcohol and drugs to control their hysteria or will resort to suicide if they cannot find some kind of peace again.

The Direction of Integration: The Nine Goes to Three

When healthy Nines integrate to Three, they become self-assured and interested in developing themselves and their talents to the fullest extent possible. They move from self-possession to making something more of themselves, from a just-being-born presence in the world to an active, inner-directed force. Because they are already healthy and extremely balanced, they no longer live through someone else, nor do they need to conform to conventional roles as sources of self-esteem and identity. Instead, integrating Nines create themselves by asserting themselves properly. They no longer fear change, becoming more flexible and adaptable, entirely capable of dealing with reality as persons in their own right.

Integrating Nines have connected with their vitality. In Freudian terms, they have gotten in touch with their id, the aggressive and instinctual side of themselves. Nines have always feared their aggressive impulses, and now they realize that they no longer have to, since these impulses are not necessarily destructive, but rather can lead to self-development.

Their peace becomes less fragile because Nines discover that they can assert themselves without being aggressive toward others, and hence without jeopardizing their relationships. As their self-esteem increases, their relationships become more mature and satisfying. Integrating Nines find that they no longer have to be self-effacing to find someone with whom they can have a relationship. By being (and becoming) themselves, they attract others who find integrating Nines more interesting and desirable than ever before. It may surprise them, but others may even begin to identify with them, to seek them out, to accommodate themselves to them. While integrating Nines will likely discourage others from being dependent upon them, it will please them nonetheless, as well it should.

THE MAJOR SUBTYPES OF THE NINE

The Nine with an Eight-Wing: "The Comfort Seeker"

The traits of the Nine and those of the Eight conflict with each other: Nines are passive and desire harmony with others, while Eights are aggressive, asserting themselves and following their self-interest. Since Nine is the basic personality type, people of this subtype tend to be fundamentally oriented to others, receptive, unselfconscious, agreeable, and so forth, while some part of them asserts itself strongly, at least at times. There is a "mellow," outgoing quality about them. They are sociable, like to tell jokes and stories, and spend time with their friends. Nines with an Eight-wing are more sensual and instinctive than the Nines with a One-wing, and tend to operate more on feelings and hunches. They tend to embody more the easygoing demeanor associated with Nines, but also give the impression of being more "physical," more grounded. This is one of the most difficult subtypes to understand because the component types are in such diametrical opposition to each other. Noteworthy examples of this subtype include Ronald Reagan, Dwight Eisenhower, Gerald Ford, Kevin Costner, Gary Cooper, Woody Harrelson, Keanu Reeves, Ingrid Bergman, Geena Davis, Sophia Loren, Ringo Starr, Whoopi Goldberg, Janet Jackson, Bing Crosby, Perry Como, Walter Cronkite, Hugh Downs, Lady Bird Johnson, and Marc Chagall.

In healthy persons of this subtype, the Eight-wing adds an element of inner strength and willpower, as well as an expansive, passionate quality to the overall style of the personality. Healthy Nines with an Eight-wing combine the comforting, positive qualities of the Nine with the endurance and strength of the Eight, resulting in a subtype at once powerful and gentle. Despite their unselfconsciousness, healthy people of this subtype are able to assert themselves effectively; despite their graciousness and concern for others, they can be quite strong and forceful; despite their ability to subordinate themselves to others and to common goals, they can be courageously independent; despite an easygoing manner, they can have formidable tempers, although these are rarely resorted to. Thus, healthy persons of this subtype give the impression of strength and good nature, sensuality, and power. The Nine with an Eight-wing wants to engage with people and things in the world more than the other subtype. They enjoy socializing, have a wonderfully dry sense of humor, and may have numerous skills, although they tend not to promote themselves. They are concerned with their immediate needs and circumstances, and more accepting of people as they are. Nines with an Eight-wing often enjoy the helping professions, consulting, sales, and services, and can be very effective in business, especially in negotiations or working in human resource capacities.

Average people of this subtype compartmentalize their emotions completely. While their self-image is one of peacefulness, they may occasionally be quite aggressive without realizing the extent of it. Unfortunately, the Nine with an Eight-wing is more likely than the other subtype to get caught up in a kind of sensual indolence which can interfere with their ability to stay directed. They can be complacent, even lazy, about achieving success in some areas of their lives, while being extremely competitive in others. If they are not intellectually gifted, they may seem slightly slow-witted— good-natured but thickheaded—because neither the Nine nor the Eight is a particularly intellectual or thinking component. These people have strong elemental drives for psychological and sexual union with the other. Their self-interest is bound up with material comfort. They can be more stubborn and defensive than Nines with a One-wing, and although usually easygoing and pleasant, people of this subtype can have bad tempers. Others cannot predict what will set them off, but usually can see their anger building. Typically, people of this subtype lose their tempers when others interfere or interrupt their sense of well-being and peace of mind. They can be blunt and explosive, but just as suddenly, they return to their "normal," placid self. When their protective instincts are aroused, they do not wish to hurt others so much as protect themselves and their property. Average persons of this subtype can become belligerent and confrontational toward others, but with little long-lasting personal animosity. Their greatest ire is aroused against those who attack their families, their beliefs, or their way of life. But once the crisis has passed, they are apt to sue for peace, making allies of their former enemies. As they deteriorate, Nines with an Eight-wing tend to dig in their heads, refusing to listen to or cooperate with anyone threatening to disturb their safe routines.

Unhealthy Nines with an Eight-wing often resemble unhealthy Fours: they are usually depressed and have very little energy. Unlike the Four, there is a general flatness and lack of emotional affect, with occasional tremors of tearfulness and anxiety. The fear of control in the Eight-wing adds to the Nine's resistance to help. Unhealthy Nines with an Eight-wing are capable of violence with little concern about the consequences of their actions. Aggressions and id impulses are strong in people of this subtype, and when they are emotionally unstable, there is little ego strength left to regulate these forces. Their aggressions may be particularly aroused by sexual jealousy of their spouses. Separation from a loved one through the alienation of affections is devastating to the Nine's sense of self, and inflames the Eight's rage out of wounded pride. As a result, Nines with an Eight-wing can be physically dangerous, striking out impulsively. They may retaliate against those with whom they have come into conflict while dissociating themselves emotionally from the harm they do. Chronic depression, extreme dissociation, and addiction are also possible.

The Nine with a One-Wing: "The Dreamer"
The traits of the Nine and those of the One tend to reinforce each other. Nines repress their emotions to maintain their peace, while Ones repress their emotions to maintain self-control. Thus, this subtype tends to be more cerebral than the Nine with an Eight-wing—more interested in ideas, symbols, and concepts. In this subtype we see people who are more emotionally controlled and cooler than those in the other subtype, although they may well dis-

play moments of anger and moral indignation. Out of the blue, the complacent, agreeable Nine becomes critical and sarcastic. Both subtypes of the Nine are attracted to questions of philosophy and spirituality, but in the Nine with a One-wing there is a distinctive idealistic quality to their beliefs. Noteworthy examples of this subtype include Abraham Lincoln, Queen Elizabeth II, Rosalynn Carter, Cyrus Vance, Henry Fonda, Jimmy Stewart, Garrison Keillor, Princess Grace of Monaco, Rose Kennedy, Joseph Campbell, Carl Jung, George Lucas, Jim Henson, Walt Disney, Norman Rockwell, Dame Joan Sutherland, Ralph Waldo Emerson, "Desdemona," "Edith Bunker," and "Marge Simpson."

Healthy persons of this subtype possess enormous integrity and are extremely principled. Their great common sense helps them to be wise in their judgments, particularly about others. They are alert to issues of fairness and objectivity when they are called on to act or to judge situations. Healthy Nines with a One-wing are wonderful at synthesizing different schools of thought and sorting out the common threads between them. They can be highly imaginative and creative, seeking to express and share their visions of an ideal world. Healthy people here are interested in sharing what they know, and appreciate the ideas and discoveries of others. They tend to be sunny, friendly, and reassuring, but with a certain seriousness about their ideals. They enjoy teaching, and may be moral leaders, teaching most effectively by their example. The Nine's openness is combined with the One's objectivity; the result is simplicity and guilelessness toward others, peacefulness and moderation toward themselves. This subtype makes a good friend (or therapist), balancing the Nine's nonjudgmental listening with the One's wisdom and desire to give helpful advice.

Average persons of this subtype may be crusaders of some sort, because they have an idealistic streak which makes them want to improve the world in whatever ways they can. They are sure of their opinions and usually have fixed ideas about everything that touches on their basic beliefs. People of this subtype tend to be orderly and self-controlled, particularly more emotionally controlled and less openly passionate than Nines with an Eight-wing. At the same time, however, average Nines with a One-wing tend to get caught up in nonessential activities. They remain active and even energetic, but with a degree of detachment and uninvolvement that derails their ability to stay on track with their long-range goals. They can be quite busy within their sphere, although many of their activities are geared toward maintaining order and the status quo in their environment. They are less adventurous, but are perhaps more thoughtful and reserved than Nines with an Eight-wing. Complacent and disengaged, they want to avoid all personal conflicts and antagonisms, but may be easily moved to anger since there is a testiness and edginess in this subtype. They often restrain the expression of their anger more Nines with an Eight-wing, and are more likely to become indignant and to smolder through clenched teeth rather than to raise their voice or cause a scene, especially in public. In such cases, they can be indirect, sarcastic, and scolding. Average Nines with a One-wing are concerned with propriety and respectability, and often feel morally superior to others (of different classes, cultures, lifestyles, and so forth). There is a puritanical streak to them, and in some, a "prim and proper" quality. They may rationalize, moralize, or appeal to political or religious ideologies to bolster their arguments. Individuals of this subtype tend to be perfectionistic, at least in some areas, although more important aspects of their lives may be severely neglected. They can also be surprisingly impersonal and callous in their disregard for others, since average persons of this subtype abstract from the real world a great deal in favor of their idealistic notions.

Unhealthy Nines with a One-wing are often extremely withdrawn and can resemble unhealthy Fives. There is a detached, schizoid quality to them, with little affect. They can become extremely angry, although in a highly compartmentalized way, acting impulsively, as if out of the blue. They are more resentful than Nines with an Eight-wing, stewing over wrongs and injustices, and may feel that it is their duty to punish or condemn others' wrongdoings. If they act, unhealthy Nines with a One-wing can become quite arbitrary, contradicting their more ordinary behavior. Obsessive-compulsive tendencies are among their neurotic traits, and unhealthy persons of this subtype may become obsessive about their apparent troubles while dissociating themselves from either their compulsive actions or their real problems. They may, for example, decide to forget what has just been the focus of their obsession as if nothing had happened. Because defense mechanisms are less global than in the other subtype, neurotics here will tend to feel their conflicts more, and therefore be more likely to have more severe emotional problems or break-downs if they become very unhealthy. If left untreated, they tend to retreat into highly dissociated states that resemble autism. They feel helpless and despairing but may suddenly respond to others with bursts of frustration and rage.

SOME FINAL THOUGHTS

Looking back at the deterioration of Nines, we can see that average to unhealthy Nines have brought about the very thing they most fear, the fear of loss and separation. Now that they are fragmented personalities, they are not only separated from others, they are separated from themselves. They are profoundly alienated from and terrified of their own lives. Only with the greatest difficulty will the core personality which remains be able to begin to reconstruct itself.

It seems that relatively few Nines deteriorate to this state of neurosis. Probably what happens in most cases is that they deteriorate into unhealthy states (denial, dissociation) after a crisis, but are able to bounce back to some degree of normal functioning. Their defenses are very powerful because they are so all-encompassing, and for better or worse, Nines are able to repress most traumas and go on living. Nevertheless, their ability to endure is always purchased at the price of leading an emotionally and personally impoverished life.

From this perspective, we can also see that their central problem has been how to awaken to themselves and how to maintain self-possession once they have attained it. The answer is that Nines must learn to accept suffering, especially the suffering involved with anxiety. Suffering, consciously accepted, has the ability to catalyze people, shocking them into awareness. Suffering also compels us to choose what meaning it has for us. When we choose a meaning for our experiences, we create ourselves. When Nines actively use suffering as a positive force in their lives, they not only give meaning to their lives, they sustain their awareness of themselves. The person who is able to give meaning to his or her suffering is both the self who suffers and the self who transcends suffering. In that moment, the self is aware and unified.

Chapter 12

Type One: The Reformer

THE ONE IN PROFILE

Healthy: Conscientious, with strong personal convictions: they have an intense sense of right and wrong, personal and moral values. Wish to be rational, reasonable, and self-disciplined, mature and moderate in all things. / Highly principled, strive to be fair, objective, and ethical: truth and justice are primary values. Sense of responsibility, personal integrity, and of having a higher purpose often make them teachers and witnesses to the truth. *At Their Best:* Become extraordinarily wise and discerning. By accepting what is, they become transcendentally realistic, knowing the best thing to do in all circumstances. Humane, inspiring, and hopeful: the truth will be heard.

Average: Dissatisfied with reality, they become high-minded idealists, feeling that it is up to them to improve everything. Crusaders, advocates, critics, they embrace "causes" and point out how things "ought" to be. / Afraid of making a mistake: everything must be consistent with their ideals. Become orderly and well-organized, but impersonal, rigid, emotionally constricted, keeping their feelings and impulses in check. Often workaholics—"anal-compulsive," punctual, pedantic, and fastidious. / Highly critical both of self and others: picky, judgmental, perfectionistic. Very opinionated about everything: correcting people and badgering them to "do the right thing"—as they see it. Impatient, never satisfied with anything unless it is done according to their prescriptions. Moralizing, scolding, abrasive, and indignantly angry.

Unhealthy: Can be highly dogmatic, self-righteous, intolerant, and inflexible. Begin dealing in absolutes: they alone know "the Truth"; everyone else is wrong. Make very severe judgments of others, while rationalizing their own actions. / Become obsessive about imperfection and the wrongdoing of others. Begin to act in contradictory ways, hypocritically doing the opposite of what they preach. / Become condemnatory, punitive, and cruel in order to rid themselves of whatever they believe is disturbing them. Severe depression, nervous breakdowns, and suicide attempts are likely.

Key Motivations: Want to be right, to have integrity and balance, to strive higher and improve others, to be consistent with their ideals, to justify themselves, to be beyond criticism so as not to be condemned by anyone.

Examples: Pope John Paul II, Mahatma Gandhi, Margaret Thatcher, Al Gore, Elie Wiesel, Barbara Jordan, Bill Moyers, Katharine Hepburn, Harrison Ford, Ralph Nader, Sandra Day O'Connor, William F. Buckley, Noam Chomsky, George Bernard Shaw, Joan of Arc, and "Mr. Spock."

AN OVERVIEW OF THE ONE

Voicing the common theme of evangelical consciousness of the self before regeneration, John Greene, a New England Puritan of the mid-seventeenth century, acknowledged that God had let him "see much of the wretchedness" of his heart, and he "thought none so vile as I none so evil an heart so proud so stubborn so rebellious and I thought God would never show mercy to so vile a miserable wretch as I was." This vision of the inward self, a vision experienced in greater and lesser degree by most evangelicals, was the source of the despair and hopelessness that so often preceded conversions. . . . Not until individuals could bring themselves, or be brought by God, to reject their very selves as worthless, sinful, and justly damned creatures, could they ever hope to be born again. (Philip Greven, *The Protestant Tempera-ment*, 75.)

The Puritans' desire for self-regeneration by striving after ideals is an expression of the personality type One. Not content to be as they are, Ones and Puritans alike feel the obligation to be better. They must somehow rise higher, beyond human nature, into the realm of the Absolute.

To this personality type, the advice of "Desiderata" sounds foolish and dangerous: "Beyond a wholesome discipline, be gentle with yourself. You are a child of the universe, no less than the trees and the stars; you have a right to be here. And whether or not it is clear to you, no doubt the universe is unfolding as it should." As far as average to unhealthy Ones can tell, the universe is emphatically *not* unfolding as it should. People are not trying hard enough to improve either the universe or themselves.

What Ones typically do not see is that, given their fundamental premise, they are locked in conflicts between opposing forces that cannot be reconciled either in themselves or in the universe. They keenly feel the struggle between good and evil, the flesh and the spirit, the ideal and the real. For Ones, the battle lines are sharply drawn between the chaotic, irrational side of their natures and the clarity of their convictions, between their dark, libidinous impulses and their self-control, between their metaphysical aspirations and their human needs—between their heads and their hearts.

In the Instinctive Triad

Ones are the type in the Instinctive Triad who "underexpress" instincts and drives. Ones, like Eights, are people of action, who respond at a gut level to the situations they encounter, but while Eights give free reign to their instincts, and Nines are "out of touch" with them, Ones try to pull them in, to limit and direct them toward the goals which their superegos deem worthy. Ones are full of passions, mostly expressed as a strong sense of convic-tion in their beliefs and actions, but they feel compelled to keep their instincts in check lest they be overwhelmed by them.

Anger, in particular, is a powerful motivation for Ones. When they are confronted with circumstances which disappoint or dis-please them, anger becomes a form of fuel which launches them into action. Indeed, anger, rightly understood, is an instinctual response to a situation we are not satisfied with. It is the energy that allows us to say no. Some Ones become conscious of this and use their anger constructively.

> I have learnt through bitter experience the one supreme lesson: to conserve my anger, and as heat conserved is transmuted into energy, even so our anger controlled can be transmuted into a power which can move the world. (Mohandas K. Gandhi, *The Words of Gandhi*, 13.)

It is striking, however, that Ones are often unaware of their anger, and almost always underestimate the degree of it. When their anger is brought to their attention, Ones often respond with a disclaimer. ("I'm *not* angry! I'm just trying to get this right.") Whatever Ones may wish to call their intense feelings, and under whatever guise they may appear, their angry feelings are the force which truly directs a One's actions. Ones often portray themselves as rational, but they are rational in the way that common sense is rational, not in the exploratory, intellectual sense. Ones do like ideas, but they like *practical* ideas, and unlike Fives, will not be long interested in ideas or concepts that do not lead them directly into constructive action.

Instinctive energy has much to do with a person's ability to assert himself, and accordingly, Ones appear to be very sure of themselves, although their self-confidence lies less in themselves than in the rightness of their ideals. Despite appearances, Ones relate to the world by seeing themselves as "less than" an ideal toward which they strive. They subordinate themselves and their powerful instinctive drives to an abstraction—usually an intangible, universal value such as truth or justice—and strive to be as perfect as it is. Unlike Nines, who are also idealistic but are often detached from the inner drive to attain their vision, Ones are determined to make their ideals a reality. Ironically, by definition, the ideal is something they must work toward but can never fully attain. Nevertheless, as we shall see, average to unhealthy Ones certainly feel lifted above the run of ordinary mortals by the attempt to do so.

This is where Ones begin to have problems. As they deteriorate toward neurosis, average Ones begin to identify with the ideal so completely that if they become unhealthy, they think they have attained it—and that everyone who has not should be condemned. On one level of awareness, even unhealthy Ones know they are not perfect, yet on another level they think and act as if they were already perfect to avoid being condemned either by their consciences or by anyone else. Average to unhealthy Ones are convinced that the more zealously they strive for perfection, the more they are made righteous by the attempt. They think that by aligning themselves with the ideal, they will always be in the right, no matter how badly they fail. The mere act of identifying themselves with the ideal makes them feel that they are better than the rest of the world. They are among the saved because they know the right way, the way everything ought to be.

Problems with Repression and Aggression

Like the other two personality types in the Instinctive Triad, Ones have a problem with the repression of some part of their psyches. Ones repress the more irrational side of their natures, their instinctual impulses and personal desires, attempting to sublimate them in a quest for perfection. Their normal human desires gradually become more and more repressed as Ones are caught in conflicts between striving after ideals and implementing them in the real world. The picture is further complicated, however, because Ones relate to the world dualistically: they see themselves as less than the ideal, while giving the impression that they are also greater than the environment, which they are obligated to improve. They constantly measure not only the distance between themselves and the ideal, but also the distance between their present perfection and their past imperfection. Simply put, Ones feel that they and their world must be "making progress." Anything that is perceived as blocking or frustrating progress toward the ideal is met with anger and criticism.

Actually, there is a double dichotomy in Ones. The first is the external dichotomy we have just seen: the pressure of living up to an ideal versus the conviction that the One is perfectly right, that the One knows better than others what is needed in any situation. The second is an internal dichotomy, which is less obvious: a split between the tightly controlled, rational side of themselves, which they present to the world, versus their repressed drives and feelings. Ironically, Ones are often emotional and passionate about their convictions, but they are not always aware of this. They like to see themselves as rational and balanced, but they are nevertheless keenly aware of their emotions, particularly their aggressive and sexual impulses. Although they attempt to keep their impulses in check as much as possible, they are never as successful in this as they would like.

Because of these dichotomies, average to unhealthy Ones always feel caught in conflicts: between the perfection of their ideal and their own imperfections; between feeling virtuous and feeling sinful; between their actions and their consciences; between their desire for order and the disorder they see everywhere; between good and evil; between God and the Devil.

The personality type One corresponds to the extroverted thinking type in the Jungian typology; it is one of Jung's clearest descriptions.

This type of man elevates objective reality, or an objectively oriented intellectual formula, into the ruling principle not only for himself but for his whole environment. By this formula good and evil are measured, and beauty and ugliness determined. Everything that agrees with this formula is right, everything that contradicts it is wrong. . . . Because this formula seems to embody the entire meaning of life, it is made into a universal law which must be put into effect everywhere all the time, both individually and collectively. Just as the extroverted thinking type subordinates himself to his formula, so, for their own good, everybody round him must obey it too, for whoever refuses to obey it is wrong—he is resisting the universal law, and is therefore unreasonable, immoral, and without a conscience. His moral code forbids him to tolerate exceptions; his ideal must under all circumstances be realized. . . . This is not from any great love of his neighbor, but from the higher standpoint of justice and truth. . . . "Oughts" and "musts" bulk large in this programme. If the formula is broad enough, this type may play a very useful role in social life as a reformer or public prosecutor or purifier of conscience. . . . But the more rigid the formula, the more he develops into a martinet, a quibbler, and a prig, who would like to force himself and others into one mould. Here we have the two extremes between which the majority of these types move. (C. G. Jung, *Psychological Types*, 347.)

From our point of view, we can see that Jung is describing various points along the Levels of Development of the One: average Ones are reformers and public prosecutors, whereas unhealthy Ones intolerantly try to force others into their mold, and so forth. As we will see, the full spectrum of the One's traits encompasses some of the most noble and least admirable aspects of human nature. When they are healthy, Ones can be the most objective, principled, and wise of all the personality types. As much as humanly possible, they try not to let their personal feelings get in the way of dealing fairly with others. They are deeply concerned with justice, not merely for themselves but for everyone.

But to contrast this, when they are unhealthy their lives are a relentless application of their ideals to every conceivable situation. Unhealthy Ones become extremely intolerant of anyone who disagrees with them, and since they are convinced that they alone know THE TRUTH (writ large, in capital letters), everything follows from that. What does not is to be condemned and severely punished. The problem is, however, that human nature keeps cropping up: unhealthy Ones find that they cannot control themselves as perfectly as they feel they must. Their impulses can be repressed for only so long. The flesh will have its day.

Parental Orientations

Ones develop as they do because as children they were disconnected from their protective-figure, that adult in their early childhood who was responsible for setting limits, giving guidelines, and disciplining the child when necessary. This is the person who occupies the traditional patriarchal role in the family. Often the protective-figure is the father, but not always. In many families, the mother is the protective-figure, while in other families, a grandparent or sibling may play this role in the child's development. The disconnection from the protective-figure, and what that person symbolized, was of central importance to the development of the superego: these children felt that they could not rely on the structure and guidelines provided by their family of origin. They may have experienced the rules of the family as arbitrary and unfair, or too strict, or too unstable. Whatever the particulars, Ones were dissatisfied and frustrated with the structure and limits that they received from the protective-figure and so felt that they had to develop their own guidelines. Ones tried to transcend the rules of their family of origin by creating a code of ethics that is even more rigorous than what is expected of them. In this way, Ones came to believe that they can avoid condemnation by always attempting to be blameless.

This created in Ones a relentless superego mechanism whose constant message is "You are not acceptable as you are; you must be better, always better." In more authoritarian or chaotic family systems, these superego messages could have become severe and inflexible. In such situations, their own wishes and feelings were rarely if ever countenanced; instead, these children felt that they always had to toe the line to avoid being criticized or condemned. As a result, their emotions and other impulses were repressed by forces symbolized by an internalized punishing father. (Freudians see toilet training as the arena in which the anal traits of the obsessive-compulsive type which correspond to the One were learned. While the Freudian anal traits of orderliness, parsimony, and obstinacy are seen in Ones, especially those with a Nine-wing, we do not have to restrict ourselves to toilet issues alone to understand the origins of this personality type.)

As children, Ones may have become disconnected from the protective-figure for any number of reasons. The protective-figure may have been absent from the family, or been abusive, or have treated the child unfairly. Or as a result of a stern moral and religious upbringing and the threat of eternal punishment, the child may have feared offending God the Father and being condemned. The child may have feared being sent to hell for being impulsive, pleasure seeking, or selfish, or for other actions which were, after all, merely the natural behavior of a child. In other cases, the One may have experienced a fairly peaceful and normal childhood, but still felt that there was something more to strive for—some higher ideal than was part of the values of the child's family or peers. Often, Ones felt uncomfortable being children, or were not allowed to behave as children, and thus struggled to become little adults before their time. For one reason or another, Ones decided that they had to rely on themselves for guidance, structure, and discipline. They would have to parent themselves, and they would have to do a better job of it than their protective-figure.

It is also worth noting that they did not rebel against strictures on themselves; rather, they internalized control in their consciences by feeling guilty for their transgressions. Nevertheless, they felt angry that the burden of perfection was placed on them, and more angry still when they saw others who were not subject to the same control of their feelings and impulses. The freedom of others (to Ones, the license which others grant themselves) antagonizes them and makes them chafe under the weight of their own prohibitions.

Problems with Anger and Perfection

Ironically, Ones vent their anger most unfairly at others when they are primarily angry with themselves for not being perfect. Instead of resolving their own disordered feelings, average to unhealthy Ones find fault everywhere else. Their self-righteous anger makes Ones aggressive; however, the One is not an aggressive personality type as such. Actually, Ones are compliant to their ideals, to their superego, since the ideal is the yardstick by which they measure everything, including themselves. The aggression in their personalities is an expression of anger at themselves and others for not complying perfectly with the ideal.

Moreover, their anger signals the fact that they put too great a load upon themselves and others: perfection is a burden that human nature cannot bear. What is difficult for Ones to accept is the interdependence of flesh and spirit which is the natural state of man. The irrational part of themselves cannot be perfected or controlled in the same way that the rational part of themselves can be. Nevertheless, they try to control their irrational selves, denying all that is base, all that is human in themselves, in order to conform to the ideal. Ultimately, Ones feel guilty for being human. They fear being condemned because they are not angels.

When Ones are healthy, however, their objective orientation to life allows them to remain firmly in touch with human realities, including their own. They are the most discerning, moral, and reasonable of all the personality types, tolerant of others and of themselves. They recognize that their ideals may not apply equally to everyone in all circumstances. When they are unhealthy, however, their behavior is a twisted caricature of their virtues because their humanity has become perverted. Unhealthy Ones punish others for their least faults while absolving themselves of their greater sins. They are completely without mercy, because they have lost contact with humanity. If ideals do not serve human beings, what purpose do they serve?

ANALYZING THE HEALTHY ONE

Level 1: The Wise Realist

Very healthy Ones allow the full range of their humanity to surface, discovering that their impulses are not as chaotic or threatening as they feared. They do not repress their needs and feelings,
except to the degree necessary for healthy functioning, just as
everyone must. Thus, the parts of themselves banished by their
superegos as irrational or chaotic come into balance with the rest of
their psyches and are integrated into their total personalities. Their
subjective side comes into alignment with objective reality, and
they become exceptionally realistic and accepting of life, even of
themselves.

Because they are so realistic about themselves, very healthy
Ones are unusually mature and well-balanced. Although they are
still attracted to ideals, very healthy Ones do not see them as uni-
lateral, stifling commands but as something which they personally
find fulfilling. They do not feel the need either to make everything
perfect or to become absolutely perfect themselves. Further, as
Ones release the rigid rules and categories of their superegos, they
see that they cannot come up with a single set of ideals and rules
applicable to every situation. It is a hopeless enterprise, and therefore not a proper moral imperative. Becoming a full human being
is sufficiently challenging. And, paradoxically, by becoming full
human beings, Ones will come as close to perfection as is humanly
possible. When they are this healthy, Ones are "a little less than
the angels," embodying great nobility of spirit.

Very healthy Ones are the wisest of the personality types because of their extraordinary discernment. Their judgment is superb
because Ones are grounded in the real rather than the ideal. They
go beyond logical reasoning to discern the best thing to do in whatever circumstance they are in. Just as very healthy Fives have the
most penetrating vision and understanding of the world, very
healthy Ones have the clearest sense of right and appropriate action
in the world, prompting others to seek them out for guidance.

Just as they are tolerant and accepting of themselves, very healthy
Ones are also accepting and tolerant of others. When most people
use the word *tolerance*, they usually mean *permissive*, that people
should be allowed to do whatever they like. However, tolerance
and acceptance of others is not the same as permissiveness. True

tolerance is the ability to respect the differences of opinion well-informed people of good will have arrived at. The tolerant One who is a Protestant allows the Jew and the Catholic, the Muslim and the Hindu, the same freedom to worship God which he himself enjoys. This does not necessarily mean that tolerant Ones think that all of the religious beliefs of others are correct, or that religious differences do not matter, but that Ones allow others the freedom to discover the truth on their own, in their own way. They can see the deeper truths underlying opposing positions and views and communicate these truths without getting caught up in any particular way of expressing the truth. Further, very healthy Ones can speak the truth in a way that others can easily hear. Others are not threatened by the One's ideals.

Very healthy Ones are able to be this tolerant because they keep ultimate values before their minds. By keeping the transcendental, spiritual realm in view, healthy Ones attain a larger perspective on reality, which endows them with the ability to see everything in its proper context. The depth of their discernment is such that healthy Ones are able to focus on what is truly most important in any situation. They know virtually at a glance what "the greater good" is. (And if they do not know, their ignorance does not cause healthy Ones alarm because they are able to wait until reality presents them with an answer.)

They are so convinced of the reality of truth and the objectivity of transcendent values that they recognize the right of others to be wrong. The faith which very healthy Ones have in the moral order is so deep that they allow others, in their view, to be wrong all of their lives because they believe that error will not ultimately prevail over truth. They believe that what is true will always prevail because truth is of the nature of reality itself. This is why to be completely realistic is to be wise. Wisdom goes beyond reason, encompassing the irrational, taking it into account. It is to see the real order of things, and hence always to know what is right and good.

Thus, very healthy Ones are transcendental realists because they have transcended their own personal understanding of reality to see that, on some profound level which cannot be comprehended or expressed, all is well—"the universe is unfolding as it should."

Level 2: The Reasonable Person

Unfortunately, healthy Ones are not always this healthy. They may succumb to the fear of being imbalanced, corrupted, or "bad," and compensate for this fear by desiring to be right in everything. They want to have total integrity, to be in right relations with the world, with others, and with themselves. Their sense of self is based on being reasonable and conscientious at all times.

Healthy Ones are indeed the soul of reason. They are extremely sensible and prudent, exemplars of rational good sense. And even though Ones at Level 2 are somewhat less healthy than at the previous stage, they still possess exceptionally good judgment, enabling them to know what is more or less important in virtually every circumstance. They are able to sort out issues clearly (moral issues in particular) because they can see the consequences of whatever decisions are being made. They are also not afraid to make value judgments, to say "This is right or wrong," "That is good or bad," and to take responsibility for their judgments and for the actions that follow from them. To describe their judgment this way makes it sound more logical than it actually is. In fact, their judgment comes from a deeply felt sense of conviction—from their gut. For Ones, right and wrong are not abstract categories: they are passionate matters, and central to living a good and balanced life. Ones believe that living a balanced life is absolutely necessary in order to maintain the objectivity they need to make sound judgments. Healthy Ones do not want their personal whims and feelings to stand in the way of objectively discerning what is right and wrong.

Healthy Ones are so objective that they can stand aside from themselves and evaluate their own actions, attitudes, and feelings. They do not want to be in error but are glad to admit their mistakes as soon as they are aware of them. They feel that nothing is to be gained by clinging to mistaken notions. Righteousness and truthfulness are important to them, not holding erroneous opinions out of pride.

Within the limitations of personality and culture, Ones know right from wrong and good from bad because they have healthy consciences. Their consciences motivate them to do what they believe is right. Healthy Ones are aware of whatever selfishness, pettiness, and wayward passions they may harbor in themselves, and they would like to see these kinds of feelings come more into balance.

They are at peace with themselves when they are virtuous and, of course, feel remorse when they fail.

Above all, Ones want to be righteous, and when they are healthy, they are. Further, they are righteous without being self-conscious about it—and certainly without being self-righteous. Being righteous does not necessarily mean being religious in a traditional sense. It is more encompassing than that: Ones want to be upright, responsible people, aligned with the Divine Law and natural order, however they may see that. The righteousness of healthy Ones is perhaps best expressed in the ideal of Chinese Taoist philosophy: a person in whom Heaven, Earth, and Humanity are balanced. To achieve this goal, healthy Ones want to live a life of moderation and integrity.

Understanding how valuable reason, moderation, temperance, and impartiality are in their lives, healthy Ones do not feel that the restraints they have internalized limit them in any way. Indeed, they believe that without constraints of conscience, human society would not be possible. Many of the most worthwhile gains of civilization result from their willingness to delay personal rewards for long-term, higher goals.

Nor do Ones feel that whatever virtue they possess, or even the fact that they desire to be good, spares them from evil and suffering in life. They have not made a pact with God to bless them for being virtuous; they do not feel exempt from the conditions of life because of their attraction to the good. For example, healthy Ones do not see anything happening to others which could not also happen to them. Instead of asking "Why me?" when suffering strikes, they are as likely to ask "Why not me?" They do not expect that life will be easy or carefree, but on the other hand, healthy Ones are not pessimists. They are simply being realistic.

Level 3: The Principled Teacher

Having a conscience enables healthy Ones to lead outstandingly moral and useful lives because they not only want to be right, they want to do what is right. They want to put objective values into practice and to be unswayed by their passions, so that, as much as is humanly possible, they can do what is objectively right.

Whereas righteousness was the primary virtue at the previous stage, truth and justice now enter the picture. Thus, healthy Ones are extremely concerned that others be treated fairly. They hate injustice wherever they find it, whether it is their friends, total strangers, or they themselves who are harmed by injustice. Healthy Ones are on fire for justice and righteousness—these are not arid principles, they are their passions. More than those of any other personality type, healthy Ones willingly put themselves on the line for their moral beliefs and would rather suffer injustice themselves than act unjustly toward anyone else. (In this respect, healthy Ones can be mistaken for healthy Eights.)

Healthy Ones have enormous integrity and are extremely ethical: to lie or to cheat someone is virtually unthinkable. They are extremely principled, having personal standards from which they will not deviate, making decisions based on what they see as objective, rational foundations, doing things regardless of their immediate self-interest. They possess a healthy self-discipline and an ability to look at the long-range implications of their actions. In civic life, for example, they vote their consciences rather than their pocketbooks. As parents, they decide issues on the basis of what will benefit the entire community rather than what will favor only their own children. As religious persons, they act on their religious principles, even if it means disobeying civil authorities. However, Ones can be extremely courageous in this regard, jeopardizing themselves, their possessions, their reputations, even their lives for their principles. They do not want to sacrifice their principles because to do so would corrupt their integrity, and by violating their integrity, they would ruin something essential, their capacity for goodness and virtue, sources of deep satisfaction to them. Indeed, Ones want to feel more than anything else that they have made some positive contribution to the world, and often experience themselves as having a sense of mission—a serious purpose.

Their integrity, truth, and sense of mission combine to create individuals who are highly responsible and reliable. In this respect, they strongly resemble healthy Sixes, but whereas Sixes tend to look outside themselves for reassurance that they are doing the right thing, Ones return again and again to their own inner moral compass. Their sense of responsibility stems from an inner drive to fulfill their ideals, their mission in life. This also gives them great focus and drive to accomplish their goals (like healthy Threes). Healthy Ones are nothing if not self-disciplined. They are able to stay on track, putting distractions, comforts, and the temptation of easy solutions aside to accomplish their purposes.

Ones at this stage stand up for what is right, appealing to the conscience, good will, and fairness of others, fearlessly and articulately expressing their beliefs, no matter whom they please or displease. Thus, not the least good that healthy Ones do for society is to be moral teachers and "witnesses to the truth," communicating their principles and moral vision to others. This is perhaps the highest form of teaching, not limited to merely passing on a body of knowledge but communicating a vision of a balanced way to live. Without a clear notion of right and wrong, and of the consequences of acting rightly or wrongly, Ones fear that they would have no direction in life and no means of finding one.

The hallmark of healthy Ones, however, is that their consciences speak primarily to *them* — they are not obligations laid on the whole world. Healthy Ones teach by personal example, not by preaching to others. They are confident that, whether or not others listen to them, the truth will ultimately be heard because the truth speaks to the soul in a voice which cannot be ignored.

ANALYZING THE AVERAGE ONE

Level 4: The Idealistic Reformer

Increasingly guided by their superegos, Ones are always subject to guilt and anxiety when they disobey. If for some reason they begin to fear that others are indifferent to their principles, that their efforts are not even "making a dent," they begin to strive after an even higher standard of excellence in everything. They want to make everything better. They become idealists, reformers, and crusaders, people with a cause, exhorting themselves and others toward perpetual improvement.

The difference between healthy Ones and average Ones is that average Ones become convinced that they alone have the answer for everyone. They alone can "fix up" the disorder they see around them. Personal conscience has intensified into a feeling of obligation to strive after the ideal in everything. Thus, average Ones begin to relate to the world from a position of moral superiority, as if they were saying, "I know the way things ought to be, so you should listen to me." They begin to experience others as less organized and directed than themselves and feel a sense of noblesse oblige by virtue of the loftiness of their ideals.

What average Ones personally define as the ideal becomes the norm for everyone else. They are convinced that they know the way everything ought to be. The weight of moral "shoulds" and "oughts" makes itself felt: not only should Ones do or not do this or that, but so should everyone else. They feel it is up to them to right wrongs, to educate the unlettered, to guide the aimless, and to instruct others in the "correct" view. The problem is, they do not trust other people to do the right thing. ("If I don't do it, who will?")

Average Ones take an Olympian view of human nature, seeing themselves as more levelheaded and sensible than others. Thus, they feel obligated to be the lawgivers and legislators of humanity, making rules which everyone should follow. Nothing is too small or too personal to escape their notice or their value judgments. Smoking, drinking, seat belts, the quality of television, pornography, and rock music are just a few of the subjects about which average Ones will debate others. Ones at this stage are not necessarily aggressive about this, but they frequently feel compelled to "point out" things to others, or explain the ramifications of others' actions. (Of course, they may well be right in their opinions, but they do not trust people to find out for themselves.)

They are ever mindful of how they are approximating their ideals, so progress is an important concept for them: they very much want to measure—at least by their moral yardstick—their improvement in whatever spheres concern them. Thus, they are extremely purposeful, always having a higher goal in view. They may feel that they should never watch television for entertainment, only for education, since they should always be improving themselves and doing something worthwhile. This is also why average Ones associate themselves with, and often lead, high-minded causes, whether it be picketing for migrant workers, or organizing the neighborhood for a political party, or rallying for environmental concerns, or organizing voters to pass a levy for the local schools.

As reformers and crusaders, average Ones know precisely where they stand on every issue, and they argue for their positions with the zeal of a missionary. Usually quite articulate, they love to debate and are able to propound their views effectively. And because they truly believe that their position is correct, they have an enormous amount of self-confidence, taking on the world like sculptors eager to get their hands on a shapeless mass of clay. Of course, therein lies the beginning of their real difficulties—and the difficulties of others with them. The world, and particularly other people, are not lumps of clay to be molded according to their re- forming impulses. Reality already has its own shape, although aver- age Ones want to give it another.

Level 5: The Orderly Person

Since by this stage Ones have made public stands and assertions of some sort, if only among family or friends, they do not want to have any inconsistency between their private feelings and their official idealistic positions. They want to have control over every area of their lives, particularly over their own impulses and emotions.

Their healthy self-discipline has deteriorated into brisk effi- ciency and orderliness. Average Ones want their sense of order to rule everything. Their strict superego is pitted against their feelings and desires, revealing the dualistic nature of their psyches. They see everything as black or white, right or wrong, good or bad, done correctly or incorrectly. There is and can be no room for subjective preferences, which they view as mere self-indulgence. Impersonal discipline and order become the principal ways in which average Ones attempt to control themselves, others, and the environment.

Meticulous and thorough, they attempt to organize the world into neat categories (as strictly as they control, or would like to control, their own inner life). They are sticklers for detail, planning and working out every conceivable contingency so that "everything will be under control," a favorite phrase. (Flow charts are virtually symbolic of their approach to reality.) Although not all Ones are compulsively neat, by this point all are constantly concerned with being organized. Orderly everywhere, they make lists and plan their schedules carefully so they will not waste time. Time is ex- tremely important to them, and average Ones are always able to account for their use of it. They are always on time and insist that others be equally punctual. No other personality type so personifies the Protestant work ethic, the person who feels that life is serious business. There are few vacations from their obligations, rarely a moment during which they feel they can relax and do whatever they want.

The way they think is highly orderly, too. Methodical and al- ways precise, they are adept at making logical distinctions. They find ambiguities troubling, and so strive to have a clear, black-and-white understanding of things. Unfortunately, few things in reality can be so readily categorized, but average Ones are determined that reality not be vague. They develop hierarchies in their minds, ways of judging everything and automatically assigning a ranking or evaluation to it, as if to say, "This is better than that"—as if they were schoolteachers on holiday who cannot stop grading everything. Average Ones believe that there must be a logical reason for every occurrence and bristle when someone presents them with information which contradicts their views. They seek concrete explanations for events, because without clear and direct causes, how can people be held accountable for their actions? How can reward and blame be assigned?

In sum, average Ones at this stage are the referees, accountants, and critics of reality—Freud's anal type. They have clear priorities, and those areas of their lives which are less important to them get fewer of their organizing impulses. To areas of high priority, however, average Ones will give a great deal of attention. In these matters they want everything to be tidy, clean, and neat; nothing should be out of place, and there should be no loose ends. Clock-like precision is their goal. Of course, the orderliness of Ones can have many positive effects, especially for the organizations in which they work, and for society as a whole. Everything runs more smoothly if things are organized, from business meetings to railroad schedules to wrapping Christmas gifts. Very little would get done if people could not count on a certain amount of order in the world and on those who provide it.

However, as with anything else, orderliness is a matter of appropriateness and degree. It would be good for average Ones to relax. They seldom allow themselves to be spontaneous, but even when they do, there is a stiff, forced quality about it, as if they had decided that it was time to be spontaneous. In interpersonal relationships, they tend to be proper in a slightly stuffy, "correct" way, relying on propriety and etiquette to express themselves. Having proper manners allows average Ones to function socially without reference to their personal feelings.

Since self-control is their desire, average Ones take sides against their impulses, doing the opposite of what they would like to do, as if their personal inclinations were somehow suspect. If Ones want to do something, like going to a movie, they will give it up, because they feel that they must devote their time to more serious projects.

On the other hand, if they do not want to do something, such as work on the weekend, they will force themselves to do so, because they feel obliged to. The irony is that average Ones begin to be more controlled than ever by their impulses because of their constant resistance to them.

Although much depends on which wing they have, there is, in general, an ascetic, austere, antiseptic quality about average Ones, especially in matters pertaining to pleasure and their desires. In some Ones, sexual impulses can be particularly threatening, since these impulses are not only irrational, but may be of a forbidden nature, contrary to their strict consciences. Their musculature is frequently tight: lips pursed, teeth clenched, neck and face stiff. *Tense, taut, stiff,* and *rigid* are words that can be applied to much of their behavior, as well as to their emotional world at this stage.

Although they are self-controlled, they seldom see themselves that way. Average Ones are very much aware that they have irrational impulses and forbidden desires. From their point of view, they are doing the world a favor by being orderly and efficient. But not only that, they are protecting the world from their passions — which would wreak havoc if they ever let them loose. They fear that if they ever allowed themselves to do as they please, their emotions would get out of control and they would be swept away by their wildest impulses, inevitably falling into the darkest sins of the heart. Who knows what lives in the unconscious? Ones think it wise not to tamper.

This stage is a turning point in their deterioration along the Levels of Development because life is not as orderly as Ones would have it, and they are not as orderly as they would like to be. Their restrained impulses keep breaking through the barricades of repression. From this stage onward, Ones attempt to control themselves and the environment ever more tightly so that their prohibitions will keep their irrational impulses in place. Not lessening their desire for internal and external order, they begin to become obsessed with rooting out disorder everywhere.

Level 6: The Judgmental Perfectionist

The more tightly they try to control their impulses, the more average Ones feel that they cannot let go. On top of this, they begin to fear that others will "mess up" the order and balance they have worked so hard to achieve. Their inner voice of guidance and idealism has become shrill and critical. Now orderliness is not enough. Perfection is required.

They become extremely threatened if the orderliness and self-control they desire for themselves and the environment does not materialize. Although it is difficult to perceive, Ones at this stage are often harder on themselves than they are on others. Their superegos have become harsh and demanding, and their overall attitude can be summarized as "nothing is ever good enough," an echo of what their protective-figures once told them. They constantly pick at things, not able to let well enough alone, and over-compensating for the fear of being judged by others, they become "judges" themselves. The one emotion they regularly allow themselves is anger in its many forms: impatience, irritation, resentment, and indignation. Strangely though, Ones are usually unaware of the degree of their anger or sometimes even that they are angry at all. To be angry is to be disordered and irrational, and their severe superegos will not allow them to acknowledge these feelings.

Highly critical of everything, they interfere with others, brusquely interrupting them, constantly telling them what to do, pointing out their mistakes, and preaching about how they can improve themselves. "I told you so" and "If you had only listened to me, this would not have happened" are often heard from judgmental Ones. They are critical of everything—didactic, pontificating, lecturing, and scolding. They lose their tempers easily over trivialities and are stern disciplinarians, impatient and faultfinding, quick to slap a wrist, literally or figuratively. Average Ones view others around them as lazy and irresponsible. ("Why are they fooling around while I'm working so hard?") They have an opinion about everything which they present as the Truth, not merely as a personal opinion. It does not occur to judgmental Ones that they could be wrong. (Out of politeness or false modesty, they may occasionally allow that it is possible they could be wrong, but at this stage Ones really do not believe their disclaimers of infallibility.)

Moreover, they almost never change their opinions because their opinions are based on their ideals, and their ideals are fixed, like compass points enabling them to know where "right" lies in any matter. Life thus becomes a never-ending application of the ideal to particulars, the constant fixing of mistakes, the unending redoing of what was first done badly by someone else.

They become indignant and resentful about the errors and lack of perfection of others, as if they were personally injured by every-one's behavior. It is a personal affront if someone litters the street or if someone they know does not pay taxes or is having an affair. Even if they are right in their criticisms of others, their manner is so abrasive and irritating that it practically invites defiance or dis-obedience. From impersonal efficiency they have deteriorated into ascerbic dogmatism. But no matter: critical Ones are concerned not with pleasing others, but with making them do what is right.

In their own lives, they are workaholics, feeling guilty if they are not being productive all the time. But perfectionistic Ones are so concerned with minutiae that, ironically, their efficiency is often reduced and they frequently accomplish less than their less driven counterparts. (They may, for instance, rigorously polish furniture to repair a few small flaws and end up removing the finish.) They constantly make specious improvements not because something really needs it, but because they have to improve things to justify their existence. Of course, their perfectionism also drives others crazy, making Ones difficult to work for (never "with"). They are very thin-skinned, and take criticism badly. They do not like to delegate work and decisions to anyone because they feel that no one would do as good a job as they. They feel it would take them longer to train someone else than it would take them to do the job right in the first place.

Naturally their perfectionism takes the enjoyment out of what they do, since nothing is ever good enough. Things are never fin-ished until they are perfect, and it takes a lot of time to make them perfect, if they can be. Thus, workaholic Ones are caught in a con-flict: even though they do not enjoy working, they do not enjoy not working. They are afraid to stop.

Interpersonal conflicts increase because Ones have all the an-swers and no one can tell them anything. Moreover, they get into the habit of making pronouncements about things they actually know little about, and highhandedly condescend to others, explain-ing things as if others were children who would do nothing right without guidance. They presume to tell people what they can and cannot do, putting prohibitions on them, like a priest who instructs couples about married life or a well-heeled columnist who lectures the poor about thrift.

At this stage, their superegos have become almost impossible to placate. Almost nothing Ones do can get the relentless inner voice of criticism off their backs. They are desperate to demonstrate that they have met the standards that have fallen on them, but the standards keep rising. Under such constant self-reproach, it is little wonder that Ones become impatient and critical with others, if only to displace some of the nasty condemnation they are heaping on themselves.

At the same time, Ones need a vacation from their perfectionism and self-criticism, but rather than do so in a constructive way, they begin to find secret sources of solace in the very pleasures their superegos most condemn. Ones may take to drink, raucous nights on the town, increased spending, sexual activity or pornography, or other "indulgences" as a way of reducing the pressure their superegos are putting on them. As much as possible though, Ones will hide these activities from others, lest they be seen as contradicting their strongly stated views.

As we saw in the Overview, Ones resent that they must be perfect. It seems unfair to them that the burden of perfection has fallen on their shoulders more than on others'. Of course, striving for perfection and having moments of feeling perfect still offer some relief to them because their sense of self depends upon feeling right and knowing where perfection lies. But still, something in Ones chafes over the freedom of others. Since they are not having much fun, why should anyone else?

ANALYZING THE UNHEALTHY ONE

Level 7: The Intolerant Misanthrope

Unhealthy Ones cannot allow themselves to be proved wrong, either by objective facts or someone else's better arguments. They are utterly convinced that they are always right about whatever they say or do. Ideals have become severe and forbidding absolutes, and unhealthy Ones are completely inflexible about them.

Their ideals are rigid dogmas from which they cannot deviate. They see everything and everyone in the light of absolutes—right or wrong, good or evil, saved or damned. There is no middle ground, no gray area, no possibility of exceptions being made. They refuse to consider any circumstances which would call for a compromise with absolute perfection. As they see it, the slightest imperfection ruins the whole, and must therefore be mercilessly rooted out. However, living according to absolutes necessarily involves a corresponding negation of their own humanity. The higher they climb, the more of humanity they leave behind. They become misanthropes who love humanity but hate individuals.

The difference between perfectionistic average Ones and intolerant unhealthy Ones is that the former, at least occasionally, include themselves in their own criticism and feel guilty when they fail to attain perfection. This is no longer the case with unhealthy Ones, who exclude themselves from condemnation. Unhealthy Ones are supremely self-righteous, feeling that their adherence to the strictest ideals of perfection justifies them, whether or not they put the ideal into practice. ("I am right, therefore everything I say and do is right.")

In fact, the One's superego has become so toxic and destructive at this stage that the One must displace its vitriol onto others in order to survive psychologically. If nothing Ones can do is good enough, seeing the greater "evil" and disorder in others may be the only relief. Thus, unhealthy Ones increasingly focus their attention on the wrongdoings of others as a way of escaping the wrath of the internalized protective-figure.

Anger remains their most prominent, and perhaps only, emotion. Unhealthy Ones would like to think that they are completely impersonal about administering justice to wrongdoers, but an unmistakable element of vindictiveness is beginning to motivate them, although they cannot admit it to themselves, much less to anyone else. Their fragile self-image depends upon seeing themselves as entirely good and righteous as a compensation for their extremely negative superego. They simply cannot admit anything less than a perfect motivation.

The fact is that they are completely intolerant of the beliefs and behaviors of others, considering anyone who disagrees with them as immoral and evil. Angrily forcing their views on others, unhealthy Ones feel that others must be made to do the right thing, as defined by them, of course. Religion, justice, truth—any or all of their ideals—may be invoked to bolster their position and make others feel wrong or sinful. But in doing so, unhealthy Ones ironically get themselves into strange positions, propounding doctrines which can be defended only by sophistry. They will argue that to save a village, it may be bombed into annihilation. To convert people to their religion, they may be sold into slavery. To protect the lives of unborn fetuses, the lives of adults may be taken. Realizing that they may be using sophistry does not deter unhealthy Ones for a moment, since their psychological survival depends on rationalizing whatever they do, no matter how much their actions conflict with their stated beliefs.

However, they are so enraged at others that the irrationality of their anger disturbs even unhealthy Ones themselves, although, of course, they feel their anger is justified. Even so, they attempt to increase self-control lest their anger get out of hand. The irony is, however, that unhealthy Ones are becoming less self-controlled than ever. They are so tightly wound that their very tightness acts as a lightning rod for repressed feelings and desires to erupt unexpectedly.

The powerful repression of their feelings and impulses also leads to periods of prolonged and severe depression, which appears in marked contrast to their angry, driven qualities. Try as they might, unhealthy Ones are not entirely able to displace their superego attacks and rage onto others. Some of it is turned against the self as well, leaving Ones disillusioned and exhausted. Alcohol and drug abuse and a precipitous decline in the maintenance of their homes and professional lives are not uncommon.

Level 8: The Obsessive Hypocrite
Unhealthy Ones now become obsessed (neurotically preoccupied) with whatever has become the focus of their fury, but which, because of their need to control themselves, they cannot act on directly. As a result, they act compulsively, controlled more than ever by their irrational impulses.

At this stage, the double dichotomy, noted in the Overview, becomes more apparent. On one hand, there is a split between their impulses and the strength of the forces necessary to maintain the repression of those impulses. On the other hand, there is a split between their need to control themselves and moments when their control utterly breaks down. Obsessions and compulsions are both attempts to control, respectively, their irrational thoughts and actions, as well as symptoms of the fact that the control they seek is crumbling.

Obsessive thoughts go repeatedly through their minds. Obsessions are extremely threatening to their consciously held beliefs, however, since they may be obscene, sacrilegious, or brutally violent. The intensity of their obsessions may be so troubling to neurotic Ones that they may feel possessed by demons. In a certain sense neurotic Ones *are* possessed, although their demons are the repressed feelings and impulses they have not allowed themselves to deal with. These obsessions are often normal needs and desires that have become twisted or distorted through constant and extreme repression. But now Ones lack the basic ego strength to hold back the torrent of repressed impulses—their vanquished desires will have their day. Moreover, neurotic Ones are unable to resolve their obsessive thoughts because they are not able to acknowledge what is really disturbing them: their bitter resentment and hatred of others—particularly the people they feel are responsible for their torments. As a result, they spend a great deal of time trying to control their thoughts so that even more upsetting ones do not overwhelm them.

To focus their thoughts on something other than their real problems, neurotic Ones may become obsessed with cleanliness or rooting out other kinds of "dirt" and disorder associated with impulses and feelings they have repressed. Obsessions about sexual feelings and control of the body may be displaced onto food, possibly resulting in anorexia or bulimia, or compulsive "cleansings" of their systems with fasts and enemas. Or they may throw themselves into obsessive-compulsive cleaning or counting, the compulsive nature of their actions ironically contradicting their normal orderliness and self-control.

Obsessions are strangely adaptive, however, because neurotic Ones neither completely admit them into consciousness nor wholly act on their impulses. On the other hand, their obsessions profoundly disturb them, and they act out just enough of them to become compulsive, and thus arbitrary, contradictory, and hypocritical.

When neurotic Ones are unconsciously controlled by their erupting impulses, they may act contrary to their stated beliefs, for example, preaching the virtues of absolute sexual purity while falling into the grip of compulsive sexual activity. They do what they condemn, like a censor who is "forced" to watch pornography, or a sex researcher who must hear the lurid stories of rapists, or a judge who is a shoplifter. Compulsive Ones may even put themselves in the way of temptation to prove that their moral strength is so solid that it can withstand testing. Thus, they can have it both ways: they can flirt with, and occasionally succumb to, vice in the name of virtue. This, of course, further threatens their position, as such compulsive behaviors will eventually be scrutinized by others, leading to scandal and ruined reputations.

Corruption of any sort is always more shocking in the Lord High Protector of Public Morals than it is in the ordinary person. Neurotic Ones are drawn into perversity because, having repressed their feelings so thoroughly, they have denied and twisted their emotions until they have become deformed. The deformity of their emotional lives is what makes neurotic Ones and their impulses dangerous, not necessarily the original impulses themselves.

Level 9: The Punitive Avenger

Someone or something has stirred up such unacceptable feelings that neurotic Ones cannot deal with them directly. Neurotic Ones are now no longer even remotely motivated by ideals, but by their overriding need to restore self-control before their obsessions and compulsions get completely out of hand. But they cannot resolve obsessions by being obsessive, or compulsions by being compulsive. They therefore "solve" their neurotic conflicts by attempting to do away with the apparent cause of their disturbances, whipping themselves into a fury over what they see as the evildoing of others, although what is really at stake is their own sanity.

Their contradictions are so deep, their obsessions so intense, and their compulsions so threatening, that neurotic Ones cannot back down. The possibility that they may have been wrong is too much for their disintegrating ego to take. More than ever, they must justify themselves. Not only must others be proved wrong, they must be punished. And since others are hideously evil, they can be condemned and destroyed without guilt.

No love, no mercy, no human sympathy can be shown to those who have become the focus of their righteous retribution. Neurotic Ones become inhumanly cruel and, with whatever power they have, they make sure that others suffer. "They are only getting what they deserve!" is the rallying cry, and since the end justifies the means, any means can be used.

Completely unmerciful and unforgiving, they set in motion injustices and atrocities while trying to portray them as the work of an impersonal agent. Neurotic Ones act as if justice itself were responsible for their sadistic punishment of others. Because their twisted mortality now sanctions it, they are capable of having others thrown into prison, tortured, or burned at the stake.

The personality type which fears being condemned, condemns others mercilessly. The personality type which once may have been so concerned with justice has become the perpetrator of gross injustices. The personality type which was once the soul of reason is now completely unreasonable.

THE DYNAMICS OF THE ONE

The Direction of Disintegration: The One Goes to Four

Starting at Level 4, under conditions of increased stress and anxiety, Ones will begin to act out some of the traits of average to unhealthy Fours. Average Ones are perhaps the most strict and self-controlled of all of the nine types, thus the move to Four signals a hidden desire to be free of the burden of their responsibilities. They want to relieve some of the pressure of their relentless superego demands and allow the backlog of repressed desires some time to "play." Having done so, however, without having examined the sources of their self-criticism, Ones will feel guilty for being "irresponsible" and become even more strict with themselves.

When Ones go to Four, they begin to fantasize about being someone else, being free of the burdens of their obligations. They seek out things of beauty and try to surround themselves with an aesthetically pleasing environment as a refuge from the pressures of their work. A certain "aesthetic elitism" develops. Average Ones see themselves as people of taste, and defend this sense of themselves all the more when they are under pressure. They may harbor romantic longings for unavailable others in their life, but, as Ones, would be very unlikely to inform the object of their admiration of their interest. Such fantasies and desires are soon attacked and repressed by the One's vigilant superego.

By Level 5, Ones begin to tire of the constant pressure to meet their ideals, and become moody and temperamental in their move to Four. They often experience periods of melancholy, feeling that no one understands how hard they are trying and how important their contributions have been. Their discipline and restraint give way to turbulent feelings, and Ones become much more emotionally reactive and self-doubting. The aestheticism of Level 4 can give way to a more forced, affected quality at Level 5. The Four's drama and hypersensitivity combine with the One's heightened sense of propriety and manners to create an individual who is extremely awkward and self-conscious in social situations. This only heightens the One's stress and desire to "measure up."

If the pressure continues, at Level 6 average Ones will begin to pick up behaviors from the Four at Level 6. Their relentless super-ego provides few rewards for their efforts, so Ones become self-indulgent, giving themselves a few exceptions to the rules: perks and pleasures that provide ways of escaping the strain of living up to their impossible ideals. If they have been extolling the virtues of sobriety, they will begin to have a drink once in a while — while no one is looking, of course. If they've been shocked at promiscuity, they may seek out anonymous sex or have an affair. Ones are desperately looking for a way to escape their cruel superegos, but at this Level, they are unable to find healthy and balanced ways of doing so. Their superego is so extreme that they unconsciously seek extreme pleasures to compensate for it.

At Level 7, under increased stress, unhealthy Ones begin to behave like unhealthy Fours. When they are unable to maintain the intensity of their rigid intolerance and rage, Ones collapse into depression. Their depression can be severe and long-term, and in this regard, Ones with strongly dysfunctional family backgrounds where stress was a constant factor may mistake themselves for Fours. The depression acts as a means of containing the One's rage, but can also be a strong indicator to Ones that something is seriously wrong with the views they have developed about life.

At Level 8, the obsessive concerns and behaviors of the One are joined by additional compulsions from the unhealthy Four. This can include irrational self-hatred, morbidity, and turbulent feelings of hatred and sexual desire. Although unhealthy Ones tend to focus on the wrongdoings of others or on exaggerated views of imperfections in their environment, at Four they also turn against themselves with equal fury.

They increasingly come under the spell of their unconscious processes, although they are completely unprepared to be plunged into the maelstrom of the unconscious. They are strangers to that territory, and what they discover about themselves fills them with horror, disgust, and self-loathing. With appalling clarity, they suddenly see the extent of their emotional chaos and the evil they have done. They begin to panic that the ideals by which they have lived and controlled themselves are no longer of any help.

At Level 9, when deeply neurotic Ones go to Four, their last moorings break loose. The hideousness of their punitive attitudes and actions crashes down upon them. They see their own corruption and are horrified. ("Oh my God, what have I done?") They fear that they have transgressed so grievously that they cannot be forgiven.

Their convictions now convict them. But while deteriorated Ones rightly are aghast at their hatred, intolerance, and cruelty, they go overboard and condemn themselves as harshly as they have condemned others. From a position of finding nothing good in others, they now find nothing good in themselves.

They become profoundly depressed, hopeless, and emotionally disturbed. Deteriorated Ones are prey to extreme guilt, self-hatred, and emotional torment from which it is difficult to reemerge. There seems to be nothing worthwhile outside themselves to which they can reattach, no ideals with which they feel worthy of associating. Now the only way to resolve what is tearing them apart is to do away with the self. An incapacitating breakdown or suicide becomes very real possibility.

The Direction of Integration: The One Goes to Seven

As we have seen, Ones exercise too much control over their feelings and impulses. The essence of the move to Seven is that integrating Ones relax and learn to take delight in life. They learn to trust themselves and reality, becoming life-affirming rather than controlled and constricted. They discover that life is not always grim and serious: happiness is a legitimate response to existence. Pleasure can be taken without sinking into the morass of sensuality; people can please and fulfill themselves without becoming irresponsible or selfish.

Integrating Ones no longer feel that they must make everything perfect. Thus they progress from obligation to enthusiasm, from constraint to freedom of action. They are more relaxed and productive, and are able to express their feelings spontaneously. Integrating Ones are more responsive to the world, more playful, and much happier.

A great burden has been lifted from them, the burden of unnecessary perfection. They realize that they can enjoy what is good in life without constantly feeling obligated to improve it, especially in those areas in which perfection is not an issue. Things do not have to be perfect to be good. ("This is good, but so is that.") They realize that much in life is already very good, even wonderful. Integrating

Ones marvel at nature, the beauty of the arts, or the extraordinary accomplishments of others who, like they, are imperfect, yet have been able to make valuable contributions.

Moreover, they discover that it is frequently possible for them to be flexible without compromising genuine values. The old adage "The good is not the enemy of the better" becomes meaningful. They stop preaching from the abstract and experience life as it is. Integrating Ones have come down from Olympus to join the human race.

THE MAJOR SUBTYPES OF THE ONE

The One with a Nine-Wing: "The Idealist"

In people of this subtype, the idealism of the One is heightened and reinforced by the Nine-wing. Both component types tend to be removed from the environment: the One because it relates to ideals, and the Nine because it tends to relate to idealizations of people rather than to people themselves. The result is that Ones with a Nine-wing are somewhat disconnected from others, and more cerebral, remote, and impersonal than Ones with a Two-wing. The main type and wing are also somewhat in conflict in that Nines want to avoid stirring things up while Ones definitely want to provoke change. On the other hand, both types share idealism and a resistance to being affected by others. In this wing subtype there is a distancing, a sense of being an outside evaluator of culture. Because of their apparent detachment and logical orientation, Ones with a Nine-wing are often mistyped as Fives. Noteworthy examples of this subtype include Al Gore, Sandra Day O'Connor, Michael Dukakis, Carl Sagan, Dr. Joyce Brothers, Katharine Hepburn, George Harrison, George F. Will, Noan Chomsky, Eric Severeid, William F. Buckley, Jeane J. Kirkpatrick, C. S. Lewis, Thomas Jefferson, Cotton Mather, Saint Ignatius of Loyola, and "Mr. Spock."

When they are healthy, people in this subtype are unusually objective and moderate in their judgments and dealings with others, since they have a special interest in remaining dispassionately involved. They are civilized in the best sense of the word, and often display a "scholarly" quality and erudition. There is a spiritual, mystical side to people of this subtype, and an attraction more to nature, art, and animals than to humans. Their emotional self-expression is restrained, but they are often generous and loyal friends. As Ones, they strive to be exemplars of their principles, teaching by embodying what they believe in, yet the Nine-wing gives them a more gentle, retiring approach to life than Ones with a Two-wing. They can be gifted, articulate speakers and writers and frequently use their talents to raise awareness of society's ills.

Average persons of this subtype actively campaign for their beliefs, although they can be pessimistic about whether people will take their advice and improve. This subtype is also more idealistic than the other, and because of the withdrawn qualities of the Nine-wing, is less likely to engage in the politics and sweat necessary to bring about the reforms they believe in. Although they have a heightened sense of public responsibility, their withdrawn tendencies often cause them to be perceived as elitists. The impersonalness of Ones and the disconnectedness of Nines produce people who preach to others almost entirely from abstract notions while trying to exclude anything personal in their behavior. Their emotions are subdued, and they have a tendency to be unconcerned and even obtuse about human motivations and human nature in general. The anger of the One is also harder to detect in this subtype, tending to be expressed in stiffness, impatience, and sometimes biting sarcasm. They increasingly prefer being alone and look for situations where they can work by themselves—again, like Fives—in order to avoid dealing with the messiness of interpersonal relationships.

Unhealthy people of this subtype are almost completely dissociated from their emotions and contradictions. They resist seeing what does not fit into their worldview. They tend to be inaccessible emotionally and intellectually, barricading themselves behind stubbornly held opinions. They may also literally distance themselves from others, "heading for the hills," and leading a hermitlike existence. They can be bitter and misanthropic because their severe judgments are not checked by any real compassion for or identification with other human beings. Unhealthy Ones with a Nine-wing tend to abstract themselves and others completely, seeing them as problems to be solved or eradicated. They readily become obsessed with what they see as the evildoing of others and compulsive about taking measures to rectify it, while dissociating themselves from contradictions in their own behavior. They can cause others a great deal of harm because they do not understand the nature or extent of the suffering they inflict upon others in the name of their ideals.

The One with a Two-Wing: "The Advocate"

The traits of the One and those of the Two support each other in many ways. Both the One and the Two strive to comply with the dictates of the superego—to be "good" according to the lights of their internalized values. Ones want to be righteous and balanced, Twos want to be selfless and all-loving. On the other hand, Ones are rational and impersonal, while Twos are emotional and involved with people. Although One is the basic personality type, there is a noticeable degree of warmth as well as an interpersonal focus in people of this subtype, compensating for the One's emotional control. The Two-wing also makes them more fiery and action-oriented than Ones with a Nine-wing. Ones with a Two-wing want to roll up their sleeves and get involved, whereas the other subtype tends to have more of an "ivory tower" quality. Noteworthy examples of this subtype include Pope John Paul II, Mahatma Gandhi, Albert Schweitzer, Mario Cuomo, Bill Moyers, Tom Brokaw, Leslie Stahl, Jane Fonda, Vanessa Redgrave, Ralph Nader, John Bradshaw, Jerry Brown, Gene Siskel, Margaret Thatcher, Alistair Cooke, Joan Baez, Joan of Arc, Saint Thomas More, and Anita Bryant.

The Two-wing softens the One's tendency to be overly harsh and judgmental. To the extent that thoughtfulness and love of neighbor are among their ideals, Ones with a Two-wing will attempt to be caring and personal; they try to temper the rigor of their ideals so they can take the needs of individuals into consideration. Healthy people of this subtype mix tolerance with compassion, integrity with concern about others, objectivity with empathy. They can be generous, helpful, kind, and rather good-humored, markedly offsetting the One's more rigid demeanor. They are more willing to "get into the trenches" to bring about the changes they desire and are often found in many of the helping professions (such as teaching, ministry, and medicine), since their idealism is much more effective when it has an interpersonal focus.

Average people of this subtype are well-intentioned and seek to educate others, both from a feeling of idealistic obligation and a desire to exert a personal influence over them. They are convinced not only that they are right, but that they are well-meaning. They are frequently involved in idealistic public causes and reforms of one sort or another out of a sense of personal responsibility for the welfare of others. Average Ones want to control themselves, while average Twos want to control others: these motives reinforce each other, making it difficult for those around Ones with a Two-wing to break away from their influence. People of this subtype allow themselves clearly defined emotional outlets as a reaction to their self-control. Tendencies to perfectionism, a strict conscience, self-satisfaction with their own goodness, and self-importance are also possibilities here. They tend to be more vocal about their discontents than Ones with a Nine-wing, since other people, rather than abstractions, are the focus of their attention. They are prone to anger and resentment when others do not follow their "suggestions." But they tend to be thin-skinned, and do not like their ideals, their motives, or their lives to be questioned.

Unhealthy Ones with a Two-wing may be intolerant of and condescending to those who disagree with them. They may attempt to manipulate others emotionally, making them feel guilty for being less perfect than they should be. These people have a tendency toward self-deception about their own motives, and self-righteousness when their motives or actions are questioned. Like Ones with a Nine-wing, they are also prone to depression, but with the Two-wing, are more likely to act out sexually or with drugs or alcohol, in ways that are completely contrary to their expressed values. Self-deception and feelings of entitlement make their defenses particularly difficult to break. There is a tremendous amount of covert aggression in persons of this subtype, both from the repressed aggression of the One and the indirect aggression of the Two. Unhealthy Ones with a Two-wing may have physical problems (conversion reactions), compulsive habits, or nervous breakdowns as a result of the anxiety generated by their contradictions.

SOME FINAL THOUGHTS

Looking back on their deterioration, we can see that neurotic Ones have brought about the very thing they most fear. They are so intolerant and cruel that they are certain to be condemned by others — and condemned even by their own consciences. They have done something so contrary to their principles that they can no longer rationalize their actions. Justice now works against them rather than for them.

We can also see that many of the propositions which average to unhealthy Ones preached as objective truths were at least partially personal predilections. The truth of many of their dogmas is not usually as self-evident as Ones think it is. This does not mean that they should not act on what they believe, but that they should recognize the role which the subjective and the irrational play in their lives. After all, reason is not the only faculty human beings possess, and once Ones pit reason against their feelings, they begin to get into trouble. Reason alone is a trap which leads to unreasonable behavior, because it does not take other parts of human nature into account.

At the heart of the One's dilemma is a fundamental contradiction. More than anything else, Ones want to have integrity congruency of thought, word and deed. But to have integrity is to be integrated, that is, whole. Integrity means oneness; however, as soon as Ones have judged some part of themselves unacceptable and repressed it, they have already lost their wholeness, their integrity. The way out is not by judging and evaluating themselves. This leads only to more and more internal conflict and division. To return to wholeness, Ones need acceptance of themselves—to see that here and now, who they are is good enough.

Unless they are very healthy, however, Ones are motivated by an underlying fear that they must constantly adhere to the strictest ideals or they will precipitously and calamitously fall into the depths of depravity. Life to them is like walking a tightrope over a chasm: one slip and they are doomed. There is so little hope or joy in this view of life that Ones should not be surprised if others do not follow them more readily. When Ones understand that there is no foolproof set of rules to guide them through life, and that even the best principles they have learned do not apply in every situation, they may discover that beyond the rules and dictates of their superego is a deeper, quiet wisdom. It is a living relationship to the truth of each moment, and a wisdom that transcends all principles. As Ones begin to accept themselves and reclaim those parts of their psyches that their superegos have banished, they find that this wisdom is always available to them. And as they live from this deeper truth, they find that they no longer need to convince people of the rightness of their way of life. Others are eager to learn and to be touched by the One's true wisdom.

Part III

Chapter 13

Advanced Guidelines

In this chapter, we hope to answer whatever remaining questions you have about how the Enneagram works. We will go into more detail about most of the topics already covered in the Guidelines. Now that you have read at least some of the descriptions, you probably have a good working sense of the Enneagram, so refinements will be more meaningful to you. We will examine three major areas in some detail: the Directions of Integration and Disintegration, the wings, and the Levels of Development. We will also touch briefly on the instinctual variants of the nine types.

THE DIRECTIONS OF INTEGRATION
AND DISINTEGRATION

As you know from the Guidelines, each personality type has a Direction of Integration and a Direction of Disintegration, as indicated on the Enneagram on the following page. Each type's *wing* also has a Direction of Integration and Disintegration. The wing's directions follow the same patterns we have already seen. For example, in a Nine with a One-wing, the Direction of Integration for the One-wing is to Seven, and its Direction of Disintegration is to Four. Likewise for all the wings of all the subtypes.

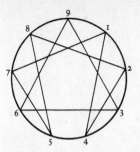

The Direction of Integration   **The Direction of Disintegration**

1–7–5–8–2–4–1   1–4–2–8–5–7–1
9–3–6–9   9–6–3–9

One point of confusion sometimes arises about four subtypes in particular—the One with a Two-wing, the Two with a One-wing, the Seven with an Eight-wing, and the Eight with a Seven-wing—because the same type seems to be the Direction of both Integration and Disintegration for that subtype. For example, it is unhealthy for a person who is a One with a Two-wing to move to Four. However, Four is also the Two-wing's Direction of Integration. So, it seems to be contradictory that someone would be going to Four in both integration and disintegration.

The confusion arises because Four represents unhealthy tendencies in the One, while Four also represents healthy tendencies in the One's Two-wing. The solution to this apparent contradiction lies in remembering that if a person is healthy, his or her unhealthy tendencies are not active. So while Four represents a One's unhealthy direction, a healthy One who is integrating will move to Seven, and only the Two-wing will integrate to Four.

Remember that the basic personality type and the wing both move in their respective Directions of Integration and Disintegration. To return to the example, the One would integrate to Seven, and the Two-wing would integrate to Four. If the person is unhealthy, the One would disintegrate to Four, and the Two-wing to Eight.

If you reflect on yourself, you will see that your wing actually does integrate or disintegrate just as your basic type does. However, it is not feasible to give a description for the development or deterioration of the wing for all the personality types, since there are too many possible states in which this happens. Once you get used to seeing how your basic personality type integrates or disintegrates, you will be able to recognize the movement of your wing as well.

It is important to realize that the personality type in the Direction of Disintegration is not unhealthy in any absolute sense since it is, after all, another personality type—and no type is fundamentally unhealthy. The type lying in the Direction of Disintegration is considered "unhealthy" only because it embodies what we most need for our personal development, but for a reason inherent in the character structure of our basic type, we cannot yet deal with. Therefore, the type which lies in the Direction of Disintegration is only *relatively* unhealthy because we cannot immediately integrate into ourselves the psychological capacities it symbolizes. The unhealthy type represents those aspects of ourselves which are the most difficult for us to come to terms with.

Eight, for example, lies in the Direction of Disintegration for Two. There is nothing inherently unhealthy about Eight, although going to Eight immediately is unhealthy for Twos because they must first resolve their aggressions. The move to Eight symbolizes the eruption of dangerously aggressive impulses into a neurotic Two's behavior.

Similarly, for the remainder of the personality types, we can see why it is unhealthy to move in the Direction of Disintegration. In brief, Threes most need to deal with dissociating from their feelings, symbolized by Nine. Fours most need to deal with their feelings of entitlement, symbolized by Two. Fives most need to deal with impulsiveness, symbolized by Seven. Sixes most need to deal with hostility toward those whom they fear, symbolized by Three. Sevens most need to deal with obsessiveness, symbolized by One. Eights most need to deal with their denied fear of being overwhelmed by others, symbolized by Five. Nines most need to deal with denied anxiety (hysteria), symbolized by Six. And Ones most need to deal with their feelings and unconscious impulses, symbolized by Four.

We are often tempted to move in our Direction of Disintegration because the normal and neurotic conflicts we get into impel us to find a quick solution to our emotional needs. The type which is in the Direction of Disintegration seems to hold out the promise of being just such a solution, although it never is. To return to the above example for a moment, a move to Eight is tempting because, as Twos become increasingly unhealthy, they become more resentful toward those they feel have been ungrateful to them and have ignored their needs. A "solution" to their aggressive feelings toward others is to lash out at people, coercing a response through openly aggressive behavior. But if unhealthy Twos succumb to the temptation to go to Eight, their anger is certain to do more harm than good, driving away the very people whose love they want by destroying the relationship. A move to the Direction of Disintegration never solves anything; at best it buys some time and sometimes it even makes everything worse.

Let us consider another refinement about the Directions of Integration and Disintegration.

You may have noticed that Threes, Sixes, and Nines have to move only two places in their Direction of Integration before returning to their basic type. The remaining types have to move six places in the Direction of Integration before returning to their basic type. It may seem unfair that six types have twice as far to go on the Enneagram as the Three, Six, and Nine.

We have already used the terms "primary" and "secondary" types in the descriptions. The primary personality types—the Three, Six, and Nine—are most seriously affected by—most out of touch with—the characteristic problem of their Triads. As you recall, Three is the primary type of the Feeling Triad, Six of the Thinking Triad, and Nine of the Instinctive Triad. The secondary types are the six remaining personality types—One, Four, Two, Eight, Five, and Seven. They are somewhat less affected by the corresponding problems of their Triads.

It may seem that there is an advantage to being one of the primary types, since there is less distance to go to integrate around the Enneagram. A Three, for example, has to integrate only to Six and then to Nine before it returns to Three. But because the goal of psychological development is to become a fully functioning person, being a primary or a secondary type is neither an advantage nor a disadvantage. The psychological agenda for both the primary and secondary types comes to the same thing—developing all their potentials in a balanced way. From a deeper perspective, all of the positive potentials of the types already exist in us, but our egos identify with a few particular personality patterns which do not allow us to experience or express the full range of our Being. The process of Integration enables us to see through the illusions and limitations of our personality pattern so that we can let go of them. When we do so, new potentials (represented by the type in the Direction of Integration) emerge and naturally fall into place.

There is nevertheless an important difference between the primary and the secondary personality types: the primary types have a more difficult time integrating because they are more seriously blocked by the root problem of their respective Triads. The primary types, although they do not have as far to go, so to speak, find it more difficult to overcome their characteristic problems. But when they do, their development is revolutionary—they make an abrupt change for the better. The development of the secondary types is more gradual, or evolutionary, as they move around the Enneagram. The secondary types have farther to go, but they change less abruptly as they integrate from type to type in their Direction of Integration.

The reason for this apparent imbalance is that the primary types contain the issues of both of the other types in their Triad. This is also why they are the most blocked with the psychological function in question. In the Thinking Triad for example, the primary issue is fear and anxiety. We have seen that Fives are fearful about the external world, and so retreat away from it into the safety of their minds, while Sevens are fearful about their inner world, thus fleeing their inner pain and anxiety by engaging in activities and experiences in the world. The Six, however, the primary type of the Triad, has both fears. Sixes are anxious both about the external world and about their inner turmoil as well. Thus, in order to move beyond their own issues toward type Nine in their Direction of Integration, they must resolve both the fears of the environment symbolized by type Five, and the fears of their own inner pain and anxiety symbolized by type Seven. Thus, all nine types must ultimately integrate the issues of each of the three Triads. They simply do so in a different sequence and in a different "rhythm."

So, from one point of view, there is an advantage to being one of the primary types since they can potentially become integrated more quickly than the secondary types. But from another point of view, there is an advantage to being a secondary type, because integration is more gradual and therefore less daunting. However, no matter how you look at it, there is no absolute advantage to being either a primary or secondary type, since the goal for everyone is the same: to integrate all of their healthy potentials. It does not matter where on the Enneagram you begin this process.

The process of integration is never ending: the Enneagram is as open-ended as human nature itself. We are able to grow constantly in an upward spiral of transformation without ever reaching a final point of perfection or complete wholeness, something which this interpretation of the Enneagram certainly does not promise. Perfection and wholeness are ideals which beckon us onward; they are not states we can ever fully attain.

On the other hand, while we can continue to integrate as long as we live, it seems that no one goes through all the stages of deterioration in the Direction of Disintegration. Before an individual could do so, he or she would have had such a complete breakdown that a profound psychotic break with reality, or death, would probably have occurred first. In other words, deterioration is self-limiting, because when people disintegrate psychologically, and usually physically as well, they simply cannot go on endlessly getting worse. Schizophrenics finally burn out, exhausting themselves mentally and physically; depressives may well commit suicide; hysterics may have serious accidents. In different ways and for different reasons they all reach dead ends, and if they do not get the help they need, they either languish in the vacuum of psychosis or die.

Happily, however, the potential for healthy development is not so limited: as long as we live we can become more integrated persons. While it is highly unlikely that we will ever become totally free from the limitations of human nature, we can become less oppressed by them.

THE WING

We have seen that no one is a pure personality type. Everyone is a mixture of two types—the basic type and the wing—which are adjacent on the circumference of the Enneagram. The wing's influence accounts for a great deal of the variety which we see in daily life among different people.

You may also recall that the wing is usually only one of the two types on either side of your basic personality type. For example, a Five usually has either a Six-wing or a Four-wing, but seldom both. A Three has either a Four-wing or a Two-wing, but again, generally speaking, not both. Additionally, it has been our experience that in those cases where a person actually seems to have both wings, the influence of both tends to be relatively weaker and less important, thus the basic type is stronger. Once you have determined your basic personality type (or that of someone else), the next step is to determine which wing you have. You can do this by the process of elimination: one of the two possible wings will be a better fit than the other.

There are several refinements we can now make about the wing. The wing is one of the two personality types *adjacent* to the basic type—the wing does not lie somewhere else on the Enneagram. A person cannot be a Nine with a Four-wing or a Seven with a Two-wing. In real life, people are not an arbitrary combination of psychological components. If they were, there would be no overall pattern to their personalities. They would be like characters in a badly written novel whose traits conflict in nonsensical ways. (Traits can be, and are, in conflict with each other, but they cannot be mutually exclusive, like being an honest man and a thief at the same time.) For instance, a combination of the traits of a Seven and a Three in the same person is contradictory, like simultaneously having sight and being blind. Such random mixtures of traits and types do not occur in human beings, and they do not occur in the personality types of the Enneagram. The structure of the Enneagram itself, the nine personality types, and the interrelationships of the personality types are not arbitrary. They are unified in a system of amazing complexity and simplicity.

Another point about the wings is worth discussing in some detail. Close observation indicates that among persons *of the same basic type and wing*, the proportion of the wing to the basic type varies significantly. In analyzing someone, it is necessary to identify the wing and to estimate the proportion of the wing to the basic type. For example, two individuals who are Eights with a Nine-wing will have similar personalities, but there will still be noticeable differences between them. These differences are partially attributable to the "amount" of Nine which each of the Eights has in his or her overall personality. One of the Eights with a Nine-wing may have virtually a 51 percent to 49 percent split (speaking in crude numerical terms) between Eight and Nine, which means that the person has a very high proportion of wing to the basic type. The other Eight may have very little Nine-wing, say 85 percent to 15 percent, in which case the Nine component, while discernible, is not a very significant part of the overall personality.

The exact proportion of the wing to the basic type is probably impossible to measure objectively. It is possible, nevertheless, to make gross estimates of the proportion of the wing to the basic type along the following lines: if an individual has a high proportion of wing to basic type, we can say that he or she has a "heavy" wing. If the wing is discernible but the basic type markedly dominates the overall personality, we can say that the person has a "moderate" wing. And if the basic type so dominates the overall personality that the wing is negligible, we can say that the person has a "light" wing. Note that in every case, the basic type must, by definition, make up at least 51 percent of the overall personality. One of the two types *always* dominates the personality as a whole. In cases where the basic type and wing are extremely close in their proportions—nearly 50/50—one can usually determine the basic type by observing the individual under stress. Which way does the person act out in their Direction of Disintegration? For instance, a person who could not determine whether she was a Four with a Five-wing or a Five with a Four-wing could observe her behavior during times of increased anxiety and see whether she behaved more like an average Two, which would indicate that the basic type was Four, or like an average Seven, which would indicate that the basic type was Five. The self-sacrificing, emotionally needy behavior of Twos is quite distinct from the hyperactive, distracted restlessness of average Sevens.

It is worth making these sorts of distinctions about the wing because when you look at the eighteen major subtypes of the Enneagram—the nine basic types with two wings per type—you can see that we are actually no longer talking about eighteen subtypes, but about fifty-four subtypes when we consider heavy, moderate, and light wing proportions to the basic type. And if you were to take the wing's precise influence into consideration—99 percent to 1 percent, 98 percent to 2 percent, 97 percent to 3 percent, and so forth—you can see that the Enneagram can account for literally hundreds of subtypes, far more than in any other typology.

Theoretically, the most accurate way to describe the personality types would be to describe each major subtype as a discrete category. Instead of nine descriptive chapters in this book there would be eighteen, because there is no such thing as, for example, a pure One. There are only Ones with a Two-wing and Ones with a Nine-wing, and so forth. But because the proportion of the wing to the basic type can vary so widely, describing all the subtypes would be nearly impossible. No book can take every variation into account. This is why it is so important for you to personalize the descriptions yourself.

THE LEVELS OF DEVELOPMENT

As noted in the Guidelines and the descriptions, there is an overall structure to each personality type. Our analysis of each type began with a description of its healthy traits, then moved to its average traits, and then to its unhealthy traits. That structure, which is not part of traditional interpretations of the Enneagram, is made up of the Levels of Development which form each type. The great fluidity of human nature—the way people change from day to day and even from moment to moment—can, at least in part, be attributed to the fact that we constantly move along the Levels of our personality type.

Although psychologists have thought that personality traits could be arranged along a continuum of some sort, since the basic personality types themselves were not clear, it was impossible to know where to assign most of the traits. With the help of the Enneagram, we are now in a position to do so with some accuracy. We will now make a few refinements to the Levels of Development, one of our major discoveries.

You will recall that the continuum of the Levels of Development for each of the basic personality types looked like this:

```
        ___
        X
        X   Healthy
        X
        ___
        X
        X   Average
        X
        ___
        X
        X   Unhealthy
        X
        ___
```

The Levels of Development

The nine different Levels are numbered in the descriptions, and if you go back to those chapters, you will see that they are clearly marked and that they serve as signposts for what is happening to the personality type as it deteriorates along the continuum. To be specific, if you start at the beginning of the analysis, you will find nine Levels of Development, namely, Levels 1 to 3 in the healthy part of the analysis, Levels 4 to 6 in the average part, and Levels 7 to 9 in the unhealthy part. The ability to specify which Level someone is at is helpful for a number of reasons.

First, the precision it is possible to achieve with the Levels of Development enables us to distinguish further subtypes within each personality type. People of the same personality type (and wing and proportion of wing) can still be quite different because they are functioning at different Levels. For example, a contentious, provocative Five (the Five at Level 6) is quite different from the healthy, perceptive Five (at Level 2). Or a domineering Two (at Level 8) is quite different from the nurturing Two (at Level 3).

Each of the nine Levels of Development produces nine distinct variations which are closely interrelated, since they comprise the personality type as a whole. As we will see in the Theory chapter, other personality typologies describe many of the same personality variations as those found in our interpretation of the Enneagram. But because of similarities among these different variations, other theorists have often confused them. For example, Karen Horney describes one personality type as a "resigned type" and another as the "well-adjusted automaton." From our point of view, we can see that these are not actually two distinct personality types, but two variations of personality type Nine—the "well-adjusted automaton" is the average Nine ("the passively disengaged person" at Level 5), while the "resigned type" is also the average Nine ("the resigned fatalist" at Level 6). Many of the categories used by psychologists are really descriptions of one or two Levels of a personality type rather than the type as a whole. Thus, for example, the "depressive personality disorder" is really the Four at Levels 7 and 8, "The Alienated Depressive" and "The Emotionally Tormented Person."

Second, keeping the Levels of Development in mind helps us to understand and describe people more accurately. People are constantly shifting along the continuum. Different things happen at each of the Levels; different traits and defense mechanisms emerge and combine with already existing traits. Each personality type is constantly changing as it spirals down the continuum toward neurosis or moves upward toward health and further integration. And as you might expect, there is an internal symmetry among the traits of each type. Each personality type is not an arbitrary collection of traits but a dynamic whole having an internal structure with many interrelated parts.

It is important to understand that the personality types are not made up of a static group of arbitrary traits. There is an enormous amount of internal coherence within each type, and that coherence is provided by the fact that traits metamorphose into each other as the person shifts up and down the Levels of Development in response to fears and desires, anxiety, and defense mechanisms.

For example, in healthy Fours self-awareness emerges at Level 2. But by Level 5, self-awareness has deteriorated into self-absorption, and by Level 8, self-absorption has deteriorated into self-hatred. Or, to give another example from Fours, we can trace their healthy sensitivity into the vulnerability of average Fours, and finally to the emotional torment of neurotic Fours. These are but two of many traits in Fours which we can follow down the continuum, tracking them as they deteriorate into related but different forms. And, of course, we can do this for all the personality types.

Moreover, there are so many interrelationships within each type, as well as symmetries and interrelationships among the nine personality types themselves, that it would be impossible to provide an adequate commentary on them here. However, to give you a better idea of some of the most important activities at each Level, we have included the following short explanations. If you review any of the analytic sections of the descriptions, you will see how they fit the following patterns.

In the Healthy Levels
AT LEVEL 1: The type at its very healthiest, a state of psychological balance, freedom, and the emergence of special spiritual capacities or virtues. The ideal state for the type, reflecting the essential qualities of the type.
AT LEVEL 2: The type is still healthy, but the ego and its defenses begin to emerge in response to basic anxieties from childhood. Deepest fears and desires emerge, the result of relationships with

parents. Sense of self and the type's cognitive style as a whole manifest themselves.

AT LEVEL 3: Still healthy, but less so. The ego is more active, producing a characteristic persona. The healthy social characteristics which the type brings to others and society appear.

In the Average Levels

AT LEVEL 4: The type has begun to become subtly imbalanced by drawing on its characteristic source of psychic energy, which is different for each type. Each type's unwitting psychological dead end emerges, which, if followed, will create increasing intrapsychic and interpersonal conflicts.

AT LEVEL 5: The ego inflates as the type tries to control the environment in characteristic ways. Defense mechanisms become more serious. A marked turning point in the deterioration of the type; traits noticeably less healthy, more negative. Conflicts with others increase.

AT LEVEL 6: The person begins to overcompensate for conflicts and increasing anxieties. Characteristic forms of self-centeredness emerge here. Conflicts with others escalate, as various forms of ego-defense are acted on.

In the Unhealthy Levels

AT LEVEL 7: The person employs highly dysfunctional and ultimately self-defeating survival tactics, different for each type, in a desperate attempt to bolster the ego, which is assailed by increasing anxiety. Serious interpersonal conflicts now.

AT LEVEL 8: Serious intrapsychic conflicts and resulting delusional defenses employed. Attempts to remake reality rather than succumb to it and anxiety. A deeply neurotic state: person getting out of touch with reality in some way, different for each type.

AT LEVEL 9: A fully pathological state. Person out of touch with reality, willing to destroy self and/or others to save illusions and to spare self from the anxiety of realizing what he or she has done. Different forms of immediate or remote self-destructiveness manifest themselves, resulting in serious violence, breakdown, or death.

This short description of what happens at each of the nine Levels of Development does not begin to do justice to them. (For a much more detailed exploration of the the Levels of Development and the clusters of traits and motivations that comprise the continuum for each type, please see the appendix and UTE, pages 89–119.) We might take as an example the personality types to illustrate how that type flows from Level to Level. If you review personality type Eight, you will see that the Eight at its best is the magnanimous heart, then becomes the self-confident person, the constructive leader, the enterprising adventurer, the dominating power broker, the confrontational adversary, the ruthless outlaw, then the omnipotent magalomaniac, and finally the violent destroyer. You can see how self-confidence deteriorates into the drive for power, and then into delusional megalomania. You can also see that, at its best, the Eight has an enormously positive effect on a large number of people, and that, when the Eight is unhealthy, it has just the reverse effect. These and many other interrelationships are discernible when you review the descriptions with these sorts of structural ideas in mind.

It can be absolutely riveting to follow each personality type from its healthiest Level downward as it succumbs to the influence of its fears and desires, conflicts and defenses, spiraling into the grip of neurosis. Like a morality play, the dissolution of each type has a certain inevitability about it. If each type is not both wise and fortunate, it knowingly and unknowingly falls into the hands of its fears and illusions until it ends in disaster. Thus, the Levels of Development help us have a clarity about human nature which we do not always have in life. The accuracy of its predictions is nevertheless something we can all recognize from our own experience.

The Levels of Development are among the most significant aspects of the personality types. The more you appreciate the fluidity and movement within and between each of the types, the more you will have a sense of the Enneagram as a dynamic symbol, and as a reflection of human nature itself.

It is also necessary to take the Levels of Development into consideration because by doing so we can appreciate just how sophisticated and nuanced the Enneagram is as a typology. As you recall, we are able to delineate 18 subtypes from the nine basic personality types and two wings. Adding the three degrees of wing proportion—heavy, medium, and light—to those subtypes gives us 54 subtypes (18 × 3). When we add the nine Levels of Development, it is clear that the Enneagram can account for 486 "subtypes" (the nine pure types times two wings times heavy, moderate, and light wing proportions times nine Levels of Development). The differences among these 486 variations of the types are probably too subtle to describe precisely—although they exist. You will be able to sense them intuitively as you recognize the vast combinations of traits which compose them.

As you can see, the Enneagram is a unified whole. Each of its parts—the nine personality types—modifies and balances the others in highly complex ways. The view of human nature presented here is not static. Human beings are infinitely variable, and the Enneagram takes this fact into account as much as any intellectual system can.

THE INSTINCTUAL TYPES

Wings are one form of Enneagram subtype, and have been discussed here at some length. In his original presentation of the Enneagram material, Ichazo described another form of subtype, based on three primary "instincts" of human behavior: Self-Preservation Instinct, Social Instinct, and Sexual Instinct.

In our view, these three components are a valuable addition to Enneagram theory, although they are not technically subtypes. A subtype, by definition, is dependent on being part of a type. For instance, you could say that blackbirds and sparrows are both "subtypes" of birds. The quality of what distinguishes them is dependent on the qualities of "birds." However, male birds and female birds would not exactly be subtypes, because you could classify male and female things separately without taking birds into account. "Male and female" would be an additional, independent variable, and the instinctual types function this way. In other words, one could divide a room full of people into three groups, Self-Preservation types, Social types, and Sexual types, simply by knowing the definitions of these categories, and *without knowing the Enneagram types of the individuals.* On the other hand, wings are a true subtype in that it would be meaningless to talk about Five-wings or Seven-wings without talking about Sixes. Very succinctly, wings are a dependent variable; the Instinctual types are an independent variable. For this reason, when used with the nine Enneagram types, we call them the "Instinctual variants."

The Instinctual types can exist as a separate typology, but can also be combined with the Enneagram types in ways that explain some of the variations we see in real people that cannot entirely be accounted for by wings or Levels of Development. Thus, a type Five could be a Self-Preservation Five, a Social Five, or a Sexual Five. Further, it is possible to have a Social Five with a Four-wing versus a Sexual Five with a Four-wing. If one were to combine these two kinds of "subtype," the wings and the Instinctual types, it would yield six "subtypes" per type for a total of fifty-four subtypes. These distinctions can actually be made, but for most people, this is a finer analysis than is needed.

As of this writing, the Instinctual types have been discussed by several Enneagram authors, although the material has been sketchy and sometimes contradictory. Much of what has been written has been based on twenty-seven single words or phrases that Ichazo offered as brief names or descriptors for these variants in combination with the nine Enneagram types. We feel that some of these descriptors are more accurate than others, but that more research needs to be done before the overlay of Instinctual and Enneagram types will be as useful and clear as the Enneagram types are by themselves. This is not to say that the Instinctual variants do not shed new light on the types, far from it. But the study of them is in relatively early stages, and so far has not crystallized into a coherent picture. Thus far, we have not devoted a great deal of time to exploring them, but we have seen enough to convince us of their probable validity and hope to investigate them more fully in the near future.

What is clear is that the three Instinctual types are representative of natural energies or drives that are innately part of the human organism. Personality, as we have seen in the previous discussion of the nine types, is highly engaged with, and often dependent on, the libidinal, instinctive energies to give it its life, its spark. Thus, the Instinctual types tell us in which of life's domains the personality will exert itself most powerfully. However, to the degree that the personality is neurotic, that is, the further down the Levels of Development a person is functioning, *the more the personality type will interfere with the natural expression of the instinct.* Hence, the lower levels of the Instinctual variants often produce the opposite of the normal function of the Instinct: Self-Preservation types become destructive of their health and security; Social types become antisocial, alienating others; and Sexual types develop problems with the expressions of their sexuality, perhaps as promiscuity or psychologically based sexual dysfunction.

We offer here only a brief definition of the instincts, and for now, we leave it to the reader's observation to conceive of how the motivations of the Enneagram types might play themselves out in the arena of concerns described by the Instinctual variants. As with the nine Enneagram types, a single individual will have some degree of all three Instinctual type behavior, but, on closer inspection, we will perceive that one Instinctual variant will be somewhat more developed than the others. It remains to be determined whether Instinctual types can change in the course of a life.

Self-Preservation: The focus here is easy to understand from the name. People of this Instinctual type are preoccupied with basic survival needs as they translate in our contemporary society. Thus, Self-Preservation types are concerned with money, food, housing, health, physical safety, and comfort. Being safe and physically comfortable are priorities. These people are quick to notice any problems in a room such as poor lighting or uncomfortable chairs, or to be dissatisfied with the room temperature. They often have issues connected with food and drink, either overdoing it or having strict dietary requirements. In the healthy to average Levels, of the three Instinctual types, they are the most practical in the sense of taking care of basic life necessities—paying bills, maintaining the home and workplace, acquiring useful skills, and so forth. When these types deteriorate, they tend to distort the instinct to the degree that they are poor at taking care of themselves. Unhealthy Self-Preservation types eat and sleep poorly or become obsessed with health issues. They often have difficulty handling money and may act out in deliberately self-destructive ways. In a nutshell, no matter what Enneagram personality type is involved, Self-Preservation types are focused on enhancing their personal security and physical comfort.

Social: This variant is focused on their interactions with other people and with the sense of value or esteem they derive from their participation in collective activities. These include work, family, hobbies, clubs—basically any arena in which Social types can interact with others for some shared purpose. The instinct underlying this behavior was an important one in human survival. Human beings on their own are rather weak, vulnerable creatures, and easily fall prey to a frequently hostile environment. By learning to live and work together, our ancestors created the safety necessary for human beings not only to survive but to thrive. Within that social instinct, however, are many other implicit imperatives, and primary among them is the understanding of "place" within a hierarchical social structure. This is as true for dogs and gorillas as it is for human beings. Thus, the desire for attention, recognition, honor, success, fame, leadership, appreciation, and the safety of belonging can all be seen as manifestations of the Social instinct. Social types like to know what is going on around them, and want to make some kind of contribution to the human enterprise. There is often an interest in the events and activities of one's own culture, or sometimes of another culture. In general, Social types enjoy interacting with people, but they avoid intimacy. In their imbalanced, unhealthy forms, these types can become profoundly antisocial, detesting people and resenting their society, or having poorly developed social skills. In a nutshell, no matter what Enneagram personality type is involved, Social types are focused on interacting with people in ways that will build their personal value, their sense of accomplishment, and their security of "place" with others.

Sexual: Many people originally identify themselves as this type, perhaps confusing the idea of a Sexual Instinctual type with being a "sexy" person. Of course, "sexiness" is in the eye of the beholder, and there are plenty of "sexy" people in all three of the Instinctual types. Furthermore, lest one think this type more "glamorous" than the other two, one would do well to remember that the instinct can become distorted in the type, leading to the area of life causing the greatest problems. In healthy to average Sexual types, there is a desire for intensity of experience—not just sexual experience, but any activity having a similar "charge." This intensity could be found in a great conversation or an exciting movie. Much has been said about this type preferring one-on-one relationships versus the Social type's preference for larger groups, but a quick poll of one's acquaintances will reveal that almost all people prefer communicating one-on-one rather than in a group. The question is more one of the intensity of contact and the strength of the desire for intimacy. Sexual types are the "intimacy junkies" of the Instinctual types, often neglecting pressing obligations or even basic "maintenance" if they are swept up in someone or something that has captivated them. This gives a wide-ranging, exploratory approach to life, but also a lack of focus on one's own priorities. In their neurotic forms, this type can manifest with a wandering lack of focus, sexual promiscuity and acting out, or just the opposite, in a fearful, dysfunctional attitude toward sex and intimacy. Sexual types, however, will be intense, even about their avoidances. In conclusion, no matter what Enneagram personality type is involved, Sexual types are focused on having intense, intimate interactions and experiences with others and with the environment to give them a powerful sense of "aliveness."

Experience has shown that ... personalities ... may be grouped into various major categories, and for purposes of studying them this is a helpful device. Classifications must never be taken too seriously—they ruin much thinking—but the fear to use them has prevented much more thinking.

—Karl A. Menninger, *The Human Mind*

Chapter 14

The Theory of the Enneagram

The Enneagram is by no means the first personality typology. The search for an accurate typology has gone on for thousands of years, beginning with the Greek philosophers, if not earlier. Galen (A.D. 130?–200?) is credited with popularizing Hippocrates' theory of the four bodily humors: the melancholic, choleric, phlegmatic, and sanguine temperaments, depending on the predominance of one of the major fluids of the body, black bile, yellow bile, phlegm, and blood, respectively. The theory of the four temperaments was used for fifteen hundred years, until the scientific inquiries of the Enlightenment gradually discredited it. Nevertheless, this ancient system continues to play a role in our language and culture because it conveys a useful insight into human nature.

Popular intuition and an informal consensus among psychologists have always maintained that personality types exist in some form. The problem for psychologists has been to find the proper categories for each fundamental type, however many there may be, so that each is discrete, meaningful, useful, and comprehensive. Traits from one type should not overlap with traits from another, yet there are obviously similarities between types which must be accounted for. Each basic personality type must describe people in ways meaningful to them, or at least meaningful to specialists, and where possible, it should be scientifically verifiable. A useful personality typology would be one which laymen as well as professionals could use in daily life and in therapeutic situations. A comprehensive typology would account for as much of the variety in human personality as possible, from healthy, to average, to neurotic, and to psychotic states.

The Enneagram's remarkable properties suggest that this symbol presents us with discrete, meaningful, useful, and comprehensive fundamental categories. The Enneagram seems to divide personality types in the categories which we find in daily life. It is so comprehensive that it can act as a framework for other typologies, in many cases completing them. The fundamentals of the Enneagram as a system are easy to grasp and meaningful: people see themselves and their friends in it. And the Enneagram is useful because it helps deepen our self-understanding and our understanding of others.

In short, the Enneagram rings true. The more accurate a typology is, the more we are justified in feeling that the categories it employs are not artificially imposed on human nature but reflect something real in human nature itself. We feel that the categories have been discovered rather than invented.

If this is so, what explanation do we have for the Enneagram? How can we account for its accuracy? Is it really the typology psychology has been searching for? Because the answers to these questions are abstract and complex, we have waited until now to examine the theory of the Enneagram in some detail.

We will look at the theory of the Enneagram in two parts: first, to compare the Enneagram with other typologies, and second, to examine some of the abstract reasons for why the Enneagram works as it does.

THE ENNEAGRAM AND OTHER TYPOLOGIES

The Enneagram's remarkable properties will become even more evident when we compare it with the typologies of Karen Horney, Sigmund Freud, Carl Jung, and the pathological categories employed in psychiatry. Although these comparisons are necessarily brief, we hope to indicate that the Enneagram is not only consistent with modern psychological systems, but suggests ways to clarify some of the obscurities in those systems.

Karen Horney and the Enneagram

On the basis of her clinical observations, the psychoanalyst Karen Horney (1885–1952) suggested that there are three general neurotic "solutions": "moving away from people" (the *withdrawn* types), "moving against people" (the *aggressive* types), and "moving toward people" (the *compliant* types). We have maintained the basic emphasis of Horney's categories, with a few significant modifications. Basically, we have expanded these three "solutions" by looking at how each type responds not just to people, but to other elements of the total environment, both outer and inner. Thus, aggressive types may assert themselves against nature or against their own fears, and withdrawn types may withdraw from activities as well as from people. Most importantly, we have seen that compliant types are not necessarily compliant to other people, but they are compliant to the dictates of their superego, which had its genesis in other people, mainly their parents. Once these clarifications have been made, these general neurotic solutions become a helpful way of categorizing personality types in a very broad, yet accurate way.*

We have seen that the Triads are dialectically related to each other as problem areas of feeling, thinking, and instinctive functioning. Another dialectical relationship exists at the level of analysis introduced by Horney's interpersonal concepts. We can correlate her three solutions with the nine personality types of the Enneagram. If we place her three designations on the Enneagram, we see that each Triad is a mixed group of personality types. Each Triad is a "mixed Triad," with each Triad having one of Horney's three solutions represented in it. Each Triad is composed of an aggressive type (that is, it "moves against others"), a compliant type (that is, it "moves toward others"), and a withdrawn type (that is, it "moves away from others"), as illustrated below.

In each Triad, we can interpret these designations as follows:

In the Feeling Triad

TWOS are compliant to the superego's dictate to be always selfless and loving.

---

*See Karen Horney, *Our Inner Conflicts*, 14–18. Horney devotes one chapter to each solution. We also highly recommend her *Neurosis and Human Growth*, in which she develops these three styles under the headings "the expansive solution" (corresponding to the "moving against" or aggressive types); "the self-effacing solution" (corresponding to the "moving toward" or compliant types); and "resignation" (corresponding to the "moving away from" or withdrawn types).

THREES are aggressive in the pursuit of their goals and in their competition with others.

FOURS are withdrawn to protect their feelings and their fragile self-image.

In the Thinking Triad

FIVES are withdrawn, away from action, into the world of thought.

SIXES are compliant to the superego dictate to do what is expected of them.

SEVENS are aggressive about engaging the environment and satisfying their appetites.

In the Instinctive Triad

EIGHTS are aggressive in asserting themselves against others and the environment.

NINES are withdrawn so that others will not disturb their inner peacefulness.

ONES are compliant to the ideals after which they strive.

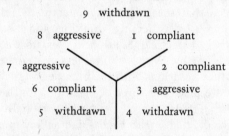

Horney's Neurotic Solutions and the Enneagram

In looking at the nine Enneagram personality types, we can see that three are *withdrawn*: Fours, Fives, and Nines. Three are *compliant*: Ones, Twos, and Sixes. And three are *aggressive*: Threes, Sevens, and Eights. Grouping the nine personality types this way reveals a *new set of symmetries*, new groups of three, which have properties in common. What is significant about this is that the Triads of Feeling, Thinking, and Instinct are not the only "triadic" relationships in the Enneagram. There are others which we will begin to discover, as illustrated on page 436.

We will see these new groups later in this chapter in different contexts. It is worth noting in passing that while Horney did not work out nine personality types herself, her clinical observations brought her to the brink of doing so. She briefly described the three subtypes in the "expansive solution" (the aggressive types which "move against" others and the environment) as the "narcissistic," the "perfectionistic," and the "arrogant-vindictive" types.*

Horney did not work out the subtypes of the "self-effacing solution" (the compliant types which "move toward" others, essentially searching for love). Nevertheless, her discussion includes elements of what we would consider to be Enneagram types Two, Six, and Nine. While we agree that the Two and Six are compliant types, the Nine is more accurately conceived of as a withdrawn rather than as a compliant type, although there are superficial elements of apparent compliance to others in the Nine, as our description of this type indicates. Again, this matter is simplified if one views the types in a context wider than that of how they deal with people. Also, Nines may not physically withdraw from others, like Fours or Fives, but may remove themselves from "contact" through dissociation, "absenting themselves" without physically withdrawing.

Horney also attempted to work out the subtypes of the "resigned solution" (the withdrawn types which "move away from" others in a search for inner freedom). She discusses what we would consider to be the personality type Nine (the "persistently resigned" subtype), the Five ("the rebellious group"), and the Four (the "shallow living" group). This last group she subdivides further into three other forms: one "with the emphasis on fun" (corresponding to Enneagram type Seven), one where the "emphasis is on prestige or opportunistic success" (which corresponds to Enneagram type Three), and a third form called "the well-adapted automaton" (which corresponds to the average to unhealthy Nine).†

It would take a much longer analysis to compare and contrast Horney's types with those of the Enneagram thoroughly. Since space does not allow this, we will only repeat our belief that Horney was independently on the way to discovering a three-times-three personality typology. Unfortunately, she was inconsistent about the

---

*See Horney, *Neurosis and Human Growth*, 193 ff. These three types correspond to the Enneagram Three, One, and Eight, respectively. We differ with Horney's listing of the "perfectionistic" type (the One) as aggressive. While the perfectionistic type has aggressive elements, its compliance to its superego forms the basis of its motivation, not the aggrandizement of its ego or its aggressive behavior as such. If we view the compliant types as compliant to the superego, then there can be little question that type One belongs in this group, being perhaps the most superego-driven type in the Enneagram.
†See ibid., 281 ff.

number of subcategories she employed, and she created separate categories for what is really the same personality type at different Levels of Development. Nevertheless, we believe that the correspondence between the Enneagram types and her "withdrawn," "compliant," and "aggressive" types is very much worth noting, since it reveals useful insights.

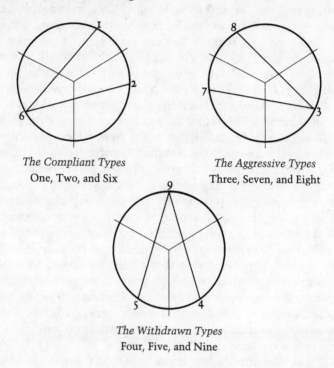

The Compliant Types
One, Two, and Six

The Aggressive Types
Three, Seven, and Eight

The Withdrawn Types
Four, Five, and Nine

Other Triadic Relationships

Freud and the Enneagram
The nine personality types of the Enneagram correlate to Freudian categories and to character types based on Freudian concepts. Naturally, a full discussion of Freud's ideas, and those of his many followers, is beyond the scope of this book. Nevertheless, two approaches to the Enneagram based on Freudian concepts are worth exploring in some detail, since Freud is so important to psychology and psychiatry.

Freud theorized that there are three areas of fixation for libido—psychic energy of a specifically sexual nature—during our childhood development, which he called the three "psychosexual" stages. He maintained that libido could be fixated around the mouth (the "oral" stage), or around the anus during toilet training (the "anal" stage), or around the genitals (the "phallic" stage). What happens at these stages has not been fully worked out, and the language used to describe each resulting "character type" varies from writer to writer. There are also some inconsistencies in the basic categories themselves. Some authorities give only two subtypes at the oral stage, while others describe three subtypes at the anal and phallic stages. Some talk of the "oral-dependent" type for those who are fixated with sucking, and the "oral-sadistic" type for those at the oral-biting stage. Thus, we are given dependent and sadistic oral types, but no anal-dependent or anal-sadistic types. Among the anal types, there are the "anal-expulsive" and the "anal-retentive" types—but no "anal-receptive" type, and so forth. It becomes very confusing.

The problem is that while Freud and others agreed upon three psychosexual stages (oral, anal, and phallic), they were inconsistent about the other variables involved. There was no consistency about whether the oral, anal, or phallic fixation points were modified by dependent, retentive, expulsive, receptive, or sadistic traits. Perhaps the Freudian categories may be clarified as follows. In Freudian terms, there are three general dispositions of psychic energy at each of the libidinal stages: receptive, retentive, and expulsive— that is, we can think of them as a dialectic of three dispositions of energy. The oral, anal, and phallic points of libidinal fixation also form a dialectic among themselves. Thus, we have two dialectical groups of three, producing nine "Freudian" character types. Had they been worked out in this manner, these neo-Freudian psychosexual dialectics would consist of the categories shown in Table 14.1.

Table 14.1.   **Neo-Freudian Psychosexual Categories**

oral		receptive
anal	X	retentive
phallic		expulsive

If we go through the permutations, the resulting nine personality types are the oral-receptive (corresponding to the Nine), the oral-retentive (corresponding to the Four), and the oral-expulsive (corresponding to the Five); the anal-receptive (corresponding to the Six), the anal-retentive (corresponding to the One), and the anal-expulsive (corresponding to the Two); the phallic-receptive (corresponding to the Three), the phallic-retentive (corresponding to the Seven), and the phallic-expulsive (corresponding to the Eight). If we arrange them in the order of the Enneagram, as below, we can see the patterns which emerge.

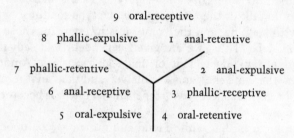

9 oral-receptive

8 phallic-expulsive   1 anal-retentive

7 phallic-retentive   2 anal-expulsive

6 anal-receptive   3 phallic-receptive

5 oral-expulsive   4 oral-retentive

Neo-Freudian Fixations and the Enneagram

It is difficult to see how these designations can be taken as more than vaguely symbolic language for psychological processes and not as literal fixations of libido around the mouth, anus, or genitals. Nevertheless, many orthodox Freudians take these designations literally, which may be why they have so much trouble applying them to real life. If, however, we take these designations as *metaphors*, they do hold clues to the traits of the personality types involved. Furthermore, if we consider the Freudian terminology metaphorically, we do not get into the problem of applying phallic terminology to women, nor do we have to find a literal meaning for a peculiar designation such as the phallic-receptive type.

To give a few examples, our so-called phallic-receptive type actually corresponds to a character type (the urethral character*) proposed by Ernest Jones, a close associate of Freud's, as well as to the Enneagram personality type Three. This type of male narcissistically invites admiration of his body (phallus) from others, and is often sexually exhibitionistic. It is clearly preferable to use the

*Otto Fenichel, *The Psychoanalytic Theory of Neurosis*, 492.

Enneagram designation, personality type Three, rather than the phallic-receptive type or even the urethral character for women or for anyone whose problems involve narcissism rather than a fixation of libido around the genitals. Is narcissism better understood as the unconscious desire to have one's genitals admired, or to have one's self admired? Even if a strictly Freudian interpretation could be shown to be the ultimate truth, such an interpretation is usually so far out of the range of normal awareness and behavior as to be all but meaningless. It seems better to work on overcoming one's inflated self-love, for example, than to reduce narcissism to the desire to have one's genitals admired.

The classic Freudian anal type (or more properly, the anal-retentive type) is characterized by frugality, obstinacy, and orderliness, which aptly describe elements of the personality type One, although they are more accurately traits of a One with a Nine-wing. However, certain elements of frugality are also found in the Six—another anal type—resulting from its caution and insecurity. The Six is also obstinate—negativistic and passive-aggressively blocking others—although, in a different way, so is the Nine—stubbornly refusing to deal with reality. Thus, there are a number of personality types in which the classic anal traits can be distinguished.

To give one last example, the oral-receptive type corresponds to the Nine, the type which optimistically believes that the environment will provide its needs like milk flowing from its mother's breast without much effort on its part. Freudians call this the oral-dependent type, although Nines can be so self-effacing and accommodating to others that, more than "depend" on others, they virtually live through them—so "receptive" is a more accurate designation.

These and other subtle but useful distinctions can be helpful to clarify the Freudian categories so commonly used in psychology and psychiatry. Other useful meanings can be worked out if you think of the Freudian psychosexual designations as a symbolic shorthand for the overall style of the personality types rather than as categories which result from libidinal fixation points occurring during early childhood. If you review our descriptions of the personality types with this in mind, you will see how our reworking of the Freudian psychosexual designations applies to the other types of the Enneagram.

You will also note that the new triadic relationships we pointed out among Horney's types correlate to our neo-Freudian libidinal types. The three oral types (the Enneagram Four, Five, and Nine) in our neo-Freudian system are the withdrawn types according to our modification of Horney's typology. The anal types (the Enneagram One, Two, and Six) in our neo-Freudian system are the compliant types in Horney's typology, and the phallic types (the Enneagram Three, Seven, and Eight) in Freud's system are the aggressive types in Horney's typology.

Freudian Structural Concepts

Freudian "structural" terminology can also be applied to the Enneagram types depending on whether the ego, id, or superego in each of the nine basic personality types is the focus of its problem area. We have added Horney's terms to the Freudian structural terms in the illustration below.

Notice that the types whose principal imbalance is in their egos also corresponds to Horney's aggressive types, that the types whose imbalances are in their ids are the withdrawn types, and that the types whose imbalances are in their superegos are the compliant types. These interrelationships can be further interpreted as follows.

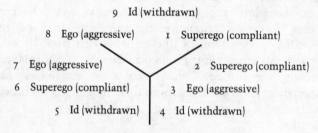

9 Id (withdrawn)

8 Ego (aggressive)   1 Superego (compliant)

7 Ego (aggressive)   2 Superego (compliant)

6 Superego (compliant)   3 Ego (aggressive)

5 Id (withdrawn)   4 Id (withdrawn)

Structural Concepts and the Enneagram

Fours, Fives, and Nines are all *withdrawn* from the direct expression of their id impulses and especially their ability to assert themselves in the environment, compensating in characteristic ways: Fours by dissociating from reality through their imaginations, Fives by dissociating from reality through their all-engrossing thought processes, and Nines by dissociating from reality through an intense idealization or identification with the other. Moreover, all three of these types have ego boundaries which are extremely permeable and open to direct influence from subconscious id-related material.

Ones, Twos, and Sixes are all *compliant* to an internalization of someone or something in their superegos which exerts a dominant influence in their behavior. Ones are compliant to their idealistic obligations which are impressed on them by their superegos (the inner judge). Twos are compliant to the demand of their superegos that they always be loving (the inner martyr); and Sixes are compliant to various authority figures they have internalized through their superegos (the inner committee).

Threes, Sevens, and Eights are all *aggressive*, that is, they respond to challenges and threats by expanding and asserting their egos in the environment. Threes are aggressive (competitive) and assert their self-image while comparing it with that of others. Sevens are aggressive (acquisitive) toward their environment, from which they try to obtain more satisfaction for themselves; and Eights are aggressive (self-assertive) toward their environment, constantly trying to project themselves in the environment so that it will become a reflection of their egos.

The Freudian structural concepts of ego, id, and superego will appear again in the next section of this chapter when we analyze why the Enneagram works.

Jung and the Enneagram

The nine personality types of the Enneagram can also be correlated to the eight "psychological types" of the Jungian typology. In the descriptions of each personality type, we correlated a Jungian type to the Enneagram type and gave a relevant quotation from Jung.

To review Jung's system for a moment, Jung posited that there are two general psychological *attitudes* (extroversion and introversion) and four psychological *functions* (thinking, feeling, intuition, and sensation). This two-times-four scheme produces eight psychological types—the extroverted thinking type, the introverted thinking type, the extroverted feeling type, the introverted feeling type, and so forth.

As you can see, the problem with correlating the eight Jungian types to the nine types of the Enneagram is that the Enneagram has one more personality type than the Jungian typology, so a one-to-one equivalence might not exist between the two systems. However,

Table 14.2   **The Jungian Correlations**

The One corresponds to the extroverted thinking type.

The Two corresponds to the extroverted feeling type.

The Three does not correspond to any Jungian type.

The Four corresponds to the introverted intuitive type.

The Five corresponds to the introverted thinking type.

The Six corresponds to the introverted feeling type.

The Seven corresponds to the extroverted sensation type.

The Eight corresponds to the extroverted intuitive type.

The Nine corresponds to the introverted sensation type.

---

a careful reading of Jung's descriptions indicates that these two systems broadly correspond, some elements very closely, some only in part, as Table 14.2 shows.

If you consult Jung's *Psychological Types*, you will see how his eight types correspond to the descriptions of the Enneagram types, except for the Three. A close reading of Jung will reveal, however, that sections of the descriptions of several of his types do in fact correspond to the Enneagram type Three. While Jung did not have a separate category for the Three, he must have been aware of this personality type from his clinical and personal experience. In a sense then, Jung inadvertently described some elements of the Three without considering this type as a separate psychological entity, something which would have thrown off the symmetry of his two-times-four theoretical framework.

It is also interesting to note the fact that the Three (whose personality is so malleable and changeable) does not correspond to one of the Jungian types. As the most adaptable of the personality types, the Three is treated in several of the Jungian types without having a category of its own.

Besides its not being comprehensive enough, there are several other problems with Jung's descriptions which we can only mention briefly here. Unfortunately, not all of Jung's descriptions seem equally worked out, and it is not always easy to understand what he is trying to describe. It is something of a paradoxical truism to say that once you understand what Jung means, you know what he means. You have to get "inside" each of his descriptions to know what he is talking about. Here again the Enneagram can help.

From the point of view of the Enneagram, we can see that Jung usually describes some of the traits of the average person of each psychological type, freely ranging around what we would consider to be the Levels of Development. He intuitively shifts to the Direction of Disintegration at the end of each of his descriptions when he mentions neurotic and psychotic developments. Occasionally, however, he confuses traits of one type with those of another—as when, for example, he describes elements of Enneagram type Nine as if they belonged to the introverted feeling type (Enneagram type Six). There are also confusions between other types, for example, between elements of the extroverted and introverted thinking types (Enneagram types One and Five, respectively). There are other confusions as well.

These are fine points, but they are significant. While people have sensed that Jung's descriptions are pointing to something true, they have also found it difficult to translate his descriptions into fuller accounts of each type, which is not surprising, because Jung was unclear about several of them himself.

Psychiatric Designations and the Enneagram

The Enneagram personality types also correlate with the "personality disorders" of the fourth edition of the *Diagnostic and Statistical Manual of Mental Disorders*, informally referred to as DSM-IV. This highly technical book is considered the primary reference work for psychiatrists and others in the mental health field, bringing together the current state of the art about personality syndromes from the clinical point of view. As you would expect, the terminology adopted in the DSM-IV is pathologically oriented and, as you might *not* expect, it sometimes seems rather arbitrary. There has been a lot of disagreement within the psychiatric community about the DSM-IV categories for the personality disorders, although there is little agreement about how they can be revised. Perhaps the Enneagram can throw light on the psychiatric personality disorders by sorting out the basic personality types, which, after all, are what become disordered when people become neurotic.

One of the main problems with the DSM-IV is that its compilers erroneously, albeit understandably, combined traits from one personality type with another, with the result that the brief schematic descriptions they offer are sometimes confusing. For example, the DSM-IV designates a "histrionic" type in order to get away from the older designation of the "hysterical" type. However, the description the DSM-IV offers of the histrionic personality disorder combines elements of Enneagram personality types Two and Seven, both of which are clearly histrionic, although in different ways and for different reasons. The Two may best be thought of as histrionic in the ordinary sense of the word, because it displays its emotions theatrically. If neurotic, the Two deteriorates into hysterical conversion reactions in which anxiety is translated directly into physical symptoms and illnesses. On the other hand, the Seven is histrionic in the sense that it is flamboyant and impulsive, acting out its emotions rather than processing them. The Seven also becomes hysterical, but as the result of panic reactions to anxiety attacks. Thus, while there are genuine similarities between these two types, a review of the descriptions of them in this book indicates that they are two distinct personality types. Their traits should not be lumped together into the single histrionic type of the DSM-IV.

Table 14.3   **The DSM-IV Correlations**

Type One corresponds to the compulsive and depressive personality disorders.

Type Two partly corresponds to aspects of the histrionic personality disorder.

Type Three corresponds to narcissistic personality disorder.

Type Four corresponds to the aspects of the avoidant, depressive, and narcissistic personality disorders.

Type Five corresponds to aspects of the schizoid, avoidant, and schizotypal personality disorders.

Type Six corresponds to aspects of the paranoid, dependent, and passive-aggressive* personality disorders.

Type Seven corresponds to aspects of the histrionic and the manic-depressive personality disorders.

Type Eight corresponds to the antisocial personality disorder.

Type Nine corresponds to aspects of the dependent, schizotypal, and passive-aggressive personality disorders.

(The Borderline Personality Disorder corresponds to aspects of many of the types and seems to be less type specific.)

---

*Former DSM-III category.

Space limitations prevent us from going into a full comparison between the official DSM-IV psychiatric types and the Enneagram personality types. For the sake of completeness, however, and to indicate from yet another viewpoint how the Enneagram personality types are not only reinforced by modern psychiatry, but how the Enneagram can help psychiatry, we have simply listed the general correspondences between the "personality disorders" in the DSM-IV and the personality types of the Enneagram. The correspondences in Table 14.3 should be taken only as the roughest of approximations, since a great many distinctions would have to be made to sort out the correspondence in any clear-cut way.

ANALYZING THE ENNEAGRAM

What, then, is the theoretical basis for the Enneagram as a psychological system? Why, for example, are there nine basic personality types and not eight, ten, twelve, or some other number? What is the basis for each of the individual personality types? Is the Enneagram an ancient typology which is a precursor to essentially Freudian ideas? Or is it really a Jungian typology or one which foreshadows the ideas of Karen Horney or some other psychologist? A complete discussion of these questions is so complex and abstract that we can examine only some preliminary answers at this time.

Let us give you our conclusion first. Even though we will give several explanations of the Enneagram, it seems that, in the final analysis, there is no single theoretical explanation why the Enneagram works as it does. No one underlying theory is the sole basis for the Enneagram. It cannot be reduced solely to Freudian, Jungian, or Hornevian concepts. If you approach the Enneagram from a Freudian point of view, you will find that it can accommodate Freudian ideas. If you look at the Enneagram from a Jungian or a Hornevian viewpoint, you will find that it can be used to represent those ideas as well. This in itself suggests that the Enneagram is a universal psychological symbol, one which can accommodate many different interpretations while retaining its unique character.

True, not everything in other psychological systems can be placed on the Enneagram, and some aspects of modern psychological systems contradict each other and cannot be reconciled. Nevertheless, the Enneagram is able to organize many common discoveries because it operates at a number of levels of abstraction while allowing a great deal of specificity. We can approach the Enneagram on many different levels, and each approach we make to it yields some new insight.

Human beings can be analyzed from a broad spectrum of viewpoints, each revealing and illuminating one facet of the whole. Human beings can be interpreted biologically, psychologically, sociologically, historically, as physical objects by physicists, and as spiritual beings by theologians. But just as there is no one all-encompassing explanation for human nature, there is no one all-encompassing explanation for the Enneagram. We cannot say that the Enneagram is a Freudian system, since it accounts for more than Freudian ideas. Nor is it a Jungian or a Hornevian system or a system belonging to any other school of thought. It is itself: a comprehensive, dynamic symbol of the human psyche based on a number of philosophical and psychological antecedents that have come together in a powerful new synthesis.

Since we cannot reduce the Enneagram to any single psychological explanation, we will look at several different approaches by which we can understand it better. We will interpret the Enneagram from a dialectical approach, a developmental approach, and a Freudian dynamic approach.

A Dialectical Approach

The reason there are nine personality types in the Enneagram is that its structure is the result of a three-times-three arrangement, or two dialectically related groups of three. No matter which level of analysis we may wish to take toward the Enneagram, we find that the dialectically related factors produce nine distinct personality categories.

If there is a single explanation of why the Enneagram works as it does, and why it is such a comprehensive system, it is because the Enneagram is a dialectical system, and as such it can be used to analyze different aspects of human nature dialectically.

On this, the most basic level of analysis—one which has been seen in the Guidelines and throughout the descriptions—the Enneagram can be thought of as an arrangement of three Triads containing three different personality types. Each Triad is a dialectic of the problem of that Triad. In each Triad, one type has overdeveloped the characteristic faculty of the Triad, another has underdeveloped the faculty, and a third is most out of touch with the faculty.

When we apply this pattern to the types in the Feeling Triad, we see that Twos overexpress their feelings, emphasizing only their positive emotions while repressing their negative ones. Threes are most out of touch with their feelings, projecting an image to others as a substitute. And Fours underexpress their feelings, revealing themselves through some form of art or aesthetic living.

In the Thinking Triad, Fives overexpress their capacity for thought, imagination, and conceptualization. They substitute thinking for doing. Sixes are the most out of touch with their ability to think for themselves, not trusting their own ability to know and decide things without the reassurance of an authoritative framework of thought, or at least a "second opinion." Sevens underexpress their ability to think, by not completing or following through with an idea before being captivated by another one. Also, the thinking of Sevens is stimulated by, and to some degree dependent on, what they want to do.

In the Instinctive Triad, Eights overexpress their instinctive drives, asserting themselves and their needs against the environment. Their instincts are unrestrained, and lead quickly to action. Nines are the most out of touch with their instinctive drives, fearing that the intensity of them would destroy the inner calm and equilibrium they are trying to maintain. Ones underexpress their instinctive drives, sublimating them instead to an ideal which they constantly strive to attain.

When we consider dialectic patterns (thesis, antithesis, and synthesis), we are always considering interrelated groups of three. In the comparison of the Enneagram types with the typologies of Horney and Freud, we saw several different dialectical groups: Horney's withdrawn, compliant, and aggressive types; Freud's ego, id, and superego; and his oral, anal, and phallic types. It seems that the dialectic patterns reflect something in the patterns of the mind itself. If there is a single reason why the Enneagram works, this is it.

A Developmental Approach
We can understand why there are nine basic personality types in the Enneagram if we consider them from yet another point of view, that of a child's earliest orientation with its parents.

From a developmental point of view, the Enneagram is a universal typology that applies to all people at all times and in all cultures, because it delineates the nine possible relationships which everyone can have with his or her parents. Everyone, without exception, has two parents, whether those parents are living or dead, present or absent, good or bad. There are nine basic personality types because there are only nine fundamental orientations which every child can take to his or her parents. Because of the sum total of childhood experiences, including genetic predispositions and environmental factors, everyone eventually adopts one of the following nine general orientations and therefore develops into one of the nine basic personality types.

Everyone's basic personality type is the result of having had a primary orientation to his or her nurturing-figure (usually the mother or a mother-substitute), or a primary orientation to his or her protective-figure (usually the father or a father-substitute), or a primary orientation equally to his or her nurturing-figure *and* protective-figure (mother and father). (Note that this set of three orientations forms a dialectic.) Second, the primary orientation may have been essentially *connected, disconnected,* or *ambivalent.* (Note that this set of three attitudes is yet another dialectic.) Nine discrete personality types are generated, depending on which parent the child relates to and the quality of that orientation.

Taking this developmental approach, we have another three-times-three pattern which results in nine basic personality types. For example, given the different necessary temperamental predispositions, one child may have been connected to her nurturing-figure, while another child may have had an ambivalent relationship to her nurturing-figure, and a third child may have been disconnected from her nurturing-figure (who, of course, may be the same person in all

Table 14.4   **Parental Orientations**

	Parental Orientation		
Parent	Connected	Ambivalent	Disconnected
Nurturing-Figure	3	8	7
Protective-Figure	6	2	1
Both	9	5	4

three instances). The first child would develop into a personality type Three, the second child into an Eight, and the third into a Seven. These relationships can be seen more clearly in Table 14.4.

As it turns out, this grouping of the personality types is extremely revealing. Reading the table horizontally, you will notice similarities with Horney's system which we have already seen. The Three-Eight-Seven group (the nurturing-figure-oriented types) are the personality types which defend themselves aggressively (Horney's "moving against" types). From developmental psychology, we know that the early bonding and mirroring experiences between the mother and child result in the development of the self-image, thus these are the ego-oriented types. They are then motivated to assert their egos into the environment and to find direct ways of gratifying their ego needs. Threes want attention, so they actively pursue those situations which will get them recognition. Sevens want to be satisfied and stimulated, so they do things that they find satisfying and stimulating. Eights want to be in control of their environment, so they obtain the means they need to be in control of their world.

The Six-Two-One group (the protective-figure-oriented types) are the personality types which defend themselves by being compliant (Horney's "moving toward" types). In general, these are the should-and-must personality types. While compliance dominates the overall picture, they are in fact a mixture of aggressive and compliant tendencies. Under pressure either from others or from anxiety, the should-and-must types tend to explode in destructive behavior. The influence of the protective-figure or patriarch and of internalized superego prohibitions symbolized by this person create the highly superego-driven types One, Two, and Six. All three types feel obligated to engage in certain behavior, often at the expense of other things they would like to do, and often take the role of authority figures themselves in different ways, since they have internalized many of the prevailing mores of society.

Last, the Nine-Five-Four group (the types oriented to both figures) are the personality types which defend themselves by withdrawing (Horney's "moving away" types). They are the loners, intellectuals, and dreamers of society. Because their childhoods produced an orientation to both parents, they have problems interacting with others, since they tend to be overwhelmed by forces either inside or outside themselves. All three types tend to dissociate themselves from reality in different ways, constructing elaborate "inner realities" which they use as a defense against their actual environment. In Freudian terms, they have problems expressing and sustaining their own immediate id impulses, especially those involving self-assertion and aggression.

It cannot be surprising that a child's orientation to his or her parents is one of the major determinants of personality and that personality types ultimately influence cultural changes, which in turn influence how parents raise their children, thus perpetuating the cycle. The person, the family, and the culture are interdependent: there cannot be one without the others. Freudian schools and interpersonal schools may not be so far apart regarding the interrelationship between the individual and society: they simply operate at different levels of analysis.

A Dynamic Freudian Approach

Freud represented the dynamics of the mind as the interaction of the id, the ego, and the superego. This has been called his "structural hypothesis," which was illustrated on page 440. These character types were never fully described either by Freud or his followers, perhaps for the following reason.

> It would be advantageous if psychoanalytic characterology were to give us a dynamic classification. However, none of the attempts made hitherto seems to have been successful. Choosing one aspect as the criterion of the division necessarily neglects other aspects.
>
> The most important of these attempts were instituted by Freud himself. After having subdivided the mind into the categories of id, ego, and superego, he asked whether it would not be possible to distinguish types of human characters according to which of these three authorities is dominant. There may be "erotic" types whose lives are governed by the instinctual demands of their id; "narcissistic" types who feel so dominated by their sense of ego that neither other persons nor demands from the id or the superego can touch them much; and there may be "compulsive" types whose entire lives are regulated by a strict superego that dominates the personality. Freud also described "mixed" types in which a combination of two forces outweigh the third one. . . .
>
> Besides the question whether Freud's descriptions of an "erotic"

and a "narcissistic" type correspond to persons whose id or ego is accentuated, there is a more important objection to his suggested typology: Psychoanalysis is essentially a *dynamic* discipline. It evaluates given phenomena as a result of conflicts. . . . A categorization of "id persons," "ego persons," and "superego persons" is not a dynamic concept. What would be characteristic for dynamic types would not be either id or ego or superego but the various interrelationships of id, ego, and superego. That is why Freud's typology has not been used much for the comprehension of neurotic character disorder. (Otto Fenichel, *The Psychoanalytic Theory of Neurosis,* 525–526.)

But this is precisely why the Enneagram is able to represent the full range of character, or personality, types. The Enneagram types represent a dynamic interrelationship of the id, ego, and superego. In each of the resulting nine types, all three of the Freudian functions of the mind interact with each other. It is not necessary to choose "one aspect as the criterion of the division," as Fenichel points out, to the neglect of other aspects. All three aspects of the mind are simultaneously taken into account in each personality type and in the Enneagram as a whole.

Each Triad is dominated by one of the three Freudian categories of the mind, which is why the Triads are characterized as having problems with feeling (ego-dominated types), thinking (superego-dominated types), or instinct (id-dominated types). In other words, there is a core problem in each Triad: the types of the Feeling Triad have common problems stemming from their egos, the types of the Thinking Triad have common problems stemming from their superegos, and the types of the Instinctive Triad have common problems stemming from their ids. The Freudian designations are shown at the center of the illustration below, within their respective Triads.

In addition to a core problem in each Triad, we discover that each personality type is dominated by one of the Freudian functions of the mind which is in conflict with the core problem of the Triad. For example, the personality type Two is dominated by its superego. If you will recall, the Two's self-esteem was conditional to feeling that it was loved by others for its good works and good intentions. The Two feels guilty when it is unloving, selfish, or aggressive, and so forth. While its superego dominates its mental life, its ego (its need for validation, self-esteem, and consistent self-image) is also an important part of the picture.

So, to interpret the Freudian dynamics, we would say that the Two's superego and ego are in some sort of potential conflict with each other. The Two needs to bring its id into balance with its superego and ego by going to Four (where "id" is on the circumference of the illustration). On the other hand, if the Two becomes more neurotic and moves to its Direction of Disintegration, it goes to Eight, adding more ego expansion to its already inflated and distorted self-image, with the result that it becomes further out of touch with potentially dangerous aggressive impulses from the id.

Putting these relationships on the Enneagram illustrates them more clearly.

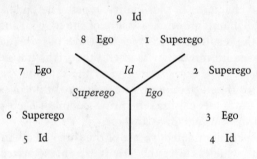

The Freudian Dynamics of the Enneagram

Several other brief examples might help to clarify the usefulness of this interpretation. The Five's id is in conflict with its superego and needs to go to Eight to bring its psyche into balance with the aid of a healthy, confident ego structure. But of course, if the Five goes to Seven, it also comes in contact with the ego—so there appears to be a problem with ego in both of the Directions of Integration and Disintegration for the Five. This is accurate because the ego is precisely what the Five needs to develop in some positive way. Of all types, Fives have the least developed interpersonal skills, and have difficulty balancing their superego and id forces because their ego structure is too weak. When a healthy Five integrates to Eight, its ego is developed and comes into balance with its conflicting id and superego, so that Fives are able to disengage from their constant inner monologues, connect more confidently with others, and move forward with productive activity. But when the Five deteriorates and goes to Seven, it becomes increasingly aggressive and impulsive until it virtually flies to pieces. This analysis points out that the ego and id are what the Five most needs to balance in either direction on the Enneagram.

Last, you can see that the particular problem in each Triad is reinforced for the Three, Six, and Nine. These primary types have the most problem with feeling, thinking, or instinctive functioning, and therefore with the ego, superego, or id, respectively. For example, the Three can be characterized as having some sort of special problem with its ego, the Six with its superego, and the Nine with its id.

The Three's ego and self-image problems result in its being most out of touch with its feelings. Because Threes are not well-connected with their authentic affect, they must get their "cues" from others, leading to a preoccupation with image. The Six's superego problems result from internalizing the superego dictates of various authority figures, resulting in confused thinking, indecisiveness, and a reliance on external guidance to settle their doubts. The Nine's problems result from its being most out of touch with its id drives, its ability to assert itself, and its needs in the environment, eventually becoming passive, resigned, and ineffectual.

Let us look at the Three more closely. As you know, the Three is the personality type in the Feeling Triad which is most out of touch with its feelings. The Three needs to go first to Six (superego) and then to Nine (id) to bring its psyche into balance. The Three's ego tends to be overdeveloped (narcissistic and exhibitionistic), so a move to Nine would be too threatening because of the emotional material Threes are suppressing in order to function. Clearly, the Three needs to balance its superego (removing some of the prohibitions against feeling and corresponding drives for recognition) first, before it can bring its ego into balance with the rest of its psyche.

This interpretation of the Enneagram accounts for several things: why each type is different, why the Directions of Integration and Disintegration are as they are, and why the Enneagram as a whole is a symbol of each of us. The Enneagram is a universal symbol because our fundamental problems can be thought of as id-related problems, ego-related problems, and superego-related problems. All human beings are affected by all three problem areas, whether we call them by their Freudian names or by the Enneagram names of feeling, thinking, and instinct.

There is much more to say about all of this—more about the descriptions and more about the theory. Several significant areas of Enneagram theory and practice—the centers, spirituality, therapeutic and business applications, relationships, and so forth— will be explored in future works. Nevertheless, even with this brief exposition, you can see that we can approach the Enneagram types from a number of different avenues.

The reason the Enneagram encompasses so many different psychological viewpoints is that it operates at various levels of abstraction simultaneously—psychosexual stages of fixation, structural areas within the psyche, object relations theory, developmental origins, interpersonal styles, and so forth. There seems to be no one theoretical explanation for why the Enneagram works as it does. It comprehends them all.

The Enneagram is an extraordinary framework for understanding more about ourselves. No matter from which point of view we approach it, we discover fresh conjunctions of new and old ideas. As we mentioned at the beginning of this chapter, this is highly suggestive that the Enneagram is a universal psychological symbol, something discovered rather than invented. What Mendelev's periodic table is to chemistry, the Enneagram may be to psychology—a way of organizing vast complexities in more understandable ways.

Just as the interrelationships between the families of atoms are too complex to have been designed by anyone, the Enneagram is too complex to have been designed by the human mind. Its immense intricacies and suggestiveness—and its paradoxical simplicity—could not have been engineered from a checklist of elements needed for a typology. Rather, the Enneagram seems to be a symbol which reflects the symmetries and irregularities of the mind itself.

Chapter 15

Postscript:
Moving Toward Wisdom

To face the world and the terrifying insecurity of human existence naked and defenseless seems like an overwhelming situation for anyone to be in. Each person's ego attempts to buffer itself from the full realization of the insecurity of its existence in different ways. Each type adopts different strategies for inflating the ego as a defense against being insecure and alone.

The paradox is that our ego cannot exist without defending itself from the full awareness of existence. Our personality is threatened by the mystery of our existence, whether we affirm it in hope or recoil from it in despair. And yet, as we have seen in the descriptions, if each of the personality types pushes its defenses to an extreme, it brings destruction on itself. Indeed, the life of the personality seems tenuous at best and always seems to be in danger of being destroyed by something. Too much openness to life and it runs the risk of being overwhelmed; too little, and it destroys itself from within. Too much freedom is as threatening to it as no freedom at all. When all is said and done, existential anxiety may be the proper response for beings who are aware of their own mortality. Like Moses before the burning bush, we quake with terror in the realization that we ultimately stand before the vastness of being.

There seems to be only one way out of the conundrum: to hope to find a meaning for our lives, a meaning that connects with something real beyond the concerns of our personality.

However, we are in the insoluble position of trying to find a meaning for our lives without being able to understand our lives as a whole. There is no way to know with certainty what that meaning is without being able to step outside of our lives to find their ultimate context. Being able to step outside of our existence may happen at the moment of death, when this life has come to an end. If we still exist in some form beyond that moment, we will know whether our life has had meaning—and what that meaning is. So much of the mystery and tragedy of existence comes about because we cannot know with certainty what our life means before that decisive moment.

Although the ultimate meaning of life is mysterious, it affects every moment that we live. What we believe about the meaning of life influences what we value and every choice we make. In considering these realities, we move from the psychological to the metaphysical, where the human context ultimately will or will not have meaning. It may be that human existence is absurd and meaningless because there is only the endless recycling of matter and energy in an indifferent universe. Or it may be that the ultimate context of human life is personal and that there is a God whose existence is the reason for our own. Or it may be that there is a divine intelligence that is not personal in any form that we could recognize. For most of us, the ultimate nature of the universe is beyond our personality's ability to know. This is why the meaning of life always involves "faith," whether we call it that or not.

In the absence of a direct experience of our own nature and of divinity, we must rely on beliefs. Mystics of various spiritual traditions insist that such direct knowledge is possible but that it requires that we transcend our personalities. If we do not have direct experiences of our true nature which form the foundation of faith, then we must have "faith" in something else. Because we cannot live without meaning, without reference to something outside ourselves, we inevitably create idols as substitutes for faith in the transcendent and the meaning which it supplies.

Of course, the supreme and universal idol is pride, the ego inflating itself, attempting to be the cause of its own being, attempting to find its own meaning within its own resources. Pride sees no reason to look beyond itself for help or guidance. It is satisfied with itself. Each of the personality types is tempted toward a particular form of pride as a way of defending itself from the anxieties involved with its existence. The Nine's temptation is to believe that its tranquillity is an ultimate value, the Eight's is to believe in its own strength and will, the Seven's is to believe that it will find fulfillment in exciting experiences, the Six's is to believe that it can create ultimate security for itself, the Five's is to believe in knowledge as a source of power, the Four's is to believe that all of its feelings and subjective states are significant, the Three's is to believe in its own excellence, the Two's is to believe in its own indispensability, and the One's temptation is to believe in its own righteousness. While these temptations are characteristic of each of the personality types, they are all our own temptations, too.

If there is a theme in this book, or a lesson to be learned by studying the personality types, it is that while we legitimately look for happiness by seeking our personal fulfillment, we often seek it wrongly. Every personality type creates a self-fulfilling prophecy, bringing about the very thing it most fears while losing what it most desires as it looks for happiness. If, when we search for happiness, we inflate our ego at the expense of recognizing and properly valuing our Essential Self, we may be sure of failing in our search. The pursuit of identity, security, and happiness without reference to our essential spiritual nature leads us into a maze of apparent goods and seductive idols. It is not so much that we do not see who we are as much as that we see only a small part of who we are. We are blinded to the fullness and magnificence of our ultimate nature by the trance of our personality. Our true nature exists only now, in this very moment. It includes all of the concerns and motivations of our personality while also transcending all of them.

Each personality type contains within itself a source of self-deception which, if played into, invariably leads us away from the direction of our real fulfillment and deepest happiness. This is an irrevocable law of the psyche, something of which we must become convinced if we are to have the courage to look for happiness where it truly resides. This requires courage, because to fully reside in that place, we must be willing to experience our deepest fears, the full extent of the falseness of our personality, and the multidimensional mystery of the human heart.

Looking at each of the personality types as a whole teaches us that the agendas of our egos are ultimately self-defeating. Each type's fears do not go away by attempting to resolve them through the mechanisms of the personality. By depending on our personality instead of realizing that our essential nature already contains all that we seek, we fail to achieve our heart's desire. Thus, Twos spend their whole lives searching for love from others and still feel that they are unloved. Threes endlessly pursue achievement and recognition but still feel worthless and empty. Fours spend their entire lives trying to discover the meaning of their personal identity and still do not know who they are. Fives endlessly accumulate knowledge and skills to build up their confidence but still feel helpless and incapable. Sixes toil endlessly to create security for themselves and still feel anxious and fearful about the world. Sevens look high and low for happiness but still feel unhappy and frustrated. Eights do everything in their power to protect themselves and their interests but still feel vulnerable and threatened. Nines sacrifice a great deal to achieve inner peace and stability but still feel ungrounded and insecure. And finally, Ones strive to maintain personal integrity but still feel divided and at war with themselves. The way out of these self-defeating patterns is to see that they cannot bring us the happiness that we seek because our personality does not have the power to create happiness. As wisdom has always recognized, it is only by dying to ourselves — that is, to our ego and its strategies — that we find life.

Thus, a related lesson can be drawn from these pages, one which we call the law of psychic economics. It is in the nature of the psyche that we inevitably pay a price for every choice we make. In each moment a certain amount of mental, emotional, and physical energy is available. When we spend that energy in an activity, it cannot be spent on something else. In addition, different choices that we make can produce widely different results. An hour spent meditating produces a very different result from an hour spent drinking beer and watching television. This is not to say that one is necessarily better than the other, but that they lead to vastly different results — which may affect the whole of our lives. Moreover, the price we pay may well not be immediately apparent, which is why we so easily fool ourselves into thinking that there will be no consequences for our actions. But the cost to ourselves is always paid in the kind of person we become. By our choices we create ourselves and shape our future, whether that future is ultimately one of happiness or unhappiness.

How, then, can we go about transcending the ego? What would motivate us to do so? How can we know what will really make us happy?

People always seek what they think will be good for them, even if they turn out to have been mistaken in their choice. Some seek wealth, others fame, others security, as each desires to possess that which he or she thinks will bring happiness. But unless we find what is truly good by learning to orient ourselves to our essential nature, we will be sidetracked into the pursuit of empty substitutes. If we fall into the trance of our personality, we turn the objects of our desires into idols which cannot satisfy us. Then we suffer and wonder why.

The strange thing is that, as with our quest for the meaning of life, we are in the difficult position of searching for what is truly good for us without having a clear understanding of what that might be. Each of the personality types seeks what it thinks will be good for it in the wrong places, or in the wrong ways, or both. Twos think that they will be happy if they are loved sufficiently by others, Threes if they are admired by others and outstanding enough, Fours if they are totally free to be themselves, Fives if they can have all the knowledge and skills they want, Sixes if they have enough security, Sevens if they can experience all they want, Eights if they can completely protect themselves, Nines if they can have total peace of mind, and Ones if they can only be perfect enough. We can see that these desires will never be fully satisfied. External conditions will never fulfill them in the way that each type wants. Without realizing it, each type is postponing happiness (and the realization of its true nature) until its demands are met. Thus, each type is doomed to frustration by searching for happiness where it cannot be found. All of these strategies fail because they are only partial goods which have been raised to the status of the prime good in life.

How, then, can the Enneagram help us know what is really good for us? The answer is simple: what each personality type genuinely needs lies in its Direction of Integration.

The difficulty is that in order to move in the Direction of Integration, we must be willing to transcend the habits of our personality. We must be willing and able to go beyond ego, to reach out to something more, to experience the parts of ourselves that have nothing to do with the agendas of our personalities. At the same time, we must also be willing to fully experience the limitation and pain that our ego's habits are causing us.

Self-transcendence is difficult and frightening because it entails going into unknown territory, feeling, thinking, and acting in ways foreign to our personality, contrary to our past habits, at odds with our old attitudes and identity, and free of the old wounds and defenses of our childhood. In a sense, self-transcendence is a rebirth, a true transformation, the coming into being of a new person who is learning to leave the old ways behind and strike out into a new world.

Yet this is precisely what each personality type must do if it is ever to find real happiness. Twos need to overcome their tendency to deceive themselves about their needs, feelings, and motives by moving toward the self-understanding and emotional honesty of the healthy Four. Threes need to overcome their desire to surpass others and draw attention to themselves by moving toward the commitment and humility of the healthy Six. Fours need to overcome their moodiness and self-indulgence by moving toward the integrity and self-discipline of the healthy One. Fives need to overcome their detachment and cynicism by moving toward the practicality and courage of the healthy Eight. Sixes need to overcome their pessimism and suspicion of others by moving toward the hopefulness and receptivity of the healthy Nine. Sevens need to overcome their superficiality and impulsiveness by moving toward the depth and focus of the healthy Five. Eights need to overcome their emotional armoring and egocentricity by moving toward the compassion and concern for others of the healthy Two. Nines need to overcome their complacency and self-forgetting by moving toward the energy and self-investment of the healthy Three. And Ones need to overcome their criticalness and rigidity by moving toward the joy and enthusiasm of the healthy Seven.

In the last analysis, learning how to transcend the ego involves nothing less than learning how to be open to love. Only love has the power to save us from ourselves. Until we learn to truly love ourselves and others — and to accept the love of others — there can be no hope of lasting happiness or peace or redemption. It is because we do not know how to love ourselves properly that we lose ourselves so easily in the many illusions ego sets before us.

This is what much of present-day psychology must take into account if it is to become less sterile. After all, Freud's own goal of therapy was to help a person "to work and to love." Modern psychology seems to have lost sight of how to accomplish this because it has abjured the transcendent, ignored the heart's deepest yearnings, and has not recognized the existence of Being, the very ground of our humanity. Unless acquiring the ability to work (and hence to re-create the world) and to love (and hence to re-create the self) becomes one of the main goals of psychology, then it will ultimately be a vain and empty enterprise. Therapeutic techniques can do little lasting good unless they help us toward a recognition of where human fulfillment really lies. About that, the testimony of the greatest human beings who have ever lived bears witness that fulfillment lies in reconnecting with the ground of our being and by living in a way that gives testimony to our spiritual nature.

This is as easy to say as it is difficult to practice. It seems to be part of the human condition for us to learn the most valuable lessons in life the hard way. However, only by suffering from our mistakes does knowledge become our own. Who would believe that happiness lies in the direction of self-transcendence unless he found this out for himself? We seem to need to forget what we require for happiness until we discover the truth for ourselves.

> According to the proverb, the longest way round is the shortest way home. It seems to be necessary to try to discover the secret by going somewhere in order to learn that [you already possess it]. The path always takes you round in a circle, back to the place where you stand. (Alan Watts, *The Meaning of Happiness*, 119–120.)

To put this in terms of the Enneagram, the movement we make in the Direction of Integration brings us full circle back to ourselves—"the longest way round is the shortest way home." Our truest fulfillment does not lie in the direction of a jealously guarded self but in the direction of self-transcendence as we learn to open to others and to reality. Alan Watts expands on this. He says that even after we have applied all the psychological techniques at our disposal, we are still left unsatisfied, because we have been looking in the wrong place for happiness.

> There is always something it [psychological technique] leaves unsolved, for there remains a subtle, indefinable and elusive inner discontent. . . .
>
> This is truly a "divine discontent" for I believe it to be what the mystics describe as the yearning of the soul for God; as St. Augustine says, "Thou hast made us for Thyself, therefore we may not rest anywhere save in Thee." By a hundred different techniques we can adjust the details of our lives and make ourselves happy in the superficial sense of having nothing specific to be unhappy about. But techniques can only deal with details, with separate parts; something different is required to transform one's attitude to life as a whole, and to transform the whole of one's life. Without this transformation the real unhappiness remains, expressing itself in all manner of disguises, finding innumerable substitutes for God which do not work because they are always *partial* things. They are, as it were, the parts of God, but not the whole of Him. Techniques can find these parts; it can find acceptance, wealth, pleasure, experience, knowledge, and all the . . . unknown realms of the soul. But even when all these many parts are brought together, there is still something which no technical trick or device can discover, and this is the whole which is greater than the sum of its parts. (Ibid., 120–121.)

Psychology, self-help books, and the Enneagram cannot save us. They cannot make us genuinely happy or, at any rate, happy for very long, because they present partial views of human nature, each groping toward the truth in its own limited way. Of course, psychological insights can help us be more perceptive about what we are afraid of and the recurrent sources of our unhappiness. Psychology can help us sort out how we behave, what we typically desire, and how much of what we desire leads us into wasteful conflicts and illusions.

Although they are complicated and subtle, the personality types delineated by the Enneagram remain but crude reflections of human nature. While it is valuable to reflect on them to understand ourselves more objectively, using the Enneagram cannot provide us with any ultimate answers, since that belongs to another realm. It cannot work magic, nor can it transform us into perfectly realized beings.

But by helping us to understand ourselves *as we really are*, at our best and at our worst, the Enneagram reaffirms some age-old insights into human nature. In the end, however, the Enneagram is merely a tool, something useful up to a certain point, whereupon we arrive at the threshold of the spirit—both the wellspring and the fulfillment of the mystery of human nature.

Appendix

THE MEANING OF
THE LEVELS OF DEVELOPMENT

To provide a fuller explanation of what happens at each level, the short explanations given in the Advanced Guidelines (pp. 423–424) have been expanded here. The descriptions and profiles found in each of the individual type chapters fit the following patterns.

In the Healthy Levels:
AT LEVEL 1: *The Level of Liberation.* By confronting and surmounting the Basic Fear (which arose in early childhood in the process of ego development), the person becomes liberated and moves into a state of ego transcendence where he or she begins to actualize the essential self. Paradoxically, the person also attains his or her Basic Desire, and therefore begins to fulfill his or her real needs. (For more on Basic Fear and Basic Desire, see chapter 2 of *Understanding the Enneagram*.) In addition, particular spiritual capacities and virtues emerge, different for each type. This is an ideal state, and the individual is at his or her healthiest, attaining balance and freedom. The person has begun shifting his sense of self from "personality" to "essence," and may have also begun incorporating many of the healthy qualities from the type in the Direction of Integration.

AT LEVEL 2: *The Level of Psychological Capacity.* If the person succumbs to his or her Basic Fear, a Basic Desire arises at this level to compensate. The person is still healthy, but as a result the ego and its defenses begin to develop in response to anxieties created by succumbing to the Basic Fear. The person's sense of self (see chapter 2 of *Understanding the Enneagram*) and "cognitive style" (which can be correlated to Jung's attitudes and functions) manifest themselves at this stage. The Basic Desire is a universal psychological human need, which if acted on rightly both provides what each person needs and is a key to transcending the self.

AT LEVEL 3: *The Level of Social Value.* In response to succumbing to secondary (derivative) fears and desires, the person's ego becomes more active, producing a characteristic persona, with its social and interpersonal qualities. The person is still healthy, although less so, because both ego and the persona are protected by defense mechanisms (see chapter 2 of *Understanding the Enneagram*). At this Level, we see the healthy social characteristics that the type brings to others. The ego takes the positive qualities it has identified with at Level 2 and attempts to reinforce them through action. While the personality, ego, and defenses are operative, the person is not seriously imbalanced and is capable of attaining (or regaining) Level 1 functioning by overcoming the Basic Fear and by acting properly on the Basic Desire.

In the Average Levels:

AT LEVEL 4: *The Level of Imbalance.* As a result of the person's succumbing to a significant Characteristic Temptation (see chapter 2 of *Understanding the Enneagram*) that violates his or her own best interests and development, the ego is inflated, defenses increased, and imbalances introduced. Imbalances are maintained by drawing on the type's source of psychic energy. This Level marks a descent into the person's psychological "dead end" which, if not resisted, will create increasing intrapsychic and interpersonal conflicts. The person strongly identifies with a particular social role which must then be defended.

AT LEVEL 5: *The Level of Interpersonal Control.* The ego inflates significantly as the person tries to control the environment (especially other people) in characteristic ways. (In the withdrawn types [see page 433], "ego inflation" is negative, marked by the deflation of the persona and a characteristic withdrawal of the person from social interactions.) The person must now get others to accept and reinforce the self-image and fulfill ego needs. Defense mechanisms cause interpersonal and intrapsychic conflicts and increasing anxiety if they fail. The traits emerging at this Level are noticeably more negative than any seen prior to this stage. This Level is a turning point in the deterioration of the type, since from here downward, the traits become more egocentric, defensive, and conflicted.

AT LEVEL 6: *The Level of Overcompensation.* The person begins to overcompensate for conflicts and anxieties brought about by the increasing inflation of the ego, as well as by the failure of the behavior seen at Level 5 to provide the person with what he or she has wanted. A characteristic form of self-centeredness emerges (different for each type), as well as overcompensated, extreme forms of behavior, usually found by others to be highly objectionable (although not pathological). Conflicts with others arise as the person acts on self-centeredness to maintain ego inflation. At this Level, each type tends to inflict on others actions related to the type's Basic Fear.

In the Unhealthy Levels:

AT LEVEL 7: *The Level of Violation.* For various possible reasons, the person's defenses have not worked and serious reactions occur. Each type employs a different survival tactic, an unhealthy "self-protective" response, in a desperate attempt to bolster the ego (now assailed by seriously increased anxiety). This response violates the integrity of the self or that of others (or both), creating serious interpersonal conflicts. This state is severely neurotic and imbalanced although not fully pathological yet. Typically, the unhealthy Levels are a response to extreme environmental stressors and/or a history of severe and chronic childhood abuse.

AT LEVEL 8: *The Level of Delusional Thinking and Compulsive Behavior.* As anxiety increases, very serious intrapsychic conflicts occur, and the person attempts to remake reality rather than succumb to anxiety. Thinking and perceiving, feeling and behavior all become severely distorted and unfree; hence, this is a fully pathological state. The person begins to lose touch with reality (becoming delusional in some way), different for each type; the resulting behavior can be characterized as "compulsive." Note that the psychological capacity that emerged at Level 2 and became inflated at Level 5 has become delusional by this Level.

AT LEVEL 9: *The Level of Pathological Destructiveness*. This is the final pathological state, in which openly destructive behavior is expressed. Having become delusionally out of touch with reality, the person becomes willing to destroy the self, others, or both to defend the ego structure and whatever delusions have arisen to buffer it from further anxiety or threat. Different forms of immediate or remote, conscious or unconscious destructiveness (including latent self-destructiveness) manifest themselves, resulting in serious breakdown, violence, or death.

These brief descriptions of the meaning of the Levels still do not do them justice. Nevertheless, with even such a brief explanation, it should be possible to understand the overall rationale of the Levels and therefore to understand the patterns presented by each type. Note that the ego emerges at Level 2, becoming increasingly inflated and destructive by Level 9. Note also that a reverse process happens with personal freedom: the person is most free at Level 1 and becomes increasingly unfree ("compulsive") as he or she deteriorates into deep pathology at Level 9. Neurosis is fundamentally unfree, while health is marked by freedom—and further integration is marked by the increasing personal freedom.

THE CORE DYNAMICS

The Core Dynamics are a schematic representation of the types which includes descriptive clusters of terms for the behaviors and attitudes at each of the nine Levels of Development as well as the key fears and motivations at each Level which drive the personality toward health or neurosis. Thus, the Core Dynamics, as the name suggests, represent the dynamic component of the Levels of Development, and offer far more information about the inner tensions and movements of each type.

Because of their energetic qualities and their specificity, the Core Dynamics enable students to use the Enneagram with much greater precision. Those using the Enneagram for their own self-discovery will be able to better comprehend the states they find themselves in, as well as the obstacles to their growth. Therapists will be able to identify the specific layers of fears and desires which may be holding a client in a dysfunctional pattern. People in general will be able to reduce interpersonal conflicts and tensions because of their increased insight into what the other person may be feeling. Once they have been mastered, the Core Dynamics make the Enneagram a much more powerful tool.

The Levels of Development were discovered by Don Richard Riso in 1977 and he further developed them over the next fourteen years. In 1991, Russ Hudson began collaborating with Don Riso to bring the Levels and the Core Dynamics to their current state of refinement. The Levels, the Core Dynamics, and virtually all of the descriptions of the types in this book represent the original work of the authors. While we are deeply indebted to the seminal insights of Oscar Ichazo, Claudio Naranjo, and their forerunners in various traditional schools of thought, the material in this book, like that in all of the contemporary teachings of the Enneagram, is a modern development.

From a technical point of view, the field of Enneagram studies will be greatly enriched by this first publication of the Core Dynamics of the personality types because the Core Dynamics reveal the inner logic of each type. It is widely recognized that many contradictions and disagreements exist between different interpretations of the Enneagram. The Core Dynamics will provide the theoretical framework for definitively sorting out the appropriate traits and motivations for each type. They will reveal which traits properly belong to each type and which traits are misattributed, as well as direct us to new areas for research and exploration.

The Layout

It is best to think of the Core Dynamics as a map of the personality type, showing the whole range of possible attitudes and behaviors, from the healthiest aspects to the most painful, pathological ones, as well as the road in between. If you turn to page 471, you will see a diagram which presents the basic skeleton of the Core Dynamics, which can be filled in with the particulars of any one type. It is a template which all of the nine personality types follow with their own variations of the basic theme.

At the top of the page, the type's number (1–9) is given along with its name. This is followed by the type's parental orientation (see Parental Orientation sections of chapters 4 through 12 for more details). Beneath this, you will see a line, over which are written four terms: B-term (Behaviors), A-term (Attitudes), Desires, and Fears. You will also notice that beneath these headings are four columns of "blanks" which proceed from the headings, through the nine Levels, to the bottom of the page. This is because, as we will see, there are corresponding clusters of attitudes, behaviors, fears, and desires (motivations) at each of the nine Levels of Development. Do not confuse the nine Levels with the nine types. The numbered Levels reading vertically down the following pages are numbered 1 through 9 and represent the internal Levels of the continuum for each type.

The diagram begins in the upper right-hand corner with the term *Basic Fear*. This fear is the fundamental insecurity that the type is trying to "solve" or at least repress. There is one specific Basic Fear for each type, expressed in the best language for it that we can find at this time. To a large degree, the Basic Fears are universal—we have all nine of them in us—but the Basic Fear for our own type is more powerful, more entrenched, and more responsible for most of our behavior, as we will soon see. Often, a person will not be conscious of her Basic Fear, but will recognize some secondary fears layered over it more readily. But if you contemplate the Basic Fear of your own type, you will begin to see its effect in your life. You can also see these Basic Fears as variations of a more central and pervasive fear found in all of the types—the fear of nonbeing, of not existing. In a way, each Basic Fear can be viewed as a particular variation of this deeper, more general fear.

You will then notice an arrow moving diagonally down from the Basic Fear to the Basic Desire. The Basic Desire is the central motivation for the type: it is the way that the type tries to manage its Basic Fear, and so can be seen as directly related to it. Again, the Basic Desires are universal and represent things that everyone wants: to feel loved and valuable, to know who one is, to feel competent, to be secure and happy, to be free, to be good, and to be at peace. The Basic Desires represent fundamental human needs, and as such are legitimate and worthwhile goals. The problem is that as a person gets more caught up in the mechanisms of his or her type, he or she will begin to pursue this desire to the detriment of many other important areas of life, and sometimes to the detriment of other people's lives.

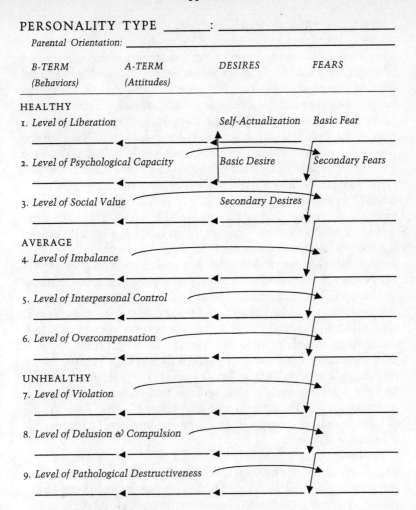

PERSONALITY TYPE _____: _____

Parental Orientation: _____

| B-TERM (Behaviors) | A-TERM (Attitudes) | DESIRES | FEARS |

HEALTHY

1. *Level of Liberation* — Self-Actualization — Basic Fear

2. *Level of Psychological Capacity* — Basic Desire — Secondary Fears

3. *Level of Social Value* — Secondary Desires

AVERAGE

4. *Level of Imbalance*

5. *Level of Interpersonal Control*

6. *Level of Overcompensation*

UNHEALTHY

7. *Level of Violation*

8. *Level of Delusion & Compulsion*

9. *Level of Pathological Destructiveness*

The Basic Desire also represents a significant turning point. Notice that there are two arrows leading away from the Basic Desire, one leading up to the Self-actualization term, and the other leading left to a blank under the "A-term" column. This is because there are two ways of "acting on" the Basic Desire, one leading to freedom and the true self of Essence at Level 1, the other leading into the world of the ego at Level 2. We will explore the latter first.

If we follow the arrow to the left, we come to the first "A-term" or Attitude at Level 2, the "Level of Psychological Capacity." In the Core Dynamics sheets for each type that follow this discussion, you will see a list of five or six words in this area with a boldfaced word at the top which is the "key term" for the cluster. These represent the psychological capacities and qualities which that type "draws on" to achieve its Basic Desire and which form the foundation of the person's ego structure. For example, type Two's Basic Fear is "of being unwanted, unworthy of being loved." This leads to a compensating Basic Desire, "To be loved unconditionally" or one could say "to be loved for one's self alone." To accomplish this desire Twos become "Empathetic," as well as "concerned, other-oriented, forgiving, compassionate," and so forth. They focus on, and are sensitive to, the feelings of others in the hope of being loved themselves. This is the basis of type Two's ego structure.

Next, the cluster of Attitudes at Level 2 leads to a cluster of Behaviors. On the diagram, this is represented by an arrow going to the left to a blank under the "B-term" column. At Level 2, however, unlike all of the other Levels, the B-term has a different significance. The B-term column at Level 2 represents the person's self-image; thus, the terms here could be called "I am" terms because they represent the way that the type sees itself. To continue with the example of type Two, at Level 2 under the B-term column we find the words "Loving, caring, selfless, thoughtful, warm-hearted, and passionate." These are the "I am" terms for type Two. People of this type would have little difficulty saying, "I am loving, caring, selfless," and so forth.

However, once a type has identified itself with a certain self-image, another fear must arise, because in truth, the qualities that the person has used to define himself do not represent the entire person. Thus the qualities that contradict the self-image must be defended against. On the diagram, you will see an arrow leading from the B-term column at Level 2, arcing to the right, back to the Fear column and to a space marked "Secondary Fears." This indicates a new fear which has arisen in response to the self-image terms at Level 2. The Secondary Fear is more immediately felt, and sometimes obscures the Basic Fear. Using our example of type Two again, we see the Secondary Fear, "That their own needs and negative feelings will harm their relationships." In other words, once type Twos have established the self-image of being loving, selfless people in the hope of getting love, they begin to fear ever being unloving, or selfish—whatever that may mean to them. Certain real feelings that they may have will contradict their self-image, and the result will be more anxiety.

If a type succumbs to this Secondary Fear, they must reinforce their self-image with definite behavior, and this is represented by the arrow leading from the Secondary Fear at Level 2 diagonally down to the Secondary Desire at Level 3. Subsequently, another layer of ego is established, strengthening and reinforcing the one at Level 2, but at the price of less freedom and greater anxiety. As you may recall from the description on page two of this appendix, Level 3 is still healthy, but is clearly within the world of ego. At this Level, each type engages in constructive behavior to prove to itself and others that it really possesses the qualities delineated by their self-image at Level 2. Looking again at type Two, we see that if Twos succumb to the Secondary Fear at Level 2, "That their own needs and negative feelings will harm their relationships," they turn to the compensating "Secondary Desire" at Level 3, seeking "To do good things for others (to reinforce their positive feelings and self-image)." This leads to the A-term or Attitude at Level 3 of being "Supportive" (along with the other terms in the Attitude cluster: "appreciative, sympathetic, nurturing," and so on) and further left to the B-term or Behavior of "Giving" (along with the other terms of the Behavior cluster, "generous, encouraging, helpful," etc.).

Note that at Level 3, and in all subsequent Levels, the A-terms represent attitudes or internal states of consciousness which are generally invisible to other people. The B-terms represent behaviors, actions, or styles of self-expression which generally *are* visible to other people. Thus, attitudes, like those of type Two at Level 3 — supportive, appreciative, and sympathetic—are expressed in specific behavior described in the B-terms at Level 3 —giving, encouraging, being helpful, and so forth.

Of course, once a person becomes identified with the behaviors and attitudes at Level 3, they too must be defended, causing yet another fear to arise. This, again, is represented by the arrow arcing right from the B-term column back to the Fear column. In the case of type Two, being helpful, generous, and encouraging causes a new fear: "That whatever they have been doing for others is not enough to gain their love (others will not come to them, they must go out more to others)." If a type succumbs to the fear at Level 3, they will pursue a compensating desire at Level 4, leading to yet another cluster of attitudes and behaviors which must also be defended, thus causing new fears, and so on. The entire process then repeats itself all the way to Level 9.

By now, you may well be able to observe the spiral structure of the Core Dynamics. A fear sets a desire in motion, leading left to internal attitudes, then to external behaviors, then back around to a new fear and down to the next Level to compensate for it. From this perspective, all ego development or disintegration can be seen as moving up or down this spiral structure.

If you turn to the example of type Two in the appendix again on pages 476–477, you will see in the A-term and B-term columns, beginning at Level 4, the "Level of Imbalance," an italicized word at the bottom of each cluster. These italicized words represent qualities from the type's Direction of Disintegration that begin to occur at Level 4. Thus they serve as a reminder of the "parallel track" of the Direction of Disintegration, and give an indication of attitudes and behaviors that will arise at each Level during periods of heightened stress.

Looking at the structure as a whole, we can see that it is fear, again and again, that drives us deeper and deeper into restrictive, painful ego states, and farther and farther from a direct experience of our true nature. We can also see that children developing in dysfunctional environments will often have more fears to contend with and therefore more ego defenses layered on. Thus, adults who are functioning in the lower end of the Levels of Development can be seen as individuals who as children were forced to develop more elaborate systems of defense.

It then follows that the way to lighten the burden of one's more painful, defended states is to follow the spiral up against the arrows. This means allowing one's self to experience the fear at the Level in which one finds one's self, and all the subsequent fears above it. It also means allowing one's self to let go of the behaviors, attitudes, and desires that one may be clinging to, by recognizing that there are more effective means to realize what one really wants—the Basic Desire.

Our discussion then, has led us back to the "turning point" at the Basic Desire at Level 2. If you recall, there were two arrows leading from the Basic Desire. The one that led left toward the

A-term leads into the world of ego, with all of the costs we have just described. The other arrow leads up to Level 1, and a space marked Self-Actualization. This means that if a person truly wants to achieve his Basic Desire, he must confront his Basic Fear at Level 1, but also let go of his Self-Image, the definition of himself formed at Level 2, seeing that it is not the whole truth of who they are. In the example of type Two, this would mean that Twos would need to confront their fear of being unwanted and unworthy of being loved, but also the self-image described under "Self-Actualization"— "that they are not allowed to take care of themselves and their own needs." This frees Twos to acknowledge the full range of their feelings and motivations without seeing themselves as "selfish," leading to the A-terms and B-terms of Level 1, "the Level of Liberation."

Level 1, however, is not the end of the road, but the beginning of another. It is the beginning of the world of the True Self, the Essence, which is not defined in the ways that the ego is. Once a person has become liberated from the trap of his own personality type, he will begin to experience all kinds of wonderful impressions of themselves, the world, and of life. Moreover, such a person would be able to integrate the positive qualities of all nine types, since they are no longer attached to behavior and beliefs connected with only one of them. There is much that could be said about Level 1, and the expanding horizons of Essence, but that is for another time.

PERSONALITY TYPE **TWO**: The Helper

Parental Orientation: Ambivalent to the Protective-figure

B-TERMS	A-TERMS	DESIRES	FEARS

HEALTHY

1. *Level of Liberation* — *Self-Actualization* — *Basic Fear*

Loving Uncon-ditionally ◄	**Altruistic**	◄ Let go of their	Of being
joyous radiant	self-nurturing	identification with	unwanted,
truly charitable	disinterested	a particular self-	unworthy of
constant	unselfish	image, that they are	being loved
"tough love"	humble	not allowed to take	
	gracious	care of themselves	
		and their own	
		needs	

2. *Level of Psychological Capacity* — *Basic Desire* — *Secondary Fears*

Loving ◄	**Empathetic**	◄ To be loved ►	That their own
caring	concerned	unconditionally	needs and negative
selfless	other-oriented		feelings will harm
thoughtful	forgiving		their relationships
warm-hearted	compassionate		
passionate	sincere		

3. *Level of Social Value* — *Secondary Desires*

Giving ◄	**Supportive**	◄ To do good things ►	That whatever
generous	appreciative	for others (to	they have been
encouraging	sympathetic	reinforce their	doing for others is
helpful	nurturing	positive feelings	not enough to gain
expressive	dedicated	and self-image)	their love (others
guiding	admiring		will not come to
serving	affectionate		them, they must
			go out more to
			others)

AVERAGE

4. *Level of Imbalance*

Demonstrative ◄	**Well-Intentioned**	◄ To be wanted— ►	That the people
approving	sentimental	to be close to	they love will love
flattering	solicitous	others	someone else more
flirtatious	familiar		than them
people-pleasing	yearning		
cultivating	needing physical		
"sharing"	contact		
persuasive	religious/psychic		
	no-nonsense		

5. *Level of Interpersonal Control*

Intrusive	◄ **Possessive**	◄ To be needed—	That they and their
"intimate"	"self-sacrificing"	to make themselves	help are being
accosting	worrying	necessary to others	taken for granted
seductive	ulterior motives		
unwanted advice	thin-skinned		
hovering	jealous		
gossiping	classic codependency		
enabling	"stuffing feelings"		
dominating	*self-centered*		

6. *Level of Overcompensation*

Overbearing	◄ **Self-Important**	◄ To be acknowl-	That they are
patronizing	self-satisfied	edged, to have their	driving others
high-handed	vainglorious	virtue and goodness	away
insincere	sanctimonious	recognized	
indiscreet	presumptuous		
terms of	self-congratulatory		
endearment	hypochondriacal		
complaining/	*confrontational*		
martyr			
undermining			

UNHEALTHY

7. *Level of Violation*

Manipulative	◄ **Self-Justifying**	◄ To maintain the	That they have
blaming	self-deceptive	belief that they	permanently
guilt-instilling	rationalizing	haven't done any	estranged their
smothering	histrionic	thing selfish/wrong	loved ones
discouraging	despondent	(holding on to	
eating disorders	enraged	people at all costs)	
somatizing	*vengeful*		
violent			

8. *Level of Delusion & Compulsion*

Coercive	◄ **Entitled**	◄ To get love from	That they are bad,
indiscriminate	insatiable	anyone in any	selfish and have
sexually act-out	desperate	way they can	violated others
voracious	obsessive "love"		
reckless	heartbroken		
molesting	demand repayment		
predatory	*no boundaries*		

9. *Level of Pathological Destructiveness*

Parasitic	◄ **Feel Victimized**	◄ To vindicate	Basic Fear is
burdensome	feel abused	themselves by	realized: they have
diseased	psychosomatic	falling apart	become unwanted
physically broken	disorders	and suffering	and unlovable
down	emotionally		
invalids	consumed		
destructive	*remorseless*		

PERSONALITY TYPE **THREE**: The Motivator

Parental Orientation: Connected to the Nurturing-figure

B-TERMS	A-TERMS	DESIRES	FEARS

HEALTHY

1. *Level of Liberation* — *Self-Actualization* — *Basic Fear*

Authentic ◀	**Inner-Directed** ◀	Lets go of their	Of being worthless
genuine	self-accepting	identification with	
affecting	modest	a particular self-	
esteemed	contented	image, that their	
self-deprecatory	tender	value is dependent	
benevolent	charitable	on the positive	
		▲ regard of others	

2. *Level of Psychological Capacity* — *Basic Desire* — *Secondary Fears*

Admirable ◀	**Adaptable** ◀	To feel valuable ▶	That they will
desirable	other-directed	and worthwhile	be rejected
attractive	realistic	(because they	
charming	self-assured	disappoint others)	
well-adjusted	purposeful		
poised	"unlimited potential"		

3. *Level of Social Value* — *Secondary Desires*

Self-Improving ◀	**Goal-Oriented** ◀	To develop them-	Of falling behind,
outstanding	ambitious	selves (to be "all	of being over-
effective	confident	that they can be")	shadowed by
competent	high-spirited		others
capable com-	diligent		
municators	focused		
motivating	persistent		
industrious	self-investing		

AVERAGE

4. *Level of Imbalance*

Performing ◀	**Success-Oriented** ◀	To distinguish ◀	Of losing the
achieving	comparing	themselves from	positive regard
career-oriented	status-conscious	others; to be	of others
self-enhancing	competitive	noticed, valued	
organized	exclusive	by others	
diplomatic	driven		
presentable	seeking recognition		
conforming	*conciliatory*		

5. *Level of Interpersonal Control*

Expedient	◄ **Image-Conscious**	◄ To create a	That others will
meet expectations	"rehearsed"	favorable	see through
chameleonic	premeditated	impression of	them—they will
packaged	impersonal	themselves	be humiliated, lose
efficient	emotionally	(to impress)	face
pragmatic	detached		
professional	"reading" others		
"friendly"	intimacy problems		
complacent	self-doubting		
	disengaged		

6. *Level of Overcompensation*

Self-Promoting	◄ **Grandiose**	◄ To convince	That they are
"showing off"	self-involved	themselves and	failing, that their
inflating accom-	narcissistic	others of the	claims are empty,
plishments	contemptuous	reality of their	fraudulent
openly competitive	arrogant	image	
mocking/sneering	jealous		
seductive	secretly needy		
"attitude"	*unrealistic*		
placating			

UNHEALTHY

7. *Level of Violation*

Deceptive	◄ **Unprincipled**	◄ To preserve the	Of being caught,
concealing	covetous	illusion that	of losing any
"cutting corners"	hostile	they are still	reason for others to
surreptitious	inner emptiness	superior, still	think well of them
detracting	affectless	okay	(that there is
divisive	feeling insignificant		nothing about
inadequate	*numb*		them people will
			admire)

8. *Level of Delusion & Compulsion*

Opportunistic	◄ **Duplicitous**	◄ To do whatever	That their
exploitative	suppressed panic	is necessary to	falseness and
betraying	remorseless	support their	emptiness will be
sabotaging	desperate	false claims	exposed—they
scheming	feel cornered	(while covering	will be ruined
pathologically	detached from self	their tracks)	
lying	*dissociated*		
depersonalized			

9. *Level of Pathological Destructiveness*

Relentless	◄ **Monomaniacal**	◄ To destroy whoever	Basic Fear is
monstrous	malicious	or whatever	realized: they are
vicious	vengeful	threatens them or	rejected as
psychopathic	sadistic	reminds them of	worthless
fragmented	*self-abandoning*	what they lack	

PERSONALITY TYPE **FOUR**: **The Individualist**

Parental Orientation: Disconnected from Both Parents

B-TERMS	A-TERMS	DESIRES	FEARS

HEALTHY

1. *Level of Liberation* — — *Self-Actualization* — *Basic Fear*

Life-Enhancing	◄ **Life-Embracing**	◄ Let go of their	That they have
redemptive	self-renewing	identification with	no identity
inspired	revitalized	a particular self-	or personal
engaged	spontaneous	image, that they	significance
truly original	connected	are more inherently	
revelatory	bountiful	flawed than others	
		—that they are	
		missing something	
		that others have	

2. *Level of Psychological Capacity* — *Basic Desire* — *Secondary Fears*

Sensitive	◄ **Introspective**	◄ To find themselves	Of losing touch
different	self-aware	and their signifi-	with their inner
gentle	intuitive	cance (to create an	states, their
quiet, warm	emotional	identity out of their	sense of self
unique	feeling-oriented	inner experience)	
honest with self	impressionable		

3. *Level of Social Value* — — *Secondary Desires*

Creative	◄ **Self-Revealing**	◄ To express their	That their
personal-	accessible	individuality to	changing feelings
universal	emotionally strong	themselves and	won't sustain them
expressive	dedicated	others (through	and their creativity
subtle	authentic	creative action)	
humane	inner-directed		
eloquent, witty			

AVERAGE

4. *Level of Imbalance*

Individualistic	◄ **Romanticizing**	◄ To cultivate and	That others will
special	fantasizing	prolong selected	not appreciate
aesthetic/exotic	dramatizing	feelings (Fantasy	the significance
symbolic	idealizing	Self)	of their identity
indirect	past-oriented		and feelings
create	infatuated		
atmosphere	creating		
"elegant"/arch	expectations		
demonstrative	*sentimental*		

5. *Level of Interpersonal Control*

Temperamental	◄ **Self-Absorbed**	◄ To be reassured	That life's
withholding	self-referential	of others' interest	demands will force
moody, aloof	self-conscious	and concern for	them to give up
hypersensitive	melancholy	them (playing	their Fantasy Self
brooding, sulking	vulnerable	"hard to get")	(others will not
precious/mannered	feel misunderstood		rescue them)
"mysterious"	self-doubting		
uninvolved	uninterested		
hovering	*possessive*		

6. *Level of Overcompensation*

Decadent	◄ **Self-Indulgent**	◄ To be absolutely	That they are
sensual	feel exempt	free to "be	ruining their lives,
pretentious	dismissive	themselves"	wasting their
unproductive	disdainful, petty		opportunities
"difficult"	self-pitying		
demanding	envious		
identity problems	petulant		
high-handed	*resentful*		

UNHEALTHY

7. *Level of Violation*

Alienated	◄ **Deeply Resentful**	◄ To reject everyone	▶ That they are
self-inhibited	emotionally	or anything that	cut off from others
mourning	blocked	does not support	and from life
morbid/hateful	ashamed of self	their emotional	(abandoned)
self-neglecting	apathetic	demands	
fatigued	detesting		
guilt-instilling	confused		
	rationalizing		

8. *Level of Delusion & Compulsion*

Clin. Depressed	◄ **Self-Rejecting**	◄ To punish them-	▶ That their
self-sabotaging	self-hating	selves (and,	situation is
self-mutilating	guilt-ridden	indirectly, others)	hopeless—
accusatory	tormented		everything is
turbulent	seething		futile
addictive	death-obsessed		
coercive	*enraged*		

9. *Level of Pathological Destructiveness*

Life-Denying	◄ **Despairing**	◄ To escape their	▶ Basic Fear is
self-destructive	hopeless	crushingly negative	realized: they have
"broken down"	feel defeated	self-consciousness	lost their identity
crimes of passion	utterly worthless		and personal
strangely calm	dissociated		significance
suicidal	desolate		
parasitic	*feel victimized*		

PERSONALITY TYPE **FIVE**: **The Investigator**

Parental Orientation: Ambivalent to Both Parents

B-TERMS	A-TERMS	DESIRES	FEARS

HEALTHY

1. *Level of Liberation* · *Self-Actualization* · *Basic Fear*

Visionary	◄ **Participating**	◄ Let go of their	Of being helpless,
pioneering	immediately	identification with	useless, incapable
enraptured	apprehending	a particular self-	
profound	comprehending	image, that they	
revolutionary	awed	are separate from	
compassionate	clear-minded	the environment	
knowing	trusting	(an outside observer)	

2. *Level of Psychological Capacity* · *Basic Desire* · *Secondary Fears*

Perceptive	◄ **Observant**	◄ To be capable	That their
"smart"	attentive	and competent	perceptions are
curious	sensory acuity	(to have something	insufficient to
insightful	fascinated	to contribute)	give them an
playful	unsentimental		orientation to life
alert	objective		(life will over-
unusual	self-contained		whelm them)

3. *Level of Social Value* · *Seondary Desires*

Innovative	◄ **Focused**	◄ To master some-	That they have
original	exploratory	thing to gain	nothing valuable
skillful	open-minded	confidence (to	to contribute
inventive	patient	create a niche for	(unprepared)
communicative	whimsical	themselves)	
creative	uncompromising		
learning	independent		

AVERAGE

4. *Level of Imbalance*

Expert	◄ **Conceptualizing**	◄ To feel safer and	That others will
knowledgeable	encyclopedic	more confident by	demand too much
acquiring	model-building	retreating into their	from them, their
technique	analytic	mind & imagination	inner world will
collecting	uncensored	("Tinkertoy")	be threatened
studious	preparing		
practicing	avaricious		
delay closure	*acquisitive*		
dilettantish			

5. *Level of Interpersonal Control*

Preoccupied	◄**Detached**	◄To shut out	That others are
creating worlds	abstracting	intrusions (by	attacking their
secretive	intense	intensifying	niche/competency
speculative	ignoring needs	their mental	
high-strung	complexifying	activity)	
offbeat/impractical	absent-minded		
compartmentalized	agitated		
flighty	*indiscriminate*		

6. *Level of Overcompensation*

Provocative	◄**Extreme**	◄To scare off anyone	That they are
argumentative	cynical	who threatens	never going to find
scornful	intellectually	their niche/	a place in the
antagonistic	arrogant	inner world	world or with
contentious	distrusting		people
far-fetched	pessimistic		
subversive	jumping to		
insensitive	conclusions		
	stingy		
	impatient		

UNHEALTHY

7. *Level of Violation*

Eccentric	◄**Nihilistic**	◄To cut off all	That the world is
isolated	retreating	connections with	closing in on them
unstable	devaluing	the world and	
rejecting	dark fantasies	people ("to hell	
emptying	feel besieged	with everything")	
burn bridges	no expectations		
dissipated	*impulsive*		

8. *Level of Delusion & Compulsion*

Delirious	◄**Schizoid**	◄To fend off their	That they can no
hallucinating	distorting	terrors	longer defend
projecting	weird perceptions		themselves (from
repelling	horrified		outside or inside
sinister	overheated/		influences)
insomniac	nauseous		
erratic	resisting all help		
	manic-depressive		

9. *Level of Pathological Destructiveness*

"Psychotic"	◄**Seeking Oblivion**	◄To leave "reality,"	Basic Fear is
deranged	imploded	to cease all sensory	realized: they are
suicidal	split off	input, to break	helpless, useless,
annihilating	inner chaos	away from their	and incapable
"autistic"	feel damned	own consciousness	
paralyzed	*panic-stricken*		

PERSONALITY TYPE SIX: The Loyalist

Parental Orientation: Connected to the Protective-figure

B-TERMS	A-TERMS	DESIRES	FEARS

HEALTHY

1. *Level of Liberation* — *Self-Actualization* / *Basic Fear*

Courageous	◄ **Self-Reliant**	◄ Let go of their identification with a particular self-image, that they must rely on someone or something outsidethemselves for security	Of being unable to survive on their own, of having no support
intrepid	self-affirming		
synergistic	independent		
indefatigable	positive-thinking		
self-expressive	grounded		
decisive	secure		

2. *Level of Psychological Capacity* — *Basic Desire* / *Secondary Fears*

Reliable	◄ **Engaging**	◄ To find security and support (to belong somewhere)	Of losing their security — their feeling of belonging
dependable	bonding		
trustworthy	identifying		
likable	faithful		
careful	trusting/ questioning		
have foresight	vigilant		
"regular"	connecting		

3. *Level of Social Value* — *Secondary Desires*

Cooperative	◄ **Committed**	◄ To create and sustain "social security" (to form systems and alliances with others)	Of doing anything to jeopardize their security systems (groups, authorities, or affiliations)
persevering	responsible		
meticulous	disciplined		
egalitarian	practical		
hardworking	action-oriented		
community builder	self-sacrificial		
thrifty	respectful		
craftsmanship	methodical		

AVERAGE

4. *Level of Imbalance*

Loyal	◄ **Dutiful**	◄ To reinforce their support systems— to strengthen their alliances and/or their position with authorities	That they cannot meet conflicting demands (of different allies or authorities)
investing	obligated		
organizing	"covering bases"		
analyzing	seeking approval		
camaraderie	convinced		
safeguarding	believing/doubting		
troubleshooting	insecure		
ingratiating	attached to systems, beliefs		
performing	competitive		

5. *Level of Interpersonal Control*

Defensive	◀ **Ambivalent**	◀ To resist having	That they are
evasive	cautious	any further	losing the support
passive-aggressive	feel pressured	demands or	of their allies and
indecisive	anxious	obligations	authorities
unpredictable	reactive	placed on them	
complaining	negative	(to assert them-	
testing	skeptical	selves without	
moody	suspicious	appearing to do so)	
chameleonic	*image-conscious*		

6. *Level of Overcompensation*

Blaming	◀ **Authoritarian**	◀ To prove their	That their actions
belligerent	cynical	value and strength	have harmed their
sarcastic	defiant	(to themselves, to	security
scapegoating	mean-spirited	their allies, and	
conspiratorial	prejudiced	to their enemies)	
overzealous	short-tempered		
fear-instilling	stubborn phobic/		
substance abuse	counterphobic "flips"		
self-promoting	*contemptuous*		

UNHEALTHY

7. *Level of Violation*

Clingingly	◀ **Submissive**	◀ To elicit the	That others will
Dependent	panicky	protection of a	destroy whatever
conform	inferiority feelings	stronger ally	security they
completely	feel helpless	(to be rescued)	have left
cowardly	depressed		
self-humiliating	emotionally needy		
self-punishing	masochistic		
"bad company"	*unscrupulous*		
unreliable			
untrustworthy			

8. *Level of Delusion & Compulsion*

Lashing Out	◀ **Paranoid**	◀ To remove all	That they will
fanatical	hateful	threats to their	be punished for
irrational	desperate	security (to attack	what they have
ranting	anxiety-ridden	whomever they	done
violent	obsessive	believe threatens	
betraying	*duplicitous*	their security)	

9. *Level of Pathological Destructiveness*

Self-Destructive	◀ **Self-Abasing**	◀ To escape	Basic Fear is
inviting disgrace	hysterical	punishment	realized: they
suicidal	guilt-ridden	(and atone	are not able to
dropping out	tormented	for their	survive on their
"skid row"	self-condemnatory	guilt)	own; they are
heedless	self-hating		abandoned
vicious	*sadistic*		

PERSONALITY TYPE **SEVEN**: The Enthusiast

Parental Orientation: Disconnected to the Nurturing-figure

B-TERMS	A-TERMS	DESIRES	FEARS

HEALTHY

1. *Level of Liberation*

Self-Actualization / *Basic Fear*

Satisfied	◄ **Appreciative**	◄ Let go of their	Of pain and
content	assimilating	identification with	deprivation
ecstatic	receptive	a particular self-	
nourished	grateful	image, that they	
spiritual	savoring	require specific	
truly free	bountiful	objects and	
		experiences to	
		▲ feel fulfilled.	

2. *Level of Psychological Capacity*

Basic Desire / *Secondary Fears*

Enthusiastic	◄ **Anticipating**	◄ To be satisfied	That their freedom
free-spirited	excitable	and content — to	and happiness will
spontaneous	stimulated	have their needs	be lost, their needs
cheerful	responsive	fulfilled	will not be met
eager, outgoing	quick, avid		
adventurous	resilient		
energetic	positive		

3. *Level of Social Value*

Secondary Desires

Productive	◄ **Realistic**	◄ To do those things	Of missing out
practical	self-confident	which will ensure	on other worth-
accomplished	future-oriented	that they will	while things and
gregarious	engaged	have what they	experiences (that
versatile	passionate	need	what they have
prolific	vivacious		isn't enough)
entertaining	bold		

AVERAGE

4. *Level of Imbalance*

Consuming	◄ **Acquisitive**	◄ To increase the	That they will be
seeking variety	keep options open	number of sources	bored or frustrated
experiencing	pleasure-oriented	of stimulation (to	(and negative
occupied/busy	appetitive	do more)	feelings will arise)
dilettantish	materialistic		
stylish	worldly-wise		
talkative	trendy, sensation-		
proselytizing	seeking		
	driven		

5. *Level of Interpersonal Control*

Hyperactive	◄ **Uninhibited**	◄ To keep them-	That the environ-
attention-grabbing	indiscriminate	selves excited and	ment will not
superficial	thrill-seeking	occupied — to	provide them
scattered	irreverent	stay "up"	with what they
outspoken	distractible		want ("scarcity
outrageous	restless		thinking")
exaggerating	tangential		
opinionated	*impatient*		

6. *Level of Overcompensation*

Excessive	◄ **Self-Centered**	◄ To get whatever	That their actions
demanding,	dissatisfied	they want	are bringing
pushy	jaded, callous	immediately	them pain and
insensitive	greedy	("instant	unhappiness
wasteful	hardened	gratification")	
addictive	denying guilt		
cavalier	*uncompromising*		
perfectionistic			

UNHEALTHY

7. *Level of Violation*

Escaping	◄ **Insatiable**	◄ To avoid their	Of losing their
dissipated	impulsive	pain and anxiety	capacity for
abusive, rude	irresponsible	at any cost	pleasure and
infantile	extremely anxious		happiness (that
debauched	bitter		they cannot
corrupting	joyless		enjoy anything)
intolerant	*vindictive*		

8. *Level of Delusion & Compulsion*

Reckless	◄ **Manic (Depressive)**	◄ To do anything	That they have
erratic	acting-out	in order to feel	irreparably ruined
unstable	hysterical	something	themselves and
unpredictable	heedless		their lives
out of control	death defying		
sadomasochistic	"numb"		
cruel	*obsessive*		

9. *Level of Pathological Destructiveness*

Paralyzed	◄ **Overwhelmed**	◄ To give up their	Basic Fear is
burned out	panic-stricken	struggle — to not	realized: they are
tortured	claustrophobic	go on anymore	in pain and are
wrecked	overloaded		deprived of what
debilitated	trapped		they need to be
punitive	*condemnatory*		satisfied and happy

PERSONALITY TYPE EIGIIT: The Leader

Parental Orientation: Ambivalent to the Nurturing-figure

B-TERMS	A-TERMS	DESIRES	FEARS

HEALTHY

1. *Level of Liberation* — *Self-Actualization* — *Basic Fear*

Heroic ◄	**Self-Surrendering** ◄	Let go of their identification with a particular self-image, that they must always be in control of their environment	Of being harmed or controlled by others
inspiring	compassionate		
courageous	merciful		
empowering	magnanimous		
selfless	forgiving		
gentle	faithful		

2. *Level of Psychological Capacity* — *Basic Desire* — *Secondary Fears*

Strong ◄	**Self-Reliant** ◄	To protect themselves (to be in control of their own life and destiny)	Of becoming weak or vulnerable — of losing their strength and independence
assertive	independent		
resourceful	strong willed		
action oriented	self-determining		
direct	resolute		
tenacious	impassioned		
robust	vigorous		

3. *Level of Social Value* — *Secondary Desires*

Leading ◄	**Self-Confident** ◄	To prove their strength through action or achievement	That they do not have enough resources at their disposal to carry out their role as leader/provider
providing	self-mastering		
constructive	honorable		
have vision	authoritative		
challenging	initiating		
championing	decisive		
tough decisions	strategic		
protective	seeking justice		

AVERAGE

4. *Level of Imbalance*

Enterprising ◄	**Pragmatic** ◄	To acquire the resources they need to maintain their position	That others do not respect them or recognize their efforts
hardworking	competitive		
risk-taking	seeking advantage		
straight-talking	shrewd		
businesslike	"no nonsense"		
rugged	self-interest		
"street smart"	driven		
knowledgeable	*analytic*		

5. *Level of Interpersonal Control*

Dominating	◄ **Self-Glorifying**	◄ To convince	Of losing con-
controlling	expansive	themselves and	trol of their
boastful/bossy	swaggering	others of their	environment
blunt	willful	centrality and	(others are not
bluffing	proud	importance	backing them up)
big promises	insistent	(to feel important)	
demand loyalty	egocentric		
"daredevils"	territorial		
secretive	*preoccupied*		

6. *Level of Overcompensation*

Intimidating	◄ **Confrontational**	◄ To pressure	That others are
combative	defiant	others to do	turning against
unreasonable	"chip on shoulder"	what they want,	them
forceful/	bad-tempered	to make others fall	
aggressive	lustful	in line with their	
threatening	cynical	agenda	
pushing limits	repressing hurt		
undermining	contempt for		
oppressive	weakness		
provocative	*extreme*		

UNHEALTHY

7. *Level of Violation*

Dictatorial	◄ **Ruthless**	◄ To survive, to	Of retaliation
"outlaw"	feel betrayed	protect themselves	
violent, brutal	antisocial	and stay in control	
treacherous	predatory	at any cost	
scheming	immoral		
untruthful	vengeful		
reclusive	*cutting off*		

8. *Level of Delusion & Compulsion*

Terrorizing	◄ **Megalomaniacal**	◄ To be invincible,	That their
rapacious	overreaching	unassailable,	resources cannot
raging	unrestrained	invulnerable	hold out any longer
devastating	"omnipotent"	(without fear)	
overrextended	no boundaries		
projecting	*phobic*		

9. *Level of Pathological Destructiveness*

Destructive	◄ **Sociopathic**	◄ To destroy every-	Basic Fear is
murderous	inhuman	thing rather than	realized: they are
monstrous	cruel	be forced to submit	harmed and/or
barbarous	remorseless	or surrender	controlled by
ruinous	*inner chaos*		others
psychotic			

PERSONALITY TYPE NINE: The Peacemaker

Parental Orientation: Connected to Both Parents

B-TERMS	A-TERMS	DESIRES	FEARS

HEALTHY

1. *Level of Liberation*   *Self-Actualization*   *Basic Fear*

Indomitable	◀ **Self-Possessed**	◀ Let go of their	Of loss and
all-embracing	"present"	identification with	separation
self-determining	self-aware	a particular self-	(impermanence)
independent	awake, alert	image, that their	
connected	serene	participation in the	
dynamic	exuberant	▲ world is unimportant	

2. *Level of Psychological Capacity*   *Basic Desire*   *Secondary Fears*

Peaceful	◀ **Unselfconscious**	◀ To have inner	Of losing their
relaxed	receptive	stability ("peace	peace of mind
steady, stable	optimistic	of mind")	
kind, gentle	humble		
natural	guileless		
sensual	contemplative		
easygoing	impressionable		

3. *Level of Social Value*   *Secondary Desires*

Comforting	◀ **Unselfish**	◀ To create and	Of conflicts
mediating	inclusive	maintain peace and	(internal and
supportive	patient	harmony in their	external)
healing	forgiving	environment	
reconciling	steadfast		
levelheaded	uncritical		
synthesizing	"balanced"		
imaginative	unpretentious		

AVERAGE

4. *Level of Imbalance*

Agreeable	◀ **Self-Effacing**	◀ To avoid conflicts	Of any significant
compliant	accommodating	(by acquiescing	changes/disrup-
conventional	idealizing others	to others: "Inner	tions in their
philosophizing	sentimental	Sanctum")	world
respectable	discounting self		
pleasant	simplifying		
"fitting in"	unquestioning		
loyal	*dutiful*		

5. *Level of Interpersonal Control*

Complacent	◄ **Disengaged**	◄ To maintain things	Of having to exert
comfort-seeking	selective attention	as they are — to be	themselves in any
habitual	passive-aggressive	undisturbed (out	way, of leaving
woolgathering	unresponsive	of the flux of life)	their comfortable
busywork	stoical		patterns
"autopilot"	resistant		
into routines	unreflective		
puttering	beliefs as defense		
defensive	*anxious*		

6. *Level of Overcompensation*

Appeasing	◄ **Resigned**	◄ To downplay	Of being forced
ignoring	minimizing	the importance	by reality to
sins of omission	unrealistic	of problems in	deal with their
deflecting	indifferent	their world	problems
suppressive	wishful thinking		
dismissing	suppressing anger		
"killing time"	apathetic		
stubborn	"peace at any price"		
belligerent	*short-tempered*		

UNHEALTHY

7. *Level of Violation*

Neglectful	◄ **Repressed**	◄ To defend their	Of acknowledging
irresponsible	unavailable	illusion that	reality at all —
ineffectual	obstinate	everything is	particularly their
low-energy	stonewalling	okay	own role in
addictive	willfully blind		problems
"doormats"	depressed		
listless	feel powerless		
clingingly	*feel inferior*		
dependent			

8. *Level of Delusion & Compulsion*

Disoriented	◄ **Dissociating**	◄ To block out of	That what has
"shut down"	complete denial	awareness anything	happened cannot
helpless	affectless	that could affect	be undone — fear
depersonalized	desolate, numb	them	of reality itself
amnesiac	"lost"		
irrational	*feel persecuted*		

9. *Level of Pathological Destructiveness*

"Disappearing"	◄ **Self-Abandoning**	◄ To eliminate	Basic Fear is
empty shells	catatonic	their awareness	realized: they
fragmenting	shattered	(to save their	have become lost
wasted, inert	devastated	illusions)	and separated from
subpersonalities	vacant		self and others
self-punishing	*self-abasing*		

PERSONALITY TYPE **ONE:** **The Reformer**

Parental Orientation: Disconnected from the Protective-figure

B-TERMS	*A-TERMS*	*DESIRES*	*FEARS*

HEALTHY

1. *Level of Liberation* · *Self-Actualization* · *Basic Fear*

Wise	◄ **Accepting**	◄ Let go of their	Of being
humane	life-affirming	identification with	corrupt, evil,
noble	tolerant	a particular self-	defective
generous	truly realistic	image, that they are	(imbalanced)
uplifting	hopeful	in a position to judge	
kind, pure	accept ambiguity	anything objectively	

2. *Level of Psychology Capacity* · *Basic Desire* · *Secondary Fears*

Reasonable	◄ **Conscientious**	◄ To be good, to	That their sub-
objective	moral	have integrity,	jective feelings
moderate	rational	to be in balance	and impulses will
sensible	discerning	with everything	lead them astray
prudent	evaluating		(impair their
modest	composed		reason)

3. *Level of Social Value* · *Secondary Desires*

Responsible	◄ **Principled**	◄ To act in accordance	That others are
truthful	sense of mission	with their con-	indifferent to
self-disciplined	ethical	science and reason	their principles
articulate	impartial		
just, fair	purposeful		
teach by	impassioned		
example	have convictions		
civilized			

AVERAGE

4. *Level of Imbalance*

Striving	◄ **Idealistic**	◄ To "fix"/improve	That they will be
reforming	obligated	themselves and	condemned for
debating	driven	their world	deviating from
remedying	should/must		their own ideals
"pointing out"	elitist		
explaining	have certainty		
advocating	"making progress"		
refined	serious		
longing	*creating*		
	expectations		

5. *Level of Interpersonal Control*

Orderly	◄ **Self-Controlled**	◄ That everything in	That others will
impersonal	impatient	their lives be	"mess up" the
opinionated	irritable	consistent with	order and balance
rigid	"narrow"/dry	their ideals	they have achieved
punctual	scrupulous		
brusque/"short"	self-critical		
methodical	feel guilty		
precise/"clipped"	emotionally		
moody	constricted		
	melancholy		

6. *Level of Overcompensation*

Critical	◄ **Judgmental**	◄ To reproach others	► That their ideals
badgering	angry	for not meeting	are actually wrong
correcting	perfectionistic	their ideals/	
argumentative	picky, demanding	standards	
sarcastic	uncompromising		
moralizing	unsympathetic		
strident	stern, strict		
workaholic	condescending		
self-indulgent	*self-pitying*		

UNHEALTHY

7. *Level of Violation*

Inflexible	◄ **Intolerant**	◄ To justify them-	That they are
vitriolic	self-righteous	selves and silence	becoming
no negotiations	rationalizing	criticism (from self	irrational
closed-minded	absolutistic	and others)	
unreasonable	bitter		
severe, harsh	misanthropic		
alienated	*depressive*		

8. *Level of Delusion & Compulsion*

Contradictory	◄ **Obsessive**	◄ To consciously	► That they are
hypocritical	compulsive	control their	losing all control
fetishistic	"possessed"	unconscious/	of themselves
untruthful	displacing	irrational impulses	
arbitrary	fixated		
self-flagellating	*tormented*		

9. *Level of Pathological Destructiveness*

Punishing	◄ **Condemnatory**	◄ To rid themselves	► Basic Fear is
cruel	hateful	of the apparent	realized: that they
wrathful	merciless	cause(s) of their	are corrupted,
attacking	furious	obsessions and	"evil," and
sadistic	hysterical	emotional disorder	defective/
self-destructive	*despairing*		imbalanced

Bibliography

Because of the unique historical transmission of the Enneagram and the nature of the personality types, there were very few sources to which we could go for material for this book. Because we wanted to ground the Enneagram personality types in modern psychology, we consulted books on psychoanalytic psychology and psychiatry. In many ways, this body of literature has been the most helpful, since it is based not only on theory but on clinical observations.

We have also consulted popular self-help books to see how other writers have approached the problem of describing personality types from different points of view. Rather than being an exhaustive bibliography of all these sources, what follows is a selected list of books we have found of interest. We recommend them to any reader who would like to know more about personality types and related areas. To one degree or another, we are indebted to them all.

Becker, Ernest. *The Denial of Death*. New York: The Free Press, 1973.
Bennett, J. G. *Enneagram Studies*. York Beach, Me.: Samuel Weiser, 1983.
———. *Gurdjieff: Making a New World*. New York: Harper and Row, Colophon Books, 1973.
Cameron, Norman. *Personality Development and Psychopathology*. Boston: Houghton Mifflin, 1963.
DeChristopher, Dorothy. Reprinted from *The Movement Newspaper* (May

1981) in *Interviews with Oscar Ichazo*. New York: Arica Institute Press, 1982.

Diagnostic and Statistical Manual of Mental Disorders, 4th ed. Washington, D.C.: American Psychiatric Association, 1994.

Fenichel, Otto. *The Psychoanalytic Theory of Neurosis*. New York: W. W. Norton & Company, 1945.

Fine, Reuben. *A History of Psychoanalysis*. New York: Columbia University Press, 1979.

Freud, Sigmund. *Character and Culture*. New York: Collier Books, 1963. Collection of articles which were originally published between 1907 and 1937.

———. *The Ego and the Id*. New York: W. W. Norton & Company, 1960. Originally published in 1923.

———. *A General Introduction to Psychoanalysis*. New York: Washington Square Press, 1952. Originally published between 1915 and 1917.

———. *The Interpretation of Dreams.* New York: Avon Books, 1965. Originally published in 1900.

Fromm, Erich. *Man for Himself.* New York: Fawcett, 1965. Originally published in 1947.

Galbraith, John Kenneth. *The Anatomy of Power*. Boston: Houghton Mifflin, 1983.

Gandhi, Mahatma. *The Words of Gandhi* (Selected by Richard Attenborough). New York: Newmarket, 1982.

Goldenson, Robert M. *The Encyclopedia of Human Behavior*. New York: Dell Publishing Company, 1970.

Greenberg, Jay R., and Stephen A. Mitchell. *Object Relations and Psychoanalytic Theory*. Cambridge: Harvard University Press, 1983.

Greven, Philip. *The Protestant Temperament*. New York: New American Library, 1977.

Hinsie, Leland E., and Robert J. Campbell. *Psychiatric Dictionary*, 4th ed. New York: Oxford University Press, 1970.

Horney, Karen. *Neurosis and Human Growth*. New York: W. W. Norton, 1950.

———. *The Neurotic Personality of Our Time*. New York: W. W. Norton, 1937.

———. *Our Inner Conflicts*. New York: W. W. Norton, 1945.

Jung, Carl. *Psychological Types*. New Haven: Princeton University Press, 1971. Originally published in 1921.

Keen, Sam. Reprinted from *Psychology Today* (July 1973) in *Interviews with Oscar Ichazo*. New York: Arica Institute Press, 1982.

Keirsey, David, and Marilyn Bates. *Please Understand Me*. Del Mar, Calif.: Prometheus Nemesis Books, 1978.

Kernberg, Otto. *Borderline Conditions and Pathological Narcissism*. New York: Jason Aronson, 1975.

Korda, Michael. *Power!* New York: Random House, 1975.

Leary, Timothy. *Interpersonal Diagnosis of Personality*. New York: Ronald Press, 1957.

Lilly, John C. *The Center of the Cyclone*. New York: Bantam Books, 1972.

———, and Joseph E. Hart. "The Arica Training," in *Transpersonal Psychologies*, ed. Charles T. Tart. New York: Harper and Row, 1975.

Lowen, Alexander. *Narcissism*. New York: Macmillan, 1983.

Maccoby, Michael. *The Gamesman*. New York: Simon and Schuster, 1976.

Maddi, Salvatore R. *Personality Theories*. Homewood, Ill.: Dorsey Press, 1968.

Malone, Michael. *Psychetypes*. New York: E. P. Dutton, 1977.

Meisser, W. W. *The Borderline Spectrum*. New York: Jason Aronson, 1984.

Metzner, Ralph. *Know Your Type*. New York: Doubleday, 1979.

Millon, Theodore. *Disorders of Personality*. New York: John Wiley, 1981.

Moore, James. *Gurdjieff: The Anatomy of a Myth*. Rockport, Mass.: Element, 1991.

Mullen, John Douglas. *Kierkegaard's Philosophy*. New York: New American Library, 1981.

Myers, Isabel Briggs, and Peter B. Myers. *Gifts Differing*. Palo Alto, Calif.: Consulting Psychologists Press, Inc., 1980.

Nicholi, Armand M., ed. *The Harvard Guide to Modern Psychiatry*. Cambridge: Harvard University Press, 1978.

Nicoll, Maurice. *Psychological Commentaries on the Teaching of Gurdjieff and Ouspensky*, vol. 2. Boulder, Colo.: Shambala, 1952.

Offit, Avodah. *The Sexual Self*. New York: Lippincott, 1977.

Ouspensky, P. D. *In Search of the Miraculous*. New York: Harcourt, Brace and World, 1949.

Rycroft, Charles. *A Critical Dictionary of Psychoanalysis*. Harmondsworth: Penguin Books, 1972.

Shapiro, David. *Neurotic Styles*. New York: Basic Books, 1965.

Speeth, Kathleen Riordan. *The Gurdjieff Work*. Berkeley, Calif.: And/Or Press, 1976.

Speeth, Kathleen Riordan, and Ira Friedlander. *Gurdjieff, Seeker of the Truth*. New York: Harper and Row, 1980.

Stone, Michael H. *The Borderline Syndromes*. New York: McGraw-Hill, 1980.

Storr, Anthony. *The Art of Psychotherapy*. New York: Methuen, 1979.

———. *The Dynamics of Creation*. New York: Atheneum, 1985.

Tart, Charles, ed. *Transpersonal Psychologies*. New York: Harper and Row, 1975.

Waldberg, Michel. *Gurdjieff, An Approach to His Ideas*. London: Routledge and Kegan Paul, 1981.

Watts, Alan. *The Meaning of Happiness: The Quest for Freedom of the Spirit in Modern Psychology and the Wisdom of the East*. New York: Harper and Row, 1979.

Webb, James. *The Harmonious Circle: The Lives and Work of G. I. Gurdjieff, P. D. Ouspensky, and Their Followers*. New York: G. P. Putnam, 1980.

Index

Abuse, experience of
  in Eights, 305, 323, 325
  in Nines, 362, 365
Abzug, Bella (Eight), 332
Addictions
  in Fives, 200
  in Nines, 372
  in Ones, 399
  in Sevens, 260, 281–83, 283, 285–86, 287
  in Sixes, 245, 249
Aggression
  in Eights, 40–41, 298, 300, 302–04, 308, 317–27, 434
  in Fives, 195, 199–201
  in Fours, 35, 99, 142–43, 160–61
  in Nines, 41, 302, 341, 343, 353–54, 359, 361, 362–63, 364–65, 371–72, 374
  in Ones, 41, 302, 377, 378–79, 380–82, 384, 390, 395, 398–99
  in Sevens, 266–67, 283–84, 290–91, 434
  in Sixes, 217, 221, 239–42, 246–48, 252–53, 305
  in Twos, 415
  in Threes, 35, 96, 99–101, 116, 119, 123–25, 434

Aggressive types (Hornevian), 433–34
Alcohol abuse (see Addictions)
Alda, Alan (Two), 90
Ali, Muhammad (Eight), 332
Allen, Woody (Six), 217
Altman, Robert (Eight), 334
Ambivalence
  in Eights, 304–05
  in Fives, 179, 194, 214, 304
  In Sixes, 217–18, 219, 223, 235–39
Ambiverts, 223
Amin, Idi (Eight), 327, 332
Anal personality types (Freudian), 6, 383, 437 (see also, Freud, Superego)
Anatomy of Power, The (Galbraith), 298–99
Anderson, Laurie (Five), 174, 210
Andrew, Prince of England (Three), 128
Anger (see Aggression)
Antisocial personality disorder (DSM-IV), 444
Anxiety
  in Eights, 300–04, 308, 312–13, 317–18, 321–22, 326
  in Fives, 38–39, 175–78, 184, 189–91, 194, 195, 214–15, 220, 263

Anxiety (*cont.*)
  in Sevens, 38–39, 220, 263–65, 270,
    273, 278, 282, 286–88
  in Sixes, 37–39, 49–50, 219–24,
    227–28, 232, 236, 243–48, 250–52,
    258, 389, 417
Arabic mathematics, 12–13
Arendt, Hannah (Five), 210
Arica Institute, 17, 19, 20
Asimov, Isaac (Five), 212
Attitude (Jung), 6–7, 441, 442–43
Autonomy (*see* Dependency issues)
Average personality levels
Avoidant personality disorder
    (DSM-IV), 444

Bacall, Lauren (Seven), 294
Baez, Joan (One), 407
Barker, Clive (Five), 174, 210
Barr, Roseanne (Eight), 298, 332
Baryshnikov, Mikhail (Six), 256
Basic personality types (*see individual
    personality types*)
Bates, Kathy (Two), 92
Belushi, John (Seven), 260, 292
Bergen, Candice (Six), 217, 256
Bergman, Ingmar (Four), 135, 170
Bergman, Ingrid (Nine), 339, 370
Bernstein, Leonard (Seven), 260,
    292
Bibliography, 495–97
Blake, William (Four), 170, 269
Boone, Pat (Two), 60, 92
Bradshaw, John (One), 407
Brando, Marlon (Eight), 298, 334
Brezhnev, Leonid (Eight), 334
Brodie, Jean (Two), 90
Brokaw, Tom (One), 407
Bronowski, Jacob (Five), 174, 212
Brooks, Mel (Seven), 292
Brothers, Joyce (One), 405
Brown, Helen Gurley (Seven), 294
Brown, Jerry (One), 407
Bryant, Anita (One), 407
Buckley, William F. (One), 377, 405
Bunker, Archie (Six), 217, 256
Bunker, Edith (Nine), 339, 373
Burnett, Carol (Seven), 292
Burton, Richard (Eight), 332
Burton, Tim (Five), 174, 210
Buscaglia, Leo (Two), 60, 92
Bush, Barbara (Two), 92
Bush, George (Six), 217, 254

Caesar, Sid (Seven), 292
Cage, John (Five), 174, 210
Callas, Maria (Four), 135, 168
Campbell, Joseph (Nine), 339, 373
Campbell, Robert J., 249–50
Camus, Albert (Four), 168
Capone, Al (Eight), 332
Capote, Truman (Three), 96, 130
Carrey, Jim (Seven), 260, 292
Carroll, Lewis (Two), 90
Carson, Johnny (Six), 217, 256
Carter, Jimmy (Three), 130
Carter, Lillian (Two), 92
Carter, Rosalynn (Nine), 373
Cash, Johnny (Eight), 334
Castro, Fidel (Eight), 298, 334
Cavett, Dick (Three), 130
Chagall, Marc (Nine), 339, 370
Childhood influences (*see* Parental
    Orientation *and individual
    personality types*)
Chomsky, Noam (One), 405
Chopin, Frederick (Four), 168
Clark, Dick (Three), 96, 128
Clinton, Bill (Three), 96, 128
Cobain, Kurt (Five), 210
Cohen, Leonard (Four), 135
Collins, Joan (Seven), 260, 294
Como, Perry (Nine), 339, 370
Compliant types (Hornevian), 433–34
Compulsive personality disorder
    (DSM-IV), 444
Connery, Sean (Eight), 298, 332
Continuum of Traits, 24
Cooke, Alistair (One), 407
Cooper, Gary (Nine), 370
Core Dynamics
  for individual personality types,
    476–93
  how to read, 468–75
Corleone, Don Vito (Eight), 298, 334
Costanza, George (Six), 217
Costner, Kevin (Nine), 339, 370
Coward, Noel (Seven), 260, 294
Cowardly Lion, the (Six), 256
Cronkite, Walter (Nine), 339, 370
Crosby, Bing (Nine), 370
Cruise, Tom (Three), 96, 130
Cuomo, Mario (One), 407

Darwin, Charles (Five), 212
Davis, Bette (Eight), 298, 332
Davis, Sammy Jr. (Two), 60, 92

Deadly sins, as personality construct, 14, 19
deGaulle, Charles (Eight), 334
DeLorean, John (Eight), 332
Delusional behaviors, 247–48, 285–86, 298, 326–27
Denver, John (Two), 92
Dependency issues, 341
  in Eights, 297, 313, 341
  in Fives, 173, 174, 179–80, 183–84, 185
  in Nines, 338, 341, 347
  in Ones, 341
  in Sixes, 217, 219–20, 224, 226–27, 233, 237, 344
  in Threes, 101, 105
  (*see also* Interpersonal relationships)
Dependent personality disorder (DSM-IV), 444
Depp, Johnny (Four), 135, 170
Depression
  in Fours, 54, 99, 142–43, 159–63, 422, 423
  in Ones, 377, 399
  in Nines, 363, 364–65, 372
  in Sevens, 284, 285–86
  in Sixes, 245–46
Depressive personality disorder (DSM-IV), 442, 444
Desdemona (Nine), 373
Desert Fathers, 14
Detachment (*see* Withdrawal)
Development, Levels of, 45–47, 421–26, 422–23 (*see also individual personality types*)
Developmental psychology, 449
Diagnostic and Statistical Manual of Mental Disorders (DSM-IV), 443–45
Dialectics, in Enneagram analysis, 28–29, 446–47
Diana, Princess of England (Six), 217, 256
Dickinson, Emily (Five), 174, 210
Dietrich, Marlene (Seven), 294
Diller, Phyllis (Seven), 294
Directions, 46–51, 413–18, 452–54, (*see also* Disintegration, Direction of; Integration, Direction of; *and individual personality types*)
Disney, Walt (Nine), 339, 373
Disorders of Personality (Millon), 238
Dissociative behaviors (*see* Withdrawal)

Dole, Bob (Six), 254
Donahue, Phil (Six), 217, 254
Downs, Hugh (Nine), 370
Drug abuse (*see* Addictions)
DSM-IV (*see Diagnostic and Statistical Manual of Mental Disorders*)
DuBois, Blanche (Four), 135, 168
Dukakis, Michael (One), 405
Dylan, Bob (Four), 135, 170
Dynamics of Creation, The (Storr), 135–36

Eco, Umberto (Five), 210
Ego (Freudian), 6, 416–17, 440–41, 450–53, 455–56, 458, 459–61 (*see also* Egocentrism, Selftranscendence *and individual personality types*)
Egocentrism
  in Eights, 297–98, 301–02, 314–17, 319, 321, 326–28
  in Fives, 192–93
  in Fours, 137, 153–56, 156–59, 162, 316, 423
  in Nines, 346, 361
  in Ones, 53–54, 376–78, 382, 384, 387–88, 390, 392–94, 395, 397–401, 408–09
  in Sevens, 260, 266, 277, 279–81, 283–84
  (*see also individual personality types*)
Ego fixations (Ichazo), 19–20
Eight personality type (The Leader), 7, 30, 33, 39, 297–337, 298–99, 336–37, 342
  abuse, experience of, 305, 323, 325
  aggression in, 40–41, 298, 300, 302–04, 308, 317–27, 434
  ambivalence in, 304–05
  anxiety in, 302–04, 313, 317–18
  average personality levels, analysis of, 297–98, 312–22
  as confrontational adversary (Level 6), 319–22
  as constructive leader (Level 3), 309–11
  control, need for, 314, 320
  Core Dynamics, 488–89
  courage (strength) in, 297, 298, 302, 306–07
  criminal behavior in, 298, 323–25
  death, fascination with, 327
  delusions, problems with, 298, 326–27

Eight personality type (*cont.*)
  Disintegration, Direction of, 328–31,
    415
  as dominating power broker (Level 5),
    315–19
  DSM-IV personality disorders in, 444
  egocentrism in, 297–98. 301–02,
    314–17, 319, 321, 326–28
  as enterprising adventurer (Level 4),
    312–15
  environment, resistance to, 300
  extroverted intuitive type (Jungian),
    300–01, 442
  guilt (superego) in, 324–35
  healthy personality levels, analysis
    of, 297, 306–11
  honor, importance of, 310
  impulsive behaviors in, 313, 315
  independence, need for, 297, 313, 341
  in the Instinctive Triad, 39–41,
    299–302, 342, 378
  Integration, Direction of, 331–32
  interpersonal relations, 303–04,
    318–19, 320–22
  intuition (vision) in, 308–09, 310–11
  leadership abilities in, 297, 299, 302,
    306–08, 309–11, 319–20
  as magnanimous heart (Level 1),
    306–08
  megalomania in, 298, 326–27
  money, importance of, 312, 314, 316,
    320–21
  as omnipotent megalomaniac
    (Level 8), 326–27
  parental orientations of, 304–06, 448,
    449
  as phallic-expulsive type
    (neo-Freudian), 438–39
  power issues (willfulness), 53, 297,
    298–99, 300, 302, 303–04, 308, 314,
    315–19, 320–22, 324, 328
  protective behaviors in, 313
  respect, importance of, 310
  as ruthless outlaw (Level 7), 323–25
  self confidence in, 297, 299, 309,
    307–309, 312, 336
  as self-confident person (Level 2),
    308–09
  self-destructive behaviors in, 298,
    299, 302, 326–28
  self-protection (armoring) in,
    302–304, 305, 312, 326, 328
  sexual behavior of, 318–19

  trust issues in, 305, 312–13
  unhealthy personality levels, analysis
    of, 298, 323–28
  as violent destroyer (Level 9), 327–28
  vulnerability (helplessness), fear of,
    300, 303–04, 308, 312–313, 321–22,
    326
  with a Nine-wing, 334–36
  with a Seven-wing, 332–34
Einstein, Albert (Five), 174, 210
Eisenhower, Dwight (Nine), 370
Elizabeth II, Queen of England (Nine),
    339, 373
Emerson, Ralph Waldo (Nine), 373
Enneagon, 19
Enneagram, the
  and the Freudian fixations, 438–41,
    450–454
  and the Freudian structural concepts,
    440–41
  and the Hornevian Neurotic
    Solutions, 433–36, 440–41
  and the Jungian personality types,
    62–63, 147, 177, 222–23, 262–63,
    300–01, 345–46, 381–82, 441–43
  and the neo-Freudian psychosexual
    categories, 437–440
  defined, 12
  Gurdjieff's contributions to, 14–17
  Ichazo's contributions to, 17–20
  inconsistencies in, 24
  Kircher's, 16
  as map of human nature, 5–6
  mathematical symbolism in, 12–13
  organizing principles of, 7–8, 27–55
  sources for, 11–26, 431
  structure of, 19, 27–30
  symbolism of, 5, 12, 15
  theoretical basis for, 445–46
  transmission of, 5–6, 11–26
  unbiased nature of, 32–33
  universality of, 30, 32–33, 447–48
Enneagram analysis
  accuracy of, 6, 8, 10, 25–25, 432
  basic personality types, 31
  complexity of, 8–9, 27, 420–21,
    425–26, 445–46, 454
  change in, 8, 31
  developmental approach to, 447–50
  dialectical approach to, 28–29, 446–47
  dynamic Freudian approach to,
    450–54
  gender distinctions in, 32

lack of bias in, 32–33
limitations of, 9–10, 462–63
negativity of traditional approaches
  to, 24
parental orientation in, 447–50
in relation to DSM-IV personality
  disorder, 443–45
in self-understanding, 3–5, 9–10, 12,
  32–33, 432
theory of, 431; 445-
triads in, 7, 16–17, 28–30, 446–47
  (*see also* Levels of Development,
  Personality types *and individual
  personality types*)
Enthusiast, The (*see* Seven personality
  type)
Escapism (*see* Withdrawal)
Expulsive behaviors (neo-Freudian),
  437–38
Extroverted types (Jungian), 6, 62–63,
  262–63, 300–02, 381–82

Faith, role of, 10
Fallaci, Oriana (Five), 210
False self-image, 35
Fear (*see* Anxiety)
Feeling Triad, the, 7, 28; 29, 34–37, 433,
  447, 451 (*see also* Two, Three and
  Four personality types)
Feldman, Silvia, 327
Fellini, Federico (Seven), 260, 294
Fenichel, Otto, 324–25, 451
Feynman, Dr. Richard (Seven), 260, 292
Field, Sally (Six), 256
Fine, Reuben, 145
Fischer, Bobby (Five), 174, 212
Five personality type (The Investigator)
  7, 29, 33, 37, 173–78, 214–15, 405
  action, problems with, 175, 178,
    186–87, 189, 197–98
  aggression in, 195, 199–201
  ambivalence (dichotomies), 179, 194,
    214, 304
  anxiety (insecurity) in, 38–39, 175–78,
    184, 189–91, 194, 195, 214–15, 220,
    263
  attachment difficulties, 194–95, 199,
    214
  average personality levels, analysis of,
    186–98
  competence, need to demonstrate,
    174, 178, 182, 184, 188–89, 190, 263
  Core Dynamics, 482–83

Disintegration, Direction of, 206–08,
  415
DSM-IV personality disorders in, 444
extremist (eccentric) behaviors in,
  196–98, 199
as focused innovator (Level 3), 184–86
genius in, 174–75, 181
healthy personality levels, analysis
  of, 180–86
humor, sense of, 185–86
knowledge, importance of, 182–83,
  184–85, 186, 187
as imploding schizoid (Level 9),
  204–06
incompetence, fear of, 175–78, 182,
  187, 195–96, 198, 214
independence (detachment) in, 173,
  174, 179–80, 183–84, 185
insight in, 180–82, 427
Integration, Direction of, 208–09
intense conceptualizer as (Level 6),
  189–95
as introverted thinking type
  (Jungian), 177, 442
as isolated nihilist (Level 7), 198–201
madness in, 174–75, 201–06
as oral-expulsive type (neo-Freudian),
  438
parental orientations of, 178–79, 448,
  449–50
perceptions, need to test, 173, 176–77
as perceptive observer (Level 2),
  182–84
pessimism in, 174, 195, 197
phobia in, 180, 417
as pioneering visionary (Level 1),
  180–82
power, fascination with, 191, 214–15
as provocative cynic (Level 6), 195–98
schizophrenia (psychotic breakdowns)
  in, 174, 180, 204–06
secrecy in, 191–92
self-absorption (egocentrism) in,
  192–93
sentimentality, lack of, 183–84
as studious expert (Level 4), 186–89
substance abuse in, 200
suicide in, 174, 204
as terrified alien (Level 8), 201–03
thinking, emphasis on, 175, 192–93
in Thinking Triad, 37–39, 175, 417
unhealthy personality levels, analysis
  of, 198–206

Five personality type (*cont.*)
  vision in, 173, 180–82
  with a Four-wing, 209–12
  with a Six-wing, 212–14
  withdrawal (isolation) in, 174, 176,
    180, 190–92, 198, 200, 201–02,
    434
Fixations, 6, 436–40 (*see also* Ego
    fixations)
Fonda, Henry (Nine), 373
Fonda, Jane (One), 407
Forbes, Malcolm (Seven), 260, 294
Ford, Gerald (Nine), 370
Forster, E.M. (Four), 168
Four personality type (The
    Individualist), 7, 29, 33, 35, 134–36,
    171–72
  abusive behaviors in, 158–59
  aggression (hostility) in, 35, 99,
    142–43, 160–61
  as alienated depressive (Level 7),
    159–61, 422
  average personality levels, analysis of,
    149–59
  Core Dynamics, 480–81
  compassion in, 148
  creativity in, 134, 135–36, 138,
    144–45, 149–50
  depression in, 54, 99, 142–43, 159–63,
    422, 423
  Disintegration, Direction of, 164–66,
    415
  DSM-IV personality disorders in, 444
  as emotionally tormented person
    (Level 8), 161–62, 422
  feelings, identification with, 135, 137,
    139–40, 146, 150–51, 172
  in Feeling Triad, 34–36, 136–38
  healthy types, analysis of, 143–49,
    423
  humor, sense of, 149
  hypersensitivity in, 152, 154–55
  identity problems in, 35–36, 136,
    139–40, 141, 146
  imagination (fantasy life) in, 134, 139,
    141, 151–52
  as imaginative aesthete (Level 4),
    149–52
  immobility (enervation) in, 159–61
  as inspired creator (Level 1), 143–45
  integration direction of, 166–67
  interpersonal relationships in, 151,
    152–53

  as introverted intuitive type
    (Jungian), 147, 442
  intuition in, 134, 146–48
  love, problems with, 172
  moodiness in, 155–56
  ordinary, the, fear of, 141
  oral-retentive type (neo-Freudian),
    438
  parental orientations of, 140–42, 448,
    449–50
  schizophrenia in, 171
  as self-absorbed romantic as (Level 5),
    152–56, 423
  self-absorption (egocentrism) in, 137,
    153–56, 156–59, 162, 316, 423
  as self-aware intuitive as (Level 2),
    145–47, 423
  self-awareness (self-consciousness) in,
    35–36, 134, 136–37, 139–41, 141,
    145, 149, 423
  as self-destructive person as (Level 9),
    162–63, 423
  self-doubt in, 142, 143, 155, 156, 162,
    171, 423
  self-expression in, 147–48
  as self-indulgent "exception" as
    (Level 6), 156–59
  self-pity in, 158
  as self-revealing individual as
    (Level 3), 147–49
  sexual behaviors, 158–59
  suicide by, 162–63
  unhealthy types, analysis of, 159–63
  victim mentality in, 36
  with a Five-wing, 169–71
  with a Three-wing, 167–69
  withdrawal and isolation in, 137–38,
    140, 143, 152–54, 171, 434
Freud, Sigmund (Five), 6, 212, 461
  dialectic patterns in, 447
  personality constructs, 6–7, 8, 383
  psychosexual categories, 436–40, 447
  structural concepts, 440–44, 447,
    450–54
  in relation to Enneagram, 438–41,
    445, 450–54
  in relation to Horney's types, 439–40
Fulghum, Robert (Two), 60
Functions (Jungian), 7, 441

Gabler, Hedda (Three), 128
Gabor, Zsa Zsa (Seven), 292
Galbraith, John Kenneth, 298–99

Gandhi, Indira (Eight), 298, 334
Gandhi, Mohandas K. (Mahatma
    Gandhi) (One), 377, 379, 407
Garland, Judy (Four), 135, 168
Gates, Bill (Five), 174, 212
Gender in Enneagram, 32
Genetics, role in personality, 31
Gere, Richard (Three), 96, 130
Gifford, Kathy Lee (Three), 96, 128
Goldberg, Whoopi (Nine), 339, 370
Gorbachev, Mikhail (Eight), 298, 332
Gore, Al (One), 377, 405
Gould, Glenn (Five), 174, 210
Grace, Princess of Monaco (Nine), 339,
    373
Graham, Billy (Six), 254
Graham, Martha (Four), 135, 168
Grant, Cary (Seven), 294
Greek philosophy, as source of
    Enneagram, 6, 12-13
Green, John, 377
Greven, Philip, 377-78
Growth, psychological (*see* Integration,
    Direction of)
Gumbel, Bryant (Three), 96, 130
Gurdjieff, George Ivanovich (Eight), 13,
    14-17, 25-26, 298, 332

Haig, Alexander (Six), 254
Hanks, Tom (Six), 217, 256
Happiness, 4-5, 9-10, 54-55, 457
Harrelson, Woody (Nine), 339, 370
Harrison, George (One), 405
Hawking, Stephen (Five), 174, 212
Hazlitt, William, 299
Healthy personality levels, 45, 422-24,
    466 (*see also*, Integration, Direction
    of, *and individual personality
    types*)
Heisenberg, Werner, 210
Helmsley, Leona (Eight), 298, 332
Helper, The (*see* Two personality type)
Hemingway, Ernest (Eight), 298, 332
Henning, Doug (Two), 60, 92
Henson, Jim (Nine), 339, 373
Hepburn, Katherine (One), 377, 405
Heredity (*see* Genetics)
Hesse, Hermann (Four), 170,
Heston, Charlton (Eight), 298, 334
Hillel, 328
Hinckley, John Jr. (Six), 254
Hinsie, Leland E., 249-50
History of Psychoanalysis (Fine), 145

Histrionic personality disorder
    (DSM-IV), 444
Hitchcock, Alfred (Five), 212
Hoover, J. Edgar (Six), 217, 254
Hope, Bob (Seven), 292
Horney, Karen, 7, 123, 244, 422, 433-36
    dialectic patterns in, 447
    interpersonal typology, 7, 433
    neurotic "solutions," 87, 433
    personality subtypes, 435, 447
    in relation to Enneagram, 8, 433-34,
        435, 449
    in relation to Freudian/neo-Freudian
        categories, 439-40
Houston, Whitney (Three), 128
Hudson, Rock (Six), 254
Hudson, Russ, 469, 500
Hughes, Howard (Five), 212
Human Mind, The (Menninger), 431
Huston, John (Eight), 334

Iacocca, Lee (Eight), 298, 332
Iago (Three), 130
Ichazo, Oscar, 14, 17-20; 426,
    interpretation of Enneagram, 18
Id (Freudian), 6, 440-41, 450-51, 452
Identification of personality types
    (*see individual personality types*)
Identity problems
    in Fours, 35-36, 136, 139-40, 141,
        146
    in Nines, 341-47
    in Threes, 35-36, 344
    in Twos, 35-36
    (*see also* Ego, Egocentrism)
Ignatius of Loyola, Saint (One), 405
Individualist, The (*see* Four personality
    type)
Insight (*see* Enneagram, Self-
    understanding)
Instinctive Triad, 7, 28-30, 39-41, 433,
    447, 451 (*see also* Eight, Nine and
    One personality types)
Instinctual types (Ichazo), 426-30
Institute for the Harmonious
    Development of Man, 15
Integration, Direction of, 46-51
    process of, 417-18
    and self-transcendence, 459-63
    (*see also individual personality types*)
Interpersonal relationships, 4-5, 7
    in Eights, 303-04, 318-19, 320-22
    in Fours, 151, 152-53

Interpersonal relationships (*cont.*)
  in Nines, 341–42, 344–45, 352, 358–59, 363
  in Ones, 389, 393, 395–96
  in Sevens, 272, 275, 276–77, 278–79, 281, 286
  in Sixes, 216–19, 222, 226, 228, 232–34, 235–36, 243, 389
  in Threes, 101, 105
Interpersonal typology (Hornevian), 433
Introverted personality types (Jungian), 6, 177, 222–23, 345–46
Intuitive type (Jungian), 147
Investigator, The (*see* Five personality type)
Irons, Jeremy (Four), 135, 168
Islam, as possible source for Enneagram, 11, 12, 13
Ives, Charles (Five), 174

Jackson, Janet (Nine), 339, 370
Jackson, Michael (Four), 135, 168
Jackson, Reggie (Six), 256
James, William, 144
Jealousy, 19, 281, 372
Jefferson, Thomas (One), 405
Jesuits, role in Enneagram transmission, 21–23
"Jewish Mother" (Two), 60, 90
Joan of Arc (One), 377, 407
John, Elton (Seven), 260, 292
John Paul II, Pope (One), 377, 407
Johnson, Lady Bird (Nine), 370
Johnson, Lyndon (Eight), 298, 332
Jones, Ernest, 438
Jones, Jim (Eight), 298, 332
Jordan, Barbara (One), 377
Joyce, James (Five), 174, 210
Judeo-Christian tradition, as source for Enneagram, 13–14
Jung, Carl G. (Nine), 6–7, 8, 339, 373
  psychological typologies, 6–7, 62–63, 147, 177, 222–23, 381–82, 262–63, 274–75, 300–02, 345–46, 441–43
  in relation to Enneagram, , 62–63, 147, 177, 222–23, 262–63, 300–01, 345–46, 381–82, 441–43

Kabbala, as source of Enneagram, 14, 17–18
Kaczynski, Theodore (Five), 212
Kafka, Franz (Five), 210
Kahane, Meir (Six), 254

Keaton, Buster (Five), 210
Keaton, Diane (Six), 217, 254
Keillor, Garrison (Nine), 339, 373
Keitel, Harvey (Eight), 332
Kemp, Jack (Three), 128
Kennedy, John F. (Seven), 260, 294
Kennedy, Robert F. (Six), 217, 254
Kennedy, Rose (Nine), 373
Kennedy, Ted (Six), 256
Kerrigan, Nancy (Nine), 339
Kierkegaard, Soren (Four), 3–4, 10, 170
Kierkegaard's Philosophy (Mullen), 261
King, Larry (Seven), 260, 294
King, Martin Luther, Jr. (Eight), 298, 334
King, Stephen (Five), 174, 210
King Lear, (Eight), 334
Kircher, Athanasius, 16
Kirkpatrick, Jeane J. (One), 405
Kissinger, Henry (Eight), 332
Korda, Michael, 218
Krantz, Judith (Seven), 294
Kubrick, Sternly (Five), 174, 210

Landers, Ann (Two), 60, 90
Landon, Michael (Three), 96
Lang, K.D., (Five), 210
Lange, Jessica (Six), 217, 254
Larson, Gary (Five), 174, 210
Lawrence, D.H. (Four), 135, 170
Leader, The (*see* Eight personality type)
Leary, Timothy (Seven), 260, 292
LeGuin, Ursula (Five), 212
Lennon, John, 210
Leno, Jay (Six), 217, 256
Lessing, Doris (Five), 212
Levels of development
  in Eights, 301–28, 488–89
  in Fives, 180–206, 482–83
  in Fours, 143–63, 480–81
  in Nines, 347–66, 490–91
  in Ones , 385–402, 492–93
  in Sevens, 267–88, 486–87
  in Sixes, 226–50, 484–85
  in Threes, 103–25, 478–79
  in Twos, 67–87, 476–77
Lewis, C.S. (One), 405
Liberace (Seven), 260, 292
Libido (Freudian), fixation points of, 427, 437, 439 (*see also* Instincts)
Lilly, John, 19
Limbaugh, Rush (Six), 217, 256
Lincoln, Abraham (Nine), 339, 373

Loren, Sophia (Nine), 339, 370
Love, 460–61
  in Fours, 172
  in Twos, 60–61, 64, 66–68, 75, 76, 89–90, 93–94
  (*see also* Healthy personality levels, Integration, Direction of)
Loyalist, the (*see* Six personality type)
Lucas, George (Nine), 339, 373
Lucci, Susan (Seven), 260, 294
Lynch, David (Five), 174, 210

Macbeth, Lady (Three), 128
Mahler, Gustav (Four), 168
Mailer, Norman (Eight), 298, 332
Malcolm X (Six), 217, 254
Mame, Auntie (Seven), 260
Manic-depression (*see* Depression)
Manic-depressive personality disorder (DSM-IV), 444
Manilow, Barry (Two), 60, 92
Mao Tse-tung (Eight), 332
Marcos, Ferdinand (Eight), 332
Martha (in *Who's Afraid of Virginia Woolf?*) (Seven), 260, 294
Marx, Karl (Five), 212
Masochistic behavior, 249–50
Mather, Cotton (One), 405
Maugham, Somerset (Three), 130
McCarthy, Joseph (Six), 254
McCartney, Paul (Three), 96, 128
McLaine, Shirley (Three), 96, 128
Meaning, search for, 456–57, 459–63
    (*see also*, Integration, Direction of *and individual personality types*)
Meaning of Happiness (Watts), 461
Meir, Golda (Eight), 334
Menninger, Karl A., 431
Mertz, Fred (Six), 256
Midler, Bette (Seven), 260, 292
Millon, Theodore, 237–38
Minnelli, Liza (Seven), 260, 292
Mishima, Yukio (Four), 135, 170
Mitchell, Joni (Four), 135, 170
Mondale, Walter (Six), 217, 254
Money issues
  in Eights, 312, 314, 316, 320–21
  in Sevens, 279–80
Monk, Meredith (Five), 174
Monroe, Marilyn (Six), 217, 256
Montana, Joe (Three), 128
More, St. Thomas (One), 407
Mostel, Zero (Seven), 292

Mother Theresa (Two), 60
Motivator, The (*see* Three personality type)
Moyers, Bill (One), 377, 407
Mozart, Wolfgang Amadeus (Seven), 260, 292
Mullen, John Douglas, 261
Multiple personality disorder, 339, 365–66

Nader, Ralph (One), 377, 407
Napoleon (Eight), 298
Naqshbandi Brotherhood, 12
Naranjo, Claudio, 19, 20–23
Narcissistic personality disorder (DSM-IV), 444
Neo-Platonism, as source of Enneagram, 12, 14, 18
Neuroses
  in relation to Instincts, 427
  source of, 24
  (*see also* Disintegration, Direction of; DSM-IV; *and individual personality types*)
Neurosis and Human Growth (Horney), 87
Neurotic "solutions" (Hornevian), 433
Newman, Paul (Eight), 334
Nicholson, Jack (Seven), 260
Nietzsche, Frederick (Five), 174, 210
Nightingale, Florence (Two), 60
Nine personality type (The Peacemaker), 7, 30, 39–40, 338–75, 339–40, 375
  abuse, experience of, 362, 365
  accommodating (balancing) behaviors in, 338, 344, 353–55, 358–59, 360,
  as accommodating role-player (Level 4), 353–55, 425
  addictive behaviors in, 372
  aggression (anger) in, 41, 302, 341, 343, 353–54, 359, 361, 362–63, 364–65, 371–72, 374
  autism in, 365
  average personality levels, analysis of, 338–39, 346, 353–62, 371, 373
  awareness/denial, problems with, 299, 339, 340, 341, 343, 345–47, 357–58, 359–60, 362, 364–66, 375, 378
  change, fear of, 347, 355–56
  communications in, 338, 350, 352
  conservative nature of, 355

Nine personality type *(cont.)*
  Core Dynamics, 490–91
  creativity in, 352–53
  depression in, 363, 364–65, 372
  Disintegration, Direction of, 366–69,
    415
  as dissociating automaton (Level 8),
    364–65, 425
  dissociative (withdrawing) behaviors
    in, 338, 340–343, 347, 356–58, 360,
    364, 379
  DSM-IV personality disorders in,
    444
  fantasies, domination by, 339, 343,
    347, 357, 361, 425
  fatalism in, 359–61
  guilt feelings in, 363–64
  harmony, need for, 344–45
  healing abilities of, 338, 351–52
  healthy personality levels, analysis
    of, 338; 347–53, 371, 373, 425
  hysterical behaviors in, 365
  idealizing behaviors in, 341, 354–54
  identity (self-definition), problems
    with, 341–47
  independence and autonomy needs,
    338, 341, 347
  in the Instinctive Triad, 39–41,
    340–42, 378
  Integration, Direction of, 369–70
  interpersonal relations in, 341–42,
    344–45, 352, 358–59, 363
  as introverted sensation type
    (Jungian), 345–46, 442
  multiple personality disorder in, 339,
    365–66
  as oral-receptive type (neo-Freudian),
    437–39
  parental orientations of, 343–45, 448,
    449–50
  passive-aggressive behaviors, 339
  as passively disengaged person
    (Level 5), 355–59, 422, 425
  peace, importance of, 339, 340,
    344–45, 346–47, 349, 351
  power drives in, 425
  as primary personality type, 416–17
  productivity problems, 357
  psychotic, schizoid behaviors, 365–66
  as receptive person (Level 2), 349–51,
    425
  receptivity and openness in, 338, 340,
    347, 349–50

  repression problems, 342–43, 359,
    362–64, 374
  as resigned fatalist (Level 6), 359–62,
    422, 425
  responsibility problems, 339
  self, oneness with, 338, 339, 347–48,
    375, 425
  self-deception in, 343
  self-effacement in, 354
  selfishness (egocentrism) in, 346,
    361
  as self-possessed guide (Level 1),
    347–48, 425
  sexual behaviors, 351, 372
  suicidal behaviors, 363
  as supportive peacemaker (Level 3),
    351–53, 425
  trust issues, 338, 349
  unhealthy personality type, analysis
    of, 339, 347, 362–66, 371, 374–75,
    425
  with an Eight-wing, 370–72
  with an One-wing, 372–75
Niven, David (Seven), 294
Nixon, Richard (Six), 217, 254
Normal behavior, 24
North, Oliver (Six), 217, 254
Numbers, symbolism of, 12–13; 15, 32
Nureyev, Rudolf (Four), 135, 168

Obsessive-compulsive behaviors, 374,
    377, 383, 399–401
Ochs, Robert, 21
O'Connor, Sandra Day (One), 377, 405
O'Keeffe, Georgia (Five), 178, 210
Onassis, Aristotle (Eight), 332
One personality type (The Reformer), 7,
    30, 40, 376–409, 377–78, 405,
    408–09
  aggression (anger) in, 41, 302, 377,
    378–79, 380–82, 384, 390, 395,
    398–99
  as anal-retentive type (neo-Freudian),
    438–39
  autonomy, need for, 341
  average personality type, analysis of,
    376–77, 390–97
  as compliant type (Hornevian), 434
  Core Dynamics, 491–92
  cruelty in, 384, 401–02; 408
  depression in, 377, 399
  dichotomies in, 378, 380–81
  Disintegration, Direction of, 402–04

dogmatism (intolerance) in, 377,
  390–92, 397–98, 408–09
DSM-IV personality disorders in, 444
as extroverted thinking type
  (Jungian), 381–82, 442
guilt in, 390, 401–02
healthy personality levels, analysis
  of, 376, 385–90
as idealistic reformer (Level 4),
  390–92
in the Instinctive Triad, 7, 378–80
Integration, Direction of, 404–05
integrity in, 376, 382, 387, 389–90
interpersonal relationships in, 389,
  393, 395–96
as intolerant misanthrope (Level 7),
  397–99
judgmental behaviors in, 376–77, 382,
  387–88, 390, 395, 397–99, 408–09
as judgmental perfectionist (Level 6),
  394–97
nervous breakdowns in, 377
obsessive behaviors in, 377, 399–401
order and control, need for, 53–54,
  376, 378, 384, 392–94, 395, 397–98,
  399–401
as orderly person (Level 5), 392–94
parental orientations of, 382–84
perfectionism in, 299, 376–77, 378,
  379–80, 384, 386, 394–97, 398
perverse behaviors, attraction to, 377,
  401
as principled teacher (Level 3)
as punitive avenger (Level 9), 401–02
as reasonable person (Level 2), 397–88
responsibility (obligation), sense of,
  389, 390–91
righteousness in, 377, 384, 388
self-acceptance in, 385, 390, 409
self-control (repression) in, 342, 376,
  380–82, 383, 385, 387–88, 389, 390,
  392–96, 397–399, 438, 439
self-indulgence in, 382, 390
sexual behaviors in, 394, 397, 401
substance abuse in 399
suicide in, 377
tolerance in, 385–86
truth, concern with, 376, 382,
  388–89, 395
unhealthy personality levels, analysis
  of, 377, 397–402
values (ethics), importance of, 376,
  384, 385–386 387, 388–89, 396

as wise realist (Level 1), 385–86
  with a Nine-wing, 405–06
  with a Two-wing, 407–08
Oral behavior stage (Freud), 6, 437
Orbison, Roy (Four), 135
Origins of the Enneagram, 11–26
Ozick, Cynthia (Five), 212

Panels of exemplars, 20
Paranoid delusions (paranoia), 247–48,
  444
Paranoid personality disorder
  (DSM-IV), 444
Parental orientations, 31, 448 (see also
  Enneagram, developmental
  approach to, *and individual
  personality types*)
Passions (Ichazo), 19
Passive-aggressive behaviors, 237–39,
  251, 339, 343
Passive-Aggressive personality disorder
  (DSM-III), 444
Pauley, Jane (Three), 96, 128
Pavarotti, Luciano (Two), 60, 92
Peacemaker, The (*see* Nine personality
  type)
Perot, Ross (Eight), 298
Personality types
  change in, 31, 43
  childhood origins of, 31
  complexity of, 6, 8, 27
  cultural preferences for, 33
  in the Enneagram, 7–8, 16–17, 25,
    31–34
  and essence, 17
  Freud's, 6–7, 8, 383
  Gurdjieff's, 16–17
  Horney's, 7, 433, 435, 447
  Ichazo's, 18–20
  identifying, guidelines for, 7–8,
    33–43, 53–55
  interrelationships between, 47–51
  Jung's, 6–7, 433–34
  as key to self-understanding, 4–5
  Levels of Development in, 8, 45–47
  reasons to study, 3–5, 8–9, 431–32,
    445–46
  as self-fulfilling prophecy, 457–49
  wing subtypes, 43–44
  (*see also* Enneagram *and individual
    personality types*)
Pfeiffer, Michelle (Six), 254
Phallic stage (Freud), 6, 437

Philbin, Regis (Seven), 260, 292
Piaf, Edith (Four), 168
Picasso, Pablo (Eight), 298, 334
Piggy, Miss (Seven), 292
Pinter, Harold (Four), 168
Plimpton, George (Seven), 294
Poe, Edgar Allen (Four), 135, 170
Porter, Cole (Seven), 294
Pound, Ezra (Five), 212
Power (Korda), 218
Presley, Elvis (Three), 128
Pride, 19, 456–57 (*see also individual personality types*)
Primary personality types (*see also personality types Three, Six, and Nine*), 416–17
Prince (The Artist Formerly Known as) (Four), 168
Protestant Temperament, The (Greven), 377–78
Proust, Marcel (Four), 135, 168
Psychiatric Dictionary (Hinsie and Campbell), 249–50
Psychiatric terminology, judgmental nature of, 32
Psychic Economics, Law of, 458–59
Psychoanalytic Theory of Neurosis, The (Fenichel), 324–25, 450–51
Psychological integration, 416–18
Psychological Types (Jung), 62–63, 147, 177, 222–23, 263, 274–75, 300–01, 345–46, 381
Psychotic behaviors, 365–66
Puritanism, 377–78

Qaddafi, Muammar (Eight), 332

Radner, Gilda (Six), 217, 256
Rank, Otto, 144–45
Reagan, Ronald (Nine), 339, 370
Receptive behaviors (Freudian), 437–38
Redford, Robert (Six), 254
Redgrave, Vanessa (One), 407
Reeve, Christopher (Three), 96
Reeves, Keanu (Nine), 339, 370
Reformer, The (*see* One personality type)
Reich, Wilhelm, 249–50
Reno, Janet (Eight), 334
Resigned type (Hornevian), 422
Retentive behaviors (Freudian), 437–38
Rice, Anne (Four), 135
Richards, Ann (Eight), 298, 332

Riso, Don Richard, 21–25, 421, 469, 500
Riso-Hudson Wing Subtypes, 44
Rivera, Geraldo (Seven), 260, 294
Rivers, Joan (Seven), 260, 294
Robbins, Tony (Three), 96, 128
Roberts, Julia (Six), 217, 256
Rockwell, Norman (Nine), 339, 373
Rooney, Andy (Six), 217, 256
Rooney, Micky (Seven), 292
Roosevelt, Eleanor (Two), 60, 90
Roosevelt, Franklin Delano (Eight), 298, 332
Rubinstein, Arthur (Seven), 260, 267, 292

Saddam Hussein (Eight), 298
Sagan, Carl (One), 405
Salinger, J.D. (Four), 135, 170
Sarman (Sarmoun) Brotherhood, 12, 13
Sartre, Jean-Paul, 174, 210
Schizoid and schizotypal personality disorder (DSM-IV), 444
Schizophrenia, 205
Schwarzenegger, Arnold (Three), 96, 128
Secondary personality types, 30, 416–17
Seekers After Truth (SAT), 20
Self-confidence (*see individual personality types*)
Self-deception (*see individual personality types*)
Selfishness (*see* Egocentrism)
Self-Preservation Instinct, 426–428
Self-transcendence (*see* Ego)
Self-understanding, attainment of, 4–5, 9–10, 19, 30, 54–55, 457–62
Selleck, Tom (Six), 256
Serkin, Peter (Five), 210
Seven personality type (The Enthusiast), 7, 30, 37–38, 259–96, 260–61, 296
  as accomplished generalist (Level 3), 270–72
  acquisitiveness in, 259, 266–67, 273–75, 279–82, 296
  addictions in, 260, 281–82, 283, 285–86, 287
  aggression in, 266–67, 283–84, 290–91, 434
  anxiety problems in, 38–39, 220, 263–65, 270, 273, 278, 282, 286–88
  appetites (greed) in, 272–73, 275

average personality levels, analysis of, 259–60, 266, 272–82
boredom, fear of, 259, 260–61, 273, 276, 278
as comedian/performer, 277
controlling behaviors in, 54, 268–69
Core Dynamics, 486–87
creativity in, 270–72
delusional behavior in, 285–86
depression in, 284, 285–86
deprivation, fear of, 270, 272–73, 296, 417
Disintegration, Direction of, 288–90, 415
DSM-IV personality disorders in, 444
as ecstatic appreciator (Level 1), 267–68
egocentrism and greed in, 260, 266, 277, 279–81, 283–84
enthusiasm in, 259, 269–70, 272
escapism (withdrawal) in, 282–86
as excessive hedonist (Level 6), 279–82
as experienced sophisticate (Level 4), 272–75
as extroverted sensation type (Jungian), 262–63
as free-spirited optimist (Level 2), 268–70
happiness in, 261, 265, 266, 267–68, 282
healthy personality levels, analysis of, 259, 266, 267–72
as hyperactive extrovert (Level 5), 275–79
hysteria in, 7, 286–88
as impulsive escapist (Level 7), 282
impulsiveness in, 259, 262, 276–79, 284
Integration, Direction of, 291
interpersonal relationships in, 272, 275, 276–77, 278–79, 281, 286
jealousy, 281
joy and wonder in, 259, 291
as manic compulsive (Level 8), 285–86
mental abilities, 261, 269, 271
money, importance of, 279–80
oral behaviors in, 276
as panic-stricken hysteric, 265, 286–88
parental orientations of, 265–66, 448, 449

as phallic-retentive type (neo-Freudian), 438
physical vitality, 270
productivity in, 266, 274
self-control, problems with, 266–67, 282–84, 286–87
self-indulgence (hedonism) in, 260–62, 263, 266–67, 275, 276–77, 279–81
sensation (stimulation), need for, 261, 262, 265, 269, 285
sexual excess, 281, 283
skills, ability to learn, 270–71
substance abuse, 281, 283
superficiality in, 277–78
in the Thinking Triad, 37–39, 261–62, 417
unhealthy personality levels, analysis of, 260, 266–67, 282–88
with an Eight-wing, 294–96
with a Six-wing, 291–94
Severeid, Eric (One), 405
Sexual behavior
in Fours, 158–59
in Nines, 351, 372
in Ones, 394, 397, 401
in Sevens, 281, 283
(*see also* Addictive behaviors)
Sexual Instinct (Ichazo), 426, 427–28, 430
Shaw, George Bernard (One), 377
Shields, Brooke (Three), 96, 128
Simmons, Richard (Two), 60, 92
Simon, Paul (Four), 168
Simpson, Marge (Nine), 339, 373
Simpson, O.J., (Three), 96, 128
Sinatra, Frank (Eight), 298, 332
Siskel, Gene (One), 407
Six personality type (The Loyalist), 7, 29–30, 33, 37, 216–18, 216–58, 258
aggression in, 217, 221, 239–42, 246–48, 252–53, 305
as ambivalent pessimist (Level 5), 235–39
as anal-receptive type (Freudian), 438, 439
anxiety (insecurity) in, 37–39, 49–50, 219–24, 227–28, 232, 236, 243–48, 250–52, 258, 389, 417
approval and support needs of, 216–19, 222, 226, 228, 232–34, 235–36, 243, 389

Six personality type (*cont.*)
  as authoritarian rebel (Level 6),
    239–43
  authority problems in, 218, 221, 226,
    233, 236, 240–41, 248–49
  average personality levels, analysis of,
    216–17, 232–43
  commitment (loyalty) in, 216,
    230–32, 235
  as committed worker (Level 3),
    230–32
  contradictions (ambivalence) in,
    217–18, 219, 223, 236–39
  controlling behaviors in, 54, 434
  cooperation, importance of, 216,
    231–32
  Core Dynamics, 484–85
  depression in, 245–46
  Disintegration, Direction of, 250–53,
    415
  DSM-IV personality disorders in,
    444
  as dutiful loyalist (Level 4), 232–35
  emotional confusion in, 220, 223,
    238–39
  as engaging friend (Level 2), 228-
  family, importance of, 231–32
  healthy personality levels, analysis
    of, 216, 226–32
  humor in, 239
  indecision, problems with, 233–35,
    237, 244
  independence/dependency in, 217,
    219–20, 224, 226–27, 233, 237, 344
  Integration, Direction of, 253–54
  as introverted feeling type (Jungian),
    222–23, 442
  masochistic behaviors in, 249–50
  as overreacting dependent (Level 7),
    243–46
  as paranoid hysteric (Level 8), 246–48
  parental orientations of, 224–26, 448,
    449
  passive-aggressive behaviors, 237–39,
    251
  phobic/counterphobic behaviors,
    220–21, 239–40
  as primary personality type, 416–17
  reactive behaviors, 223–24, 226, 232
  responsibility in, 234–35, 236–37
  scapegoating by, 241–42
  as self-defeating masochist (Level 9),
    248–50

  structure, need for, 218, 219–20,
    230–31, 234–35
  substance abuse by, 245, 249
  testing behaviors in, 236
  in Thinking Triad, 7, 37–39, 218–20,
    417
  trust issues (paranoia) in, 218, 222,
    228–30, 233, 244–45, 246–48
  unhealthy personality levels, analysis
    of, 217, 243–50
  as valiant hero (Level 1), 226–28
  vigilance in, 221–22, 229, 230, 247
  with a Five-wing, 254–56
  with a Seven-wing, 256–58
Skinner, B.F. (Five), 212
Social Instinct (Ichazo), 426, 427,
  428–29
Spielberg, Steven (Seven), 260, 292
Spock, Mr. (One), 377, 405
Springsteen, Bruce (Six), 217, 254
Stahl, Leslie (One), 407
Stalin, Joseph (Eight), 332
Stallone, Sylvester (Three), 96, 128
Stanwyck, Barbara (Eight), 334
Starr, Ringo (Nine), 339, 370
Steinberg, Saul (Four), 170
Stendhal, 147
Stephanopoulos, George (Three),
  130
Stern, Howard (Seven), 260, 294
Stewart, Jimmy (Nine), 373
Sting (Three), 96, 130
Stone, Sharon (Three), 96
Storr, Anthony, 135–36
Streep, Meryl (Three), 130
Streisand, Barbra (Three), 130
Substance abuse (*see* Addictions)
Subtypes (*see* Wings)
Sufi tradition, as source of Enneagram,
  11–14, 18
Suicide
  in Fives, 174, 204
  in Fours, 162–63
  in Eights, 162–63
  in Ones, 377
  in Nines, 363
  in Sevens, 290
Superego (Freudian), 6, 440, 450–53
  compliance with, 433
  in Enneagram, 440–41
Susann, Jacqueline (Seven), 294
Sutherland, Dame Joan (Nine), 373
Swayze, Patrick (Six), 217, 256

Taylor, Elizabeth (Seven), 260, 292
Tchaikovsky, Peter Ilich, 168
Thatcher, Margaret (One), 377, 407
Therapy, limitations of, 461–63
Thinking Triad, the, 7, 28–30, 37–39,
    417, 433, 447 (*see also* Five, Six, and
    Seven personality types),
Thomas, Danny (Two), 90
Thomas, Michael Tilson (Three), 130
Three personality type (The Motivator),
    7, 29, 33, 34–36, 95–133, 96–97,
    132–33
  abuse, experience of, 124
  aggression (hostility) in, 35, 96,
    99–101, 116, 119, 123–25, 434
  attractiveness of, 107, 108–09
  as authentic person (Level 1), 103–05
  average type, analysis of, 109–19
  catatonia in, 127
  competitiveness in, 100,
    107–08,109–11, 389
  as competitive status-seeker (Level 4),
    109–11
  Core Dynamics, 478–79
  deceptive behaviors in, 99, 119,
    120–22
  dependencies of, 101, 105
  as dishonest opportunist (Level 7),
    119–21
  Disintegration, Direction of, 125–27,
    415
  DSM-IV personality disorders in, 444
  egotism (narcissism), problems with,
    96–97, 99–101, 115–19, 120–22, 132
  emptiness, inner, 99, 132, 121
  failure, fear of, 119–20
  feelings, repression of (self-deception),
    98–99, 111–12, 115, 120
  in Feeling Triad, 7, 34–36, 97–99
  healthy personality levels, analysis
    of, 103–09
  image/identity, importance of, 35–36,
    96, 98, 99, 100–01, 110–17, 132–33,
    313, 389
  as image-conscious pragmatist
    (Level 5), 111–15
  inner-direction in, 95, 98, 103–04, 105
  Integration, Direction of, 127–28
  integrity, problems with, 96, 132
  jealousy in, 96, 123
  in Jungian typology, 442
  as malicious deceiver (Level 8),
    121–22

  opportunism in, 96, 98, 120–21
  as outstanding paragon (Level 3),
    107–09
  parental orientations of, 101–03,
    448–49
  as phallic-receptive type
    (neo-Freudian), 438–39
  pragmatism in, 96, 99, 108, 119–20
  as primary personality type, 416–17
  self-acceptance (self-esteem) in,
    36–37, 95, 97, 98–99, 100–01,
    104–05, 106–07, 119
  as self-assured person (Level 2),
    105–07
  as self-promoting narcissist as
    (Level 6), 115–19
  sensitivity to others, 105, 106
  superiority, sense of, 95–96, 100, 117,
    120–1
  unhealthy personality levels, analysis
    of, 119–25
  vindictiveness (maliciousness) in, 96,
    99–100, 123–25,132
  as vindictive psychopath (Level 9),
    122–25
  with a Four-wing, 130–32
  with a Two-wing, 128–30
  worthlessness, fear of, 98, 99, 109,
    115–16, 122–23
Triadic relationships (Hornevian),
    435–36
Triads, 7, 16–17, 28–30, 446–47
    (*see also* Thinking Triad, Feeling
    Triad, Instinctive Triad)
Truman, Harry, 310
Trump, Donald (Eight), 298, 332
Truth, seeking of, 10
Tune, Tommy (Two), 92
Tutu, Desmond (Two), 60, 90
Two personality type (The Helper), 7,
    29, 34; 59–61, 59–94, 93–94, 223
  abuse, experience of, 84–85
  aggression (hostility) in, 35, 63,
    77–78, 81, 84–85, 87, 88–89, 99,
    415–16
  ambivalence in, 63, 304
  as anal-expulsive type (neo-Freudian),
    438
  average personality levels, analysis of,
    59–60, 72–80
  care-taking behaviors in, 61, 65, 66,
    70–71, 82, 94, 304
  as caring person (Level 2), 69–70

Two personality type (*cont.*)
codependency/commitment, problems with, 77, 81–83
as coercive dominator (Level 8), 83–85
control issues in, 34, 54, 433
Core Dynamics, 476–77
Disintegration, Direction of, 87–89, 415–16
as disinterested altruist (Level 1), 67–68
DSM-IV personality disorders in, 444
as effusive friend as (Level 4), 72–74
egocentricity in, 63–64, 66, 73–74, 77, 79–80, 94
empathy in, 69, 106
as extroverted feeling type (Jungian), 62–63, 442
in Feeling Triad, 34–36, 61–63
healthy personality levels, analysis of, 59, 67–71, 89–90
identity, problems with, 34–36, 65, 81–83, 89–90
Integration, Direction of, 89–90
love in, 60–61, 64, 66–68, 75, 76, 89–90, 93–94
manipulative (attention-getting) behaviors in, 61, 62, 72–3, 74–75, 81–83, 93–94
as nurturing helper as (Level 3), 70–71
obsessive, compulsive behaviors in, 61, 67, 84
parental orientations of, 65–67, 448, 449
as possessive "intimate" (Level 5), 74–78
possessiveness in, 74–76
psychosomatic problems in, 64, 86–87
as psychosomatic victim as (Level 9), 85–87
as self-deceptive manipulator (Level 7), 81–83
as self-important "saint" as (Level 6), 78–80
sexual problems in, 84, 85
substance abuse by, 80
suffering (masochism) in, 83, 86–87
unhealthy personality levels, analysis of, 60, 81–89
with a One-wing, 90–92
with a Three-wing, 92–93

Unhealthy personality levels, 7, 47, 415, 424, 467–68 (*see also,* Disintegration, Direction of, *and individual personality types*)
Ustinov, Peter (Seven), 292

Vader, Darth (Eight), 334
Van Gogh, Vincent (Five), 174, 210
Vance, Cyrus (Nine), 373
Violence (*see* Aggression)

Wagner, Richard (Eight), 298, 332
Wallace, Mike (Eight), 298, 332
Walters, Barbara (Eight), 298, 332
Warhol, Andy (Three), 130
Washington, Denzel (Three), 96, 128
Watson, James (Five) 212
Watts, Alan, 461
Wayne, John (Eight), 298, 334
Webb, James, 15–16
Weil, Simone (Five), 174, 212
Well-adjusted automaton type (Hornevian), 422
White, Vanna (Three), 96, 128
Whitman, Walter (Four), 168
Wiesel, Elie (One), 377
Wilde, Oscar, 122
Wilkes, Melanie Hamilton (Two), 60
Will, George F. (One), 405
Williams, Robin (Seven), 260, 292
Williams, Tennessee (Four), 135, 168
Williamson, Marianne (Seven), 260, 292
Willis, Bruce (Seven), 260
Wilson, Edward O. (Five), 212
Windsor, Duchess of (Seven), 280, 294
Wingfield, Laura (Four), 135, 170
Wings, 418–21
subtypes, 43–44
variability in, 419–21
(*see also individual personality types*)
Winnicott, D.W. 135–36
Winters, Jonathan (Seven), 292
Withdrawal/isolation:
in Fives, 174, 176, 180, 190–92, 198, 200, 201–02, 434
in Fours, 137–38, 140, 143, 152–54, 171, 434
in Nines, 338, 340–343, 347, 356–58, 360, 364, 379, 434
in Sevens, 282–86
Withdrawn types (Hornevian), 433–34
Woolf, Virginia (Four), 135, 170
Words of Gandhi, The (Gandhi), 379

YOUR LOCAL BOOKSTORE can provide you with copies of all of Don Richard Riso's books: *Personality Types* (1987, 1996), *Understanding the Enneagram* (1990), *Discovering Your Personality Type: The New Enneagram Questionnaire* (1995), and *Enneagram Transformations* (1993). You can also order them from the publisher by calling (800) 225-3362.

To obtain multiple copies for use in Enneagram Workshops as well as in business and organizational settings, please contact Houghton Mifflin Company, Special Sales Department, 222 Berkeley Street, Boston, Massachusetts, 02116, or call (617) 351-5919. Special discounts are available for sixteen copies or more.

To contact Don Richard Riso and Russ Hudson for information about their Enneagram Workshops, Professional Training Program, new publications, and business seminars, or to have your name added to their mailing list for workshops in your area, please contact The Enneagram Institute at the address below.

To have the *Riso-Hudson Enneagram Type Indicator* interpreted by an Enneagram teacher trained and certified by Don Richard Riso and Russ Hudson, please contact The Enneagram Institute for a free referral to a teacher in your area.

To order the self-scoring offprint of the *Riso-Hudson Enneagram Type Indicator* or audiotapes by Don Richard Riso and Russ Hudson, please call The Enneagram Institute at the number listed below.

The Enneagram Institute
222 Riverside Drive, Suite 10
New York, NY 10025
Telephone: (212) 932-3306
Fax: (212) 865-0962
E-mail: ennpertype@aol.com